HANDBOOKS

IRELAND

CAMILLE DeANGELIS

IRELAND

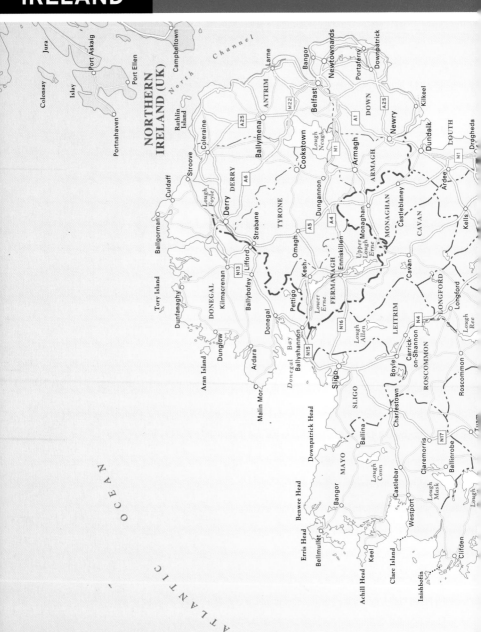

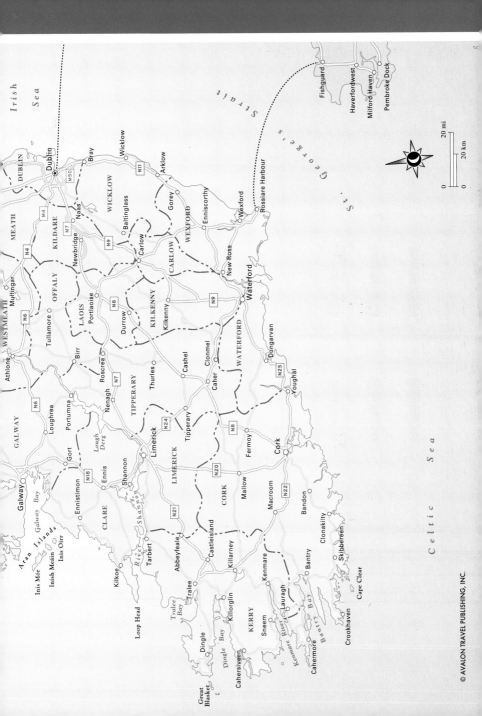

DISCOVER IRELAND

Ten years from now you'll find yourself daydreaming on a busy day, remembering the trip you're about to take. Your mind will take you back to some charming village in the west of Ireland on a clear night, walking down a narrow winding street with the sweet smell of peat-smoke tickling your nose, a smudge of rosy-pink behind the western hills, and a pleasant chill in the air. You'd just taken leave of the liveliest pub in town, and as you walked you were humming one of the reels played at a traditional music session earlier in the evening. There were a couple of fiddles, a bodhrán, maybe an accordion, tin whistle, or banjo. Perhaps there was even a set of uilleann pipes – and if there was, one of the locals told you what a rare treat this was, as there are so few uilleann pipers left. Then he bought you a pint.

Whether your drink of choice was Guinness or Bailey's, whether you were staying in a Victorian country manor or the humblest of hostels, as you were walking down that narrow winding street on that

Ha'penny Bridge over the River Liffey, Dublin

clear evening, it occurred to you under a star-flecked sky that it had been years since you felt so content, so unequivocally happy.

It rains, yes. Sometimes the sun won't show itself for days. But try not to complain about it; that privilege is reserved for the natives, whether they hail from one of the Republic of Ireland's 26 counties or the six counties of Northern Ireland (Antrim, Armagh, Derry, Down, Fermanagh, and Tyrone). Just think of the mud on your shoes as the price you pay for all that gorgeous greenery.

Inspired by the island's fertile valleys, lofty crags, and lonesome bogs, the richness of Irish legend knows no parallel, from the epic adventures of Cuchulainn and Fionn mac Cumhaill to the miraculous deeds of obscure early Christian saints. The holy men who first recorded these stories in illuminated manuscripts and meticulous annals became a legend unto themselves, as Ireland developed a reputation for scholarship and high culture during the "dark ages" of mainland Europe. Ghosts of the past haunt the landscape — great

Dunluce Castle, County Antrim

© CAMILLE DEANGELIS

monasteries and remote abbey ruins, fairy-tale castles and ancient stone circles – providing a precious link to myth and history.

Though the country is still as proud of its rebels, saints, and bards as it ever was, in the last two decades Ireland has seen rapid change and unprecedented prosperity. The Ireland of today isn't the Ireland of 10 or even five years ago, as all the suggestive advertising, Golden Arches, and ubiquitous cell phones can attest. Many Irish have mixed feelings about the "Celtic Tiger," the economic boom of the 1990s, aided much by Ireland's membership in the European Union. It has allowed their emigrant brothers and sisters to return home to work, but it has also permeated their culture with the ever-lengthening shadow of modern consumerism.

The Celtic Tiger also encouraged a gourmet trend, so don't believe anyone who tells you Irish food is terrible; the days of gristly lamb stew at the "best" restaurant in town are long gone. "Modern Irish" cuisine applies creative Continental touches to local, often organic meats, seafood, and produce. Unless you happen to be staying in a very remote locale, there's no reason why you can't have

the rhododendron garden at Howth, County Dublin

yourself a three-course feast. You may pay handsomely for it, like everything else here – have you heard that Ireland is the second-most expensive country in Europe? – but if you know where to go, you can eat like royalty.

All over the island you'll find a sometimes strange mix of old and new, like the crusty old farmer driving his tractor at 20 kilometers an hour down a busy highway with a cell phone tucked between ear and shoulder; stylish women's clothing boutiques in 16th-century shopfronts along a narrow cobblestoned street; or the sleek glass-and-steel visitor-center architecture at the country's most important archaeological sites. Dublin, Ireland's vibrant capital, has plenty of such remarkable juxtapositions. The city's museum of modern art is located in a sprawling neoclassical military hospital, and many of its hippest pubs, eateries, and concert venues have been reincarnated out of disused industrial spaces.

But no amount of modernization will blot from the countryside its romantic, often melancholy ruins. The more sobering parts of the landscape (rural farmsteads rendered bleak by the lashing rain,

Teach Synge, playwright J. M. Synge's summer cottage in the Aran Islands

statues of the Madonna in roadside niches, derelict houses and forlorn shopfronts painted what novelist Richard Condon termed "poorhouse gray") reveal one layer after another of this country's dark but utterly fascinating history. These glimpses of a vanished Ireland will only add to the texture of your visit.

It's safe to say many of Ireland's most beloved attributes will never change: Potatoes are still the fifth food group, stout is still considered a meal in a glass, and the Irish are as hospitable a people as ever. No doubt you heard this long before you planned your visit to the isle of saints and scholars, but still nothing will prepare you for the complete strangers who all but offer you the shirt off their backs – on the whole, the Irish are still some of the most generous folks on the planet. In its people, legends, and landscapes, Ireland ignites the imagination in a way few other earthly places can.

the stunning Harry Clarke window at St. Mary's Church, Cong, County Mayo

Contents

14

MAP CONTENTS

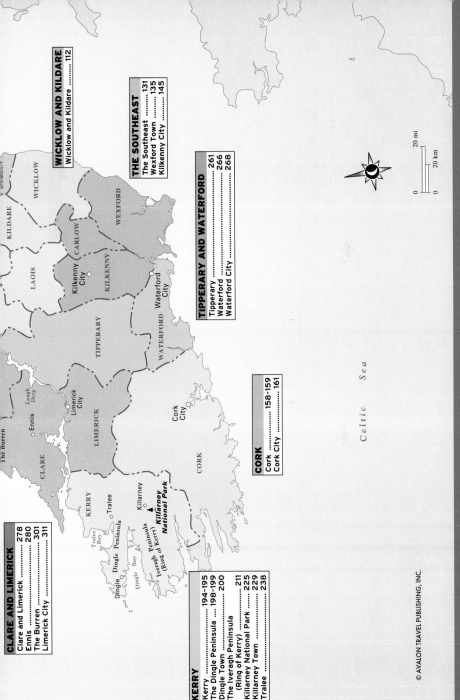

CLARE

The Burren

Ennis

Lough
Derg

Limerick
City

LIMERICK

LAOIS

KILDARE

WICKLOW

CARLOW

KILKENNY

Kilkenny
City

WEXFORD

TIPPERARY

WATERFORD

Waterford
City

KERRY

Tralee

Tralee
Bay

Dingle

Dingle Peninsula

Dingle Bay

Iveragh Peninsula
(Ring of Kerry)

Killarney

Killarney
National Park

Cork
City

CORK

Celtic   Sea

0   20 mi

0   20 km

© AVALON TRAVEL PUBLISHING, INC.

The Lay of the Land

DUBLIN

Unless you're flying into Shannon, the fast-paced, cosmopolitan capital of the Irish Republic will be your first stop. Many visitors tour the Guinness Brewery and go for afternoon pub crawls in the Temple Bar neighborhood—be sure to seek out Dublin culture *outside* the pubs, too. Art, architecture, archaeology, and book lovers can occupy themselves for days at **Trinity College,** where the magnificent **Book of Kells** is on display; the **Chester Beatty Library;** the **National Gallery;** the splendidly neo-Gothic **Christ Church Cathedral.** A visit to the **National Museum** is a must as well. It's worth passing an hour or two on **St. Stephen's Green** just watching most of Dublin go by. It's a bus ride from the city center, but **Phoenix Park** is a good place to check out a hurling or Gaelic football match on a Sunday afternoon. Pause in the fishing village of **Howth** on your way north to Belfast, and walk through a gloriously overgrown hillside rhododendron garden with a stunning sea panorama.

MEATH AND LOUTH

The first Neolithic farmers settled in the fertile Boyne River valley in what is now County Meath, and the awesome megalithic monuments they left behind are archaeologists' primary source of info. The best-known passage tomb at the necropolis of **Brú na Bóinne** is **Newgrange,** which predates the Great Pyramid at Giza by half a millennium. The guided tour and slick-but-informative interpretive center are no less worthwhile for their popularity. For a glimpse of unexcavated, unrestored, downright spooky hilltop passage tombs, visit the more remote **Loughcrew Cairns.** "Wee" County Louth offers two of the country's more distinguished monastic sites at **Mellifont Abbey** and **Monasterboice,** and a cruise on **Carlingford Lough** is another highlight. You can also go on a guided tour of the **Battle of the Boyne site** outside Drogheda.

WICKLOW AND KILDARE

County Wicklow is often called the "Garden of Ireland" for its green vales and Italianate terraces, most notably at **Powerscourt.** It's amazing how you can drive less than half an hour south from Dublin and find yourself in the gorse-dotted mountains of **Wicklow Mountains National Park.** After the big city, you'll feel like you're in another country altogether. The gem of the park is the early Christian monastery at **Glendalough,** "Glen of the Two Lakes," which began as St. Kevin's hermitage in the 6th century. The national park also has some of the oldest walking trails in the country. The flat plains of County Kildare are pretty uninteresting in comparison. This is horse-breeding country, though the vast **Bog of Allen,** Ireland's largest, stretches across northern Kildare. You'll find Ireland's most spectacular Palladian manor at **Castletown,** built for the Donegal-born Speaker of the Irish House of Commons, William Conolly.

THE SOUTHEAST

County Wexford in Ireland's southeast corner is the sunniest in the country; it also boasts Europe's oldest **lighthouse** at **Hook Head,** which you can climb for a fantastic view over the Waterford estuary to the distant Comeragh and Galtee mountains. Just north of laid-back Wexford Town is the country's longest beach, **Curracloe,** and there's another Blue Flag strand at **Rosslare** to the south. Wexford saw the most fighting in the 1798 uprising that led to the Act of Union with Britain; Enniscorthy's **National 1798 Centre** provides a fine introduction to this chapter in Irish history. County Carlow is pretty nondescript in comparison, though the gargantuan **Browne's Hill Dolmen** is worth a detour. Kilkenny City offers plenty of medieval atmosphere in its narrow winding streets, the wonderfully restored **Kilkenny Castle,** and **St. Canice's Cathedral** with its climbable round tower. The county is dotted with quiet, picturesque villages along the River Nore, and **Jerpoint Abbey,** a short drive south of the city, is one of the country's finest monastic ruins.

CORK

Cork is Ireland's largest county, and its (however industry-heavy) capital city has enjoyed a cultural renaissance in recent years. Climb the tower and play a tune on the bells of **St. Anne's Church.** Admire the Harry Clarke windows and whimsical floor mosaics at the neo-Hiberno-Romanesque **Honan Chapel** at University College Cork. Then, if you're not churched out, visit the neo-Gothic **St. Fin Barre's Cathedral,** Cork's own version of Notre Dame. **Kinsale** is one of Cork's most touristy towns for its reputation as "Ireland's Gourmet Capital"; if serenity is what you're after, head out to West Cork with its three lovely peninsulas—the **Beara, Sheep's Head,** and **Mizen Head,** where you can go sea-kayaking or hill-walking to your heart's content. The forest park/nature reserves at **Gougane Barra** and **Glengarriff** are lovely, too, and from Glengarriff you can board a ferry for the sumptuous Italianate garden on **Garnish Island.**

KERRY

It may be Ireland's most touristy county, but that's because it's also one of the most breathtakingly beautiful places on God's green earth. The rugged **Dingle Peninsula** is sprinkled with prehistoric and monastic ruins, among them the mortarless-yet-watertight **Gallarus Oratory,** and Dingle Town offers plenty of gourmet restaurants and lively musical pubs. The **Iveragh Peninsula,** looped by the famous **Ring of Kerry,** has a few hidden places you'll want to seek out, from the Skellig Ring to the quiet highlands. A visit to the 6th-century monastery perched atop jagged **Skellig Michael** is well worth the nausea of a rough ferry ride. Surely Kerry is a slice of heaven; you just have to do a little extra planning to escape the crowds.

THE MIDLANDS

The Midlands get a bad rap from tourists and natives alike, as though there's nothing worth seeing amid these fertile fields and boggy hills. The monastic city of **Clonmacnoise** on the River Shannon is the biggest exception, and there are plenty of other places worth a small detour en route to the southwest. What the Midlands region lacks in high-voltage tourist attractions, it more than compensates for in opportunities to veer well off the beaten track—be it on signposted **hill-walking routes** or in truly **authentic pubs,** nary a shamrock in sight, where the occasional out-of-towner is greeted with pleasant surprise.

TIPPERARY AND WATERFORD

The fields of Counties Tipperary and Waterford are some of the island's most fertile; at the center of Tipperary's "Golden Vale" is the awe-inspiring **Rock of Cashel,** where Patrick baptized the king of Munster. This hilltop ecclesiastical complex consists of a round tower, Romanesque chapel, Gothic cathedral, and 15th-century tower house. Tipperary's rich farmlands were prized by English settlers, and there are castles in various states of repair. The most remarkable of these are the still-impregnable **Cahir Castle** and the Elizabethan **Ormonde Castle.** The highlights of the sunny Waterford coast are the breathtaking ruins of **St. Declan's Monastery** at the start of a bracing cliff walk, and the pretty village of **Dunmore East,** perfect for an afternoon or golfing or windsurfing. Dunmore East is a short drive or bus ride from Waterford City, home of the world-famous crystal factory.

CLARE AND LIMERICK

County Clare on the west coast is best known for the **Cliffs of Moher,** alternatively known as Tour Bus Central. The view is pretty, though it's by no means the country's finest vista. Try to visit in low season if you can. West of here stretches a deceptively barren-looking limestone plateau, the **Burren,** where you'll find another famous sight, **Poulnabrone,** Ireland's best-known Neolithic portal tomb, along with various other ring forts and castles. Just north of the cliffs is lively **Doolin,** renowned for its musical pubs, though ongoing holiday home construction is starting to spoil its charm. On the Burren's southern fringe is **Dysert O'Dea,** a ruined church with one of Ireland's most striking Romanesque doorways, plus a remarkable high cross in the pasture beyond. Other monastic sites here include the sprawling castle-cum-friary at **Quin Abbey,** an even more remarkable set of high crosses at **Kilfenora,** and St. Molua's Oratory in pretty Shannonside **Killaloe.** Limerick City is the republic's third-largest, and it's also the least attractive; never-theless, it's worth passing through for the **Hunt Museum,** the finest collection of antiquities outside Dublin. South of the city is placid **Lough Gur,** its shores dotted with the remains of pre-historic settlements. The Shannon Airport is in Clare near the Limerick border, and nearby **Bunratty Castle** falls into the touristy-but-fun category; a kitschy medieval banquet here's a fine way to spend your last night in Ireland.

GALWAY

Sparkling Galway City draws nearly as many tourists as Dublin, yet the place manages to keep from feeling "touristy." Still, its medieval **Shop Street** is wall-to-wall people during the city's many summer festivals. Head west to the brooding heather-covered mountains and glittering black lakes of **Connemara,** not so much the bastion of traditional Irish culture it once was, but still a must-see region. Highlights include the early Victorian manor house **Kylemore Abbey,** now an exclusive boarding school; and **Killary Harbour,** Ireland's only fjord, which attracts outdoorsy travelers to its excellent adventure center outside the laid-back village of Leenane. Reachable from Rossaveal in south Connemara or Doolin in County Clare, the three **Aran Islands** in Galway Bay—a Gaeltacht (Irish-speaking) region—are just as enchanting. South Galway near the Clare border offers its own delights: **Dunguaire Castle** in the postcard-perfect seaside village of **Kinvara;** the poet Yeats's restored summer home, a 16th-century tower house he christened **Thoor Ballylee;** and the sprawling monastic site at **Kilmacduagh** with its leaning round tower. Eastern Galway is mostly flat farmland, though the fascinating Romanesque doorway at **Clonfert Cathedral** is certainly worth a detour en route to Galway City from the Midlands.

THE NORTHWEST

Far less traveled than Galway, Mayo feels—in the shoulder and low seasons, anyway—like you have the county to yourself. Whether climbing **Croagh Patrick** (one of Ireland's most popular pilgrimages), surfing on **Carrownisky Strand,** or exploring **Achill Island** (Ireland's largest at 145 square kilometers), most visitors base themselves in the pleasant Georgian town of **Westport.** Northern Mayo is far wilder, with the **Mullet Peninsula,** often blanketed in haze, and the dramatic blowhole and rock stack at **Downpatrick Head.** County Sligo is touted as "Yeats country" because it was the home of the poet's mother. Though Yeats didn't spend much time here, he often mentioned places like **Innisfree** on **Lough Gill** in his poetry, and he asked to be reburied in the parish churchyard at **Drumcliffe** where his great-grandfather had been rector. Lively **Sligo Town** is on the upswing, with a few funky pubs and a terrific avant-garde theater company. Sligo also has several important megalithic burial sites, including **Carrowmore** a short bike ride from town and **Creevykeel** north on the Donegal road; creepiest of all is the necropolis at **Carrowkeel** in the south near the Roscommon border. Make time for a long soak at one of Sligo's **seaweed baths;** there's one in Strandhill near Sligo Town and another in Enniscrone on the scenic route west to Mayo.

DONEGAL

Ireland's northernmost county, Donegal is nearly cut off from the republic by the six counties of Northern Ireland (it's only bordered by a slice of County Leitrim republic-side); also, Donegal is one of three Ulster counties in the Irish Republic (along with Cavan and Monaghan). Weekenders from Derry or Belfast appreciate its remote beauty more than the average international traveler. Since it's so far north, most tourists never make it up here. It's their loss: Donegal's **rugged landscapes** are every bit as dramatic as the far more touristy Connemara or Dingle, and the scenery is all the more delightful when you have fewer tourists to share it with. Make the tough five-hour slog across the **Slieve League** sea cliffs in the Gaeltacht parish of **Glencolmcille,** home to one of Ireland's more established language summer schools. You'll hear plenty more Irish spoken farther north in **Gweedore,** where crimson sunsets stain the so-called **Bloody Foreland.** East of here is **Glenveagh National Park** with its "poisoned glen," Victorian castle, and Donegal's highest peak, **Mount Errigal.** Near the Derry border is the county's most important archaeological site, an early Christian ring fort known as **Grianán of Aileách.**

BELFAST, ANTRIM, AND DERRY

Along with Kerry in the southwest, County Antrim is generally considered Ireland's most picturesque. **Giant's Causeway** is the myth-inspired name for a series of 40,000 hexagonal basalt columns extending into the ocean; though it's certainly a natural wonder, it isn't as dramatic as it looks in tourist board photographs. The coastal drive from the clifftop **Mussenden Temple** in eastern Derry to the Giant's Causeway, to the exhilarating **Carrick-a-Rede rope bridge,** and along the fabled **Nine Glens of Antrim** is a highlight of any trip to the Emerald Isle. Though the cities of **Derry** and **Belfast** have endured horrific acts of terrorism from both unionist and republican paramilitary groups in past decades, both are perfectly safe these days. Just be forewarned that the sectarian graffiti, marches, and other divisive political displays might leave you feeling pretty uncomfortable. For an unvarnished history lesson in two hours or less, take a **Black Taxi tour** through Belfast's working-class neighborhoods; and of course, be sure to check out Derry's **Bogside peace murals** after you've made the nine-furlong circuit around the intact **city walls.**

ATLANTIC OCEAN

Celtic Sea

DOWN AND ARMAGH

The pretty coastline of County Down is overshadowed by Antrim's Causeway Coast and Nine Glens, but it's every bit as enjoyable. Wander through spooky **Grey Abbey** or the formal gardens at **Mount Stewart House** on the Ards Peninsula, or go scuba diving in **Strangford Lough.** Near the border with the republic are the **Mourne Mountains,** perfect for walking or cycling. Nestled within is Belfast's reservoir, the **Silent Valley,** so called for the eerie absence of birds. It's said that all the noise and drilling involved in building the dam and reservoir frightened them off. The city of Armagh is considered Ireland's ecclesiastical capital for two reasons: Not only did Patrick use it as his base in the mid-5th century, but the city is also the headquarters of both the Catholic and Protestant primates. If you ask the way to **St. Patrick's Cathedral,** you'll have to specify which one; the Anglican cathedral is on the site of Patrick's original church, and the ornate, twin-spired neo-Gothic Catholic cathedral is up a long flight of steep stairs. Northern Armagh is known for its roses and apple blossoms; May and June are the best times to visit, when both are in full bloom.

ATLANTIC OCEAN

Celtic Sea

TYRONE AND FERMANAGH

Two of Northern Ireland's three landlocked counties, Tyrone and Fermanagh are relatively untouristy. Tyrone's primary attraction is the excellent **Ulster-American Folk Park,** which provides a glimpse of 19th-century everyday life for kids and an engaging refresher course in American history for adults. Northern Tyrone features the isolated, rather eerie **Sperrin Mountains.** The easygoing riverside market town of Enniskillen makes a good base for exploring the **holy islands of Lough Erne,** of which **Devenish Island** is the best known and most substantial. There's also **Enniskillen Castle** with its fairy-tale, Scottish-style water gate (and over-the-top military museum), and near the Fermanagh-Donegal border is the famous **Belleek Pottery,** which has been producing porcelain ornaments since 1857.

Planning Your Trip

If you take only one piece of advice regarding this trip, let it be this: Relax! Don't try to see seven counties in as many days. If you do that, you'll spend half of each day behind the wheel of a rental car. It's worth noting that when the Irish go on vacation, they tend to pick one place and stay put. So choose two or three places you really want to see—say, Mayo and Galway—and see them properly. Savor them. And be sure to factor in a couple more days for poor weather conditions (particularly if you want to take a ferry to any offshore islands) or a case of love at first sight: "If we can't buy a holiday cottage here then can we at least spend one more night?" That happens a lot. Keep your itinerary flexible. Granted, it's not so easy to do in high season when you've got to book accommodations well in advance and canceled bookings still show up on your credit card, but in the off or shoulder seasons, to a great extent, you can afford to plan as you go.

WHEN TO GO

July and August are peak months, but the sheer volume of tourists in Kerry, Clare, and other popular destinations can be downright irritating. Ireland can be beautiful at any time of year, but it's best to examine your own proclivities before you purchase your tickets. Planning to do any water sports or camping? Crowds or no, June through August is your window (though May and September may also suit, depending on the activity). Do those smog-spewing tour buses really get on your nerves? Visit during the spring or autumn—the "shoulder seasons"—or in wintertime, better yet. Want to get off the beaten track? Late spring or early autumn is best, because transportation can be limited to more remote locales (especially the various islands off the west coast) between November and April. Note that late autumn can be the rainiest time of year.

© CAMILLE DEANGELIS

Dún Chonchúir on Inis Meáin, the least traveled of the three Aran Islands

There is much to be said for a wintertime visit. New Year's is a good choice; listening to a live traditional music session with a pint in hand sure beats watching the ball drop (which, incidentally, is made from 485 kilograms of Waterford crystal). Irish winters are milder than those of New England—the low/high temperatures run 0–11°C (32–52 °F)—and the rare snowfall wreaks both magic and chaos (the former in both schoolchildren and landscape; the latter in the national bus system). Aer Lingus and other airline carriers post their lowest fares in January and February, and many hotels, B&Bs, and hostels offer better off-season rates, though many others close altogether. Visiting a touristy destination in the dead of winter, when you feel like you have the place all to yourself, can be strangely exhilarating—and there are some winter days that dawn sunny and mild.

You may also wish to time your visit to coincide with a particular event or festival—there's one for every interest, and attending events while you're in town can really enhance your vacation. For instance, there's the Dublin Theatre Festival in early October (a must for drama buffs), the International Jazz Festival in Cork in late October, and the Cúirt International Festival of Literature in Galway in late April.

WHAT TO TAKE

Bring lots of comfortable clothing to wear in layers, as well as a waterproof jacket. Pack a couple of sweaters even in summertime—but don't let the threat of rain keep you from applying sunblock. On lucky days when the temperature's in the high 20s C (80s F), you'll find the beaches (or "strands") crowded with pasty-skinned locals of all ages reveling in the sun.

Dress is quite informal, even in the fancier pubs and restaurants. Though raingear is obviously sensible, you will find that the Irish don't wear galoshes unless farming is their business. Getting soaked on your way home is something of an Irish ritual, followed by the ritual of tea-drinking while warming and drying oneself by the fire. Throw a few Kleenex travel-packs in with your skivvies.

But if you plan to do a lot of hill-walking or other outdoor activities, you might want to bring a pair of Wellingtons along with your hiking boots. If you don't mind the occasional case of damp feet, however, keep your load light. Umbrellas are nearly useless, as the wind can make the rain seem like it's falling sideways from every direction. But be optimistic, like the Irish, and pack your sunglasses.

Hill-walkers and cyclists should also bring the usual compass, flashlight, medical mini-kit, pocketknife (in your checked luggage), and so forth.

If you bring a digital camera, laptop, cell phone, or other device, be sure to purchase a plug adapter at an electronics store before you leave. (The Irish plug has two horizontal prongs and one vertical.)

With the advent of the worldwide ATM there is little need for traveler's checks (though your bank will charge a nominal conversion fee, with traveler's checks you're charged both on purchase and redemption).

Explore Ireland

THE 21-DAY BEST OF IRELAND

Three weeks might seem like a long time, but it's not nearly long enough! Starting and ending in Dublin, this whirlwind "best of" itinerary leaves out plenty of other worthwhile places. You'll need a rental car, since there's no time left over for waiting around for Bus Éireann. And if you aren't fortunate enough to have three weeks' vacation time, this strategy has been subdivided into northern and southern legs.

THE NORTHERN LEG

Day 1

Drive from Dublin Airport to **Brú na Bóinne** and take the **Newgrange** tour. Then check out the **Hill of Tara** and **Trim Castle** before heading north to Louth to see the exquisite high crosses at **Monasterboice**. Spend the night in medieval **Carlingford,** with its imposing, inaccessible castle ruins overlooking the harbor.

Day 2

Take a scenic drive through the **Mourne Mountains** in County Down, have lunch in **Strangford,** a lovely village on an eponymous lake, and spend the night at Anna's House in **Lisbane,** a short drive south of Belfast—unofficially the best B&B on the island, with an exquisite two-acre garden.

Day 3

Arrive in Belfast and take the famed **Black Taxi tour.** Spend the afternoon at the **Botanic Gardens** or **Cave Hill Country Park** if the weather's fine, but if not, take the **Belfast City Hall** tour. After a terrific meal at one of the city's many outstanding restaurants and gastro-pubs, see what's on at the **Grand Opera House** or **Ulster Orchestra.**

Day 4

Head north from Belfast on the A2, driving past the **Glens of Antrim** to the **Carrick-a-Rede rope bridge,** once traversed daily by local salmon fishermen but now a worthwhile tourist draw. Spend the night in quiet **Ballintoy** or cheerful, family-friendly **Ballycastle.**

Day 5

Drive the **Causeway Coast** route today, spending about two hours at the **Giant's Causeway** with its 40,000 hexagonal basalt columns. Have lunch at The Nook, then proceed west to **Downhill** to check out the ruins of Bishop Hervey's estate and the charming **Mussenden Temple.** End the day in **Derry City,** at quirky Peadar O'Donnell's pub.

Day 6

Walk the **Derry City walls,** then the **Bogside peace murals.** Continue west into Donegal, pausing at the hilltop ring fort of **Grianán of Aileách** before driving north to

Killarney National Park

the **Inishowen Peninsula.** Spend the evening at the fabulous McGrory's pub in **Culdaff,** where you can catch a well-known musical act any night of the week.

Day 7

Another long but rewarding day's drive: Travel from Inishowen southwest to **Gweedore,** with its dramatic "Bloody Foreland" viewing point, and **Glenveagh National Park,** where you can traipse through the mistakenly named "Poisoned Glen." Pull into **Donegal Town,** home to Donegal Castle, once the seat of the powerful O'Donnell clan.

Day 8

Before leaving town, visit the **Donegal Craft Village,** which offers loads of excellent gifts from handloomed tweed scarves to funky bog sculptures. Pause in County Sligo for a **seaweed bath,** then proceed south into Mayo. Spend the night in lively **Westport.**

Day 9

Drive five minutes west to **Murrisk** and climb **Croagh Patrick,** which offers stunning views on a clear day, then reward yourself with lunch at The Tavern (probably the best restaurant in the county, both food- and service-wise). Drive through the haunting **Doolough Valley** to **Leenane,** tucked at the end of Killary Fjord.

Day 10

Do the **Connemara** tour, hitting neo-Gothic **Kylemore Abbey** and lovely **Connemara National Park** before having lunch in **Clifden.** Drive east to **Galway City** and revel in the nightlife.

Day 11

Make a day trip to **Inis Mór,** the largest Aran Island, driving to Rossaveal for the ferry. Once on the island, rent a bike and pedal out to **Dún Aengus** and the **Seven Churches.** Have a late lunch at Lios Aengus, a friendly café with excellent stuffed spuds, in the port village of **Kilronan;** save room for the banoffee pie. Back in Galway, enjoy dinner at Nimmo's Winebar and Restaurant (informal, but reservations are smart).

© CAMILLE DEANGELIS

view from Croagh Patrick

Day 12

Rise early, pack a picnic lunch, and drive east to **Clonmacnoise** in County Offaly (making a quick detour at **Clonfert Cathedral** to check out the magnificent Romanesque doorway). Go on the excellent guided tour at St. Ciarán's monastic city, then have your picnic. Drive west again to the **Burren** in County Clare, and base yourself in **Doolin** or **Corofin.** Depending on your interests, you can visit **Dysert O'Dea,** a church ruin with another astounding Romanesque doorway and nearby high cross; vast **Quin Abbey,** built on the foundations of an earlier castle; **Knappogue Castle,** museum by day and medieval banquet venue by night; the **Craggaunowen Project,** with replicas of Neolithic dwellings; the **Burren Perfumery and Floral Centre,** where local scent-makers distill the fragrances of indigenous flowers; or the dramatic **Cliffs of Moher**—and whatever you don't have time for, you can always visit tomorrow morning. The famous Cliffs will probably be at the top of your list, but if the weather is bad you should skip them (as you won't be able to see anything in the rain and mist). The best foul-weather options are Knappogue, Craggaunowen, and the Burren Perfumery, but unless you *really* aren't into monastic ruins, Dysert O'Dea and Quin Abbey are arguably the most worthwhile destinations.

If you've only got two weeks for your trip, end it here, departing from **Shannon Airport** (in southern Clare).

THE SOUTHERN LEG
Day 13

Rise early to finish up yesterday's sightseeing; or if you're just doing the southern leg, arrive at the Shannon and head for the Cliffs of Moher, a 75-minute drive from the airport. Take the car ferry from Killimer in south Clare to Tarbert in north Kerry, and proceed south through Tralee to the **Dingle Peninsula.** Drive **Slea Head,** visit **Gallarus Oratory** and the **Riasc Monastic Settlement,** and spend the night in **Dingle Town** after a fine meal and some live trad.

Day 14

Drive from Dingle to **Killarney National Park** and go for a walk or bicycle ride—this is one of Ireland's most popular tourist destinations, and you'll see why as soon as you arrive. Spend the night in **Killarney Town,** and have yourself a fine meal at Lord Kenmare's.

Day 15

From Killarney, do the **Ring of Kerry** counterclockwise; the earlier your start, the fewer tour buses you'll get stuck behind. Have another lovely dinner in **Kenmare,** one of Kerry's two unofficial gourmet capitals (the other being Dingle, of course!).

Day 16

Do the **Beara Peninsula** today, driving the dazzling **Healy Pass** from Lauragh in Kerry to Adrigole in Cork, all relatively quiet little places even in summertime. End up in **Glengarriff,** rambling through the forest park and up the steep steps to **Lady Bantry's Lookout.** Or take the ferry to **Garnish Island** with its formal Italianate garden.

Day 17

Drive from Glengarriff to **Kinsale** for lunch at one of its famed gourmet restaurants. Finish the day in **Cork City,** climbing the tower at **St. Anne's Church** to ring the bells. Also make a point of visiting the lovely **Honan Chapel** at University College Cork. Take in a play or concert at one of Cork's many fine theaters.

Day 18

Head east to **Ardmore** in County Waterford, and take a short walk uphill from the village's main street to the spectacular ruins of **St. Declan's Monastery.** Then go for the gorgeous five-kilometer cliff walk all around the headland, ending up back on the main street.

Day 19

Drive north to **Cashel** in County Tipperary, and visit the **Rock of Cashel** ("St. Patrick's Rock"); don't miss the spooky Romanesque Cormac's Chapel. Have dinner at the atmospheric Chez Hans, a worthwhile splurge if there ever was one.

Day 20

Drive east from Cashel to **Kilkenny City** and visit **Kilkenny Castle.** Have lunch in Kilkenny, then head south to Thomastown to see **Jerpoint Abbey.** Then drive through Carlow and Wexford north to **Wicklow Mountains National Park;** stay near **Glendalough.**

Day 21

Spend the early morning on one of Glendalough's shorter walking trails, take one last stroll through the monastic city, and then head north for **Powerscourt House and Gardens.** Spend your last night back in **Dublin.**

WILD AND RUGGED IRELAND

This two-week sports sampler includes a couple of days at one of Ireland's best adventure centers, a diving excursion, a day's surfing, a five-hour cliff walk, and a climb up Mount Errigal in Donegal's Glenveagh National Park, with an occasional lie-in day to rest up. There are two routes up Errigal: a relatively easy one for "tourists" and another for serious hikers. This travel plan includes a few opportunities for getting off the beaten track, particularly in Mayo and Donegal—and it's one itinerary for which you don't need a rental car (just note that several of the Bus Éireann routes you'll be relying on operate only between late June and early September). There are fine hostels at each destination.

Day 1

Destination #1 is **Killary Adventure Company** outside **Leenane** in Connemara. Fly into Shannon and take the Citylink bus to Galway City. (Bus Éireann service in Connemara is pretty spotty.) Even if you've arranged for accommodations at the center, take the cheap-and-cheerful Sleepzone shuttle bus from Bothar na mBán to Sleepzone Connemara in Leenane; the adventure center is a stone's throw away. Stock up on groceries before leaving Galway.

Day 2

Spend the better part of the day in a kayak on **Killary Harbour.**

Day 3

You've got plenty more options for your second day at Killary: sailboarding, abseiling (rappelling), rock-climbing, water-skiing, clay pigeon shooting, archery…you can even sail a Hobie Cat.

Day 4

Go diving with **Scuba Dive West** in **Renvyle,** west of Leenane. (You may be able to get a ride from Killary, but if not, you can always ring for a taxi.) Stick with your Leenane accommodation for simplicity's sake.

Day 5

Take Bus Éireann route #61 from Leenane to **Westport.** Chill out here and arrange your transport (by taxi) and equipment rental with **Surf Mayo** (at Carrownisky Strand near Louisburgh) for the following day.

Day 6

Pack a lunch and head for the strand. Mayo five-oh! Back in Westport in the evening, treat yourself to a meal at the excellent Mediterraneo restaurant across the street from Matt Molloy's pub.

Day 7

So long, Westport. Head north on Bus Éireann route #66/64 to **Donegal Town** (changing buses at Sligo) and spend the night there, since you probably won't make the last bus to Glencolmcille.

Day 8

Ride the Bus Éireann route #490 (on McGeehan coaches) to **Glencolmcille,** where you can stay at either the modern Malinbeg Hostel

a Connemara sunset

© GENEVIEVE HANDY

or the quirky Dooey Hostel (though it's not as convenient for hiking Slieve League, the best pub in the parish is just down the road). Go for an easy walk—tomorrow's going to be challenging.

Day 9

Walk **Slieve League,** Europe's highest sea cliffs. You'll need a lift to get to Bunglás, the start of the five-hour hike; if you stay at the Dooey Hostel, you'll need a ride both ways. William O'Brien provides a minivan taxi service in the area, and he's accustomed to taking hikers. Spend another night in Glencolmcille.

Day 10

This is where spotty bus service necessitates an annoyingly circuitous route. Take Bus Éireann (routes #490/480) from Glencolmcille to Letterkenny via Donegal Town. The tiny village of **Dunlewey** has two hostels in the shadow of Mount Errigal in the **Glenveagh National Park** but no bus service apart from the Donegal Airport Bus (between Letterkenny

and the airport just south of Gweedore). Ring Cronan Mac, the shuttle operator, to see if he can take you from Letterkenny to Dunlewey; otherwise you can ride the Lough Swilly bus from Letterkenny to Gweedore and hire a taxi from there.

Day 11

Climb **Mount Errigal**—and if you've got energy to spare, go for an easy ramble through the park. Spend another night in Dunlewey.

Day 12

Treat yourself to a B&B in **Gweedore,** and kick back and enjoy some of the country's best traditional music in one of the pubs in **Bunbeg.**

Day 13

Save yourself the long bus ride to **Dublin** and fly there on Aer Arann from the Donegal Airport near Gweedore (you can get there with the Donegal Airport Bus). Spend your last night in Dublin.

OF CASTLES AND KINGS

This itinerary features a cross-section of the most exemplary medieval fortresses, tower houses, neoclassical manors, and other structures that fall into the "castle" catch-all. A few of the castle museums are filled with period furnishings (of questionable accuracy at times, but the furniture, tapestries, and so forth can still give you a sense of how the castle's original inhabitants lived). Admission charges (usually benefiting a restoration or maintenance fund) can be pricey, but if the architecture, archaeology, and history of Irish castles interest you then it's well worth the cost. So as not to wear you out traveling, this list concentrates on castles in the southern half of the country, but you could easily make an alternative plan for Ulster.

You'll need a car to do the whole itinerary, but it can be easily tweaked for bus travel; while all the castles covered here are accessible by bus, you'll have to factor in wait time. Keeping in mind, too, that bus journeys inevitably take longer than traveling by car, plan to visit only the five or six castles that seem the most interesting to you. To follow the full itinerary by bus will take several extra days.

Day 1

Arrive in **Dublin** and take it easy, visiting **Dublin Castle** after lunching at Chez Max just outside the castle gates. Do the **Chester Beatty Library** while you're here (it's on the castle grounds).

Day 2

From Dublin, make a day trip to **Trim Castle,** the country's largest Anglo-Norman fortress, in County Meath. Administered by Dúchas, Trim boasts some of the best-informed tour guides in the Republic.

Day 3

Rise early and depart Dublin for **Castletown** in County Kildare. Then head to **Birr Castle Demesne** in County Offaly for an afternoon ramble through the formal gardens as well as a demonstration of the Great Telescope. Eat and sleep (or at least eat) at the excellent Spinners Townhouse, and be sure to have a pint at the Chestnut.

Day 4

Head south to **Kilkenny City** to visit the exquisitely renovated and refurnished **Kilkenny Castle,** the highlight of which is the Long Gallery with its tableau of ancestral portraits. Budget travelers should stay at **Foulksrath Castle,** an An Óige hostel 11 kilometers north of the city (it has family rooms as well).

Day 5

Head south from Kilkenny to **Ormonde**

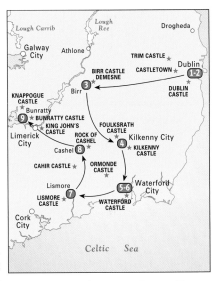

Castle in Carrick-on-Suir, County Tipperary, pausing at the fortified ruin of **Kells Priory** if time allows. Continue south to **Waterford City**—and if budget allows, stay at **Waterford Castle.** It's very formal, but of all the castle-hotels in Ireland this one is the best by far.

Day 6

Spend the day in Waterford, visiting the pepperpot-shaped **Reginald's Tower** (now a historical museum) and the famous **crystal factory.**

Rock of Cashel

© CAMILLE DEANGELIS

Day 7

Head west from Waterford to **Lismore Castle** and enjoy a stroll through the gardens. Then check out the nearby gate towers at **Ballysaggartmore,** "the castle that never was," surrounded by eerily quiet woodland.

Day 8

Head north to **Cahir Castle,** and afterward visit the **Swiss Cottage** for a glimpse at how the Anglo-Irish gentry played at living quaintly. Drive north again to **Cashel** and enjoy a gourmet meal at Chez Hans (ring ahead for a reservation).

Day 9

Visit the **Rock of Cashel,** originally the seat of the kings of Munster. If you have time, stop by **King John's Castle** in Limerick on your way to **Bunratty.**

Day 10

First thing in the morning, purchase a banquet-tour combo ticket for **Bunratty Castle,** which will save you four euros off the regular admission charge (if you're visiting in high season, be sure to buy this ticket on the website a couple months in advance, and just pick it up when you get there). Since you'll be leaving in the morning from Shannon Airport, you'll probably want to attend the first dinner at 5:45 P.M. Then take the castle tour. In the afternoon, drive to **Knappogue Castle** (and **Quin Abbey**) in Quin village, and if you have time left over visit the ruined church at **Dysert O'Dea** and the nearby museum of antiquities in a 15th-century tower house. Drive back to Bunratty for the medieval banquet—and enjoy the kitsch!

SACRED SITES AND PILGRIMAGES

Whether your interest is religious or archaeological, this itinerary covers some of the most important cathedrals and monastic ruins in Ireland. The Skellig Islands—which offer the remains of an early Christian monastery atop a jagged peak jutting out of the ocean—will be the highlight of your trip, but be sure to factor in an extra day (or two) in case the weather's bad on the morning you wish to visit. A rental car is pretty much essential for this one.

Day 1

Fly into **Dublin** and visit **Christ Church Cathedral, St. Patrick's Cathedral,** and **St. Michan's Church,** three Anglican churches (all but the last have pre-Reformation histories, and thus may be of interest to Catholics as well). True pilgrims will want to visit the shrine of St. Valentine at **Our Lady of Mount Carmel.**

Day 2

Make a day trip to County Louth to visit **Mellifont Abbey,** once one of the most prosperous Cistercian abbeys on the island (guided tours available in high season) and **Monasterboice,** which offers scant ecclesiastical ruins and Ireland's two most important high crosses.

Day 3

Quit Dublin for **Glendalough** in the **Wicklow Mountains National Park.** Spend the night here so you can experience the site first thing in the morning, before the arrival of the tour buses. St. Kevin's monastic city is even more memorable when few others are around to share the experience.

Day 4

Rise early and take a walk along Glendalough's **Upper and Lower Lakes.** Then make the drive to **Kilkenny City,** where you'll base yourself while visiting the area's monastic remains.

Day 5

South of the city, tour **Jerpoint Abbey** and examine its intricate carvings. Also visit **Kells Priory** and other smaller, more secluded ruins like the **Kilfane and Kilree Churches.**

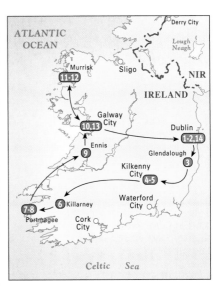

Day 6

A couple days from now, weather permitting, you'll visit Skellig Michael off the coast of the Iveragh Peninsula in County Kerry. To break up the journey from Kilkenny, spend the night in **Killarney.** Pop inside the austere, cavernous, Catholic **St. Mary's Cathedral.**

Day 7

Rise early and visit **Muckross Abbey** in **Killarney National Park.** Before skipping town, check out the Harry Clarke studio window and ornate Flemish-style altar at the **Franciscan Friary.** Spend the night in **Portmagee.**

Day 8

Take the ferry from Portmagee to **Skellig Michael.** Bring a picnic lunch to enjoy on a grassy peak outside the monastery, with its beehive huts and tiny whitewashed chapel, and take the excellent tour. Spend another night in Portmagee.

Day 9

Head through northern Kerry and take the Tarbert–Killimer ferry to County Clare. Visit **Quin Abbey,** the Franciscan **Ennis Friary,** and the church at **Dysert O'Dea,** and spend the night in **Ennis** or **Corofin.** Guided tours of Quin Abbey and the Ennis Friary are available in the summer months.

Day 10

Keep driving north to **Galway City,** stopping at the **Kilmacduagh** monastic site en route, with its tall, complete, but precariously tilted round tower. Take time to enjoy the Galway nightlife.

Day 11

Drive through northern Connemara into County Mayo. Spend the night in **Murrisk** and enjoy a wonderful meal at The Tavern, just across the road from the ruins of 15th-century Murrisk Abbey.

Day 12

Climb **Croagh Patrick.** It's two hours up and an hour and a half down—it's a challenging climb if you aren't in great shape. Stay another night in Murrisk, but spend the evening listening to a trad session at one of Westport's many musical pubs.

Day 13

Return to Galway and visit its **cathedrals,** both named for St. Nicholas: the Catholic cathedral just over the Salmon Weir Bridge and the Anglican church on Lombard Street.

Day 14

Your last day brings another highlight: **Clonmacnoise.** Head east from Galway, and if you have time, stop at Clonfert to admire the medieval cathedral's stunning Romanesque doorway. Then proceed to Clonmacnoise. Founded by St. Ciarán, this was once Ireland's greatest monastic city, and its ruins alongside the Shannon are truly fascinating. Administered by Dúchas, Clonmacnoise always has guided tours available. Be sure to take a walk down to the **Nuns' Church,** which has another remarkable Hiberno-Romanesque doorway. Drive back to Dublin.

St. Kevin's Church, Glendalough

© CAMILLE DEANGELIS

GHOSTS OF ANCIENT IRELAND

Amateur archaeologists can have a field day on the Emerald Isle—pun intended! If you don't have a rental car, you can still do much of this itinerary (Loughcrew and Carrowkeel being the only places you'll have to skip, as public transportation is nonexistent and taxis unfeasible). You'll be flying into Dublin and out of Shannon for this one (which typically isn't any more expensive).

Day 1

Spend your first day in **Dublin** at the **National Museum of Archaeology and History,** which houses the vast majority of the country's treasures from prehistory to the present.

Day 2

Base yourself in County Meath for the next two nights. Visit **Brú na Bóinne** today, Ireland's most important Neolithic site. Newgrange is the most famous passage tomb here, though Knowth is also accessible by guided tour, and you can take a walk around unexcavated Dowth.

Day 3

Visit the **Loughcrew Cairns** for a sense of what Newgrange might have been like before it was excavated and turned into the country's most popular attraction.

Day 4

From Meath, drive northwest to County Sligo, stopping first at **Carrowkeel** just over the Roscommon border. This one vies with Loughcrew for Ireland's creepiest megalithic cemetery. Spend the night in **Sligo Town.**

Day 5

Visit the **Carrowmore** and **Creevykeel** sites outside Sligo Town; these prehistoric tombs aren't as dramatically situated as Carrowkeel or Loughcrew, but they are interesting in their own right. Spend a second night here.

Day 6

Drive west from Sligo to northern Mayo to visit the excellent interpretive center at **Céide Fields.** Heck, why not stop in **Enniscrone** first for a seaweed bath? Then you can spend

the night in **Ballycastle,** a very quiet one-street town (and the closest to Céide Fields).

Day 7

Drive south from Ballycastle to **Galway City.** This is going to be the least interesting day of your trip, but no matter—tomorrow, Inis Mór is going to be the #1 highlight. This, the largest of the Aran Islands, is rich in prehistoric and early Christian ruins (the clifftop fort of Dún Aengus is the most popular, though there's plenty more to see besides) and still surprisingly traditional in attitude.

Day 8

Take the ferry from Rossaveal to **Inis Mór** and spend the afternoon at **Dún Dúbhchathair** (The Black Fort). This ruin is much less popular than Dún Aengus, but just as picturesque.

Creevykeel Court Cairn

© CAMILLE DEANGELIS

Day 9

Rise early and get to **Dún Aengus** before the morning ferries arrive full of day-trippers. Spend the afternoon exploring the less popular destinations, like **Dún Eochla.**

Day 10

Take morning ferry back to Galway. Drive south into the **Burren,** checking out dramatically situated **Poulnabrone,** which marks a prehistoric burial site, in the early dusk when the site is spookiest. Stay in the **Doolin** area (you can rise early and hightail it to Shannon for your early afternoon flight; if this isn't feasible, stay in Ennis).

DUBLIN

It's not just the world's best Guinness (it's the freshest!) that brings tourists to Ireland's capital city at all times of year. They come to observe the ubiquitous reminders of the city's checkered history: from its Viking origins, through the long centuries of British domination, into a nationalist tinderbox during the second decade of the 20th century, and its eventual emergence as the capital of a free and independent state in December 1922.

Today Dublin is as fast, modern, and style-conscious as any European capital—and it feels more fast-paced and cosmopolitan every time you visit. Any of the 12 genuine Dublin accents are increasingly rare to hear; the city has become like New York in that most of its 505,700 residents (within the city limits) were born and raised elsewhere. It's also a remarkably youthful place, with more than half its population under the age of 26.

Like a number of other European metropolises, the city has an abundance of neoclassical architecture mixed with fast food places, clothing chains, and souvenir shops—and increasingly exorbitant admission and accommodation prices (it's reached "gouging" level in some places). It was perhaps inevitable that the "Celtic Tiger" economic boom of the 1990s and the continued economic prosperity would turn the capital city into a mixed bag of excellent gourmet restaurants and Mickey D's, chic nightclubs and tacky tourist traps. But the city is truly what you make of it. Load up on life-altering cultural experiences, spend your afternoon drinking Guinness and talking "sport"—or better yet, do a little bit of both.

© CAMILLE DEANGELIS

DUBLIN

HIGHLIGHTS

◖ **The Book of Kells:** Two pages at a time of Ireland's most famous illuminated manuscript are on display under glass (page 43).

◖ **National Gallery:** Check out great paintings by Irish and international artists from the 16th century to the present; Caravaggio's *The Taking of Christ* is the highlight of the European collection (page 45).

◖ **National Museum of Archaeology and History:** Once discovered, every Irish treasure from every period in history – including the Tara Brooch, Ardagh Chalice, and Cross of Cong – has wound up in the country's most important museum (page 46).

◖ **St. Stephen's Green:** Europe's largest city square features colorful parterres, interesting sculptures and memorials, and many opportunities for people-watching and bird-feeding (page 46).

◖ **The Chester Beatty Library:** This well-presented collection of priceless manuscripts, donated to the republic by an American businessman, is housed on the grounds of Dublin Castle (page 47).

◖ **Christ Church Cathedral:** Wander down the central aisle of the city's grandest Gothic edifice, with its precariously tilting columns and strange artifacts (page 48).

◖ **St. Michan's Church:** The medieval limestone crypt of this Anglican church offers the city's most macabre sights, and Handel used the organ upstairs to practice his *Messiah* for its first performance in 1742 (page 52).

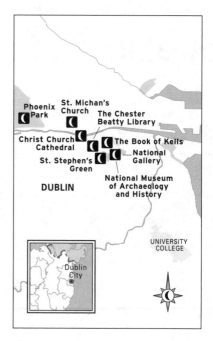

◖ **Phoenix Park:** Visit the residence of the President of Ireland or catch a hurling match on a Sunday afternoon inside Europe's largest walled park (page 55).

◖ **Dublin City Walking Tours:** Whether you're interested in history, ghost stories, or whiskey, the city's various walking tours offer something for everyone (page 58).

LOOK FOR ◖ TO FIND RECOMMENDED SIGHTS, ACTIVITIES, DINING, AND LODGING.

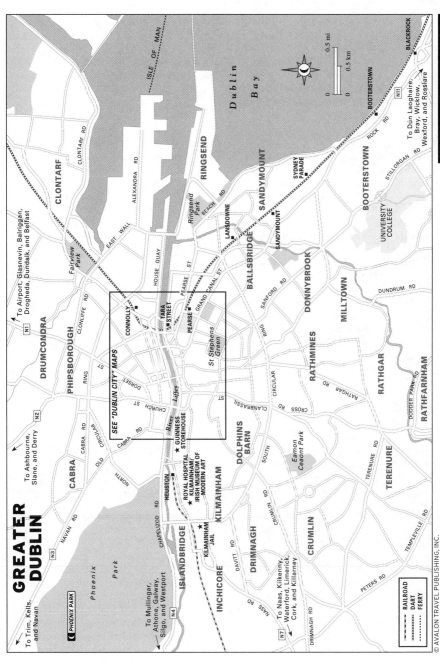

GREATER
DUBLIN

PHOENIX PARK

To Trim, Kells,
and Navan

To Ashbourne,
Slane, and Derry

To Mullingar,
Athone, Galway,
Sligo, and Westport

To Naas, Kilkenny,
Waterford, Limerick,
Cork, and Killarney

To Airport, Glasnevin, Balriggan,
Drogheda, Dundalk, and Belfast

Phoenix Park

NAVAN RD
N3

N2

N1

N4

N7

ISLANDBRIDGE

INCHICORE

KILMAINHAM

DRIMNAGH

CRUMLIN

TERENURE

RATHFARNHAM

RATHGAR

RATHMINES

MILLTOWN

DONNYBROOK

BALLSBRIDGE

SANDYMOUNT

BOOTERSTOWN

BLACKROCK

RINGSEND

CLONTARF

DRUMCONDRA

PHIPSBOROUGH

CABRA

DOLPHINS BARN

CHAPELIZOD RD

DAVITT RD

NAAS RD

DRIMNAGH RD

PETERS RD

TEMPLEVILLE RD

TERENURE RD

CRUMLIN RD

SOUTH CIRCULAR

CLANBRASSIL ST

CROSS RD

RING

SANFORD RD

CIRCULAR

RATHGAR RD

DODDER PARK RD

DUNDRUM RD

STILLORGAN RD

ROCK RD

N11

To Dún Laoghaire,
Bray, Wicklow,
Wexford, and Rosslare

BOOTERSTOWN

SYDNEY PARADE

LANSDOWNE

SANDYMOUNT

BEACH RD

Ringsend
Park

EAST WALL

ALEXANDRA RD

HOUSE QUAY

PEARSE ST

GRAND CANAL ST

St Stephens
Green

River Liffey

CHURCH ST

DORSET ST

CABRA RD

RING

OLD CIRCULAR

CABRA RD

NORTH CIRCULAR

CLONLIFFE RD

CLONTARF RD

Fairview Park

CONNOLLY

TARA STREET

PEARSE

GUINNESS STOREHOUSE

ROYAL HOSPITAL
KILMAINHAM/
IRISH MUSEUM OF
MODERN ART

KILMAINHAM JAIL

HEUSTON

Eamon
Ceaont Park

UNIVERSITY
COLLEGE

Dublin Bay

ISLE OF MAN

0.5 mi

0.5 km

0

0

SEE "DUBLIN CITY MAPS"

RAILROAD
DART
FERRY

© AVALON TRAVEL PUBLISHING, INC.

Most of the greater county is made up of sprawling commuter suburbs, though there are a few seaside towns worth an afternoon excursion in fine weather. The fertile plains of Meath to the north and the verdant hills and valleys of Wicklow Mountains National Park to the south provide opportunities for unforgettable day trips as well.

Though Dublin originates from the Irish "Dubh Linn" ("Dark Pool"), today its official name in Gaelic is Baile Átha Cliath ("Town of the Hurdles"), the name of an adjoining settlement north of the Liffey.

HISTORY

Actually, the Vikings didn't found Dubh Linn. Ptolemy recorded the existence of a settlement here on his famous map of A.D. 140; he called it *Eblana Civitas*. It's said that St. Patrick arrived in 448 and got busy making converts. Then the Vikings came in 841 with the intent of setting up a trading post (trading human cargo, that is) using the existing native Irish settlement. They were driven out by Brian Boru at the Battle of Clontarf in 1014.

But that wasn't the end of the foreign invaders—far from it. The Normans arrived in the 12th century at the plea of the deposed king of Leinster, Diarmuid Mac Murrough. Mac Murrough was only hoping to reclaim his throne, but one imagines he lived to regret his actions when the Normans cast their eyes over the entire island. Henry II, who had sent his troops under the ambitious and opportunistic Strongbow to "aid" the Leinster king, established a court in Dublin to keep an eye on his power-hungry knights—and thus was British domination established. Greater Dublin became known as "the Pale" for its complete subjugation to English government control.

The Norman adventurers settled into their confiscated lands and after a few generations considered themselves Irish—though they still swore loyalty to the British Crown, and those who rebelled swiftly lost their holdings through bloodshed. Still more Plantationers arrived to claim territories allotted by Elizabeth I (the native Irish farmers were forced to work as tenants on what had been their own land). Dublin City was the stronghold of this British Ascendancy, where the Anglo-Irish landowners usually kept townhomes. For them, city artisans—furniture-makers, silversmiths, and architects—kept up a busy practice. Dublin in Georgian times would have been quite an exciting place for all its wealth and prestige.

As a consequence of the failed island-wide rebellion in 1798, the 1801 Act of Union stripped Dublin of its independent Parliament. A Kerry lawyer, Daniel O'Connell, was sent to London to represent County Clare, and he succeeded in rolling back the Catholic-oppressive Penal Laws in 1829. He was elected the first Catholic Lord Mayor of Dublin in 1841 but died six years later feeling like a failure for having left so much unaccomplished. History would judge him otherwise, but the struggle for civil rights and political independence for Irish Catholics continued.

The city bore the fruits of the Irish Literary Revival with the establishment of the Abbey Theatre, the world's first English-speaking repertory theater, in 1904. Auspiciously enough, the venue on Lower Abbey Street (purchased for the company by Annie Horniman) was on the site of a morgue. Not all Dubliners were open-minded enough to appreciate the efforts of Lady Augusta Gregory and William Butler Yeats; the use of the word "shift" (as in a ladies' undergarment) during a performance of John Millington Synge's *The Playboy of the Western World* led to a riot in the theater in January 1907. The original theater burned down in July 1951 and was rebuilt and reopened in 1966. (Despite its ugly new premises, the Abbey is still showcasing the finest in classic and contemporary Irish drama.)

One of the most crucial events in Irish history took place in Dublin on a single day, Easter Sunday 1916, when a nationalist guerrilla group, the Irish Republican Army, took over the General Post Office and declared Ireland a free and independent republic. The British attacked, and citywide chaos and bloodshed ensued. The rebellion was eventually suppressed, and 77 participants (including future Taoiseach and president Eamon de Valera) were sentenced to death. (Only de Valera's American citizenship saved his neck.) Ultimately, 15 of those 77 were executed at Kilmainham Jail, and the nationalist papers declared them martyrs for the cause.

Since the country asserted its freedom from constitutional monarchy in the Republic of Ireland Act of 1949, Dublin's history has been marked by economic stagnation. Membership in the European Economic Community (later European Union) starting in 1973 slowly began to turn things around, however, and since the mid-1990s the city has enjoyed an economic boom.

PLANNING YOUR TIME

As in all European capitals, no amount of time in Dublin will allow you to see everything worth seeing—not even if you stay a month. Rather than exhaust yourself on a one- or two-day visit, be selective in what you choose to see, and spend a bit of time just watching the world go by in a pub, café, or on a park bench in St. Stephen's Green. You'll soak up as much "culture" in those places as you would in the National Museum.

Many attractions (especially churches and small museums) close for lunch, so be sure to arrive early enough in the morning to get the most out of your visit. For maximum efficiency, the more ambitious visitor should divide the city into sections and explore one area per day. For instance, plan to visit Kilmainham Jail, the Irish Museum of Modern Art at the Royal Hospital Kilmainham, and the Guinness Storehouse on the same day, since they're all on the western end of the city. Hop-on, hop-off bus tours are a popular means of seeing a lot of places in just a few hours.

As for day trips out of Dublin, there are several possibilities, whether you join in on a bus tour or rent a car. Nestled in the Wicklow Mountains in County Wicklow is Glendalough, one of Ireland's most important monastic sites; Newgrange, part of the Brú na Bóinne funerary complex in County Meath, is one of the most significant Neolithic sites on the whole continent. Other worthwhile excursions include Trim Castle, the largest Anglo-Norman fortress in the country, also in County Meath, and Castletown, Ireland's grandest Palladian manse, in County Kildare, accessible by Dublin Bus. All these places are within an hour and a half of the capital. Or you could just take the DART to one of the county's seaside towns for the afternoon; Killiney south of the city has a great beach, and Howth and Malahide to the north each have several attractions as well.

Sights

Though Dublin sprawls for miles, almost everything you'll want to see is concentrated within an easily walkable area on either side of the River Liffey, wedged between the city's two major train stations (Heuston on the west side and Connolly on the east). North of the Liffey, or "Northside," is a grittier neighborhood, traditionally blue collar and of less interest to tourists; this characterization is becoming somewhat less apt, however, as widespread commercial redevelopment progresses. The Northside's main thoroughfare is O'Connell Street.

South of the river are Temple Bar, Trinity College, St. Stephen's Green, Dublin Castle, Christ Church and St. Patrick's Cathedrals, and many other attractions. Dame Street runs parallel to the river, linking Christ Church with Trinity, and hungry visitors should turn south onto South Great Georges Street for its array of great eateries. Grafton Street, the famous pedestrian shopping hub, links the Trinity College campus to the north with St. Stephen's Green to the south. Wedged between St. Stephen's Green and Merrion Square, a couple of blocks east of Grafton Street, are lots of important buildings within one square block—the National Library, Museum, and Gallery, along with Leinster House (the Irish equivalent of the U.S. Capitol Building).

SIGHTSEEING PASSES

The Dúchas **Heritage Card** (tel. 01/647-6587, www.heritageireland.ie, €21, students €8), available for purchase at all Dúchas sites, will get you into Kilmainham Jail, Phoenix Park Visitor Centre (Ashtown Castle), and the Casino Marino. If you're up for a really ambitious round of sightseeing, though, it's wise to have more than the Heritage Card on hand. The **Dublin Pass** (contact the tourist office for details, tel. 01/605-7700, www.dublinpass.ie, 1/2/3/6-day pass €29/49/59/89) gets you into Dublin Castle, the Dublin Writers Museum, Kilmainham Jail, the Jameson Distillery, the Guinness Storehouse, and several other places. (Though it advertises free admission to the Irish Museum of Modern Art, the National Museums, and the Chester Beatty Library, note that there is no charge to these places anyway!) One free Aircoach ride is also included in the pass, though this isn't of much use unless yours is a fly-by-night visit, and there are "special offers" available at many shops and restaurants. Compare a list of the places you want to see with the list of covered attractions on the website, and if the admission charges exceed the price of a pass, pick one up at the tourist office.

TRINITY COLLEGE

Chartered in 1592 by the Virgin Queen for "the planting of learning, the increasing of civility, and the establishment of the true religion"—that's Protestantism—"within the realm," Trinity College Dublin (TCD) remains the island's most prestigious university. The college was opened in 1594 on the grounds of the Augustinian Priory of All Hallows, which wa s dissolved under Henry VIII's decree in 1537; the oldest extant buildings date to the early 18th century. Though the college had permitted the admission of Catholics since the late 18th century (provided they converted to Protestantism), it was not until 1970 that the Catholic Church officially permitted it. Now, of course, a majority (roughly 70 percent) of TCD's 12,500 students are Catholic.

The **guided campus tour** (tel. 01/608-1724, departs the main gate every 40 minutes 10:15 A.M.–3 P.M. daily mid-May to Sept., ticket €10) is pricey but worthwhile: The tour itself is informative but entertaining, and your ticket includes admission to see the Book of Kells, in the Old Library. Even if you don't have time for the Book of Kells exhibition or a guided campus tour, take 10 or 15 minutes to wander around the perimeter of the immaculate campus green (known as Parliament

© CAMILLE DEANGELIS

Prestigious Trinity College was founded by the charter of Queen Elizabeth I.

Square) lined with dignified Georgians (you might even want to duck into the campus chapel, on your left after you pass through the main gate).

◖ The Old Library and the Book of Kells

The Old Library, which dates to the 1720s, houses the Book of Kells (tel. 01/608-2308, www.tcd.ie, open 9:30 A.M.–5 P.M. Mon.–Sat. all year, 9:30 A.M.–4:30 P.M. Sun. June–Sept., noon–4:30 P.M. Sun. Oct.–May, admission without campus tour €7.50), the best known of all Ireland's illuminated monastic manuscripts. A different two-page spread is on display each day, under thick glass of course; with so much company, you'll be lucky to get a close extended look. Before you get to the viewing room, there's an engaging exhibition, "Turning Darkness into Light," that puts the book into historical and religious context.

The Old Library also houses the Book of Armagh, the Book of Dimma, the Book of Durrow, and the Yellow Book of Lecan, which contains a partial version of the *Táin Bó Cúailnge* ("The Cattle Raid of Cooley"), one of Ireland's greatest medieval epics. Try to get here early in the day; you don't want to waste your afternoon in the queue to get in. The Book of Kells is cool, but not *that* cool!

Douglas Hyde Gallery of Modern Art

Named for the first president of Ireland, the Douglas Hyde Gallery of Modern Art (entrance on Nassau St., tel. 01/608-1116, http://douglas-hydegallery.com, open 11 A.M.–6 P.M. Mon.–Fri., until 7 P.M. Thurs., 11 A.M.–4:45 P.M. Sat., free admission) is in the Arts and Social Science Building, south of the Old Library. Two temporary exhibitions are on at a time in separate galleries, and feature paintings, sculpture, and textile arts from an international roster of artists.

SOUTH OF TRINITY

Dublin's political hub, as well as the National Gallery, Library, and Museum, is contained

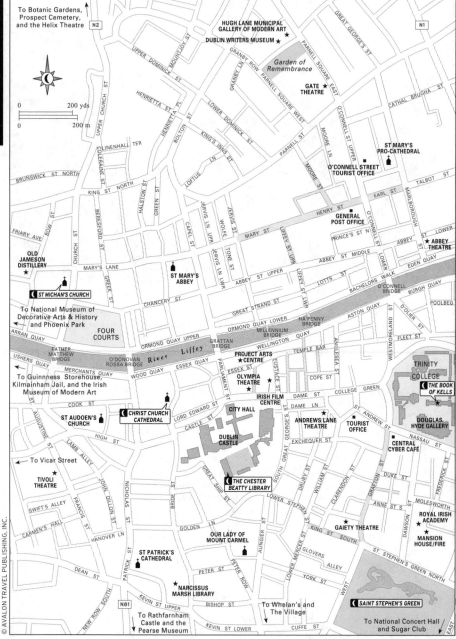

© AVALON TRAVEL PUBLISHING, INC.

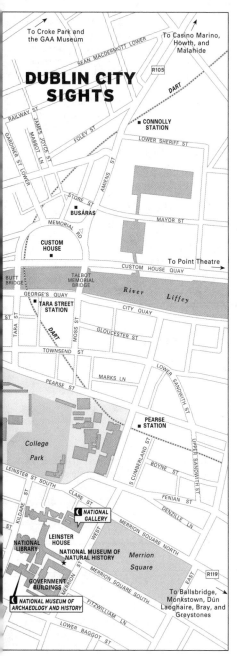

DUBLIN CITY SIGHTS

within a single block northeast of St. Stephen's Green, between Kildare and Merrion Streets. One block west, on Dawson Street, is the early Georgian Mansion House, the official home of the Lord Mayor of Dublin since 1715. Dawson Street is lined with other grand old buildings with interesting architectural details; several ground floors have been converted into chic bars and eateries.

Leinster House

Leinster House (entrance on Kildare St., tel. 01/618-3271, www.irlgov.ie/oireachtas, free admission), once home of the 20th Earl of Kildare (and later Duke of Leinster), now houses the Irish Parliament, the Oireachtas na hÉireann. The Parliament comprises a lower house, the Dáil (pronounced "doll"), and an upper house, the Seanad ("SHAN-add"); meetings (only 90 days out of the year Nov.–May) are open to the public. Tickets are available at the entrance on Kildare Street. Guided tours are also available occasionally; ring for more information.

For a free tour of the Irish **Government Buildings** (Upper Merrion St., tel. 01/645-8813, open 10:30 A.M.–1:30 P.M. Sat., free admission), head to the National Gallery lobby first for a ticket. Built between 1904 and 1911 and renovated to the nines in the late 1980s, the Government Buildings house the Taoiseach's offices as well as the Council Chamber (where the cabinet meets) and the Department of Finance. It's a worthwhile stop if you're interested in the Irish government or Edwardian architecture. Another item of interest is the huge stained glass window with nationalist motifs by Evie Hone in the entrance hall, which was commissioned for the New York World Trade Fair in 1939.

◖ National Gallery

The National Gallery of Ireland (Merrion Sq. W., tel. 01/661-5133, www.nationalgallery.ie, open 9:30 A.M.–5:30 P.M. Mon.–Sat., until 8:30 P.M. Thurs., noon–5:30 P.M. Sun., free admission) is well worth a visit for its comprehensive collection of Irish art (plan to linger in the Yeats hall—bet you had no idea the whole family was so talented!) as well as works by Caravaggio, El Greco, Goya, Rembrandt, Vermeer, and Picasso. Other highlights include *The Marriage of Strongbow and Aoife,* a humonguous tableau scene painted by Daniel Maclise in the 1850s, and the Millennium Wing, which houses a permanent collection of contemporary works as well as visiting exhibitions. There's also a quality bookshop and an airy, modern café with pretty good food.

National Library

Check out the main reading room with its coffered dome at the National Library of Ireland (Kildare St., tel. 01/603-0200, www.nli.ie, open 10 A.M.–9 P.M. Mon.–Wed., 10 A.M.–5 P.M. Thurs.–Fri., 10 A.M.–1 P.M. Sat., free admission), which usually has a downstairs exhibition featuring scribbled pages from first drafts of beloved works and other interesting tidbits.

National Museum of Natural History

A better official name for the National Museum of Natural History (Merrion St., tel. 01/677-7444, www.museum.ie, open 10 A.M.–5 P.M. Tues.–Sat., 2–5 P.M. Sun., free admission) might just be the Victorian Taxidermy Museum—it's already commonly known as the "Dead Zoo." Most visitors will probably end up skipping this one, but for those with antiquarian taste this quirky museum will provide an hour's diversion.

◖ National Museum of Archaeology and History

There's more than one National Museum, but this one (Kildare St., tel. 01/677-7444, www.museum.ie, open 10 A.M.–5 P.M. Tues.–Sat. and 2–5 P.M. Sun., free admission) is the one you hear most about, for its phenomenal collection of artifacts from every period in Irish history: prehistoric tools and pottery; stunning gold torcs and other jewelry from the Bronze Age; ornate chalices, crosses, crosiers, bells, and brooches from the early Christian and medieval eras; Viking jewelry and weaponry;

18th- and 19th-century lace, silver, and musical instruments; and clothing and wooden sculptures—even a body!—found preserved in the bogs. The museum's three most important medieval artifacts are the Tara Brooch, an exquisite example of Celtic gold and silver metalwork dating to the beginning of the 8th century; the early 9th-century Ardagh Chalice, made of silver, gold, and bronze, found with other smaller treasures in a Limerick potato field in 1868; and the 12th-century Cross of Cong, an ornate silver reliquary that supposedly houses a splinter of the True Cross. Basically everything of archaeological importance found anywhere in the country is brought here and put under glass (even the bog man, and the effect is disconcerting to say the least). Visiting exhibitions complement a permanent collection of ancient Egyptian, Cypriot, Roman, and Byzantine artifacts.

Dawson Street

The first meeting of the Dáil took place on January 22, 1919, in the early-18th-century **Mansion House,** around the block from Leinster House on Dawson Street, as did the adoption of the Declaration of Independence and signing of the Anglo-Irish Treaty in 1921. The Mansion House is the official residence of the Lord Mayor of Dublin, elected by the city council for a one-year term, and is not open to the public.

Bibliophiles, take note: The **Royal Irish Academy** (19 Dawson St., tel. 01/676-2570, www.ria.ie, open 10 A.M.–5:30 P.M. Mon.–Thurs., 10 A.M.–5 P.M. Fri., free admission) has a trove of priceless medieval illuminated manuscripts, including *The Cathach,* the oldest Irish psalter (dating to the 6th century, and associated with St. Columba). Generally only one manuscript is on display at a time, though.

◖ ST. STEPHEN'S GREEN

Probably Europe's largest city square, St. Stephen's Green is tranquil and immaculately kept. All these verdant walkways, duck ponds, and tidy flowerbeds (nine hectares in all) belie a dark history, however: Before the mid-17th century the area was commonly used for rowdy public executions (including burnings). The space was closed off from "rabble" in 1663 and gradually spiffed up for use by Dublin's elite. In 1877 Arthur Guinness introduced an Act of Parliament to open the green to the public, and this finally happened in 1880. The main entrance is through the **Fusiliers' Arch** at the northwest corner; modeled after the Arch of Titus in Rome, it memorializes the 200-plus Royal Dublin Fusiliers killed in the Boer War. The park is dotted with smaller memorials to 1798 rebels Theobald Wolfe Tone and Robert Emmet, William Butler Yeats, Constance Markievicz, nationalist poet and translator James Clarence Mangan, and several other luminaries. The park is perfect for a leisurely stroll at any time of day, or just pick a bench and watch half of Dublin go by on their lunch breaks.

DUBLIN CASTLE AND AROUND

Dublin Castle (Dame St., Cork Hill, tel. 01/677-7129, www.dublincastle.ie, tours 10 A.M.–4:45 P.M. Mon.–Fri., 2–4:45 P.M. Sat.–Sun. and holidays, admission €4.50), built by order of King John in 1204, served as the seat of British power in Ireland for more than 700 years. In his book *Castles of Ireland,* Brian de Breffny notes that "the medieval castle had never been a source of pride to the Viceroys after the Middle Ages. They found it shabby, unsuitable and ugly, despite desultory attempts to improve it, and their comments about it were invariably derogatory." De Breffny offers the following sample from the Lord Deputy of Dublin Castle in 1633: "I have been forced to take down one of the great Towers which was ready to fall and the rest are so crazy as we are still in fear part of it may drop upon our heads as one tower did whilst my Lord Chancellor was here…[the castle is] little better than a very prison."

Little of the original castle survives due to those half-hearted refurbishments and a widespread fire in 1689; today you can tour the excavations of the 13th-century foundations (called the "Undercroft," where the old castle joined the city walls), but otherwise it's just the Record Tower, finished in 1258, that remains. Most of the current structure dates from the mid-1700s. Despite its dank and crumbling walls, the castle continued to be used for official balls and banquets into the 20th century. During the Victorian era as many as 15,000 people were entertained there in the five-week period culminating in the annual St. Patrick's Ball (a festivity that, it is safe to say, the holy man would have scarcely approved of). In 1907 the Irish Crown Jewels were filched from Bedford Tower and never seen again.

Today Dublin Castle is home to many government offices and a neo-Gothic chapel, which was converted to Catholicism in 1943. Guided tours usually include the state apartments, Undercroft, and chapel, but if the state rooms are unavailable due to official business the abridged tour will cost you a euro less.

City Hall

Opposite the castle entrance is Dublin City Hall (Dame St., tel. 01/222-2222, www.dublincity.ie, exhibition open 10 A.M.–5 P.M. Mon.–Sat., 2–5 P.M. Sun., admission €4, free admission to lobby and rotunda). Built for the Royal Exchange in the 1770s, this neoclassical edifice boasts a gold-leaf dome supported by a dozen fluted columns, as well as plasterwork crafted by one of Dublin's mayors, Charles Thorp. Unless you're in the mood for a history lesson at the exhibition in the downstairs vaults, just pop inside to admire the rotunda with its statue of Daniel O'Connell.

◖ The Chester Beatty Library

Bibliophiles and art lovers should put The Chester Beatty Library (on the grounds of Dublin Castle, signposted from the car park through the front gates, tel. 01/407-0750, www.cbl.ie, open 10 A.M.–5 P.M. Mon.–Fri., 11 A.M.–5 P.M. Sat., 1–5 P.M. Sun., closed Mon. Oct.–Apr., free admission) at the top of their sightseeing list. Arthur Chester Beatty (1875–1968), a prosperous American businessman living in London, moved his exquisite collection of illuminated manuscripts (and plenty of other treasures) to Dublin in 1950. The shrewd but soft-spoken Beatty spent the remainder of his life here, and he was the first person to be made an honorary Irish citizen. After a 10-minute audiovisual on Beatty's life and times, you make your way up to the galleries to peruse the collections of Chinese snuff bottles and embroidered garments, Japanese inro (lacquered wood containers suspended from a kimono sash), and a wealth of Islamic, Indian, and Asian manuscripts, working your way to the rooms of medieval and Renaissance books and engravings (including several by the late-15th/early-16th-century German master Albrecht Dürer). It's worth lingering in several rooms to watch the demonstration videos on illumination, book-binding, engraving, and other arts. The top-floor exhibits analyze three world religions (Christianity, Islam, and Buddhism) through manuscripts and other sacred objects. Behind glass are fragments of letters written as early as the second century B.C., epistles that would eventually be included in the New Testament. There's also a rooftop garden and a classy café on the ground floor. The Beatty collection would be a mustsee even if admission weren't free; it's just all the more worthwhile because it is!

TEMPLE BAR

Probably named for a local family in the late 17th century, this area stretches between Dame Street (which turns into Lord Edward Street) and the river, the western and eastern boundaries being Fishamble Street, where Handel first conducted his *Messiah* in 1742, and Trinity College, respectively. Temple Bar—what *The New York Times* called "that dilapidated medieval neighborhood"—underwent an ambitious government-sponsored facelift in the 1990s using the designs of several local cutting-edge architectural firms. Today it's a hyper-commercialized hive of pubs, clubs, restaurants (often mediocre), and atmospheric alleyways.

Tucked between Sycamore and Eustace Streets just a couple of blocks south of the river, Meetinghouse Square is the hub of the neighborhood, buzzing at all hours with locals and tourists alike. The **Temple Bar Food Market** (tel. 01/671-5717, 9:30 A.M.–5:30 P.M.) transpires here on Saturdays.

You can traverse Temple Bar's alleyways after nightfall without a backward glance, though the proliferation of (albeit harmless) drunken rowdies late at night can sure get on one's nerves. Unless you believe this…shall we say, *festive* atmosphere is an integral part of the Dublin experience, you might want to avoid the area after 10 or 11 P.M.

CHRISTCHURCH AND AROUND
Christ Church Cathedral

Though the marvelous Christ Church Cathedral (Christchurch Place, west end of Lord Edward St., tel. 01/677-8099, www.cccdub.ie) has its origins in the late 12th and early 13th centuries, much of the building was structurally unsound, and it was almost entirely rebuilt through the generosity of Henry Roe in the 1870s. Roe's chosen architect, George Edmund Street, preserved as much of the original edifice as possible and faithfully replicated the rest in the Romanesque and Early English Gothic styles.

In the yard are the foundations of a 13th-century chapter house, and in the southern aisle you'll spot the tomb of a knight whose nose is worn off; though it is identified as Strongbow's, we know for a fact that his tomb was destroyed when the south wall collapsed in 1562. Cathedral literature states this tomb is a replica of the original, but it's more likely someone else's tomb entirely. A reliquary in the Peace Chapel contains the heart of 12th-century archbishop Laurence O'Toole, patron saint of Dublin. The cathedral offers a few more weird surprises, like the mummified cat-and-rat pair found in a pipe of the church organ and the massive arches on the north side of the aisle leaning at an unnerving angle. Creepy statues of Charles I and II greet you as you enter the crypt, where you can watch a 12-minute audiovisual on the cathedral's history and check out the ornate silver plate presented to the cathedral by William of Orange in celebration of his victory at the Battle of the Boyne.

The cathedral is open daily (9 A.M.–6 P.M. weekdays June–Aug., 9:45 A.M.–5 P.M. or 6 P.M. weekdays Sept.–May, open 10 A.M.– 4:30 P.M. Sat. and 12:45–2:45 P.M. Sun. all year, admission €5). Evensong, which features music dating to the Reformation period, is performed in the cathedral at 3:30 P.M. Sunday, 6 P.M. Wednesday and Thursday, and 5 P.M. Saturday.

Patrick Street and Around

Dublin's second Anglican cathedral is **St. Patrick's** (Patrick St., tel. 01/475-4817, www. stpatrickscathedral.ie), built in the Early English Gothic style at the turn of the 13th century near a well where Ireland's patron saint was said to have performed baptisms. St. Patrick's is the largest of Ireland's medieval cathedrals, though it has no crypt because it was built above the trickly River Poddle. Jonathan Swift, who served as Dean from 1713 to 1745, is entombed here beside his mistress, Esther Johnson. Come at the end of the day (weekdays excepting Wednesday) to hear the choir perform evensong; their 18th-century predecessors were the first to sing Handel's *Messiah.* St. Patrick's is open daily (9 A.M.–6 P.M. Mon.–Sat. and 9–11 A.M., 12:45–3 P.M., and 4:15–6 P.M. Sun. Mar.–Oct.; 9 A.M.–6 P.M. weekdays, 9 A.M.–5 P.M. Sat., 10–11 A.M. and 12:45–3 P.M. Sun. Nov.–Feb., admission €5).

Down the street is the **Narcissus Marsh Library** (St. Patrick's Close, tel. 01/454-3511, www.marshlibrary.ie, open 10 A.M.–1 P.M. and 2–5 P.M. Mon. and Wed.–Fri., 10:30 A.M.– 1 P.M. Sat., admission €2.50). Ireland's first public library was established in 1701 by Narcissus Marsh, who was the Anglican Archbishop of Cashel, Dublin, and Armagh (though not all at once). The archbishop opened the library with 10,000 volumes from his personal collection, and today there are more than 25,000 ancient (and somewhat moldy-looking) tomes arranged carefully on the original shelves in two cathedral-ceilinged galleries. Rotating exhibits under glass feature centuries-old books

with hand-painted illustrations, and another case houses Jonathan Swift's death mask. The library staff are very friendly and informative, the volunteers delightfully quirky and garrulous; bibliophiles will find the Marsh library well worth a visit.

Catholics and lovebirds might want to step inside **Our Lady of Mount Carmel** (entrance at 56 Aungier St., tel. 01/475-8821), which houses "some of" the remains of St. Valentine in a niche on your right as you walk up the aisle.

St. Audoen's Church

The Anglican St. Audoen's Church (Cornmarket, High St., tel. 01/677-0088, open 9:30 A.M.–5:30 P.M. daily June–Sept., free admission) is only remaining medieval parish church in Dublin, flanked by a chunk of the old city wall. St. Audoen's Arch here is the last extant city gate. The Catholic St. Audoen's around the corner on High Street is an imposing neoclassical edifice with a huge and hideous Corinthian portico. The two churches form a somewhat amusing study in architectural contrasts. Here too is **St. Mary's Abbey** (Mary's Abbey St., Meetinghouse Ln., off Capel St., tel. 01/833-1618 and 01/647-6587 in winter, open 10 A.M.–5 P.M. Mon.–Sat. midJune–mid-Sept., free admission), once the richest Cistercian monastery in the country. Here "Silken Thomas," Lord of Offaly, had the chutzpah to renounce his allegiance to Henry VIII in 1534, thus sparking a yearlong, nationwide insurrection.

NORTHSIDE

Head north of the Liffey for a glimpse of everyday life in the capital city. The "Northside" neighborhood consists of everything north of the river and south of the M50 motorway skirting the city, and the word is used to refer to a blue-collar attitude as often as it is indicative of urban geography. The "post-code snobbery" of the Dublin elite has eased in recent years as developers have erected sparkling new shopping centers, and every just-opened eatery is hipper than the one before it. There is plenty

a monument to Daniel O'Connell on the street of the same name

in the way of sightseeing north of the Liffey as well: the Writers Museum, Jameson Distillery, and St. Michan's Church are just a few of the highlights.

O'Connell Street

The Northside's primary thoroughfare, O'Connell Street is a transportation hub where you'll find the General Post Office (headquarters of the ill-fated Easter Rising in 1916) as well as a few decorations of hilariously questionable taste: the "Floozy in the Jacuzzi" (you'll see!), a statue of James Joyce to which locals chain their bicycles, and the "Dublin Spire," a 120-meter light-up metal spoke Dubs know better as the "stiffy by the Liffey."

Erected in 1854 in memory of "the Great Liberator," the **O'Connell Monument** is flanked by four winged figures representing patriotism, fidelity, eloquence, and courage. Farther up O'Connell Street (formerly Sackville), the **General Post Office,** or **GPO** (tel. 01/705-7000, open 8 A.M.–8 P.M. Mon.–Sat., free admission), an imposing neoclassical edifice built between 1815 and 1817, served as a

rebel stronghold during the Easter Rising of 1916. Here Patrick Pearse (also spelled Pádraic or Pádraig) read the Proclamation of the Irish Republic from the front steps, and the shell marks are still visible on the facade.

Just off O'Connell Street is **St. Mary's Pro-Cathedral** (83 Marlborough St., 01/874-5441, www.procathedral.ie, open 7:30 A.M.–6:45 P.M. Mon.–Fri., 7:30 A.M.–7:15 P.M. Sat., 9 A.M.–1:45 P.M. and 5:30–7:45 P.M. Sun., 10 A.M.–1:30 P.M. public holidays, free admission), the seat of the Catholic Archbishop of Dublin ("pro" indicating the church is an "acting cathedral"; Dublin has two Anglican cathedrals, St. Patrick's and Christ Church, but the Catholic Church still recognizes the latter as its official cathedral because it was designated as such in the 12th century). "The Pro," as locals call it, was designed by amateur architect John Sweetman in 1816 with a Greek revival facade and a richly decorated interior evocative of the great basilicas of Rome.

At the top of O'Connell Street is the **Parnell Monument,** an obelisk pillar topped with a bronze statue by Augustus St. Gaudens.

Parnell Square

At the **Dublin Writers Museum** (18 Parnell Sq., tel. 01/872-2077, fax 01/872-2231, www.writersmuseum.com, open 10 A.M.–5 P.M. Mon.–Sat., 11 A.M.–5 P.M. Sun. year-round, closing at 6 P.M. Mon.–Sat. June–Aug., admission €6.70), you can peruse exhibition boards (presenting Ireland's literary heritage in chronological order, with plenty of biographical details) and glass cases containing typewriters, first editions, original correspondence, and other stuff; an audio guide is included in the admission price. The foyer and upstairs rooms feature portraits and bronze busts of luminaries from Yeats and Beckett to Elizabeth Bowen and Mary Lavin, and there is generally a rotating exhibit upstairs as well.

A couple doors down is the **Hugh Lane Municipal Gallery of Modern Art** (22 N. Parnell Sq., tel. 01/874-1903, www.hughlane.ie, open 10 A.M.–6 P.M. Tues.–Thurs., 10 A.M.–5 P.M. Fri.–Sat., 11 A.M.–5 P.M. Sun., free admission), in the erstwhile townhome of the first Earl of Charlemont and designed by William Chambers in the 1760s. The fantastic permanent collection includes works by Monet, Renoir, Degas, Corot, Millais, and Burne-Jones, and native works by Sean Keating, Harry Clarke, Paul Henry, and Jack B. Yeats, most of which was collected by Sir Hugh Lane before his demise on the *Lusitania* in 1915. The gallery also includes an authentically chaotic re-creation of **Francis Bacon's studio** (admission €7, half-price on Tuesday before noon) in London.

Across the street is the **Garden of Remembrance** (Parnell Sq. E., tel. 01/874-3074). Opened in 1966 to commemorate the 50th anniversary of the Easter Rising, it features a sculpture by Oisin Kelly depicting the legend of the Children of Lir (who were turned into swans by their sorceress stepmother).

Croke Park

Those interested in **Gaelic football** and **hurling** should check out the **GAA Museum** (Gaelic Athletic Association, New Stand,

the Four Courts, headquarters of the Irish judicial system

© CAMILLE DE ANGELIS

Croke Park, Clonliffe Rd., north of the Royal Canal, tel. 01/855-8176, http://museum.gaa.ie) for a high-tech history of the games, including a 15-minute audiovisual. In addition to visiting the museum (open 9:30 A.M.–5 P.M. Mon.–Sat. and noon–5 P.M. Sun. Apr.–Oct., 10 A.M.–5 P.M. Tues.–Sat. and noon–4 P.M. Sun. Nov.–Mar., admission €5.50), you can take a one-hour stadium tour (€9.50). The museum is at Croke Park, the country's largest stadium (with 84,000 seats). The All-Ireland finals take place here every September. To get here, take Dublin Bus (route #3, #11/A, #16/A, or #123) from O'Connell Street.

Four Courts

Notice that striking (not to mention humongous) green-domed neoclassical structure on the quay? It's the Four Courts (Inns Quay, tel. 01/872-5555, open 11 A.M.–1 P.M. and 2–4 P.M. weekdays, free admission), home of the Irish law courts since 1796; the name comes from the four traditional divisions of the judicial system (Chancery, King's Bench, Exchequer, and

© CAMILLE DEANGELIS

Handel rehearsed his *Messiah* here at St. Michan's in 1742.

Common Pleas). Designed by James Gandon in the 1780s, the building was bombarded by provisional forces and gutted by republican "irregulars" during the Civil War; the restoration work dates to 1932. Note that the public is admitted only when court is in session.

◖ St. Michan's Church

Named for a Danish bishop who built the original church on the site of an ancient oak grove, the Anglican St. Michan's Church (Church St., tel. 01/872-4154, stmichan@iol.ie) houses the organ on which Handel practiced the *Messiah* before its first performance at the old Dublin Music Hall on Fishamble Street on April 13, 1742. That's not why teenagers come here in droves, though—it's to see the uncannily preserved remains in the medieval crypt—a phenomenon caused by a combo of methane gas and the limestone foundations, which absorb the moisture in the air. This is, bar none, the most macabre sight in the city, and not for the faint-hearted. Hours vary seasonally (10 A.M.–12:45 P.M. and 2–4:30 P.M. weekdays and 10 A.M.–12:45 P.M. Sat. mid-

Mar.–Oct., 12:30–3:30 P.M. weekdays and 10 A.M.–12:45 P.M. Sat. Nov.–mid-Mar., admission €3.50).

Access to the crypt is by guided tour, which takes place whenever there are enough visitors. Stringy cobwebs dangle from the rough stone ceiling in these dimly lit subterranean vaults, each one belonging to a different aristocratic Dublin family. The first cell on your right displays the death mask of Theobald Wolfe Tone as well as the gruesome execution order of John and Henry Sheares, all of whom were patriots in the 1798 rebellion. (The brothers' remains are here too.) You'll pass family vaults on either side, a couple of which have been illuminated to show you how the coffins have been stacked upon those of the previous generation—many of which have collapsed, with undecomposed limbs poking through the splintered wood. You can see the fingernails and everything.

The amusingly theatrical guide will lead you to the last cell (whose coffins are open and on display), make a show of deliberating—he oughtn't let you inside, you see—then ask if you'd like to touch the hand of the so-called

"Crusader" in the box at the back of the vault, who has been dead for at least 600 years. Not only was he almost two meters tall, but his feet were actually sawn off to fit him in the coffin. Don't feel too sorry for him, though; at least people are still coming to visit him, while his fellow soldiers are long since forgotten.

Jameson Distillery

If you have time for only one tipple tour, go for the Jameson Distillery (Bow St., Smithfield, 1 block north of Arran Quay, tel. 01/807-2355, www.whiskeytours.ie, open 9:30 A.M.–5:30 P.M. daily, admission €8.75) rather than the Guinness Storehouse; it's less expensive and more engaging, and unlike at Guinness you get a real guided tour (departing every half hour). And of course, a whiskey-tasting is included in the price of admission.

Collins Barracks

The **National Museum of Decorative Arts and History** at the Collins Barracks (Benburb St., one block north of Wolfe Tone Quay, tel. 01/677-7444, open 9:30 A.M.–5:30 P.M. Mon.–Sat., until 8:30 P.M. Thurs., noon–5:30 P.M. Sun., free admission), opened in 1999, may not be as exciting as the National Museum of Archaeology & History, but it's still worth a visit. Here you'll find collections of silver, coins, period clothing and furniture, ceramics, glassware, and weaponry. There's a special gallery devoted to long-stored items just recently dusted off. On a darker note, the 14 executed Easter rebels were buried on Arbour Hill directly behind the barracks.

WEST OF THE CITY CENTER
Guinness Storehouse

Perhaps the biggest tourist trap in Dublin is the Guinness Storehouse (St. James' Gate, tel. 01/408-4800, www.guinness-storehouse.com, open 9:30 A.M.–5 P.M. daily, admission €14, 10 percent discount with online booking). It's one thing if you're a devoted stout drinker, but don't feel like you ought to go just because everyone else is. Note that the tour is self-guided—and even cheekier, you have to pay the admission fee even if you just want to have lunch in the restaurant (which, admittedly, serves up some really good traditional meals like shepherd's pie and Irish stew, all liberally laced with the black stuff). But at least your ticket includes the best pint you'll ever taste in the upstairs, all-glass "Gravity Bar" with a panoramic city view. The walk is doable (about 15 minutes from Trinity), but you could also take Dublin Bus route #51B or #78A from Aston Quay or #123 from O'Connell or Dame Street; the trip will take 10 minutes.

Kilmainham Jail

Another very popular attraction, Kilmainham Jail (or "Gaol," Inchicore Rd., tel. 01/453-5984, open 9:30 A.M.–6 P.M. daily Apr.–Sept., 9:30 A.M.–5:30 P.M. Mon.–Sat. and 10 A.M.–6 P.M. Sun. Oct.–Mar., admission €5.30) is a late 18th-century prison that is open to the public essentially to commemorate the 15 nationalists executed in early May 1916 for their leading roles in the Easter Rising. You can enter the stonebreakers' yard where Patrick Pearse, his brother William, and 12 other patriots were shot at daybreak. Over the course of a fascinating (if crowded) hour-long tour, you'll hear plenty of heart-tugging stories. One concerns Joseph Plunkett, who married his long-time sweetheart, Grace Gifford, inside the jail just four hours before his execution on May 4, 1916.

The Easter Rising nearly eclipses the rest of the jail's history, which the guide discusses only briefly; during the Great Famine there were as many as 9,000 people crowded into 188 cells. It's said that people often committed crimes because they knew they'd be fed in prison. You can peep into these cells, many of which are labeled with their most famous occupants. Another highlight of the tour is a trip to the "panopticon," the all-seeing eye, the cavernous open-plan cell block where scenes from several Irish movies (including *Michael Collins* and *In the Name of the Father*) were filmed.

After the tour, head to the upstairs exhibition and look out for a red-lighted side hallway, which is lined with display cases of poignant

THE WRAITHS OF KILMAINHAM

The long, dark history of Kilmainham Jail – Ireland's largest uninhabited prison – and its tragic association with the Easter rebellion, make a variety of ghost stories nearly inevitable. Along with the doomed patriots, the jail housed everyone from common criminals to ordinary citizens who'd fallen on especially hard times. In fact, many victims committed crimes simply because they knew they'd be fed in prison. Even children were incarcerated here. Records indicate that Kilmainham saw approximately 150 executions in its 128-year history, and many of those prisoners were buried in the stonebreakers' yard (where 14 Easter rebels met their deaths). Furthermore, the jail was built on the site of a gallows.

So it comes as no surprise that many folks, visitors and employees alike, will testify that Kilmainham has quite an accumulation of restless spirits. Those volunteers who set about restoring the jail during the 1960s had plenty of chilling stories to share: lights turning on by themselves in remote sections of the building late at night, inexplicable gusts of wind, and heavy phantom footsteps. According to the Paranormal Research Association of Ireland, most of the supernatural activity occurs in the west wing, where you'll find the political prisoners' dark, dank cells.

During the tour your guide will draw your attention to an excerpt of a poem by Patrick Pearse, "The Rebel," scrawled on the wall above a doorway:

Beware of the thing that is coming,
  beware of the risen people,
Who shall take what ye would not give.
Did ye think to conquer the people,
Or that law is stronger than life and
  than men's desire to be free?
We will try it out with you, ye that have
  harried and held,
Ye that have bullied and bribed,
  tyrants, hypocrites, liars!

Pearse, one of the leaders of the Easter rebellion, was among those executed in May 1916, and his words are as much a contribution to the spooky atmosphere as they are a reminder of Ireland's centuries-old political struggle.

© CAMILLE DEANGELIS

Kilmainham Jail

personal effects of the 14 Easter rebel-martyrs. It's the best part of the visit. To get to the jail, take Dublin Bus route #51/B, #78A, or #79 from Aston Quay.

Royal Hospital Kilmainham and the Irish Museum of Modern Art

Just up the road is the Royal Hospital Kilmainham (Military Rd., Kilmainham, tel. 01/612-9900, open 10 A.M.–5:30 P.M. Tues.–Sat., noon–5:30 P.M. Sun. June–Sept., admission €3.50), a late 17th-century neoclassical edifice that many at the time grumbled was far too grand for its inhabitants, who were retired soldiers. In summer you can tour the hospital's baroque chapel, great hall, formal gardens, and burial grounds, and there are often concerts held here.

On the premises is the Irish Museum of Modern Art (tel. 01/612-9900, www.imma.ie, open 10 A.M.–5:30 P.M. Tues. and Thurs.–Sat., 10:30 A.M.–5:30 P.M. Wed., noon–5:30 P.M. Sun., free admission), with an intriguing collection of works by lesser-known Irish painters, sculptors, and printmakers. Guided tours are available on Wednesday, Friday, and Sunday at

2:30 P.M. To get here, take Dublin Bus route #51/A/B, #78A, or #79 from Aston Quay, #123 from Dame Street or O'Connell Street, or #26 from Wellington Quay.

◖ PHOENIX PARK

Long before it was Europe's largest enclosed park, Phoenix Park served as the largest Viking cemetery outside Scandinavia—surely a fact no one's thinking of while playing or watching any of the soccer, hurling, cricket, or horse racing going on here! The name "Phoenix" has nothing to do with that mythical bird (though it appears on an eponymous monument near the middle of the park); it's just the anglicization of Fionn Uisce, "Clean Water," a reference to a stream running through the park. At seven square kilometers, Phoenix Park is roughly twice the size of Central Park in Manhattan; like Central Park, it has several busy through-roads. Every day as many as 20,000 cars travel through the park, and the Office of Public Works hopes eventually to eliminate all through traffic.

Once inside, it's quite easy to orient yourself by a 63-meter obelisk, the **Wellington Monument,** at the southeastern corner. Across Chesterfield Avenue is the **People's Garden,** laid out in 1864, and **The Hollow,** where a bandstand in a natural amphitheater hosts brass and swing bands in the summertime.

On the far side of the park, the **Phoenix Park Visitor Centre** (tel. 01/677-0095, phoenixparkvisitorcentre@opw.ie, open 10 A.M.–5 P.M. Wed.–Sun. Nov.–Mar., 10 A.M.–5:30 P.M. daily late Mar. and Oct., 10 A.M.–6 P.M. daily Apr.–Sept., admission €2.90) offers a 20-minute audiovisual on the park's history, certainly worthwhile if you've purchased the Dúchas Heritage Card. It's also your point of entry for nearby 17th-century **Ashtown Castle.** This restored tower house is rather small and unfurnished, though, so the half-hour tour is of only moderate interest.

The park holds several official buildings, including the residence of the U.S. ambassador and Garda Síochána headquarters. There's also the home of the Irish president, **Áras**

an Uachtaráin (tel. 01/670-9155, hourlong tours on Sat. 10:30 A.M.–4:15 P.M. summer, 9:30 A.M.–3:30 P.M. winter, free admission). The "Irish White House" is in the northeastern section of the park, and you can sign up for a visit on a Saturday morning at the visitors center. After an introductory audiovisual presentation, you'll be whisked off to the president's house in a minibus for an hour-long tour of the main state reception rooms and gardens. There are no reservations and spots are limited, so it's wise to arrive when the Phoenix Park Visitor Centre opens at 9:30 A.M. to obtain tickets for the first tour at 10:30. Note that state business can sometimes lead to cancellation of all tours, and that backpacks and cameras aren't permitted. To get to the visitors center by Dublin Bus, the route that drops you the closest (Ashtown Gate) is #37, which you can board from Lower Abbey Street (Northside).

In the southeast corner is **Dublin Zoo** (tel. 01/677-1425, www.dublinzoo.ie), established in 1830—making it the second-oldest zoo in Europe. Dublin Bus route #10 from O'Connell Street will get you here. Hours vary seasonally (9:30 A.M.–6 P.M. Mon.–Sat., 10:30 A.M.–6 P.M. Sun. May–Sept., 9:30 A.M.–4 P.M. Mon.–Fri., 9:30 A.M.–5 P.M. Sat., and 10:30 A.M.–5 P.M. Sun. Oct.–Apr., admission €13.50).

GLASNEVIN

An erstwhile suburb three kilometers north of the Liffey, Glasnevin is home to Dublin City University (DCU) as well as two of the city's most important attractions.

National Botanic Gardens

The 19-hectare National Botanic Gardens (Botanic Rd., 3.5 km north of Trinity College, tel. 01/837-7596 or 01/837-4388, www.botanicgardens.ie, open 9 A.M.–6 P.M. Mon.–Sat. and 10 A.M.–6 P.M. Sun. in summer, 10 A.M.–4:30 P.M. daily in winter, free admission, guided tour €2, parking fee €2) are home to more than 20,000 plant species, 300 of which are endangered and 6 of which are already extinct in the wild. Established in 1795,

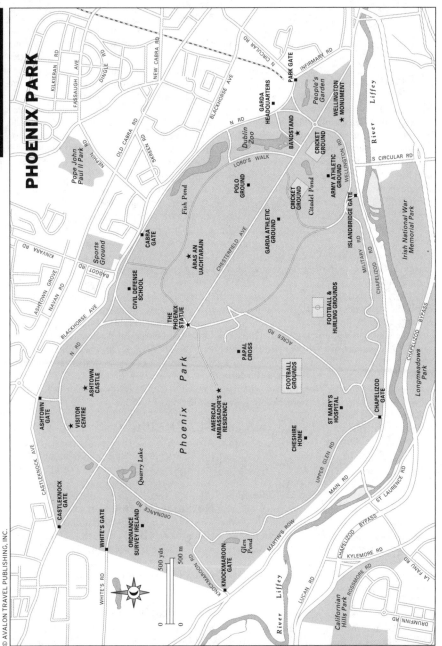

PHOENIX PARK

KILKIERAN RD
FASSAUGH AVE
DINGLE RD
NEPHIN RD
KINVARA RD
ASHTOWN GROVE
NAVAN RD
BAGOT RD
BLACKHORSE AVE
N RD
CASTLEKNOCK AVE
CASTLEKNOCK GATE
WHITE'S GATE
WHITE'S RD
ORDNANCE RD

NEW CABRA RD
OLD CABRA RD
SKREEN RD
BLACKHORSE AVE

N CIRCULAR RD
INFIRMARY RD
PARK GATE

Pope John Paul II Park
Sports Ground

ASHTOWN GATE
★ VISITOR CENTRE
★ ASHTOWN CASTLE

Quarry Lake

Fish Pond

CABRA GATE
CIVIL DEFENSE SCHOOL

★ ARAS AN UACHTARAIN

THE PHOENIX STATUE ★

CHESTERFIELD AVE

LORD'S WALK

POLO GROUND ■

GARDA ATHLETIC GROUND ■

CRICKET GROUND ■

Dublin Zoo

Citadel Pond

BANDSTAND ★

GARDA HEADQUARTERS

People's Garden
WELLINGTON MONUMENT ★

CRICKET GROUND

ARMY ATHLETIC GROUND ■

WELLINGTON RD

ISLANDBRIDGE GATE

MILITARY RD

S River Liffey
S CIRCULAR RD

Irish National War Memorial Park

Phoenix Park

PAPAL CROSS ★

★ AMERICAN AMBASSADOR'S RESIDENCE

ACRES RD

FOOTBALL GROUNDS

FOOTBALL & HURLING GROUNDS

CHAPELIZOD RD
CHAPELIZOD BYPASS

Longmeadows Park

CHESHIRE HOME
ST MARY'S HOSPITAL

CHAPELIZOD GATE

UPPER GLEN RD
MAIN RD
ST LAURENCE RD

MARTIN'S ROW

KNOCKMAROON GATE
Glen Pond
KNOCKMAROON RD

River Liffey

LUCAN RD
CHAPELIZOD BYPASS
KYLEMORE RD
ROSSMORE RD

Californian Hills Park

DRUMFINN RD
LA FANU RD

500 yds
500 m
0

© AVALON TRAVEL PUBLISHING, INC.

the gardens feature superb Victorian glasshouses by Richard Turner. It was here in August 1845 that the then-curator, David Moore, first noted the potato blight and correctly predicted its devastating consequences.

To get to the gardens, catch Dublin Bus #13/A from Merrion Square or O'Connell Street, or #19 from O'Connell Street (4/hour daily, 15-minute trip, fare €0.95).

Glasnevin Cemetery

Just west of the botanic gardens is Glasnevin Cemetery, also known as Prospect Cemetery (Finglas Rd., 3.5 km north of Trinity College, tel. 01/830-1133, www.glasnevin-cemetery.ie, open 9:30 A.M.–6 P.M. Mon.–Sat. and 9:30 A.M.–5 P.M. Sun., closes earlier in winter, free admission), the largest in the country at 124 acres. Here is the final resting place of many of Ireland's most beloved patriots: Daniel O'Connell (just look for the faux round tower), Charles Stewart Parnell, Michael Collins, Eamon de Valera, Maud Gonne MacBride, Constance Markievicz, Patrick Pearse, and Arthur Griffith. Much of the statuary here bears overt republican and patriotic motifs, apt considering it was established as a Catholic burial ground in 1832, after the Act of Emancipation. Note the watchtowers in the graveyard's southeastern section, which were used to keep an eye out for bodysnatchers. A free 90-minute guided tour departs the main gate at 2:30 P.M. every Wednesday and Friday. Alternatively, there's a map-and-guide available from the flower shop at the front gate for €3.50.

The cemetery is on Dublin Bus route #40 from Parnell Street (5/hour daily, 35-minute trip).

EAST OF THE CITY CENTER

The Dúchas-run **Casino Marino** (Cherrymount Crescent, off the Malahide Rd., 4 km east of the city center, tel. 01/833-1618, open 10 A.M.–5 P.M. daily May and Oct., 10 A.M.–6 P.M. daily June–Sept., noon–4 P.M. weekends Nov.–Mar., noon–5 P.M. weekends Apr., admission €2.90) is, in the words of *Irish Times* writer Frank McDonald, "surely our most peculiar national monument. It was designed by an English architect who never set foot in this country for an Irish aristocrat and aesthete who almost went bankrupt trying to recreate Italy in Ireland." These men were William Chambers and James Caulfield (the first Earl of Charlemont), respectively. As a young man, the earl had dragged his Grand Tour of Europe into a nine-year odyssey, and he became good friends with Chambers while both were staying in Rome. He later had Chambers design his "summer home," what is still widely considered one of the best examples of small-scale neoclassical architecture; difficult as it is to picture now, this section of Dublin was still part of the boonies back in the 18th century, and the casino (as in "small house") had a great view of Dublin Bay and the surrounding countryside. Now it's something of an oasis amid the urban sprawl.

Ironically, Chambers never laid eyes on one of his very finest achievements, which is larger and grander than it appears from the exterior. Ingenious touches abound, like chimneys disguised as decorative urns on the roof and rainwater pipes hidden in columns, and the nearly hour-long guided tour offers plenty more interesting historical and architectural tidbits.

The building was taken into state care in 1932, but the 10-year restoration effort commenced only in 1974. To preserve the original flooring, visitors are asked to wear disposable booties over their shoes. To get here, take Dublin Bus route #123 from O'Connell Street (4 or more/hour daily, 20-minute trip, single fare €0.95), or ride the DART from Connolly to Clontarf Road (4/hour daily, 4-minute ride, single/return fare €1.35/2.45).

RATHFARNHAM

South of the city, in the "village" of Rathfarnham, is **Rathfarnham Castle** (Rathfarnham bypass, between Rathfarnam Rd. and Grange Rd., Dublin 14, tel. 01/493-9462, open 9:30 A.M.–5:30 P.M. daily May–Oct., admission €2), an impressive 16th-century structure with 18th-century interiors by two of England's most prominent architects,

William Chambers and James "Athenian" Stuart (to distinguish him from the actor, you know...actually, he got that moniker after publishing *Antiquities of Athens,* which greatly influenced the neoclassical movement in late-18th-century British architecture). Conservation work is ongoing in the castle itself, where access is by a guided tour of 45 minutes to an hour. Take Dublin Bus #16/A from South Great Georges Street.

Patrick Pearse, one of the Easter rebels executed in May 1916, was a devoted learner and teacher of the Irish language. The nearby **Pearse Museum and St. Enda's National Historic Park** (Grange Rd., Rathfarnham, Dublin 16, tel. 01/493-4208, open 10 A.M.–1 P.M. and 2–5:30 P.M. daily May–Aug., until 5 P.M. Feb.–Apr. and Sept.–Oct., until 4 P.M. Nov.–Jan., free admission) is housed on the premises of the school he founded in 1909; it features an exhibition on Pearse's life and work with a collection of letters and photographs and a 20-minute audiovisual. The adjacent St. Enda's Park includes a waterfall, walled garden, and self-guiding nature trail. Take bus route #16/A to get here.

TOURS

All tours are bookable through the tourist office on Suffolk Street.

◖ Walking Tours

Get some exercise, learn a lot, and maybe even have yourself a tipple on one of Dublin's many excellent guided walking tours. The best known, running since 1988, is the **Dublin Literary Pub Crawl** (tel. 01/670-5602, www.dublinpubcrawl.com, tours at 7:30 P.M. daily and noon Sun. late Mar.–late Nov., only Thurs.–Sun. in low season, €11), hosted by local actors who'll perform the work of Ireland's most beloved poets and playwrights at each of the four pubs on the itinerary. The two-hour, 15-minute tour starts at The Duke pub on Duke Street off Grafton Street. The performances come between frequent 20-minute beer breaks.

If you love a good old-fashioned ghost story, try the **Ghost Walk Macabre** (tel. 087/677-1512 or 087/271-1346, advance booking essential, 75-minute tour €12), led by similarly theatrical guides (they're all members of the Trapeze Theatre Company). The walk departs the Fusiliers' Arch at St. Stephen's Green at 7:30 P.M. daily.

Want something a little more serious? Then you'll admire your hardworking guides on the **Historical Walking Tour** (tel. 01/878-0227 or 087/688-9412, www.historicalinsights. ie, 11 A.M. and 3 P.M. daily Apr.–Sept., noon Fri.–Sat. Oct.–Mar., €10), all postgraduate history students. The two-hour walk departs from the Trinity College entrance. Themed tours, available between May and September, include "Architecture and Society," the "Sexual History of Ireland," and another focusing on the Easter Rising. Another reputable company does an **Easter Rising Walk** (tel. 01/707-2493 or 087/830-3523, www.1916rising.com, 11:30 A.M. and 2:30 P.M. Mon.–Sat. and 1 P.M. Sun. Apr.–Sept., tickets €10), which departs the International Bar on Wicklow Street and also lasts two hours.

City Bus Tours

Dublin Bus (59 O'Connell St., tel. 01/873-4222, www.dublinbus.ie) offers tours in and around the city. The **Hop-On Hop-Off Tour** (buses every 15 minutes 9:30 A.M.–4:30 P.M. daily, €14) is a 90-minute circuit that includes pretty much all the city center attractions, plus Phoenix Park and the Guinness Storehouse, and your ticket entitles you to discounts at several places. The **Ghost Tour** (7 P.M. and 9 P.M. Sat.–Sun., 8 P.M. Tues.–Fri., 2-hour tour €25) offers, among other grisly tidbits, a "crash course in body-snatching." The **Coast and Castles Tour** (10 A.M.–2 P.M. daily, 3-hour tour €22) covers the National Botanic Gardens, Casino Marino, Malahide Castle, and Howth Harbour. You can book any of these tours at the Dublin Bus office on O'Connell Street or at the Bus Éireann counter at the Suffolk Street tourist office; all tours depart the O'Connell Street office.

Boat Tours

One of the most fun and original (if touristy) ways to see more of the city is on a **Viking Splash Tour** (tel. 01/707-6000, www.viking-splashtours.com, tours generally every half hour 10 A.M.–5 P.M. daily Mar.–Oct., open Wed.–Sun. in Feb. and Tues.–Sun. in Nov., tickets €16, €18.50 June–Aug.). Tours depart 64-65 Patrick Street (near St. Patrick's Cathedral) and St. Stephen's Green North (at Dawson Street). You'll spend the first 50 minutes on this 75-minute tour walking around the city wearing "Viking" hats and behaving outrageously in public at the behest of your guide. In between, of course, you'll learn a lot of historical tidbits. The tour culminates in a 20-minute boat trip on the Grand Canal Basin in a "Duck"—a reconditioned WWII amphibious military vehicle. There is not much "splashing" involved, however.

Day Trips from Dublin

Brú na Bóinne (Newgrange and two other passage tombs), Powerscourt, and Glendalough in Wicklow Mountains National Park are commonly experienced on a day tour out of the city. (For more information, see *Brú na Bóinne* in the *Meath and Louth* chapter and *Powerscourt* and *Glendalough* in the *Wicklow and Kildare* chapter.)

Want to take a pass on the cheesy commentary? The **Newgrange Shuttlebus** (freephone tel. 1800/424-252, departs Suffolk St. tourist office at 8:45 A.M. and 11:15 A.M. and O'Connell St. outside the Royal Dublin Hotel at 9 A.M. and 11:30 A.M. daily, departs Brú na Bóinne at 1 P.M. and 4 P.M., 45-minute trip, €15 return) is a great option if efficient transportation to and from the site is all you're looking for (and the price is less in accordance, though site admission is not included). In low season there is only one departure, at 11:15/11:30 A.M.

Bus Éireann does a "Wicklow panorama" day tour that includes Powerscourt and Glendalough (tel. 01/836-6111, departs Busáras on Store St. at 10:30 A.M. Wed., Fri., Sun., returns 4:30 P.M., ticket €22, includes admission fees). Bus Éireann also does a Boyne Valley tour that includes the Brú na Bóinne admission fee (departs bus station 10 A.M. Thurs. and Sat., returns 4:15 P.M., ticket €22).

Over the Top Tours (tel. 01/838-6128 or 087/259-3467, freephone tel. for reservations 1800/424-252, www.overthetoptours.com, departs O'Connell St. outside Gresham Hotel at 9:20 A.M. and Suffolk St. tourist office at 9:45 A.M. daily, returning 5:30 P.M., ticket €26) offers a smaller (max. 14 people) tour of Glendalough and Wicklow National Park.

Entertainment and Events

TRADITIONAL PUBS

There're always traditional music sessions on at the chintzy tourist traps of Temple Bar, but you're better off seeking out more low-key venues. Nothing's quite "authentic" in this town—you'll have to go out to the boonies for a session that doesn't have a heavy element of tourist-driven theatricality to it—but some spots are certainly more "authentic" than others. Avoid any place that charges a cover for entry.

Tucked away behind the Four Courts, **Hughes'** (19-20 Chancery St., tel. 01/872-6540) offers live trad nightly into the wee

hours and is far less touristy than the musical pubs of Temple Bar. Similarly atmospheric is the upstairs bar at **Cobblestones** (N. King St., tel. 01/872-1799), where you'll also find trad or folk on a nightly basis. It's a bit more touristy, but that's because **O'Donoghue's** (15 Merrion Row, tel. 01/661-4303) offers (arguably) the city's best trad. The walls are covered with pictures of The Dubliners, the '60s folk group that got its start here, and the courtyard/alleyway leading to the entrance is always packed with a youngish crowd more interested in chat than music.

© JOHN M. KEATING/PHOTO BY VINCENT VIDAL

Dublin's coolest Northside bar, John M. Keating, is in an 18th-century Methodist church.

It claims to be Ireland's oldest pub, a hotbed of seditious activity in rebellions gone by, but the **Brazen Head** (Bridge St., tel. 01/677-9549, www.brazenhead.com) is pushing the limits on tourist-kitsch with its silly castellated facade and extremely overpriced drinks (even for Dublin). The nightly session is meant to be traditional, but the guys here play a lot of Van Morrison or Thin Lizzy, with only the occasional jig or reel thrown in. Having said all this, there's still a fair bit of *craic* to be found, especially in the spacious courtyard beer garden.

A delightfully "crusty old man's pub" (it used to sell groceries as well), **James Toner's** (Lower Baggot St., tel. 01/676-3090) hums with an after-work crowd of all ages. This is believed to be the only pub in Dublin William Butler Yeats ever visited.

A classy yet understated Victorian pub with all the period details, **William Ryan's** (28 Parkgate St., tel. 01/677-6097) is in a residential neighborhood off the tourist circuit, which means the ambience is refreshingly workaday. The same goes for **The Long Hall** (51 S. Great Georges St., tel. 01/475-1590), though weirdly enough, it's smack-dab in the middle of touristville. After a satisfying meal at one of the great restaurants on or near South Great Georges, you can chill out here to the strains of Annie Lennox—another nice surprise, in a place like this. Another great Victorian snug-lined pub is **John Kehoe's** (9 S. Anne St., tel. 01/677-8312), where you can have a drink upstairs in the late proprietor's old living room.

BARS AND CLUBS

Dublin has amassed a reputation for one of the hottest club scenes in Europe, though it's difficult to party properly when even the hippest places close their doors at 3 A.M.! Cover charges vary from €5–10 during the week to €15–20 at weekends. Check *inDublin* (www.indublin.ie), a free weekly, for a listing of what's on when that's as comprehensive as it gets. Not into grinding? The city center offers plenty of trendy bars—some you might call "novelty"—where you can kick back with a fancy cocktail and let the night slip by in a whirl of funky lighting and stimulating conversation.

FESTIVALS AND EVENTS IN DUBLIN

Naturally, Dublin's **St. Patrick's Festival** (01/676-3205, www.stpatricksday.ie) is Ireland's largest: The parade attracts as many as 1.5 million spectators, and there's everything from concerts to street theater to fireworks over the four days leading up to St. Paddy's Day. Environmentalists might want to time their visit for the **Convergence Sustainable Living Festival** (15-19 Essex St., tel. 01/674-6415, www.sustainable.ie), taking place over 10 days in April.

Summer brings the music fests. The **Anna Livia International Opera Festival** (01/661-7544, www.operaannalivia.com) and **Pipeworks** (43-44 Temple Bar, tel. 01/633-7392, www.pipeworksfestival.com) – formerly known as the Dublin International Organ and Choral Festival – both take place in June; the opera fest is seven days long, and most events are on at the Gaiety or the National Concert Hall; the latter festival takes place over 10 days at the city's finest churches (St. Patrick's, Christ Church, and others) and the National Concert Hall. If opera or organ music isn't your thing, don't fret. It may not be *in* Dublin, but the high-profile rock and indie artists performing at the Heineken-sponsored **Oxegen** (www.oxegen.ie) over a weekend in early July draw a youthful, international crowd. The venue is Punchestown Racecourse outside Naas, County Kildare (37 km west of Dublin), tickets sell out quickly (the box office opens in November), and most people camp outside the racecourse (though sleep, unlike booze, is a precious commodity here).

One of the biggest and most exciting events on the city's calendar, the **Dublin Theatre Festival** (01/677-8899, www.dublintheatrefestival.com, tickets €10-35) takes place over the first two weeks in October. Productions are Irish and international, classic and avant-garde, and plays are put on at theaters all over the city. The well-established **fringe festival** (01/872-9016, www.fringefestival.com) offers comedy as well as more experimental work.

And the last weekend in October brings the **Dublin City Marathon** (01/623-2250, www.dublincitymarathon.ie), established in 1979 and sponsored by Adidas. This race is widely known as the "friendly marathon" for the especially supportive crowds it attracts.

It's within spitting distance of the Trinity College gates, but **The Bank** (20-22 College Green, tel. 01/677-0677, www.bankoncollegegreen.com) is more popular with 20- and 30-something professionals. The stunning Victorian details—polished mahogany, plasterwork, mosaic flooring, open fireplaces, a wrought-iron mezzanine above the horseshoe bar—belie a relaxed atmosphere and down-to-earth staff. Somewhat trendier is the **Market Bar** (Fade St., off S. Great Georges St., tel. 01/677-4835, tapas €6–10), in an old sausage factory. It's an atmospheric space to that end, with tall walls of exposed brick, a ceiling made all of skylights, comfortable seating, and another wall of shelves lined with wooden shoe-trees thrown in for quirky good measure. The only less-than-cool thing about this place is the inexplicably brusque barstaff.

With an absolutely breathtaking, impeccably assembled interior, the commodious art nouveau **Café en Seine** (40 Dawson St., tel. 01/667-4567) draws a youngish, well-heeled crowd of those who don't mind the high drink prices. Get here early, order your cocktails, score a couple of plush armchairs by an ornate period fireplace, and people-watch to your heart's content. Or for a taste of the Middle East, try the equally popular **SamSara** (35-36 Dawson St., tel. 01/671-7723) a couple doors down.

Here's one to write home about: an 18th-century Methodist church converted into a swanky new bar and restaurant, complete with original pipe organ, stained glass windows, and marble wall memorials. Ask the bartender at **John M. Keating** (Mary St. at Jervis St., tel. 01/878-0223 or 087/636-3738, www.jmk.ie) how the eponymous owner achieved this

GAY DUBLIN

Ireland has made leaps and bounds in the tolerance department since homosexuality was legalized in 1993, but Dublin is really the only place where you can hold hands with your partner without feeling self-conscious. And you're spoiled for choice entertainment-wise; May is a great time to be here, for the **Dublin Gay Theatre Festival** (tel. 01/677-8511, www.gaytheatre.ie), when you'll spot Oscar Wilde's mug hanging on banners all over town (though the plays put on are mostly contemporary). Another event worth planning a trip for is the **Gay Pride Parade,** established in 1992; the parade is the culmination of the **International LGBTQ Pride Festival** (www.dublinpride.org), a two-week event toward the end of June. There's also the city's Lesbian and Gay Film Festival, **Look Out** (6 Eustace St., tel. 01/679-3477, www.irishfilm.ie), for four days in early August, where international flicks are screened at the Irish Film Institute.

There are a few all-gay clubs in Dublin: The oldest, **The George** (89 S. Great Georges St., tel. 01/478-2983), offers bingo on Sunday nights, and **Gubu** (7-8 Capel St., tel. 01/874-0483) and **Pod** (Harcourt St., at the Old Railway Station, tel. 01/478-0225) play live shows; all three draw eclectic crowds. Gubu is a good place to go for a drink any night of the week. Many quality nightclubs offer special LGBT

nights, like Monday-night "Strictly Handbag" at **Rí-Rá** (Dame Ct., tel. 01/677-4835, www.rira.ie). Strictly Handbag is so much fun that a lot of straight Dubs attend it regularly as well. As for pubs, **Out on the Liffey** (27 Upper Ormond Quay, tel. 01/872-2480) is popular with biker dudes; if you're looking for something posh, try **Front Lounge** (33 Parliament St., tel. 01/670-4112).

Now on to the practical stuff. Stop by the **Outhouse** (105 Capel St., Northside, tel. 01/872-1055, www.outhouse.ie), the city's most established resource center, and peruse the notice boards before checking your email or having lunch at the café (open 1:30–5:30 P.M. Mon.-Fri., 1–5 P.M. Sat., plus 6:30–9:30 P.M. Tues., 7–10 P.M. Thurs. women only, 7–10 P.M. Fri. men only). The **Gay Switchboard Dublin** (tel. 01/872-1055, www.gayswitchboard.ie) also provides advice and information. **Gay Dublin** (www.gaydublin.com) is a decent source of entertainment info, and better yet is the nationwide **Gay Ireland** (www.gay-ireland.com).

Consider staying at **Frankie's Guesthouse** (8 Camden Pl., off Camden St., same as Aungier St. but three blocks south, tel. 01/478-3087, www.frankiesguesthouse.com, complimentary wireless Internet, €45–60 pp, s €40–60, credit cards accepted), Dublin's only exclusively gay and lesbian B&B.

entrepreneurial feat—isn't it sacrilegious, or something?—and the bartender will sagely point out to you that this church was fast plummeting into ruin when Keating purchased the property in the late '90s (and wouldn't the people buried beneath you prefer a swanky bar over a crumbling edifice littered with empty crisp bags?). Several years and millions of euros later, here we are in the coolest, most unusual nightspot on either side of the Liffey, though the bar's newness coupled with its Northside location means there are virtually no tourists here. The old crypt has also been converted into a second bar down a long set of stairs, but the

main bar is far more atmospheric. You might want to have your dinner up in the organ gallery, a highly unusual feature in ecclesiastical architecture regardless of the denomination.

The swanky **Mint Bar** (Westmoreland St., tel. 01/645-1322, www.westin.com) at the Westin Hotel offers salsa Fridays and "Velvet Lounge" Saturdays, with a mix of lounge, jazz, and swing; the music starts at 10 P.M. both nights, and bar nibbles are available until 10:30. The Morrison Hotel also has a superchic bar (with white leather everywhere), **Lobo** (Lower Ormond Quay, tel. 01/887-2400, www.morrisonhotel.ie); with a stylish (if pretentious) crowd, hip ambience, and titillating cocktail menu, it's perfect for "pre-clubbing."

A hip place to pass the day away with coffee and nibbles, after dark **The Globe** (11 S. Great George's St., tel. 01/671-1220, www .globe.ie) is a perennial pre-club favorite with Dublin's fashion-conscious trend-setters. There's an evening tapas menu, trip hop and acid jazz on the stereo, and a collection of faux-classical marble statues. There's also live jazz on Sunday afternoon. After closing, the Globe becomes part of **Rí-Rá** (Dame Ct., tel. 01/677-4835, www .rira.ie, open at 11:30 P.M. Mon.–Sat., free before midnight during the week, cover €5–10), probably the best nightclub in the city for its eclectic crowd, Monday-night '80s theme (very gay-friendly), great funk and lounge tunes, and astonishingly friendly bouncers.

Friday nights bring "Salsa Palace" and Saturdays "The Soul Stage" (jazz, soul, hip-hop, and motown) at the **Gaiety Theatre** (King St. S., tel. 01/677-1717, www.gaietytheatre.com, open at midnight, Fri./Sat. cover €15/20). Both nights feature live bands, four different bars, and old films playing on the main stage until 4 A.M. The motto is "sweets for the sweet" at the classy **Sugar Club** (8 Lower Leeson St., tel. 01/678-7188, www.thesugarclub.com, cover €10/15 before/after 10 P.M.), where a live show prefaces a night of dancing. The lineup is eclectic, from indie rock bands to ska, blues, or Latin. The acoustics are fab, the seats slouchy velour, and the cocktails killer. Fridays are reserved for cabaret, and Wednesday has a Las Vegas theme.

LIVE ROCK VENUES

There's something on every night of the week—rock, jazz, blues, trad, you name it—at **Whelan's** (25 Wexford St., tel. 01/478-0766, www.whelanslive.com, tickets €10–23) and at its "sister" venue, the **Village** (26 Wexford St., tel. 01/475-8555, www.thevillagevenue.com). Featuring some high-profile performers (Damien Rice, Rodrigo y Gabriela, and the Flaming Lips just for starters), **Vicar Street** (58-59 Thomas St., tel. 01/454-5533, www.vicarstreet

.com, tickets €20–35) is a cozy enough place to catch a show—with its main level dotted with round tables and theater-style balcony, it holds only 1,000.

The city's largest pop/rock venue is **Point Theatre** (East Link Bridge, North Wall Quay, tel. 01/836-3633, www.thepoint.ie, tickets €40–70), which has hosted Prince, Pearl Jam, Diana Ross, Paul Simon, and many other greats over the years in this converted railway depot that seats up to 8,500.

The **Olympia Theatre** (72 Dame St., tel. 01/677-7744) sometimes offers experimental or unusual drama (like, say, Shakespeare's *Twelfth Night* by a Russian company, in Russian), but it's better known for its eclectic range of concerts at the weekend. The Goo Goo Dolls, Lyle Lovett, Bic Runga, and Sufjan Stevens have all played here.

If you're not looking for a concert as such, another option is a dimly lit Northside pub, **Sin É** (which means "That's it"; 14-15 Ormond Quay, tel. 01/878-7009), which has live pop/indie/rock music nightly. There's no cover and the bartenders are nice as can be.

OTHER MUSIC VENUES

Venues abound for the listener with more refined tastes as well. The National Symphony Orchestra performs nearly every Friday night at the **National Concert Hall** (Earlsfort Terrace, just south of St. Stephen's Green, tel. 01/475-1666, www.nch.ie, performances usually start at 8 P.M., tickets €8–25), and on other nights there are international bands and orchestras, jazz ensembles, and traditional music performances. Northside, the **Hugh Lane Municipal Gallery of Modern Art** (22 N. Parnell Sq., tel. 01/874-1903, www.hughlane.ie) also hosts classical concerts.

Serious jazz fans should check out **Jazz on the Terrace** (www.jazzontheterrace.com), which "represents Irish jazz artists abroad and international jazz artists in Ireland." There's a listing of upcoming concerts, gigs, and festivals as well as links to local band websites. One of the city's best jazz venues is the **Boom Boom Room,** upstairs at **Patrick Conway's**

(70 Parnell St., tel. 01/873-2687, www.the-boomboomroom.tv, cover €5–8). Conway's has been open for business since 1745.

Founded in 1951 in an attempt to preserve the country's musical traditions, **Comhaltas Ceoltóiri Éireann** (32 Belgrave Sq., Monkstown, tel. 01/280-0295, www.comhaltas.com, performances at 9 P.M. Mon.–Thurs. July–Aug., tickets €10) offers a *seisiún* of top-notch singing and dancing along with the jigs, reels, and airs you'd hear in a pub session. Friday nights all year there's a "country set dance" starting at 9:30 P.M., where the €8 admission fee basically gets you an informal lesson (and a lot of *craic*). To get here, take the DART from Tara Street in the city center southbound to Seapoint Road.

THEATER AND CINEMA

Ireland's national theater, the **Abbey** (Lower Abbey St., tel. 01/878-7222, www.abbeytheatre.ie, tickets €15–30) commissions new works from Irish playwrights and occasionally revives classic plays by O'Casey, Beckett, Behan, and many lesser-known dramatists. In addition to the rather out-of-date main theater, there's a smaller venue downstairs, **The Peacock.** Afterward, if you feel like chatting about the play with random strangers, the pub to head to is the **Flowing Tide** (9 Lower Abbey St., tel. 01/874-0842).

Other Dublin mainstays include the **Gaiety Theatre** (King St. S., tel. 01/677-1717, www.gaietytheatre.com, tickets €17–55), opened in 1871, which puts on everything from Riverdance to Mother Goose to the more mainstream productions of the annual Dublin

Theatre Festival; and the **Gate Theatre** (1 Cavendish Row, tel. 01/874-4045, www.gatetheatre.ie, tickets €15–30), founded by the flamboyant duo of Hilton Edwards and Micheál MacLiammóir in 1928, which offers a range of Irish classics—from Oscar Wilde to Brian Friel—as well as quirkier works along the lines of Harold Pinter.

Opened by President Mary McAleese in 2002, **The Helix** (Collins Ave., Glasnevin, DCU campus, tel. 01/700-7000, www.thehelix.ie, tickets €15–25) sports an art gallery and three separate venues for an eclectic (but fairly mainstream) calendar of plays and concerts. Take Dublin Bus route #4, #11/A/B, #13/A, or #19 to Ballymun Road.

If you're more into the experimental side of things, see what's on at the **Tivoli Theatre** (135-136 Francis St., tel. 01/454-4472) or **Andrew's Lane Theatre** (9-17 St. Andrew's Lane, tel. 01/679-5720, www.andrewslane.com, tickets €10–26). The **Project Arts Centre** (39 E. Essex St., tel. 1850/260-027, www.project.ie, tickets €12–20) is another solid venue.

For arthouse and classic film screenings, the place to go is the **Irish Film Centre** (6 Eustace St., tel. 01/679-3477, www.fii.ie, tickets €6–8).

COMEDY

One of the best comedy venues in the city is the **Comedy Cellar** at the **International Bar** (23 Wicklow St., tel. 01/677-9250, cover €8), which has shows on Monday, Wednesday, and Thursday nights starting at 9 P.M. As many as 10 jokemeisters will pass the evening, which lasts until closing time.

Shopping

GRAFTON STREET

Though everyone thinks Grafton Street is the best place to shop in Dublin, if you take a walk down the crowded pedestrian street you'll notice that most of the shops are midscale women's clothing boutiques (and the same goes for the huge, glass-domed **St. Stephen's Green Shopping Centre** where Grafton meets the park). You can skip Grafton altogether if you're looking for souvenirs; head for **Powerscourt Townhouse** (59 S. William St., one block west of Grafton St. and signposted, tel. 01/679-4144), which includes several smallish but classy clothing and jewelry shops and a great vegetarian restaurant, **Café Fresh,** on the top floor.

Just around the corner from Grafton Street is a spacious **Avoca Handweavers** shop (11-13 Suffolk St., tel. 01/677-4215, www.avoca.ie, café open 9:30 A.M.–5 P.M. weekdays, 10 A.M.– 5 P.M. Sat., 10 A.M.–5:30 P.M. Sun., open 30 minutes later in summer, mains under €12), full of delightful gifts—blankets, sweaters (colorful and modern, not the old-fashioned Aran kind), jewelry, along with household items (aerodynamic spatulas, spice racks, hardcover cookbooks, and so forth) downstairs and a top-floor café, a nice spot for lunch or tea despite the lack of windows.

Another gem just off Grafton Street is **Cathach Books** (10 Duke St., tel. 01/671-8676, www.rarebooks.ie), which rightly bills itself as "Ireland's leading antiquarian bookshop." Serious bibliophiles should note that its catalog is available online.

SOUTH GREAT GEORGES STREET

Full of delights is the **Market Arcade** on South Great Georges Street (at Exchequer), with a variety of shops and stalls of secondhand books and vintage clothing. The **Farm Shop** sells

© CAMILLE DEANGELIS

fun with neon on South Great Georges Street

DUBLIN

fruit, olives, Turkish delight, and other goodies perfect for noshing as you watch the world go by from a park bench on St. Stephen's Green.

SOUTH OF TRINITY COLLEGE

There is a wealth of sweater and knickknacky shops along Nassau Street, just east of Grafton Street and south of Trinity, but most of them aren't worth browsing. If it's an Aran sweater you're after, try **Cleo** (18 Kildare St., tel. 01/676-1421), which has an exquisite selection (and, as at those shops selling machine-knit ganseys, you do get what you pay for). Then spend an hour or two at **Kilkenny Design** (5-6 Nassau St., tel. 01/677-7066), an upscale chain store renowned for its stock of cutting-edge Irish fashion, housewares, pottery, silverware, jewelry, sculpture, and framed art. There's also a fantastic upstairs café.

TEMPLE BAR

This area's better known for its tourist-trap pubs, but a couple of small stores are worth seeking out (especially if you're an "alternative" type). The shop at **Cultivate** (15-19 Essex St. W., tel. 01/674-6396, www.cultivate.ie), Dublin's "sustainable living and learning centre," sells eco-friendly produce, detergents, and other items along with a selection of environmental books and magazines. Check out the "permaculture" garden in the courtyard out back. This is also the place to go for more info on the **Convergence Sustainable Living Festival** (www.sustainable.ie), held annually in April.

Anthology Books (Meeting House Sq., tel. 01/635-1422, www.anthologystore.com) has a great selection of feminist, gay and lesbian, art and architecture, and Irish-interest titles.

Sports and Recreation

IN THE CITY

Be a temporary Dubliner and stretch your legs on the nine-hectare **St. Stephen's Green** (tel. 01/475-7816), or go for a run or longer walk at the seven-square-kilometer **Phoenix Park** (tel. 01/677-0095) on the western perimeter of the city center.

Built for the 2003 Special Olympics summer games, the **National Aquatic Centre** (Snugborough Rd., Blanchardstown, Dublin 15, tel. 01/646-4364 or 01/646-4367, www.nac.ie, open 9 A.M.–8:45 P.M. weekdays, 9 A.M.–7:45 P.M. weekends, admission €12) features plenty of kiddie delights (slides, wave and surf machines, the works) as well as the official Olympic-size pool. Dublin Bus route #38A from Hawkins Street (or Berkeley St., outside St. Joseph's Church) will get you here.

In addition to a regular roster of five-week courses and retreats, the **Dublin Buddhist Centre** (42 Leeson St. Lower, in the basement, tel. 01/661-5934, www.dublinbuddhistcentre.org) offers one-day yoga, meditation, and spirituality workshops for all experience levels. This nonprofit center is part of the FWBO, or Friends of the Western Buddhist Order.

OUTSIDE THE CITY

Don't stay in the city center if the weather's fine! There are several sandy beaches in the Dublin 'burbs; some of them, like **Killiney** (kill-EYE-nee, 16 km south of the city), **Portrane** (24 km north), and **Donabate** (21 km north), have even been awarded the coveted Blue Flag. Killiney is particularly attractive; some say it even has a vaguely Mediterranean vibe on fine summer days. Many Irish celebs (Bono, Enya, and director Neil Jordan, among others) have homes here. Fortunately, you can reach all these beaches via the DART (tel. 01/805-4288, www.dart.ie, 2–3/hour daily from Connolly Station, 20-minute trip, get off at Donabate for Portrane as well, single/day return fares about €2.50/4). **Dollymount,** another Blue Flag beach (and UNESCO Biosphere Reserve, for its web-footed population), is immediately north of Dublin Harbour. The strand is linked to the Dollymount neighborhood by an old wooden bridge. Get here via Dublin Bus route #130 from Lower Abbey Street (4–6/hour daily).

Want to experience the wild and wonderful Wicklow Mountains National Park, but don't have time for an overnight trip? **Dirtyboots Treks** (tel. 01/623-6785, www.dirtybootstreks. com, full-day trek including packed lunch and transportation €45) will take you on a four- or five-hour hike, giving you bits of info on the natural history of the mountains along the way. The tour departs Trinity College gates at 9 A.M. almost daily; groups are limited to eight, making this a more intimate (not to mention far more strenuous) sightseeing option. No worries if you haven't brought hiking boots or raingear—you can rent them for €9.

Not many folks can say they've sailed over Ireland in a hot air balloon. Want bragging rights? Contact **Irish Balloon Flights** (80 Cypress Grove Rd., Templeogue, Dublin, tel. 01/408-4777 or 087/933-2622, flight-check line 087/743-7575, www.balloons.ie, 1/2/3 or more passengers €240/220/210 pp). Most flights depart Rathsallagh House in Wicklow (60 km south of Dublin) or Trim Castle in Meath (55 km northwest), though there are other launch locations around the country. The hefty ticket price includes a glass of champagne after a one-hour flight.

SPECTATOR SPORTS

Catch a **hurling** or **Gaelic football** match at the country's largest stadium, **Croke Park** (Clonliffe Rd., north of the Royal Canal in Drumcondra, tel. 01/836-3222, tickets €20–55), on Sunday afternoons May–September. Except for playoff games (when tickets can be mighty hard to come by), you can purchase admission at the door. For more background on these native sports, be sure to check out the **Gaelic Athletic Association** website (www.gaa.ie).

Dublin Bus routes #3, #11/A, #16/A, and #123 frequently link O'Connell Street with Croke Park.

Football (i.e., soccer) and rugby matches are played at **Lansdowne Stadium** (Ballsbridge, tel. 01/668-9300, www.lrsdc.ie) on the south side of the city. A major redevelopment means that the stadium won't be hosting any more sporting events until 2009. The revamped stadium will have a capacity of 50,000, though local residents, understandably, are vehemently opposed. To get here, take the DART to the Lansdowne Road Station, a short walk from the park, or ride Dublin Bus route #7, #8, #45, or #84.

Accommodations

Securing decent accommodations in Dublin can be a real headache; rooms are hard to come by at peak times, especially budget beds, and as you will hopefully never have to discover firsthand, it isn't just hostel dormitories that can be dirty and otherwise unpleasant. Even "four-star" hotels can have nasty surprises in store. Aside from the Irish Tourist Board seal of approval, your best bet is word of mouth (from someone who's stayed at the place in question in the last year); don't place much stock in an establishment's website. That may seem obvious, but it's even more important here; an awful lot of guesthouses manage to make dumpy rooms look luxurious.

TEMPLE BAR

It's central, but accommodations in Temple Bar can be noisy. Don't stay in this section unless you're planning to be out pubbing every night.

Despite an inefficient reception area and a rather inexperienced staff, **Four Courts Hostel** (15-17 Merchants Quay, tel. 01/672-5839, www.fourcourtshostel.com, dorms €18–25, private rooms €28–36 pp, Internet access

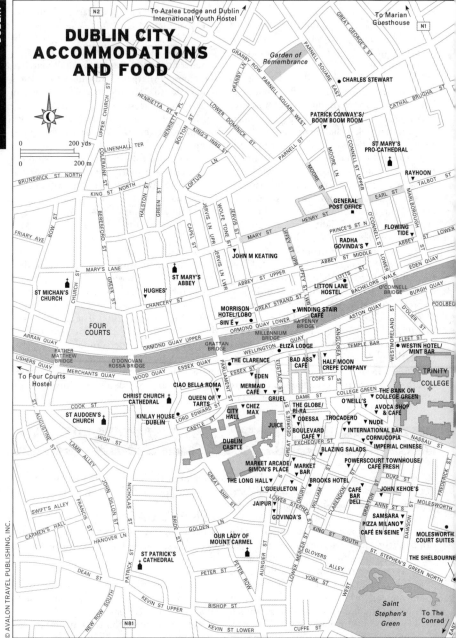

DUBLIN CITY ACCOMMODATIONS AND FOOD

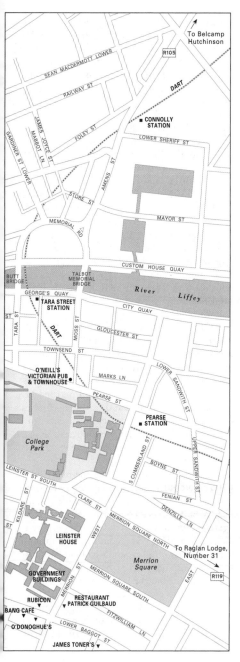

€4/hour, credit cards accepted) is still one of the best hostels in the city. The location is superb, security is adequate, the rooms are clean and the mattresses comfortable, and there are separate rooms for socializing and quiet pastimes. This place isn't quite as bohemian as it likes to think it is (there are cartoon murals along the staircase spouting random statistics—did you know that lefties live an average of nine years less than right-handers?—and the impossibly buxom blonde carrying a U.S.A. tote bag annoys you more every time you pass her), but the Four Courts still attracts a fun crowd. Basic continental breakfast (i.e., vending-machine coffee is extra) is included in the price.

The top guesthouse/hotel in this neighborhood is the **Eliza Lodge** (23-24 Wellington Quay at Eustace St., tel. 01/671-8044, www. dublinlodge.com, rooms €110–228, s €76–95), You can expect friendly and accommodating staff, mod but comfortable rooms (with in-room safes), and an outstanding breakfast in Elizablues, the downstairs restaurant. Some of the rooms have Jacuzzis and/or balconies overlooking the Liffey and Millennium Bridge.

Owned by Bono and The Edge, **The Clarence** (6-8 Wellington Quay, tel. 01/407-0800, www.theclarence.ie, rooms €340–370, suites €700–900, penthouse suite €2,500) is unsurprisingly a favorite with celebrities. The individually designed rooms are luxuriously furnished with king-size beds with Egyptian cotton sheets, Shaker-style furniture, wireless Internet, a CD and DVD collection, and laptop-sized safes. Check out the website for last-minute deals as low as €179. Needless to say, this hotel is definitely worth maxing out the credit card for.

CHRISTCHURCH

You can see the cathedral out your dorm room window at another of Dublin's most reliable hostels, **Kinlay House** (2/12 Lord Edward St., tel. 01/679-6644, www.kinlaydublin.ie, dorms €17–25, private rooms €30–40 pp, credit cards accepted). It's big, sure, but not overwhelmingly so. Atmospheric yet well-maintained, Kinlay House has ample kitchen and dining facilities, comfy beds, and professional staff. You can't go wrong booking a bed here.

AROUND TRINITY COLLEGE

Owned and run by the O'Neill family for more than 100 years, **O'Neill's Victorian Pub and Townhouse** (36-37 Pearse St., tel. 01/671-4074, www.oneillsdublin.com, €35–65 pp, s €55–120) offers comfortable new mattresses, hearty breakfasts, and fine period details in both the rooms and the delightful downstairs pub. Street noise from the DART passing nearby can be a problem, so this one is not recommended for light sleepers, and though the location is pretty central, just north of Trinity College, the immediate neighborhood is not especially nice.

Built in 1865 to house the Allied Irish Bank, the five-star **Westin Hotel** (Westmoreland St., tel. 01/645-1000, www.westin.com, rooms €320–600, package deals from €180 pp) retains its Victorian elegance in the reception areas, though the bedrooms are thoroughly modern: in-room massage treatments, laptop safes, minibars, private balconies, and so forth. The Westin is especially known for its trademarked "Heavenly Bed," featuring the most sumptuous bedclothes in all Dublin. Cheekily, there is a charge for wireless Internet access, and breakfast is extra (€25) unless you've booked a package deal.

AROUND ST. STEPHEN'S GREEN

You'll pay handsomely for the central location, but the range of top-quality accommodations near and around the green is well worth a splurge. Popular with families, **C Molesworth Court Suites** (35 Schoolhouse Ln., off Kildare St., tel. 01/676-4799, www.molesworthcourt. ie, 1/2-bedroom suite €160/200, 2/3-bedroom penthouse suite €280/350) offers swanky, spacious self-catering apartments in a stellar location with the attentive service of a five-star hotel. Each apartment comes equipped with wireless Internet, CD and DVD players, and a kitchenette.

If you appreciate finding mints on your pil-

low when you return to your hotel room, try the small, plush, and friendly **C Brooks Hotel** (Drury St., tel. 01/670-4000, www.brookshotel.ie, €85–130 pp sharing, singles charged at double rate), where you'll also find plasma TVs in the bedroom—*and* bathroom! The in-room foot spa and pillow menu (from which to select your pillow of choice) are other nice touches. Delicious full breakfasts are cooked to order and included in the room price.

One of Dublin's best guesthouses is **Number 31** (31 Leeson Close, Lower Leeson St., tel. 01/676-5011, www.number31.ie, €75–120 pp, s €115–160), with individually designed bedrooms in two wings: the retro-'50s coach house (with its sunken sitting room and mirrored bar) and the more staid Georgian townhouse. A top-notch breakfast menu, served in the conservatory, features homemade breads and salmon and kippers cooked to order. Top this off with a friendly staff, big comfy beds, and relaxing vibe, and you have a hotel with significant repeat business.

A five-star Hilton hotel, **The Conrad** (Earlsfort Terrace, 01/602-8900, www.conradhotels.com, rooms €250–525) is conveniently located across the street from the National Concert Hall. Rooms are comfortable and well appointed, if a bit on the sterile business-class side, and feature bathrobes and slippers, minibar, wireless Internet, and HiFi with CD player, ergonomic desk chairs, and converter plugs in case you've forgotten yours.

Closed for restoration at time of writing, **The Shelbourne** (27 St. Stephen's Green, tel. 01/663-4500, www.marriott.co.uk, rooms €325–600) offers incomparably elegant Georgian reception rooms, and the modern bedrooms (featuring down comforters, bathrobes and slippers, minibar, and suchlike) have historically inspired touches. Now owned by Marriott, the Shelbourne is likely to remain at the cream of the crop when it reopens in 2007. The complimentary on-site parking is a major plus; you won't find this at other city five-star hotels. The full-size swimming pool's kinda nice to have, too.

NORTHSIDE

Accommodations north of the Liffey are generally less expensive. The An Óige **Dublin International Youth Hostel** (61 Mountjoy St., tel. 01/830-1766, www.irelandya.org, dorms €18–21, twins/triples €23–26 pp, credit cards accepted) is huge and therefore utterly chaotic with so many school groups coming and going, so obviously it isn't your #1 choice. That said, the security is tight, the dorms and bathrooms are so clean they're sterile (not a bad thing, considering all the horror stories you hear about the hostels in this city), and continental breakfast in the lovely chapel-turned-dining hall is included in the price. You can also "upgrade" to a reasonably priced fry (€4 full Irish, €3 vegetarian).

No self-respecting U2 fan should pass up the chance to stay in their old recording studio, the IHH **Litton Lane Hostel** (2-4 Litton Ln., tel. 01/872-8389, www.irish-hostel. com, dorms €13–25, private rooms €25–45 pp, weekly rate €95, credit cards accepted), where there are concert videos playing 24/7 in the common room. The facilities are all adequate, the dorms clean though predictably cramped.

Looking for no-frills B&B? Try the **Charles Stewart** (5-6 Parnell Sq., tel. 01/878-0350, www.charlesstewart.ie, €32–45 pp), which offers clean but nondescript en-suite rooms with television and hostess tray. The 24-hour reception is handy, and the rate includes a full breakfast. Check the website for even better specials, usually at midweek. The rooms are homier at the **Marian Guesthouse** (21 Upper Gardiner St., tel. 01/874-4129, www.marianguesthouse. ie, €27–45 pp, s €35–45), though not all are en suite. The full Irish fry will keep you going 'til dinnertime.

With a great riverside location, the **Morrison Hotel** (Lower Ormond Quay, tel. 01/887-2400, www.morrisonhotel.ie, rooms €325–590, penthouse €1,500) has recently opened a new wing with 48 additional bedrooms (the total's now 138). Rooms are high-tech, featuring CD players or iPod docking stations along with free wireless Internet, and there's a safe and minibar in every room. Six new "studio" rooms have flatscreen Apple computers and sunken bathtubs with leather head- and footrests. The hotel also has one of the most sophisticated bars in the city. Headspace, a new spa featuring Turkish baths, seaweed wraps, and aromatherapy, is slated to open in 2007.

OUTSIDE THE CITY CENTER

You'll often find better value for your money outside the city center. Here are a few top guesthouses in Drumcondra and Glasnevin (both a couple kilometers north of the city center), Balgriffin (near Malahide), and Ballsbridge (south of the center).

Recommended for its bright, spotless, homey rooms, **Azalea Lodge** (67 Upper Drumcondra Rd., tel. 01/837-0300 or 087/243-4589, www.azalealodge.com, €45 pp, s €60, credit cards accepted) has a kind and accommodating owner who'll serve you tea and biscuits in the back garden. This place is reachable by Dublin Bus #40, or it's about a half-hour walk south to the city center.

Convenient for a morning stroll through the National Botanic Gardens, **Botanic View** (25 Botanic Ave. at Iona Rd., Glasnevin, tel. 01/860-0195, www.botanicview.com, €40–60 pp, s €50–60) offers immaculate (if a bit pink and frilly) rooms with cable television, a friendly and helpful proprietor, and the full fry at the breakfast table. Take Dublin Bus #13, #19/A, or #83; otherwise it's a brisk 35-minute walk to/from the city center.

Built in 1786 by the third Earl of Donoughmore, stately ivy-clad **Belcamp Hutchinson** (Carrs Ln., off the Malahide Rd., Balgriffin, Dublin 17, tel. 01/846-0843, www.belcamphutchinson.com, €75 pp sharing, no single occupancy) is set in almost two hectares of gardens, including a restored walled garden and circular hedge maze. Rooms are spacious and comfortable, the owners bend over backward to provide information and ensure your comfort, and the top-notch breakfasts feature homemade jams and produce from the garden. For those with a rental car, Belcamp is a good choice for your first or last night in Ireland since it's so close to the airport.

Another excellent B&B is south of the city center, in the prestigious Dublin 4. Dating from 1861, **Raglan Lodge** (10 Raglan Rd., Ballsbridge, tel. 01/660-6697, €60–80 pp, s €66–88) is an elegant brick home on "Embassy Row" with private parking and a wealth of period details. All rooms are en suite (three with shower, four with bath), and the breakfast menu is truly excellent, with freshly squeezed O.J., porridge, homemade muesli, fresh and stewed fruits, and smoked salmon and kippers. There's free wireless Internet, too; just ask for the access code. Because it's only a block from the American embassy, you can get here via the same Dublin Bus route (#4, #5, #7/A, #8, #45, #63, or #84 to Lansdowne Road), though the B&B is also within walking distance of the city center.

Food

Whether you want a (relatively) cheap, no-frills meal or a lavish three-course affair, Dublin's eateries run the gamut. So long as you know where to go, you might just end up eating better here than you did in Paris. Plus, finding good-value eats in this city isn't as difficult as you might think.

Note that some restaurants have started tacking a 10–15 percent "service charge" onto your bill (regardless of the number in your party). If you weren't satisfied with your meal in any way, don't hesitate to ask your server to deduct it.

AROUND GRAFTON STREET

You'll find the best pub grub in the area at **O'Neill's** (2 Suffolk St., tel. 01/679-3656, food served 3:30–9:30 P.M. Mon.–Thurs. and noon–9:30 P.M. Fri.–Sun., mains €9–12), a commodious, old-fashioned watering hole—open more than three centuries—with excellent carvery lunches that call to mind a Thanksgiving feast (though there's a vegetarian quiche on the menu as well).

The upstairs café at **Avoca Handweavers** (11-13 Suffolk St., tel. 01/677-4215, www .avoca.ie, café open 9:30 A.M.–5 P.M. weekdays, 10 A.M.–5 P.M. Sat., 10 A.M.–5:30 P.M. Sun., open 30 minutes later in summer, mains under €12) is an incredibly popular lunch spot for ladies-who-lunch. As at every Avoca café, the fare is a comforting mix of the traditional and the innovative, with terrific wholegrain breads and fresh vegetable soups to warm your weary bones on rainy afternoons.

It's a bit overwhelmingly trendy, but **Nude** (21 Suffolk St., tel. 01/675-5577, www.nude.ie, 8 A.M.–10 P.M. Mon.–Sat. and 11 A.M.–7 P.M. Sun., lunches €6–10)—owned by Bono's older brother—is otherwise a great option for lunch (eat in or takeaway), serving up fruit smoothies, paninis, and veggie wraps (all organic) to young health-conscious Dubs. Try the goat's cheese, sundried tomato, spinach, and garlic wrap (though Nude isn't all vegetarian; there are chicken, beef, and bacon wraps as well).

Perpetually bustling █ **Café Fresh** (Powerscourt Townhouse shopping center, top floor, S. William St., tel. 01/671-9669, www.cafe-fresh.com, open 10 A.M.–6 P.M. Mon.–Fri., 9 A.M.–6 P.M. Sat., mains €4–11) is arguably the city's best (non-Indian) vegetarian eatery. This airy cafeteria-style café serves up thoroughly delicious savory tarts, nut loaf, risotto, deluxe salads, and droolworthy daily specials like coconut pancakes. Wash down your lunch with a cup of organic Fair Trade java. Another busy cafeteria-style veggie-house is **Cornucopia** (Wicklow St., open noon–8 P.M. Mon.–Sat., noon–7 P.M. Sun., mains €9–12), which also offers so much choice—something vegetarians just aren't used to!—that your inevitable hesitation will irritate the harried-looking man behind the counter. It's pretty cramped, too, so try not to come here with your big backpack, or after a spell of retail therapy.

Calling the **Imperial Chinese** (12a Wicklow St., off Grafton, tel. 01/677-2580, open

12:30–2:30 P.M. and 5:30 P.M.–midnight daily, mains €10–18) the best Chinese in Dublin isn't saying all that much—but don't let that stop you. It's deservedly popular with locals, and you can choose a lobster from the tank at the front of the restaurant.

The old Bewley's Café is now a **Café Bar Deli** (Grafton St., tel. 01/672-7720, www.cafebardeli.ie, open noon–11 P.M. Thurs.–Sat., noon–10 P.M. Sun.–Wed., mains €8–14), which does quick and reliably good pizzas, salads, and pasta. Respectfully, the new owners have left the charming old facade and interior untouched. Another chain restaurant well worth a mention is the classy-yet-informal **Pizza Milano** (38 Dawson St., tel. 01/670-7744, open noon–midnight Mon.–Sat., noon–11 P.M. Sun., mains €10–15), which does good-value pastas and gourmet pizzas using really fresh produce. You'll have no qualms about ditching your diet when you see the dessert menu, and it's all as delish as it sounds. This is one of the most kid-friendly restaurants in the city, and there's live jazz on Wednesday nights, too.

Looking for a special gourmet meal before you head to the Gate Theatre? You've got a couple of choices. Part of the Mansion House, **Fire** (Dawson St., tel. 01/676-7200, www.mansionhouse.ie, open 5:30–10 P.M. Mon.–Sat. and 1–4 P.M. Sat., mains €14–38, 2/3-course early-bird special €20/25) has attracted plenty of local admirers with its eye-popping fusion of classical details and cosmopolitan funk. Neopolitan flatbreads flecked with chicken and prosciutto emerge from the wood-burning oven (a novelty here), but otherwise the menu's heavy on steaks and seafood. The **Trocadero** (3 St. Andrew St., tel. 01/677-5545, www.trocadero.ie, open 5–11 P.M. Mon.–Sat., mains €16–30) is a romantic Continental eatery lined with plenty of red velvet and headshots of legendary Irish actors. The pre-theater menu is something of a Dublin institution. Those who partake of the €23 two-course early-bird special (5–7 P.M. daily) are expected to "vacate by 7:45 P.M. sharp."

TEMPLE BAR

Don't leave lunch to chance in Tourist Central; far too many pubs here do a bustling business with overpriced, mediocre grub. In fact, avoid eating in any Temple Bar pubs if you can help it.

Sinead O'Connor once waited tables at the **Bad Ass Café** (9-11 Crown Alley, tel. 01/671-2596, open 11:30 A.M.–11 P.M. daily but can close earlier, lunches €8–10, dinners €12–18), but she's not this cheerfully grungy eatery's only claim to fame: It does a range of super-tasty pizzas, burgers, and Mexican grub, attracting a chilled-out, quasi-hippie crowd who'd otherwise steer clear of this touristy strip. Bummer this place closes so early though—not quite as "bad ass" as we'd like!

Got a case of the late-night munchies? It may be lacking in atmosphere, but a sweet or savory pancake from the **Half Moon Crêpe Company** (5A Crown Alley, no phone, www.halfmoon.ie, open 8 A.M.–11 P.M. Mon.–Thurs., 8 A.M.–2 A.M. Fri., 9:30 A.M.–2 A.M. Sat., 9:30 A.M.–11 P.M. Sun., light meals €3–6), across the street from the Bad Ass, will more than do the trick. Another more upscale crêperie and deli (this one with a hipster vibe, good coffee, and outdoor seating) is **Lemon Jelly** (10-11B E. Essex St., tel. 01/677-6297, open 8 A.M.–midnight Mon.–Thurs., 8 A.M.–4 A.M. Fri., 10 A.M.–4 A.M. Sat., 10 A.M.–midnight Sun., meals under €8).

Ciao Bella Roma (25 Parliament St., tel. 01/677-0004, open noon–11 P.M. Mon.–Sat., 1–10 P.M. Sun., mains €10–15) offers a two-course lunch and early-bird dinner (including a glass of house wine) for an incredible €9.

Temple Bar's top restaurant is the aptly named, two-story **Eden** (Meeting House Sq., tel. 01/670-5372, www.edenrestaurant.ie, open noon–2:30 P.M. and 6–10:30 P.M. weekdays, noon–3 P.M. and 6–11 P.M. weekends, 2/3-course lunch €20/24, €25 3-course pre-theater menu 6–7 P.M. Sun.–Thurs., dinner mains €18–29), with boughs of ivy dangling from the ceiling and sinfully delicious modern Irish.

SOUTH GREAT GEORGES STREET

You'll find heaps of good restaurants along South Great George's Street, which turns into Aungier Street farther south, and tucked away on its narrow side streets. After browsing for vintage duds or secondhand books at the Market Arcade, pop by the pleasantly hole-in-the-wall **Simon's Place** (S. Great George's St., beside the arcade, tel. 01/679-7821, open 8:30 A.M.–6 P.M. Mon.–Sat., mains €5–8) for a hefty sandwich and a cup of Fair Trade brew.

Smoothies, salad bowls, pizza by the slice, and freshly baked cakes and breads are on offer at the tiny, all-vegetarian **Blazing Salads** (42 Drury St., tel. 01/671-9552, www.blazingsalads.com, open 9 A.M.–6 P.M. weekdays, 9 A.M.–5 P.M. Sat., mains under €8), all of which is available for takeaway only.

Juice (73-83 S. Great Georges St., tel. 01/475-7856, www.juicerestaurant.ie, open 11 A.M.–11 P.M. daily, mains €12–16, 2/3-course lunch €10/13, 3-course early-bird special €15 5–7 P.M. Mon.–Fri., 15 percent service charge), Dublin's only full-service vegetarian restaurant, is a bit of a hit and miss: While the menu is relatively innovative, every so often you'll get a dish that's an absolute dud (avoid the lasagna), and some folks have complaints about small portions. You'll find better value and consistency in the city's cafeteria-style veggie restaurants, though it's certainly worth trying if you'd like a more formal meal (or want to dine after 9 P.M.). Reservations are smart, even if you just stop by earlier on in the day.

For a hefty portion of vegetarian heaven, try cafeteria-style **Govinda's** (4 Aungier St., tel. 01/475-0309, www.govindas.ie, open noon–9 P.M. Mon.–Sat., mains €6–10). Linger at a table by the window watching all of Dublin go by while you dig into your *mattar paneer* (or one of many vegan options). Unless the hunger of the world's on you, the small lunch portions (€6) will keep you going until dinnertime.

But if you're a carnivore—or just looking for a swanky table setting—try **Jaipur** (41-46 S. Great Georges St., tel. 01/677-0999, open 5–11 P.M. daily, mains €9–21). The two-course €20 early-bird menu (5–7 P.M.) is a pretty good value for Dublin, and the waitstaff are super-polite.

Ersatz balconies brimming with silk flowers, walls sponge-painted a certain shade of rust—the decor at the **Boulevard Café** (27 Exchequer St., tel. 01/679-2131, open 10 A.M.–midnight Mon.–Sat., lunch mains €7–10, 2-course lunch €14, dinners €13–23) looks the way a wealthy suburban housewife might redecorate her "great room" after a trip to Cinqueterre (and Harry Connick Jr. on the stereo reinforces the impression). The sandwiches and salads here are pure bliss, though, the vegetables roasted to perfection, and the toffee ice cream is a must.

Brunch at **Odessa** (13 Dame Ct., off Exchequer St., tel. 01/670-7634, open 6 P.M.–late daily, 11:30 A.M.–4:30 P.M. Sat.–Sun., mains €14–22) is a modern legend. It's been so popular for so long that calling Odessa "trendy" doesn't quite fit, but it's still true this loungy eatery attracts a come-to-be-seen crowd (that there's an adjacent "supper club" says something, doesn't it?).

There's a completely new menu on offer daily at 🅒 **L'Gueuleton** (1 Fade St., tel. 01/675-3708, open 12:30–3 P.M. and 6–10 P.M. Mon.–Sat., plat du jour plus wine €15, lunch €10–17, dinner €20–30), which doesn't actually have a sign out front. No reservations are taken, so if you didn't know better you'd find a queue of Dubliners-in-the-know on the pavement outside on weekend evenings and wonder what the heck they were waiting for. Divine French fare that doesn't take itself too seriously, that's what, and in a wonderfully relaxed dining room with exposed brick walls and tasteful yet funky modern art. As always, lunch is a much better value (the portions are generous), and you don't have to worry about getting a table if you show up around two. Oh, and the token vegetarian dish is excellent as well.

DAME STREET

It's a shame the **Queen of Tarts** (Dame St. at Parliament St., tel. 01/670-7499, open 7:30 A.M.–6 P.M. weekdays, 9 A.M.–6 P.M.

Sat., 9:30 A.M.–6 P.M. Sun., lunches €6–9) is in such a tiny space; you can keep passing by, squinting through the window, and noting with disappointment there *still* isn't a table free. This bakery-café is utterly charming and deservedly popular; along with a dazzling array of gourmet desserts, you can order from an extensive breakfast menu, or a sandwich or savory tart at lunchtime. The only drawback, besides the cramped digs, is the burnt-tasting coffee.

You'll feel like you're back on the Lower East Side in New York City at **Gruel** (68a Dame St., tel. 01/670-7119, open 11:30 A.M.–9:30 P.M. Mon.–Wed. and Fri., 11:30 A.M.–10:30 P.M. Thurs., 11 A.M.–10:30 P.M. Sat., 11:30 A.M.–9 P.M. Sun., mains €8–14, 10 percent service charge), a narrow, bustling café frequented by Dublin's hip young things (and the too-cool waitstaff to match). Forget the self-consciously ironic name—the fare is imaginative, freshly prepared, and reasonably priced, and the brunch is one of the best you'll find in Dublin. The perennially (and deservedly) popular, posh-but-friendly **Mermaid Café** (69-70 Dame St., tel. 01/670-8236, www.mermaid.ie, open 12:30–2:30 P.M. and 6–11 P.M. Mon.–Sat., 12:30–3 P.M. and 6–9 P.M. Sun., 2/3-course lunch €22/26, dinner mains €21–29) next door is arty-American in a completely different way. It's owned by the same people, but the clientele is a bit older. With an emphasis on organic produce, the menu generally features inventively prepared veal, venison, monkfish, and salmon, and naturally the lone veggie option (gorgonzola polenta served with figs and mushrooms, say) is excellent too. Brunch is a popular option, and reservations (at any time) are pretty much essential.

Less pricey than L'Gueuleton, but far more predictably French, **Chez Max** (1 Palace St., tel. 01/633-7215, open 8 A.M.–midnight weekdays, 11 A.M.–midnight weekends, mains €13–22) has a fabulous location right beside the entrance to Dublin Castle (and the outdoor seating to take full advantage of it). The food is lovely, but vegetarian Franco-

philes (oxymoronic as they are) should head for L'Gueuleton instead.

Fortunately for hungry cocktail lovers, the food at ♦ **The Bank** (20-22 College Green, tel. 01/677-0677, www.bankoncollegegreen.com, food served 10 A.M.–10 P.M. daily, mains €11–23) is far more creative than the name (though fittingly there's an ATM in the lobby). Even if you're planning to have dinner elsewhere, order a plate of tasty bruschetta to take the edge off your Multiple Orgasm cocktail.

MERRION SQUARE

This area is humming with white-collar professionals by day, so as you'd expect there are several top-notch eateries with impeccable service to meet the demand for business-lunch and dinner options; reservations are recommended across the board. One of these is **Rubicon** (6 Merrion Row, tel. 01/676-5955, www.rubiconrestaurant.net, open noon–2:30 P.M. Mon.–Fri., 5:30–10:30 P.M. Mon.–Thurs., 5:30–11 P.M. Fri.–Sat., 5:30–10 P.M. Sun., 2/3-course lunch €18/22, 2-course early-bird special €18 5–7 P.M., dinner mains €14–29), an inventive mod-Irish restaurant with refreshingly minimalist decor, a great-value lunch menu, and desserts for which you'd gladly trade your firstborn child. Across the street is the even more celebrated **Bang Café** (11 Merrion Row, tel. 01/676-0898, www.bangrestaurant.com, open 12:30–3 P.M. and 6–10:30 P.M. Mon.–Sat., until 11 P.M. Thurs.–Sat, lunch mains €13–22, dinner €17–28), which offers fresh twists on traditional dishes like bangers and mash along with divine Continental fare (using seafood from West Cork). Treat yourself to a drink off the marvelous (and reasonably priced) cocktail menu.

Widely praised as Dublin's best, **Restaurant Patrick Guilbaud** (21 Upper Merion St., tel. 01/676-4192, www.restaurantpatrickguilbaud.ie, open 12:30–2:15 P.M. and 7:30–10:15 P.M. Tues.–Sat., 2/3-course lunch €33/45, dinner mains €30–80) has been doing exquisite French fare using local meats and produce for more than 25 years. There's a nine-course "tasting menu" (€130) featuring

French twists on traditional Irish dishes like colcannon and braised crubbeens (that's pig's feet, for the uninitiated) as well as a separate vegetarian menu with mains around €30. And if 20 quid for a chocolate fondant induces a gasp, be assured you'd give your first- *and* secondborn children for it.

NORTHSIDE

There are fewer notable restaurants north of the Liffey, though this is slowly beginning to change. For very good pizzas and pastas that won't kill your wallet, try **Rayhoon** (8 Talbot St., tel. 01/874-7901, open noon–11 P.M. Mon.–Sat., 5–11 P.M. Sun., mains €10–20).

Love Govinda's vegetarian Indian grub, but prefer table service? Head north across the bridge to **Radha Govinda's** (83 Middle Abbey St., beside Eason Books just off O'Connell St., tel. 01/872-9861, www.radhagovindas.com, open noon–9 P.M. Mon.–Sat., mains €10–16), where you'll find essentially the same delicious menu.

Named after a Yeats poem, the legendary **Winding Stair Café** (40 Lower Ormond Quay, tel. 01/872-7320, www.winding-stair.com, open 12:30–3:30 P.M. and 6–10:30 P.M. daily, mains €12–20) was once the perfect spot to while away the afternoon with a cup of coffee and a good book, but it closed in early 2005 amid the wailing of legions of regular customers. Now there's mostly-good news for old fans: It was reopened in the fall of 2006 as an upscale modern Irish restaurant. Gone are the murals and checkered tablecloths, but the food is delicious (if fancy), the wine list is exhaustive, and the waiters are nice. Reservations are a good idea. It's not quite as cool as the original Winding Stair, but better a new, posh version than none at all.

See *Bars and Pubs* under *Entertainment and Events* for the full low-down on the fabulously unusual 🄲 **John M. Keating** (Mary St. at Jervis St., tel. 01/878-0223 or 087/636-3738, www.jmk.ie, bar food served noon–9:30 P.M. Mon.–Wed., noon–10 P.M. Thurs.–Sat., and 12:30–8 P.M. Sun., gallery restaurant open noon–10 P.M. Mon.–Wed., noon–11 P.M. Thurs.–Sat., and 12:30–10 P.M. Sun., bar meals €6–8, restaurant mains €12–22), a bar-cum-restaurant in a converted Methodist church.

Information and Services

INFORMATION

As you would expect, Dublin's central **tourist office** (St. Andrew's Church, 2 Suffolk St., tel. 01/605-7700, www.visitdublin.com, open 9 A.M.–7 P.M. Mon.–Sat. and 10:30 A.M.–3 P.M. Sun. July–Aug., 9 A.M.–5:30 P.M. Mon.–Sat. Sept.–June)—which does not accept inquiries by phone—is so busy you could spend all afternoon in line. There is a secondary office at 14 Upper O'Connell Street (tel. 01/605-7700, open 9 A.M.–5 P.M. Mon.–Sat.). You're best off just stopping by to pick up flyers and free listings of upcoming events; *inDublin* (www.indublin.ie) is a great free weekly magazine you can find here or in many hostels and cafés.

Other sources for entertainment info are the twice-monthly *Dublin Event Guide* (www.eventguide.ie) and the *Evening Herald* (along with its freebie sister paper, the *Herald AM*), which is published every day but Sunday.

Dublin's city-center **public library** (Ilac Shopping Centre, Henry St., 01/873-4333, www.dublincitypubliclibraries.ie, open 10 A.M.–8 P.M. Mon.–Thurs., 10 A.M.–5 P.M. Fri.–Sat.) is located on the Northside, two blocks west of O'Connell Street.

SERVICES
Banks

Bureaux de change abound in the city center, but the commission charges are lowest at the banks: **Bank of Ireland** (2 College Green or 6 Lower O'Connell St.), **AIB** (40-41 Westmoreland St. or 1-3 Lower Baggot St.), or **Ulster Bank** (33 College Green or George's Quay). There's an **American Express** desk (Andrew's St., tel. 01/605-7709, open 9 A.M.–5 P.M. Mon.–Sat.) at the central tourist office.

Embassies

The **U.S. Embassy** (42 Elgin Rd., Ballsbridge, tel. 01/668-8777, http://dublin.usembassy. gov) is on Dublin Bus routes #4, #5, #7, #7A, #8, #45, #63, and #84 to Lansdowne Road. The **Canadian Embassy** (65/68 St. Stephen's Green, 4th floor, tel. 01/417-4100, www. dfait-maeci.gc.ca) is more conveniently located. For a complete embassy listing, visit the Irish **Department of Foreign Affairs** online (http://foreignaffairs.gov.ie/embassies).

Emergency and Medical Services

Dial 999 for an emergency. Crime against tourists is relatively rare, though pickpocketing is a problem. Ring the 24-hour **Tourist Victim Support Service** (tel. 01/478-5295 or freephone tel. 1800/661-771) if you need any assistance. The fastest way to reach the Garda (the Irish police) is by dialing 999, which will connect you with the Command and Control center at Harcourt Square (tel. 01/475-5555).

Hospitals in the city center include **St. James'** (James St., tel. 01/453-7941, just south of Heuston Station and the Guinness Storehouse) and **Mater Miserichordiae** (Eccles St., between Berkeley Rd. and Dorset St., north of Parnell Sq., tel. 01/830-1122).

Both branches of **O'Connell's Pharmacy** (21 Grafton St., tel. 01/679-0467, and 55-56 O'Connell St., tel. 01/873-0427) stay open until 10 P.M. daily.

Post Office

The **General Post Office** (O'Connell St., tel. 01/705-7000) is open until 8 P.M. Monday–Saturday, and there are branches at St. Andrew's Street and South Anne Street.

Internet Access

You'll have no trouble finding an Internet café in this city, and the competition keeps prices low. The least expensive is **easyInternet** (37-39 Wellington Quay, no phone, www.easy-internetcafe.com, open daily until late, rate varies but under €2/hour), which offers new flatscreen PCs (with a prepaid vending machine system and no visible staff) along with a Subway sandwich shop. Depending on the time of day, you can pay as little as €1/hour (or less). Tops for atmosphere is **Central Cyber Café** (6 Grafton St., upstairs, tel. 01/677-8298, www .centralcafe.ie, open 9 A.M.–10 P.M. weekdays, 10 A.M.–9 P.M. weekends, €5/hour, lower rates before noon and after 8 P.M., wireless access, too), which serves smoothies, bubble tea, and cappuccinos.

While many bars and cafés offer wireless Internet access, it's almost never free: Service providers like Eircom and BitBuzz charge an arm and a leg for daily or monthly access. But you can pick up a 20-minute voucher with any purchase; buy two drinks, ask for two vouchers, and you're set for 40 minutes. Just look for the wireless sticker in the front window; try **O'Neill's** (2 Suffolk St., tel. 01/679-3656) or **Sin É** (14-15 Ormond Quay, tel. 01/878-7009), both of which are spacious and quiet during the afternoon (be sure to arrive after lunchtime at O'Neill's). Another option is **The Globe** (11 S. Great George's St., tel. 01/671-1220), that trendy Dublin mainstay.

Laundry

Laundry service is usually a couple quid cheaper than a launderette at your hostel or B&B; otherwise, drop off your duds at the **All-American Launderette** (40 S. Great George's St., tel. 01/677-2779, open daily), which also has self-service.

Left Luggage

You can leave that ungainly suitcase in a coin-operated locker at **Busáras** (Store St., €4–9 for 24 hours, open 7 A.M.–10:30 P.M. daily). Better yet, for around €6, **Connolly** (east side, north of the Liffey at Amiens St., tel. 01/836-6222, open 7 A.M.–10 P.M. Mon.–Sat. and 8 A.M.–10 P.M. Sun.) and **Heuston** (west side, Victoria Quay, same phone and hours) train stations also offer locker rooms; a (usually helpful and very chipper) attendant will squeeze your bag into the smallest locker possible to save you a couple bob.

Getting There and Around

GETTING THERE

Dublin is 217 kilometers east of Galway on the N6, 166 kilometers south of Belfast on the M1, and 256 kilometers northeast of Cork City on the N8.

Air

Flights depart **Dublin International Airport** (tel. 01/814-1111, www.dublinairport.com) for more than 140 destinations in Europe, Asia, and North America. The most commonly traveled airlines from the U.S. and Canada are **Continental Airlines** (tel. 1890/925-252, www.continental.com), **Aer Lingus** (tel. 1800/474-7424 from the U.S. and Canada, tel. 01/886-8888 for reservations, tel. 01/886-6705 for departures/arrivals, www.aerlingus.com), **Air Canada** (tel. 1800/709-900, www.aircanada.ca), and **American Airlines** (tel. 01/602-0550, www.aa.com).

An alternative to **British Airways** (tel. 1800/626-747, www.britishairways.com) is the most popular budget airline to Britain and mainland Europe, **Ryanair** (tel. 0818/303-030, www.ryanair.ie), which offers daily service from Berlin (Schonefeld), Birmingham, London (Gatwick, Luton, and Stansted), Edinburgh, Glasgow (Prestwick), Paris (Beauvais), Venice (Treviso), Milan (Orio al Serio), Rome (Ciampino), and other destinations.

Car-rental agencies on the arrivals hall lower level include **Europcar** (tel. 01/812-0410, www.europcar.ie), **Avis** (tel. 01/605-7500, www.avis.ie), and **Budget** (tel. 01/844-5150, www.budget.ie).

A **left luggage** service (tel. 01/814-4633, open 6 A.M.–11 P.M. daily) will run you €6–8 per day per item. Unlike at Shannon Airport, wireless Internet access is not complimentary; you can purchase time on the Eircom network at airport newsagents or from the website (€3/30 minutes).

Train

Iarnrod Éireann, also known as **Irish Rail** (tel. 01/836-6222, www.irishrail.ie) operates from **Connolly** (east side, north of the Liffey at Amiens St., points north) and **Heuston** (west side, Victoria Quay, points west and south); the stations are linked by the new Luas light rail line. Traveling by train is much more expensive than by bus, but the trip is also far more comfortable. Round-trip (or "return") tickets are always a much better value: single/5-day return fares are available to/from Belfast (€35/50), Galway (€29/41), Cork (€55/59), Rosslare (€19/25), and many other destinations.

Bus

Busáras (Store St., tel. 01/836-6111, www.buseireann.ie), the central bus depot, can take you anywhere you need to go via **Bus Éireann.** Buses depart regularly for Drogheda and Belfast (route #1), Kilkenny, Cahir, and Cork (#7, #8 for Cork via Cashel), Limerick and Ennis (#12), Tralee (via Limerick, #13), Killarney (#14), Athlone and Galway (#20), Westport (via Athlone, #21), Sligo (#23), Donegal (#30), and Derry (#33).

This none-too-pleasant station is made even more chaotic by frequent construction work; it's also swarming with pickpockets, so summon all your street smarts. If you plan to do three or more days of bus travel during your holiday, pick up an **Open Road** pass at the central ticket office (3 days' travel over a 6-day period €45, 4 days out of 8 €58). The **Emerald Card** (8 days' travel over a 15-day period €203, including Ulsterbus €228) is valid on both Bus Éireann and Irish Rail.

Citylink (tel. 01/626-6888, www.citylink.ie, at least 14/day daily, €14/18) offers frequent Galway–Dublin service, continuing to the airport. The Dublin city stop is at Burgh Quay, south of the Liffey, one block north of Trinity College. Citylink prices are comparable to Bus Éireann's, but the buses are newer and more comfortable (and the drivers are friendlier).

Boat

Reach Dublin by ferry from Liverpool or Holyhead. From Liverpool, take **P&O Irish Sea Ferries** (tel. 01/407-3434, www.poirishsea.com, 2/day Tues.–Sun., 1/day Mon., crossing 7.5 hours, car and driver €140–245, additional passengers €22–37), which does not carry pedestrians, or **Norfolk Line** (tel. 01/819-2999, www.norfolkline.com, 2/day Tues.–Sat., 1/day Sun.–Mon., crossing 8 hours, day sailings: car and 2 passengers €140–230, additional passengers €15–20, pedestrians €30–46, night sailings: car and 2 passengers €225–350, additional passengers €20–30, pedestrians €60–76). Meals are included in the price of passage, though there is generally a fuel surcharge of €4 per person. The Holyhead–Dublin route is served by **Irish Ferries** (tel. 01/638-3333, www.irishferries.com, 2/day daily, crossing 1 hour 50 minutes, car and driver €89, additional adult €25, pedestrians €27).

It is also possible to travel between Dublin and the Isle of Man via **Steam Packet** (tel. 1800/805-055, www.steam-packet.com, usually 2/day daily, crossing 2 hours 50 minutes, fare €159–204 for car and driver, each additional passenger €46–50).

Ferries pull into the Ferryport Terminal (Alexandra Rd., tel. 01/855-2222) at North Wall, and there are Bus Éireann shuttles to meet every incoming boat (fare €2). Buses leave Busáras for the ferry terminal 75 minutes before scheduled departures.

GETTING AROUND

The city center is easily walkable, but if you're carrying your luggage or want to get to a sight outside the center you have several options.

To and from the Airport

The airport is off the M1 12 kilometers north of Dublin, and parking in the short-term lot costs €3/hour.

Dublin Bus (tel. 01/873-4222, route #748) operates a frequent **Airlink** service from the street directly outside the arrivals hall; buy a ticket (€5) at the kiosk or on board (with exact change), and look out for the bright green-and-blue double-decker. The bus will take you to O'Connell Street, Busáras, and Connolly and Heuston Stations. The ride is more comfortable on **Aircoach** (tel. 01/844-7118, www.aircoach.ie, departures from O'Connell St. every 15 minutes, every 30 minutes midnight–5 A.M., single/return fare €7/12), which offers 24-hour service. **Citylink** (tel. 01/626-6888, www.citylink.ie, at least 14/day daily, single/monthly return ticket €19/29) offers a frequent Dublin Airport–Galway coach service.

A taxi to or from the airport will run you €25–30.

Train

Dublin's spiffy new light rail system, **Luas** (freephone tel. 1800/300-604, www.luas.ie, departures every 5–10 minutes 7 A.M.–10 P.M., runs until 12:30 A.M. Sat. and 11:30 P.M. Sun., fare within city-center zone €1.40) whisks commuters in from the 'burbs, but it's also useful for tourists looking to get from Heuston to Connolly Station or any point in between (including the National Museum at Collins Barracks, the Four Courts, Abbey Street, and Busáras). Buy a ticket at the bus stop kiosk before boarding.

For travel outside the city, you'll want to take the **DART,** or Dublin Area Rapid Transit (tel. 01/805-4288, www.dart.ie, fares under €5), which is much faster than the bus. There is frequent service (2–3 trains hourly) to Drogheda in County Louth (from Connolly, with other routes to Malahide and Howth), Kildare (from Heuston), or Dun Laoghaire, Killiney, Bray, and Greystones (from Pearse or Connolly).

Bus

For Kilmainham Jail, Phoenix Park, the National Botanic Gardens, and other attractions on the city fringe, take **Dublin Bus** (tel. 01/873-4222, www.dublinbus.ie, single ticket to most destinations €0.95–1.35). Maps and departure times (generally three or more per hour during the day) are posted at each stop. Exact change is not necessary, though notes are not accepted and if you overpay you won't get change from the driver. You can redeem your passenger change receipt (bring the original ticket as well) at the Dublin Bus office at 59 Upper O'Connell Street.

The Dublin Bus **Airlink** service is the second-least expensive way to get to the airport (route #748, fare €5, frequent departures from Ormond Quay, O'Connell St., Busáras, and Connolly and Heuston Stations, 30-minute trip). The least expensive way is to take the local bus (route #16A from O'Connell St. or #41 from Lower Abbey St., 3/hour, fare €1.75, 40-minute trip).

Car

It's possible to rent a car without returning to the airport. Rental agencies with city center branches include **Europcar** (Baggot St. Bridge, tel. 01/614-2800, www.europcar.ie), **Dan Dooley** (42 Westland Row, tel. 01/677-2733, www.dan-dooley.ie), and **Hertz** (149 Upper Leeson St., tel. 01/660-2255, www.hertz.ie).

That said, pick up the rental only when you're ready to leave the city, as driving in Dublin can be extremely confusing and stressful even for natives. Pay-and-display parking in the city center will run you €2.50/hour.

Bicycle

With so much traffic and construction work going on, getting around by bike can be pretty risky; don't forget to wear your helmet. It's also pricier to rent a bike (around €20/80 per day/week, plus a €100–200 deposit) than elsewhere in the country. Try **Irish Cycling Safaris** at the Belfield Bike Shop (near the running track on the University College Dublin campus, on Dublin Bus routes #3, #10, and #11B from O'Connell St., tel. 01/716-1697, www.cyclingsafaris.com, open until 6 P.M. weekdays and 10 A.M.–2 P.M. Sat.), which also offers weeklong themed cycling trips, or **Cycleways** (185-186 Parnell St., tel. 01/873-4748, www.cycleways.com, open until 6 P.M. Mon.–Sat., 8 P.M. Thurs., credit cards accepted).

Taxi

There are 79 **taxi ranks** (www.taxi.ie) all over the city, most of which operate 24 hours a day. Between the hours of 8 P.M. and 6 A.M., bus lanes at the following locations also serve as taxi ranks: Dame Street, outside the Bank of Ireland, near Trinity but facing Christchurch; Merrion Row, near St. Stephen's Green; Dawson Street, opposite the Mansion House; and, Northside, on Talbot Street, on the O'Connell Street side of the railway bridge.

Alternatively, ring **National Radio Cabs** (tel. 01/677-2222) or **City Cabs** (tel. 01/872-2688). There are surcharges galore across the board: late-night pick-ups, phone bookings, luggage handling per bag (even if you load it yourself), and extra passengers.

·Vicinity of Dublin City

NORTH OF DUBLIN CITY
Howth

A charming fishing village on a small peninsula north of the city, Howth (rhymes with "both," from the Norse for "headland"; Bínn Eádáir, "Hill of Eadair," after a chieftain of the mythical Tuatha de Danann) makes a fine afternoon excursion, what with its rhododendron gardens and spooky, poorly tended 14th-century abbey ruins overlooking the harbor.

Howth Castle has remained in the same family, the St. Lawrences and their descendants, for more than 800 years. The current structure dates from 1564 and has been restored and rebuilt many times since then. The most interesting story about this castle regards the pirate queen Grace O'Malley, who dropped by for dinner once in 1575 only to be snubbed by Christopher St. Lawrence. O'Malley promptly kidnapped his son and heir and sailed him back to Mayo. (He was eventually returned to his family, but not before the St. Lawrences had much humbled themselves.) Though the castle is not open to the public, the

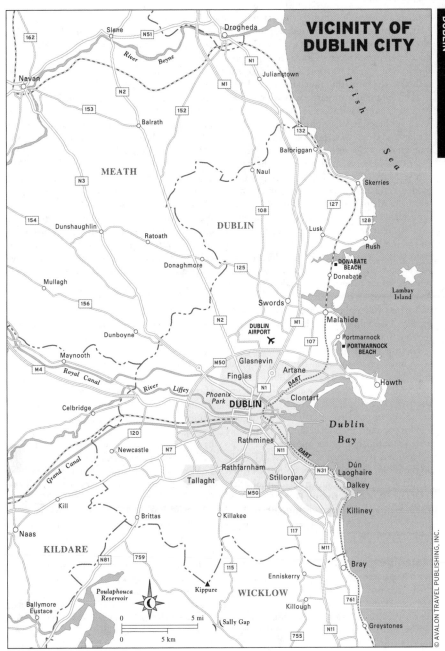

VICINITY OF DUBLIN CITY

Irish Sea

Dublin Bay

MEATH

DUBLIN

KILDARE

WICKLOW

162
Slane
N51
Drogheda
River Boyne
Navan
N1
Julianstown
M1
N2
132
153
152
Balrath
Balbriggan
N3
Naul
Skerries
154
Dunshaughlin
108
127
128
Ratoath
Lusk
Rush
Donaghmore
125
DONABATE BEACH
Mullagh
Donabate
156
Lambay Island
N2
Swords
Dunboyne
DUBLIN AIRPORT
M1
Malahide
Maynooth
M50
Portmarnock
M4
Royal Canal
Glasnevin
Artane
107
PORTMARNOCK BEACH
River Liffey
Finglas
N1
DART
Howth
Celbridge
Phoenix Park
DUBLIN
Clontarf
Grand Canal
120
Rathmines
N11
Newcastle
N7
Rathfarnham
DART
Dún Laoghaire
Tallaght
Stillorgan
N31
Kill
M50
Dalkey
Brittas
Killakee
Killiney
Naas
117
M11
N81
759
Bray
Ballymore Eustace
115
Enniskerry
761
Poulaphouca Reservoir
Kippure
Killough
Greystones
Sally Gap
755
N11

0   5 mi

0   5 km

gardens are open in summertime (try to go in May or June when the rhododendrons are in bloom), and on the grounds is a prehistoric dolmen known as Aideen's Grave (Aideen being the wife of a dead warrior, a little legend attached to the formation much later on). Access to the rhododendron gardens is via the Deer Park Hotel and Golf Course.

To get here, make a right out of the DART station and cross the street, following the main road for about five minutes. Make a left for the Deer Park Hotel entrance (passing the Anglican St. Mary's Church with its small memorial garden), and after another five minutes you'll see the castle on the right (the turnoff is here for a rather ramshackle "transport museum" as well). It's another 10-minute walk straight on for the hotel. Once there, walk along the right side of the building, past the bar, and you'll see a clearly trodden path leading you into the woods (where the rhododendrons are). A short climb up this secret-gardenesque path will afford you a phenomenal view over Dublin Bay. The dolmen is on the wooded path to the fourth tee.

Feeling peckish? Instead of risking the hotel food, try the grub at the dimly lighted, atmospheric **Abbey Tavern** (Abbey St., tel. 01/839-0307, www.abbeytavern.ie, food served noon–3 P.M. daily, lunch mains €10–13). Dinner in the upstairs restaurant is overpriced at €33 for two courses, but the simple, reasonably priced pub lunches hit the spot.

Howth is 16 kilometers northeast of Dublin on the R105, and is served by both **DART** (tel. 01/805-4288, 2/hour daily from Connolly Station, fare €1.60) and **Dublin Bus** (tel. 01/873-4222, route #31, 3/hour daily from Eden Quay, fare €1.55). The DART will get you there in 20 minutes, but the bus takes nigh an hour.

Malahide

With its pleasant promenade, Blue Flag strand, shady tree-lined avenue, and hip boutiques—not to mention the second-most haunted castle on the island—Malahide (Mullach Íde, "Promontory of St. Ita") makes another pleasant day trip.

With the exception of one lord's temporary eviction at the hands of Cromwell in the 17th century, the Talbot family lived at **Malahide Castle & Gardens** (tel. 01/846-2184, www.malahidecastle.com, open 10 A.M.–5 P.M. Mon.–Sat. year-round, 10 A.M.–6 P.M. Sun. Apr.–Sept., 11 A.M.–5 P.M. Sun. Oct.–Mar., admission €6.70) from 1174 to 1976. Though most of the present structure dates from the 17th and 18th centuries, Malahide retains the title of oldest inhabited castle. The Talbots converted from Catholicism in 1779, and the exquisitely carved Flemish panels in the Oak Room—depicting various Old Testament tales along with the Coronation of the Virgin—indicate that the room was once used as their chapel. Other rooms feature period furniture, rococo plasterwork, and an extensive portrait collection, and 35-minute guided tours leave every quarter of an hour. Outside, the botanic gardens feature more than 4,500 plant species, many of them exotic; this is a fine spot for a picnic lunch.

The Malahide Historical Society claims the castle houses at least five ghosts (whose sightings are well documented). Some may be the spirits of the 14 Talbot men who breakfasted in the banquet hall on the morning of the Battle of the Boyne—a meal destined to be their last. Another wraith is that of a 15th-century sentry named Puck who fell asleep on duty, thus allowing an enemy to storm the castle, and who hanged himself in shame; he hasn't been spotted in 30 or so years, though.

A combination ticket is available for Malahide Castle along with the **Fry Model Railway** (on the castle grounds, tel. 01/846-3779, open 10 A.M.–1 P.M. and 2–5 P.M. Mon.–Sat. and 2–6 P.M. Sun. Apr.–Sept., 2–5 P.M. weekends and holidays in low season, admission €6.70) for €11.50.

You have a choice of eateries on Malahide's main drag. For excellent Greek and Cypriot victuals, try **Cape Greko** (Unit 1, 1st floor, New St., tel. 01/845-6288, www.capegreko.ie, open 5–11 P.M. Mon., noon–11 P.M. Tues.–Thurs., noon–midnight Fri.–Sat., noon–10 P.M. Sunday, lunches €9–15, dinner mains

€15–25). The service is as quick and polite as the food is delish, and veggie-lovers are well-catered for.

Malahide is 15 kilometers north of Dublin on the R107. Get there via **DART** (tel. 01/805-4288, 2/hour daily from Connolly Station, fare €2.40). **Dublin Bus** service (tel. 01/873-4222, route #32A, 9–11/day daily from Eden Quay, or 3/hour daily on #42 from Lower Abbey St., fare €1.80) is much slower (the DART journey is 22 minutes, but the bus takes nearly an hour).

SOUTH OF DUBLIN CITY
Dún Laoghaire

Thirteen kilometers south of the city, Dún Laoghaire ("dun LEER-y") is an uneasy mix of seaside resort and industrial harbor. The town has been hyped as a lower-cost alternative regarding food and accommodation, but this seems a little like going to Paris to dine on PB&J. Most folks take the DART down here to visit the **James Joyce Tower & Museum** (1 km east of town in Sandycove, signposted on the R119, tel. 01/280-9265, open 10 A.M.–5 P.M. Mon.–Sat. and 2–6 P.M. Sun. Feb.–Oct., admission €6.50), housed in a martello tower

that features in the opening scene of Joyce's best-known work, *Ulysses*. The 22-year-old Joyce spent just a week here in August 1904 before leaving for Italy to live the life of a literary expat (teaching English, naturally) with future bride Nora Barnacle. On the seaside of the tower is a swimming hole, known as the **Forty Foot Pool** (named not for height, but for the 40th Regiment of the British Army stationed at the tower above). In years gone by the pool was forbidden to women, as men liked to bathe there in the nude. Today, alas, there are few exhibitionists carrying on the tradition.

Another reason to come to Dún Laoghaire is if you're leaving the country by ferry. The **Stena Line** (tel. 01/204-7777 or 01/204-7799 for timetable, www.stenaline.ie, 3/day daily, 2-hour trip, advance reservations recommended, single pedestrian fare €27–44, cars €180–210) links Dún Laoghaire with Holyhead in North Wales. Book online for the best rates.

Dún Laoghaire is 13 kilometers south of Dublin on the R118 coastal road. The **DART** (tel. 01/805-4288, 3–4/hour daily, get off at Sandycove for the Joyce museum, single/daily return €1.95/3.50) can get you down here in 20 minutes or less from Pearse Station.

MEATH AND LOUTH

Wedged between Dublin and Northern Ireland on the east coast, Meath (An Mhí, "The Middle") and Louth (An Lú, "The Least") boast some of the island's most important megalithic and early Christian remains. Newgrange, a Neolithic passage tomb that predates the pyramids at Giza, is arguably the country's most popular tourist attraction, but there are also lesser-known sites (but just as worthwhile) in Meath and Louth.

Ireland has plenty of dreary, humdrum towns, but these counties' proximity to the capital means an even greater proliferation of such places. Navan and Dundalk in particular are bulging with anonymous cookie-cutter estates to meet the overwhelming demand for affordable housing within an hour or so of Dublin. Keep on driving, as the few sights in these towns aren't all that worthwhile.

HISTORY

Though Ireland has more than 1,200 megalithic tombs (in varying states of preservation, of course), archaeologists have learned the most about everyday life in the Stone Age from the sites of County Meath. From remains at Brú na Bóinne—the megalithic funerary complex of which Newgrange is the centerpiece of sorts—we know plenty more than what they ate (livestock, nuts, wheat, and barley). They "cleaned" their teeth with soot, cleared tracts of forest for growing grain and raising animals brought over from England, and decorated their pottery and tomb walls with elegant tri-spiraling motifs. And the population stats are downright horrifying: The average life expectancy was 26 years for women and 29 for men, and the infant mortality rate was as high as 75 percent.

HIGHLIGHTS

◖ **Brú na Bóinne:** At this funerary complex, Newgrange, one of Europe's most famous Stone Age monuments, and two other important passage tombs, Knowth and Dowth, attract as many as 200,000 yearly visitors, who admire their astonishingly advanced architecture and striking Neolithic art (page 87).

◖ **The Hill of Tara:** Go for an outdoor guided tour of the legendary seat of the High Kings of Ireland (page 90).

◖ **Loughcrew Cairns:** Less popular than Newgrange but with an even more stunning hilltop location, these spooky Stone Age cairns are nicknamed the "Hills of the Witch" (page 91).

◖ **Trim Castle:** The huge cruciform keep of this mighty Anglo-Norman fortress has been restored with vertiginous catwalks and detailed historical models, but what really makes Trim worth your while is the excellent guided tour (page 95).

◖ **Monasterboice:** Along with the remains of a round tower and two small churches, this 6th-century monastic site features the two most magnificent high crosses in all Ireland (page 105).

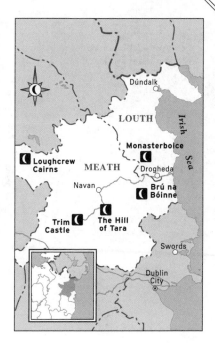

LOOK FOR ◖ TO FIND RECOMMENDED SIGHTS, ACTIVITIES, DINING, AND LODGING.

In pre-Christian times the high king of Ireland had his royal court at Tara in Meath. There is more legend than fact associated with the Hill of Tara, however; this broad grassy mound with its unimpressive ruins is more a national symbol than anything else. The same is true of the Cooley Peninsula in County Louth, setting for the 8th-century epic of *The Cattle Raid of Cooley,* an oral tradition finally set to paper by the monks of Clonmacnoise and Noughaval (in Wexford) in the 12th and 14th centuries. Thomas Kinsella's 1969 translation is the definitive one.

It was to Tara that St. Patrick sought permission to preach the new religion on this island.

St. Buite, a disciple of Patrick, founded a monastery at Monasterboice near the River Boyne in the early 6th century. "Boyne" is actually a corruption of his name. The Hill of Slane is also associated with Patrick, who according to legend lit a paschal fire here in view of King Laoghaire's palace on the hill of Tara. After a spiritual duel of sorts between Patrick and the king's druidic advisors, the enraged king reluctantly converted to Christianity. Trinity College Dublin archaeology professor George Eogan (who excavated Knowth, at Brú na Bóinne) believes the great evangelist may have actually lit the fire at Knowth, however.

But the most terrible epoch in the history of

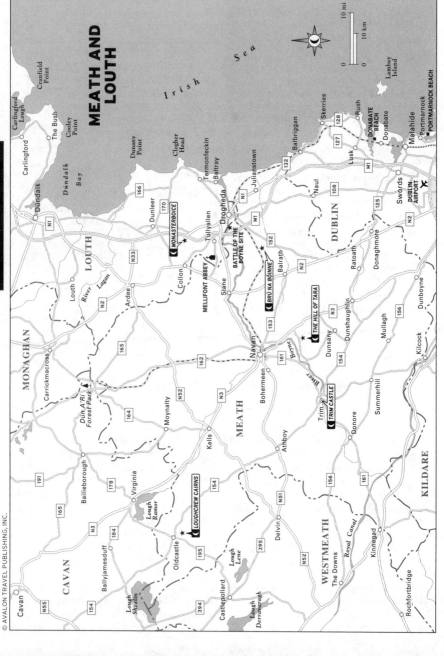

these counties concerns the attempted Jacobite revolution in 1690, when the forces of the deposed Catholic king, James II, assembled on these gentle riverside hills to fight the English Parliament's choice of monarch, the Protestant William of Orange (James's son-in-law). It is not an exaggeration to state that the fate of the island hung in the balance, and the English victory enabled hundreds of years of further social and political oppression.

PLANNING YOUR TIME

Newgrange, Meath's principal attraction, is most often done as a day trip out of Dublin, though there's more here—Loughcrew Cairns and Trim Castle especially—to warrant at least an overnight stay in the Boyne Valley. It is perhaps most efficient to experience Louth's sights—nearly all of which are in or near Drogheda, and can be visited in the span of a day—while en route to Belfast.

Meath

Meath is often referred to as "The Royal County," since the pre-Christian seat of the high kings was here, on the Hill of Tara. Originally there were five Irish provinces—Leinster, Munster, Connaught, Ulster, and Meath—but the fifth and smallest was subsumed into Leinster by an Act of Parliament under Henry VIII in 1543, which formed two new counties, Meath and Westmeath.

Navan is the county's principal town, but you don't want to waste your vacation time in an overdeveloped commuter suburb. Newgrange and the other Boyne Valley sights can be done in a day tour out of Dublin, but it's far better to base yourself in Trim or Slane and take your time. And if you're interested in the archaeology but can't stand crowds (you'll find 'em at Newgrange even in winter), consider visiting the spooky, yet-to-be-excavated Loughcrew Cairns instead of Brú na Bóinne.

THE BOYNE VALLEY

From superstitious Stone Age farming communities to the seat of royal power, home of saints and scholars and a bloody battle for the English throne: The history of the Boyne River valley is even richer than the soil. A day tour out of Dublin, such as the one offered by **Mary Gibbons Tours** (tel. 01/283-9973, www.newgrangetours.com, departs the Dublin tourist office on Suffolk St. at 10:15 A.M. Mon.–Sat., returning at 4:30 P.M., tickets €35, includes admission fees), will take you to Brú

na Bóinne, the Hill of Tara, and the Battle of the Boyne site. **Bus Éireann** also offers a Newgrange and Boyne Valley tour (Busáras, Store St., tel. 01/836-6111, www.buseireann. ie, departs bus station 10 A.M. daily and returns at 5:45 P.M., tickets €27, includes admission fees).

Locally, the village of Slane makes the most pleasant base for visiting the Boyne Valley sights, though Trim and Drogheda are good options as well.

◖ Brú na Bóinne

Opened in 1997, the very informative Brú na Bóinne Visitor Centre (2 km west of Donore village on the L21, clearly signposted from Drogheda/N1 and Slane/N2, tel. 041/988-0300, brunaboinne@opw.ie, admission €2.90 exhibition only, €5.80 with Newgrange, €10.30 exhibition and both sites) is your access point (via a brief shuttle bus ride) for three of Europe's most important prehistoric burial chambers: Newgrange, the best-known and most-visited, as well as Knowth and Dowth, the latter of which has yet to be excavated. (It's also the only monument you can check out without going through the visitors center.) Newgrange and the interpretive center are open year-round (9:30 A.M.–5:30 P.M. daily Mar.–Apr. and Oct., 9 A.M.–6:30 P.M. daily in May, 9 A.M.–7 P.M. daily June–Sept., 9:30 A.M.–5 P.M. Nov.–Feb.); Knowth is open the same hours but only May–October. On this UNESCO World Heritage

Site there are more than 90 monuments and earthworks in all.

You need only to look at the lush river valley around you to understand why the first Neolithic farmers chose to settle here between 3800 and 3400 B.C. The Boyne provided rich soil, fish, drinking water, and a means of transport, and the surrounding forests provided plenty of timber. The river attained spiritual significance as well, a symbol in their pagan religion of the sometimes-hazy boundary between the "real" and "other" worlds.

These elaborately constructed megalithic passage tombs were the product of that belief, and the 40 burial mounds at Brú na Bóinne are the first signs of human activity in this region. **Newgrange** (Sí an Bhrú) was built between 3300 and 2900 B.C., making it 500 years older than the Giza pyramids and a thousand years older than Stonehenge. This type of megalithic tomb was built all over western and northern Europe during the fourth millennium B.C., however, and it's somewhat ironic that the architects and laborers who spent at least 15 years erecting Newgrange would never be entombed there themselves. Yes, even in Neolithic times a rigid social hierarchy was firmly in place.

You may be startled at first by the tomb's spiffy white quartz facade, a reconstruction based on the findings of University College Cork (UCC) archaeologist Michael J. O'Kelly. The entry stone is carved with exquisite triple spirals, the most common interpretation being that this motif symbolizes nature's cyclicity. The mound alone weighs 200,000 tons and covers a full acre; grooved channels in the upper surfaces of the roof stones siphon off the rainwater, keeping the chamber dry. Clearly, this monument, a marvel of Stone Age technology, was built to last.

Dr. O'Kelly's discoveries between 1962 and 1975 included the cremated remains of five bodies in the niches around the cruciform central chamber, though they were not cremated inside the tomb (no soot was found on the walls). Dearly departed members of the Neolithic upper crust were probably deposited here until the next winter solstice, when the

Ireland's best-known megalithic tomb, Newgrange features an entry stone carved with triple spirals.

© CAMILLE DEANGELIS

dawning light streaming through the roof box would have, so they believed, transported their spirits to the afterlife. After the solstice these remains would have been transferred to other graves nearby, though probably not beneath the myriad "satellite tombs" around each of the three primary monuments; these would have been reserved for families lower on the social ladder.

Dr. O'Kelly also alighted—pun intended—on the roof box above the doorway and was the first person in modern times to witness the solstice illuminate the burial chamber. Today you can view a simulated version toward the end of the tour, and once back in the visitors center you can enter your name into a drawing to see it for real come December 20. Before you go, though, spend a few minutes deciphering the eerie early-19th-century graffiti.

Note that the guided tour of Newgrange is not for claustrophobics, as the passageway is very low and narrow and the central chamber is too small for the number of visitors per group.

Knowth (Cnóbha), roughly the same size as

© CAMILLE DEANGELIS

A scene from *Braveheart* was filmed in the gloomy, labyrinthine Bective Abbey.

Newgrange, is accessible by a second shuttle bus. Excavated by George Eogan from Trinity College Dublin in 1967 and 1968, this passage tomb is encircled by 127 large curbstones, and the two chambers within see the light of the spring equinox. Knowth alone contains 45 percent of Irish tomb art, and more than 25 percent of the tomb art in all Europe, so it's a real disappointment that you can't actually enter either of its two passages (you can only take a peek inside). According to UCC archaeologist Elizabeth Shee Twohig, many motifs in megalithic art were probably "derived from altered states of consciousness." A replica of a carefully carved phallic stone found at Knowth is on display in the exhibition; whatever their intention in building such monuments, clearly these Stone Agers were having their fun.

Though **Dowth** (Dubhadh)—with its 115 curbstones and two westward-facing tombs—is comparable in size to Newgrange and Knowth, it has never been properly excavated. Archaeologists believe that, like Knowth, this site was still a hive of activity in early Christian times. The crater at the center of the mound is the result of excavations in the 1840s; like Newgrange, Dowth's west face was quarried by local builders. You can walk around the site, though entrance to the mound is not possible.

The Brú na Bóinne interpretive center is kid-friendly without being dumbed down, featuring replicas of Neolithic clothing, tools, and tchotchkes. Birdcalls play on a speaker above a full-scale model of a circular thatched hut, a speculative reconstruction based on the post holes and foundation trenches uncovered during the excavation. There's also a seven-minute audiovisual inside an ersatz planetarium, and a low stone doorway on the far side leads into a full-scale model of the inner chamber at Newgrange. Along with the usual tearoom and gift shop, the center also houses a full-fledged tourist office.

Brú na Bóinne is one of Ireland's top tourist attractions, which means you need to be strategic in planning your visit. In high season it's wise to arrive at opening to beat most of the coach tours and school groups. Come in the afternoon and you may not be able to visit the sites at all—spaces on the tours fill up extremely quickly. Purchase a combo ticket for the interpretive center and both monuments, and consider buying the Dúchas Heritage Card if you'll be visiting other OPW sites on your trip.

Brú na Bóinne is 55 kilometers northwest of Dublin off the N2, and the site is also clearly signposted from Slane and Drogheda on the N51. Those not driving can do Brú na Bóinne as a day trip out of Dublin.

Bective Abbey ·

The substantial ruins of Bective Abbey (7 km north of Trim, signposted off the Navan road/ R161) are well worth seeking out. This is Ireland's second Cistercian monastery, founded in 1147 as a "daughter house" of Mellifont Abbey in County Louth and converted into a mansion after minions of Henry VIII forcibly dissolved it. Romantically labyrinthine, the abbey's highlight is a lovely arcaded cloister—and if it seems familiar, it may be because one of the scenes in *Braveheart* (with Sophie Marceau and Jeanne Marine) was filmed here. The site itself is not signposted, so keep an eye out for the gate on your left. (If the gate's locked, the wire fence a few paces down the road is easily hoppable.) Though at time of writing visitors had to leave their cars along the narrow road, the OPW is planning a new entrance and small car park.

◖ The Hill of Tara

As with Rome, all roads once led to the Hill of Tara (12 km south of Navan off the N3, tel. 046/902-6222, open 10 A.M.–6 P.M. daily mid-May–mid-Sept., admission €2.10), legendary seat of the high kings of Ireland from the 3rd through the 10th century A.D. Here St. Patrick obtained permission from King Laoghaire to preach Christianity on the island after explaining the concept of the Holy Trinity using a shamrock plucked from the grass. For this reason the site is often called the **Ráth of the Synods** (a synod being, essentially, a religious assembly). The 20-minute guided tour takes you by the **Mound of the Hostages,** a Bronze Age passage tomb built between 2500 and 2000 B.C.; remains of several ring forts and earthenworks, including a "banquet hall" more likely used as another burial site, and **Fort of King Laoghaire,** supposedly entombed standing up and in full armor; and the **Lia Fáil,** the overtly phallic "Stone of Destiny," where the kings were crowned—suspiciously Arthurian, eh? The tour, coupled with a 20-minute audiovisual at the visitors center, will give you a sense of the historic importance around this sheep-dotted hill.

In more recent history, Tara was the site of an Irish defeat in the rebellion of 1798, and in 1843 "the Great Liberator," Daniel O'Connell, held a mass rally on this hill. It's said as many as a million people turned up to hear his call for the repeal of the Act of Union. Even if that figure is exaggerated, most agree at least half a million people were there that day—still a stunning statistic, considering the pre-famine population was somewhere in the neighborhood of eight million.

To get to Tara from Dublin (40 km), head north for Cavan on the N3. The **Bus Éireann** (tel. 01/836-6111) Dublin–Navan route (#109, at least one departure per hour daily) can leave you off at Tara Cross within easy walking distance of the site, if requested.

The Battle of the Boyne

The largest battle in Irish history was fought on July 1, 1690, between supporters of William of Orange and the Jacobites, who sought to restore the Catholic king he had deposed. There were more than 61,000 troops amassed on the **Battle of the Boyne site** (Oldbridge Estate, 3 km north of Donore village off the L21, tel. 041/988-4343, battleoftheboyne@duchas.ie, open 10 A.M.–6 P.M. daily May–Sept., free admission) on that fateful morning. The date of the battle is still seared on the Irish national psyche, especially in the north, where Protestant schoolboys continue to celebrate the "marching season" with truly frightening zeal.

As at the Hill of Tara, you really need the guided tour (45 minutes long) to get anything out of a visit to the battle site; otherwise it's just an ironically peaceful riverside stroll. To get here, take the N51 west from Drogheda (5 km) or east from Slane (13 km), or take the N2 or M1 motorway out of Dublin; the site is clearly signposted from the N51. If you're relying on public transport, the **Bus Éireann** route out of Drogheda (#163, 6/day Mon.–Sat., 5/day Sun.) stops in the nearby village of Donore. From Dublin, take the #110 bus (6/day Mon.–Sat., 5/day Sun.) and transfer in Drogheda. It's much more efficient to take one of the Boyne Valley day tours, however.

Loughcrew Historic Gardens

The complex at Loughcrew Historic Gardens (Loughcrew House, 5 km south of the village of Oldcastle, signposted off the R195/Mullingar road, tel. 049/854-1060, www.loughcrew. com, open 12:30–5 P.M. daily mid-Mar.–Sept., 1–4 P.M. Sun. and bank holiday Mon. in low season, admission €6) is yet another example of 21st-century big-house enterprise: You can wander through the restored 17th- and 19th-century gardens (which include the ruin of St. Oliver Plunkett's family church), spend the night in period style at the early-19th-century neoclassical **Loughcrew House** (tel. 049/854-1356, €75 pp, s €90, evening meal €40), and give your Visa some exercise in the furniture and gift shops. Since 2000 a charity benefit opera has been held annually on a circular stage in the garden (tickets €70–95), and a weekend **jazz festival** (day/weekend tickets €30/55) in late June attracts some pretty high-profile performers. Visit the website for more details on both events.

You'll need to pick up the key here if you wish to pop inside one of the Neolithic passage tombs at the Loughcrew Cairns.

Loughcrew House is 106 kilometers northwest of Dublin. To get to the house, garden, and cairns, take the N3 from Dublin to Kells and pick up the westbound Oldcastle road, the R154, and follow the signs for Loughcrew Gardens from the village.

Unfortunately, Bus Éireann's Drogheda–Oldcastle service is too infrequent and convoluted to be of any use to the tourist (though there are three buses direct from Kells Monday–Saturday, the last return bus leaves too early in the day). Consider renting a car if Loughcrew is at the top of your destination list.

◖ Loughcrew Cairns

If the prospect of elbowing through the crowds at Newgrange in summertime gets you seriously queasy, consider a visit to the relatively quiet (and "undeveloped") necropolis of the Loughcrew Cairns (Corstown, 3 km east of Oldcastle off the R154, tel. 049/854-2009 or 041/988-0300 for off-season inquiries, open 10 A.M.–6 P.M. mid-June–mid-Sept., admission €1.60), constructed around 3000 B.C. These 30 megalithic tombs (scattered on three neighboring hills) are known as the Hills of the Witch, for legend claims a beldam jumped from one hill to the next, dropping stones from her pocket to form them. Sliabh na Caillighe (meaning "Hill of the Witch") is the highest at 280 meters, and supposedly provides a view of 17 counties. The other two hills are known as Carnbane East (195 meters) and Carnbane West (205 meters). (You don't need to be a mountaineer to scale these hills, but for heaven's sake, put on sensible footwear!) The Neolithics decorated the largest tomb, Cairn T (on Carnbane East), with their trademark stone carvings; as at Newgrange (which was erected around the same time), New Agers flock here on the equinoxes to watch the morning light stream inside.

To borrow the key to Cairn T from the Loughcrew Gardens visitors center, you are required to leave your passport or driver's license, a laundry list of contact details, and a €50 deposit. Contact Loughcrew House directly (tel. 049/854-1356, info@loughcrew.com) should you wish to borrow the key outside visitors center opening hours (key available 10 A.M.–4 P.M. only). Bring a flashlight. There are guides onsite during official opening hours, from whom you can obtain the key to Cairn L (on Carnbane West).

To get to the cairns, take the N3 from Dublin to Kells and pick up the westbound

MEATH AND LOUTH

An astonishingly well-preserved belfry crowns the Hill of Slane.

Oldcastle road, the R154; follow the signs for Loughcrew Gardens from the village. You'll have to double back on that road once you've picked up the Cairn T key (though you can still wander around the site without it, of course).

SLANE

If you're planning to do the Newgrange–Tara–Battle of the Boyne circuit, Slane (Baile Shláine) is far and away the most pleasant base—it's only 9 kilometers northwest, 24 kilometers northeast, and 12 kilometers west of those respective sites. Despite the occasional high-profile concert at Slane Castle, the village is delightfully quiet, friendly, and down-to-earth, priding itself on its illustrious sons: the early 20th-century poet Francis Ledwidge and John Boyle O'Reilly, a Fenian who became editor of a Boston newspaper, the *Pilot,* after escaping an Australian penal colony in the late 1880s.

Sights

Slane Castle (on the N51 just west of the village, tel. 041/988-4400, www.slanecastle.

ie, open noon–5 P.M. Sun.–Thurs. May–July, admission €7), on whose grounds a natural amphitheater is now the country's coolest concert venue, was built in the 1780s using several prominent British and Anglo-Irish architects. Today you can tour several of the drawing rooms and bedrooms, among them the chamber in which King George IV enjoyed the occasional rendezvous with the lady of the house. The current Lord Conyngham, an enterprising chap, seems to be squeezing a profit out of his ancestral home in every manner feasible.

The **Hill of Slane,** where St. Patrick lit his paschal fire in a sort of religious competition with the druids at Tara in 433, is crowned with the atmospheric ruins of the 15th-century **Slane Abbey.** Above a gorgeous mullioned window rises a dramatic belfry—look up and you'll find you can see up all the way to the roof. To get here, take Chapel Street away from the river (past George's Patisserie) to the signpost on your left, just beyond the modern Celtic cross that serves as a 1798 monument. The road winds gently uphill for another kilometer, and at the crest you'll find lovely panoramic views of the Boyne River valley.

Francis Ledwidge, a tremendously promising poet who grew up just outside Slane, was killed in the first World War. He was just shy of 30. **The Ledwidge Museum** (Janeville, Slane, tel. 041/982-4544, ledwidgemuseum@eircom.net, open 10 A.M.–1 P.M. and 2–5:30 P.M. daily, admission €2.50) commemorates Ledwidge's life and poetry in a small exhibition and garden. In a piece on walking the Boyne with Seamus Heaney in the early '80s, Anthony Bailey mentions that a certain British publisher actually had the effrontery not to invite Ledwidge's own brother (then in his 80s, and still living in Slane) to the local book launch. Ninety years after the poet's death, that edition of Francis Ledwidge's work is still displayed prominently in local bookstores.

A two-hour **Slane historical walking tour,** led by Mick Kelly (tel. 087/937-7040), departs the Conyngham Arms every evening at 7.

THE TÁIN TRAIL AND THE CATTLE RAID OF COOLEY

The Táin Trail cycling route is 504 kilometers long, a loop that extends from Roscommon to Carlingford on the Cooley Peninsula – hitting Longford town, Athlone, Trim, Slane, and Kells, and plenty of sleepy midland villages along the way. County Louth includes 150 kilometers of this route, which hits the various settings of the medieval epic *Táin Bó Cúailnge* (literally "The Driving-Off of Cows of Cooley," but the anglicized title is *The Cattle Raid of Cooley*).

The epic follows the exploits of the teenaged Ulster warrior Cuchulainn and his nemesis, Maeve (queen of Connaught). In an attempt to best her husband's wealth, Maeve (also spelled "Medb") plots to steal the finest bull in Ulster, and because the rest of the Ulster army is incapacitated by a mysterious curse, Cuchulainn is the only one who can stop her. Drawn-out battles ensue, some pitting Cuchulainn against his own loved ones.

If you're planning to cycle the Táin Way, contact **Irish Cycle Hire** (Enterprise Centre, Ardee, tel. 041/685-3772, www.irishcyclehire.com, weeklong packages approximately €300-460 pp), which takes care of your equipment rental as well as your dining and accommodations along the way. More information is available through the **East Coast & Midlands Tourism** office (tel. 044/934-8761, www.eastcoastmidlands.ie).

Sports and Recreation

Slane is on the **Táin Trail** cycling route (see the sidebar *The Táin Trail and the Cattle Raid of Cooley*). Since there's no bike shop in the village proper, pedaling to Newgrange isn't really an option unless you've brought one with you. Climbing the Hill of Slane (it's a leisurely kilometer) is a nice way to pass an afternoon, as both the monastic ruins and the view at the top are eminently picture-worthy; alternatively, you might head over the bridge (just south of the square) and pick up the path along the Boyne. Otherwise, there's always the **Stackallen Tennis and Pitch and Putt Club** (Stackallen, Pig Hill, 2 km from Slane on the Navan-bound N51, tel. 041/982-4279 or 087/977-3213, info@stackallen.com).

Accommodations

Whether you're looking for budget beds or charming self-catering digs, head on over to the IHH **Slane Farm Hostel and Cottages** (Harlinstown, 2 km from the village on the Kells road, the R163, tel. 041/988-4985, www.slanefarmhostel.ie, open Feb.–mid-Dec., dorms €16–20, doubles €25 pp, singles €30, credit cards accepted), a converted 18th-century stablehouse all done up in cheerful green trim. The kitchen, sitting room, and dormitories are amazingly clean and homey, stocked and decorated with far more care than most people give their own living spaces. The only downside here is the strangely chilly reception.

Nearly right next door is **Hillview House** (Gernonstown, 2 km from town on the R163, tel. 041/982-4327, hillview@02.ie, €30–35 pp, s €42–45), a small white bungalow with friendly owners and the sweet smells of hay and manure greeting your nose should you crack your bedroom window. Not such an appealing prospect? Try the stately **Boyne View** (tel. 041/982-4823, heveyboyneview@eircom.net, €30–35 pp, s €42–45), a lovely stone Georgian just off Main Street overlooking the river.

As far as hotels go, the **Conyngham Arms Hotel** (Main St., tel. 041/988-4444, www.conynghamarms.com, rooms €115–150) is about as old-fashioned as it gets, with cathedral ceilings, four-poster beds (not in every room, though), and that certain air of faded gentility. The restaurant fare is far better than average, too—but don't plan on an early night, as the noise from the pub can be heard even on the top floor.

Food and Entertainment

There are few dining options in Slane. If you

have a car and it's a Friday, Saturday, or Sunday evening, consider driving to the superb **Rainy Lane Bistro** for dinner, in a rural setting between Navan and Kells (see *Kells*).

The Old Post Office Restaurant (Main St., tel. 041/982-4090, www.theoldpost-office.com, open 9 A.M.–5:30 P.M. daily, 6:30–9:30 P.M. Wed.–Sat., daytime mains €4–10, dinner €13–25, B&B €35 pp, s €40) does excellent fry-ups in a bright, cheerful, casual atmosphere, and in the evening you can dine by candlelight on duck, lamb, salmon, or an inspired plate of pasta. Otherwise, the **Conyngham Arms** (Main St., tel. 041/988-4444, food served noon–8 P.M. daily, meals €15–25) does pub grub as well as more formal meals in the restaurant.

Savor a pain au chocolat and a café au lait at **George's Patisserie** (Chapel St., tel. 041/982-4493, www.georgespatisserie.com, open 9 A.M.–6 P.M. Tues.–Sat., snacks under €6). The ornate three-tier cakes on display conjure daydreams of a grand old-fashioned wedding. Though the café offers only sweet things, there's a delicatessen on the premises featuring local meats and cheeses.

The old-style tearoom is no more, but the dark, spacious, comfortable **Boyle's** (Main St., tel. 041/982-4195) is still the best spot in town for an afternoon drink. The friendly bartenders show plenty of traditional Irish hospitality, too. Both Boyle's and the **Slane House Bar** (Main St., tel. 041/982-4706) are popular with sport fans, though the televisions aren't as intrusive as in other bars. **The Village Inn** (Main St., tel. 041/982-4230) has a fun collection of pictures and posters from castle concerts gone by. There's also good *craic* to be found at the old-school pub at the Conyngham Arms.

Information
You'll find the local **tourist office** (Main St., tel. 041/982-4010, www.meathtourism.ie, open 9:30 A.M.–5 P.M. Mon., Thurs., and Sat.) across the street from the Conyngham Arms Hotel.

Services
There was no bank or ATM in Slane at time of writing, so be sure to make a withdrawal before leaving Dublin.

Pick up cough drops at **Breen's Pharmacy** (Main St., tel. 041/982-4222). The **Spick and Span Laundrette** (3 Newgrange Mall, tel. 041/982-0959) does dry cleaning as well. The **post office** (tel. 041/982-4922) is also in Newgrange Mall.

Getting There
Slane is 15 kilometers west of Drogheda on the N51 and 48 kilometers northwest of Dublin on the N2. **Bus Éireann** passes through Slane on the following routes out of Dublin: Letterkenny (#32, 5/day daily), Derry (#33, 3–4/day daily), Portrush (#36, 3–4/day daily), and Clones in County Monaghan (#177, 6/day daily). There is also direct service from Drogheda (#183 or #188, at least 6/day Mon.–Sat.).

Getting Around
Newgrange Bike Hire (Drumree, tel. 086/069-5771, kevinohand@eircom.net, ring for rates) is 300 meters from the Brú na Bóinne visitors center.

For a taxi in the Slane area, ring **M&L Cabs** (tel. 087/214-3088 for a cab, tel. 086/360-1338 for a minibus).

TRIM
Dominated by the fascinating ruins of an Anglo-Norman castle, Trim (Baile Átha Troim) is a tidy little town on the River Boyne 40 minutes northwest of Dublin. It's a quiet place—some may find it a bit too quiet, especially after dark—but its medieval attractions and a couple of delightfully scruffy pubs make Trim a pleasant spot to spend the night.

Between the humongous castle and the town's smallish size, orienting yourself is fairly easy. The street that hugs the castle ruins changes names from the New Dublin Road to Castle Street to Bridge Street—here crossing the Boyne—to High Street to Navan Gate Street as it curves northward. Most of the town's amenities are on Market Street, which shoots westward off the main drag where Castle meets Bridge Street. Turn off the west end of Market Street onto Emmet Street, home to several pubs offering live trad.

◖ Trim Castle

Granted the land by Henry II, Hugh de Lacy and his son Walter built a motte-and-timber tower in 1172 on the site of the Boyne-side Trim Castle (tel. 046/943-8619, open 10 A.M.– 6 P.M. daily Apr.–Oct., 10 A.M.–5 P.M. weekends Nov.–Mar., admission with/excluding the keep €3.70/1.60), only to burn it down the following year to prevent the Irish from taking it by force. They rebuilt the castle over the following three decades, and it was—and remains—the largest Anglo-Norman castle in the country. Before its restoration in the late '90s, Trim was partially rebuilt (and filled with various livestock and ragamuffin extras) for the filming of *Braveheart,* and you can flip through a photo album available from the admission desk.

Only the service tower is missing from the imposing, three-story, cruciform keep, accessible by guided tour only; it's an informative-but-interesting 45 minutes. On the ground level, three large and wonderfully detailed models of the castle at three different periods in its history highlight many notable architectural features, like the "roof scars" that are all that remain of a double A-framed, red-tiled roof, or the squinches that still lend structural support. Metal catwalks allow visitors to peruse the upper levels, and the view from the parapet is worth the vertigo on the spiral stairs.

Elsewhere on the castle grounds, the Barbican Gate has five parallel murder holes (there are also two in the town gate, from which you enter the grounds), and the jail features an oubliette.

Other Sights

Just across the Boyne are the **yellow steeple,** once the bell tower of the Augustinian Abbey of St. Mary (its present ruined state thanks, yet again, to Cromwell), and the **Sheep's Gate,** the only extant gate from the old town walls. The early 15th-century **Talbot Castle** (High St., tel. 046/943-1213, guided tours available June–Aug., call for an appointment) incorpo-

rates a portion of the old abbey and was once owned by Jonathan Swift (he lived there for only one year, though his mistress spent much more time there). The Millennium Bridge at the end of Castle Street connects the medieval ruins on either side of the river.

Newtown Abbey (Lackanash Rd., 1.5 km east of town, always accessible, free admission) contains the ruins of the **Cathedral of Saints Peter and Paul,** remarkable for its well-worn double tomb effigy of a knight and his wife. The sword that separates them has inspired locals to refer to them as "the jealous man and woman." The rainwater that collects in the carvings is said to have curative properties— for warts, that is—and the space between the effigies is littered with rusted safety pins. To get here, take the New Road/Navan exit at the roundabout at the end of New Dublin Road (just east of the castle), cross the Boyne, and make the first right onto Lackanash Road, a residential street. It's a 20-minute walk or a 3-minute drive from town.

Trim is also a viable base for the Boyne Valley's prime attractions (Tara is 23 km, Newgrange 34 km). Need a break from driving, or don't have wheels? Contact Anne Leavy at **Tours na Mí** (tel. 046/943-2523, abirdyleavy@iol.ie).

Entertainment and Events

You can't leave Trim without taking a pint at **Marcie's,** a.k.a. **David's Lad** (Lackanash Rd., Newtown, tel. 046/943-6103, open at 9 P.M. Thurs.–Tues.), which claims to be Ireland's second-oldest pub. Granted, with the rough stone walls, grungy chairs, and cement floors it feels like drinking in your uncle's basement, but the fact that everybody knows everyone here means an authentically Irish night out. The half dozen snow-haired gents who play traditional music here on Friday nights (starting a bit after 10:30) have been jamming together longer than you've been alive. To get here, follow the same directions for Newtown Abbey; the pub is directly across the road.

Another delightfully old-fashioned pub is **James Griffin's** (High St., tel. 046/943-1295), but if it's more trad you want, check out **The Emmet Tavern** (Emmet St., tel. 046/943-1378), with sessions Thursday–Saturday; **The Olde Stand** (Emmet St., tel. 046/943-1286) Friday–Sunday; or **The Steps** (Emmet St., tel. 046/943-7575) on Thursday. **Brogan's** (High St., tel. 046/943-1237) has sessions every other Saturday, so ask at the bar if you're in luck this weekend. The **Castle Arch Hotel** (Summerhill Rd., tel. 046/943-1516, www.castlearchhotel.com) offers trad every Saturday night, however.

Shopping

Trim doesn't have much in the way of gift shops, but you could try **Tobin's** (4-5 Market St., tel. 046/943-6265), which has the usual range of jewelry, crystal, pottery, and knitwear, though not all of it's Irish in origin.

Sports and Recreation

Tee off at the **County Meath Golf Club** (Newtonmoynagh, 1.5 km outside town, tel. 046/943-1463, www.trimgolf.net), which has an 18-hole parkland course.

You have a choice among equestrian centers in the area (no more than a 10-minute drive): There's the **Kilcarty Horse Riding Centre** (Kilcarty, Dunsany, tel. 046/902-5877 or 086/088-7841), the **Pelletstown Riding Centre** (Pelletstown, Drumree, tel. 01/825-9435), or the **Moy Riding Centre** (Summerhill, Enfield, tel. 04/055-8115).

Accommodations

There is a hostel on Bridge Street, but it's on the sketchy side (not to mention the lockout until 6 P.M.). In the town center, your best bet is the family-run **Brogan's Guesthouse** (High St., tel. 046/943-1237, www.brogans.ie, €36–40 pp, s €45–55), whose 14 comfy but no-nonsense bedrooms are divided between the original townhouse and the converted stables. The best reason to stay here is, of course, the downstairs pub; outside of David's Lad in Newtown, it's the best watering hole in Trim.

Built in 1810, the marvelous **Highfield House** (Maudlins Rd., tel. 046/943-6386, www.highfieldguesthouse.com, €36 pp, s

€50) was once a maternity hospital. The house is situated on a hill a couple minutes' walk from the castle, and its imposing stone facade, with bright flowers tumbling from the window boxes, matches the amazingly authentic decor. Gilded mirrors, cathedral ceilings and ornate plasterwork, high windows and sumptuous curtains, original oil paintings of young ladies in powdered wigs—it might sound on the stuffy side, but the rooms are actually quite comfortable (with new showers), and Internet access (on a standing console in the foyer) is included. Just keep in mind you're staying here for the atmosphere, not the breakfast.

For the full fry done up right, try **Tigh Cathain** (Longwood Rd., 1 km from town on the R160, tel. 046/943-1996, www.tighcathaintrim.com, €33–35 pp, s €45–50), a Tudor-style bungalow surrounded by carefully tended gardens, or **Crannmór Country House** (Dunderry Rd., 1.5 km northeast of the town center, tel. 046/943-1635, www.crannmor.com, €34–36 pp, s €46–48), a spacious, ivy-clad farmhouse in equally tranquil surroundings.

Trim's swankiest beds are found at the **Castle Arch Hotel** (Summerhill Rd., on the southern end of town, tel. 046/943-1516, www.castlearchhotel.com, €75–95 pp). Formerly known as Wellington Court (there's a monument to the duke of Waterloo fame nearby, on the corner of Emmet St. and Patrick St.), the town's only hotel often has terrific weekend packages up for grabs (two nights B&B plus dinner for only €99 per person, even at the height of summer!), so be sure to check the website before you go.

Food

Trim falls surprisingly short in the culinary category. It's too bad **Brogan's** (High St., tel. 046/943-1237, food served noon–2:30 P.M. weekdays, mains under €12) only serves weekday lunch.

It may be cafeteria-style, but **Bennini's** (French's Ln., tel. 046/943-8409, open 9 A.M.–4:30 P.M. and 6–9 P.M. daily, opening at 10 A.M. weekends, lunch €5–10) serves fresh sandwiches and stuffed potatoes in a surprisingly spiffy outfit, though it tends to attract families with lots of noisy young'uns. Don't be fooled by the faux-Italian name, though—the coffee is no good.

Next door is the absurdly named **Franzini O'Brien's** (French's Lane, tel. 046/943-1002, open 6:30–10 P.M. Mon.–Sat., 5–9 P.M. Sun., mains €12–26), the best restaurant in Trim. The menu is strangely eclectic: You can order a burger, pasta…or duck glazed in peach sauce! You have a choice of fun cocktails too. Franzini's is overpriced, however—the food is good, but by no means exceptional. When eating out in Trim, though, this is your only respectable option.

Information

The **tourist office and heritage center** (Mill St., tel. 046/943-7111 or 046/943-7227, www.meathtourism.ie, open 9:30 A.M.–5:30 P.M. Mon.–Sat., noon–5:30 P.M. Sun. May–Sept., 9 A.M.–5 P.M. Mon.–Sat. Oct.–Apr., exhibit admission €3.50) offers a 20-minute audiovisual show on Trim's medieval history (unfortunately, not included in the castle admission price).

Services

The **AIB** (Market St., tel. 046/943-6444), **Bank of Ireland** (Market St., tel. 046/943-1230), and **Ulster Bank** (High St., tel. 046/943-1233) all have ATMs. The **post office** (tel. 046/943-8870) is also on Market Street.

There are two pharmacies on Market Street, **Kelly's** (tel. 046/943-1279) and **Farrell's** (tel. 046/943-6600). **The Laundry Basket** (Loman St., 943-8558) offers an express service for tourists.

Getting There and Around

Trim is 56 kilometers northwest of Dublin off the N3, picking up the R154 in the hamlet of Black Bull 26 kilometers outside the city. **Bus Éireann** (tel. 01/836-6111) operates a local service from Dublin (#111, 9/day Mon.–Fri., 8/day Sat., 4/day Sun.), though to get here from anywhere else by bus, you'll have to head back to Dublin first.

If you need a taxi, ring **Donal Quinn** (tel. 046/943-6009 or 087/222-7333), who offers 24-hour service; **John's Taxi Service** (tel. 085/124-1732, minibus with wheelchair access); or **Martin's Cabs** (tel. 087/913-2000 or 086/834-6366).

KELLS

Kells's (Ceanannas Mór, "Great Ford") claim to fame, the 6th-century **Book of Kells** (which was illuminated on the Scottish island of Iona by St. Columba and brought here at a later date), is on display at Trinity College Dublin, so a visit to this humdrum little town isn't exactly a must. It does make a viable base for exploring the attractions of the Boyne River valley, however. There are several excellent accommodation options and the county's best restaurant is within easy driving distance.

Sights

Housed in the old courthouse, the **Kells Heritage Centre** (Headfort Pl., tel. 046/924-7840, kellsheritagecentre@eircom.net, open 10 A.M.–5:30 P.M. Mon.–Sat. and 2–6 P.M. Sun. May–Sept., 10 A.M.–5 P.M. Mon.–Sat. Oct.–Apr., admission €4) offers a thorough historical exhibition, a small trove of religious artifacts, and an audiovisual show. Outside, protected from the elements by a sturdy Plexiglas roof, is the 10th-century **Market Cross**, which has a strange history. The English hanged local participants in the 1798 rebellion from its arms. Having stood in the same location on Cross Street in the center of town since the monastery was founded, it was toppled in 1996 by a careless motorist. Most visitors will want to skip the exhibition (with its replica cross) and just check out the original for free out front.

You'll find what's left of Kells Abbey—established by St. Columba in A.D. 559—on the grounds of the Protestant **Church of St. Columba** (on the R163/Oldcastle road, just west of town, open 10 A.M.–5 P.M. Mon.–Fri. and 10 A.M.–1 P.M. Sat.). The present edifice dates to 1778, and its rather austere facade belies a Victorian Gothic interior teeming with ostentatious funerary monuments; a copy of the Book of Kells is in the old baptistry. A 15th-century belfry and a sundial of uncertain origin accompany a 10th-century, 26-meter roofless round tower and a small 12th-century oratory known as St. Colmcille's House. There are four more high crosses in the churchyard, all of which date to the 9th century and depict scenes from the Gospels. Two are in horrible condition due to the destructive whims of Cromwell's soldiers. The South Cross is by far the best preserved, but shockingly little remains of the North Cross—you could hardly even call it a stump.

Sports and Recreation

Contact the McGowans at **White Gables** (Headfort Pl., tel. 046/924-0322, kelltic@eircom.net) for a guided walk of the Kells environs.

Golfers can get a sweet sleep-eat-and-putt package through the Headfort Arms Hotel and the **Headfort Golf Club** (on the N3/Dublin road just outside of town, tel. 046/928-2001, www.headfortgolfclub.ie).

For a leisurely jaunt down the backcountry roads of County Meath, contact the **Kells Equestrian Centre** (Normanstown, just over 3 km outside Kells on the Ardee road, signposted off the N52, tel. 046/924-6998, www.kellsequestrian.com).

Accommodations

Kells does have an IHH hostel, but at time of writing it was being used as accommodation for immigrants. Fortunately, the area is awash in great midrange accommodations.

It may be a stately Georgian farmhouse, but **Lennoxbrook** (Carnaross, signposted 5 km north of Kells on the N3/the Cavan road, tel. 046/924-5902, mullan.lennoxbrook@unison.ie, €33 pp, dinner €15) doesn't sacrifice comfort for polish; proprietor Pauline Mullan really wants you to kick back and enjoy yourself. The elegant rooms, peaceful surroundings (forest, stream, gardens, the works), and

excellent meals at such modest prices make this one a fantastic value.

If you don't have a car, though, stay at **White Gables** (Headfort Pl., tel. 046/924-0322, kelltic@eircom.net, €35 pp, s €40), which is far and away the best B&B accommodation in town: You can expect top-notch breakfasts (owner Penny McGowan is a cordon bleu chef), linen sheets, sauna privileges, and a wealth of tourist info—the McGowans also host walking tours.

Classy in a small-town way, the **Headfort Arms** (John St., tel. 046/924-0063, www.headfortarms.ie, €80 pp, s €105, suites €195–225) has staff so kind, efficient, and accommodating that they could rival those at the fanciest five-star hotels. The extensive breakfast menu at the Vanilla Pod, with a delicious array of fresh pastries and fruit salad, is the perfect way to start off a long day of sightseeing. All rooms have wireless Internet access. Check out the website for midweek and weekend packages including B&B, dinner, and two rounds at the Headfort Golf Club.

Food and Entertainment

The safest bet for a pub lunch or dinner is **Monaghan's** (The Carrick, the Cavan road, a two-minute walk from the center, tel. 046/924-9995, food served noon–8 P.M. daily, mains €8–12). The **Blackwater Inn** (Farrell St., tel. 046/924-0386) has trad sessions on Monday night and soft rock or American country musicians on Wednesday and Friday. Or chill out in the backyard beer garden any night of the week.

The restaurant at the Headfort Arms Hotel, **Vanilla Pod** (John St., tel. 046/924-0084, open 5:30–10 P.M. Mon.–Fri., 5:30–11 P.M. weekends, mains €14–23), is generally considered the best eatery in town. It can be hit-or-miss, though one must give props for the emphasis on local meat and produce—and the fun cocktail menu.

Only locals know about the **◖ Rainy Lane Bistro** (Bohermeen, Navan, a 15-minute drive from Kells, tel. 046/902-2639, open

5 P.M.–late Fri.–Sun., mains €14–24, no credit cards), and doubtless they'd prefer to keep it that way. Everything about this romantic little restaurant is extraordinary, from its rural location (way, *way* off the beaten track) to the inventive, mostly organic menu—even the wines are biodynamic. The steaks are divine (whether you like yours well done or practically still mooing), the seafood specials are often organic, and the few vegetarian options are delicious as well. Even if you have no room left for a homemade dessert (Tia Maria fudge ice cream, anyone?), your tea or coffee is served with a plate of scrumptious petits fours, also homemade. The food is fantastic and the service second-to-none, but you'll enjoy it even more for having ventured down a series of narrow winding roads in the dusk to reach this charming house with candles flickering in the windows. All in all, this is truly one of the most special dining experiences in Ireland. Reservations are essential, since you'll need to get detailed directions over the phone anyway.

Information and Services

The **tourist office** (Headfort Pl., tel. 046/924-9336) is with the Kells Heritage Centre in the old courthouse and has some hours.

Both the **Bank of Ireland** (John St., tel. 046/924-0032) and **AIB** (John St., tel. 046/924-0610) have ATMs.

The **post office** (tel. 046/924-0598) is on Farrell Street, as is **Lynch's Pharmacy** (tel. 046/924-0515).

Getting There and Around

Kells is 60 kilometers northwest of Dublin on the N3, and the **Bus Éireann** (tel. 01/836-6111) stop is outside the Parochial House on John Street. There are at least two buses an hour (6:15 A.M.–10 P.M.) on the Dublin–Cavan route (#109) as well as a less frequent service from Dublin to Cavan and Donegal (#30, 7/day daily). You can also get to Enniskillen or Belleek on this route. To get to Athlone (#70) or Drogheda (#188), you must make a connection in Navan (also #30 or #109, at least 2/hour, a 15-minute ride). All other destinations require a connection in Dublin.

For a taxi, ring **Martin Cumiskey** (tel. 087/250-4242) or **Kells Cab Hire** (tel. 046/924-0415).

DUNSANY

Remarkably, the lands of **Dunsany Castle** (Dun Samhnaigh, 5 km south of Tara off the N3, tel. 046/902-5198, www.dunsany.net, open 9 A.M.–1 P.M. weekdays May–Aug. and Oct.–Nov., and by arrangement, admission to downstairs/two floors €6.35/10.20) have remained in the same family since the Anglo-Norman invasion of the 12th century. Very little remains of the medieval castle (though a significant church ruin from the 15th century stands in the adjacent park), and most of the current structure dates from the late 18th century. The 20th Baron of Dunsany opens several rooms of the ancestral home to small groups in the summer months and on the weekends leading up to Christmas. A vaulted hall—a kitchen in the 12th century—now displays locally made table linens and other swanky items from the Dunsany Home Collection (www.dunsany.com), designed by the lord himself. His grandfather, the 18th Lord Dunsany (otherwise known as Edward Plunkett), was a fantasy novelist whose works are still in print; he also supported the Slane poet Francis Ledwidge and the short story writer Mary Lavin. Their writing desks are on display in the castle.

If you enjoy studying private collections of art, antiques, and relics (for Saint Oliver Plunkett was a relation), a visit to Dunsany is certainly worth making the advance arrangements (although some of the more important pieces in the collection have been removed due to security concerns). To get here, exit the N3 at Dunshaughlin onto the R125, heading toward the village of Kilmessan. The castle is signposted from there. Dunsany is 11 kilometers west of Trim off the R154.

Louth

Considering it's the smallest county on either side of the border, Louth has quite a fair bit to offer the visitor, including the truly magnificent high crosses of Monasterboice and the remains of once-powerful Mellifont Abbey with its unusual octagonal lavabo. Pass through the county's principal town, Dundalk, to reach the Cooley Peninsula, with its thoroughly lovely medieval heritage town of Carlingford. Base yourself here or in far less touristy Drogheda, a pleasantly workaday place in the throes of citywide redevelopment.

DROGHEDA

A gritty-but-lively industrial town about an hour's drive north of Dublin, Drogheda ("DROH-heh-duh," Droichead Átha, "Bridge of the Ford") is slowly shedding its dormitory town image. Ongoing construction may be unsightly, but it definitely adds to the sense that this is a city on the upswing. It's delightfully untouristy, and your best choice for a base if you want to sample the local nightlife after a day at Newgrange and all the other Boyne Valley attractions. There are plenty of sights in Drogheda proper as well, including **Millmount,** a folk and archaeology museum and craft complex, and a liberal sprinkling of vivid historical reminders—after all, Drogheda was one of Ireland's most important medieval walled towns 600 years back. The city was devastated more than any other by the advent of Oliver Cromwell in 1649; his forces slaughtered more than 2,700 members of the town's garrison on September 11 of that year. Sir Arthur Aston, commander of the resistance, was beaten to death with his own wooden leg by Cromwell's henchmen.

Sights

Drogheda's medieval heritage allows for a full day of sightseeing. Seven hundred years ago the town wall was a mile and a half long, and the area enclosed was twice that of medieval Dublin. There were eight defense gates, of which the 13th-century **Butter Gate** (Barrack St., just north of Millmount) and **St. Laurence's Gate** (between Laurence St. and Cord Rd. at Francis St.) remain (though the Butter Gate is nearly a century older). An even more dramatic sight is the **Magdalene Tower** (on the northern end of town, at the end of Magdalene St.), which is said to be haunted by the spirit of a nun—though there is very little left to haunt! The belfry is all that remains of a 13th-century Dominican friary, though the tower itself probably dates from the following century: downright precarious, and downright eerie. But wait, there's more: excavations unearthed a skeleton of a woman who must have stood seven feet tall!

The town's primary tourist attraction is the **Millmount Museum** (Millmount, on the southern end of town, clearly signposted from town center, tel. 041/983-3097, www.millmount.net, open 10 A.M.–6 P.M. Mon.–Sat. and 2:30–5:30 P.M. Sun., admission €4.50), housed within an early-18th-century military complex that also includes a martello tower (offering a nice panoramic view of the river valley). The museum itself is a motley assortment of religious artifacts, rare rocks, and cottage industry antiques, and the pre-1800 guild banners are supposedly the only ones left in the country.

On the site of a Franciscan monastery and center of learning founded in the early 15th century, the **Highlanes Gallery** (56-57 West St., tel. 041/983-7869, www.highlanes.ie, open daily) now houses Drogheda's civic art collection as well as traveling exhibitions from Ireland and abroad. The building itself dates from 1829.

Before the construction of the **Boyne Viaduct** in the 1850s, northbound passengers had to disembark at Drogheda and secure alternative transportation to the next station 10 kilometers away. No wonder the architect, a Louth man named John Mac Neill, was considered a genius in his day. At 427 meters long, with 18 arches each 18 meters wide, this bridge

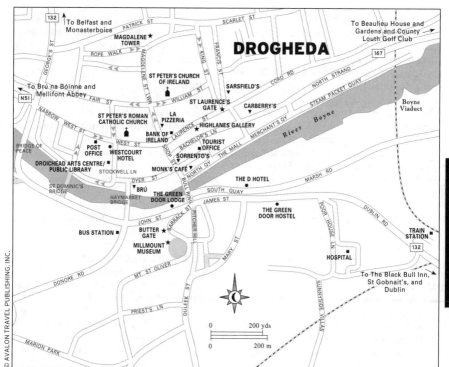

MEATH AND LOUTH

spanning the river on the eastern side of town is still a formidable sight.

St. Peter's Roman Catholic Church (West St.) is the final resting place of St. Oliver Plunkett's head. Tried for "treason" (having allegedly taken part in the "Irish Popish plot") and martyred in 1681, Plunkett's noggin was "rescued" and brought to Drogheda by a group of French nuns. What remains is now on display—a truly frightening sight—in a tall, ornate brass-and-glass case. Another glass reliquary nearby holds three of the saint's ribs, a scapula, and other carefully labeled bones. This is the most morbid attraction in Louth, if not the entire eastern seaboard.

Still more morbid attractions are to be found at the mid-18th-century **St. Peter's Church of Ireland** (William St.). In the churchyard you will find a relatively rare cadaver tomb (depicting the departed in a decayed state, something

of a fad in the century or so after the bubonic plague). Furthermore, the previous edifice had a wooden steeple, where as many as 100 people took refuge during Cromwell's rampage in 1649. Cromwell set fire to the tower, and no one survived.

Take in Plunkett's head along with a load of other historical sights—the old town walls, St. Mary's Catholic and Protestant churches, Millmount, and more—on the **Medieval Drogheda** walking tour (tel. 041/983-7070, departs the tourist office on Mayoralty St. at 2 P.M. Mon.–Sat., tickets €5). The tour lasts about an hour and a half.

Entertainment and Events

Drogheda has a pretty happenin' arts scene, the prime venue being the **Droichead Arts Centre** (Stockwell St., tel. 041/983-3946, www.droichead.com, tickets €6–12). This is the place for film screenings, plays, concerts, and art exhibitions. The city hosts several festivals throughout the year, the two most popular being the **Drogheda Arts Festival** (tel. 041/987-6100) in April and the **Drogheda Samba Festival** (tel. 041/983-8332) in July. The arts fest is a feast for the eyes and ears, with plenty of street theater, concerts, comedy acts, film screenings, dance performances, and visual art and crafts exhibits. The samba festival gets up free outdoor concerts featuring international samba bands. There's also the **Irish Steel Guitar Festival** (tel. 041/984-5684), which attracts musicians from Nashville and the U.K., in October.

Many of Drogheda's hip young things can be found at **Brú** (the Haymarket, Unit 8, North Bank, tel. 041/987-2784), a posh riverside bistro, which has a DJ on Friday and Saturday nights. Another hot spot is the super-chic bar at **The d Hotel** (Scotch Hall, tel. 041/987-7700), which also has a DJ on the weekends.

Not into "hot spots"? Fair enough. Far and away the best pub in town is **Tí Chairbre,** better known as **Carberry's** (North Strand, no phone). With a fire burning brightly in the grate, layer upon layer of concert posters pasted to the walls and ceiling, and scratchy old recordings of American "Memphis blues" on the stereo, the atmosphere here is second to none—all in all, one gets the impression that very little has changed here since even your granddaddy was in diapers. The drinks are relatively cheap, the bartender's friendly, and the trad sessions are wonderful (*sean nós* Tuesday night, traditional music Wednesday, and another trad session on Sunday afternoon around 2–4 p.m.). Come even if it isn't a music night—the locals are great fun.

If you're not in the mood for trad, you can catch an outdoor jazz session starting at 4 p.m. on Sunday at the **Black Bull Inn** (Dublin Rd., tel. 041/983-7139, blackbullinn@eircom.net). Another worthwhile watering hole is the family-run **Sarsfield's** (Cord Rd., near St. Laurence's Gate, tel. 041/983-8032), which sponsors several local sports teams (ladies', too!). In decades past several Drogheda pubs would open at 7:30 in the morning so dock and factory workers could have a pint before work, and until quite recently Sarsfield's was continuing that tradition.

Shopping

Drogheda is by no means a shopper's mecca; the best place for high-quality gifts is the **Millmount Design Store** (Millmount Craft Centre, tel. 041/984-1960, elainejeweldesign@eircom.net), featuring work coming out of the Millmount Centre craft studios: knitwear, quilts, ceramics, silver, glassware, and suchlike.

For OS maps, local interest books, or vacation reading, visit the **Wise Owl Bookshop** (The Mall, tel. 041/984-2847).

Sports and Recreation

In fine summer weather, there's no better diversion than a leisurely garden stroll. **Beaulieu House and Gardens** (Beaulieu, Drogheda, 5 km east of town on the Baltray road, signposted off the R167, tel. 041/983-8557, www.beaulieu.ie, open 11 a.m.–5 p.m. Mon.–Fri. May–mid-Sept., admission to house or garden €6, combo ticket €12) was erected on the site of a Plunkett castle in the 17th century. The admission price includes a guided tour (departing on the hour) of the big house in all its Georgian splendor. The walled garden dates from 1732, and there's also an early-19th-century church on the grounds that features some spooky tomb effigies. June and July are the best times to visit, as the roses are in full bloom.

Established in 1892, the **County Louth Golf Club** (Baltray, 7 km east of Drogheda on the R167, tel. 041/988-1530, www.countylouthgolfclub.com) is rated in the top six courses on either side of the border.

The more ambitious can cycle to nearby attractions—Mellifont Abbey and Monasterboice (both about 8 km), the Battle of the Boyne site (5.5 km), or Brú na Bóinne (11.5 km).

Accommodations

Budget travelers' only option is **The Green Door Hostel** (13 James St., the Dublin road, tel. 041/983-4422, www.greendoor-ireland.com, large dorms €16.50, small dorms €22.50, private rooms €25 per person, credit cards accepted), an IHH hostel with a new location in a recently refurbished Georgian townhouse. The management is easygoing, friendly, and helpful, the facilities are adequate, and the proximity to the train station is a definite plus. **The Green Door Lodge** (47 John St., tel. 041/983-4422, www.greendoorireland.com, €35–40 pp), in the hostel's original location, now does B&B. You just have to pick up your keys at the new hostel, which is a five-minute walk down the busy Dublin road.

Head down that road too if you're looking for a B&B, as there are very few to be found within the city limits. There are plenty of places signposted a kilometer or two outside. Named after the original 6th-century "nun on the run," **St. Gobnait's** (1 km out of Drogheda on the Dublin road/R132, tel. 041/983-7844, €35–40 pp, s €50) is a handsome ivy-clad brick home with an elegant-but-homey atmosphere and cheery, helpful proprietors.

But if a central location is what you're after, try the **Westcourt Hotel** (West St., tel. 041/983-0965, www.westcourt.ie, €60 pp, s €65, weekend discounts available). The rooms and atmosphere are standard business class, though the staff are friendly and the pub grub offers great value. On the weekends this hotel isn't a good choice for the early-to-bed set, as the bar and nightclub noise seeps up into most of the bedrooms.

Brand-spanking new, with all the trimmings of a four-star cosmopolitan establishment, **The d Hotel** (Scotch Hall, south of the Boyne, tel. 041/987-7700, www.monogramhotels.ie, €95–130 pp) offers mod-yet-comfy bedrooms, a trendy bar with plenty of fun cocktails to choose from, complimentary Internet access and laundry service, friendly staff, and an awesome breakfast menu. The d Hotel is part of a slick new shopping complex, Scotch Hall—all of which exemplifies the city's mostly admirable push for redevelopment and renewal. Check the website for special deals.

Food

Drogheda has never enjoyed a reputation for fine dining, though fortunately that's beginning to change with all the ongoing hubbub of "urban renewal."

Monk's (1 N. Quay, tel. 041/984-5630, open 8:30 A.M.–6 P.M. Mon.–Sat., 10 A.M.–5 P.M. Sun., mains €4–13, all-day breakfast €6) is on the bland side as cafés go, but it's still Drogheda's best, with fresh produce, tasty open sandwiches, decent coffee, and the likes of Sade on the stereo.

For a hearty meat-and-potatoes kind of lunch, head to Bridie Mac's pub at the **Westcourt Hotel** (West St., tel. 041/983-0965, www.westcourt.ie, food served noon–9 P.M. daily, lunches under €10). Unless the hunger of the world is on you, you won't even be able to finish the half-size portion. For something more gourmet, head to the **Black Bull Inn** (1 km outside the city center on the Dublin Rd., tel. 041/983-7139, blackbullinn@eircom.net, food served noon–10 P.M. daily, mains €10–17), which is on every local's list of favorites. Asian-inspired dishes are a specialty, and all the burgers are made with local beef.

Two of the most popular eateries in town are Italian: **La Pizzeria** (15 St. Peter's St., open 10 A.M.–11 P.M. Thurs.–Tues., mains €10–15) and the more upscale **Sorrento's** (41 Shop St., tel. 041/984-5734, open 6:30–11 P.M. Tues.–Sun., mains €10–16). As with most Italian eateries in this country, keep low expectations and you may be pleasantly surprised!

With a great location right on the Boyne, **Brú** (the Haymarket, Unit 8, North Bank, tel. 041/987-2784, www.bru.ie, open 1–10 P.M. or later daily, lunches €8, dinner mains €11–23) would get the business even if the food were only half as nice as the view (and the floor-to-ceiling panoramic windows take full advantage). The Continental fare here is excellent, however, and the sticky toffee pudding's the best in the county. Perhaps surprisingly for a place this chic, the waitstaff let you linger for as long as you like. All in all, no one would disagree with the owners that "a new era in urban dining has arrived in Drogheda."

Information and Services

The very helpful **tourist office** (Mayoralty St., tel. 041/983-7070, www.drogheda.ie, open 9 A.M.–5:30 P.M. Mon.–Sat.) is just off the North Quay, behind the Sound Shop.

You'll find plenty of ATMs and bureaux de change along Drogheda's main drags: **Bank of Ireland** (14 St. Laurence St., tel. 041/983-7653), **Ulster Bank** (104 West St., tel. 041/983-6458), or **AIB** (Dyer St., tel. 041/983-6523). The main branch of the **post office** (West St., tel. 041/983-8322) is beside the Westcourt Hotel.

Hickey's Pharmacy (10-11 West St., tel. 041/983-8651) is open Sundays and holidays. Get your duds sudsed at **Shirley's Laundrette** (5 Dublin Rd., tel. 041/984-5220).

Check your email at the **public library** (Stockwell St., tel. 041/983-6649), which allows one hour of free Internet access on slow but serviceable PCs.

Getting There

Drogheda is on Ireland's east coast between Dublin (50 km south) and Belfast (120 km north), reachable by the M1 motorway (which becomes the A1 in the U.K.) linking those two cities.

Drogheda is on the main Belfast–Dublin bus route (#1, 7/day Mon.–Sat. from both cities, 6/day Sun.). The Dublin–Dundalk route (#100 or #101, departures from Drogheda every 30 minutes), popular with commuters, is the quickest way to get back to Dublin. Other direct routes include Athlone and Galway (#70, departing Galway 12:30 P.M. Mon.–Sat., and Fri. and Sun. at 6 P.M.), and Slane (#188, 6/day Mon.–Sat.). You can also reach Drogheda from Kells (#188, 3/day Mon.–Sat., transfer at Navan). Beware that the **Bus Éireann** station (John St. and Donore Rd., tel. 041/983-5023) is popular with pickpockets.

If you haven't purchased a Rover pass, however, you might want to take a slightly less expensive coach service: **Matthews Coaches** (tel. 042/937-8188, www.matthewscoach.com, single/return ticket €7/10) buses depart Parnell Street in Dublin 22 times a day Monday–Friday, 10 times on Saturday, and 9 times on Sunday, with equally frequent return service.

Drogheda is also on the Belfast–Dublin **Irish Rail** line (Dublin Rd., about half a kilometer east of the city center, tel. 041/983-8749, at least 5 express departures daily, frequent local service), which is perhaps the country's most popular commuter service.

Getting Around

Drogheda is small enough to walk everywhere; if driving, prepare yourself for major congestion and pay-and-display. There are taxi ranks on West Street at Duke Street and just opposite St. Laurence's Gate. Or ring **Paddy Clarke's Cabs** (tel. 041/983-7890 or 087/247-2635).

For bike rental, contact **Quay Cycles** (11 N. Quay, tel. 041/983-4526, €14/day) or **P.J. O'Carolan** (77 Trinity St., tel. 041/983-8242, €15/day).

MELLIFONT ABBEY

Ireland's first Cistercian monastery, Mellifont Abbey (from *mellifons,* Latin for "honey fountain"; Tullyallen, 1.5 km off the R168, the main Drogheda–Collon road, tel. 041/982-6459 or 041/988-0300 for info in winter, mellifontabbey@opw.ie, open 10 A.M.–6 P.M. daily May–Oct., accessible without charge in winter, admission €2.10) was established in 1142 by St. Malachy, the Archbishop of Armagh. (Incidentally, Malachy was the first native of Ireland to be canonized. He also prophesied that the world would end soon after the reign of Pope John Paul II.) Malachy planned with St. Bernard of Clairvaux to open a stricter, more rigorous religious order, a community made up of both French and native monks. Though the French and Irish failed to gel, the Cistercian ideology (and architecture) caught on in this country, and Mellifont became the "mother house" for many smaller monasteries.

The abbey's most unusual feature is its lavabo, an octagonal building used as a communal washing-place before meals, which was completed in 1157 (or nearer to the year 1200, depending on whom you ask). Otherwise, stumps of arches are most of what remain here, but never fear—if you can't restore this place in your imagination, there are several artists' renderings that can do it for you.

The focus of the visitors center is an exhibition on medieval masonry, but otherwise it's a bit short on the features one expects from Dúchas sites (no audiovisual, and no tearoom). Visit Mellifont before Monasterboice, because the abbey ruins frankly aren't all that impressive compared to the exquisite high crosses at the latter site. Also note that in low season there won't be anyone to charge you an admission fee (but then again, you won't get the guided tour).

Unfortunately, there is no public transportation to Mellifont, but it's worth hiring a taxi from Drogheda to take you to both monastic sites. Biking it is also an option.

◖ MONASTERBOICE

Established in the 6th century by St. Buite, a disciple of Patrick, Monasterboice (Mainistir Bhuithe, signposted off the M1 10 km north of Drogheda, tel. 041/982-6459, always accessible, free admission) is the only Irish monastery to bear the name of its founder. This secluded site in lovely pastoral surroundings consists of an incomplete round tower (now 33.5 meters high), two small churches (built in the 14th or 15th century), and, most important, a group of absolutely breathtaking 10th-century high crosses. These were no doubt used to teach the Gospel at a time when only scholars and holy men could read.

The 5.5-meter-high **Muiredach's Cross,** named for an abbot who died in the year 923, is widely considered the finest high cross in all Ireland, and it features both Old and New Testament scenes. It must have been carved before his death, however, as an inscription on the base reads, "a prayer for Muiredach, under whose auspices the cross was made." On the eastern face, the Last Judgment is the central panel, with St. Michael weighing souls toward the bottom, and St. Paul on the smaller panel above. On the shaft are the Adoration of the Magi, Moses striking the rock (to bring water to the Israelites), David and Goliath,

You'll find Ireland's most exquisite high crosses at Monasterboice.

Cain and Abel, and Adam and Eve. The central scene on the western face is of the Resurrection, with Moses and Aaron on the smaller panel above; Christ's mission to the apostles, doubting Thomas, and Christ's arrest are on the shaft. Though the carvings on the base are more difficult to discern, they are probably the signs of the zodiac. The cross is topped with a miniature church, the scenes with St. Paul and Moses comprising its sides.

The carvings on the other two high crosses, designated North and West, were surely just as magnificent at one time, but these two have suffered the weather more acutely. Of the 50 panels on the **West Cross,** only a dozen are still discernible. In the lee of the tower, the West Cross is one of the tallest in the country at 6.5 meters high (some say it's as tall as 7 meters), and its central panels also depict the Crucifixion and Last Judgment. Flanking this Crucifixion scene, however, are two small scenes showing sheep-shearing and -milking—allusions to Christ's traditional role as the "Good Shepherd." The shaft's eastern face depicts scenes from the Old Testament (David killing a lion, the sacrifice of Isaac, David with the head of Goliath, and David and Samuel), just as the western face is devoted to scenes from the Gospels (Christ's baptism, the ear-cutting scene in the garden of Gethsemane, and the kiss of Judas); like the Muiredach Cross, the West Cross also has a "house cap" on top.

Damaged by Cromwell's troops, the **North Cross** isn't quite as remarkable as the others; it features another Crucifixion scene on the western face and an abstract geometric design on the eastern face.

Monasterboice is about a 10-minute drive north of Drogheda. If you don't have a car, the best thing to do is to hire a taxi, as there is no public transportation to the site.

CARLINGFORD

The substantial seaside village of Carlingford (Cairlinn), a listed medieval heritage town in the shadow of Slieve Foy (a.k.a. Carlingford Mountain), is the focal point of the Cooley Peninsula in northern Louth. The locals take tremendous pride in the romantic stone ruins that make a ramble down the main streets so enjoyably atmospheric, and ongoing development on the outskirts of town hasn't so far diminished that laid-back medieval vibe. Various seafood, music, and sporting festivals transform this quiet place during the summer months, but the fun is thoroughly infectious—even if you don't like oysters.

Most of Carlingford's shops, pubs, and eateries are on the Market Square and the Dundalk road on its southern side. Walking past the 15th-century, weed-dappled Taaffe's Castle from the tourist office and bus stop by the water will bring you to Newry Street; turn right at the Carlingford Arms pub and you've found the square. To your left is the atmospheric Tholsel Street, and through the arch in the gate tower you'll come to the old Holy Trinity Church, now the town's heritage center.

Sights

Carlingford's medieval architecture is unsurpassed in any other Irish town of its size. On the aptly named Tholsel Street you'll find the **Tholsel,** the gate tower, which was used by customs officials to monitor the influx of goods in medieval times. Just up that cobblestoned lane is **The Mint,** established in the mid-15th century by royal charter (though no coins ever came out of it). Pause here to check out the small but elegant ogee arches flanked by intricately carved Celtic motifs.

The town center is dominated by the 15th-century **Taaffe's Castle,** a tower house chock-full of interesting architectural features: Note the murder holes, crenellated battlements, and slit windows used by archers all those centuries ago.

As far as monastic ruins go, the early-14th-century Dominican **Carlingford Friary** (Dundalk Rd., signposted from the heritage center) isn't terribly remarkable. The OPW takes good care of these ruins, but the graffiti and mold-speckled masonry create an air of neglect that will attract the romantically inclined.

On a rocky cliff overlooking the harbor on the western end of town, the eerie and imposing early Norman **King John's Castle** is so named for the king's visit to Carlingford in 1210—though building had commenced about 20 years before that, under the auspices of Hugh de Lacy (who, rather ironically, King John was heading off to fight at Carrickfergus Castle in Antrim). The castle's interior is closed off because it's no longer structurally sound, though hopefully conservation work will commence soon. In the meantime it's still worth climbing the steps for a brief walk-around and peek through the barred doors.

Go for a one-hour walking tour covering Carlingford's medieval history, a worthwhile alternative to wandering around the town's ruined castles and monastery learning only what's on the OPW signposts; call **Carlingford Walks** (tel. 086/352-2732, tours at 11 A.M., 2 P.M., and 5 P.M. Wed., Thurs., and Sat., 11 A.M. and 2 P.M. Fri. and bank holidays, 2 P.M. and 5 P.M. Sun. Apr.–Sept., appointments available Oct.–Mar., four-person minimum, ticket €5).

If you're interested in learning more on Carlingford's medieval history but can't make the walking tour, head to the **Holy Trinity Heritage Centre** (tel. 042/937-3454, heritagetrust@eircom.net, open 10 A.M.–12:30 P.M. and 2–4:30 P.M. Mon.–Fri., noon–4:30 P.M. weekends, admission €2).

Entertainment and Events

The **Carlingford Arms** (Newry St., tel. 042/937-3418) and **McKevitt's** (Market Sq., tel. 042/937-3116) are both sure bets for live music in summertime. Otherwise, pop in for a pint at the delightfully old-fashioned **P.J. O'Hare's** (Market Sq., tel. 042/937-3106).

Ah, what a magical combination! Time your visit for the **Oysters, Jazz & Blues Festival** (mid- to late August, ring the tourist office for details), the biggest event on the Carlingford social calendar: live bands, oyster-tastings, kiddie amusements, and plenty more. Needless to say, book your accommodations well in advance. The **Carlingford Maritime Festival** in June is another big draw, with a regatta and boat races, walking tours, and seafood cookery demonstrations. Contact the tourist office or the **Carlingford Marina** (North Commons, tel. 042/937-3073, www.carlingfordmarina.ie) for more information.

Shopping

Carlingford has a few cute boutiques. **Serene Silver Jewellers** (Dundalk St.) stocks vintage-look jewelry, handbags, fairy dolls, and other girlie goodies. If your idea of "girlie goodies" is chic-and-dainty lingerie and stiletto heels, however, you can spend a rainy afternoon inside **The Pink Room** (Dundalk St., tel. 042/938-3669, www.thepinkroom.ie). Just check the balance on your credit card before you go!

Sports and Recreation

The 40-kilometer **Táin Way** walking route encircles the peninsula and the Cooley mountains, including plenty of scenic forest paths. Pick up an OS map at the tourist office before you leave. There's also a more adventurous 500-kilometer cycling route, the **Táin Trail,** which takes you through five counties, taking in all the legendary sites mentioned in *Táin Bó Cúailnge* ("The Cattle Raid of Cooley"). See the sidebar *The Táin Trail and the Cattle Raid of Cooley* for details.

The **Carlingford Adventure Centre** (Tholsel St., tel. 042/937-3100, www.carlingfordadventure.com) offers a dizzying variety of day and weekend activities for all age groups—rock-climbing, archery, sailing, kayaking, volleyball, and plenty more—and packages include meals and housing in the center's hostel.

If you've ever wanted to learn how to sail, contact the **Carlingford Yacht Charter & Sea School** (tel. 042/937-3879, www.beauforthouse.net). The **Dundalk & Carlingford Sailing Club** (tel. 042/937-3238, www.dcsc.ie) also offers sailing lessons and boat hire on weekends March–November. But if you feel like kicking back and watching it all go by, you can take a cruise on the lough with **Carlingford Pleasure Cruises** (tel. 042/937-3239, daily departures May–Sept. subject to weather, tickets €6).

Or would you rather be playing golf? The **Greenore Golf Club** (signposted off the R175, tel. 042/937-3212) is an 18-hole championship course five kilometers east of Carlingford, on the northern tip of the peninsula.

Accommodations

Since the IHH **Carlingford Adventure Centre and Holiday Hostel** (Tholsel St., tel. 042/937-3100, www.carlingfordadventure.com, dorms €17–22, private rooms €28–35 pp, credit cards accepted) exists primarily to house people going windsurfing and whatnot, you may feel out of the loop if you aren't participating. You can expect clean dorms, en suite private rooms, and fine facilities.

There are several rather posh B&Bs along Ghan Road (in full view of Carlingford Lough and County Down beyond), but the stylishly designed and lavishly landscaped **¢ Shalom** (Ghan Rd., signposted on the R173 opposite the tourist office, tel. 042/937-3151, www.jackiewoods.com, €29 pp, s €39.50) is recommended for its free Internet access (including wireless), accommodating proprietor, and electric heating pads. All in all, it's an excellent value even if you're traveling on your own. Self-catering apartments are also available in the adjacent building.

With lots of Georgian character, a picturesque setting, and a top-notch restaurant and cookery school, 18th-century **Ghan House** (tel. 042/937-3682, www.ghanhouse.com) is arguably Carlingford's most popular accommodation. Just be forewarned that the housekeeping isn't always on par with the food.

You have a choice of guesthouses in the center of town. Though the atmospheric pub at McKevitt's Village Hotel is one of the locals' favorite watering holes, the accommodation is a relatively poor value. The rooms are very comfortable and the location is super-convenient at **The Oystercatcher Lodge & Bistro** (Market Sq., tel. 042/937-3922, www.theoystercatcher. com, €40–45 pp during the week, €50–55 Fri., €65–70 Sat., s €60–70 during the week only), though the significantly higher weekend rates and stiff single supplement are a bummer. Ring ahead for special midweek and low-season rates.

There's also the brand-new **Four Seasons Hotel and Leisure Club** (just east of the village on the R173, tel. 042/937-3530, www.4seasonshotel.ie, rooms €180–220), startlingly out of place in a town with such a low-key medieval character. It's your typical hotel, right on down to the mediocre, over-priced bar and restaurant food, though the pool, sauna, and other leisure facilities are certainly a plus.

Food

Looking for lunch? Then head to **Food for Thought** (Trinity Mews, Dundalk Rd., tel. 042/938-3838, open 9 A.M.–7 P.M. daily, lunches €5–10), a café-cum-deli-cum-gourmet store lined with shelves of loose teas and berry cordials. Here you can order a pizza, tortilla, a plate of crab cakes, or plenty of other tasty options for eat-in or takeaway. It's just a shame the store's cheerful ambience doesn't inspire the staff to crack a smile.

Seafood gourmands could linger in Carlingford for a full week, as the town's best restaurants share a deservedly good reputation. Oysters are a local specialty. (Never fear: Vegetarians and hard-core carnivores will find something on every menu to suit them, too.) If oysters aren't your thing, you can order a lovely leg of lamb at **The Oystercatcher** (Market Sq., tel. 042/937-3989, www.theoystercatcher.com, open 6:30–9:30 P.M. Mon.–Sat., 5–8:30 P.M. Sun., 2/3-course dinner €25/35). Tucked at the back of a charming courtyard in an old stone edifice off the Dundalk road, the smaller **Kingfisher Bistro** (McGees Court, tel. 042/937-3716, open 6:30–9 P.M. Tues.–Fri., 6:30 P.M.–late Saturday, 5:30–8:30 P.M. Sunday, mains €15–26) offers the most adventurous menu in town and is also the best choice for vegetarians. But ask a random local for a recommendation, and more often than not you'll be told to go to **Magee's Bistro** (Tholsel St., tel. 042/937-3751, www.mageesbistro.com, open 10 A.M.–4 P.M. and 6–9 P.M. weekdays, 6:30–9 P.M. or later Sat., noon–4 P.M. and 6:30–9 P.M. or later Sun., mains €16–25, 2/3-course Sunday lunch €18/22 12:30–3:30 P.M.). You can't beat the medieval ambience on the patio out front when the weather's good. Be sure to ring for a reservation on summer weekends.

If none of these eateries are open (hours can be irregular in low season), try the pub food at the **Carlingford Arms** (Newry St., just off Market Sq., tel. 042/937-3418, food served noon–9 P.M. daily, mains €14–24)—it's pretty good, if pricey. The portions are generous, however, and the barstaff are quite pleasant. Another option in the dead of winter is the restaurant at **McKevitt's Village Hotel** (Market Sq., tel. 042/937-3116, food served noon–9 P.M. daily), which usually has a three-course €20 menu on offer 7–9 P.M.

Information and Services

For pointers, postcards, and plenty more, head to the **Cooley Peninsula Tourist Office** (Old Dispensary, on the water, tel. 042/937-3033, www.carlingford.ie, open

10 A.M.–5 P.M. Thurs.–Mon. Nov.–Mar.,
10 A.M.–5:30 P.M. Mon.–Sat. and 11 A.M.–
5:30 P.M. Sun. Apr.–Oct.).

There's an **AIB** ATM on Newry Street, directly opposite the Carlingford Arms pub and restaurant, but no bank as such. The **post office** (tel. 042/937-3171) is on the Dundalk road, just north of the Market Square.
Murphy's Laundry (Dundalk Rd., tel. 042/938-3891) offers same-day service for tourists. Need cough drops? Try **Bradley's Pharmacy** (Market Sq., tel. 042/937-3259).

Getting There and Around

Carlingford is 24 kilometers east of Dundalk on the R173, just 10 kilometers southeast of the border with County Down in Northern Ireland and 108 kilometers north of Dublin. **Bus Éireann** offers a Monday–Saturday service on the Dundalk–Newry route (#161), with five departures from Dundalk but only two from Newry. For departure times, ring the bus station in Dundalk (tel. 042/933-4075) or Newry (tel. 028/3062-3531).

Need a taxi? Call **Paul Woods** (tel. 042/937-3149).

RAVENSDALE

Inland, the Cooley Peninsula is surprisingly developed, and the hamlet of Ravensdale (on a minor road, signposted off the R173 about 10 kilometers east of Dundalk) isn't a real tourist attraction as such. Ravensdale is on the **Táin Way** walking route, and there are a couple of other diversions to note. The grounds of the mansion of the Earl of Clermont are now part of the lovely **Ravensdale Forest Park,** the "big house" in question having burned like so many others in the Irish Civil War. Those interested in going horseback riding through these woods should contact **Ravensdale Lodge Equestrian & Trekking Centre** (Ravensdale, signposted off the N1, tel. 042/937-1034, www.ravensdalelodge.com).

WICKLOW AND KILDARE

Counties Wicklow (Cill Mhantáin, "Church of Mantáin," a disciple of Patrick) and Kildare (Cill Dara, "Church of the Oak Wood") are something of a study in contrasts. Half an hour due south of Dublin and you're in another world entirely, verdant hills and winding backroads: That's Wicklow, aptly nicknamed the "Garden of Ireland." Half an hour west and you're in Kildare, marked by a chain of commuter suburbs and flat green pastures—racetrack country.

More movies have been filmed in Wicklow than in any other county in Ireland: *King Arthur* most recently, as well as *Excalibur, Michael Collins, Ella Enchanted, Far and Away, Into the West,* and plenty more. A scene in the 2002 *Count of Monte Cristo* remake was filmed in the Italianate garden at Powerscourt, and *Brave-*

heart was filmed in both Wicklow and Kildare (as well as Trim Castle in County Meath).

To put it bluntly, County Kildare doesn't have much to offer the visitor (unless you're interested in horse breeding). Flat fertile farmland aside, its principal geographical features are an enormous peat bog (950 square kilometers) in the county's northern reaches, known as the Bog of Allen, which spreads into Counties Laois, Offaly, and Westmeath; the bog surrounds the Hill of Allen (200 meters), a scenic viewpoint topped by a lookout tower and rich in folklore (it's said the Irish hero Fionn mac Cumhaill lived here and buried his treasure somewhere along its slopes). In recent years the hill has been badly scarred by quarrying and pollution. Two canals cross the Bog of Allen: The 212-kilometer Grand Canal, used

© CAMILLE DEANGELIS

HIGHLIGHTS

◖ Powerscourt House and Gardens: Exquisitely manicured Italianate gardens and statuary, leisurely walking trails, gourmet eats, retail therapy – it's all here (page 113).

◖ The Wicklow Way: Hike all or part of this 132-kilometer trail from southern Dublin through the Wicklow Mountains and placid green farmlands north of Carlow (page 116).

◖ Glendalough: Nestled in the gorse-dotted hills of the Wicklow Mountains National Park around two placid lakes, this fantastic 6th-century monastic site was once one of Ireland's most important centers of learning (page 116).

◖ Glenmalure: The country's longest glacial valley is far removed from the manicured gardens Wicklow is renowned for, but this quiet, utterly remote locale has an appeal all its own (page 119).

◖ Castletown: Enjoy a guided tour of Ireland's grandest Palladian mansion, built for William Conolly, Speaker of the Irish House of Commons, in the early 18th century (page 126).

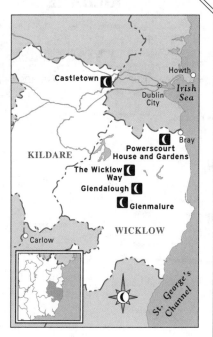

LOOK FOR ◖ TO FIND RECOMMENDED SIGHTS, ACTIVITIES, DINING, AND LODGING.

WICKLOW AND KILDARE

to transport both cargo and passengers from Dublin to points west, is still open for recreational vessels, and the less commercially successful Royal Canal is undergoing restoration for the same purpose.

HISTORY

Both Wicklow and Kildare were hives of early Christian activity. The early 6th-century St. Brigid is the unofficial patron of Kildare, though the county had strong pre-Christian ties to a goddess of the same name (leading many to speculate that a "Saint Brigid" never actually existed). Yet another Patrick legend has the saint, at the beginning of his evangelist mission, desiring to land on a beach just south of Wicklow Town. The locals were less than friendly, and in a scuffle on the beach one of his disciples, Mantáin, lost a few teeth. For this reason the county's Irish name, Cill Mhantáin, can be more loosely translated as "Church of the Toothless One." ("Wicklow" is Anglo-Norman, and has no such story to explain it.) The region's most important monastic site, Glendalough, was founded in the 6th century as well, by the hermit St. Kevin.

These counties' proximity to the capital meant that English forces were omnipresent throughout the darkest periods in Irish history; the Penal Laws and other anti-Catholic legislation were easiest to enforce by simple geography. It's a pretty drive today, but at the turn of the 19th century the Military Road through the Wicklow mountains was built to facilitate

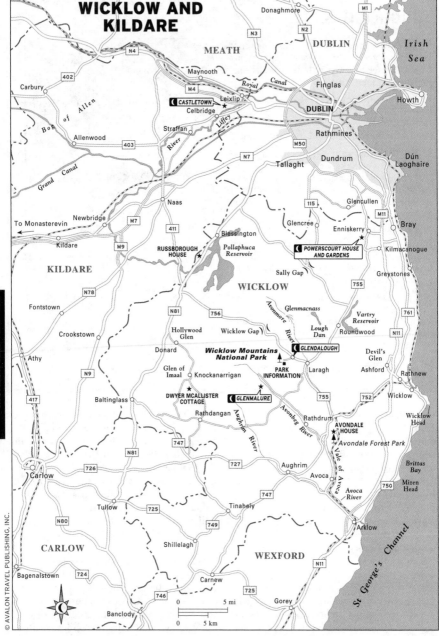

the English army in its pursuit of the 1798 rebels. And the English Pale, a 32-kilometer fortified radius around Dublin City, encompassed much of County Kildare.

PLANNING YOUR TIME

Kildare's attractions can be visited in passing (from Dublin to the sights of the Midlands, the Rock of Cashel in Tipperary, or Birr Castle in Offaly, perhaps), but you will certainly want to linger in Wicklow. The county's most important (and most popular) sight, Glendalough, can be done in a day trip from Dublin, but it's better to spend the night; ideally you should spend two or three, since there are great hiking opportunities in the national park. If you don't have time for an overnight visit, make a day trip here, to Powerscourt, or to the slightly shabby seaside town of Bray for an exhilarating cliffside walk. Those walking the whole Wicklow Way should bank on a week and a half.

Wicklow

There's something for everyone in County Wicklow (www.visitwicklow.ie), especially outdoor enthusiasts. The **Wicklow Way** (see sidebar) is the most popular walking trail in the country, so there are plenty of accommodation and dining options along the route. You'll not have to sacrifice comfy mattresses and scrummy steak dinners for this weeklong adventure! Even the less-athletic visitor will enjoy a stroll through the gardens at Powerscourt, Kilruddery, or Avondale. Idyllic Glendalough, one of the country's most important monastic sites (just behind Clonmacnoise, in fact), offers at least nine different trails, whether you're out for a casual ramble or an all-day mountain climb.

ENNISKERRY

Just 18 kilometers south of Dublin, Enniskerry (Áth na Sceire, "Ford of the Reef") is a charming planned village, a perennial favorite with Dublin day-trippers for one reason: the magnificent Powerscourt House and Gardens. This tiny, tidy town—essentially just the one central square, marked with a small clock tower and lined with houses and a smattering of shops—was designed by the Earl of Powerscourt in the mid-18th century to house his staff. Most visitors just pop by for the afternoon, but several fine accommodation options make it worth an overnight stay, especially if you're planning on heading farther south into the vales of Wicklow.

◖ Powerscourt House and Gardens

No one could argue that Powerscourt House and Gardens (signposted from the village, tel. 01/204-6000, www.powerscourt.ie, open 9:30 A.M.–5:30 P.M. daily, admission to gardens €7.50, house €2.50, combined ticket €9) aren't the finest in the country. The estate's 19 hectares include a breathtaking Italianate garden designed in the early 19th century; the terraces were laid in the 1840s using granite and pebbles from the beach at Bray, and took more than 100 men a dozen years to complete. Lovely mid-19th-century garden sculptures— Apollo, Diana, cherubs, and so forth—bear obvious Italian and French influence. Indeed, it's easy to forget you aren't taking a ramble through some Florentine villa; only the temperature and Great Sugarloaf Mountain (501 meters) looming beyond remind you that the Mediterranean is a plane ride away. Beyond the terrace is a large lake guarded by a pair of fantastic winged horses cast from zinc in 1869.

There's more: a Japanese garden teased out of old boglands; winding paths flanked by rhododendrons and towering trees of North American origin; a tower shaped like a pepper urn, built in 1911 in anticipation of a royal visit, which you can climb for a fairly panoramic view; a huge walled garden with resplendent gates and an ivy-covered memorial to the seventh Viscountess of Powerscourt, which incorporates busts of four

© CAMILLE DEANGELIS

The lake at Powerscourt features a pair of winged horses cast in shimmery zinc.

Renaissance masters; and a pet cemetery including some strangely poignant epitaphs ("faithful beyond human fidelity").

Since the devastating fire of November 1974, the house is a shadow of its former self—and, frankly, a combined house-and-garden ticket isn't worth the extra €1.50 unless you're *really* interested in the succession of gentry who lived here. (The best story concerns the garden's designer, Daniel Robertson; though still in his 20s, he had to be taken around in a souped-up wheelbarrow to inspect the landscapers' progress, as he suffered continually from the gout—no wonder, seeing as he drank a bottle of sherry a day.) The house exhibit includes a 15-minute audiovisual, a series of informative history panels, old marble sculptures brought inside for preservation, and the ballroom upstairs (a thoroughly disappointing restoration, that is).

Powerscourt is also an ideal spot for retail therapy; there's an Avoca shop (including delectable, if pricey, foodstuffs for takeaway), an interior design gallery, and a huge conservatory offering more practical souvenirs in addition to the usual potted plants. And of course, you can have lunch here, too—on a patio overlooking the Italian garden.

The famous **waterfall** (open 9:30 A.M.–7 P.M. in summer, 10:30 A.M.–dusk in winter, admission €4.50) is five kilometers away (signposted from the Enniskerry square), and, cheekily enough, the €9 combined ticket doesn't cover your admission. The cascade was created in 1821 for King George IV's visit to Powerscourt, but it was a lucky thing he never made it out of the house to see it; the bridge built to view it was washed away as soon as the waterfall was "turned on." Even today it's the highest waterfall in the country at 121 meters.

Powerscourt is one of the most popular tourist attractions in the country, so you'd better skip it if you prefer to keep off the beaten track—Secret Garden, this isn't. And gorgeous as they are, the only things Irish about these gardens are the labor and rain that nurture them daily.

Powerscourt also has a **golf club** (signposted from the house and gardens entrance, tel.

01/204-6033, www.powerscourt.ie) with two different courses, both of them ultra-scenic.

Accommodations

The **Knockree Hostel** (Lacken House, 7 km west of Enniskerry on the road to the hamlet of Glencree, signposted from Enniskerry, tel. 01/286-4036 for info, tel. 01/830-4555 to book, www.anoige.ie, dorms €14–15), in a converted farmhouse with lovely pastoral and mountain views, is old-school An Óige right on down to the 10 A.M.–5 P.M. lockout.

For accommodations in the village proper, try **Ferndale** (on the square, tel. 01/286-3518, www.ferndalehouse.com, open Apr.–Oct., €35–40 pp, singles charged at double rate), a cheerful, immaculately maintained Victorian townhouse.

For something much grander, book a room at the **Summerhill House Hotel** (half a km south of the village, signposted off the N11, tel. 01/286-7928, www.summerhillhousehotel.com, room €90–140), with extensive and perfectly manicured grounds in the shadow of Sugarloaf Mountain. Though Summerhill doesn't have its own leisure facilities, guests are entitled to use the small fitness center (sans pool) at its sister hotel in Bray (six kilometers east), the Esplanade.

Food and Entertainment

The **Terrace Café** (tel. 01/204-6070, open 10 A.M.–5 P.M. daily, mains €8–13) on the mansion's ground floor offers a fantastic view and sophisticated, high-quality lunch fare—quiches, salads, and the like. Alternatively, you can head back into the village for an equally tasty (and somewhat less expensive) meal at **Poppies Country Cooking** (The Square, tel. 01/282-8869, open 8:30 A.M.–6 P.M., mains €8–10), a warm, always-bustling café with hearty portions and friendly staff.

Wingfield's Bistro (Church Hill, tel. 01/204-2854, former opening hours 7–9 P.M. Mon.–Sat., 1–8 P.M. Sun., mains €15–25) was closed for renovations at the time of writing, but locals seem confident its reputation for fine food and service will continue upon reopening.

There's not much of a nightlife here, though the **Enniskerry Inn** (on the square, tel. 01/286-3513, lunch served 12:30–2:30 P.M. daily), formerly known as the Glenwood Inn, has set dancing on Tuesday nights and karaoke on weekends.

Information and Services

Enniskerry doesn't have a tourist office, but the Powerscourt staff can answer any questions on the surrounding area. Check out the helpful community website (www.enniskerry.ie) before you go.

There is an **ATM** (but no bank) on the square, as well as the **post office** (tel. 01/286-2561).

Getting There and Around

Enniskerry is 18 kilometers south of Dublin. Traveling by car, take the M11 out of the city and take the Enniskerry exit onto the R117; both house and waterfall are clearly signposted from the square.

Day excursions to Powerscourt as well as Glendalough are available through **Bus Éireann** (tel. 01/703-2574, departing Busáras 10:30 A.M. daily mid-Mar.–Oct., returning 5:45 P.M., tickets €27, including admission fees). Powerscourt Waterfall is five kilometers from the house as the crow flies, so if you'd like to visit both sites ride Bus Éireann or take the **DART** (tel. 01/805-4288, up to 12 departures from Connolly Station per hour, single/return ticket €2.30/4) to Bray and pick up the **Alpine Coaches** shuttle service (tel. 01/286-2547 or 087/257-2973, alpinecoaches@eircom.net, departs station at 11:05 A.M., 11:30 A.M., 12:30 P.M., and 1:30 P.M. July–Aug., 11:05 A.M., 12:30 P.M., 1:30 P.M. and 3:30 P.M. Sept.–June, return ticket to waterfall €5, both sites €9) from the station there. From the Bray DART station, you can also reach Enniskerry via Dublin Bus route #184 or #185 (3/hour daily, €1.35).

A slower but less convoluted way to go (to the house and gardens only) is a 60-minute ride on **Dublin Bus** (tel. 01/873-4222, www.dublinbus.ie, 3/hour, €1.90 one-way), route #44 or #44C from Townsend Street in Dublin.

◖ THE WICKLOW WAY

The country's most popular walking route, the 132-kilometer Wicklow Way, begins in Marlay Park in suburban Dublin and winds south into Wicklow Mountains National Park, passing through Glendalough and down the western flank of the monster-mountain Lugnaquilla in Glenmalure, and ending just over the Wicklow-Carlow border in Clonegal. The Wicklow Way walking trail info site (www.wicklowway.com) is by far the best resource in planning your hike: scope out the route, book accommodations and evening meals, arrange luggage transfer, and plan for appropriate clothing and equipment.

The way is dotted with original An Óige hostels (www.anoige.ie), some of which have been around since the 1940s, and plenty of B&Bs that cater especially for walkers. The route is less frequently traveled south to north, so if you're planning to walk it in high season it's worth considering starting off in Carlow instead of Dublin. In general, expect plenty of company if you're walking in it in June, July, or August. Those who only have time to walk part of it generally start in Roundwood and walk south to Glendalough, a distance of approximately 12 kilometers. **St. Kevin's Bus Service** (tel. 01/281-8119, www.glendaloughbus.com) can get you back to Dublin from either place.

To get to Marlay Park (also known as Marley Grange) in Dublin, take the Ballinteer-bound **Dublin Bus** (tel. 01/873-4222, www.dublinbus.ie, #16, 3/hour, fare €1.35) from O'Connell Street. If starting in Carlow, take the Dublin-Waterford **Bus Éireann** (tel. 01/836-6111, #5, 2/day Mon.-Sat. at 9 A.M. and 5:30 P.M., 3/day Sun. at 11 A.M., 4:30 P.M., and 6 P.M.) to Kildavin (3 km southwest of Clonegal on a local road, request stop) or, if you need to do any last-minute shopping, the larger town of Bunclody (5 km south of Clonegal on the R746); there is no bus service to Clonegal.

WICKLOW MOUNTAINS NATIONAL PARK

Much of northern Wicklow has been designated a national park, approximately 20,000 hectares (or 200 square kilometers)—that's 10 percent of the county in all. The park is a delight whether you're walking the Wicklow Way or just driving through, with a load of astonishingly isolated glens and hollows; the views from the Sally Gap, the lofty intersection of the R759 and Military Road (the R115) are splendid, as is the view from the road that bends around the Glenmacnass Waterfall on the Military Road just north of Glendalough. These gorse-dappled hills also include sizable tracts of mountain blanket bog and a wealth of indigenous flora, fauna, and birdlife. Though Glendalough is the best-known hamlet within the park, there are other villages in which you could base yourself: Laragh is just a kilometer and a half east of Glendalough, and there's also Roundwood 11 kilometers up the road. Also inside the park, Glenmalure is popular with hikers on the Wicklow Way.

For tidbits on local geography and botany as well as navigational advice, head to the national park **information office** (Bolger's Cottage, tel. 0404/45656, tel. 0404/45425 for guided walks, off-season tel. 0404/45338, educationcentrewicklow@environ.ie, open 10 A.M.–6 P.M. daily May–Aug., weekends in Apr. and Sept., free admission), which is located at Glendalough, 100 meters west of the Upper Lake car park and two kilometers west of the Glendalough Visitor Centre. The info office hosts a summer lecture program and "sensory garden" as well.

◖ GLENDALOUGH

Perhaps Ireland's most famous monastic site, Glendalough (Gleann dá loch, "Glen of the Two Lakes") is an utterly enchanting spot—no less so, miraculously enough, for all the coach buses and cheesy food and souvenir stands clustered outside the stone gateway to the old monastery and modern graveyard. This is a lush, glacier-carved valley dotted in yellow gorse,

mained stock-still until it hatched. Another legend claims a local woman became smitten with Kevin and visited him in his cliff-top cave, known as **St. Kevin's Bed;** angered by her advances, he pushed her off the ledge and she drowned in the lake below. (That place is now known, rather inaccurately it seems, as **Lady's Leap.**) This much is true, however: Once word got around of an extraordinary hermit in an idyllic situation, other monks were joining him in droves, and a community was formed.

You can take in most of the monastic ruins (aside from **Temple na Skellig** on a ledge over the Upper Lake, accessible only by boat—though you can't hire one!) on a leisurely walk along the south shore of the Lower Lake. The old monastery grounds hold a small priest's house in the shadow of the round tower, the **Cathedral of Saints Peter and Paul** (dating from the 10th and 12th centuries), and the 12th-century **St. Kevin's Church**—this one is quite unusual, having its original stone roof. The miniature round tower in the west gable resembles a chimney, which is why it's better known as "Kevin's Kitchen."

A visit to the Dúchas-run **Glendalough Visitor Centre** and **tourist office** (tel. 0404/45325, open 9:30 A.M.–6 P.M. daily mid-Mar.–mid-Oct., 9:30 A.M.–5 P.M. mid-Oct.–mid-Mar., admission €2.90) isn't tremendously informative if you've been to other monastic sites, since the exhibit (including the 15-minute audiovisual) covers early Irish monasteries in general—the construction and function of round towers, manuscript illumination, everyday life, and so forth. There's not a lot of info about St. Kevin, and the legends told in an automated storytelling nook for the kiddies are 100 percent sanitized. That said, it's a worthwhile stop if the weather's bad, especially if you've purchased the Dúchas Heritage Card. The exhibit also includes a collection of early grave slabs and a bullaun stone, a primitive crucible carved out of a larger rock. (Initially used for crushing grain and herbs, later folklore claimed rainwater collected in the bullaun had curative properties—warts, of course.)

You can also pick up a scale map of the nine

© CAMILLE DEANGELIS

St. Kevin's Church is one of Glendalough's most memorable ruins.

with walking trails skirting two placid lakes and the substantial remains of a holy community founded by St. Kevin in the 6th century: a 10th- or 11th-century **round tower,** one of the tallest in the country at 30 meters, with a cap rebuilt from fallen stones in 1876; a badly weathered high cross; and the ruins of seven churches. By the 9th century Glendalough was second in size and prestige only to Clonmacnoise in County Offaly. (There are several illuminated manuscripts associated with Glendalough housed at Oxford and the British Library. Most interesting is the passage in the 11th-century Book of Glendalough that tells of a UFO sighting in unequivocal terms.)

One of Ireland's most beloved saints (after Patrick and Brigid, of course), Kevin's life is shrouded in intriguing (and sometimes dark) legends. It's said that after Kevin cured the high king's pet goose, he asked for the land under the bird's flight path as a reward. Many stories tell of his love of animals: Once, while he was praying with arms outstretched, a bird laid an egg in his open palm, and Kevin re-

Glendalough walking trails (2–11 kilometers in length, from easy strolls to hill walks requiring navigational skills) for 50 cents. A walk in any direction is glorious, though the path along the Upper Lake at sunrise or sunset offers the most breathtaking views of all (and you'll enjoy them in utter solitude). An easy climb to **Poulanass Waterfall** begins at the national park information office on the eastern shore of Upper Lake, as does a far more strenuous hike up Spinc Mountain (490 meters). Alternatively, the fit and adventurous can scale **Camaderry Mountain** (700 meters) on the northern side of Upper Lake; the path begins at the Upper Lake car park. The **Wicklow Way** also skirts the eastern flank of Spinc Mountain.

For more information on outdoor activities and other topics, check out the Glendalough community website (www.glendalough.connect.ie).

Accommodations

There are accommodations to suit every budget in and around Glendalough. It's big enough to attract a lot of school groups, and some of the mattresses could use replacing, but the **Glendalough International Youth Hostel** (The Lodge, on the Upper Lake road, signposted off the R756, tel. 01/882-2563, glendaloughyh@ireland.com, dorms €18–21, kiosk Internet access €2/40 minutes, credit cards accepted) is still adequate for the backpacking set. All the rooms are en suite.

Considering the awesome lakeside location and comfortable rooms filled with gorgeous antiques, **Derrymore** (the Upper Lake road, about a kilometer past the monastery entrance, tel. 0404/45493, http://homepage.eircom.net/~derrymore, €33 pp, s €50) offers excellent value. There's a discount if you stay two or more nights (the four-night rate is €28 per person, €43 for a single), and packed lunches are available for walkers with prior notice. You'll find the same gorgeous view from the bedrooms at **Pinewood Lodge** (signposted on the Upper Lake road, tel. 0404/45437, pwlodge@gofree.indigo.ie, €35 pp, s €50, credit cards accepted). You can rent bikes through

the B&B and chill out in the garden after a long day's pedal.

It's on the stodgy side, and the food won't wow you, but the family-run **Glendalough Hotel** (tel. 0404/45135 or 0404/45391, www.glendaloughhotel.com, €75–95 pp, s €97–117) is situated right outside the old monastery gate. Between the location and the size (with 44 rooms, it's on the large side for a rural inn), it's a very popular wedding venue, so consider yourself warned. (If you stay here, you might consider walking down the road to Laragh to eat at the Wicklow Heather.)

Getting There

Glendalough is 60 kilometers south of Dublin; you can take the N11 out of the city as far as Ashford before turning away from the coast (onto the R763), though the route south from Enniskerry (on the R755), passing Great Sugar Loaf to the east, is far more scenic. **St. Kevin's Bus Service** (tel. 01/281-8119, www.glendaloughbus.com, single/return €11/18) operates a daily bus service from Dublin to Glendalough via Bray and Roundwood, departing St. Stephen's Green North (at Dawson St., opposite Mansion House, at 11:30 A.M. and 6 P.M. Mon.–Sat. and 11:30 A.M. and 7 P.M. Sun. Sept.–June, 11:30 A.M. and 6 P.M. Mon.–Fri. and 11:30 A.M. and 7 P.M. Sat.–Sun. July–Aug.). There are at least two daily return buses from Glendalough (three on weekdays in July and Aug.).

LARAGH

A hamlet less than two kilometers east of Glendalough, Laragh is a vital stop for eats (whether dining out or stocking up on groceries) and gas (but no ATM). There are a few B&Bs in and around the village, but the views just can't measure up to those in Glendalough proper. One to try is the relatively new **Trooperstown Wood Lodge** (on the R755, the Roundwood/Annamoe road, 2.5 km north of the village, tel. 0404/45312 or 086/263-1732, www.trooperstownwood.com, €30–35 pp, credit cards accepted). While the rooms are fairly standard, you can expect an old-fashioned welcome in the form of a tea-and-biscuit tray, and the owners (who also run the grocery-slash-gas station in the village) will be a big help in getting your bearings in the area.

Pilgrims may want to stay in one of the self-catering *cillíns* (small churches) at the **Glendalough Hermitage** (signposted from the R756 just west of Laragh village, tel. 0404/45777, www.hermitage.dublindiocese. ie, twin room €30–33 pp, s €40–45, discount for 3 or more nights), a prayer retreat run by St. Kevin's Parish Church. Each cottage (the architecture inspired by the Glendalough church ruins) has its own kitchenette, bathroom, sitting area, and open fireplace.

Open for breakfast, lunch, and dinner, the ◖ **Wicklow Heather** (on the main road, the R756, tel. 0404/45157, open 8 A.M.–10 P.M. daily, dinner mains €14–24) serves up a refreshingly eclectic menu (and good coffee) in a romantic, if slightly quirky, dining room (the pitched wood roof with head-bangingly low crossbeams is decked out in white lights and bric-a-brac: kettles, farm implements, even lacrosse sticks). The service is pleasant, too—and you might even get a free half shot of Bailey's with your check.

Lynham's of Laragh (Main St., tel. 0404/45345, food served noon–7 P.M. daily, mains €12–18) is the kind of place that leaves the Christmas decorations up year-round. There's live trad most nights in summertime and on Friday and Saturday nights in low season. The pub grub's hearty but quite basic; the Wicklow Heather should be your first choice.

St. Kevin's Bus Service (tel. 01/281-8119, www.glendaloughbus.com, single/return €10/16) passes through Laragh en route to Glendalough. For a taxi, ring **Philip Davis** (tel. 087/614-1297).

ROUNDWOOD

There's not a whole lot going on in Roundwood, which advertises itself as the highest village in the county. The **Wicklow Way** passes less than two kilometers west (by the shore of Lough Dan, which unfortunately is surrounded by private land), accounting for most of the buzz in this sleepy one-street village on summer afternoons. Tired walkers doff their boots at **Tochar Cottage** (Main St., tel. 01/281-8129, tocharcottage@hotmail.com, open Mar.–Nov., €30 pp, s €40, dorms €20), a basic B&B with a hostel annex at the center of town, or at **Ballinastoe Beg** (Ballinastoe, tel. 01/281-8940, www.ballinastoe.com, open Apr.–Oct., €35 pp, s €40), which claims to be the highest B&B in the country. Truth or no, the awesome mostly organic breakfast will keep you full 'til dinnertime. Evening meals are available with advance notice (€20), the owners can give you a lift back onto the walking trail (it's about 3.5 km west of here), and you can check your email. To get to Ballinastoe from town, head up the R755 (the Dublin road) and you'll see it signposted on your left in about four kilometers.

A unique fusion of Irish and German cuisine makes the **Roundwood Inn** (Main St., tel. 01/281-8107, bar food served noon–9:30 P.M. daily, meals €10–20) a favorite with locals, and it should be your top choice for dinner if you're spending the night in Glendalough (though the Wicklow Heather in Laragh comes a very close second). Reservations are required at the adjoining restaurant (tel. 01/281-8107, open 7:30–9:30 P.M. Fri.–Sat., 1–2 P.M. Sun., mains €15–25), though fortunately the full menu is available in the pub. Meat-lovers are expertly catered for here—enjoy your venison, lamb, or suckling pig with a bottle of obscure German wine—though the quality of the seafood dishes can be a bit inconsistent. (Vegetarians are better off dining at the Wicklow Heather.) The inn dates from the 1750s, and the decor is a queer mix of hunting lodge and mock Tudor.

Roundwood is nine kilometers north of Laragh on the R755 and is clearly signposted from the eastern end of the village. It's also a stop on **St. Kevin's Bus Service** Dublin–Glendalough route (see *Glendalough*).

◖ GLENMALURE

Ireland's longest glacial valley, Glenmalure will probably remind Pennsylvanians of the

© CAMILLE DEANGELIS

Go for a long ramble through the isolated, gorse-dotted Glenmalure Valley.

Poconos. Between the hills clad in evergreens and yellow gorse, the nonexistent cell-phone service, the horse-drawn caravans on shady backroads, and the mobile library in the parking lot of the Glenmalure Lodge, you might be forgiven for thinking you've entered a time warp (in the very best sense). **Glenmalure Lodge** (11 km west of Rathdrum on a local road, tel. 0404/46188, glenmalurelodge@ yahoo.com, food served noon–9 p.m., meals €10–20, B&B €35 pp, s €45) was established in 1801 and has a really cozy, amiable vibe; even if you're just passing through, do stop by for a pint at one of the picnic tables out front. (Too bad that time warp doesn't cover the drink prices.)

Pass the lodge, and after five or six kilometers the road terminates at a car park beside the River Avonbeg, where you'll find a modern monument to those patriots who perished in the 1798 rebellion. Just cross the small cement bridge and take off in either direction for a scenic ramble. The more ambitious can climb **Lugnaquilla,** the tallest mountain out-

side County Kerry at 924 meters. Approaching the mountain from Glenmalure (on the eastern side) is the easiest route; provided you're in good shape, the return trip will take about six hours. Glenmalure is also halfway along the **Wicklow Way.**

Public transport is nonexistent in this area, and even getting here by car can be tricky; the winding, pothole-riddled local roads are frustratingly lacking in signposts (accurate or otherwise!). The surest way to reach the Glenmalure Valley is via Rathdrum, which is 11 kilometers east. From Laragh, the village just east of Glendalough, take the R755 south to Rathdrum (also 11 kilometers), or take the N11 south out of Dublin and pick up the Rathdrum road (the R752) from the town of Rathnew. Then from Rathdrum, Glenmalure is clearly (and correctly) signposted at a T junction beside the town square.

THE GLEN OF IMAAL

The Glen of Imaal (Gleann Ó Máil), named after the brother of a 2nd-century high king, is the prettiest part of western Wicklow—though the area doesn't attract many visitors because the northeastern section is blighted by a (however clearly marked) military firing range. Unfortunately, since the closing of the An Óige hostel five kilometers south of the village of Donard in 2006, backpackers have no place to spend the night (and after all, who in their right mind would open a B&B near an artillery range?). If by chance you find yourself driving down a shady backroad west of Glenmalure, however, you might want to make a stop at the Dúchas-run **Dwyer McAllister Cottage** (Derrynamuck, on the local Knockanarrigan–Rathdangan road, signposted from Knockanarrigan, tel. 0404/45325, open 2–6 p.m. daily mid-June–mid-Sept., free admission), a small folk museum in a thatched cottage of historical importance. During the 1798 rebellion several Irish leaders were surrounded in this cottage by British troops, and one of them, Samuel McAllister, burst out of the cottage to meet his death so his comrade Michael Dwyer could escape out the back.

© CAMILLE DEANGELIS

Avoca was the setting for the beloved TV series *Ballykissangel*.

AVOCA

A darling little village just beyond the southeastern border of the national park, Avoca (Abhóca) was put on the map by the popular BBC television series ***Ballykissangel,*** which ran six seasons between 1996 and 2001.

Based on writer and creator Kieran Prendiville's childhood memories of holidays in County Kerry, pretty much all of "Bally-K" was filmed here in real-life shops and pubs (well, *pub*). Just north of the village, the **Meeting of the Waters** is a verdant spot immemorialized in a sentimental poem by Thomas Moore. Here the Avonbeg and the Avonmore merge to form the River Avoca, making it a popular hangout for local anglers.

Avoca Handweavers

"Bally-K" aside, most visitors are here for Avoca Handweavers (Old Mill, up Main St. just beyond the village, tel. 0402/35105, www. avoca.ie, open 9:30 A.M.–6 P.M. daily), a craft complex that includes Ireland's oldest working mill (opened in 1723). This is where the Avoca mohair-tweed-and-gourmet-goodies empire began—or began again, to be more precise—in the 1970s, when a couple of Dublin businesspeople reinvested and reopened the mill. Today you can still pop into the weaving shed and watch the artisans at their looms. The shop isn't as spacious as you would expect, but the prices are a bit better than in the gift shops, and there's also an upstairs bargain room worth checking out. You can expect a gourmet meal at the **◖ café** (mains €10–13)—savory tarts, Guinness pie, and some of the most delicious brown bread you'll find anywhere to go along with your vegetable soup. Indeed, it's by far the best lunch spot in the area.

Accommodations and Food

At **◖ Ashdene** (Knockanree Lower, less than 1 km from the village past the Avoca Handweavers shop, tel. 0402/35327, www.ashdeneavoca.com, open Apr.–Oct., €30–35 pp, s €40–45, credit cards accepted), proprietor Jackie Burns greets you with tea and apple pie with fresh cream. This B&B is exceptionally homey, with plenty of pink and tranquil, un-spoiled views of the surrounding hills and forest, along with thoughtful touches like Q-tips in the bathroom and herbal teas on the hostess tray. The breakfast is as outstanding as the welcome: real brewed coffee, fresh-squeezed orange juice, deluxe fruit salad, and Nutella for your toast (ah, heaven!).

Another option is **Greenhills** (tel. 0402/35197, burnsgreenhills@yahoo.ie, open May–Sept., €33–35 pp, s €42–45), another bungalow right next door. **The Old Coach House** (Meeting of the Waters, 4 km north of Avoca on the R752/Rathdrum road, tel. 0402/35408, avocacoachhouse@eircom.net, €35 pp, s €50, 4-course dinner €28), built in 1840 to accommodate coaches traveling from Dublin to Wexford, is a two-minute drive, is open year-round, and provides excellent value across the board. The restaurant is open to Coach House guests only.

Get your fill of traditional pub grub (shepherd's pie, fried cod, and suchlike) at **Fitzgerald's** (Main St., tel. 0402/35108, food served noon–8:30 P.M. daily, mains €10–15), where the two televisions alternate between sport and soap. (There's a decent vegetarian option, too.) The *Ballykissangel* pub scenes were filmed here; check out the cast photos on the walls. There's live folk and trad on weekends year-round. Another option for hearty lunch or dinner grub, and live trad on Friday and Saturday nights in the summer, is **The Meetings** (4 km north of Avoca on the R752, tel. 0402/35226, food served noon–9 P.M. daily, mains €12–18), a mock-Tudor pub so named for its location at the Meeting of the Waters. April–October you might also find an outdoor ceilidh—a rollickin' music and dance session—on Sunday afternoons starting around 4 P.M.

Information and Services

You'll find the library, tourist office, and Internet point in one teeny building: the **Avoca I.T. Centre** (Main St., tel. 0402/35022, www .avoca.com, open 9 A.M.–1:30 P.M. and 2– 5 P.M. Mon.–Fri., 10 A.M.–2 P.M. Sat., Internet access €3.80/30 minutes). Across the bridge, the **post office** (tel. 0402/35211) is still advertising its claim to fame: It, too, was often featured on the television series.

Getting There and Around

Avoca is 65 kilometers south of Dublin, with various possible routes; you could take the N11 and turn off for Avoca at Rathnew, though the routes through the national park (the R115 or the R755) are, of course, much more scenic. Avoca is 23 kilometers south of Glendalough on the R755 (picking up the R752 in Rathdrum). The Dublin–Arklow route (#133) of **Bus Éireann** (tel. 01/836-6111) stops in Avoca as well as the Meeting of the Waters twice a day (once on Sunday), the two departures being at 9 A.M. and 5:30 P.M. Monday–Saturday (arriving 11:05 A.M. and 7:35 P.M.) and 2 P.M. on Sunday (arriving 4:20 P.M.). Note that this bus departs the Connolly Luas station on the eastern side of the city center during the week, and from Busáras on Sunday. Return buses pass through Avoca at 8:15 A.M. and 1:15 P.M. Monday–Saturday and 5:45 P.M. Sunday.

RATHDRUM

Like Blessington, Rathdrum is a humdrum town made noteworthy by another "big house": the Parnell family home and birthplace of Charles Stewart Parnell, Ireland's greatest tragic hero of the modern age. Surrounded by a forest park of more than 200 hectares is **Avondale House** (2 km south of town on the R752, tel. 0404/46111, open 11 A.M.–6 P.M. daily mid-Mar.–Oct., house admission €5.50, additional €5 parking fee), purchased by the state in 1904. Nearly a hundred years after the (small-scale) Wicklow gold rush of 1795, Parnell made an unsuccessful attempt at panning for gold near Avondale in hopes of finding enough to make a wedding ring for his mistress, Kitty. His elegant Georgian home still houses much of the Parnell family's furniture and artwork and is well worth a visit even if the sun's shining. Then spend an hour or two rambling through the forest park, which includes a Continental-style arboretum and plenty of shady walking trails—it's open year-round.

Avondale is signposted at the crossroads on the eastern end of Rathdrum, which is 58 kilometers south of Dublin off the N11 (picking up the R752 at Rathnew) and 10 kilometers northeast of Avoca on the R752; Avoca makes the most pleasant base for visiting Avondale. It is possible to reach Rathdrum via **Bus Éireann** (tel. 01/836-6111) on the Dublin–Avoca–Arklow route (#133), though service is infrequent enough to pose a logistical challenge (i.e., you've got to get to the Dublin Connolly Luas stop to board the bus for a 9 A.M. departure, as the only other daily bus that stops in Rathdrum leaves too late in the day). And once you get to town, it's still a two-kilometer walk to Avondale.

THE WICKLOW COAST

The gardens and mountains of Wicklow generally attract more attention than the county's beaches. There's little to bring the visitor to Wicklow Town (the beach is rocky and littered with broken beer bottles), though the tourist office tries its darnedest with the Wicklow Gaol; the exhibition is downright cheesy, and not worth your time. All things considered, Wexford's seaside towns—Kilmore Quay, Duncannon, and Arthurstown in particular—are quite a bit nicer, though the coastal walk from Bray to Greystones along with the pristine strand at Brittas Bay are well worth stopping for.

Bray

Though this seaside town 20 kilometers south of Dublin has certainly spiffed itself up in recent years, Bray's ongoing shortage of quality cafés, restaurants, and accommodations puts a damper on any plans for an overnight visit. If, when walking the streets here, you get the sense that this isn't the best the east coast has to offer, you'd be hitting the nail on the head.

Having said all this, the **coastal walk** from the Bray promenade eight kilometers south to Greystones is a deservedly popular activity with Dublin day-trippers, and it's easy as pie to get

down here on the DART, walk the route, and then return on the DART from Greystones. Bray itself is small enough to get the hang of in a few minutes; Strand Road hugs the promenade (or "esplanade," as it's locally known), to which Main Street runs briefly parallel; continuing down the main drag will eventually get you to Glendalough (30 km southwest). Turning off the northern end of Main Street onto Sea Point Road or Quinsborough Road will get you to the seafront the quickest.

Bray has its share of cultural attractions, namely **Kilruddery House & Gardens** (3 km south of town on the Greystones road/R761, tel. 01/286-3405, www.killruddery.com, gardens open 1–5 P.M. Sat.–Sun. in Apr., 1–5 P.M. daily May–Sept., house open 1–5 P.M. May, June, and Sept., gardens/combined admission €5/8), a late-17th-century manor with a stunning domed greenhouse and Elizabethan-style architectural detail (all of which was added in the 19th century). The estate has been in the family of the earls of Meath since 1618, and the formal garden, laid out in the 1680s, is one of the oldest in the country. There's also an aquarium on the waterfront, **National Sealife** (Strand Rd., tel. 01/286-6939, www.sealife.ie, open 9:30 A.M.–6 P.M. Mon.–Sat., admission €7), which places as great an emphasis on marine conservation as it does on entertaining the kiddies.

The town's best pub, for live music and general *craic,* is the **Harbour Bar** (Seapoint Rd., tucked away on a side road just north of the promenade, tel. 01/286-2274). This pub-cum-lounge is popular with all sorts, from hardcore sea anglers to the town's small "alternative" population. It's also worth stopping by the **Mermaid Arts Centre** (Main St., tel. 01/272-4030, art gallery open 10 A.M.–6 P.M. Mon.–Sat.) to see what's playing in its theater and art house cinema.

ACCOMMODATIONS AND FOOD

Most accommodations in Bray have a time-warp feel to them—clean, tidy, and otherwise adequate, but certainly in need of an interior facelift. Just pretend you're spending the night at Great-Aunt Mildred's. Try **Ulysses** (Strand Rd., tel. 01/286-3860, €37 pp sharing) right on the promenade, or ivy-clad **Iveragh** (44 Meath Rd., tel. 01/286-3877, iveragh@hotmail.com, €30–33 pp, s €45) one block up from the water—heading south on Strand Road, make a right onto Convent Avenue, and Iveragh is on the corner to your left. Do think twice before saying "thanks, but no thanks" to Great-Aunt Mildred, because Bray's "top" accommodation, the Royal Hotel, is in major need of a change in management; other hotels in town are similarly run-down and overpriced.

Ironically, Bray's best restaurant is directly opposite the local McDonald's. The commodious **Cape Greko** (51 Main St., tel. 01/286-0006, www.capegreko.ie, open 5–11 P.M. Mon., noon–11 P.M. Tues.–Thurs., noon–midnight Fri.–Sat., noon–10 P.M. Sun., mains €16–25) serves up tasty victuals from Greece and Cyprus. The music and decor (painted plaster reliefs and suchlike) may be a bit predictable, but the service is good, the produce super-fresh, and the extensive menu offers something for everyone. The €20 three-course early-bird menu (available 5–7 P.M. Mon., 3–7 P.M. Tues.–Fri., 3–6 P.M. Sat.) is a terrific value.

PRACTICALITIES
The **tourist office** (Main St. at Seapoint Rd., tel. 01/286-7128, www.bray.ie, open 9:30 A.M.– 1 P.M. and 2–5 P.M. Mon.–Sat. June–Sept., 2– 4:30 P.M. Mon.–Sat. Oct.–May) is located in the town's old courthouse.

Getting to Bray from Dublin is easy, with frequent service from Pearse and Connolly Stations on the DART. The **Irish Rail** station (tel. 01/236-3333, trains every 5 minutes at peak, 2–3 off-peak departures/hour, single/return ticket €2.30/4) is off Quinsborough Road, about 500 meters east of Main Street. From here you can travel farther south to Wexford and Rosslare Harbour, or north to Dublin and Howth. If driving, you have a choice between the M11 motorway and the coastal road, the R119, though both get seriously congested at peak periods.

Greystones

The eight-kilometer Bray coastal walk will leave you off in Greystones, another fishing village-turned-resort town-turned-commuter suburb. Worked up an appetite? The best spot for an informal meal is **Bels Bistro** (Church Rd., tel. 01/201-6990, open noon–10 P.M. daily), whether you're in the mood for something traditional (like fish and chips), relatively exotic (Thai fish cakes), or vegetarian (try the grilled portobello wrap).

Though Greystones boasts a Blue Flag beach, there's not a whole lot going on here otherwise, so you're best off heading back to Dublin on the **Irish Rail** (Church Rd., tel. 01/888-0343, 2–3 departures/hour) suburban service.

Brittas Bay

A pristine five-kilometer Blue Flag strand, Brittas is the county's nicest beach. Located 18.5 kilometers south of Wicklow Town on the R750, it's predictably popular with Dublin day-trippers. There isn't anyplace to stay or eat in the area, though, strangely enough, so it makes the most sense to pack a picnic lunch in the morning and spend the afternoon here before driving down to Wexford (or to the lovely hamlet of Avoca, 18 km southwest) in the evening. Oh yes—and beware that cheeky €2 parking fee!

BLESSINGTON

Another ho-hum town in the northwestern corner of the county, Blessington is noteworthy for **Russborough House** (tel. 045/865-239, open 10 A.M.–5 P.M. Mon.–Sat. and 10:30 A.M.–5:30 P.M. Sun. Apr.–Sept., admission €6), a grand Palladian villa erected in the 1740s—and best known for a veritable parade of art heists, the most recent of which (in 2001) left a gaping hole in a drawing room wall after a duo of brazen thieves rammed through the veranda doors in a jeep, making off with millions of dollars' worth of paintings (all were eventually recovered). A guide (who has dutifully memorized the date and origin of every stick of furniture in the place) will lead you through the house on a tour that lasts just shy of an hour and includes four bedrooms and a fine collection of porcelain figurines upstairs. The most interesting item in the house is an ornate gold microscope dating to 1772, which was supposedly a wedding gift to Marie Antoinette. The house isn't quite as impressive as its reputation attests, especially since the painting collection was moved to the National Gallery after that last robbery (those pesky art thieves sure have a way of spoiling we aesthetically inclined tourists' fun). Thus, unused wall outlets and unfaded rectangles of velvet wallpaper are all that remain here of a tremendous trove of works by Goya, Gainsborough, and other artis-

tic heavyweights. The Beit ("bite") Foundation was upgrading security at time of writing, and they hope to bring the collection back to the house in the near future.

Sheep roam the space where the gardens once stood, but you can still take a ramble through a small hedge maze out back in high season. Bottom line: If you enjoy examining elaborate plasterwork and fine furniture and objets-d'art from all over Europe, by all means pay a visit.

Blessington is 30 kilometers southwest of Dublin on the N81, and Russborough is 5 kilometers farther south on the same road.

Kildare

Traveling through County Kildare feels a bit like walking a treadmill in purgatory. The landscape is flat and uninteresting (and presently treeless, despite the name Kildare, which means "Church of the Oak Wood"), dominated by sprawling suburban commuter estates, and thoroughbred horses far outnumber the human population. This last bit may sound like heaven to champion equestrians (in that case, be sure to visit the National Stud Museum in Kildare Town), but the rest can pass on through.

KILDARE TOWN
Kildare Town is associated with two things: St. Brigid (behind only the Virgin Mother and St. Patrick in Irish Catholic devotion), who was said to have founded a monastery here in the 5th century, and the **Irish National Stud** (Tully, 1.5 km south of Kildare, signposted from the town center, tel. 045/521-617, www.irish-national-stud.ie, open 9:30 A.M.–6 P.M. daily mid-Feb.–Oct., admission €9). The Stud was founded in 1900 by an eccentric Scotsman named Colonel William Hall-Walker, whose family made its fortune in whiskey (Johnnie Walker, anyone?). Though he was ridiculed for such practices as having natal horoscopes drawn for all his horses, the colonel was clearly doing something right, and The Stud was

taken over by the state in 1946. There's a small museum in addition to the guided tour of the stables, during which time you can admire all the newborn foals. If you're lucky, you might even be able to witness a birth.

Adjacent are the **Japanese Gardens,** laid out between 1906 and 1910, and **St. Fiacra's Garden,** which opened in 1999. St. Fiacra was the patron saint of gardeners, and this newer garden offers an hour's worth of tranquil lakeside and woodland strolls. Admission to both gardens is included in The Stud ticket. Though the gardens are certainly lovely, they aren't truly worth a special visit. You've got to be *really* into horses to warrant the stiff admission price.

Planning to spend a little more time here in horse country? **Silken Thomas** (The Square, Main St., tel. 045/522-232, food served noon–9 P.M. daily, mains €10–22, B&B €35 pp), named for the 10th Earl of Kildare, is the town's best pub-cum-restaurant; the steaks are so tasty you won't mind if the atmosphere is on the stodgy side. There's B&B upstairs, or try the **Curragh Lodge Hotel** (the Dublin road, tel. 045/522-144, clhotel@iol.ie, €50 pp, s €60), a pretty standard small-town hotel with friendly, accommodating management and better-than-average pub and restaurant fare.

Kildare is 56 kilometers southwest of Dublin on the new M7 motorway. **Bus Éireann** (tel. 01/836-6111) offers frequent service from Dublin (#126, 14/day Mon.–Sat., 8/day Sun.), and another route passes through Kildare on the way to Ennis (#12, 14/day daily). A speedier option is **Irish Rail** (tel. 01/836-3333, departures from Heuston Station every 30 minutes).

⨀ CASTLETOWN

Yet another ho-hum commuter suburb, Celbridge is on the map for Ireland's largest, most glorious Palladian country house: the unimaginatively named Castletown (tel. 01/628-8252, open 10 A.M.–6 P.M. Mon.–Fri., 1–6 P.M. weekends Easter–Sept., 10 A.M.–5 P.M. Mon.–Fri. and 1–5 P.M. Sun. in Oct., admission €3.70). It was built in the 1720s for William Conolly, Speaker of the Irish House of Commons, a Donegal man of humble beginnings who was eventually considered the wealthiest man in the country. Construction was ongoing for decades after Conolly's death under a veritable parade of architects. The Guinness family purchased the house in the late 1970s and began the arduous process of restoration. Now the estate is run by Dúchas, and the hour-long tour of Castletown is well worth the schlep out of Dublin. As a general rule, if you've toured one "big house" you've toured them all—grand sweeping staircases, intricate plasterwork, marble busts and gilt furniture don't seem quite so splendid after a while—but if you visit only one Irish manse, let it be this one.

Castletown is 20 kilometers from Dublin; if driving, begin on the N4 west and take the Celbridge exit (putting you on the R403 for a few more kilometers). Otherwise, the **Dublin Bus** will get you here from either the Pearse Street or Wood Quay stop in the city center (tel. 01/873-4222, www.dublinbus.ie, route #67 or #67A, 2–3 departures/hour Mon.–Sat., hourly on Sun., single ticket €1.85, trip takes 70 minutes).

MAYNOOTH

Considering the presence of a national university, one might expect Maynooth (Maigh Nuad, "New Plain") to be full of hot-and-

happenin' cafés and bars. Not quite. Perhaps the seminary—Ireland's largest—has something of a dampening effect on even ordinary students' social aspirations. That said, the pleasant tree-lined Main Street has a few shops and pubs worth checking out, and the National University of Ireland (NUI) Maynooth campus boasts some stunning neo-Gothic architecture. Thackeray may have dismissed Maynooth as a "miserable village" in his *Irish Sketch Book of 1842,* but the writer would certainly have better things to say of it now. All in all, it's the most worthwhile stop in County Kildare.

An overnight visit isn't necessary, though, especially considering the dearth of accommodations in the area. One has to wonder where all the parents stay come graduation time!

Orienting yourself in Maynooth is a snap: Everything you need is on (or just off) Main Street, with the university's southern campus, the Manor Mills Shopping Centre, and Mill Street all on the western end; from this side of town, you can also turn south onto Leinster Street to reach the train station and the Royal Canal, a newly restored relic of British imperialism.

Sights

Now a branch of the National University of Ireland, **NUI Maynooth** (tel. 01/708-6000, www.nuim.ie) was opened as a seminary at the close of the 18th century. From a humble inaugural class of 40 aspiring priests, Maynooth prospered into the world's largest seminary by the year 1895.

The seminary is still here, surrounded by all the trappings of a modern university in the age of technology, though it's hardly surprising that its admissions have dropped dramatically in recent years. NUIM is divided into north and south campuses, though everything to interest the visitor is on the south campus.

It goes without saying that the most important building on campus is the cavernous **college chapel.** With its elaborate frescoes, stained glass, and miserichordia, this grand and somber church is truly awe-inspiring. The chapel is clearly signposted from the university's front gate, a two-minute walk.

Guarding the entrance to the south NUI campus, the 13th-century Anglo-Norman **Maynooth Castle** (tel. 01/628-6744, open 10 A.M.–6 P.M. Mon.–Fri. and 1–6 P.M. weekends June–Sept., 1–5 P.M. Sun. in Oct., free admission), once the primary residence of the earls of Kildare, has been in a state of ruin since the 17th century. The castle is now administered by Dúchas. Seeing as it's free, you might as well take a few minutes to check out what's left of the keep and gatehouse.

Shopping

Maynooth has some decent opportunities for retail therapy, including the **Manor Mills Shopping Centre** at the west end of Main Street. You'll find super-stylish women's duds at **Hula-Bou** (Main St., tel. 01/628-6824) or **Mystique** (Mill St., tel. 01/628-5668), while **Paul Monaghan** (3-4 Mill St., tel. 01/628-9199) takes care of the boys.

Accommodations

There isn't as great a selection of accommodations as you might expect in a college town, and B&Bs are strangely few and far between. NUI offers budget rooms, though naturally availability is much higher during the summer months. Contact **Maynooth Campus Accommodation** (tel. 01/708-6200, www. maynoothcampus.com, dorms €21 pp, s €25; en suite rooms €55 pp; apartments €31 pp sharing, s €28–36) for details.

Spiffy and new (it's purpose-built), **Hawthorn House** (Old Greenfield, beside the Maynooth rail station, tel. 01/629-0400, www. hawthornhousebandb.com, €37.50 pp, s €45, 2-person apartments €400/week) offers self-catering accommodation as well as B&B, and the common areas are lovely—there's a guest sitting room stocked with books and music as well as a deck and garden out back. Self-catering rates include Internet access.

Another option is the commodious **Ballygoran Lodge** (Old Celbridge Rd., tel. 01/629-1860 or 087/274-0801, €35 pp shar-

ing), decorated liberally with angel effigies and plaques with witty epigrams. From Maynooth, follow the signs for Celbridge, taking Mill Street past the Glenroyal Hotel on the left and the Maxol station on your right, and you'll see the B&B signposted on the left. Make the left and you'll see the house down the road on the right.

While you'll find the poshest digs in town at the very corporate **Glenroyal Hotel** (Straffan Rd., signposted from Main St., tel. 01/629-0909, www.glenroyal.ie, €65 pp, s €90, special web rates available), including two swimming pools, management can be inefficient, the pub and restaurant food is typically mediocre, and on weekends the nightclub din will keep you up. An ultra-atmospheric alternative is **Moyglare Manor** (3 km north of town on the R157, tel. 01/628-6351, www.moyglaremanor. ie, d €250, s €150, suite €330, 12.5 percent service charge), a Georgian country home with all the delightfully posh accoutrements—from king-sized, four-poster, lushly made beds to a piano lounge with a cheerful open fire. Glenroyal guests, note that the top-notch Moyglare restaurant (open 12:30–2 P.M. Mon.–Fri. and noon–2:30 P.M. Sun., 7–9:30 P.M. daily, set lunch €35, dinner €60, reservations required) is also open to nonguests. If you're lucky you might even have a pianist on hand to set the mood.

Food and Entertainment

The cafeteria-style **Coffee Mill** (Mill St., tel. 01/601-6594, open 8 A.M.–5 P.M. weekdays, 8:30 A.M.–4 P.M. Sat., lunches €5–8) is your average student hangout, offering basic sandwiches and salads. In fair weather you can sip your coffee on a pleasant stone patio out back.

Easily the best restaurant in town, **Stone Haven** (1 Mill St., tel. 01/601-6594, open 5–9:30 P.M. Tues.–Sun., mains €13–25) offers an eclectic menu in a romantic ambience. Another option is inside the Glenroyal Hotel but independently operated: **Lemongrass** (Straffan Rd., tel. 01/629-0915, www.lemongrass.ie, open noon–10 P.M. daily, lunch €8–15, dinner €15–27) may be a chain Thai restaurant, but oftentimes the great thing about chains is that you know exactly the kind of meal you can expect—and the Lemongrass restaurants do the best Thai on the island.

Caulfield's (Main St., tel. 01/628-6078, food served noon–8 P.M. daily, meals €8–14) does traditional pub grub—and is, along with **Brady's** (Main St., tel. 01/628-6225), the best watering hole in Maynooth.

Information and Services

Maynooth does not have a tourist office, though there is an **information point** on the NUI campus (tel. 01/708-3576, open 9 A.M.– 5 P.M. and 6–10 P.M. daily).

The **Bank of Ireland** (tel. 01/628-6811) and **Ulster Bank** (tel. 01/628-5533), both on Main Street, have ATMs and bureaux de change.

Maynooth Launderette & Dry Cleaning (tel. 01/628-6203) and **McCormack's**

Pharmacy (tel. 01/628-6274) are both on Main Street. Check your email at the **Tech Store** (Glenroyal Shopping Centre, Unit 5, tel. 01/629-1747, www.techstore.ie, open noon– 11 P.M. daily, €5/hour).

Getting There and Around

Maynooth is 26 kilometers west of Dublin, just off the M4 motorway. **Dublin Bus** (tel. 01/873-4222, www.dublinbus.ie, #66, #66X, #67A, #67N, or #67X, frequent daily departures, 1-hour journey, fare €2.10) can get you here from Wellington Quay in downtown Dublin. A quicker option is **Irish Rail** (Leinster St., tel. 01/836-6222, Dublin Connolly–Sligo line, at least 8/day Mon.–Sat., 4/day Sun., 25-minute journey, single/return ticket €3/5).

Express Cabs (tel. 01/628-9866 or 01/627-4222) offers 24/7 service, with both cabs and minibuses.

THE SOUTHEAST

To describe Counties Wexford (Loch gCorman, "Corman's Lake"; from Weiss Fjord, "White Ford") and Kilkenny (Cill Chainnigh, "Church of St. Canice") is an exercise in superlatives. The former is Ireland's sunniest county (just ask any meteorologist!), the latter its most medieval. Kilkenny in particular has a rich monastic history; aside from the substantial ruins at Jerpoint and Kells, the countryside is sprinkled with splendid high crosses and the remains of smaller abbeys and churches. Carlow (Ceatharlach, "Four Lakes"), on the other hand, is one of those nondescript counties with little to divert the tourist (the gigantic Browne's Hill Dolmen being the exception).

HISTORY

Traveling through Wexford, it's almost easy to forget we're more than two centuries removed from the 1798 rebellion; memorials are everywhere. Though it ended in bloody defeat, the memory of the Battle of Vinegar Hill (just outside Enniscorthy) in June 1798 would inspire the 1916 Easter Rising and the subsequent IRA guerrilla activity that led to the Anglo-Irish Treaty.

Written in the "Marble City" in 1366 and passed the following year, the Statutes of Kilkenny were intended to segregate the Anglo-Norman colonists from the native Irish, banning intermarriage and the adoption of native customs, dress, and language. These laws

WARNING
GREAT CARE MUST BE
TAKEN NEAR THE
WATERS EDGE IN THIS
AREA   FREAK WAVES
SLIPPERY ROCKS

HIGHLIGHTS

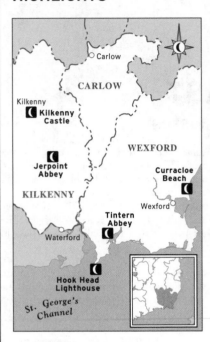

◖ Curracloe Beach: At 19 kilometers, this is the country's longest strand, and it's also one of the most pristine (page 139).

◖ Tintern Abbey: Named after the Welsh abbey of Wordsworth fame, these ruins have a checkered history all their own (page 141).

◖ Hook Head Lighthouse: There has been a beacon at Hook Head since the 6th century, and this 13th-century lighthouse is probably Europe's oldest. Climb to the top for a terrific view over Waterford Harbour (page 142).

◖ Kilkenny Castle: Once the seat of the dukes of Ormonde, this castle has been magnificently restored using authentic furniture and decor from the 1830s (page 146).

◖ Jerpoint Abbey: Examine the intricate stone carvings on the tombs, walls, altar, and cloister of this late 12th-century Romanesque priory a short drive south of Kilkenny City (page 153).

LOOK FOR ◖ TO FIND RECOMMENDED SIGHTS, ACTIVITIES, DINING, AND LODGING.

were ultimately unsuccessful, as the Normans assimilated so well they became "more Irish than the Irish themselves," and though these laws predated the Reformation by nearly two centuries, they were nevertheless the ominous forerunner of the Penal Laws.

PLANNING YOUR TIME

If you'd like to visit Kilkenny, Hook Head, and/or Wexford on the same trip, you could travel from Dublin to Kilkenny (taking in the

Browne's Hill Dolmen outside Carlow Town en route) and on to Cork, then make an eastbound loop to take in Waterford's pretty seaside towns before ferrying over Waterford Harbour to Wexford's Hook Head Peninsula. This is quite an ambitious plan, however, so unless you have loads of time, you're best off choosing between Wexford and Kilkenny. Need nightlife and fine grub in a quaint atmosphere? Do Kilkenny. Want to bypass the tour buses? Go for Wexford, Hook Head especially.

THE SOUTHEAST

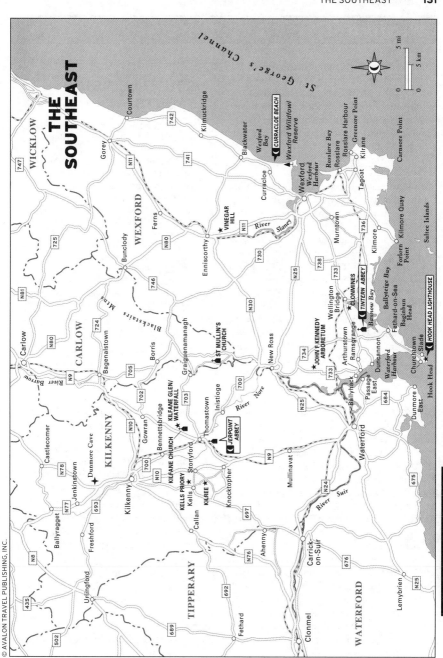

THE SOUTHEAST

Wexford

Aside from the Blackstairs Mountains on the western border, Wexford is a flat and low-lying county with a pretty but undramatic coastline. While you're here, sample the local strawberries and order a cup of coffee with crème fraîche (instead of milk)—that's the way they like their java down here.

ENNISCORTHY

Site of the biggest battle of the 1798 rebellion, Enniscorthy (Inis Córthaidh) is fairly attractive as far as market towns go, though there's more nightlife to be found in Wexford. Make an afternoon of it on your way south to Wexford Town—unless, of course, you're here in late June or early July, when you'll want to spend your time gobbling juicy berries and fresh cream at the annual **Strawberry Fair.**

The town layout is a bit confusing, so pick up a copy of the Town Trail map from the **tourist office** (Castle Hill, tel. 054/923-4699, www. virtualenniscorthy.com, open 10 A.M.–1 P.M. and 2–5:30 P.M. Mon.–Sat. mid-June–Aug., 2–5:30 P.M. Sun. Sept.–mid-June); if it's closed, check out the map posted on Abbey Quay.

Sights

There's a fair bit to see here, including the early 13th-century **Enniscorthy Castle** housing the **Wexford County Museum** (Castle St., tel. 054/923-5926, open 10 A.M.–1 P.M. and 2–6 P.M. Mon.–Sat., 2–5:30 P.M. Sun. June–Sept., 2–5:30 P.M. daily Oct.–Nov. and Feb.–May, Sun. only Dec.–Jan., admission €4.50). Another attraction is the Pugin-designed Catholic **St. Aidan's Cathedral** (Cathedral St.) in the town center.

Make the most time, however, for the **National 1798 Centre** (Mill Park Rd., signposted from the town center, tel. 054/923-7596, www.iol. ie/~98com/english.htm, open 9:30 A.M.–6 P.M. Mon.–Sat., 11 A.M.–6 P.M. Sun., admission €6); spend an hour and a half or so learning about the failed uprising that nevertheless inspired subsequent generations of patriots.

SOUTH LEINSTER SPORTS

You can go hang gliding in the Blackstairs Mountains (along the Carlow-Wexford border) in the summer months; Mount Leinster, the range's tallest peak at 795 meters, is particularly popular. For details, ring **Eamon Thompson** (tel. 01/455-6437).

The **Irish Parachute Club** (based in Edenderry, County Offaly, 61 km west of Dublin off the N4, tel. 1850/260-600 or 046/973-0204, www.skydive.ie, tandem dive €320) offers a significantly discounted rate for those wishing to jump for charity. Beginners' trips are available, as is an Accelerated Freefall certification course conducted on the weekends over a monthlong period. Experienced skydivers can take a tandem jump from an elevation of up to 4,000 meters!

Or if you prefer to keep your feet planted firmly on solid ground, there's always the 102-kilometer, infrequently traversed **South Leinster Way,** which begins in tiny Kildavin in County Carlow and ends at Carrick-on-Suir, County Tipperary. The walking route passes through the Blackstairs as well as the lovely village of Inistioge in County Kilkenny. For details on the route, accommodations, and other practical matters, check out the **South Leinster Way Walking Trail** website (www.southleinsterway.com).

Afterward, take a walk up **Vinegar Hill** (Cnoc Fíodh Na gCaor, 2 km southeast of town, signposted from the center, always accessible, free admission), where the rebels lost control of County Wexford. That day, June 21, 1798, there were 1,000 Irish casualties (and 100 British). Writing just over a century after the rebellion, William Bulfin mused: "Looking down from Vinegar Hill on the open country below, you could not help wondering how the

BROWNE'S HILL DOLMEN

If you're traveling from Dublin to Kilkenny or Waterford, you might want to make a stop in County Carlow to visit Browne's Hill Dolmen (Hacketstown Rd., 3 km east of Carlow Town on the R726, always accessible, free admission), one of Ireland's most important megalithic monuments.

The largest in Ireland, Browne's Hill Dolmen is more than 4,000 years old and has a capstone weighing a staggering 100 tons. Surrounded by pastures (and a string of car dealerships across the road), this awesome megalith is said to mark the grave of a prehistoric chieftain. Nowadays local hoodlums discard their beer cans in the low and spooky space beneath the capstone – sadly, even the cows show more respect. Spend a while between the grassy pastures, speculating how these Neolithic people could possibly have contrived to move such a gargantuan capstone into place.

Getting here from Carlow Town is a bit tricky, as the site isn't signposted from the town center. Head east on the main drag, Tullow Street, and at the end of it you'll come to a fork in the road: You'd go left for the N9 and the train station, but keep straight through the intersection – this is Pollerton

© CAMILLE DEANGELIS

The dolmen's capstone alone weighs over 100 tons.

Road. You'll soon come to a roundabout where the dolmen is signposted.

Ireland's second-smallest county, Carlow boasts few attractions for the visitor beyond Browne's Hill Dolmen, but the Blackstairs Mountains on the Wexford border make for a pretty drive (the scenic route, the R702, goes from Borris in Carlow to Kiltealy in Wexford), and on summer weekends it's even possible to hang glide from Mount Leinster, the highest peak in the province (see *South Leinster Sports* for details).

Wexfordmen of '98 kept up the fight so long… there is no protection from infantry or artillery fire…had there been even a few barrels of gunpowder on Vinegar Hill the day of the battle, the two thousand rifles of the Wexfordmen would alone have sufficed, without artillery, to change the course of history." To get there, you'll walk up a street of ugly pebbledashed houses; at the top is a small car park, a modern memorial, the ruin of a signal tower, and a panoramic view of the River Slaney and a mix of countryside and suburban sprawl.

Sports and Recreation

Go quad-biking in all weather with the **Quad Attack Adventure Centre** (Clonroche, 13.5 km west of town on the N30, tel. 053/924-4660, www.quadattack.ie), which also has an

indoor amusement ring complete with bungee jumps and sumo suits. Or if the weather holds, serious water-sporters can rent a Canadian-made canoe and paddle down the river; contact **Slaney Canoe Hire** (tel. 054/923-4526), who'll deliver your boat wherever you request.

Accommodations and Food

If you'd like to spend the night in Enniscorthy, try the **Lemon Grove** (Blackstoops, 1 km north of town off the N11, signposted from the center, tel. 054/923-6115, www.euroka.com/lemongrove, €33–40 pp sharing, credit cards accepted) for B&B or the modern three-star **Riverside Park Hotel** (the Promenade, tel. 054/923-7800, www.riversideparkhotel.com, €80 pp, s €90), which has a new leisure center with exercise pool and all the usual facilities.

THE SOUTHEAST

On your way into **The Antique Tavern** (14 Slaney St., tel. 054/923-3428, www.theantiquetavern.com, food served noon–4 P.M. Mon.–Sat., mains under €10), take a moment to read the amusing "hear ye" plaque posted by the innkeeper, which proclaims its hospitality "will not be extended to Highwaymen, Raperees, Bandits, Footpads, Thimblemen, Three-card trickers, Persons of no fixed abode, or persons whose appearance, manner or conduct might rise to offence." Provided that none of this applies, you can take your pint up to the cute-but-tiny Plexiglas-enclosed terrace pretty nearly overlooking the river. At **Shenanigans** (13 Market Sq., tel. 054/923-6272, food served noon–8 P.M., mains €6–9), the name, coupled with the red and orange walls, might make you feel like you're having a pint in some hipster nursery school. The pub grub is fairly standard—paninis, burgers, an all-day breakfast (€8)—but the fixings are fresh and tasty.

Practicalities

Before leaving town, check your email at **Softtech** (4 Castle St., tel. 054/923-0833, opening hours vary, €2/hour), which offers the cheapest rate outside the Fair City.

Enniscorthy is 20 kilometers north of Wexford Town on the N11. **Bus Éireann** stops here on the Dublin–Wexford–Rosslare Harbour (#2, 13/day Mon.–Sat., 10/day Sun.) and Dublin–Waterford (#5, 5–6/day daily) routes.

WEXFORD TOWN

With its medieval layout, wickedly narrow Main Street, and abundance of cozy pubs, Wexford has a certain timeless quality. This is the kind of place where you might overhear one local say to another, "I'm sorry for your troubles, Jim," then turn a corner onto a residential street to find a couple of 10-year-olds swinging their hurling sticks in the gathering twilight. Unlike many other Irish towns, Wexford changes little from one visit to the next—and that's just the way it should be.

The town center is laid out along the west bank of the River Slaney, which empties into Wexford Harbour. The railroad line runs between the river and the quay (which changes names, northwest to southeast, from Wellington Place to Commercial Quay, then to Custom House Quay, and finally to Crescent Quay). Crescent Quay is presided over by a statue of Commodore John Barry, Wexford native turned American revolutionary, a gift from President Eisenhower. One block west, Selskar Street, changing to North Main Street and then South Main Street, runs parallel to the quay, and the more residential John Street/School Street/Roches Road is another long block west, up an incline. At the top of Selskar Street is tidy, green Redmond Square, named for conservative nationalist Wexford MP John Redmond; roughly three blocks west is the Bull Ring, the town's historical nexus. Notice Diana's Boutique across the way? That was the home of Oscar Wilde's mother, Jane Francesca Elgee Wilde—an accomplished pro-Ireland political commentator in her own right. (She used the pen name "Speranza.")

Sights

There are a couple of cheesy folk parks in the area, but you'll learn more of local history by simply walking the streets. The **Bull Ring** has served many quotidian purposes over the years—marketplace, bull-baiters' arena—but it's also figured in every pinnacle (or low point) of Wexford's history. Here Cromwell slaughtered two-thirds of the town's population; here the 1798 rebels declared an Irish republic (and the Lone Pikeman statue is a tribute to those who died in the subsequent battle); here Daniel O'Connell and later Eamon de Valera took to the podium.

Like so many other friaries, **Selskar Abbey** (Westgate St., beside the heritage center, open during center hours, free admission) has Cromwell to thank for its present state. But the present maintenance of the old graveyard is an utter disgrace, too: grass as tall as your hips and rubbish everywhere (even inside a lidless tomb resting on the floor of the old church!). Not that they care much, wherever they are, but you can't help feeling sorry for the folks buried here.

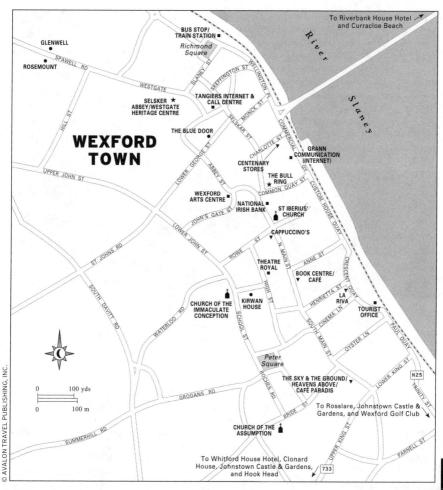

To Riverbank House Hotel
and Curracloe Beach

River

Slaney

BUS STOP/
TRAIN STATION ■

Richmond
Square

GLENWELL ●

ROSEMOUNT ●

SPAWELL RD

WESTGATE

SLANEY ST

SKEFFINGTON ST

WELLINGTON PL

TANGIERS INTERNET &
CALL CENTRE

SELSKER ★
ABBEY/WESTGATE
HERITAGE CENTRE

HILL ST

**WEXFORD
TOWN**

THE BLUE DOOR ●

SELSKAR ST

MONCK ST

COMMERCIAL QUAY

CHARLOTTE ST

CENTENARY
STORES

GRANN
COMMUNICATION
(INTERNET)

UPPER JOHN ST

LOWER GEORGE ST

ABBEY ST

THE BULL
RING ★

COMMON QUAY ST

WEXFORD
ARTS CENTRE ●

NATIONAL ■
IRISH BANK

ST IBERIUS
CHURCH

CUSTOM HOUSE QUAY

JOHN'S GATE ST

CAPPUCCINO'S ●

LOWER JOHN ST

ROWE ST

N MAIN ST

ANNE ST

ST JOHNS RD

THEATRE
ROYAL ■

BOOK CENTRE/
▼ CAFÉ

CRESCENT QUAY

SOUTH DAVITT RD

WATERLOO RD

CHURCH OF THE
IMMACULATE
CONCEPTION

KIRWAN
HOUSE

SCHOOL ST

HIGH ST

HENRIETTA ST

LA
RIVA ▼

CINEMA LN

SOUTH MAIN ST

TOURIST
OFFICE ●

OYSTER LN

PAUL QUAY

Peter
Square

ROCHES RD

THE SKY & THE GROUND/
HEAVENS ABOVE/
CAFÉ PARADIS ▼

LOWER KING ST

N25

GROGANS RD

BRIDE ST

To Rosslare, Johnstown Castle &
Gardens, and Wexford Golf Club

TRINITY ST

SUMMERHILL RD

CHURCH OF THE
ASSUMPTION ✝

UPPER KING ST

PARNELL ST

To Whitford House Hotel, Clonard
House, Johnstown Castle & Gardens,
and Hook Head

733

0   100 yds
0   100 m

It's said the first-ever treaty between the English and the Irish was signed on this site in 1169. The abbey itself was established in 1190 by Alexander de la Roche, who had just returned from the Crusades—and according to legend, there was a distraught element to this benefaction—as his sweetheart, fearing him dead, had locked herself in a convent.

The town's most interesting church is the Anglican **St. Iberius** (N. Main St., tel. 053/914-3013, open 10 A.M.–5 P.M. Mon.–Sat., free admission), built in the mid-17th century and extended in the 1760s. The dignified Georgian interior is dotted with eloquent wall memorials; the altar rail, moved here from St. George's in Dublin, saw the marriage of the Duke of Wellington in 1806. The caretaker has plenty more interesting stories about St. Iberius's history; supposedly there's been a church on this site since the 5th century, and at one time, when the water level was much higher, the river flowed up to the back door.

Climb rickety stairs to the organ loft at St. Iberius's Church.

History-wise, Wexford's Catholic "twin churches" can't compete, but the neo-Gothic **Church of the Immaculate Conception** (Lower John St. at Rowe St., tel. 053/912-2055) and **Church of the Assumption** (Bride St., off School St.) are worth a peek if you find yourself ambling down the western end of town: brilliant-hued stained glass windows, adoration statues—the usual.

Entertainment and Events

One of Wexford's best watering holes is **The Sky & the Ground** (112 S. Main St., tel. 053/912-1273), the place to go for live trad (Mon., Wed., and Thurs. nights), but pay no attention to the chalkboard out front advertising music at 9. The musicians seem to wander in when they feel like it, and not a moment before, so the session doesn't actually start until after 10. On Friday night you'll find another band playing, weirdly enough, anything from Sinatra to Incubus. You'll generally find a younger crowd at the **Centenary Stores** (Charlotte St., off Commercial Quay, tel. 053/912-4424, www.thestores.ie), which

has trad sessions on Sunday afternoon, as well as the town's most popular nightclub (open 11 P.M.–2 A.M. Tues. and Thurs.–Sun., cover €8, free before 11:30 P.M.).

As for theater, the town's got two venues: the **Wexford Arts Centre** (Cornmarket, tel. 053/912-3764, www.wexfordartscentre.ie, tickets €10–20) offers the standard lineup of plays, concerts, and art exhibitions, while the **Theatre Royal** (27 High St., tel. 053/912-2144) does opera and classical concerts (though it was being completely rebuilt at time of writing). Otherwise this is the prime venue for the town's most important annual event, the **Wexford Opera Festival** (tel. 053/912-2400, www.wexfordopera.com). Be sure to book your accommodations well in advance if you plan to attend, as Puccini-lovers from all over the globe flock here come late October. Tickets go on sale in June.

Shopping

You'll find plenty of boutiques and gift shops along Main Street, and there's also a market on Friday morning (9 A.M.–2 P.M.) in the Mallin Street car park.

Root through the secondhand stacks at **Reader's Paradise** (3 Selskar St., tel. 053/917-1886) or stop by the **Book Centre** (5 S. Main St., tel. 053/912-3543), which has a nice café upstairs.

Wexford has one of the best antiques shops in the country: **Linda Hunt Antiques** (26 Henrietta St., tel. 053/46870, www.lindahuntantiques.com), specializing in exquisite Napoleonic, Victorian, and Deco jewelry—some found locally, other pieces alighted upon in England or France. There's also a lovely dress collection (nothing newer than the early 1960s), mid-20th-century rag dolls, a sprinkling of quality furniture, even a stash of turn-of-the-20th-century glass medicine bottles (some still full!).

Sports and Recreation

Ireland's longest strand, the 19-kilometer **Curracloe Beach,** is only 8 kilometers north of town, and the nearly-as-lovely Rosslare Strand is 15 kilometers south. Rosslare is easier to get to by public transport, however. Equestrian centers near both Curracloe and Rosslare offer beach treks.

The 18-hole, par-72 course at the **Wexford Golf Club** (Mulgannon, 5 km south of town on the N25, tel. 053/914-2238, www.wexfordgolfclub.ie) features views of the Blackstairs, Wexford Harbour, and the Saltee Islands.

Accommodations

Super-friendly, with a great home-away-from-home kind of atmosphere, **Kirwan House** (3 Mary St., tel. 053/912-1208, www.wexfordhostel.com, dorms €16–20, private rooms €22–25 pp) is a fine option for budget travelers. You're sure to meet an interesting character or two passing time in the sitting room.

With a beautiful front garden on a plot the size of a postage stamp, **Rosemount** (Spawell Rd., tel. 053/912-4609, www.wexfordbedandbreakfast.ie, €30–50 pp, s €50–65, credit cards accepted) is equally classy and immaculate on the inside. It's right beside Redmond Memorial Park—within easy walking distance of the pubs, yet far enough outside the center for peace and quiet on a weekend evening. The gated private car park makes this your best option if you're driving. Just down the street is **Glenwell** (3 Glena Terrace, Spawell Rd., tel. 053/917-4516, €35 pp, s €40), a late-Victorian brick townhouse filled with antiques and period details, run by the parents of Mrs. Kelly of Rosemount. Here you can order coffee for breakfast with confidence; it's far better than the average B&B bilgewater. Closer to the action is another recommended B&B, **The Blue Door** (18 Lower George St., tel. 053/912-1047, http://indigo.ie/~bluedoor, €35 pp, s €45, credit cards accepted). This elegant Georgian townhouse does a fine breakfast as well, with smoked salmon, thoughtful meat-free options, and Fair Trade tea and coffee.

Not planning to spend the evening at The Sky & the Ground? A few minutes' drive from town is the lovely **Clonard House** (Clonard Great, 3 km southwest of town off the R733, tel. 053/914-3141, www.clonardhouse.com, open May–Nov., €35–40 pp sharing), a stately, immaculate farmhouse built in 1783. The genuinely kind and helpful owners serve Irish coffee on arrival, many of the rooms have four-poster beds and other antiques, and the setting is utterly peaceful. What's not to love?

The best (and best-value) hotel in Wexford is the family-run **Whitford House Hotel & Leisure Club** (New Line Rd., 3 km south of town off the N11, tel. 053/914-3444, weekend €70–83 pp, midweek €58–77 pp, bank holidays €80–99 pp sharing, weekend s €90–108, midweek s €78–102, €15–20 deluxe room supplement). Deluxe rooms have private balconies, huge bathrooms, and in-room safes (and the "superior deluxe" have king-size beds). The leisure facilities include a 20-meter pool, hydromassage pool, sauna and steam room, gym, and day spa with massage and aromatherapy treatments available. The bar and restaurant fare is excellent, and there's live trad in the pub three or four nights a week.

Another good choice, just over the Wexford Bridge from the town center, is **Riverbank**

House Hotel (tel. 053/912-3611, www.river-bankhousehotel.com, low/high season €40/75 pp, weekend €55/80, s €65/100, €80/105 weekend). Your euros don't go quite as far here, but some of the rooms offer pleasant river views and the restaurant fare is delicious.

Food

Get your caffeine fix at **Cappuccino's** (25 N. Main St., tel. 053/912-4986, open 8 A.M.– 6 P.M. Mon.–Sat., 10:30 A.M.–6:30 P.M. Sun., meals €5–9) or the new mod-and-airy café upstairs at the **Book Centre** (5 S. Main St., tel. 053/912-3543, open 9 A.M.–5:30 P.M. Mon.–Sat.). Cappuccino's has a range of breakfast and lunch options, and the bookstore café does prepackaged, though fresh, Italian gourmet sandwiches for €4–6.

The owner of The Sky & the Ground made a smart decision in converting the off-license next door into a faux-Parisian tapas bar (of all things!). The pizza at **Café Paradis** (S. Main St., tel. 087/052-0141, open 4–11 P.M. Wed.–Sun., mains €7–12) is just passable, but the atmosphere, wine selection, and gourmet coffees are absolutely lovely—and so are the waitstaff (who are also pulling pints next door). Looking for a chilled-out yet romantic spot where you can nurse a bottle of shiraz over an evening you don't want to end? This is your new favorite haunt. For a more formal meal, just head upstairs to **Heavens Above** (tel. 053/912-1273, open 5–10 P.M. Mon.–Sat., 4–9 P.M. Sun., mains €16–28). The downstairs pub menu isn't as gourmet, but it's also a better value.

Wexford's top restaurant is **C La Riva** (Crescent Quay, entrance on Henrietta St., tel. 053/912-4330, warrengillen@dol.ie, open 6 P.M.–late Mon.–Sat. and bank holiday Sundays, mains €14–28), in an airy upstairs dining room overlooking the harbor. The service is friendly and unpretentious (and they let you know how much they appreciate your business), and the food—modern Irish with French, Italian, and Asian touches—is otherworldly, with an emphasis on organic local produce and free-range meats. The dessert menu is fantastic, too.

© CAMILLE DEANGELIS

Posted outside a Wexford pub, the sign says it all.

Information

The **tourist office** (tel. 053/912-3111, www .wexfordtourism.com, open 9:30 A.M.–1 P.M. and 2–5 P.M. Mon.–Fri. Nov.–Mar., 9 A.M.– 1 P.M. and 2–6 P.M. Mon.–Sat. Apr.–Oct.) is in an ugly new glass-and-concrete edifice right on the waterfront, within spitting distance of its former location on Crescent Quay opposite the Commodore Barry statue.

For a couple of quid, you can watch a 30-minute audiovisual on the town's medieval history at the **Westgate Heritage Centre** (8a Westgate, tel. 053/915-2900, open 10 A.M.–5:30 P.M. Mon.–Sat. Feb.–Dec.). The building incorporates a section of the original town wall.

Services

You'll find ATM and bureau de change facilities at the **AIB** and the **National Irish Bank** on North Main Street. There are **post office** branches on Anne and North Main Streets.

Take care of your other business at **Padraig's Launderette** (4 Mary St., tel. 053/912-4677, closed Sun.) and **McCauley's**

Pharmacy (4/6 Redmond Sq., tel. 053/912-2422, open daily).

You have a choice of hole-in-the-wall Internet cafés (though "café" isn't the word): **Tangiers Internet & Call Centre** (Trimmers Lane W., off N. Main St., tel. 053/914-6404, open 9:30 A.M.–10 P.M. Mon.–Thurs. and Sat., 9:30 A.M.–1 P.M. and 2:30–10 P.M. Fri., 2–7 P.M. Sun., €4/hour) or **Grann Communication** (5 Commercial Quay, no phone, open 10 A.M.–10 P.M. Mon.–Sat., 1–8 P.M. Sun., €3/hour).

Getting There
Wexford is 138 kilometers south of Dublin on the N11 and 59 kilometers east of Waterford on the N25. Buses and trains arrive at O'Hanrahan Station at Redmond Square on the quay (tel. 053/913-3114). Wexford is a stop on the **Irish Rail** Dublin–Rosslare Harbour line (3/day), and **Bus Éireann** offers direct service from Dublin (#2, 13/day Mon.–Sat., 10/day Sun.), Rosslare Harbour (#2, 13/day Mon.–Sat., 11/day Sun.), and Tralee via Cork and Waterford (#40, 4/day Mon.–Sat., 1/day Sun.).

Getting Around
Bike hire is available from **Haye's** (108 S. Main St., tel. 053/912-2462, €12/day) and the **Bike Shop** (9 Selskar St., tel. 053/912-2514, €12/day), both Raleigh dealers.

Call **T&J's** (tel. 053/912-8168 or 087/630-1360) or **Wexford Taxis** (tel. 053/915-3999) for a cab. There's also a taxi rank outside Dunnes Stores at the Bull Ring.

NORTH OF WEXFORD TOWN
◖ Curracloe Beach
No visit to Wexford is complete without a leisurely walk along the 19-kilometer Curracloe Beach, the longest strand in Ireland—and arguably the loveliest. Remember the Normandy invasion scene at the beginning of *Saving Private Ryan*? Filmed here!

How about an early-morning canter down the strand? Contact the **Curracloe House Equestrian Centre** (Curracloe, 13 km northeast of Wexford off the R742, tel. 053/913-7582).

On the way to Curracloe, devoted birdwatchers should stop by the **Wexford Wildfowl Reserve** (North Slob, 8 km northeast of Wexford Town on the Castlebridge road/R741, tel. 053/23129, open 9 A.M.–5 P.M. daily, free admission), which hosts as many as 10,000 wintering white-fronted geese from Greenland per year. Jointly administered by Dúchas and IWC BirdWatch Ireland, the visitors center offers a 15-minute audiovisual on the history of the Wexford Slobs.

Curracloe is eight kilometers north of Wexford on the R742. Upon entering the village, make a right immediately after the Curracloe Roadhouse and bear left to reach the strand. There's Bus Éireann service on Monday and Saturday only (#379, 1/day Mon., 2/day Sat.).

SOUTH OF WEXFORD TOWN
Johnstown Castle
Though the interior serves as Irish Environmental Protection Agency HQ, the grounds of the 19th-century neo-Gothic Johnstown Castle (6 km southwest of Wexford Town, signposted off the N25, open 9 A.M.–5:30 P.M. daily, pedestrian/car admission €2/5, free Oct.–Apr.) are open to the public: 20 hectares of gardens, woods, and pretty (artificial) lakes. There's also a sizable walled garden and conservatory, and the sunken garden is an ideal picnic spot. Fortunately, the grounds' popularity with young families doesn't detract from their tranquility in the slightest. Be on the lookout for peacocks!

The manor itself was built on the site of a medieval tower house, which was incorporated into a three-story castellated mansion in the 17th century. This manor, in turn, became a portion of the current structure through decades of construction from the 1820s onward. There's also the ruin of a medieval tower house, Rathlanon Castle. If the weather turns, you can head for the **Irish Agricultural Museum and Famine Exhibition** (tel. 053/917-1247, open 9 A.M.–5 P.M. Mon.–Fri. and 11 A.M.–5 P.M. Sun.

June–Aug., 9 A.M.–12:30 P.M. and 1:30–5 P.M. Mon.–Fri. and 2–5 P.M. weekends Apr.–May and Sept.–Oct., closed weekends Nov.–Mar., admission €6), which offers a collection of Irish country furniture, replicas of artisan workshops and farmhouse kitchens, and a historical analysis of the famine—all worthwhile, though not while the sun's shining!

There is no public transportation to Johnstown, but it's an easy bike ride from Wexford Town.

Rosslare

The golden strand at Rosslare, 15 kilometers south of Wexford Town, attracts droves of young families in the summertime. There are a few rather stodgy hotels and B&Bs within short walking distance of the beach, but frankly it makes more sense to do Rosslare as a day trip from Wexford Town (especially since decent seaside dining options are all but nonexistent), picking up provisions for a picnic lunch at the Tesco grocery store on the Crescent Quay before you go.

Rent a surfboard and wet suit from the **Rosslare Windsurfing Centre** (tel. 053/913-2101), open May–September. **Loisin Riding Centre** (Kilrane, 7 km south of Rosslare, tel. 053/913-3962 or 086/609-2809, liosincentre@oceanfree.net) offers beach treks along Rosslare Strand, and accommodations are provided.

Rosslare is 15 kilometers south of Wexford off the N25, but you could also take **Irish Rail** (tel. 053/913-3114, 3/day) from O'Hanrahan Station.

Rosslare Harbour

Doing the European tour? Then you might find yourself leaving for Cherbourg in France via the ferry from Rosslare Harbour. The town itself is unequivocally unpleasant, so most people stay in Wexford and take the train down in the morning—the food and nightlife are pretty sad, as are the local hotel standards. If you want to spend the night, there're a few nice B&Bs within one kilometer of the ferry port; an early breakfast option is standard. Try **Wayside House** (Ballygeary,

Kilrane, signposted off the N25, tel. 053/913-3475, www.waysideguesthouse.com, €29–33 pp, s €42–45, credit cards accepted) or **Dungara** (on the N25, tel. 053/913-3391, unastack@eircom.net, €30–33 pp, s €45, credit cards accepted).

Ferry operators include **Irish Ferries** (tel. 053/913-3158, www.irishferries.com), which sails to Cherbourg (3/week, 18-hour trip, car and driver €99, passenger €56) and Roscoff (3–6/week Apr.–Sept., 16–24-hour trip, similar fares) in France, as well as Pembroke in Wales (2/day, 4-hour trip, car and driver €89, passenger/pedestrian €25–27); **Stena Line** (tel. 053/931-3997, www.stenaline.ie) sails to Fishguard in Wales (6/day, 3.5-hour trip, car and driver €102–192, pedestrian/passenger €24).

Rosslare Harbour is 156 kilometers south of Dublin and 18 kilometers south of Wexford on the N11 to the N25. This is the last stop on the **Irish Rail** (tel. 053/913-3114) lines from Dublin (3/day, single fare €19) and Waterford (1/day), and it's only a half-hour trip from Wexford (on the Dublin line). Or get here via **Bus Éireann** (tel. 01/836-6111) from Dublin or Wexford (#2, 13/day Mon.–Sat., 10/day Sun.) or Tralee, Cork, or Waterford (#40, 2/day Mon.–Sat., 1/day Sun.).

KILMORE QUAY

The road is still lined with whitewashed thatched-roof cottages in the fishing village of Kilmore Quay (Cé na Cille Móire). There's not much to do here aside from taking a walk along the harbor and chowing down on über-fresh seafood, but it's enough to occupy you for one glorious afternoon. You can also hop a boat to the Saltee Islands, a must for birdwatchers. Ring **Eamonn Hayes** (tel. 053/912-9723 or 087/213-5308, www.kilmoreangling.com) or **Declan Bates** (tel. 053/912-9684) for departure info. For beach treks, contact the beginner-friendly **Wavecrest Riding School** (Ballyhealy House, Kilmore, tel. 053/913-5035, www.ballyhealyhouse.com), which also provides B&B.

The great thing about **Quay House** (on the R739 on the northern end of the village, tel.

053/29988, www.kilmorequay.net, €40–50 pp, credit cards accepted) is that it's large enough to provide that ideal degree of anonymity. The bedrooms are bright and airy, and the comfortable and well-appointed guests' sitting room is an ideal spot for planning your itinerary for the following day. The four en-suite rooms at **Mill Road Farm** (on the R739, tel. 053/912-9633, www.millroadfarm.com, €30 pp, s €40) have sea views. There's a hotel here too, **Hotel Saltees** (on the R739 north of the pier, tel. 053/912-9610, www.hotelsaltees.ie, €50–60 pp, s €60–80), but it's nothing special.

Even if you stay at the hotel, you're best off eating at **Kehoe's Pub and Parlour** (on the left-hand side of the R739 as you approach the harbor, tel. 053/29830, www.kehoes.com, food served noon–8:30 P.M. daily, mains €9–25), whose nautical theme is amusingly over-the-top: There are two mannequins in old-fashioned scuba-diving gear, one of which is suspended from the ceiling. It's a great old pub, with amiable bartenders, a lively local crowd, music Friday through Sunday, and a perfectly adequate vegetarian option. Save room for the blackberry crumble.

Kilmore Quay is 20 kilometers south of Wexford Town on the R739. **Bus Éireann** provides infrequent service from Wexford Town (#382, 2 buses on Wed. and Sat.).

THE HOOK HEAD PENINSULA

Known to Wexford folk as simply "the Hook" (www.thehook-wexford.com), this 10-kilometer-long, low-lying peninsula forms the eastern boundary of Waterford Harbour and affords the county's finest scenery by far. The downside of this laid-back, untouristy atmosphere and a string of tiny, tranquil seaside villages is a dearth of public transportation—the **Bus Éireann** Wexford–Waterford route (#370) passes through on Monday and Thursday only. You'll find the area's best accommodations in Arthurstown. There's an ATM a few miles away in Ramsgrange, but be on the safe side and withdraw what you'll need before leaving Wexford.

The way south to Hook Head passes the vast, spooky, privately owned Loftus Hall; legend has it that in 1765 the devil (in the form of a handsome young man, naturally) courted Anne Tottenham, a relative and guest of Baron Loftus, and she wasted away after glimpsing his cloven feet under the card table one night. Her ghost is said to haunt the manor to this day. On the east side of the peninsula is Bannow Bay, where the Normans, led by Strongbow, first put boot to ground in 1169.

The tiny village of Slade is of interest for its ruined tower house and scuba-diving companies; contact the **Hook Sub-Aqua Club** (tel. 051/388-302 or 087/286-0648, www.divewexford.org) or the **Wexford Diving Centre & Dive Charters** (based at Riverstown Farm, Murntown, tel. 053/913-9373).

Clonmines

On Bannow Bay are the ruins of a walled Norman village called Clonmines, a veritable "medieval ghost town." The remains, most of which date from the early 1400s, are extensive: a castellated town hall, several churches and residential tower houses, and pieces of the town and harbor walls. The town was abandoned in the 17th century when shifting sands blocked the port and erosion became a serious problem, though the Irish Parliament still allowed the ghost town two representatives up until the Act of Union.

Clonmines has never been excavated, and unfortunately, the ruins are on private land and are not open to the public. But they're visible from the road: Take the R733 west from Wellington Bridge, and after you pass Wallace's Hardware Store (a big green warehouse) on your left, you'll see a small cemetery and church ruin with a strange pyramidal tower. Pull over here and view Clonmines over the inlet.

◖ Tintern Abbey

Named after the Welsh abbey immortalized by Wordsworth, the Dúchas-run Tintern Abbey (Saltmills, 16 km south of New Ross off the R734, tel. 051/562-650, open 10 A.M.–6 P.M. daily May–Sept., 10 A.M.–5 P.M. Oct., admission €2.10) has a long and checkered history.

Founded by William Marshal (Strongbow's son-in-law) at the turn of the 13th century, it was the third-richest Cistercian abbey in Ireland at the time of Henry VIII's suppression in the late 1530s. Afterward, Tintern was given to an English soldier, Anthony Colclough ("COLE-klee"), who converted it into a castle. His ancestors—a colorful lot, by all accounts—occupied Tintern continuously into the 1960s. Most colorful of all was "Sir" Vesey Colclough, who locked his wife in the tower and had five mistresses on hand at a time in the mid- to late 18th century. The exhibition on the top floor of the tower house is hilariously cheesy, and excellent guided tours are available as well. The most remarkable feature of the abbey architecture are the corbel tables high on the exterior chancel walls—individualized grotesque heads that could've inspired some of the creatures in Jim Henson's *Labyrinth*. There are (often muddy) walking trails beyond the abbey, one of which leads past an old lime kiln to the Colclough family graveyard.

Tintern is 30 kilometers southwest of Wexford on the R733, and unfortunately bus service is too infrequent to be of use.

Fethard-on-Sea

Though Fethard (Fiodh Ard, "High Wood," "FET-erd") is the largest town on the peninsula, you'd hardly know it when driving down the main street. There's not much here besides a hotel, a cute little café, and a couple of pubs. For visitor info, stop by the seasonal **tourist office** (tel. 051/397-502, open 9:30 A.M.–5:30 P.M. Mon.–Fri. July–Aug.) signposted off Main Street.

On your way out to Hook Head, stop by the **Village Kitchen** (Main St., tel. 051/397-460, open 11 A.M.–8 P.M. Thurs.–Sun., daily in high season, mains €5–10), a cheerful café doing afternoon tea as well as hearty lunches—seafood, mostly, but the veggie lasagna is also recommended.

Across the street, family-run **Hotel Naomh Seosamh** (Main St., tel. 051/397-129 or 086/353-7395, abobrien@eircom.net, €35 pp) is your typical small-town hotel, but it offers

better value than many other guesthouses in the area. It's popular with Hook Head divers.

Fethard-on-Sea is 38 kilometers southwest of Wexford Town on the R733/R734.

◖ Hook Head Lighthouse

Take in Wexford's best view atop the Hook Head Lighthouse (tel. 051/397-055, open 9:30 A.M.–5:30 P.M. daily, admission €5.50), probably the only secular medieval building still serving its original function. It's also the oldest operational lighthouse in Ireland or Britain, and one of the oldest in the world.

Built of local limestone by Anglo-Norman adventurer William Marshal in 1240, it was originally manned by monks from nearby St. Dubhan's Abbey (who had been lighting beacons back in the 6th century), and it still stands 36.3 meters high. A 20-minute guided tour takes you up the lighthouse's 115 steps, where you can see the Saltee Islands to the east, the Blackstairs and Comeragh Mountains to the north, and County Waterford across the harbor. It's really windy up here, and exhilarating indeed.

The lighthouse is south of Churchtown, at the very end of the peninsula. There's a Friday-only bus service from Wexford, but as there's only one bus it's of no use to tourists—you need a car to get down here.

Duncannon

A surprisingly quiet seaside town, Duncannon (Dún Canann, "Fort of Conan") offers a long white strand and the 16th-century, star-shaped **Duncannon Fort** (tel. 051/389-454, open 10 A.M.–5:30 P.M. daily June–Sept., guided tours at 10:30 A.M., 12:30 P.M., 2 P.M., 3 P.M., and 4:30 P.M., admission €4). It also boasts the top restaurant on the Hook, **Squigl** (Quay Rd., tel. 051/389-700, open 7–10:30 P.M. Tues.–Sat. and noon–2:30 P.M. Sun. all year, 7–9:30 P.M. Sun. July–Aug., mains €12–20)—a bit on the trendy side, but the seafood is divine. Other dishes have a French-slash-Mediterranean twist, and the veggie options are ample. The best accommodation options are in Arthurstown, however—just 3.5 kilometers north on a local road.

© CAMILLE DEANGELIS

The Hook Head Lighthouse is most likely the oldest in Europe.

Arthurstown

There's not much going on in Arthurstown either, but it does have the Hook's best guesthouses. ⟨ **Marsh Mere Lodge** (on the R733 on the north side of Arthurstown, 1 km south of the ferry dock at Ballyhack, tel. 051/389-186 or 087/222-7303, www.marshmerelodge.com, €38 pp, s €50) is an absolute delight, filled with gorgeous antique furniture, artwork, books, stained glass, even a vintage hat collection flanking the hall mirror—and you might find a set of silver-backed brushes on your Victorian dressing-table. The upstairs sitting room offers a harbor view and a baby grand piano, and the bedrooms bear whimsical names ("Poor Poet" or "Passing Glances") instead of numbers. Best of all is the welcome: (loose-brewed) tea, delectable home-baked goods, and a friendly chat. Another four-star guesthouse is an elegant, ivy-covered Georgian, **Glendine Country House** (on the R733, tel. 051/389-258, www.glendinehouse.com, open Feb.–mid-Nov., €35–55 pp, s €55–75, 10 percent discount for two or more

nights, credit cards accepted), surrounded by 50 acres of peaceful pastures. In addition to six commodious rooms overlooking Waterford Harbour, there are two self-catering cottages each sleeping up to five (low/high season €300/550 per week). Though they don't do dinner, Mr. and Mrs. Crosbie will feed you soup and sandwiches in the afternoon. Both guesthouses offer consistently better breakfasts (and value in general) than the Georgian **Dunbrody Country House Hotel** (signposted off the R733 on the east end of Arthurstown, tel. 051/389-600, www.dunbrodyhouse.com, dinner and B&B €160–230 pp sharing). Some of the rooms are in need of maintenance and refurbishment and the food quality is strangely uneven—sometimes excellent, sometimes downright poor—so you have to wonder how much you can learn in the hotel cookery classes. At least the spa gets top marks.

Arthurstown is 17 kilometers north of Hook Head on a local road and 38 kilometers west of Wexford Town on the R733. There is no bus service.

Ramsgrange

Staying in Arthurstown, and prefer to eat someplace more relaxed than the hotel restaurant (or Squigl in Duncannon)? There's a refreshingly unpretentious pub-cum-restaurant, **The Hollow** (Ramsgrange, 2 km east of Arthurstown on the R733, tel. 051/389-230, food served 10:30 A.M.–9 P.M. daily, mains €7–23) in the nearby village of Ramsgrange. Aside from a few surprises like a scrummy fried halloumi salad, the menu is fairly standard, with steak and seafood predominating. It's also a nice little spot to relax with a pint, despite the soccer on the telly—with the cement floor and '70s-era wallpaper, you know you're in genuine small-town Ireland. Pass through the village on the Wexford-bound R733 and you'll see the pub less than a kilometer down on the right-hand side.

Need cash? There's an **ATM** at the Centra (open until 10 P.M.) on the Arthurstown end of the village.

Ballyhack

Heading west to Waterford? Save time, gas, and aggravation by taking the **Passage East Ferry** (tel. 051/382-480, www.passageferry.com, frequent departures 7 A.M.–10 P.M. Mon.–Sat. and 9:30 A.M.–10 P.M. Sun. Apr.–Sept., until 8 P.M. Oct.–Mar., single/return fare €7/10 per car) across Waterford Harbour. Overlooking the tiny ferry terminal is a relatively unremarkable 15th-century tower house, **Ballyhack Castle** (tel. 051/389-468, open 10 A.M.–6 P.M. daily mid-June–mid-Sept., free admission). Ballyhack is just one kilometer north of Arthurstown on the R733.

NORTH OF THE HOOK

A somewhat grim and mostly uninteresting town 34 kilometers west of Wexford and 20 kilometers north of Arthurstown, New Ross is perhaps best experienced through your rearview mirror. There's a noteworthy attraction just south of here, however: The J. F. K. memorial gardens will be of particular interest to American visitors. They're a nice afternoon stopover when traveling to or from the Hook Head Peninsula.

The John F. Kennedy Arboretum

Go for a leisurely stroll through the Dúchas-run John F. Kennedy Arboretum (10 km south of New Ross, signposted 1 km off the R733, tel. 051/388-171, open 10 A.M.–5 P.M. daily Oct.–Mar., 10 A.M.–8 P.M. daily May–Aug., 10 A.M.–6:30 P.M. daily Apr. and Sept., admission €2.90), opened in 1968 through the contributions of several Irish-Americans. The park comprises 623 acres skirting the 270-meter Slieve Coillte, and the 15-minute audiovisual tells you more than you need to know about the arboretum's design, botany, and animal life. The visitors center's "period" architecture seems downright quaint; check out the Wicklow granite fountain in the courtyard, which has J. F. K.'s most famous words—"Ask not what your country can do for you"—inscribed in Irish as well as English. Enterprising old chaps are on hand with their pony traps, and the grounds are a-buzz with local families on weekend afternoons; the children's playground even has a small hedge maze.

The arboretum is signposted on the R733, 10 kilometers north of Arthurstown and 10 kilometers south of New Ross.

Kilkenny

Sure it's landlocked, but Kilkenny's still the most charming county in Ireland's southeast. The River Nore turns its sleepy villages into postcard-perfect scenes: 12-arched bridges, young couples walking hand-in-hand down tidy waterside paths, and local anglers casting their lines, looking like they haven't a care in the world. The county has wealth of monastic sites, from the famous (Jerpoint) to the small and secluded (Kells, Kilfane, and Kilree)—not to mention the Gothic splendor of its capital city.

Since there isn't much in terms of budget accommodation elsewhere in the county, backpackers are best off basing themselves in the city and renting a bike to explore the surrounding small towns and sights. (You could also travel by bus, but the service is infrequent enough to pose a few logistical challenges.)

KILKENNY CITY

With its winding medieval streets, narrow lanes, and ever-sociable spirit, Kilkenny is an utter delight. Its castle is magnificent, the pubs and music unsurpassed. Like the Jimmy Stewart flick you watch again and again, this city only gets better with age.

You may find yourself wondering what the deal is with all these cats—the local sports teams, the Cat Laughs Comedy Festival, the sign above Kyteler's pub. It was said that the witch of Kilkenny, Alice Kyteler, used to turn herself into a cat. (For more on Dame Alice's exploits, see the sidebar *The Witch of Kilkenny*.)

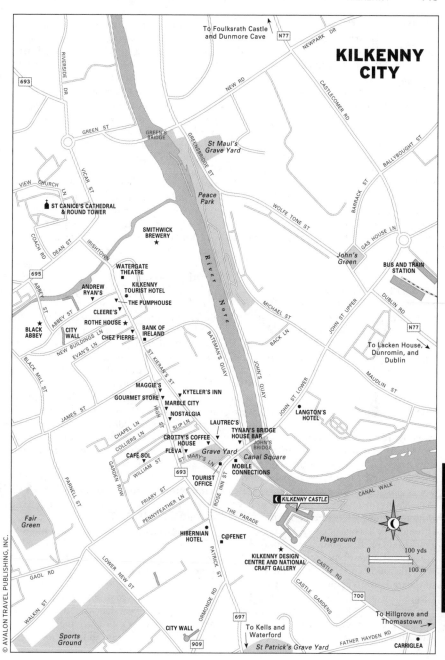

KILKENNY
CITY

To Foulksrath Castle
and Dunmore Cave
N77
NEWPARK DR

NEW RD
CASTLECOMER RD
BALLYBOUGHT ST

RIVERSIDE DR
693
GREEN ST
GREEN'S BRIDGE
GREENSBRIDGE ST
St Maul's Grave Yard

VIEW
CHURCH LN
VICAR ST
Peace Park
BARRACK ST
GAS HOUSE LN

ST CANICE'S CATHEDRAL & ROUND TOWER

COACH RD
DEAN ST
IRISHTOWN
SMITHWICK BREWERY
WOLFE TONE ST
John's Green

695
ABBEY ST
WATERGATE THEATRE
ANDREW RYAN'S
KILKENNY TOURIST HOTEL
THE PUMPHOUSE
River Nore
MICHAEL ST
JOHN ST UPPER
DUBLIN RD
BUS AND TRAIN STATION

BLACK ABBEY
CITY WALL
CLEERE'S
ROTHE HOUSE
CHEZ PIERRE
BANK OF IRELAND
BACK LN
N77
To Lacken House, Dunromin, and Dublin

BLACK MILL ST
NEW BUILDINGS LN
EVAN'S LN
ST KIERAN'S ST
BATEMAN'S QUAY
JOHN'S QUAY
JOHN ST LOWER
MAUDLIN ST

JAMES ST
MAGGIE'S
GOURMET STORE
KYTELER'S INN
MARBLE CITY
NOSTALGIA
LANGTON'S HOTEL

CHAPEL LN
COLLIERS LN
HIGH ST
SLIP LN
LAUTREC'S
TYNAN'S BRIDGE HOUSE BAR
JOHN'S BRIDGE

CAFÉ SOL
CROTTY'S COFFEE HOUSE
FLEVA
Grave Yard
Canal Square
CANAL WALK

GARDEN ROW
WILLIAM ST
ST MARY'S LN
MOBILE CONNECTIONS
693
TOURIST OFFICE

PARNELL ST
FRIARY ST
ROSE INN ST
KILKENNY CASTLE

Fair Green
PENNYFEATHER LN
THE PARADE
Playground

HIBERNIAN HOTEL
C@FENET
N
100 yds
100 m

GAOL RD
LOWER NEW ST
PATRICK ST
KILKENNY DESIGN CENTRE AND NATIONAL CRAFT GALLERY
CASTLE RD
CASTLE GARDENS
700
To Hillgrove and Thomastown

WALKIN ST
CITY WALL
909
697
ORMONDE RD
To Kells and Waterford
St Patrick's Grave Yard
FATHER HAYDEN RD
CARRIGLEA

Sports Ground

© AVALON TRAVEL PUBLISHING, INC.

THE SOUTHEAST

The 18th-century **Tholsel** on High Street, built from the black marble from which Kilkenny gets its "Marble City" moniker, stands on the site where Kyteler's loyal maid was burned at the stake in 1324.

The city is more a large town, easily walkable. As Irish streets are wont to do, the main thoroughfare changes names from Patrick to High to Parliament Street, and it's called Irishtown after that. Hang a left at the end of this main street and you'll come to St. Canice's Cathedral on a small hill. High and St. Kieran's Streets form an isosceles triangle with Rose Inn Street at the base; head east from Rose Inn and you'll cross the bridge onto John Street. Off Rose Inn is the Parade, where you'll find Kilkenny Castle and the city's prime boutique galleries in the old stables across the street.

◖ Kilkenny Castle

Its grand hallways may often be gorged with tour groups, but you can't leave this city without visiting Kilkenny Castle (tel. 056/772-1450, open 10:30 A.M.–5 P.M. daily Apr.–May, 9:30 A.M.–7 P.M. daily June–Aug., 10 A.M.–6:30 P.M. daily Sept., 10:30 A.M.– 12:45 P.M. and 2–5 P.M. daily Oct.–Mar., admission €5.30). You won't find text-laden interpretive panels or artifacts under glass in this castle; the Office of Public Works has carefully restored its principal rooms to their full 1830s grandeur, though unfortunately only 5 percent of the furniture is original to the house. The gallery and decorated rooms are accessible by guided tour only, which lasts about 50 minutes. There's also a 12-minute audiovisual you don't want to doze through—it has one or two scandalous anecdotes to share. Tuck your camera away before you enter the vestibule; otherwise, the staff will ask you to surrender it for the duration of the tour. Tours commence every half hour (beginning one-half hour after opening), but you may have to buy your ticket and wander the grounds for a bit first (there's more lawn than garden, though the rose garden is laid out in the shape of a Celtic cross, with a fountain at the center; there's also a shady, secluded path following the Nore).

From the 1390s to 1935 Kilkenny Castle was the principal seat of the Butler family. Their ancestor, James Butler, was a true-blue royalist who gained a nifty title—first Duke of Ormonde—upon the restoration of Charles II to the English throne in 1660. It was he who reimagined this early-13th-century Anglo-Norman fortress as a French chateau, having spent a decade in exile there in the company of the king. Long before this, though, the site had been occupied by an early Norman motte-and-bailey erected by the infamous Strongbow in 1172. Because Kilkenny was the second-most important city in 13th- and 14th-century Ireland, the Irish Parliament often convened at the castle, and in 1366 the Statutes of Kilkenny, presage of apartheid, were written there. Fast-forward to 1935: The combination of genteel poverty and the new Irish Free State encouraged the Butler family to quit their ancestral home for good. Thirty years of neglect ensued, and in 1967 Arthur Butler bequeathed the castle to the state for the nominal sum of £50.

The skylit Long Gallery, the last room on the tour, has tapestries on one wall, a poignant collection of Butler family portraits on the other (some clearly idealized, some clearly *not*), and wooden ceiling beams painted with colorful and intricate motifs inspired by the Book of Kells. Over the centuries the Butlers amassed a phenomenal international art collection, including works by Coreggio, Tintoretto, Murillo, Van Dyck, and it's a shame the collection is long since dispersed (at the auction in 1935). The Butler Art Gallery (free admission) in the old servants' quarters is a fitting legacy, though like all contemporary art, perhaps, the exhibitions here won't appeal to everyone.

In the courtyard, note the wonderfully vivid soldiers' heads (carved in stone, that is) flanking the Parade Tower doorways, as well as the balconies on the castle's original northern wall—all of which were added to soften the severity of the facade.

THE WITCH OF KILKENNY

Easily the most colorful character in the city's history, Dame Alice Kyteler was a businesswoman in the early 14th century who gained more money and power with each husband she acquired. There were four in all, and since each died under mysterious circumstances it was inevitable that Dame Alice should be accused of witchcraft. (Why didn't they just charge her with poisoning them? One suspects her wealth and cleverness were perhaps her greater crimes.) Though she was formally charged in 1324, her influential friends (her brothers-in-law, mostly) had the offending bishop, Richard de Ledrede, imprisoned for 17 days. The trial commenced upon his release, however, and Dame Alice and her servant girl, Petronella (or Petronilla), were sentenced to burn at the stake. Dame Alice fled the country the night before the execution, leaving loyal Petronella to her fiery fate on November 3, 1324. Alice Kyteler's firstborn son, William Outlawe, agreed to give alms to the poor and reroof the choir stalls at St. Canice's Cathedral to avoid the gallows. Dame Alice was never seen or heard of again.

If you're of a literary bent, pick up a copy of Emma Donoghue's fantastic book of "true fictions," *The Woman Who Gave Birth to Rabbits;* the final story in the collection, "Looking for Petronilla," is told from Alice Kyteler's point of view.

Other Sights

Kilkenny owes its medieval flavor to 13th-century, Anglican **St. Canice's Cathedral** (the Close, on the north end of town off St. Canice's Place/Dean St., tel. 056/776-4971, www.stcanicescathedral.ie, open 9 A.M.–6 P.M. Mon.–Sat. and 2–6 P.M. Sun. June–Aug., 10 A.M.–1 P.M. and 2–5 P.M. Mon.–Sat. and 2–5 P.M. Sun. Apr.–May and Sept., until 4 P.M. Oct.–Mar., tower/church/combo admission €2/3/4), "Canice" being the Irish version

of Kenneth. You'll find brilliant stained glass, tomb effigies and wall memorials, intricate choir-stall carvings—all the usual features of a Gothic cathedral. If you've been to others (like Dublin's Christ Church), a visit to St. Canice's shouldn't be a top priority. You can see five counties from the top of the 9th-century round tower, though the climb is not for the faint-hearted and the view is disappointingly industrial. Save a euro: A €5 combo ticket is available for St. Canice's plus Rothe House.

There are plenty more medieval churches in this town, one of which is the Dominican **Black Abbey** (Abbey St., off Parliament St., tel. 056/772-1279, free admission), now a Catholic church. Aside from an ugly altar window dating from its most recent renovation in 1976, the abbey retains much of its Gothic flavor. Built in the 13th century, it was used as a courthouse after Henry VIII's dissolution of the monasteries, laid to ruin by Cromwell's troops in 1650, and rebuilt in the 1860s.

Established in 1710, the **Smithwick Brewery** (Parliament St., tel. 056/772-1014, free admission) is still brewing some of the country's best ale, though it's now owned by Guinness. (Tip: The W is silent in "Smithwick's.") The ruin of **St. Francis' Abbey** behind the brewery owes its present condition to—you guessed it!—Oliver Cromwell. The Franciscans were renowned brewers in their day; it's no coincidence that Edmund Smithwick set up shop here! Tours take place at 3 P.M. weekdays May to September, but be sure to ring ahead.

If you have time left over, spend an hour at the Tudor-era **Rothe House** (Parliament St., tel. 056/772-2893, www.rothehouse.com, open 10:30 A.M.–5 P.M. Mon.–Sat. and 3–5 P.M. Sun. Apr.–Oct., 1–5 P.M. Mon.–Sat. and 3–5 P.M. Sun. Nov.–Mar., admission €3), the former home of a wealthy Kilkenny merchant who later lost everything in 1690 after backing James II during the Williamite war. Now under the auspices of the Kilkenny Archaeological Society, it houses a modest collection of Celtic and Viking artifacts and 16th-century costumes. A 15-minute audiovisual is included in the admission price.

THE SOUTHEAST

Jonathan Swift, philosopher George Berkeley, and dramatist George Farquhar all attended Kilkenny College on John Street, which is now the county hall.

Tours

Since there's a lot to see here, you might want to go on an hour-long walking tour so you don't miss anything. **Pat Tynan** (tel. 087/265-1745, tynantours@eircom.net) is the Marble City's undisputed #1 expert—and he's entertaining, too; tours depart from the tourist office (6/day daily Mar.–Oct., 4/day Sun., 3/day Tues.–Sat. Nov.–Feb., €6).

Entertainment

Kilkenny has the best live music scene in the east. The silver-throated ladies at **Maggie's** (60 High St., tel. 056/776-1017) Monday–Thursday night trad sessions sing the most hauntingly beautiful ballads you'll hear anywhere. Or if you can elbow your way past the chain-smoking young ne'er-do-wells loitering outside, **Andrew Ryan's** (3 Friary St., tel. 056/776-2281) also does trad sessions worth coming out for on Thursday and Friday nights. The folks at **Cleere's** (28 Parliament St., tel. 056/776-2573, www.kilkennycomedyclub.com or www.cleeres.com) claim their Sunday night trad session is the longest running in the city—and it's also the best venue for comedy shows, open mikes, blues, and rock.

Tired of trad? Popular with a young crowd for its pool table, dartboard, and cheap sandwiches, **The Pumphouse** (26 Parliament St., tel. 056/776-3924) has live blues, rock, and folk acts on Sunday nights from 9:30.

Or for a nice quiet pint in a quaint Victorian pub, gaslights and all, step inside the sympathetically renovated **Tynan's Bridge House Bar** (2 Horseleap Slip, at St. John's Bridge, tel. 056/772-1921). And it may be touristy, but you've just got to have a pint at **Kyteler's** (27 St. Kieran's St., tel. 056/772-1064); the home of the city's infamous witch hasn't changed all that much since the day she skipped town on a flying broomstick.

Whatever dramatic or musical act's touring

FESTIVALS AND EVENTS IN KILKENNY CITY

Sponsored by Smithwicks, the **Cat Laughs Comedy Festival** (Parliament St., tel. 056/776-3837, www.thecatlaughs.com) in late May/early June is the best known on the city's calendar, attracting some of the funniest performers on the planet. Another great festival is the well-established **Kilkenny Arts Festival** (9-10 Abbey Business Centre, Abbey St., tel. 056/775-2175, www.kilkennyarts.ie) in mid-August, which offers a marvelous program of jazz and classical concerts, film screenings, art exhibitions, book readings, and street theater. There's also the **Carlsberg Kilkenny Rhythm and Roots Weekend** (29 Parliament St., tel. 056/779-0057, rhythmandroots@eircom.net), a music festival focusing primarily on bluegrass and American country/western. Rhythm and Roots usually takes place the last weekend in April or first weekend in May.

Book your room well in advance even if you aren't planning to attend any events, as everyone and their uncle descends upon this little city for these three big festivals (the arts festival alone draws as many as 70,000 out-of-towners). For more info, check out **KilkennyCity.net** (www.kilkennycity.net).

---

the country is sure to play at the **Watergate Theatre** (Parliament St., tel. 056/776-1674, www.watergatekilkenny.com, tickets €12–20). The Watergate is one of the primary venues for the city's top two festivals—the Cat Laughs Comedy Festival in late May/early June and the Kilkenny Arts Festival in August.

Shopping

Kilkenny has a reputation for fine shopping thanks primarily to the flagship **Kilkenny Design Centre** (Castle Yard, tel. 056/772-2118, www.kilkennydesign.com), which is still selling the cutting edge of modern Irish design, be it jewelry, fashion, homewares, or cuisine. This upmarket store-cum-café is housed in the erstwhile stables of the castle directly across the street, where you'll also find the **National Craft Gallery** (Castle Yard, tel. 056/776-1804, www.ccoi.ie), which showcases the work of eminent Irish textile artists, woodturners, potters, silversmiths, and others.

Rightly described by its sweet-tempered shopkeeper as "a bit of a wonderland," **Butterslip** (Butterslip Ln., tel. 056/770-2502, www.butterslip.com) is a girlie paradise of French soaps and perfume, chic jewelry and handbags, and ultra-feminine garb. Ladies, don't miss this one.

Pick up paperbacks, OS maps, and maybe even a bit of lunch at the **Kilkenny Book Centre** (10 High St., tel. 056/776-2117), which has an upstairs café.

Sports and Recreation

Go for a stroll through the 50-acre **Kilkenny Castle gardens,** free of charge and open until 8:30 P.M. in the spring and summer. Or rent a bike to explore all the peaceful villages along the River Nore. Looking for something a bit more unusual? Go for a round of clay pigeon-shooting, archery, or quad-biking at the **Countryside Leisure Activity Centre** (Bonnettsrath, 2 km northeast of the city, signposted off the N77, tel. 056/776-1791).

Golfers and horse riders are catered to locally as well, at the **Kilkenny Golf Club** (2 km north of the city on the N77, tel. 056/776-5400, www.kilkennygolfclub.com) and the **Top Flight Equestrian Centre** (Warrington, 5 km south of the city, signposted off the R700/Bennettsbridge road, tel. 056/772-2682, www.topflightkilkenny.com).

Accommodations

You'll sleep well here no matter your budget. The **Kilkenny Tourist Hostel** (35 Parliament St., tel. 056/776-3541, kilkennyhostel@eircom.net, dorms €16–17, private rooms €20–21 pp) is a great spot—central, friendly, laid-back, bohemian yet clean.

But not all B&Bs are created equal, especially in the city center; some are overpriced, run-down, or (often) both. Two safe bets within a five-minute walk of the center are **Carriglea** (Archers Ave., Castle Rd., tel. 056/776-1629, www.iol.ie/~archers, open Feb.–Nov., €30–35 pp sharing), with fabulous pancake breakfasts, and **Dunromin** (Dublin Rd., just east of the train station, tel. 056/776-1387, www.dunrominkilkenny.com, open Apr.–Nov., €30–36 pp sharing, credit cards accepted), with Internet access and the deluxe full Irish breakfast. Both have homey atmospheres, comfy beds, and very hospitable owners.

It's not as convenient, but then again, the ivy-clad **Hillgrove** (2 km southeast of town on the R700/Bennettsbridge road, tel. 056/775-1453, http://homepage.eircom.net/~hillgrove, open Feb.–mid-Dec., €33–35 pp, s €40–45) is a lot quieter too. It's also an excellent value—comfortable beds with electric blankets, rooms with garden views, and a fantastic breakfast menu featuring French toast, porridge with liqueur, and other delights.

A Victorian boutique hotel and inventive gourmet restaurant, **Lacken House** (Dublin Rd., 500 m east of the train station, tel. 056/776-1085, www.lackenhouse.ie, open Apr.–Oct., €75 pp, s €100) has all the period flair and sumptuous furnishings, plus room service and in-room massage treatments. Be sure to ask for a dinner-and-B&B package deal, a great value. Two of Kilkenny's best hotels are also the most central: **Langton's** (69 John St., tel. 056/776-5133, www.langtons.ie, weekday/weekend €65/100 pp, s €65/125) and the ultra-classy Victorian **Hibernian** (1 Ormonde St., tel. 056/777-1888, www.kilkennyhibernianhotel.com, €65–95 pp sharing, suites €95–130 pp sharing). With its nightclub and modern bars, Langton's attracts a younger clientele (though one of the bars hosts trad sessions most nights of the week), and the Hibernian has a quieter, more reserved ambience. Both offer good food and top-notch service at every turn.

Food

Kilkenny has loads of quality cafés and restaurants, some of which may even send you over the moon. For scrummy (and very reasonably priced) sandwiches you can take on a long cycle, stop by the tiny **Gourmet Store** (56 High St., tel. 056/777-1727, open 9 A.M.–6 P.M. Mon.–Sat., lunches under €6). **Crotty's Coffee House** (St. Kieran's St., tel. 056/776-4877, open 9 A.M.–5:30 P.M. Mon.–Sat., mains under €9) is a favorite with the locals, owing to homebaked apple pie and plentiful outdoor seating. Another option for prime people-watching out-of-doors (not to mention pure kitsch) is **Nostalgia,** also known as **M.L. Dore** (entrances at 65 High St. and St. Kieran's St., tel. 056/776-3374, open 8 A.M.–9 P.M. Mon.–Sat., 9 A.M.–7 P.M. Sun., mains €6–12).

Kyteler's (27 St. Kieran's St., tel. 056/772-1064, food served noon–9 P.M. daily, mains €9–23) may seem like the obvious choice for pub grub—and it's very good indeed—but for something a bit less pricey, check out **Marble City** (entrances at 66 High St. and St. Kieran's St., tel. 056/776-1143, food served noon–10 P.M. daily, mains €8–14) just across the way. Unsurprisingly, groups of local students hog the outdoor tables at this one. The **Hibernia Hotel** (1 Ormonde St., tel. 056/777-1888, food served noon–8 P.M. Sun.–Thurs. and noon–5 P.M. Fri.–Sat., bar meals €10–15) has an utterly delectable array of desserts to accompany your afternoon tea—spiced ginger pudding, anyone?

Refreshingly unpretentious and very reasonably priced, **(Chez Pierre** (17 Parliament St., tel. 056/776-4655, open 10 A.M.–4 P.M. Mon.–Sat. for lunch and tea, 6:30 P.M.–late Thurs.–Sat., lunch €8–10, dinner mains €14–18) will more than satisfy your craving for simple, absolutely delicious French eats (and coffee). Plus, the owners let you know how much they appreciate your business. Another romantic spot that won't break the bank—if you order one of the gourmet pizzas, anyway—is **Lautrec's** (9 St. Kieran's St., tel. 056/776-2720, open 6–10 P.M. daily, until 11 P.M. Fri.–Sat., mains €8–25, €24 3-course early bird special 5–7 P.M.).

Kilkenny's top Italian restaurant, Rinuccini's on the Parade, consistently receives high marks, but it's also quite pretentious and bor-

derline overpriced. Though not Italian, two excellent alternatives are Café del Sol and Fléva. **Café Sol** (William St., tel. 056/776-4987, www.cafesolkilkenny.com, open 11:30 A.M.–10 P.M. Mon.–Sat., noon–9 P.M. Sun., lunch mains €7–15, dinners €16–29) is a rather small, bustling spot with all the sunny Mediterranean decor you'd expect with such a name. **(Fléva** (84 High St., tel. 056/777-0021, open 12:30–2:30 P.M. and 5:30–10:30 P.M. Mon.–Sat., 12:30–10:30 P.M. Sun., lunch mains €9–15, dinners €17–25, 2/3-course early bird special €18/22 Sun.–Fri., 3-course Sun. lunch €22) is a bright and airy upstairs eatery with a bizarre mix of classy '40s jazz and cheesy Italian pop on the stereo. These two eateries are comparable in terms of menu and price, but the service is better at Fléva—and the larger space means no one's bumping your shoulder as while passing your table.

It may be one of Kilkenny's priciest restaurants, but at **Lacken House** (Dublin Rd., 500 m east of the train station, tel. 056/776-1085, www.lackenhouse.ie, open 6–9:30 P.M. Tues.–Sat., Sun. on bank holidays, €35 4-course early bird special 6–7:30 P.M. Tues.–Fri., 5-course dinner €59) you get what you pay for: mostly organic fruit and produce, local meats and farmhouse cheeses, a separate vegetarian menu, an excellent wine list, and a "House house platter" that lets you sample a bit of everything. Gourmands will want to stay in the adjoining guesthouse.

Information
The **tourist office** is housed in the city's 16th-century poorhouse (Shee Alms House, Rose Inn St., tel. 056/775-1500, www.kilkennytourism.ie, open 9 A.M.–5 P.M. Mon.–Sat. Nov.–Mar., 9 A.M.–6 P.M. Mon.–Sat. Apr.–Oct., 11 A.M.–1 P.M. and 2–5 P.M. Sun. May–Sept., open until 7 P.M. July–Aug.).

For local news and events, pick up a copy of the *Kilkenny Advertiser* (www.kilkennyadvertiser.ie) in any bookstore, newsstand, or café.

Services
There are several banks with ATMs and bureaux de change at the Parade and High Street

intersection, and at the **Bank of Ireland** on Parliament Street. The **post office** is at 73 High Street.

If the owner of your B&B doesn't provide laundry service, ring **Drycleanit.com** (tel. 056/779-0058 or freephone tel. 1800/201-069, www.drycleanit.com), who pick up and deliver your laundry and dry cleaning (there's no actual shop). **O'Connell's Pharmacy** (tel. 056/772-1033) has two branches (4 Rose Inn St. and 89 High St.).

Kilkenny needs a nice Internet café. Until then, you can use one of the speedy terminals at **Mobile Connections** (10 Rose Inn St., tel. 056/772-3000, open 10 A.M.–10 P.M. Mon.–Sat. and 2–8 P.M. Sun., €0.08/minute) or **C@fenet** (4 Lower Patrick St., tel. 056/777-0051, opening hours vary, €2.90/hour).

Getting There

Kilkenny City is 123 kilometers southwest of Dublin (on the N9) and 48 kilometers due north of Waterford (on the N10, picking up the N9 in Knocktopher). Buses and trains pull into MacDonagh Station (on the Dublin road, tel. 056/772-2024), just under half a kilometer east of the city center, over the bridge. **Bus Éireann** passes through on the Dublin–Cork (#7, 9/day Mon.–Sat., 7/day Sun.) and Waterford–Athlone (#73, 2/day Mon.–Sat., 1/day Sun.) routes; from Athlone you can change buses for Galway and other points north. **Irish Rail** stops here on the Dublin–Waterford line (4–5 trains/day, single/return fare €22/27).

Getting Around

Driving in Kilkenny can be a real pain in the you-know-what. Free parking is nearly impossible to come by, though you can find some beside the public library on John's Quay (on the east bank of the River Nore). There's also free parking along Ormonde Road, a five-minute walk from the town center.

For bike rental, stop by **Kilkenny Cycles** (Lower Michael St., tel. 056/776-4374, €14/day) or **J.J. Wall** (88 Maudlin St., tel. 056/772-1236, €14/day).

The taxi rank is at the Patrick Street car park beside the castle. Or phone **Kilkenny Cabs** (tel. 056/775-2000).

NORTH OF KILKENNY CITY

Bus service to Foulksrath Castle and Dunmore Cave is available through **Buggy's Coaches** (tel. 056/444-1264, buggy@indigo.ie, 4 buses/day Mon.–Sat., return fare €5), which departs from the Parade in the city center (just up from Rose Inn St.).

Foulksrath Castle

Have a car, but still trying to scrimp—or just thrilled at the thought of staying in a castle without squandering your inheritance? Foulksrath Castle (Jenkinstown, signposted 12 km north of Kilkenny off the N77, tel. 056/776-7674, 10 A.M.–5 P.M. lock-out, dorms €13.50, sheet rental €2) is the oldest hostel in the country in both respects: A 15th-century tower house, it was opened by An Óige in 1938. It goes without saying that the facilities here are quite rustic—the bathrooms are attached to the original structure in an unsightly building more suitable to a construction site—but the grounds and common areas are wonderfully atmospheric, and the vertigo subsides after a few times up and down that incredibly narrow winding staircase. The rooms are actually quite toasty, though the barnyard animals might wake you come daybreak. The 11 P.M. curfew is a mite annoying, but then again, those wanting to hit the pubs won't be spending the night here anyway. It's possible to stay at Foulksrath even if you aren't driving; ring the hostel for shuttle bus info.

Dunmore

The Irish words for Dunmore Cave (Ballyfoyle, 10 km north of Kilkenny, signposted off the N78, tel. 056/776-7726) are Dearc Fearna—"Cave of the Alders"—a poetic name for one of Ireland's darkest places. Hours vary seasonally (9:30 A.M.–5 P.M. daily mid-Mar.–mid-June and mid-Sept.–Oct., 9:30 A.M.–6:30 P.M. daily mid-June–mid-Sept., 10 A.M.–5 P.M. weekends the rest of year, admission €2.90).

THE SOUTHEAST

Dark things came to pass here, too. Local monastic records tell of a devastating Viking massacre at a nearby fort in the year 928, and when the barbarians discovered refugees in Dunmore Cave, they smoked them out, carried the men off as slaves, trapped their families in the cave, and left them to suffocate. Excavations in the 1970s supported this horrible story, as the four dozen skeletons found here were nearly all those of women and children.

History aside, the cave is interesting in its own right; the centerpiece is Europe's largest freestanding stalagmite. Note that you can only visit the caves on a guided tour, and unfortunately you aren't allowed to take any pictures.

SOUTH OF KILKENNY CITY
Bennettsbridge

It's got a reputation as a shopping mecca, but there are just a couple of big-name pottery studios in quiet Bennettsbridge (Droichead Bineád): **Nicholas Mosse Pottery** (on the far side of the bridge, signposted, tel. 056/972-7105, www.nicholasmosse.com) and **Stoneware Jackson** (2 km north of town on the R700, tel. 056/972-7175, www.stonewarejackson.com). Both are open Monday to Saturday all year, and Nicholas Mosse opens on Sunday afternoons in July and August as well; there's a tearoom and do-it-yourself studio, too. Souvenir-hunters can make this a nice day trip out of Kilkenny, but there's not much of interest otherwise.

Bennettsbridge is 8.5 kilometers south of Kilkenny on the R700.

Kilfane

An early 14th-century church ruin outside the village of Kilfane (Cill Pháin, "Church of Pan," signposted 600 m off the N9) contains a truly stunning knight's effigy known as the **Cantwell Fada,** or "Long Cantwell"—most likely Thomas de Cantwell, the Welsh adventurer turned Lord of Kilfane. Complete with chain mail, sword, shield, and coat of arms, Tom's tall, skinny effigy is attached to the wall, unusually enough; the church has a castellated Norman tower as well.

the Cantwell Fada, a life-size effigy of Thomas de Cantwell

© CAMILLE DEANGELIS

One kilometer south is the **Kilfane Glen & Waterfall** (signposted off the N9, tel. 056/792-4558, open 11 A.M.–6 P.M. daily July–Aug., 2–6 P.M. Sun. Apr.–June and Sept., admission €6), with a 15-acre garden dating to the late 18th century and several shady walking trails.

Kilfane is three kilometers north of Thomastown on the N9, and you can request a stop on the Bus Éireann Waterford–Dublin route (#4, 10/day Mon.–Sat., 7/day Sun.).

Thomastown

On the main N9 road but otherwise quiet as can be, Thomastown (named for Thomas de Cantwell) is a pleasant market town full of hardware stores and farm suppliers. This is the kind of place where a truckload of pigs (their rear ends wiggling through the side-slats) could back up traffic for several minutes as the driver negotiates a sharp bend in the narrow street. You'll pass through Thomastown on your way to the magnificent Jerpoint Abbey just south of town.

Though there are a few nice B&Bs in the area, the lack of cafés and restaurants in town pretty much necessitates a trip into Kilkenny City for a nice dinner (or The Motte in Inistioge, which is excellent—and a lot closer). For the romantic Georgian farmhouse experience, look no further than **Ballyduff House** (5 km south of town off the R700, tel. 056/775-8488, €45 pp, s €55)—classy antiques, fireplaces (nonworking, but they add to the atmosphere), and commodious bedrooms and bathtubs. The house is a bit drafty (aren't they all?), but you've got an electric heating pad on that big comfy bed. Or try **Abbey House** (on the N9, 2.5 km south of town, tel. 056/772-4166, www.abbeyhousejerpoint.com, €45–80 pp, credit cards accepted), directly across the road from Jerpoint. Built in 1750, the grounds (with well-kept gardens and a small river) are delightful, and you'll receive an old-fashioned welcome of tea and scones.

Thomastown is 18 kilometers south of Kilkenny on the R700 and is on the main Dublin–Waterford road (N9). **Bus Éireann** passes through on the Athlone–Kilkenny–Waterford route (#73, 2/day Mon.–Sat., 1/day Sun.), as well as the Dublin–Waterford route (#4, 10/day Mon.–Sat., 7/day Sun.). The bus can drop you off at Jerpoint.

◖ Jerpoint Abbey

Established by the Cistercian order in the late 12th century, Jerpoint Abbey (on the N9, 2.5 km southwest of Thomastown, tel. 056/24623, open 10 A.M.–5 P.M. daily Mar.–May and mid-Sept.–Oct., 9:30 A.M.–6 P.M. daily June–mid-Sept., 10 A.M.–4 P.M. daily Nov., admission €2.90) contains some of Ireland's most exquisite tomb and altar carvings in its Romanesque church. There are more effigies to be found along the early 15th-century cloister, including those of St. Christopher and various knights (or mercenaries). You can climb upstairs to the old dormitory to observe the cloister and its trim green lawn from above.

The visitors center has on display an early 16th-century double tomb effigy (of a harper and his wife) as well as a few fragments of a high cross from Kilkieran. Unfortunately, you aren't likely to get the 45-minute guided tour unless you tag along with a larger group. If you have time to see only one abbey ruin in the southeast, let it be Jerpoint.

Inistioge

Known as one the country's most charming riverside villages, Inistioge (Inis Tíog, "in-ish-TEEG") has hosted several film crews over the years, most famously for *Circle of Friends*. It's as quiet and timeless as it looks in the movie, with just a few pubs around a small central green and an Anglican church, St. Mary's, with a small clock tower dressed in ivy. Inistioge is also on the 102-kilometer **South Leinster Way,** but those not so athletically inclined can go for a walk through the nearby **Woodstock Gardens** (1 km south of the village off the R700, signposted, tel. 056/775-8797, www.woodstock.ie, open 9 A.M.–8 P.M. daily May–Sept., 10 A.M.–4:30 P.M. daily Oct.–Apr., €3.50 parking fee)—once the demesne of a big house (burnt during the Civil War in 1922), now a state park in the lee of 520-meter Brandon Hill, with shady walking trails and picnic areas.

After your ramble, stop by the predictably quaint **Old Schoolhouse River Café** (opposite the riverside picnic green by the bridge, no phone, opening times vary, generally 11 A.M.–5 P.M. in summer, lunches €4–7) for tea and apple pie. (The outdoor seating would be even more pleasant were the main road not separating the café from the picnic green.)

Sure, the village is cute and all, but half your reason for coming to Inistioge is to dine at **The Motte** (on the R700 just north of the village, tel. 056/775-8655, open 7 P.M.–late Thurs.–Sat., open Wed. night starting March 17, 2/3-course menu €32/37, reservations essential). The cozy-cottage exterior belies a somewhat minimalist (though small and firelit) dining room, and while the modern Irish fare is top-notch, it's the we-close-only-when-you're-ready-to-leave attitude that keeps people coming back.

The dearth of accommodations in and around Inistioge is quite surprising given its

THE SOUTHEAST

© CAMILLE DEANGELIS

picturesque St. Mary's Church in the riverside village of Inistioge

enduring popularity with film producers. Your only option in town is upstairs at the **Woodstock Arms** (on the square, tel. 056/775-8440, €33 pp, s €40), which offers tidy (if small and spartan) en-suite rooms overlooking the square. The Woodstock Arms is also your best bet for dinner if The Motte is closed, and the front beer garden is the happeningest spot in town on sunny evenings.

Outside the village is the wonderfully atmospheric, slightly quirky **Cullintra House** (The Rower, 7 km southeast of Inistioge, signposted off the R700, tel. 051/423-614, http://indigo.ie/~cullhse, €30–45 pp, s €55–65, 5-course dinner €35), a 250-year-old farmhouse with 230 acres of gardens and walking trails. If you're looking for a romantic getaway, you'll find no better place, what with the tranquil, verdant setting, candlelit dinners, and rooms authentically furnished with big brass beds (two in a converted barn with A-frame ceiling

and exposed wood beams). A few catches to note: There's a two-night minimum stay, dinner is compulsory (it's excellent though, and you probably wouldn't prefer to eat elsewhere anyway), and the owner has a very specific system for bookings: You email her with your phone number and she rings you back.

Inistioge is 26 kilometers southeast of Kilkenny on the R700, and Bus Éireann service is too infrequent to be of use (one bus, Thursday only).

Kells

There's not much of architectural interest in the sprawling ruin of the Augustinian **Kells Priory** (600 m north of Kells village on the R697, always accessible, free admission), yet this place is majestic all the same. Seven towers punctuate a fortified wall featuring gates complete with murder holes, inside the high walls a vast lawn. Daisies and buttercups dapple the unmown grass. Most of what you see dates to the 15th century, though the oldest buildings are from the late 12th.

There are picnic tables just outside the gate, beside the car park, or you might rather take your lunch inside among the ruins. Kells is 13 kilometers south of Kilkenny off the N10 (the signposted turnoff at Stoneyford will take you west down a local road), and there is no public transportation.

Kilree

In an out-of-the-way spot in a small glen, **Kilree Church** features a roofless 28-meter round tower and a 9th-century high cross in the field beyond, said to mark the grave of a pagan chieftain. Hop the stone wall for a closer look at its carvings—Jacob and the angel, Daniel in the lions' den—and you'll soon have plenty of bovine company. For those interested in monastic ruins, tranquil Kilree is definitely worth the detour.

Kilree is two kilometers south of Kells, signposted off the R697.

CORK

Ireland's largest county, Cork (Corcaigh, "Marshy Place") has figured crucially in many of the nation's darkest chapters, particularly in the armed struggle for independence and subsequent Civil War of 1922–1923.

The postcard-perfect coastal scenery of West Cork's three peninsulas—Beara, Sheep's Head, and Mizen Head, from west to east—is the county's primary draw, though you'll find all three refreshingly untouristy in comparison to the Dingle and Iveragh Peninsulas of County Kerry ("in comparison" being the operative phrase, though, especially on the Beara). Outside of the infamous Blarney Castle, the upscale harbor town of Kinsale is the most popular destination of all. West Cork is a haven for artists, and you'll find galleries full of intriguing contemporary works in even the most remote villages. The seafood is tops—you'll find fish caught here in Dublin's swankiest restaurants—and so are the opportunities for scuba diving and other water sports.

Many dismiss Cork City as excessively industrial, and though it's true the city can't compete with Dublin's sophistication or Galway's bohemian sparkle, it's still well worth a visit. You'll probably want to pass on through the relatively featureless farmlands of northern Cork, however.

HISTORY

Dubbed the "City of Spires" for its distinctive skyline, Cork started out as a monastic settlement, founded by St. Finbarr (also spelled Finbar or Fin Barre) in the late 6th or early 7th century. But the city first prospered with

© CAMILLE DEANGELIS

CORK

HIGHLIGHTS

◖ St. Anne's Church: Climb the tower of this Anglican church on the north bank of the River Lee for a chance to ring the bells; the only downside is that all of Cork City can hear you if you misread the music (page 162)!

◖ Honan Chapel: Opened in 1916 on the campus of University College Cork, this exquisite "neo-Hiberno-Romanesque" chapel features stunning stained glass by Harry Clarke and the 12 signs of the zodiac in a floor mosaic by the entrance (page 162).

◖ Mizen Vision: After you've visited this newly revamped visitor center, walk carefully down a precarious path clinging to a sandstone cliff to Ireland's southwesternmost point (page 181).

◖ Bantry House and Gardens: In the family of the earls of Bantry since the 18th century, this fine manor house is full of priceless art and furnishings – the epitome of faded grandeur – and there is a formal garden with outstanding bay views along with a worthwhile historical exhibition (page 184).

◖ Glengarriff Woods Nature Reserve: An enchanted forest if ever there was one, Glengarriff offers a variety of walking trails and a dramatic scenic viewpoint, Lady Bantry's Lookout, over Bantry Bay (page 188).

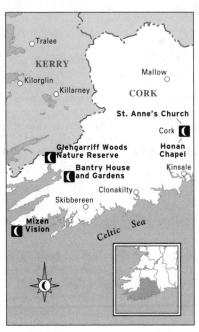

LOOK FOR ◖ TO FIND RECOMMENDED SIGHTS, ACTIVITIES, DINING, AND LODGING.

the advent of the Vikings in the 1100s. The Normans took control of their trading settlement later on in the 12th century, and the city's dozen Anglo-Norman merchant families would prosper from its well-situated port in their trade with continental Europe. Cork's breweries, distilleries, woolen factories, and shipbuilders did a booming business in the 18th and 19th centuries.

After the Reformation, Cork was a predominantly Protestant city until the late 1840s, when the native Irish began moving in from the surrounding countryside hoping to escape the famine. Others would depart for North America from the nearby port of Cobh.

With this ethno-religious shift in the population, Cork became a staunchly nationalist city. Roughly 1,000 IRA members prepared for rebellion during the Easter Rising of 1916, as in Dublin, though unlike Dublin no blood was shed in Cork that day. The Black and Tans, those notoriously brutal and undisciplined British paramilitaries, wreaked violence on rebels and civilians alike, setting fire to much of downtown Cork. Two of the city's nationalist mayors met their ends through the Black and Tans: They executed Thomas MacCurtain at his home in March 1920, and in August of that year they imprisoned his successor, Terence MacSwiney, in London. MacSwiney went on a hunger strike, and when he died after 78 days the people of Cork regarded him as a martyr for their cause.

The violence continued after the truce and Anglo-Irish Treaty, when Irish nationalists split into pro- and anti-treaty factions. Civil war ensued in the summer of 1922, and initially Cork was dominated by anti-treaty forces. Michael Collins, the IRA leader who had gone to London to bargain for the Irish Free State, was ambushed and assassinated in West Cork on August 22, 1922, by the anti-treaty IRA, his former comrades. The fighting continued until April 1923, when the anti-treaty men finally gave up their arms.

By the 1980s many of Cork's traditional industries had bottomed out, and the unemployment rate soared. The economic boom of the

© CAMILLE DEANGELIS

Go for an afternoon stroll through the tranquil Glengarriff Woods Nature Reserve.

mid-1990s brought new businesses to the area, however, and the city remains one of Ireland's busiest ports.

PLANNING YOUR TIME

Of Cork's three western peninsulas, the Beara is the most popular tourist destination (and the most picturesque). Those looking to get off the beaten track should visit Sheep's Head, which is more popular with Irish weekenders than international visitors. You could easily spend your whole vacation in West Cork, though most visitors just spend three or four days here before heading north to Killarney. Cork City merits one full day of sightseeing and two nights to sample its pubs, restaurants, and theaters.

Consider flying into Cork Airport from Dublin to save on gas and travel time, or at least flying one-way back to Dublin after a tour of Cork and Kerry (unless, of course, you have time to visit the Rock of Cashel, Kilkenny, and other places on the Dublin–Cork route).

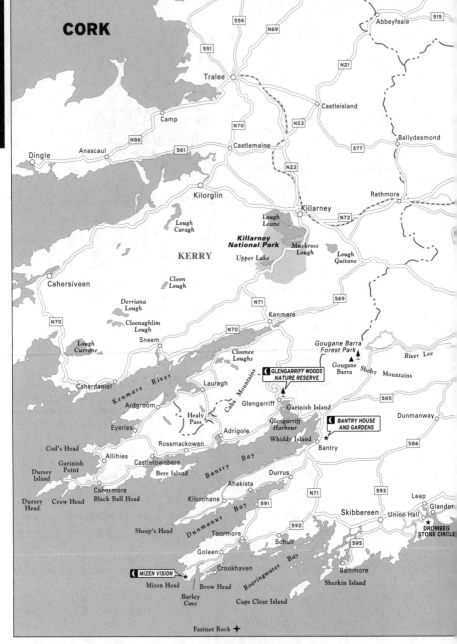

CORK

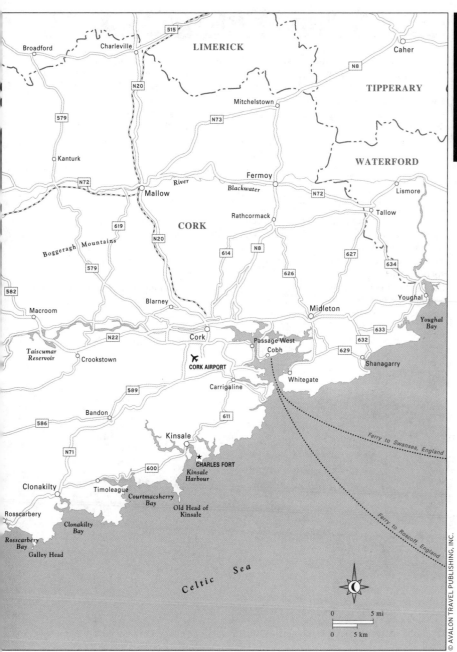

Cork City

Dublin may seem increasingly like a generic European metropolis, but Cork still feels like a genuinely Irish city, industrial warts and all. This "changeling city" (so said Kate O'Brien) has an aura of confidence, a certain *je ne sais quoi,* coming off its stint as 2005 European Capital of Culture. You've probably heard otherwise, as even Cork natives have been known to badmouth their hometown, and it's true that to spend more than a couple of days here when you could be off frolicking in beautiful West Cork would be rather silly. But a vibrant nightlife (fueled by the presence of a national university), a few excellent restaurants, and a significant arts and theater scene plead a good case for spending the night here, if not two. After all, the Beara's not going anywhere.

The city center is wedged between two channels of the River Lee. You can often see flame-throwers and other performers at the small but always-jammin' Bishop Lucey Park, which is bordered by South Main Street on the west, the Grand Parade on the east, Tuckey Street on the south (which changes names to Oliver Plunkett to the east), and Washington Street one block to the north. St. Patrick's Street, lined with chain stores, curves like a smile a couple blocks northeast of the park. Immediately north of Patrick Street, the artsier Huguenot Quarter is named for the influx of French Protestants who came to Cork to avoid religious persecution in the late 17th and early 18th centuries. And north of the Lee, the Shandon neighborhood is a quiet section—when the bells of St. Anne's aren't ringing, that is—with quaint rows of townhouses along narrow winding lanes, still the kind of place where the older locals greet you as you pass.

© CAMILLE DEANGELIS

Of all the national university campuses, the University College Cork campus is by far the most scenic.

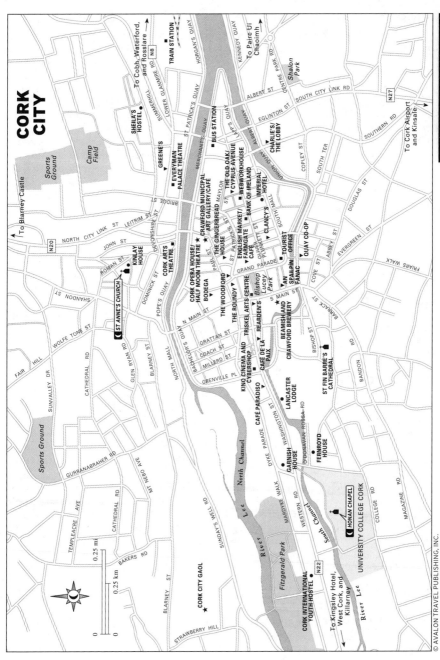

CORK CITY

To Blarney Castle

Sports Ground

Camp Field

To Cobh, Waterford, and Rosslare

TRAIN STATION

N8

To Paire Ui Chaoimh

KENNEDY QUAY

Shalon Park

SHEILA'S HOSTEL

SUMMERHILL

LOWER GLANMIRE RD

HORGAN'S QUAY

CENTRE PARK RD

GREENE'S

ST PATRICK'S QUAY

ALBERT ST

SOUTH CITY LINK RD

EVERYMAN PALACE THEATRE

MERCHANT'S QUAY

BUS STATION

MAYLOR

EGLINTON ST

CHARLIE'S/ THE LOBBY

SOUTHERN RD

N27

To Cork Airport and Kinsale

BRIDGE ST

LEITRIM ST

DEVONSHIRE ST

CRAWFORD MUNICIPAL ART GALLERY/CAFE

THE GINGERBREAD HOUSE

PAUL ST

THE OLD OAK/ CYPRUS AVENUE

WEBWORKHOUSE

ALBERT QUAY

IMPERIAL HOTEL

COPLEY ST

SOUTH TER

DOUGLAS ST

N20

NORTH CITY LINK ST

JOHN ST

ROMAN ST

KINLAY HOUSE

DOMINICK ST

POPE'S QUAY

BODEGA

CORK OPERA HOUSE/ HALF MOON THEATRE

ST PATRICK'S ST

ENGLISH MARKET/ FARMGATE CAFE

BANK OF IRELAND

GRAND PARADE

COOK ST

CLANCY'S

SOUTH MALL

EVERGREEN ST

ABBEY ST

SHANDON ST

ST ANNE'S CHURCH

CORK ARTS THEATRE

N MAIN ST

THE WOODFORD

THE ROUNDY

Bishop Lucey Park

PEMBROKE ST

TOURIST OFFICE

QUAY CO-OP

S MAIN ST

COVE ST

WOLFE TONE ST

GLEN RYAN RD

BLARNEY ST

NORTH MALL

BACHELOR'S QUAY

GRATTAN ST

COACH ST

MILLERD ST

GRENVILLE PL

TRISKEL ARTS CENTRE

REARDEN'S

CAFE DE LA PAIX

BEAMISH AND CRAWFORD BREWERY

BISHOP ST

BARRACK ST

ST FIN BARRE'S CATHEDRAL

BANDON RD

FRIARS WALK

FAIR HILL

CATHEDRAL RD

SUNVALLEY DR

KINO CINEMA AND CYBERSHOP

CAFE PARADISO

DYKE PARADE

WASHINGTON ST

LANCASTER LODGE

O'DONOVAN ROSSA RD

FERNROYD HOUSE

GURRANABRAHER RD

MT NEBO AVE

MARDYKE WALK

GARNISH HOUSE

WESTERN RD

HONAN CHAPEL

UNIVERSITY COLLEGE CORK

COLLEGE RD

MAGAZINE RD

Sports Ground

TEMPLEACRE AVE

CATHEDRAL RD

SUNDAY'S WELL RD

Lee

North Channel

River Lee

South Channel

Fitzgerald Park

0.25 mi

0.25 km

BAKERS RD

N22

CORK CITY GAOL

CORK INTERNATIONAL YOUTH HOSTEL

To Kingsley Hotel, and West Cork, and Killarney

River Lee

STRAWBERRY HILL

BLARNEY ST

© AVALON TRAVEL PUBLISHING, INC.

SIGHTS

There isn't a ton of stuff to see in Cork, but it's enough to keep you occupied for an afternoon.

◖ St. Anne's Church

The clock tower at the 18th-century Anglican St. Anne's Church (John Redmond St., tel. 021/450-5906, open 9:30 A.M.–5 P.M. Mon.–Sat., free admission to church, €6 to ring the bells) was traditionally known as the "four-faced liar" because each clock face read a different time. One of the coolest experiences you'll have in Cork is climbing the tower to play the eight "Bells of Shandon," memorialized in a popular early-19th-century song by a priest named Father Prout. You're even supplied with sheet music (the whole city's going to hear you, so you can't just ring them at random!). Afterward you can venture out onto the narrow balcony for a terrific view of the city.

◖ Honan Chapel

Consecrated in 1916, the Honan Chapel (on the UCC campus, signposted, tel. 021/490-3088, open 8 A.M.–8 P.M. Mon.–Fri., 10 A.M.–6 P.M. Sat., open for noon Mass Sun., free admission) is much more than the spiritual center of **University College Cork**. With its intricate Hiberno-Romanesque doorway, funky floor mosaics, modern sculptures and wall hangings, and exquisite stained-glass windows by Harry Clarke and Sarah Purser, the chapel (named for the local family who funded it) stunningly exemplifies Celtic revival architecture as well as the Irish Arts and Crafts movement. You could spend a good hour here admiring the windows alone, which depict several obscure Irish saints, like Ita (the "Brigid of Munster") and one of her pupils, Fachtna, a bishop whom you might easily mistake for Patrick. With his craggy face and flowing white hair, it's also hard to believe he lived only to the age of 46.

Other Sights

Art lovers should head to the **Crawford Municipal Art Gallery** (Emmet Pl., tel. 021/427-3377, www.crawfordartgallery.com, open 10 A.M.–5 P.M. Mon.–Sat., free admission). Visiting exhibitions with historical themes complement a small but outstanding permanent collection of 18th- through 20th-century sculptures, paintings, and prints. Though most of the collection is of Irish provenance, you can also check out minor works by Picasso, Dali, Braque, and Miro. The gallery, which was once the Custom House, also houses one of the city's best eateries.

The exhibition at the early-19th-century **Cork City Gaol** (Convent Ave., Sunday's Well, tel. 021/430-5022, www.corkcitygaol.com, open 9:30 A.M.–6 P.M. daily Mar.–Oct., 10 A.M.–5 P.M. daily Nov.–Feb., admission €6) does the whole wax-mannequins-and-sound-effects schtick, but it's still one of the city's top attractions.

Stout lovers, get thee to the **Beamish and Crawford Brewery** (S. Main St., tel. 021/491-1100, www.beamish.ie, tours at 10:30 A.M. and noon Tues. and Thurs. May–Sept., 11 A.M. Thurs. Oct.–Apr., admission €7) for a tour that includes an audiovisual and a pint of the black stuff. Unlike Guinness and Murphy's, Beamish is brewed exclusively in Ireland. The brewery also sponsors a historical **walking tour** (tel. 021/488-5405, olgacork@eircom.net, 90-minute tour €7) that departs the Grand Parade tourist office weeknights at 8 P.M. June–August. The ticket price includes a pint (or cuppa) at An Spailpín Fánac afterward.

The cavernous Anglican **St. Fin Barre's Cathedral** (Dean St., tel. 021/496-3387, http://cathedral.cork.anglican.org, open 9:30 A.M.–5:30 P.M. Mon.–Sat. and 12:30–5 P.M. Sun. Apr.–Sept., 10 A.M.–12:45 P.M. and 2–5 P.M. Mon.–Sat. Oct.–Mar., admission €3) feels thoroughly Gothic, though it was built between 1865 and 1870 by the English architect William Burges (who designed all the stained-glass windows, mosaics, and sculptures, of which there are more than 1,260). The city's first bishop and patron saint, St. Fin Barre is said to have established a monastery on this site in the 7th century. The windows depict scenes from the New and Old Testaments—and the clerestory windows feature the signs of the zodiac. If you come

THE "BIZARRE GENIUS" OF HARRY CLARKE

Ireland's greatest stained-glass artist (indeed, one of the world's finest), Harry Clarke, was born in 1889 in Dublin to an Irish mother and an English father, and he was educated by the Jesuits. Though Clarke was clearly influenced by Aubrey Beardsley, Gustav Klimt, and other romantic Nouveau artists, his stained-glass designs and "febrile, fantastical" illustration style (most famously exemplified in his superbly creepy watercolors and pen-and-inks for the stories of Edgar Allen Poe), his work is not derivative. Clarke's windows are informed by the classic "religious-sensual conflict," and though the artist was not a devout Catholic, his lingering guilt over his absence at his mother's death coupled with the Jesuits' fire-and-brimstone preachings contributed to a haunting, melancholy style that resonates with the viewer long after seeing his works. Clarke died in 1931 at the age of 42; he was so prolific during his relatively short career that one can only imagine how much more he might have accomplished had he lived a full life.

You'll find some of Clarke's finest work in the neo-Hiberno-Romanesque **Honan Chapel** at University College Cork (which also includes the work of a rival studio, that of Sarah Purser); in the **Seipeal Eoin agus Naomh Mhuire gan Smal** (Chapel of Saint John and Immaculate Mary) on Inis Meáin, County Galway; and the absolutely magnificent three-lighted Last Judgment altar window at **St. Patrick's Church** in Newport, County Mayo. There are many smaller works in churches across Ireland, and a couple of small windows are on display at the Crawford Municipal Gallery in Cork City as well.

© CAMILLE DEANGELIS

St. Fachtna, in one of the stunning windows at Honan Chapel, University College Cork

Stateside, you can see a series of nine windows commissioned for the **Basilica of St. Vincent de Paul** in Bayonne, New Jersey, during the last year of Clarke's life, and the *Geneva Window*, a series of illustrations of Gaelic revival works that was originally commissioned for the League of Nations, is on display at the **Wolfsonian Foundation** (www.wolfsonian.fiu.edu), a museum focusing on the "propaganda arts" at Florida International University in Miami.

For more information, check out *The Life and Work of Harry Clarke*, by Nicola Gordon Bowe, a professor at the National College of Art and Design in Dublin.

---

later in the afternoon, you might be able to catch a rehearsal of the children's choir. Even if you don't want to pay the admission fee, you can sit on the small grassy knoll out front and admire the wonderful (life-sized) statuary tableaux inspired by that of Notre Dame. Gargoyles of every shape are perched high over the wise and foolish virgins (on opposite sides of the central door).

ENTERTAINMENT

The name means "The Wandering Migrant Worker," and fittingly enough, **An Spailpín Fánac** (S. Main St., tel. 021/427-7949) hosts the occasional socialist meeting. This pub might be on the grungy side, but it's still a local favorite for rollickin'-good trad sessions nearly every night of the week.

Cork's top venue for live pop/rock is

FESTIVALS AND EVENTS IN CORK CITY

Cork's festival calendar isn't quite as busy as Dublin's or Galway's, but there's still plenty to write home about.

Founded in 1954, the five-day **International Choral Festival** (Festival House, 15 Grand Parade, tel. 021/422-3535, www.corkchoral.ie) straddles April and May with a busy lineup of competitions and concerts. Listening to a visiting children's choir perform some afternoon at St. Fin Barre's Cathedral might just be the highlight of your Cork sojourn.

Over 12 days at the end of June, the **Midsummer Festival** (15 Grand Parade, tel. 021/427-5874, www.corkfestival.com) offers a program of park, street, and traditional theater; family-oriented recreation, like boat trips on the Lee; art exhibitions; comedy shows and concerts from opera to pop/rock to cabaret.

Jazz and stout might not sound like the most natural combination, yet the city's ever-popular **International Jazz Festival** (www.corkjazzfestival.com, tickets €15–40) is sponsored by Guinness. The four-day festival takes place at the end of October and features everything from swing bands to gospel choirs at the Everyman Palace Theatre, the Opera House, the Gresham Metropole Hotel, and many other venues. Contact individual box offices to book. Murphy's, the local stout, sponsors the city's weeklong **International Film Festival** (tel. 021/427-1711, www.corkfilmfest.org) in early October.

Cyprus Avenue (Caroline St., tel. 021/427-6165, www.cyprusavenue.ie, tickets €6–20), which has hosted the likes of Luka Bloom and Claire Sproule along with plenty of up-and-coming local bands. You can buy tickets for Cyprus Avenue gigs at the bar downstairs, the **Old Oak** (113 Oliver Plunkett St., tel. 021/427-6165, www.oldoak.ie), which also hosts live bands Sunday–Wednesday and DJs Thursday–Saturday. This is a spacious, classy, comfortable old pub where you can kick back in a leather booth with a pint in the late afternoon in relative peace and quiet, your old pal Van on the stereo.

Rearden's (26 Washington St., tel. 021/427-1969, www.reardens.com), a popular UCC hangout, hosts bands or singer/songwriters Wednesday and Friday through Sunday nights. **The Lobby** (1 Union Quay, tel. 021/431-1113 or 086/260-9270, www.lobby.ie, cover €10–15) also hosts some fantastic singer/songwriter acts in the upstairs room. Across the way, the live acts at **Charlie's** (2 Union Quay, tel. 021/496-5272) are generally more Jerry-Garcia-lookalike than ambitious up-and-comer. There's trad on Sunday afternoon starting around 3 P.M. Charlie's is also noteworthy because you can start boozing it up here from 7:30 A.M. every day but Sunday (when the bar opens at 12:30 P.M.).

Or would you rather just chill out someplace hip-but-not-*too*-hip? Cork's got plenty of that kind of bar, too. There's a cool riverside wine bar, **Café de la Paix** (16 Washington St. W., tel. 021/427-9556), where you can get a bruschetta, cheese, or pâté plate for two along with a bottle of wine for €25. Or try **The Roundy** (Castle St., tel. 021/427-0433), a smart and stylish bar (with windows all around a circular room, as you no doubt surmised) attracting an equally smart and stylish after-work crowd. DJs in the upstairs bar play Thursday, Friday, and Sunday nights.

Some locals might tell you **Bodega** (46 Cornmarket St., tel. 021/427-2878) isn't quite as cool as it used to be, but don't pay them any mind. This converted warehouse has a soaring ceiling, whitewashed brick walls, two-story mirrors behind the bar, and bountiful outdoor seating (under festive canopies), all of which makes for a refreshingly laid-back atmosphere. The bar food's very good, too.

The city has a theater for every night of the week. Catch an arthouse film at **Kino** (Washington St. W., tel. 021/427-1571, www.kinocinema.net, tickets €4.50-7.50), or see whatever theater company's making the rounds at the old-fashioned, pleasantly worn **Everyman Palace Theatre** (15 MacCurtain St., tel. 021/450-1673, www.everymanpalace.com, tickets €10–30). There are generally more experimental dramas on the calendar at the **Cork Arts Theatre** (Carrolls Quay, tel. 021/450-8398, www.corkartstheatre.com, tickets €12–25), in a brand-new building (on the site of the old theater) with a cozy 100-seat auditorium. The **Triskel Arts Centre** (Tobin St., tel. 021/427-2022, www.triskelart.com, tickets €5–20) puts on film screenings, plays, photography exhibits, and international, sometimes-quirky musical acts.

As you'd expect, the **Cork Opera House** (Emmet Pl., tel. 021/427-6357, www.corkoperahouse.ie, tickets €15–50) does much more than opera, and it's not all on the conservative side: Along with ballet, classical music, Shakespeare, and suchlike, you'll find the occasional black comedy or laugh-a-minute musical. Part of the opera house, the **Half Moon Theatre** covers the lighter stuff, pop/folk/rock concerts and comedy shows mostly.

SHOPPING

St. Patrick Street is Cork's commercial thoroughfare, though you'll find smaller and more atmospheric shops on the side streets and lanes between Patrick and Paul Streets. The city's largest mall is the **Merchant's Quay Shopping Centre** near the bus station.

Two great little bookshops in the Huguenot Quarter, perfect for browsing, are secondhand **Connolly's Bookshop** (Rory Gallagher Pl., Paul St., tel. 021/427-5366) and **Mainly Murder** (2A Paul St., tel. 021/427-2413), which stocks more than whodunits. **Walnut Books** (50 Cornmarket St., tel. 021/434-0348, www.walnutbooks.com) has a focus on sustainable living, with a motto of "handpicked books for the discerning world-changer." Upstairs, **Lotus** carries Fair Trade coffee and snacks as well as clothes, accessories, and gifty things imported from Thailand.

The premises of **The Hemp Company** (Western Rd., tel. 021/427-8958, www.hemp.ie) are small but chock-full of surprisingly hip clothing and accessories, cosmetics, and hair products all made from the green stuff.

SPORTS AND RECREATION

Head west for excellent water-sporting opportunities in Kinsale, Schull, or Baltimore. The city's closest golf course is the 18-hole, par-72 **Harbour Point Golf Club** (Little Island, 10 km east of Cork on the N25, tel. 021/435-3094, www.harbourpointgolfclub.com).

Though opportunities for play are limited inside the city, you can always watch a hurling or Gaelic football game at the **Pairc Uí Chaoimh** stadium (Marina Walk, tel. 021/438-5876 or 021/496-3311, www.gaa.ie, tickets €15–25). Matches take place on Sunday afternoons in summertime; get here via Bus Éireann local route #2 from Parnell Place.

ACCOMMODATIONS

The dorms are on the cramped side, but IHH, family-run **Sheila's** (4 Belgrave Pl., Wellington Rd., tel. 021/450-5562, www.sheilashostel.ie, dorms €14–18, private rooms €22–26 pp, credit cards accepted) is still the friendliest hostel in town. Sheila's has a sauna, free Internet access, bureau de change, and bike rental, and the staff are an excellent source of information. You'll have more space and quiet (except on bank holiday weekends, of course) at the An Óige **Cork International Youth Hostel** (1/2 Redclyffe, Western Rd., tel. 021/454-3289, www.anoige.ie, €14–19, twins €21 pp sharing, credit cards accepted), located in a beautiful old brick home, but it's a 15-minute walk from the city center. Another safe bet is **Kinlay House** (Bob & Joan's Walk, Shandon, tel. 021/450-8966, www.kinlayhousecork.ie, dorms €13–16, private rooms €20–25 pp, credit cards accepted)—clean and spacious, with good facilities, just like its sister hostels in Galway and Dublin.

Most of Cork's B&Bs are dotted along Western Road near the university, all with small car parks out front. Renowned for its deluxe breakfasts (smoked salmon, pancakes,

GAY CORK

After Dublin, Cork is the island's most gay-friendly city. Over August bank holiday weekends in the past, **Cork Pride** (www.corkpride.com) has put up a series of athletic races, film screenings, and even a formal ball. It doesn't happen every year, but it's worth looking up as you plan your trip.

You might want to make your first stop **The Other Place** (8 S. Main St., tel. 021/427-8470, www.theotherplaceclub.com, open noon-10 P.M. Mon.-Sat., noon-6 P.M. Sun.), a resource center, bookstore, and café with free wireless Internet. In addition to a calendar of social events and classes, The Other Place runs the Southern Gay Health Project, which educates local gay men on HIV/AIDS and so forth. The Other Place also offers a nightclub on weekend nights. Another resource center is **L.Inc** (11A White St., tel. 021/480-8600, L.Inc@oceanfree.net, open 8-10 P.M. Thurs. and noon-3 P.M. Tues.), short for "Lesbians in Cork." There are a couple of local switchboards, too, though the hours are quite restricted: **Gay Information Cork** (tel. 021/427-1087, gayswitchcork@hotmail.com, open 7-9 P.M. Wed. and Fri.) and the **Cork Lesbian Line** (tel. 021/431-8318, open 8-10 P.M. Thurs.).

As for bars, try the laid-back **Loafers** (26 Douglas St., tel. 021/432-3550, www.loafersbar.com), which attracts a pretty eclectic crowd (though it's also one of the city's most popular lesbian hangouts). For late-night drinks, try the newer **Instinct** (Sullivan's Quay, tel. 021/496-6726, www.instinctcork.com), which offers comedy shows on Tuesday nights. Gay-friendly pubs include **The Roundy** (Castle St., tel. 021/427-0433) and **Bodega** (46 Cornmarket St., tel. 021/427-2878). For clubbing, your best bet is The Other Place Friday through Sunday. There are a few other monthly clubs around town though; check out **GayCork.com** (www.gaycork.com) for the lowdown.

Same-sex couples might want to stay at **Emerson House** (2 Clarence Terrace, Summer Hill N., tel. 021/427-1087 or 086/834-0891, www.emersonhousecork.com, €45-80 pp sharing), an exclusively gay B&B.

---

porridge with a generous dollop of Bailey's) and well-appointed rooms, **Garnish House** (Western Rd., tel. 021/427-5111, www.garnish.ie, €45–70 pp, s €60–80, credit cards accepted) has acquired a reputation as the city's top guesthouse. Rates rise considerably at peak times (bank holiday and festival weekends in particular), and single travelers will certainly find better value elsewhere. Try **Fernroyd House** (4 O'Donovan Rossa Rd., off Western Rd., tel. 021/427-1460, www.fernroydhouse.com, €35–40 pp, s €45–50, credit cards accepted), an excellent choice for its airy and immaculate rooms, genuinely kind and accommodating proprietors, free wireless Internet, and lovely garden out back. The breakfast here is top-notch as well, with homebaked breads and scones and ample vegetarian options. Western Road can be fairly noisy, but Fernroyd is situated off the main drag in a relatively quiet cul-de-sac.

Vegetarians will be thrilled to know that **℃ Cafe Paradiso** (16 Lancaster Quay, tel. 021/427-7939, www.cafeparadiso.ie, rooms €160, credit cards accepted) is now offering accommodations above the legendary restaurant. The three en-suite double rooms are individually designed and furnished with such care that you feel like you're staying in the guest room of your (very hip) best friend. And of course, breakfast is divine (and divinely healthy—no rashers or black pudding in sight!).

Directly across the street, right on the River Lee, is the excellent business-class **Lancaster Lodge** (Lancaster Quay, tel. 021/425-1125, www.lancasterlodge.com, €60 pp, s €86, 10 percent senior citizen discount). Here you can expect friendly and professional staff, comfortable queen-size beds, plasma TVs, complimentary wireless Internet, and soundproof walls and windows. Suites with Jacuzzi are available at a higher rate (€85 pp, s €110). Breakfast is included in the room price, with a buffet as well as smoked salmon and omelets cooked to order.

The five-star **Kingsley Hotel** (Victoria Cross, past Western Rd. on the west end of the city, a 25-minute walk into town, tel. 021/480-0555, www.kingsleyhotel.com, rooms €150–310) was built on the site of the old Lee Baths, an open-air public pool that kept generations of Cork schoolchildren cool on those (albeit rare) dog days. The deluxe-grade rooms feature espresso machines, mini-bars, LCD televisions, CD and DVD players, down quilts, bathrobes and slippers, in-room safes, and "walk-in" showers along with bath-tub. There's complimentary wireless Internet in all rooms as well. Opened in 2006, a new spa offers a range of ayurvedic treatments, and the leisure center has a huge pool, Jacuzzi, steam room, and sauna. Best of all, the all-around service lives up to the five-star rating. Check out the website for good-value B&B and dinner packages.

With a more central location, the newly re-furbished **Imperial Hotel** (South Mall, tel. 021/427-4040, www.imperialhotel.ie, rooms €175–215, s €135) has a similarly high standard of service (and a new Aveda salon and spa). All rooms feature Aveda toiletries and compli-mentary mineral water, and the superior-grade rooms have queen- and king-size beds, digital interactive television, bathrobes and slippers, and broadband access. Breakfast isn't included in the room price, however.

FOOD

In Cork there aren't quite as many cool restau-rants as there are great pubs, but you'll feast like a king if you know where to go.

The Gingerbread House (Paul St., tel. 021/427-6411, open 8 A.M.–10 P.M. daily, mains under €6) is an airy cafeteria-style eat-ery with a spacious loft and outdoor tables on a pedestrian brick-laid street (along with the req-uisite *Hansel and Gretel* excerpt up high on the wall). This open, chill space has a ton of po-tential, so it's kind of a shame the food's barely

serviceable. Come here for a cafetière of pretty good coffee (€2.20, a deal considering lots of cafés are charging €2 for a single cup nowa-days) and a round of people-watching, or dig into the purchase you just made at Connolly's Bookshop across the way.

Affiliated with the much-acclaimed Bally-maloe Cookery School, the **Crawford Gallery Café** (Emmet Pl., tel. 021/427-4415, open 10 A.M.–4:30 P.M. Mon.–Fri., 9:30 A.M.–4 P.M. Sat., mains €10–20) is a perennial favorite with ladies-who-lunch (and pretty much everyone else in Cork, too). It's a per-fectly classy (and convenient) spot to enjoy a gourmet quiche or salad after a morning of culture in the city art gallery.

With fresh meat, cheeses, and produce sourced from the downstairs farm market, the **Farmgate Café** (upstairs at the English Mar-ket, off Oliver Plunkett St. and the Grand Pa-rade, tel. 021/427-8134, open 8:30 A.M.–5 P.M. Mon.–Sat., mains €9–12) offers hearty, great-value traditional dishes you won't find else-where nowadays: corned beef and cabbage, lamb stew, corned mutton, and drisheen (a kind of black pudding one customarily douses with mustard before sampling). There are a few terrific meat-free choices as well.

A good choice for pub grub is **The Woodford** (Paul St., tel. 021/425-3932, www.thewood-ford.ie, food served 10 A.M.–7 P.M. daily, mains €7–12), serving sweet and savory crepes for breakfast and a fairly standard lunch menu of paninis, salads, seafood, steak, and chicken (apart from a few really tasty vegetarian op-tions, including nut loaf). The atmosphere's a bit on the bland side as far as pubs go, but the leather sofas are a comfy place to kick back with a lemon crepe and a cup of coffee while you plan your day. **Clancy's** (15-16 Princes St., tel. 021/427-6097, food served 8 A.M.–midnight weekdays, 10:30 A.M.–midnight Sat., 12:30–4:30 P.M. Sun., mains €8–20) is another popular gastro-pub, with a reputa-tion for very spicy buffalo wings and other good-value Mexican and Italian-inspired dishes. For funky atmosphere *and* scrummy eats, try **Bodega** (46 Cornmarket St., tel.

021/427-2878, food served noon–9 P.M. daily, until 10:30 P.M. Wed.–Sun., lunch €8–15, dinner mains €15–20). Vegetarians have a choice here as well.

Part of Isaac's Hotel, the wonderful **Greene's** (48 MacCurtain St., tel. 021/450-0011, www.isaacs.ie, open 12:30–3 P.M. Mon.–Sat. and 12:30–4 P.M. Sun., 6–10 P.M. daily, lunch €12–15, 3-course early-bird special €27 6–7 P.M., mains €16–30) is reached through an atmospheric stone archway and a courtyard with a waterfall floodlit by night. The modern Irish fare here is top-notch, and you won't find a tastier steak anywhere in the city. The desserts are to die for. Be sure to get here by 7 P.M. for the early bird, which is a far better value than the à la carte.

Cork has two organic vegetarian restaurants, one cafeteria-style above a whole foods store and the other a gourmand's delight. Both are city mainstays. The **Quay Co-op** (24 Sullivan's Quay, tel. 021/431-7026, www.quay-coop.com, open 9 A.M.–9 P.M. daily, mains under €9) does hearty top-value meals—lasagna, chickpea burgers, savory tarts, and heaping salads. Be sure to work up an appetite before you arrive, because the portions are gigantic. Though the same can't be said of **⬤ Cafe Paradiso** (16 Lancaster Quay, tel. 021/427-7939, www.cafeparadiso.ie, open noon–3 P.M. and 6:30–10:30 P.M. Tues.–Sat., lunches €8–16, dinner mains €22–25), you'll more than forgive the daintiness. This is undoubtedly one of the best restaurants in the country, vegetarian or otherwise (and it's better than all Dublin's veggie eateries put together); owner-chef Denis Cotter has elevated meatless cuisine to an art form. The fantastically inventive menu changes regularly; expect to spend at least half an hour deciding on a main course. The lengthy, well-chosen wine list can present a dilemma as well. Some might balk at the dessert prices (many are €10), but every option is a memorable end to a memorable meal. Though the food is heavenly, what's even better about this place is the relaxed atmosphere with attentive, down-to-earth service.

INFORMATION

Stop by Cork's **tourist office** (Grand Parade, tel. 021/425-5100, www.corkkerry.ie, open 9 A.M.–6 P.M. Mon.–Fri. and 9 A.M.–5:30 P.M. Sat. June–Aug., 9:15 A.M.–5:30 P.M. Mon.–Sat. Sept.–May) for leaflets on upcoming events. You may find the staff are more helpful at the seasonal **Cork City Information Booth** (corner St. Patrick St. and Winthrop St., open daily June–Sept.), however.

SERVICES

For ATMs or bureaux de change, visit the **Bank of Ireland** or **AIB**, both on St. Patrick Street. The **general post office** is on Oliver Plunkett Street.

Get your duds sudsed at the **Western Road Launderette** (Western Rd., opposite the UCC gate, tel. 021/427-9937, open until 9 P.M. weekdays, 6 P.M. Sat.). For a pharmacy, your best bet (it's open Sundays) is **Boots** (Merchant's Quay Shopping Centre, tel. 021/427-2230).

Check your email at **Cyberstop** (19 Lancaster Quay, tel. 021/427-3203, www.cyberstop.ie, open 10 A.M.–10 P.M. Mon.–Fri., noon–10 P.M. Sat.–Sun., €3/hour), where an hour of Internet access comes with real brewed coffee or tea, cheerfully served to your flatscreen terminal (offer valid weekdays only). Or try **Webworkhouse.com** (8A Winthrop St., tel. 021/427-3090, www.webworkhouse.com, open 24 hours, €2.50–3/hour). It's a haven for hardcore gamers and online gamblers, but night owls can get Internet access here for only €1.25/hour between 3 A.M. and 8 A.M.

GETTING THERE

The Parnell Place Bus and Train Station is at Merchant's Quay. **Bus Éireann** (tel. 021/450-8188, www.buseireann.ie) provides regular service to Cork from Galway, Ennis, and Limerick (#51, 14/day daily), Dublin (#8, 6/day daily), Cashel (#8 and #71, 9/day Mon.–Sat., 7/day Sun.), Waterford (#40, 13/day daily), Tralee and Killarney (#40, 14/day daily), Kilkenny (#7, 4/day Mon.–Sat., 3/day Sun.), and many other places. It's faster to travel from Dublin via **Irish Rail** (tel. 021/450-6766, www.irishrail.ie, 9/day daily, single/5-day return €54.50/59).

Fly into **Cork International Airport** (6 km south of the city on the N27, tel. 021/431-3131, www.corkairport.com) from Dublin (on Aer Arann or Ryanair), Belfast (on Aer Arann), Edinburgh, London (Heathrow on Aer Lingus, Stansted on Ryanair, and Gatwick on Ryanair or Easyjet), Rome, Barcelona, Amsterdam, and several other European cities. The most frequently traveled airlines are **Aer Arann** (tel. 0818/210-210, www.aerarann.ie), **Aer Lingus** (tel. 0818/365-000, www.aerlingus. ie), **Ryanair** (tel. 01/609-7800, www.ryanair. com), and **Easyjet** (tel. 1890/923-922, www. easyjet.com). Bus Éireann operates a shuttle between the airport and city center bus station (single/return fare €3.80/6.30), or a taxi will run you €10–15. Another option is **Skylink** (tel. 021/432-1020, www.skylinkcork.com, single/return fare €5/9), which departs every half hour for hotels, hostels, and guesthouses in the city center.

GETTING AROUND
You can get all over the city by foot, but if you don't feel like schlepping back to the B&B there's always the local bus service. Route #8 links Western Road with St. Patrick's Street in the city center (fare €1.20).

For a cab, ring the **Cork Taxi Co-op** (6 Washington St. W., tel. 021/427-2222) or **Shandon Taxi Cabs** (tel. 021/450-5333 or 021/450-2255).

Hire a bike from **Rothar Cycles** (55 Barrack St., tel. 021/431-3133 or 087/217-1752, www .rotharcycletours.com, closed Sun., €20/80 per day/week, €100 deposit, one-way service €30). *Rothar* means "wheel," by the way.

Around Cork City

BLARNEY
Built in the 15th century, Blarney (tel. 021/438-5252, www.blarneycastle.ie) is Ireland's most infamous castle—and its biggest tourist trap. Hours vary seasonally (9 A.M.–sunset Mon.–Sat. and 9:30 A.M.–sunset Sun. Oct.–Apr., 9 A.M.–6:30 P.M. Mon.–Sat. and 9:30 A.M.–5:30 P.M. Sun. May and Sept., 9 A.M.–7 P.M. Mon.–Sat. and 9:30 A.M.–5:30 P.M. Sun. June–Aug., admission €7). During the reign of Elizabeth I the chatelain of Blarney Castle, Cormac MacDermot MacCarthy, was a veritable master of unfulfilled promises, and his smooth talk infuriated the old Virgin Queen. A legend arose from a priest's song-poem published in 1860, which promised that whoever kissed the now filthy-black stone, located along a parapet high above the castle floor, would be infused with MacCarthy's gift for honey-tongued BS.

So you can smooch the stone, a gruff elderly man lowers you, backward and headfirst, down a gap at the edge of the wall. Many tourists find the experience exciting and count it a must-do while in Ireland, but from an anthropological standpoint it's all rather inexplicable, not to mention undignified. It's not just a rumor that British soldiers used to relieve themselves on that stone, and according to a few of the locals, disgruntled castle employees continue the tradition after hours.

Outside of that notorious stone, the castle ruins are picturesque and would be worth a visit were it not for the crowds. With so much company, it makes little sense to come here when you could enjoy a placid stroll among any of the other charmingly secluded ivy-clad ruins in this country.

Blarney is eight kilometers northwest of Cork off the N20. **Bus Éireann** (tel. 021/450-8188, route #224, 25-minute trip, return fare €5.20) provides frequent service from Parnell Station.

FOTA ISLAND
Featuring walled and Italianate gardens dating to the first half of the 19th century, the **Fota**

Arboretum and Gardens (Fota Island, Carrigtwohill, 8 km north of Cobh on the R624 and 14 km east of Cork City off the N25, tel. 021/481-2728) is laid out over 11 hectares. Hours are shorter in winter (9 A.M.–6 P.M. Mon.–Sat. and 11 A.M.–6 P.M. Sun. Apr.–Oct., 9 A.M.–5 P.M. Mon.–Sat. and 11 A.M.–5 P.M. Sun. Nov.–Mar., free admission). If the weather turns, you can take a self-guided tour through the Regency-style **Fota House** (tel. 021/481-5543, www.fotahouse.com, open 10 A.M.–6 P.M. Mon.–Sat., 11 A.M.–6 P.M. Sun., admission €5.50).

But the island's biggest draw, for families especially, is the 28-hectare **Fota Wildlife Park** (tel. 021/481-2678, www.fotawildlife.ie, open 10 A.M.–5 P.M. Mon.–Sat., 11 A.M.–5 P.M. Sun. mid-Mar.–Oct., 10 A.M.–3 P.M. Mon.–Sat. and 11 A.M.–3 P.M. Sun. Nov.–mid-Mar., admission €11.50). The wildlife park is much better than a zoo because there are no cages.

There is a €2 parking fee for both wildlife park and arboretum; Fota actually makes a better day trip from Cork City via **Irish Rail,** as there is a train an hour pulling into Fota Station.

COBH

Once the port of Cork City, Cobh ("Cove") was the *Titanic*'s final port of call in 1912 (a fact rather tackily milked by the local tourist office), and was also a common departure point for those immigrating to America and Australia. In a cringe-worthy twist of irony, Cobh was renamed Queenstown in 1849 after Victoria, who in the words of William Bulfin "never did anything for Ireland but preside over more than three-score years of its most disastrous history." After the Irish Free State was formed in 1921, the town council's first act was to change the name back again.

Frankly, Cobh is far too industrial-feeling—the row of huge and hideous factories on the far side of the estuary makes the "harbor view" boast pretty near laughable; nor are its cultural attractions quite interesting enough to merit a stopover. That said, if the Cork coast was the last your ancestors saw of Ireland, you might find the heritage center, **Cobh,**

The Queenstown Story (in the old railway station, adjacent to the new one, tel. 021/481-3591, www.cobhheritage.com, open 10 A.M.–6 P.M. daily May–Oct., 10 A.M.–5 P.M. daily Nov.–Apr., admission €6), worth a visit. Situated on a hill overlooking town and harbor is the Catholic **St. Colman's Cathedral** (Cathedral Pl., tel. 021/481-3222, open daily, free admission) in all its hyper-elaborate neo-Gothic glory. Designed by Pugin the Younger and associates, it was built over a period of 47 years (1868–1915). Much of the funds came from America and Australia.

Cobh's layout is a bit confusing at first, with narrow crisscrossing streets wedged between harbor and the hill on which St. Colman's stands. Running west to east, the waterside main drag changes names from Lower Road to Westbourne Place to West Beach to East Beach. Everything you'll need is located on (or just off) this main drag.

Accommodations and Food

For basic B&B in a handy location a block from the town center, try **Ard na Laoi** (15 Westbourne Pl., tel. 021/481-2742, €34 pp sharing). A romantic Victorian overlooking the harbor, **Seafield** (Lower Rd., a 5-minute walk west of town past the train station, tel. 021/481-1563, http://homepage.eircom.net/~allen, €38 pp, s €45) has wonderfully commodious rooms individually decorated with antiques, fully restored bathrooms with power-showers, free wireless Internet, fine filling breakfasts, and a very helpful proprietor.

Cobh's best hotel is the **Watersedge** (Westbourne Pl., tel. 021/481-5566, www.watersedgehotel.ie, €55–80 pp, s €75–100, suites €160–240); some of the rooms have balconies overlooking the water, and the hotel restaurant, **Jacob's Ladder** (food served 12:30–9 P.M. daily, mains €13–22), is one of the town's best eateries. Another (less formal) pub-cum-restaurant, **The Quays** (Wellington Pl., tel. 021/481-3539, food served noon–9:30 P.M. daily, mains €11–25) also has good food (the portobello mushroom burger hits the spot)—and a younger, hipper crowd on the harbor-facing deck.

© CAMILLE DEANGELIS

wildly ornate, neo-Gothic St. Colman's Cathedral in Cobh

Information and Services

The **tourist office** (tel. 021/481-3301, www.cobhchamberofcommerce.ie, open 9:30 A.M.–5:30 P.M. Thurs.–Tues., 1–5 P.M. Wed.) and Sirius Arts Centre are located in the old yacht club on the harbor. There's an ATM and bureau de change at the **AIB** on West Beach, just north of Kennedy Park, where there's a romantic old bandstand and a small farmers' market on Friday mornings (selling mostly prepared foods, a nice option for an alfresco lunch on a bench overlooking the water). Check your email at the **Cobh Internet Café & Call Shop** (Church St., tel. 021/485-5353, open 10 A.M.–10 P.M. Mon.–Sat., 2–10 P.M. Sun., €2/30 minutes, €3.50/hour).

Getting There

Cobh is 24 kilometers southeast of Cork City off the N25 (picking up the R624 before Carrigtwohill) and is a cinch to get to by **Irish Rail** (tel. 021/450-6766, 1/hour daily, 24-minute trip, return ticket €5).

MIDLETON

A humdrum town 20 kilometers east of Cork City, Midleton (Mainistir na Corann, "Abbey of the Choir") is only worth a stop for the **Jameson Heritage Centre** (signposted from the main street, tel. 021/461-3594, open 10 A.M.–6 P.M. daily, frequent tours Mar.–Oct., tours at 11:30 A.M., 2:30 P.M., and 4 P.M. daily Nov.–Feb., admission €6), a must for whiskey drinkers. The old distillery dates from the 1820s (though the buildings themselves date from the 1790s, as this complex was originally a woolen factory) and was turned into a tourist attraction when the new one opened in 1975. Here you'll find the world's largest pot still (with a capacity of 32,000 gallons). A 45-minute guided tour consists of an introductory audiovisual; a comprehensive tour of the old distillery with all its mills, stills, and warehouses (you'll practically be able to make whiskey at home after this); and a tasting in the bar afterward. Two volunteers in each group get to sample other Irish and Scotch varieties for comparison.

CORK

Midleton is 20 kilometers east of Cork on the N25, and there is frequent **Bus Éireann** service from the city (tel. 021/450-8188, route #40 or #41, 18/day Mon.–Sat., 13/day Sun.).

KINSALE

When William Bulfin characterized the Battle of Kinsale (Cionn tSáile, "Head of the Sea") as a "disastrous epoch" in Irish history, he might have been referring to either of the two conflicts that left the native Irish in even worse straits than before: in 1601, when the Gaelic earls of Tyrone and Tir Conaill (now part of Donegal) fought in vain to rid Ireland of the English imperialists; or in 1689, when the forces of William of Orange resoundingly defeated the Jacobites. Other local tragedies included the *Lusitania,* which sank 20 kilometers south of Kinsale in May of 1915; nine of the survivors landed here.

Kinsale's food is as rich as its history; the town has declared itself Ireland's gourmet capital, and this is only a minor exaggeration. Between all the fancy eateries and its popularity with wealthy golfers and yachters, the budget-conscious visitor can feel out of place here; that said, good-value early-bird menus abound, and though you may pay five or ten quid more for a B&B than you would elsewhere, you'll find it's money well spent.

Though the layout is medieval, Kinsale is still pretty easy to get the hang of. The town wraps itself around the harbor inlet, bordered by Pier Road to the west, Emmet Place to the north, and Pearse Street to the east. Turn north off Emmet Place onto Market Quay (not on the water, despite the name), which will lead you to the Market Square. Cork Street is another block north of the square. On the west side of the town center, Main Street and O'Connell Street run parallel to Market Quay.

Sights

Built to be Kinsale's Custom House at the turn of the 16th century, Dúchas-run **Desmond Castle** (Cork St., tel. 021/477-4855 or 021/477-2263 in winter, open 10 A.M.–6 P.M. daily mid-Apr.–Oct., admission €2.90) later

The Kinsale farmers market offers plenty of things to nibble every Tuesday.

served as a French prison and famine work-house. Today this tower house on the north side of town features a modest museum on the history of wine.

Built in 1677, the star-shaped **Charles Fort** (Summer Cove, 2 km east of town, tel. 021/477-2263, open 10 A.M.–6 P.M. daily mid-Mar.–Oct., 10 A.M.–5 P.M. daily Nov.–mid-Mar., admission €3.70) was named in honor of Charles II. James II "kept court" here before the disastrous Battle of Kinsale in 1689 (during the Williamite war, as opposed to the Battle of Kinsale in 1601 that precipitated the event known as the Flight of the Earls). The site is run by Dúchas, which offers the usual exhibition and 45-minute guided tour.

A freely accessible (and very picturesque) ruin built in 1603 on a small peninsula in Kinsale Harbour, **James Fort** offers a serene view of the town, bay, and surrounding hillside. To get here, follow Pier Road (on the west side of the harbor) south out of town and make a left when you reach the bridge; the fort is beyond the Castlepark Marina.

Tours
Don Herlihy's Historic Walking Tour (tel. 021/477-2873, ticket €7) offers a dynamic introduction to the town's crucial role in Irish (and English) history. The 90-minute guided walk departs the tourist office at 11:15 A.M. daily mid-March–mid-October.

Entertainment and Events
Calling all gourmands: Be sure to time your arrival for the **Kinsale Food Festival** (tel. 021/477-9900) in early October. Tickets for the various parties and tastings sell for as much as €75, though other events are free of charge. Other great times to be here are mid-July for **Kinsale Arts Week** (www.kinsaleartsweek.com) or the autumn bank holiday weekend (usually the last weekend in October) for the **Kinsale Jazz Festival.** Check out www.kinsale.ie for more festival info.

But if what you're looking for is good old-fashioned traditional music, head for the **Spaniard** (Scilly, follow Pearse St. south out of town and around the harbor, tel. 021/477-2436, www.thespaniard.ie), with sessions Wednesday all year and Friday night and Sunday afternoon in high season, or **An Seanachai** (6 Market St., tel. 021/477-7077) on Tuesday night.

Shopping
There are loads of opportunities for retail therapy in Kinsale (just take a stroll from the Market Square south along Main Street), but the two shops you shouldn't miss are **Kinsale Crystal** (Market St., tel. 021/477-4493, www.kinsalecrystal.ie), the workshop of a former Waterford master-cutter, and **Kinsale Silver** (Pearse St., tel. 021/477-4359, www.kinsalesilver.com), a family-run workshop that produces beautifully handcrafted, one-of-a-kind Celtic designs.

Sports and Recreation
An easy two-kilometer walk takes you south of town and over a bridge to James Fort, a romantic old ruin overlooking the harbor. Or pass the fort by boat on **Kinsale Harbour Cruises** (tel. 086/250-5456 or 021/477-8946, www.kinsaleharbourcruises.com, hourly sailings in high season, 60-minute trip €12). Cruises depart from the Kinsale Marina, 300 meters south of the tourist office on Pier Road.

Kinsale is a golfer's haven, though the €275 greens fee for 18 holes at the **Old Head of Kinsale Golf Club** (8 km southwest of town, tel. 021/477-8444, http://oldhead.com) is beyond most folks' budgets. It may not be quite as sought after (or scenic), but an alternative is the **Kinsale Golf Club** (Farrangalway, 3 km northwest of town on the R607, tel. 021/477-4722, www.kinsalegolf.com).

The **Oysterhaven Activity Centre** (Oysterhaven, 10 km southeast of town on a local road, signposted from the R600, tel. 021/477-0738, www.oysterhaven.com) offers sailing and windsurfing courses as well as canoe and kayak rental.

Accommodations
This upscale town has plenty of upscale accommodations, and though there are a couple

of hostels in the area, budget travelers should definitely splurge on a B&B. Be sure to ask about discounts in the off-season.

Everything's as comfortable as home at **The Olde Bakery** (56 Lower O'Connell St., one block west of the Pier Rd. on the west side of the harbor, tel. 021/477-3012, www.theolde-bakery.com, €35–40 pp sharing): There are real quilts on the beds, an open fire in the cozy sitting room, and hearty food and friendly banter around the communal breakfast table.

Less than a 10-minute walk from the town center, **Woodlands House** (Cappagh, tel. 021/477-2633, www.woodlandskinsale.com, open Mar.–mid-Nov., €35–45 pp, s €50–70, credit cards accepted) has a nice situation overlooking the harbor, lovely gardens, and king-size beds in its six immaculate rooms. There are in-room safes, and CD and DVD players are available if you ask. You'll be greeted with tea and cookies. To get here, head up O'Connell Street and make a left onto Church Street, passing St. Multose's Church (on your left) before bearing right; then follow the sign for Bandon, and you'll see the B&B up the road on your left.

A handsome ivy-clad Georgian, the **Old Presbytery** (43 Cork St., tel. 021/477-2027, www.oldpres.com, €50–80 pp sharing) is one of Kinsale's most popular B&Bs for its equally atmospheric yet modern rooms (some with balconies and Jacuzzis) and deluxe breakfasts (crepes, smoked salmon, cheese plates, and such-like). There's also a charming "penthouse suite" with fireplace, perfect for honeymooners.

Another top-notch guesthouse is **Friar's Lodge** (Friar's St., off Cork St., tel. 021/477-7384, www.friars-lodge.com, €60 pp, s €80), quite a good value considering how large, comfortable, and well-appointed the rooms are: DVD, radio, wireless Internet, chocolates, in-room safe—even a pillow menu so you can choose your favorite type of pillow. You can pour yourself a complimentary drink in the sitting room, too.

Kinsale's best hotels are boutiques. The carefully restored, well-maintained **Blue Haven Hotel** (3 Pearse St., by the harbor, tel. 021/477-

2209, www.bluehavenkinsale.com, €60–120 pp, s €140) has lavishly decorated rooms featuring flat-screen TVs, wireless Internet, and pillow menus, and the hotel restaurant can more than compete with Kinsale's finest eateries. A more modest option is the 10-room **White Lady Hotel** (Lower O'Connell St., one block west of Pier Rd., tel. 021/477-2737, www.whiteladyhotelkinsale.com, €50 pp, s €80), with a great small-town feel (and the personal, friendly service to go along with it). The food's good, and the rooms are comfortable but no-frills. The White Lady has Kinsale's most popular nightclub, so this isn't your place if you're planning on an early night.

Food

Kinsale has many fine restaurants, but don't let its gourmet reputation fool you into thinking you can get a great meal any old place. And some highly praised restaurants are seriously overpriced; go for the early-bird special if you can. (You might also want to note that some eateries here have an unwritten dress code even for lunch, so you'd best leave the windpants and the ballcaps at the B&B.) For more info before you go, take a look at **Kinsale's Good Food Circle** website (tel. 021/477-4026, www.kinsalerestaurants.com).

On Tuesday the **farmers market** (Market Sq., 9 A.M.–1:30 P.M.) has stalls selling baked goods, chocolate ice shakes, gourmet Fair Trade coffee, and other ready-to-eat goodies.

An atmospheric café with checkerboard floors, big mirrors, and a huge mullioned-arch window overlooking a pedestrian thoroughfare—perfect for people-watching—the **Milk Market Café** (Milk Market St., off Market St., no phone, open 10 A.M.–6 P.M. Mon.–Sat., mains €5–12) is great for a light lunch of sandwiches, pizzas, or savory pancakes. The coffee's good, too.

For Irish-French fusion (without the fancy-pants prices), try **Max's Winebar** (48 Main St., tel. 021/477-3677, open 12:30–3 P.M. and 6:30–10:30 P.M. Mon. and Wed.–Sat., 1–3 P.M. and 6:30–10 P.M. Sun., lunch €6–13, 3-course early-bird special €22 12:30–3 P.M.

and 6:30–7:30 P.M., dinner mains €16–27), where rough stone walls and wide wooden tables add to the laid-back, unpretentious atmosphere. Another Kinsale mainstay is **(Jim Edwards'** (Market Quay, tel. 021/477-2541, www.jimedwardskinsale. com, bar food served 12:30–10 P.M., restaurant open 6–10 P.M. daily, bar meals €12–18, restaurant mains €18–30), which serves up the best steaks in town.

Toddie's (Eastern Rd., just south of town on the east side of the harbor, tel. 021/477-7769, http://toddies.kinsale.tv, open 6–10:30 P.M. daily in summer, closed Mon. in low season and Jan., 3-course dinner €45, reservations necessary) offers inventively prepared seafood in a stylish gallery-cum-dining room. But perhaps Kinsale's most beloved seafood restaurant is the **Fishy Fishy Café** (O'Connell St., tel. 021/477-4453, open noon–4 P.M. daily Apr.–Sept., closed Sun. Oct.–Mar., mains €20–30), which has the best mussels you'll ever eat. You can have the catch of the day prepared however you like it, along with the requisite glass of white.

And if you'd prefer a change from seafood, there's a sleek new eatery called **Cucina** (9 Market St., tel. 021/470-0707 or 087/764-8924, www.cucina.ie, open 9 A.M.–5 P.M. Mon.–Sat., mains €8–18), where all Kinsale's hip young things come for brunch (the only thing Italian about this place is the name). Vegetarians should make this their #1 choice for lunch, as there are loads of great choices.

Information

The local **tourist office** (on the harbor, Pier Rd. and Emmet Pl., tel. 021/477-2234, open 9:15 A.M.–1 P.M. and 2:15–5:30 P.M. Mon.–Sat. Mar.–mid-Nov., daily July–Aug.) is jointly run by the Irish Tourist Board and the Kinsale Chamber of Tourism (www.kinsale.ie). Also check out the **Kinsale Advertiser** (www.kinsalenews.com), a free weekly available at most newsagents.

Services

The **Bank of Ireland** (Emmet St.) and the **AIB** (Pearse St.) each have an ATM and bureau de change; the **post office** on Pearse Street also changes money.

The **Kinsale Launderette** (Main St., tel. 021/477-2205) is only open Monday to Friday. Neither the **Collins Kinsale Pharmacy** (12 Market St., tel. 021/477-2077) nor **Moloney's** (Emmet St., tel. 021/477-2130) is open Sunday.

Unfortunately, there's no cheap Internet access available here. Try **Finishing Services Internet Bureau** (71 Main St., tel. 021/477-3571, open 9 A.M.–5:30 P.M. weekdays and until 7 P.M. June–Aug., 10 A.M.–5 P.M. Sat., €3/30 minutes).

Getting There and Around

Kinsale is 23 kilometers south of Cork City on the R600. Rather than use the pay-and-display lot near the pier, turn right and make like you're leaving town, but following the water; you'll find plenty of free parking along this eastern side of the harbor, and it's only a two-minute walk back into town. **Bus Éireann** (tel. 021/450-3399, route #249, 30-minute trip, 10/day Mon.–Sat., 5/day Sun.) offers frequent service from the city via the airport.

Need a lift? Ring **Kinsale Cabs** (tel. 021/470-0100). Bike rental is available from the **Hire Shop** (18 Main St., tel. 021/477-4884 or 086/881-2354, www.thehireshop.ie, open daily, €12/59 per day/week).

CORK

West Cork

TIMOLEAGUE

A sleepy little town on a back road to Clonakilty, Timoleague (Tigh Molaige, "House of Molaga") is worth a stop for its splendid churches as well as **Timoleague Abbey.** Still standing imposingly over Courtmacsherry Bay, this Franciscan abbey was built around 1240 on the site of the hermitage of Molaga, an obscure 7th-century saint. Though these pigeon-infested ruins are worth ambling through, there isn't much of architectural interest. Take a peek through the altar window for a nice view of the bay.

Timoleague's churches are actually neater than the abbey ruins. The Anglican **Church of the Ascension** (one block east of the friary ruins), which dates from the early 19th century, features gorgeous wall mosaics completed over a period of 30 years (1894–1926), a Crucifixion scene in the east window, and a life-size angel font, a copy of a Renaissance statue in Rome. Fortunately, unlike most Church of Ireland buildings, this one is open during the day. Timoleague's Catholic church, the Hiberno-Romanesque **Church of the Nativity of Our Lady** (a 2-minute walk up the hill, tel. 023/46185), features a three-lighted Harry Clarke window (from 1931) above the choir loft with scenes from the life of Jesus and the Ascension and Coronation of Mary.

Timoleague is 10 kilometers east of Clonakilty on the R600 and 45 kilometers southwest of Cork City (from the N71, picking up the R602 west of Bandon). **Bus Éireann** (tel. 021/450-8188) route #238 from Cork City passes through Timoleague twice a day, Monday to Friday, and it is possible to reach Timoleague from Clonakilty, via Bandon, on route #47. That said, if you don't have wheels, it makes more sense to travel the 10 kilometers by bike from Clonakilty (as the connection in Bandon is very inconvenient).

CLONAKILTY

Best known as the birthplace of IRA military leader Michael Collins, Clonakilty (Cloich na Coillte, "Castle of the Woods") is a delightful market town with a friendly, easygoing vibe and a well-earned "Ireland's Tidiest Town" distinction. (It's also Ireland's first official "Fair Trade Town.") With its fun pubs and handful of great restaurants, this is an excellent place to base yourself when exploring West Cork.

Clonakilty's main street, the N71, changes names from Pearse to Ashe to Wolfe Tone from west to east, with the small Asna Square (with 1798 monument) marking the change from Pearse to Ashe. Bridge Street intersects Pearse Street on the west end of town, leading south past the church, post office, and a statue of Michael Collins to the pretty Georgian Emmet Square.

Sights

There's not much to see in Clonakilty, though the **West Cork Model Railway Village** (Inchydoney Rd., tel. 023/33224, www.modelvillage. ie, open 11 A.M.–5 P.M. daily Feb.–Oct., open at 10 A.M. July–Aug., noon–4 P.M. weekends Nov.–Jan., admission €6.50, family ticket €20) is a popular draw for families with children. The Catholic, neo-Gothic **Church of the Immaculate Conception** (Bridge St.) features splendid wall mosaics and a rather disconcerting near-life-size wooden crucifix positioned right between the pews.

Entertainment and Events

When in Clonakilty, there's no better place to pass the evening than **Tigh De Barra** ("tee deh-BUR-ruh," 55 Pearse St., tel. 023/33381, www. debarra.ie), a veritable smorgasbord for the ears. There's live folk music here every night of the week—though Monday is trad night, and other times you might find a tribute band paying homage to some rock legend (often Jimi Hendrix). Aside from these informal "sitting room sessions," bigger gigs have featured the likes of Christy Moore, Sharon Shannon, and Luka Bloom (tickets €10–40).

But if it's just trad you're after, try "The

Little House," **An Teach Beag** (5 Recorder's Alley, off Pearse St., tel. 023/33883), with sessions nightly July–mid-September. In low season there's music on Tuesday and Friday through Sunday.

Shopping

Clonakilty has its share of chintzy souvenir emporia, but some really nice boutiques dot the main drag. An upscale craft shop and contemporary art gallery, **Etain Hickey** (40 Ashe St., tel. 023/21479) stocks ceramics and other homewares, jewelry, framed prints, and stained-glass pieces. For battery-free, delightfully old-fashioned playthings, stop by **Ecotoys** (29 Ashe St.).

Sports and Recreation

How about a pony trek along sandy **Inchydoney Strand,** four kilometers south of town? Ring the **Clonakilty Equestrian Centre** (Inchydoney Rd., signposted from town, tel. 023/33533).

The nine-hole **Dunmore Golf Club** (Muckross, tel. 023/34644) is adjacent to the Dunmore House Hotel.

The **Lisselan Golf Course** (4 km east of town off the N71, tel. 023/33249, www.lisselan.com) also has nine holes and is equally scenic (set within mature gardens along the Argideen River).

Accommodations

Backpackers have an option in the clean but smallish **Old Brewery Hostel** (Brewery Ln., just west of Emmet Sq., tel. 023/33525, wytchost@iol.ie, dorms €12, private rooms €15 pp). There are only 26 beds, so it's essential to ring ahead and confirm your reservation lest your bed be given away. There are better hostels in West Cork, but this one will do while you're here.

You can't go wrong with B&Bs in Clonakilty; they're all of a very high standard, and those outside town offer scenic views. The most central is **Wytchwood** (Old Brewery Ln., tel. 023/33525, www.wytchwood.ie, open Mar.–Sept., €35–40 pp, s €40–60, credit

cards accepted), a Georgian townhouse with a walled garden and spacious, airy rooms; the beds are just like home, with colorful Avoca mohair blankies.

Other B&Bs are signposted off the main N71 road on either end of Clonakilty, around a five-minute walk into town. The rooms at **Bay View** (Old Timoleague Rd., signposted off the N71 just east of town, tel. 023/33539, www.bayviewclonakilty.com, open Mar.–Oct., €30–38 pp, s €40–55) have very comfortable (if very pink and frilly) beds and beautiful views of sea and gardens. **Glendine** (Tawnies Upper, just north of the town center, signposted from Pearse St., tel. 023/34824, www.glendine.com, open Feb.–Nov., €33–38 pp, s €60, credit cards accepted) offers commodious rooms, accommodating owners, and an extensive breakfast menu with scrummy home-baked goods. The stiff single supplement's a bummer, though.

The most family-friendly B&B in town is **Melrose** (The Miles, signposted off the N71 on the western end of town, tel. 023/33956, www.melrosewestcork.com, closed Dec., €33–38 pp, s €45–50, credit cards accepted), with a back garden and patio with play area and barbecue, so you can self-cater here in the evenings if you don't feel like eating out. The showers are excellent, the rooms homey, the breakfasts delish (you'll sample the local black pudding), and the owners genuinely friendly and welcoming.

The **Emmet Hotel** (Emmet Sq., tel. 023/33394, www.emmethotel.com, €55–75 pp) has been offering "Georgian elegance since 1785," and though it's not posh it's friendly and well maintained, with spacious bedrooms and comfortable mattresses. Ask for a room overlooking the small town green. There's no private car park, but parking on the square is free. But if you don't need "character," then by all means stay at the new **Quality Hotel & Leisure Centre** (on the N71, Skibbereen Rd., 1.5 km west of town, tel. 023/36400, www.qualityhotelclon.com, rooms €70–150). The 20-meter pool and other fitness facilities are fine, but forgo the bar and restaurant for dinner and drinks in town. Better yet, try the

Dunmore House Hotel (Muckross, 5 km south of town, tel. 023/33352, www.dunmorehouse-hotel.com, €75–95 pp sharing) for its country-house charm, gorgeous sea views from every bedroom, and cordial, can-do reception.

Food

As for cafés, Evita's down the street might have the Internet hookup, but **Hart's** (8 Ashe St., tel. 023/35583, open 10 A.M.–5 P.M. Tues.–Sat., mains €5–7) has better food and atmosphere. Order a freshly squeezed pear-apple-lime juice to wash down your ciabatta.

One of Clonakilty's most beloved eateries is **An Súgán** (41 Wolfe Tone St., food served 12:30–10 P.M. daily, bar meals €6–12, restaurant mains €12–24), with a heavy seafood emphasis along with a couple of steak and duck dishes. A more eclectic menu is available at the classy **Malt House Granary** (30 Ashe St., tel. 023/34355, open noon–4 P.M. and 5–10 P.M. daily, mains €11–24), which elevates a hearty local specialty, black pudding, into a culinary work of art. There are several excellent vegetarian options. The wine list is small but well chosen, the service prompt and polite.

Clonakilty's newest and most exciting restaurant is the swanky-but-comfortable **◖ Richy's Bar and Bistro** (Wolftone St., tel. 023/21852, www.richysbarandbistro.com, open noon–10 P.M. daily, open at 11 A.M. weekends, €25 3-course early bird 5–7 P.M. Mon.–Thurs., mains €9–25), with that elusive combination of great food, laid-back atmosphere, and cordial and efficient service. The Mauritian owner-chef, Richy, describes his marvelously inventive cuisine as "West Cork fusion," but however you categorize the menu, there's something for everyone on it.

And if all else fails, you can dine with confidence at **O'Keefe's** (Emmet Sq., tel. 023/33394, www.emmethotel.com, restaurant open 6:30–9:30 P.M. daily, bar food served noon–9:30 P.M. daily, bar mains €10–20, restaurant mains €15–30), the restaurant at the Emmet Hotel, where the bar and restaurant fare is surprisingly high quality.

Information

The **tourist office** (25 Ashe St., tel. 023/33226, www.corkkerry.ie and www.clon.ie, open 9 A.M.–6 P.M. daily June, 9 A.M.–7 P.M. daily July–Aug., 9:30 A.M.–5:30 P.M. Mon.–Sat. Sept.–May) can give you info for anywhere you're headed in West Cork.

Services

The **AIB** at the corner of Pearse and Bridge Streets has an ATM and bureau de change. The **post office** is in a converted Presbyterian church on Bridge Street.

There are several pharmacies in town, including **Harrington's** (1 Ashe St., tel. 023/33318). Take your laundry to **Wash Basket** (Spiller's Ln., off Bridge St., tel. 023/34821).

Internet access is available at the **Talk and Internet Saloon** (Ashe St., across from the tourist office, no phone, open Mon.–Sat., €4/hour) or at the **Clon Cyber Café** at Evita's Sandwich Bar (37 Ashe St., tel. 023/21745, www.cloncybercafe.com, open 11 A.M.–9 P.M. Mon.–Sat., noon–9 P.M. Sun., €1/10 minutes, €5/hour), which also offers wireless access for the same price.

Getting There and Around

Clonakilty is 52 kilometers southwest of Cork City and 56 kilometers east of Bantry on the N71. **Bus Éireann** (tel. 021/450-8188, www.buseireann.ie, #47 or #236, 7/day daily) links Cork City with the towns on the Mizen Head Peninsula, stopping at Clonakilty en route.

Rent a bike from **MTM Cycles** (33 Ashe St., tel. 023/33584, €10/50 per day/week). For a cab, ring **Jim Kelleher** (tel. 023/34624) or **Clonakilty Hackneys** (tel. 023/34130).

GLANDORE AND UNION HALL

Linked by a causeway over a tidal estuary, the darling twin fishing villages of Glandore (Cuan Dor, "Harbour of the Oaks") and Union Hall (Bréantrá, "Foul Beach") are all abuzz with visiting yachters on warm summer evenings.

Just off the R597 three kilometers east of Glandore is the Bronze Age **Drombeg Stone**

Circle (always accessible, free admission), with a dramatic situation among the fields overlooking Glandore Harbour. Nine meters in diameter, the circle consists of 17 upright stones, and archaeological evidence indicates that alterations were made to the original stone arrangement during the Iron Age. Also dating from that period is a nearby *fulacht fiadh,* a cooking site where piping-hot stones dropped into this trough from a nearby fire would have slow-cooked the night's repast.

Unfortunately, Union Hall's reputation as a backpacker's heaven-on-earth is no longer accurate; the once-delightful Maria's Schoolhouse Hostel was up for sale again at time of writing, though the standard was on the slide pretty much as soon as Maria sold the business. She's still around, though, as her husband runs **Atlantic Sea Kayaking** (trips leave from Reen Pier, tel. 028/21058, www.atlanticseakayaking.com, 3-hour trip €45, 2.5-hour moonlight paddle €40). By day or night, this paddle trip is a must-do for anyone "from nine to 98" when in Union Hall. Reen Pier is clearly signposted from the village center (take the road uphill to the church and bear right at the Y junction).

There are several nice beaches in the area, but the prettiest of all is also the most out-of-the-way. Following the same route to the pier, you'll come to the old schoolhouse/hostel, and there's a narrow, unpaved, uphill road immediately opposite. Turn onto this road, follow it for a couple kilometers, make a left at the T junction, and follow the steep downhill switchbacks, which lead to a small but delightfully secluded beach, just the kind of place the locals don't want you to find out about. The small grassy cliff above the tiny car park is perfect for sunbathing on sunny August afternoons.

Accommodations and Food
Most of the accommodations are on the Union Hall side; a complete renovation of Glandore's hotel was just commencing at time of writing. Most convenient is **Ardagh House** (Union Hall village center, tel. 021/33571, www.ardaghhouse.com, €33 pp, s €42–45, credit cards accepted), which is also the most popular restaurant in town (not that there are many!). Here you'll have a comfy bed with an electric blanket, laundry service, and Internet access. There's a well-maintained garden out back. Serving simple but hearty meat and fish dishes, the restaurant is open nightly April–October and weekends November–March (mains €14–22).

Another option for B&B is **Shearwater** (signposted from Union Hall town center, tel. 028/33178 or 086/314-1818, www.shearwaterbandb.com, open Apr.–Oct., €35 pp, s €50), up the hill overlooking Glandore Harbour, where you'll have Internet access and a view from every room. On the Glandore side is the ivy-clad **Kilfinnan Farmhouse** (signposted off the R597 just east of the village, tel. 028/33233, kilfinnanfarm@eircom.net, €40 pp, s €50), with the charming atmosphere and incredibly fresh eggs, butter, and milk on the breakfast table you can only find inside a real farmhouse.

For steaks and seafood, try **Casey's Bar** (Main St., tel. 028/33590, food served 12:30–9:30 P.M. in summer only, mains €10–20).

Practicalities
There's no ATM in either village, though the **post office** on Union Hall's main street changes money.

Glandore is 3.7 kilometers off the N71 (on the R597), with Union Hall 1 kilometer farther west across a one-lane causeway. If driving, make the turnoff at Leap; if traveling via **Bus Éireann** (tel. 021/450-8188, route #47, at least 7/day Mon.–Sat., 5/day Sun.), you'll have to disembark at Leap and make the (albeit pleasant) walk down to Glandore.

SKIBBEREEN
A workaday, slightly rough-around-the-edges market town between Bantry and Clonakilty, Skibbereen (An Sciobairín) is worth a stop for its **tourist office** in the town hall on North Street (tel. 028/21766, open 9 A.M.–6 P.M. Mon.–Sat. June and Sept., 9 A.M.–7 P.M. Mon.–Sat. July–Aug., 9:15 A.M.–1 P.M. and 2–5:30 P.M. Mon.–Fri. Oct.–May). The

Skibbereen Heritage Centre (Old Gasworks Building, Upper Bridge St., tel. 028/40900, www.skibbheritage.com, open 10 A.M.–6 P.M. Tues.–Sat. mid-Mar.–May and Oct., daily June–Sept., open 9:30 A.M.–5:30 P.M. Mon.–Fri. Nov. and Feb.–mid-Mar., admission €5) is also worth a look for its in-depth Great Famine exhibition. You might also check out whatever visual art exhibition is on at the **West Cork Arts Centre** (North St., tel. 028/22090, www.westcorkartscentre.com, open 10 A.M.–6 P.M. Mon.–Sat.).

Make a withdrawal at the **AIB** ATM on Bridge Street before following the signs for lovely Baltimore, 13 kilometers south on the R595.

BALTIMORE

A heck of a lot prettier than its Maryland namesake, Baltimore (Dún na Séad, "Fort of the Jewels") is at the tip of its own little peninsula, punctuated by two islands to the southwest: **Sherkin** and **Cape Clear**, the latter being a Gaeltacht region of 150 people. Board a ferry from the Baltimore pier to either island (tel. 028/39159 or 086/346-5110, www.capeclearferry.info, 3–4/day daily May–mid-Sept., 1–2/day daily in low season, return fare €12).

Though Baltimore means "Town of the Big House" (Baile an Tighe Mhóir), its official Irish name refers to the ruins of an O'Driscoll castle overlooking the harbor. Unsurprisingly, this little town is a beloved haunt of yachters, scuba divers, and sea kayakers; for more info on diving excursions, contact John Kearney at the **Baltimore Diving & Watersports Centre** (tel. 028/20300, www.baltimorediving.com), which also offers hostel and self-catering accommodations, a restaurant, bike hire—even a sauna. Beginning divers are welcome, as the center specializes in PADI courses. Another diving center here is **Aquaventures** (Lifeboat Rd., tel. 028/20511, www.aquaventures.ie); for sailing lessons, contact the **Baltimore Sailing School** (tel. 028/20141, www.baltimoresailingschool.com). Five-day courses run May–September. If you'd rather keep your feet on solid ground, you can always go for a stroll

out to the Baltimore Beacon, better known as **Lot's Wife,** which was built by the British after the 1798 rebellion.

Accommodations, Food, and Entertainment

Sometimes a town becomes increasingly popular because one of its accommodations is a destination in itself, and that's definitely the case in Baltimore. It's partly a hostel, but the IHH **◖ Rolf's** (500 meters off the R595, signposted on the north side of the village, tel. 028/20289, www.rolfsholidays.com, dorms €13–15, doubles/twins €20–35 pp, credit cards accepted) is better described as a great-value B&B (with the second B extra), along with a few four- and six-bed dorms. The situation is idyllic all-around, with mature well-tended gardens and gorgeous views from the flagstone terrace and dining room. Airy, well-appointed two-bedroom cottages are available for weekly rental (low/high season €450/750). Best of all is the adjoining café–wine bar–art gallery, **Café Art,** offering everything from full breakfasts to fantastic three-course dinners (open 12:30–2:30 P.M. and 6–9:30 P.M., closing at 9 P.M. in winter, mains €11–21), also a great value. The menu is eclectic yet artfully simple.

Baltimore is surprisingly short on B&B accommodations, but one to try is **Channel View** (half a kilometer north of Baltimore on the R595, tel. 028/20440, www.channelviewbb.com, open Mar.–Oct., €28–35 pp, s €40–60, credit cards accepted), with private gardens, colorful and comfortable rooms, and fresh fish for breakfast. Planning to stay a while? Look into renting one of eight well-appointed self-catering **Inish Beg Cottages** (Inish Beg Island, tel. 028/21745, www.inishbeg.com), part of a newly restored 39-hectare estate on its own island, accessible via bridge from Baltimore. Facilities include an indoor heated 13-meter pool, steam room, and gym. Low/high-season rates start at €375/750 per week for a one-bedroom cottage, though there are larger cottages available.

There are other hotels in and near Baltimore, but **Casey's of Baltimore** (on the R595 on the north end of the village, tel. 028/20197, www.caseysofbaltimore.com, €73–87 pp, s €89–110) is far and away the best in terms of service, food, maintenance, and atmosphere. Many of the spacious, homey rooms come with sea views and/or king-size beds. Casey's also has one of the friendliest, liveliest bars in Baltimore—you're sure to catch a trad session here on summer weekend evenings, and the pub grub is faultless.

There's plenty of harborside pub action too; all the bars have picnic tables out front overlooking the bay. Aside from Casey's, you'll find the best bar meals in town at **Bushe's** (The Square, on the harbor, tel. 028/20125, www. bushesbar.com, food served 9:30 A.M.–8 P.M. Mon.–Sat., 12:30–8 P.M. Sun., meals under €10), a Baltimore institution. Sailors regularly stop in to pick up their newspaper subscriptions, shower, and grab a pint and an open-faced crab sandwich. Francophile fish-lovers will devour the shellfish platter (€50) at **Chez Youen** (on the quay, tel. 028/20136, open 6– 10 P.M. daily, closed Nov. and Feb., 3-course dinner €30–40), another local favorite.

Practicalities

There is no tourist office or ATM in Baltimore; the nearest information and banking facilities are in Skibbereen (13 km north on the R595), which you'll pass through on the way down.

Baltimore is 46 kilometers southwest of Clonakilty and 98 kilometers southwest of Cork City off the N71 (via Skibbereen). **Bus Éireann** (tel. 021/450-8188) route #47 (8/day Mon.–Sat., 6–7/day Sun.) will get you from Cork to Skibbereen, where you can change buses (route #251, 4/day Mon.–Fri., summer-only service Sat.) for Baltimore.

The Mizen Head Peninsula

Not as well traveled as the Beara, the Mizen ("MIZZ-en") isn't quite as spectacular either. Those divers and sea anglers not in Baltimore come to Schull, the Mizen's most substantial town, where on summer evenings the pleasant, tidy main drag hums with animated conversation from a line of picnic tables outside all the pubs. The Mizen Head warrants one full day, and you'll want to end it here.

Toward the very edge of the peninsula, Crookhaven is a nightmare on sunny summer weekends, when the main street is full of shirtless unsavories kicking footballs and sticky-faced children darting into oncoming traffic. You're coming here to relax (and load up on the fresh seafood), but the irony is that this place is so popular there's no peace and quiet to be found. Schull is touristy too, but it's also a whole lot classier (and it's never as crowded as that). It's certainly worth seeking out the lovely **Barley Cove** west of Crookhaven (signposted from the R591), though you'll have plenty of company.

◖ MIZEN VISION

A highlight of any trip to West Cork is an exhilarating (if wind-tossed) walk around Mizen Head, the island's most southwesterly point, and a visit to Mizen Vision, the visitors center (at the end of a local road, signposted off the R591, tel. 028/35115, www .mizenhead.net, open 10:30 A.M.–5 P.M. daily mid-Mar.–May and Oct., 10 A.M.–6 P.M. daily June–Sept., 11 A.M.–4 P.M. Sat.–Sun. Nov.–Mar., admission €6) at Mizen Head. The lighthouse was built here at Fastnet Rock in the early 1850s after an American ocean liner sank near Crookhaven, claiming 92 lives. A sturdier replacement tower was built at the turn of the 20th century. A walk down to the signal station is as memorable for the view as it is the exhibition inside. At time of writing the center had just reopened after the building of a new observation tower and gallery and renovation of the signal tower. You'll need your own set of wheels to get here.

SCHULL

Nestled between Roaringwater Bay and the 408-meter Mount Gabriel, Schull (pronounced "skull"; An Scoil, "The School") is the largest town on the Mizen Head Peninsula—but fortunately it doesn't feel like it. This one-street fishing village is a haven for scuba divers and yachting enthusiasts, as the busy harbor attests. In high season Schull is touristy but not overwhelmingly so; on summer bank holidays there are just as many Irish out-of-towners as there are international visitors, making for quite a festive atmosphere.

Sights

The **Schull Planetarium** (Schull Community College, Colla Rd., on the west side of the harbor, tel. 028/28552 or 028/28315) is the only one in the Irish Republic, with an eight-meter dome and a 70-seat auditorium. Opened in 1989 through the generosity of Josef Menke, a German industrialist who spent many holidays in Schull, the planetarium offers 45-minute "starshows" of the night sky in the Northern Hemisphere. Opening hours and showtimes vary during the summer (3:30–5 P.M. Sun. mid- to end of May and first two Sun. in Sept., show at 4 P.M.; 3:30–5 P.M. Tues., show at 4 P.M., and 7:30–9 P.M. Sat., show at 8 P.M. in June; 3:30–5 P.M. Tues., Fri., and Sat., show at 4 P.M., and Mon. and Thurs. 7:30–9 P.M., show at 8 P.M. July–Aug.; admission €5).

Food, Entertainment, and Events

Schull's eateries emphasize organic local produce, seafood, and farmhouse cheeses. Sample it all at the **Waterside Inn** (Main St., tel. 028/28203, www.watersideinnschull.com, food served 12:30–9:30 P.M. daily, bar meals under €10, restaurant mains €22–30). The restaurant fare, all seafood, is tasty but pricey; you can get a cheap bowl of the Waterside's legendary chowder at the bar. (It's not actually waterside, by the way.)

A delightful café-wine bar-deli with a fine stash of organic chocolate, farmhouse cheeses, and international wines all perfect for a picnic, the **West Cork Gourmet Store** (Main St.,

tel. 028/27613, open 9:30 A.M.–9 P.M., dinner served 7–9 P.M., mains €12–14) also does fantastic gourmet pizzas (though the pastas are on the mediocre side). Best of all, the friendly waitstaff don't rush you from your table even on busy summer weekends.

Another popular café-wine bar (plus art gallery) is the cheerful, airy **Newman's West** (Main St., tel. 028/27776, food served 9 A.M.–midnight Mon.–Sat., until 11 P.M. Sun., meals under €10), where a €5 purchase gets you wireless Internet access. The sandwich menu features fresh local ingredients and is very reasonably priced. The café is a recent addition to the town's most beloved watering hole, **T.J. Newman's.**

The week after the August bank holiday brings the **Schull Regatta,** the most important event on the local calendar since its first race in 1884.

Shopping

Schull has several cute shops along its main street, including **Pizzazz,** with gorgeous, ultramodern jewelry, and **Gwen's Chocolates** (tel. 028/27853, www.gwenschocolates.com), worth giving up your diet to sample every dainty flavor from cointreau to rum raisin. For light reading or Ordnance Survey maps, stop by **Chapter One** bookshop (tel. 028/27606). The town **farmers market** takes place every Sunday starting at 10 A.M., Easter–October.

Sports and Recreation

Waterbabies are well catered to here. **Schull Watersports Centre** (at the pier, tel. 028/28554) offers lessons and equipment rental, whether you want to go kayaking, sailboarding, deep-sea angling, or scuba diving. Other diving charter companies include **Mizen Charters** (tel. 087/251-7452), **Divecology** (Cooradarrigan, tel. 028/28946 or 086/837-2065, www.divecology.com), and **Blue Thunder** (tel. 086/386-2876). Though there aren't any beaches in Schull itself, you can drive farther west to **Ballyrisode Strand** in Toormore (9 km) or **Barley Cove** near Crookhaven (23 km).

Tee off at the nine-hole, par-30 **Coosheen Golf Club** (signposted off the R592 3 km east of town, tel. 028/28182, http://homepage. eircom.net/~coosheengc) overlooking Schull Harbour.

Accommodations

Under construction at the time of writing, **Schull Harbour View Hotel** (Main St., www .schullharbourviewhotel.com) should be open by summer 2007. The hotel will feature harbor views from many of the rooms as well as a swimming pool, Jacuzzi, and sauna.

Schull's top B&B, **Stanley House** (signposted off the western end of town, a 2-minute walk up a local road, tel. 028/28425, www. stanley-house.net, open Mar.–Oct., €33 pp, s €42–45), is one kilometer outside town. The views over Roaringwater Bay from every room are incomparable—as is the welcome—and there's a carefully tended garden out back perfect for relaxing in. On a quiet residential cul-de-sac just off Main Street is **Glencairn** (Ardmanagh Dr., tel. 028/28007, susanglencairn@yahoo.ie, €35 pp, s €40)—no view, but the location is handy. A comfortable, good-value B&B signposted from the eastern end of town, and one kilometer up a narrow road, is **Hillside** (tel. 028/28248, http://homepage. eircom.net/~hillsideaccom, open May–Sept., €30–32 pp sharing).

Those with wheels should consider staying at **Fortview House** (on the R591 9 km west of Schull, signposted from the R592/Schull–Goleen road, tel. 028/35324, www.fortview-housegoleen.com, open Mar.–Oct., €40–45 pp, s €52–57, self-catering cottages low/high season €320/650 per week, evening meal €30 by prior arrangement), a farmhouse built in 1913 with fine antiques (wrought-iron bedstands, the lot) but all mod cons, a genuinely friendly welcome, and a top-notch breakfast menu featuring eggs laid just out back.

Information and Services

Schull doesn't have a tourist office, but check out **Schull.ie** (www.schull.ie) before you go. The **AIB** on Main Street has an ATM and bureau de change; you can also withdraw funds from the ATM at the Centra supermarket across the way (open until 10 P.M.). For Internet access, your only option is **@ Your Leisure** (Main St., tel. 028/28600, open daily, €6/hour), a video store with a couple of old-school iMacs.

Getting There and Around

Schull is 55 kilometers west of Clonakilty (from the N71 to the R592), and 105 kilometers west of Cork City by the same route. Public parking (in three different lots off the main street) is free and ample. **Bus Éireann** (tel. 021/450-8188, www.buseireann.ie, #47 or #236, 7/day daily) links Cork City with the towns on the Mizen Head Peninsula, including Schull, via Clonakilty.

For taxi service, ring **Betty Johnson** (tel. 028/28410 or 086/265-6078). Rent a bike from **Cotter's Yard** (Main St., tel. 028/28165, after-hours tel. 028/35185, €12/day).

The Sheep's Head Peninsula

The least traveled of Cork's western peninsulas is Sheep's Head, a bucolic (and blissfully undeveloped) finger of land 26 kilometers long and only 4 kilometers wide. This is your best bet for getting off the beaten track in West Cork. Pick up maps for the 88-kilometer **Sheep's Head Way** or 100-kilometer **Cycle Route** from the tourist office in Bantry.

Accommodations are sparse on the peninsula; most visitors use Bantry as a base. The folks at **Seamount Farm** (Glenlough West, 12 km west of Bantry on Goat's Path Rd., signposted, tel. 027/61226, www.seamountfarm. com and www.sheepshead.ie, €30–32 pp sharing) not only cater to long-distance walkers, they organize hill-walking holidays on Sheep's

Head. This is a great-value B&B with terrific home-baked goods (tea and fresh-out-of-the-oven scones served on arrival), cozy rooms with electric blankets, and lovely sea and garden views.

Fortunately, it's possible to get out here without a rental car, even though **Bus Éireann** route #255 runs only on Saturday. **Bantry Rural Transport** (5 Church St., Bantry, tel. 027/52727, usually 2/day daily) serves Durrus and Kilcrohane (on the south side of the peninsula) via Goat's Path Road; you'll find the timetable on the Bantry community website (www.bantry.ie).

BANTRY

The sizable harbor town of Bantry (Beanntrai), the gateway to the Sheep's Head, is quickly losing whatever charm it possessed to a row of luxury harborside condominiums and other new construction. The town also has more than its share of seedy-looking grog-houses, which doesn't exactly encourage one to venture down the main drag by night with an ear cocked for the strains of traditional music. That said, **J. J. Crowley's** (The Square, tel. 027/50029) is a nice old pub with traditional music, ballads, or set dancing on Wednesday, Friday, and Saturday nights and Sunday afternoons.

The town itself is easy to get the hang of, with Wolfe Tone Square (shaped more like a narrow rectangle) just east of the pier, Marino and New Streets heading east from the square's end, and Main Street (which becomes Church Road) branching off New Street (at the intersection where New Street turns into Bridge Street). Marino Street turns into the Glengarriff road.

C Bantry House and Gardens

Come to Bantry for the stunning Italianate gardens at Bantry House (1 km southwest of town on the N71, the Skibbereen road, tel. 027/50047, www.bantryhouse.ie, open 10 A.M.–6 P.M. daily Mar.–Oct., admission to house, gardens, and Armada center €10, gardens and center €5), which has been in the same family (the descendants of the earls of

Bantry) since the 18th century. The house itself is a veritable museum of art and antiques, and admission includes a guided tour. On a fine day you might want to stick to the garden, though, which has a grand staircase of 99 steps offering a beautiful panoramic view of Bantry Bay. The French Armada exhibition focuses on a historical episode preceding the 1798 rebellion, in which a French fleet sailed to Ireland intending to overthrow the British; raging storms ruined their plans before the British could, and 10 of the 50 French warships were lost. One of them lies at the bottom of Bantry Bay, though it was only discovered in 1981.

Bantry House is also a hotel (but with the faded-grandeur routine you've got to expect the occasional maintenance issues). B&B rates start at €120 per person.

Accommodations and Food

Bantry's hostel and hotels are of a disappointingly low standard; you're better off at a B&B. Two fine ones are within easy walking distance of town. The first is **The Mill** (Newtown, 1 km north of town on the N71, tel. 027/50278, www.the-mill.net, open Easter–Oct., €32–35 pp, s €50), a lovingly maintained chalet-style place with lush gardens; homey but character-filled sitting, dining, and bedrooms; laundry service; and deluxe breakfasts. Or try **Ard na Greine** (Newtown, 1.5 km north of town on the N71, tel. 027/51169, www.ardnagreine.net, open Apr.–Sept., €32–33 pp, s €45, credit cards accepted), where you can expect comfortable beds, delicious home-baking, and a proprietor for whom nothing's too much trouble.

Bantry has several nice coffee shops, but most convenient is the **Organico Café** (2 Glengarriff Rd., tel. 027/51391, www.organico.ie, open 10 A.M.–6 P.M. Mon.–Fri. and 10 A.M.–5 P.M. Sat., mains under €10, Internet access €4/hour), an inventive vegetarian café, Fair Trade grocery, bakery, takeaway, art gallery, and Internet access point all in one. For the fresh Bantry Bay seafood you've been hearing about, head to the super-stylish, family-run **O'Connor's** (Wolfe Tone Sq., tel. 027/50221, www.oconnorseafood.com, open 12:15–5 P.M.

and 6–10 P.M. daily, lunches €6–12, dinner mains €18–28)—the best restaurant in town.

Practicalities

You'll find the **tourist office** (tel. 027/50229, open 9:30 A.M.–5 P.M. Mon.–Sat. mid-Mar.–Oct., daily July–Aug.) on Wolfe Tone Square. There's an ATM and bureau de change at the **Bank of Ireland,** also on the square.

Bantry is 44.5 km south of Kenmare and 14 kilometers southeast of Glengarriff on the N71, and 91 kilometers west of Cork on the R586. **Bus Éireann** can get you here via the Cork–Castletownbere route (#46, 4/day Mon.–Sat., 3/day Sun.). Rent a bike from the **Bicycle Shop** (the Glengarriff road/N71, on the north end of town, tel. 027/52657, €12/day).

AHAKISTA

Another blink-and-you'll-miss-it village on the south side of the peninsula, Ahakista (Átha an Chiste) has the best watering hole on Sheep's Head, the **Tin Pub** (on the local Durrus–Kilcrohane road, tel. 027/67337, www.tinpub .com, food served noon–9 P.M. daily in high season, meals under €12). Named, laconically, for its corrugated tin roof, there's a pleasantly rustic atmosphere here, indoors as well as in the rambling beer garden—a real garden!—out back. The bar menu consists of savory pies (shepherd's, chicken, salmon, or "superior fish") supplied by Ballymaloe alumni Cully & Sully. The Tin Pub has a longstanding reputation for great music, with trad sessions here on Tuesday and Sunday nights along with the occasional karaoke or samba show. More formal gigs feature some pretty high-profile musicians (like The Bridies, formerly the lead fiddlers in Michael Flatley's *Lord of the Dance*).

DURRUS

While on the Sheep's Head, be sure to stop for lunch at the **Good Things Café** (Ahakista Rd., just west of Durrus, tel. 027/61426, www.the-goodthingscafe.com, open 10:30 A.M.–5 P.M. Wed.–Mon., 7–8:30 P.M. Fri.–Mon., open daily in Aug., weekends only Oct.–Dec., closed Jan.–Mar., mains €12–23), a gourmet grocery

© CAMILLE DE ANGELIS

St. Finbarr's Oratory, a place of pilgrimage at Gougane Barra

and restaurant overlooking Dunmanus Bay. The menu features local delicacies like Durrus cheese, Bantry Bay lobster, and Gubbeen ham, all wonderfully prepared.

NORTHEAST OF BANTRY
Gougane Barra Forest Park

By far the loveliest section of inland Cork is the four-square-kilometer Gougane Barra Forest Park (Gúgan Barra, always open, free admission) tucked in the Shehy Mountains on the Cork-Kerry border. Looking at all the thick swathes of pine and spruce covering these hillsides, it's difficult to believe this area was once pretty much treeless (until the forestation program commenced in 1938). Gougane Barra's wooded walking trails have a vaguely magical feel, like you're venturing into a world where banshees and other preternatural creatures still exist. There's a tearoom and hotel overlooking the dark, glassy Gougane Barra Lake at the park entrance, and not much else. Before you enter the park, turn off onto an artificial causeway to a tiny island with a tiny chapel, **St. Finbarr's Oratory,** featuring stained-glass windows of obscure Irish saints. This is a popular pilgrimage site come September, as St. Finbarr lived a hermit's life on this little island in the 6th century; you can still see a holy well at the end of the causeway, as well as a complex of eight monks' cells just beyond the restored 18th-century Catholic chapel. The park entrance is 700 meters beyond the island causeway. In high season the park gets crowded with coach tours, so be sure to get here early in the day.

All the bedrooms at the family-run Óstan Gúgan Barra, or **Gougane Barra Hotel** (sign-posted 2 km off the R584 west of Ballingeary, tel. 026/47069, www.gouganebarrahotel.com, open mid-Apr.–mid-Oct., €60–70 pp) offer lake and/or mountain views. This is the kind of place you might hesitate about—after all, it's got no competition, and a lack of competition usually breeds mediocrity in the hotel business—but fortunately that's not the case here. Though the restaurant is fine, the fresh-and-simple bar meals are a much better value, and breakfast comes with plenty of home-baked goods (bar food served noon–9:30 P.M. Mon.–Sat., restaurant open 5:30–9:30 P.M. daily and noon–4 P.M. Sun., 3-course pre-theater menu €25 at 6 P.M. Tues.–Sun. July–Aug., set dinner €37, Sun. lunch €25, bar meals €10–20). The hotel hosts one professional dramatic production all summer as part of the **Theatre by the Lake,** a new addition in 2005 (performances at 8:30 P.M. Tues.–Sun. July–Aug., tickets €10–15, pre-booking required). A pleasant tearoom just across the car park, **Cronin's,** is named for the hotel's original owners.

For more information on the forest park, hotel, and recreational activities, visit the Gougane Barra website (www.gouganebarra. com). The park doesn't have a visitors center, so the hotel is also your best source of info once you're there.

Gougane Barra is 26 kilometers northeast of Bantry off the R584 and 71 kilometers west of Cork City on the N22, picking up the R584 a couple kilometers before Macroom. A Saturday-only **Bus Éireann** service (#255) links Bantry with the Gougane crossroads; the bus departs Bantry at 4 P.M., arriving outside the forest park at 4:40 P.M.

The Beara Peninsula

The "Ring of Beara" is Cork's prettiest peninsula, though the northeast section belongs to County Kerry. If driving, you can take the longer coastal route through the sleepy pastel-hued villages of Eyeries, Ardgroom, and Allihies before reaching the Beara's de facto capital, Castletownbere; or you can cut through the Caha mountains from Lauragh (in Kerry) to Adrigole via the gorgeously scenic Healy Pass. Bus Éireann serves the Beara only as far west as Castletownbere, and though private bus services are available they're too infrequent to be much help to the visitor who has only a couple days to spare; if you want to do the Beara right, you're best off with a rental car. For more information on the 197-kilometer **Beara Way** walking route, see the sidebar *Long-Distance Walks in County Cork.*

The nearest official Irish Tourist Board offices are in Kenmare and Glengarriff, though there's a kiosk on the square in Castletownbere, and you can visit the **Beara Tourism** website (www.bearatourism.com) before you go.

GLENGARRIFF

Popular for its enchanted-forest nature reserve, quality gift shops, friendly pubs, and speedy ferry to the garden isle of Ilnacullen, Glengarriff (An Gleann Garbh, "The Rugged Glen") is the southern gateway to the Beara. It also makes a far more pleasant base than Bantry for exploring the Sheep's Head Peninsula.

Glengarriff is a one-street town, and the fork in the road at the west end of Main Street will lead to Castletownbere if you go left and Kenmare (and the nature reserve) if you go right.

Garnish Island

Take the ferry to Garnish Island (also spelled Garinish) to visit the Dúchas-run **Ilnacullin** (1.5-km boat trip from Glengarriff pier, tel. 027/63040, admission €3.70), a lovely 15-hectare Italianate garden designed by Harold Peto in the 1910s for British MP Annan Bryce, then-owner of Garnish. It's

open 10 A.M.–4:30 P.M. Monday–Saturday and 1–5 P.M. Sunday March and October, 10 A.M.–6:30 P.M. Monday–Saturday and 1–6:30 P.M. Sunday in April, 10 A.M.–6:30 P.M. Monday–Saturday and 11 A.M.–6:30 P.M. Sunday May–June and September, 9:30 A.M.–6:30 P.M. Monday–Saturday and 11 A.M.–6:30 P.M. Sunday July–August (closed in winter). Bryce's dream of transforming this rocky little island into a paradise of flowers and shrubbery from all over the world might have seemed crazy at the time, but the dream came true after decades of nurturing his exotic plant

LONG-DISTANCE WALKS IN COUNTY CORK

Cork's longest walking route is the 197-kilometer **Beara Way,** which loops from Kenmare to Glengarriff to Castletownbere; at Allihies a path diverges toward Dursey Island, and there is also a section on Bere Island (accessible by ferry from Castletownbere). Walking the Beara Way and including this portion of the route will take approximately 10 days; without Dursey and Bere Islands, it can be completed in one week. The terrain is relatively easy, the scenery pretty but not quite as breathtaking as Dingle or the Ring of Kerry.

The **BearaWay.net** (www.bearaway. net) site was under construction at time of writing, but it will surely be as helpful as its sister sites (KerryWay.net, et al.) once it's up and running.

The Beara is much less popular than the Kerry Way, and quieter still is the 89-kilometer **Sheep's Head Way.** This route loops around the narrow Sheep's Head Peninsula, beginning and ending in Bantry, and can be completed in three days.

menagerie. Ilnacullin, or Illaunacullin, means "Island of Holly," but it's the azaleas and rhododendrons that bloom the brightest in May and June. You can also watch seals sunning themselves on the rocks on the island's southern shore.

The garden is the only thing to see on the island, though there's a tearoom at the visitors center. Note that there's a charge to reach Garnish via the **Blue Pool Ferry** (tel. 027/63333, return trip €10) in addition to the gardens admission. The pier is signposted next to Murphy's Village Hostel on Main Street.

Glengarriff Bamboo Park

There's another garden in Glengarriff you don't need a ferry to get to: Glengarriff Bamboo Park (signposted off Main St., tel. 027/63570, www.bamboo-park.com, open 9 A.M.–7 P.M. daily, admission €5) hosts 30 bamboo and 12 palm tree species on five hectares; all of the species can flourish in West Cork's frost-free Gulf Stream climate.

◖ Glengarriff Woods Nature Reserve

Three square kilometers of enchanting sylvan landscapes comprise the Glengarriff Woods Nature Reserve (entrance on the N71 1 km north of town, open daily until dusk). For a 6.5-kilometer walking route that takes in all the park's highlights, pick up a *Slí Na Slainte* route map from the tourist office. There's also a list of suggested routes on a billboard by the car park. Whichever route you take, don't miss climbing the steps to **Lady Bantry's Lookout.** The hike is short (2–3 minutes) but steep; it's well worth the effort for a fantastic panorama of the forests of the nature reserve, the village of Glengarriff, Bantry Bay, and the Sheep's Head Peninsula on the horizon.

Shopping

Looking for a pullover to bring home to Aunt Edna? You've got three quality craft emporia to choose from, all on the main street: **Quills** (ring Killarney store, tel. 064/32277, for info, www.quillsireland.com), the **Irish Craft**

Climb to Lady Bantry's Lookout for a terrific view of Bantry Bay.

© CAMILLE DEANGELIS

Centre (tel. 027/63201), and **The Spinning Wheel** (tel. 027/63347).

In keeping with West Cork's reputation for contemporary visual art, the **Catherine Hammond Gallery** (Main St., tel. 027/63812, www.hammondgallery.com) showcases exciting work by emerging and established painters from Ireland and America. No bland landscapes here, that's for sure.

Sports and Recreation

It may only have nine holes, but the views at the **Glengarriff Golf Club** (2 km east of town on the N71, tel. 027/63150 or 087/246-8071, www.glengarriffgolfclub.com) are as beautiful as you'd expect.

Accommodations

It's by no means the best hostel in West Cork (the dust-filmed windows on what was once the ground-floor restaurant hardly entice one to ring the bell), but **Murphy's Village Hostel** (Main St., tel. 027/63555, dorms €15–17, doubles €20 pp sharing) fits the bill if you're traveling on a shoestring.

Up a long, steep, switchbacked driveway is a beautifully situated B&B, **Oakfield** (on the eastern end of the village, tel. 027/63371, €34 pp). From up here you have a stunning view of Garnish Island beyond the perfectly manicured public park across the road. The rooms are comfortable, simple, and unpretentious, and Ann Barron is a genuinely kind and very helpful hostess. Be sure to ask for one of the front-facing bedrooms. There are plenty more B&Bs along the Main Street, but definitely try this one first. Another place with great views on the same side of town is **Cois Coille** ("Near the Woods," tel. 027/63202, www.coiscoille. com, open mid-Mar.–Oct., €34 pp sharing). Guests can enjoy the view from the front patio or relax in the well-tended gardens out back. (No televisions in the rooms, though.) Otherwise, the delightful **Rainbow Restaurant** also does B&B (Main St., tel. 027/63440, www. glengarriffrainbow.com, €30–40 pp sharing).

There's one hotel in town, **Casey's Hotel** (Main St., tel. 027/63010, caseyshotel@yahoo.

com, €50 pp), which boasts the distinction of having hosted Eamon de Valera. It's a typical small-town, two-star establishment in every respect, with friendly staff and quaint reception rooms but rather smallish bedrooms. The restaurant and bar menus may look appetizing, but the quality is too uneven to recommend eating here.

Food and Entertainment

Due in part to its ample outdoor seating, the **Blue Loo** (Main St., tel. 027/63167, food served 9 A.M.–6 P.M. daily, mains under €12) is the most popular pub in town. Fill up on hearty grub here or at **Johnny Barry's** (Main St., tel. 027/63315, food served 12:30–9:30 P.M. daily, mains under €12). Both pubs do reliably good steaks and seafood, and offer trad sessions on summer evenings.

The food (more or less the usual steaks and seafood) is quite good at **The Rainbow** (Main St., tel. 027/63440, food served noon–9:30 P.M. daily, mains €11–20), but it's the exceptional (and exceptionally speedy) service that really sets this place apart. The owners will ask you more than once if you're satisfied with your meal, and the waitresses are equally affable and eager to please. If you've been less than impressed with the generally mediocre standard of service in Irish restaurants, you'll find a meal here is memorable no matter what you order. The desserts are scrummy, too. The adjoining **Hawthorn Bar** offers live music (trad and folk) most nights in the summertime.

And on your way to Bantry, be sure to stop at the **Old Church Coffeehouse** (on the N71 just east of the village, by the harbor, tel. 027/63663, opening hours vary, mains under €10) for a cup of java and yummy baked goods in an atmospheric Protestant church-turned-tearoom, stained glass windows and all. (There's also a lunch menu, though the food quality is uneven.)

Information and Services

On the Bantry end of the village is a small, seasonal **tourist office** (tel. 027/63084, open 10:15 A.M.–6 P.M. Mon.–Sat. June–Aug.).

The staff here are far more friendly and helpful than the average Oifig Fáilte employee, so stop in here if you have questions about any place at all in West Cork.

There was no ATM in Glengarriff at time of writing. If you need cash, plan to stop in Bantry or Kenmare. The **post office** is inside O'Shea's supermarket on Main Street.

Getting There and Around

Glengarriff is on Bantry Bay on the south side of the Beara Peninsula, 30 kilometers south of Kenmare and 14 kilometers northwest of Bantry on the N71. The Cork–Castletownbere **Bus Éireann** route (tel. 021/450-8188, www.buseireann.ie, #46, 3–4/day Mon.–Sat., 2/day Sun.) stops in Glengarriff.

For bike rental, stop by **Jem Creations Art Gallery** (just off Main St., Castletownbere Rd., tel. 027/63113, €12/72 per day/week). For a taxi, ring **Donal Harrington** (tel. 027/63564); **Glengarriff Cabs** (tel. 027/63060) does guided tours as well.

ADRIGOLE

The southern terminus of the spectacular Healy Pass through the Caha mountain range, the widely scattered (along 10 kilometers!) village of Adrigole (Eádargoil) makes a nice base, what with its water-sporting opportunities, quality hostel and guesthouse, and charming café/gift shop/art gallery. Nearby **Hungry Hill** (685 meters) has the country's highest waterfall, dubbed the Mare's Tail.

The **West Cork Sailing Centre** (signposted off the R572, tel. 027/60132, www.westcorksailing.com) offers sailing courses and powerboat training, or you can just rent a kayak or canoe for €13.

Looking for a nice souvenir? You'll find contemporary oils, watercolors, and prints as well as giftier things (jewelry, knitwear, pottery, and such) at the **Adrigole Arts Centre** (signposted on the R572 just west of the village, tel. 027/60234, www.adrigolearts.com, open 10 A.M.–6 P.M. Mon.–Sat. Mar.–Oct. and 11 A.M.–6 P.M. Sun. May–Sept., snacks under €5). The staff are genuinely friendly and the coffee and baked goods are delish—plus there's a front terrace with a sea view on which to enjoy them.

Whether you want a campsite, dorm bed, double room, or self-catering cottage, the **Hungry Hill Lodge** (Adrigole Harbour, signposted on the R572, tel. 027/60228, www.hungryhilllodge.com, dorms €15–17, private rooms €17–23 pp, 1/2-person tent €7/13, credit cards accepted) can accommodate. There's an adjoining pub/coffee shop serving breakfast and lunch (as well as real ground coffee), and dinner is available on request.

You'll find top-quality seafood at the überclassy **Mossie's** (Ulusker House, Trafrask, signposted off the R572 on the eastern side of the village, tel. 027/60606, www.mossiesrestaurant.com, €35–65 pp, s €50–85, restaurant open noon–6 P.M. and 7–9:30 P.M. daily in summer, closed Mon.–Tues. in low season, lunches €12, dinner mains €18–23), where afternoon tea is served in the garden on sunny summer days. Given the elegant surroundings, the menu is surprisingly unpretentious. The bedrooms are wonderfully decorated, full of antiques (some with clawfoot tubs and balconies overlooking the bay), but not at all stuffy. Rates vary by the room; for instance, the deluxe Russian Room is nearly twice as much as a smaller double room with shower instead of bath.

Adrigole is 14.5 kilometers south of Lauragh on the R574 (the Healy Pass), 17 kilometers east of Castletownbere, and 19 kilometers west of Glengarriff. **Bus Éireann** (tel. 021/450-8188) stops in Adrigole on the Cork–Castletownbere route (#46, 4/day Mon.–Sat., 3/day Sun.). For more info before you go, check out the nonprofit **Adrigole.org** (www.adrigole.org).

CASTLETOWNBERE

By far the busiest town on the Beara, Castletownbere (Baile Chaisleáin Bhéarra) is something of a disappointment. You might sit for 20 minutes with your engine running on the ridiculously narrow main street, and the lack of quality restaurants is surprising considering the town has one of Ireland's largest fishing fleets (there are plenty of the Irish equivalent of a greasy spoon, though). Granted, tourism isn't a high priority here, and some folks may actually find the town's indifference rather refreshing. The town's name originated from a MacCarthy stronghold that no longer exists.

"Castletown" is the place to be for water sports. Based in Castletownbere, Frank Conroy at **Sea Kayaking West Cork** (tel. 027/70692 or 086/309-8654, www.seakayakingwestcork. com, half/full-day trips €40/70) offers kayaking trips off the Beara Peninsula from a half day to three days' duration; prices include an organic picnic lunch (generally free-range pork or seafood, but vegetarians need only ask to be accommodated), and beginners are welcome. Same goes for **Beara Diving & Watersports** (The Square, tel. 027/71682 or 087/699-3793, www.bearadiving.com, 3-hour beginner's dive €75), which caters to rookies and experienced divers alike.

A couple of art galleries are worth seeking out here: the **Sarah Walker Gallery** (at the pier, tel. 027/70387, www.sarahwalker.ie), which offers landscapes and natural images that are easy on the eye, and the **Mill Cove Gallery** (3 km east of town on the R572, tel. 027/70393, www. millcovegallery.com), which has abstract sculptures and landscapes on display.

Accommodations and Food

Castletownbere has several fine B&Bs. Try **Island View House** (Knockanroe Heights, signposted from the pier, a 3-minute walk uphill, tel. 027/70415, www.islandviewhouse. com, €40 pp, s €55, discounts for more than one night), which offers fantastic breakfasts of fresh grilled seafood (cod, hake, mackerel, or whatever's come off the boats that morning), omelets, and porridge with Bailey's. The **Old Presbytery** (less than 1 km east of town on the R572, tel. 027/70424, marywrigley@tinet. ie, €40 pp sharing) is a classy Georgian house with a 1.6-hectare garden, harbor views from the spacious front rooms (all of which are decorated with paintings by local artists), and really comfy beds. **Realt na Mara** (1 km east of town on the R572, tel. 027/70101, www.realt-

namara.org, €29–35 pp, s €39–45, credit cards accepted), a modern bungalow set high above the road, has bay views from the front rooms and offers a traditional welcome.

A wine store and whole-foods grocery, **Taste** (Main St., no phone, open Mon.–Sat.) has sushi, tiramisu, and other tasty things available for takeaway. Or if it's home baking and a cup of tea you're after, the best café in town is the **Olde Bakery** (Castletown House, West End, tel. 027/70869, oldebakerybeara@ eircom.net, open 9 A.M.–11 P.M. daily in summer, earlier closing in low season, mains under €8). For a good old-fashioned seafood platter, try **Niki's** (Main St., tel. 027/70625, open noon–9:30 P.M. daily, until 9 P.M. Sun., mains €12–20) or the more formal **Comara** (Bank Place, same as Main St., tel. 027/71111 or 086/862-9648, www.comara-restaurant. com, open 5–10:30 P.M. Wed.–Sun., 12:30– 3 P.M. Sun., early-bird menu €19 5–7 P.M., mains €15–26), which also has several respectable vegetarian options.

Practicalities

You can get on the Internet at the **Beara Action Group** (The Square, tel. 027/70880, www.bearainfo.com, open 9 A.M.–1 P.M. and 1:45–5 P.M. Mon.–Tues., 9:30 A.M.–1 P.M. and 1:45–5:30 P.M. Wed.–Fri., €4.50/hour), which also dispenses tourist information. Another option is **Beara Computers** (The Square, tel. 027/71040, open 10 A.M.–9 P.M. Mon.–Fri. and 11 A.M.–9 P.M. Sat., €4/hour). The **AIB** on the square has an ATM.

Castletownbere is 36 kilometers west of Glengarriff on the R572. This is the end of the line on the **Bus Éireann** route #46 from Cork City (tel. 021/450-8188, 4/day Mon.– Sat., 3/day Sun.).

DZOGCHEN BEARA

A Tibetan Buddhist retreat in an absolutely idyllic location overlooking the sea, Dzogchen Beara (Garranes, near Allihies, 8 km southwest of Castletownbere, signposted off the R572, tel. 027/73032, www.dzogchenbeara. org) offers spiritual retreats lasting a weekend or longer, and accommodation is available in the Garranes Farmhouse Hostel (dorms €14) or self-catering cottages (€310–560 per week, €285–375/week in low season). You can involve yourself in the meditation classes and prayer services as much or as little as you like. This is a great option for those looking for a relaxing space and time for reflection—but be sure to book ahead by phone or email.

There is no bus transport along this stretch, though you can get a taxi from Castletownbere; try **Shanahan's** (tel. 027/70116) or **Beara Cabs** (tel. 087/649-4796).

ALLIHIES

Come to tiny Allihies (Na hAilichí) for a romp on the lovely **Ballydonegan Strand,** no less enchanting for its popularity with local families. A quiet, unspoiled, one-street village once known for its copper mines, Allihies is a fine alternative to bustling Castletownbere. Another draw for international college students is the **Allihies Language & Arts Centre** (on the main street, tel. 027/73154, www.allihies. ie), housed in the old village schoolhouse.

There's no hotel in Allihies, but you have a choice of B&Bs: **Sea View** (on the R575, tel. 027/73004, www.seaviewallihies.com, open Mar.–Oct., €35–40 pp sharing) is in the village center, a five-minute walk from the beach; closer still is **Beach View** (on the R575, tel. 027/73105,

€30–35 pp sharing), a cheerful white bungalow perched right over the strand.

Your only dining option here is **O'Neill's** (Main St., tel. 027/73008, food served 12:30–9 P.M. daily, mains €10–15), offering the standard fare (paninis, steaks, and whatnot) in a standard pub atmosphere. It doesn't start serving lunch until 12:30, yet you can order a pint here at 11 A.M. There's live trad here weekends in high season.

Allihies is 18 kilometers west of Castletownbere on the R575 and 58 kilometers southwest of Kenmare in County Kerry. Unfortunately, there is no Bus Éireann service beyond Castletownbere, and private buses run too infrequently to be of use to tourists.

DURSEY ISLAND

Only a quarter of a kilometer off the peninsula's edge, 6.5-kilometer-long Dursey Island is connected to the mainland by the country's only **cable car** (runs 9–11 A.M., 2:30–5 P.M., and 7–8 P.M. Mon.–Sat., 9–10 A.M., noon–1 P.M., 4–4:30 P.M., and 7–7:30 P.M. Sun. all year, return fare €4). This is the only means of transport for Dursey's 60-odd inhabitants, who regularly send their terrified market-bound sheep and cattle across. Aside from bird-watching (there's a sanctuary here), there's not much to see on the island itself, nor are there any accommodations.

KERRY

A trip to Ireland virtually always includes a few days in Kerry (Ciarraí), whether you're backpacking or on a golfing holiday. Many consider the landscapes in this county the loveliest on the island, and it's true that Killarney National Park, the Ring of Kerry driving route (which loops the Iveragh Peninsula), and the Dingle Peninsula are all deservedly popular. Therein lies the paradox: You are a tourist annoyed by the presence of other tourists. Come to Kerry expecting otherworldly scenery but plenty of company.

There are a few opportunities for escaping the well-worn tourist track, however: The Kerry Way walking route is the country's longest at 215 kilometers, taking you through the astonishingly remote highlands, and the Beara Peninsula (most of which belongs to Cork) is another fine choice for a taste of peace and solitude even in the summertime.

HISTORY

You might say the history of County Kerry commenced with the plodding of a lizardlike creature 365 million years ago, whose fossilized footprints can be seen on the eastern edge of Valentia Island. There human activity has been traced as far back as 4560 B.C. Copper mines in the Kerry highlands date to the Bronze and early Iron Ages, and attracted entrepreneurial settlers from mainland Europe; the remains of another ancient mine can be seen on the eastern shore of Killarney's Lower Lake.

Kerry's early Christian heritage is rich indeed; some of the country's earliest monasteries

© CAMILLE DEANGELIS

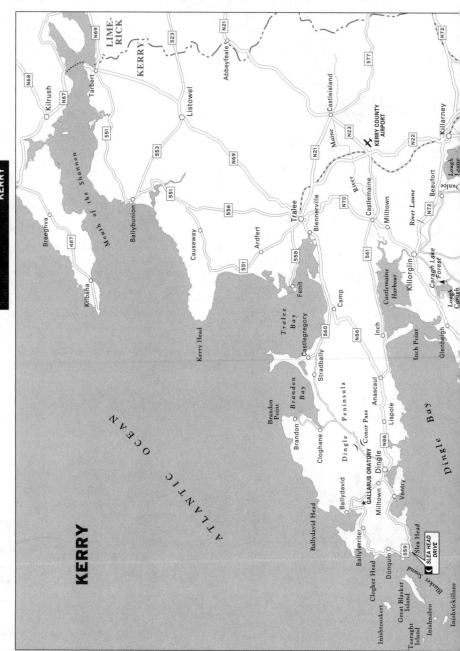

KERRY

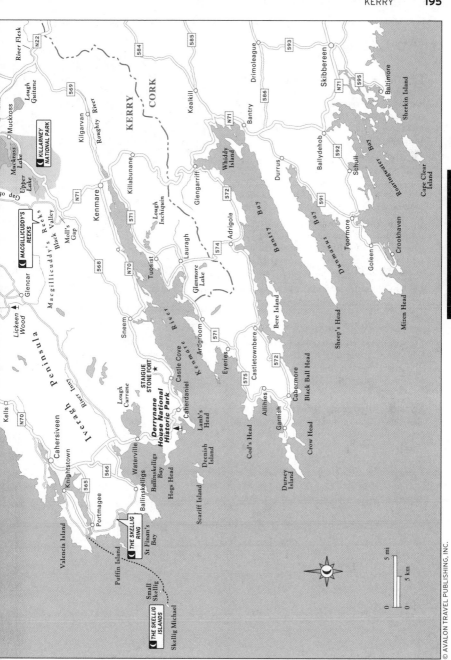

KERRY

© AVALON TRAVEL PUBLISHING, INC.

HIGHLIGHTS

The Harry Clarke Windows at Díseart: There are many fine stained-glass windows by Harry Clarke and his workshop all over the country, but the six windows in this neo-Gothic chapel are among his most exquisite (page 198).

Slea Head Drive: This is one of the country's most dramatic scenic routes, leading you west from Dingle Town to the village of Dunquin, Europe's most westerly point (page 204).

The Skellig Ring: A short detour off the well-traveled Ring of Kerry gets you great views of St. Finian's Bay and the Skellig Islands via the Coomanaspig Pass – not to mention far less traffic (page 217).

The Skellig Islands: Early Christian monks had it tough in every abbey, but none so much as the holy men of Skellig Michael off the coast of the Iveragh Peninsula (page 219).

Killarney National Park: Despite all the droves of tourists in July and August, Killarney's lakes, glens, and mountains are among Ireland's most fantastic scenery (page 223).

Macgillicuddy's Reeks: A daunting sight even for experienced climbers, these mountains include Corrán Tuathail, the country's tallest peak (page 228).

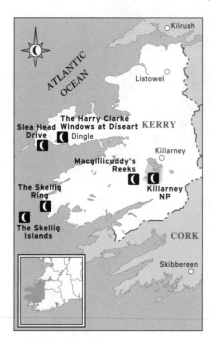

LOOK FOR **C** TO FIND RECOMMENDED SIGHTS, ACTIVITIES, DINING, AND LODGING.

were founded at Inisfallen (on Killarney's Lower Lake), Ardfert, Kilmakedar (on the Dingle Peninsula), and Skellig Michael.

In the 15th century the county was ruled by the earls of Desmond (the Fitzgerald family), who were of Norman origin but became, as the saying goes, "more Irish than the Irish themselves." They were great patrons of the Gaelic bards and poets. Better known locally as the knights of Kerry, the Fitzgeralds—never loyal to the British crown—rebelled in the late 16th century and lost their lands, title, and lives in a massacre at the northwestern tip of the Dingle Peninsula in 1580. The county was colonized anew with loyalist Protestants fresh from London. Like everywhere else, life for the native Irish became increasingly oppressive in the centuries to follow.

The county's most illustrious son was Daniel O'Connell, "the Great Liberator," whose struggle to overturn the Penal Laws in the 1820s by political means would later inspire the peaceful tactics of Gandhi and Martin Luther King Jr.

PLANNING YOUR TIME

Most visitors take in the south of Ireland in a clockwise direction from Dublin, spending several days in Killarney and Dingle before proceeding north to Clare and Galway. July and August are the worst times to visit Kerry: The roads are choked with gargantuan tour buses, accommodation prices can rise twofold (or more), and having so much company at sites best experienced in solitude can add a significant element of frustration to your holiday. April or September is ideal.

You need at least two nights and one full day on the Dingle Peninsula, though there is enough to see and do (and enough great pubs and eateries) to keep you occupied for three nights or more.

Though the Ring of Kerry may be completed in a single day, there's no reason to exhaust yourself. Spend the night in Ballinskelligs, Portmagee, or Cahersiveen (the last of which has the best pub scene) and drive back to Killarney the following afternoon. If you are planning to visit the Skellig Islands, budget two (if not three) full days in the area in case poor weather conditions prevent a sailing. Killarney National Park warrants at least one full day, two if you're doing the Gap of Dunloe as well.

The Dingle Peninsula

Like a great green finger pointing to the New World, the Dingle Peninsula (Corca Dhuibhne) stretches 65 kilometers from Tralee to Dunquin, Europe's westerly point. "It is the outsider who sees Dingle whole," Paul Theroux noted in *Sunrise With Seamonsters*. "The Irish there live in solitary villages."

It's a bit less touristy than the Ring of Kerry, but a lot of folks would tell you this peninsula offers even more beautiful scenery. "Pretty" or even "beautiful" is not the word, however; these land- and seascapes are far too dramatic and haunting for that. Base yourself in bustling Dingle Town, 14 kilometers east of the peninsula's end as the crow flies, and see as much as you can by bike. It's guaranteed to be the highlight of your vacation.

DINGLE TOWN

In recent decades Dingle (An Daingean Uí Chúis, "Fort of the Hounds") has evolved from an unassuming Gaeltacht fishing village into the sparkling gourmet capital of County Kerry. (In early 2005 the town's name was officially changed to the Irish version, An Daingean, but nobody has paid much attention.) The sheer volume of tourists who pass through every summer can be downright overwhelming for the visitor looking for a bit of peace, but there's plenty of quiet to be found farther west on the

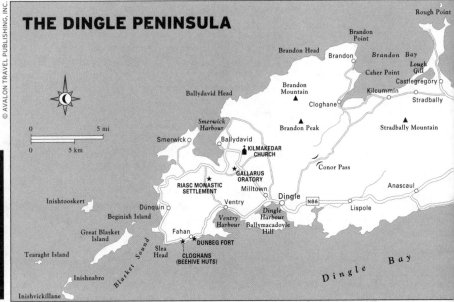

THE DINGLE PENINSULA

peninsula. For visitors looking for great food, brilliant traditional music, and boundless *craic*, Dingle's your new favorite place.

Note that most of Dingle's attractions aren't actually in Dingle Town: the Riasc Monastic Settlement, Gallarus Oratory, Dunbeg Fort, and beehive huts are all near the peninsula's western end (see *West of Dingle*).

🌙 The Harry Clarke Windows at Díseart

It's tempting to say that every window Harry Clarke ever designed was truly his "best work," and the six windows in an upstairs chapel at the **Díseart Institute of Education and Celtic Culture** ("dee-ZHART," Green St., tel. 066/915-2476, www.diseart.ie, open 9:30 A.M.– 1 P.M. and 2–5 P.M. Mon.–Fri., free admission) are no exception. Until June of 2001 only the nuns of St. Joseph's Convent could view these scenes from the life of Christ in this glorious neo-Gothic chapel, but the nuns of the Presentation order are no longer here, and the Díseart Institute has generously opened the chapel for

public viewing; a donation is appreciated but not mandatory. Commissioned in 1922, these six two-lighted mullioned windows—from the Gifts of the Magi to the Risen Christ and Mary Magdalene—are newly cleaned and renovated. And each one is utterly breathtaking. Before heading upstairs to the chapel, be sure to pick up a leaflet from the hall table—it lists the biblical excerpts corresponding to each window— and pop by the reception room if you have any questions. The Díseart staff are tremendously friendly and helpful.

Other Sights

The town's most popular attraction is a dolphin named Fungie (with a hard "g") who's been shadowing the fishing boats since early 1984. He's Dingle's most popular personality, and you can either swim or motor out to greet him (see *Sports and Recreation*). You can also catch the resident dolphin on video at the cool (but nevertheless overpriced) **Oceanworld** (Strand St., on the west side of town, tel. 066/915-2111, open 10 A.M.–8:30 P.M. daily

people know about **An Conair** (Spa Rd., tel. 066/915-2011), which is just around the corner from The Small Bridge. All three have sessions nightly in high season. Another possibility is **John Benny's** (Strand Rd., tel. 066/915-1215, www.johnbennyspub.com), with a range of live entertainment on Monday (trad with set dancing), Wednesday and Friday (just trad), and Saturday (blues and folk).

Two of what you might term "novelty pubs" are **Dick Mack's** (Green St., tel. 066/915-1070) and **Foxy John's** (Main St., tel. 066/915-1316), both full of crusty old locals. Dick Mack's, half boot repair and leather workshop, has attracted loads of celebrities over the years (just check out the star-studded walk of fame on the sidewalk outside), and Foxy John's is half hardware store. Not only is **James Ashe** (Main St., tel. 066/915-0989) the coziest spot in town to soak up a pint, but the pub grub is second to none.

The rather dumpy Hillgrove Hotel on Spa Road has the town's only nightclub—ideal for observing the mating habits of rural teenagers and bachelor farmers alike—but your choices are limited if you're looking for something more along the lines of a swanky late-night wine bar. **The Blue Zone** (Green St., tel. 066/915-0303, open 6 P.M.–1 A.M. or later daily, pizzas €9–16) fits the bill—and the pizzas are scrummy!—but it's not technically supposed to be open past 1 A.M., which means the *gardaí* sometimes come a-knocking on a Saturday night. You'll find live jazz here on Tuesday and Thursday.

Fancy Irish traditional music but don't like the 10 P.M. starting time of most pub sessions? There's an excellent thrice-weekly **folk concert** at the Anglican **St. James' Church** (Main St., tel. 087/982-9728, performance at 7:30 P.M. Mon., Wed., Fri. May–Sept., advance tickets €10, €12 at the door) featuring some of the best musicians in the country, let alone Dingle.

And if you're in the mood for rock, there's often a gig on at **McCarthy's** (Goat St., W. Main St., tel. 066/915-1205). Some big names have played here, including Damien Rice and Glen Hansard from The Frames.

July–Aug., 10 A.M.–6 P.M. daily May–June and Sept., 10 A.M.–5 P.M. daily Oct.–Apr., admission €9). There are more than 300 fishy species at this aquarium, nearly all of which are native to these waters.

Outside **St. Mary's Church** on Green Street (not of much interest in itself) is the weird-but-wonderful **Trinity Tree**, a three-trunked wooden column—a dead sycamore—carved up and down with biblical characters in a funky, South American tribal style. This is the work of Chilean wood carver Juan Carlos Lizana, who was recruited by the parish priest, Monsignor Padraig Ó Fiannachta, in 2001. The job took three months, and the Trinity Tree is clearly the single most cool thing in Dingle Town.

Entertainment and Events

Lookin' for trad? You're in for a treat no matter where you go. **An Droichead Beag** ("The Small Bridge," Main St., tel. 066/915-1723) and **O'Flaherty's** (Bridge St., tel. 066/915-1205) both have rollickin'-good trad sessions, but they're also quasi-tourist traps. Fewer

KERRY

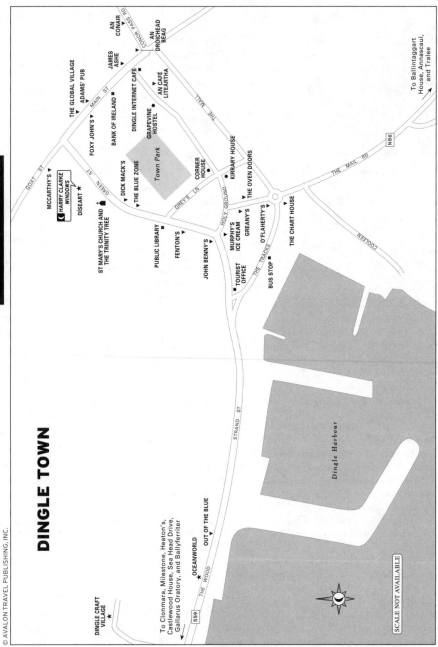

DINGLE TOWN

© AVALON TRAVEL PUBLISHING, INC.

DINGLE CRAFT VILLAGE

To Clonmara, Milestone, Heaton's, Castlewood House, Sea Head Drive, Gallarus Oratory, and Ballyferriter

559

THE WOOD

OCEANWORLD
OUT OF THE BLUE

STRAND ST

Dingle Harbour

SCALE NOT AVAILABLE

GOAT ST

THE GLOBAL VILLAGE
ADAMS' PUB

FOXY JOHN'S

MCCARTHY'S
HARRY CLARKE WINDOWS
DISEART

GREEN ST

DICK MACK'S
THE BLUE ZONE

ST MARY'S CHURCH AND THE TRINITY TREE

PUBLIC LIBRARY

FENTON'S

JOHN BENNY'S

MAIN ST

JAMES ASHE

BANK OF IRELAND

DINGLE INTERNET CAFÉ

AN CAFÉ LITEARTHA

GRAPEVINE HOSTEL

Town Park

CORNER HOUSE

GREY'S LN

HOLY GROUND

MURPHY'S ICE CREAM
GREANY'S
O'FLAHERTY'S

TOURIST OFFICE

THE TRACKS
BUS STOP

CONOR PASS RD

AN CONAIR

AN DROICHEAD BEAG

THE MALL

KIRRARY HOUSE

THE OVEN DOORS

THE CHART HOUSE

THE MAIL RD

COOLEEN

N86

To Ballintaggart House, Annascaul, and Tralee

Shopping

Dingle has plenty of opportunities for some top-notch retail therapy. The brightly painted **Ceardlann na Coille,** the **Dingle Craft Village** (The Wood, just off Strand St., tel. 066/915-1778) on the western fringe of town has a range of studios, from pottery to knitwear, woodworking, and leather goods.

Renowned goldsmith **Brian de Staic** (Green St., tel. 066/915-1298, www.briandestaic.com) has a studio and shop here; another jeweler with more innovative designs is **Niamh Utsch** (Green St., tel. 066/915-2217, www.nugoldsmith.com). Also be sure to drop by the studio-cum-shop of weaver **Lisbeth Mulcahy** (Green St., tel. 066/915-1688, www.lisbethmulcahy. com), whose husband Louis has a much-celebrated pottery farther west on the peninsula.

The **Greenlane Gallery** (Holy Ground, tel. 066/915-2018, www.greenlanegallery.com) has some pretty fun avant-garde sculpture in addition to the requisite landscape paintings.

Commodum Design (Main St., tel. 066/915-1380, www.commodum.ie) has a gorgeous selection of hand-knit sweaters and Avoca blankets (and plenty more great gift ideas). **An Gailearaí Beag** ("The Little Gallery," Main St., tel. 066/915-2976) has locally made pottery, knitwear, stained glass, and cute little children's chairs made of traditional *súgán* rope.

Bibliophiles, don't miss **An Café Liteártha** (Dykegate St., tel. 066/915-2204). Opened in 1979, this small Gaeilge-speaking café-bookshop serves up cheap and tasty lunches behind a terrific selection of Irish-interest books. It's a Dingle institution.

Sports and Recreation

No trip to Dingle is complete without cycling Slea Head Drive, a roughly 47-kilometer loop that offers otherworldly vistas and archaeological treasures in equal measure (see *West of Dingle*). A shorter cycle (sans most archaeological sites) would take you out to Slea Head, but turning east in Dunquin, after a steep climb, will send you on an exhilarating downhill ride before rejoining the R559 a couple of kilometers west of Ventry.

For scuba diving in the bay and around the Blaskets, contact the **Dingle Marina Diving Centre** (Strand St., at the harbor, tel. 066/915-2422); the **Leisure Centre** (tel. 066/915-1066) at the marina rents fishing tackle.

The peninsula's mountains and beaches make for some unforgettable pony trekking. To book, contact **Dingle Horse Riding** (Ballinaboola, Dingle, signposted on the west end of Main St., tel. 066/915-2199 or 086/813-7917, www.dinglehorseriding.com) or stop in at the **Mountain Man** (Strand St., tel. 066/915-2400, www.themountainmanshop.com). This shop also organizes guided walks, as does **Hidden Ireland** (tel. 888/246-9026 from the U.S., www.hiddenirelandtours.com); a weeklong trip, meals and transportation included, will run you €2,095 per person (€2,420 for singles).

Accommodations

There are plenty of good hostels in and around Dingle. The central **Grapevine** (Dykegate St., tel. 066/915-1434, www.grapevinedingle.com, dorms €12–15) is the place to stay if you're planning on a pub crawl. The dorms are cramped but clean, the sitting room is wonderfully cozy, and the place attracts hikers and bohemians in equal measure. Confirm your reservation the day before in high season, lest your bed be given away. If you'd prefer a private or family room (in an atmospheric 18th-century hunting lodge, no less), try IHH **Ballintaggart House** (1 km east of town on the N86, tel. 066/915-1454, www.dingle-accommodation.com, open mid-Mar.–Oct. and New Year's, dorms €13–20, private rooms €24–38 pp, credit cards accepted). The owners are lovely people, and very accommodating. The walk into town on that busy, narrow road is a bit of a bummer, but at least there's a frequent shuttle service in high season.

Your best bets for moderate accommodation are long-established, grandma's-house kind of places (and not all rooms are en suite): try **Kirrary House** (Avondale, off Dykegate St., tel. 066/915-1606, collinskirrary@eircom.net, €35 pp, s €45) or the **Corner House** (Dykegate St., tel. 066/915-1516, €40 pp, s €45). Another

THE DINGLE WAY

If you have the time and the stamina, the 179-kilometer Dingle Way is the ideal way to experience the otherworldly Corca Dhuibhne. The route begins at Tralee, heading west to the village of Camp on the north side of the peninsula; from Camp the path becomes a loop that skirts the coast. This loop is traditionally traversed in a clockwise direction, which means you'll pass through Annascaul, Dingle Town, Ventry, and Dunquin before reaching the formidable Mount Brandon on the peninsula's northwest tip. The clockwise route is easier the first few days, allowing you to prepare yourself for Brandon (of course, if you are *extremely* fit and looking for more solitude along the trail, you'd probably want to walk it counterclockwise, tackling Mount Brandon toward the beginning). The whole hike, beginning and ending in Tralee, should take about eight days, though if you start and finish in Camp you can do it in six and a half (with a total distance of 136 kilometers).

For travel advice, maps, details on hiker-friendly B&Bs, and suchlike, visit the excellent **DingleWay.net** (www.dingleway.net).

moderately priced option is **Clonmara** (Milltown, tel. 066/915-1656, clonmara@hotmail.com, €35 pp), a cheerful bungalow overlooking the harbor, a 10-minute walk west of town. It's even more cheerful on the inside, with brightly painted walls, colorful bedspreads, and a pleasant owner. The pitch-and-putt is next door. Another nice B&B a short walk from town is **Milestone** (Milltown, 1 km west of town on the R559, tel. 066/915-1831, www.iol.ie/-milstone, €35 pp, s €40–45), an extraordinarily friendly and accommodating place named for the Bronze Age standing stone in the front garden.

Dingle's posh guesthouses tend to look and feel vaguely like classy-but-bland American hotels; then again, it's nice to have hotel

amenities along with an owner who remembers your name and appreciates your business. At each of these guesthouses you can expect awesome gourmet breakfasts (smoked salmon with your scrambled eggs, fresh porridge with cream and whiskey or Bailey's, an array of pastries, all that sort of thing). The first is **Heaton's** (The Wood, 600 m west of the marina, tel. 066/915-2288, closed Jan., €65 pp, suites €90 pp, s €95), which has Jacuzzi bathtubs and spacious rooms with French furniture and white decor that feels peaceful rather than excessively minimalist. Five-star **Castlewood House** (The Wood, west of town just before the Milltown roundabout and bridge, tel. 066/915-2788, www.castlewooddingle.com, open Feb.–Dec., €70 pp, s €100) offers CD/DVD players, whirlpool bathtub-shower combos, Internet access, and individually designed and decorated bedrooms.

If you generally stay in hotels, you might consider a guesthouse while in Dingle, as the town's hotels are generally disappointing in terms of service and value.

Food

Dingle is a gourmand's joy. This is the place to break out the plastic for a truly memorable meal. For a simple, cheap, but tasty lunch, though, try the wonderful hole-in-the-wall **An Café Liteártha** (Dykegate St., tel. 066/915-2204, open 9 A.M.–6 P.M. Mon.–Sat., later summer hours, lunches under €6), with a bookshop in front. This is the only café in town that won't have a new name and owner a year or two down the road. And on a warm summer day, make straight for **Murphy's Ice Cream** (Strand St., tel. 066/915-2644, www.murphysicecream.ie and http://icecreamireland.com, open 11 A.M.–6:30 P.M. daily, desserts €4–8). It may be pricey, but you get what you pay for: heaven by the scoopful.

Most of the pubs do food. Some of the best grub can be found at the cozy **James Ashe** (Main St., tel. 066/915-0989, food served noon–3 P.M. and 6–9 P.M., mains €6–18) and **Adams** (Main St., tel. 066/915-1231, food served noon–4:30 P.M. daily, mains €6–11).

Another inexpensive lunch option is **The Oven Doors** (Holy Ground, tel. 066/915-1056, open 9 A.M.–10:30 P.M. daily Mar.–Dec., mains €5–10), a good spot for pizza or a stuffed spud. Fair Trade coffee's also on the menu, and the desserts are delish.

The fare at cozy, unpretentious **Greany's** (Holy Ground, tel. 066/915-0924, open noon–9 P.M. daily, mains €8–18) won't knock your socks off, but it's still very good—and good value. This is a fine alternative if you aren't in the mood to drop €30 on a main course at a formal eatery. The menu includes beef and Guinness stew, veggie quiche, burgers, and curries, and the desserts are tasty as well. Plus, the service is excellent.

There is no one "best" seafood restaurant in Dingle. Try the bright and airy **Out of the Blue** (Strand St., tel. 066/915-0811 or 086/169-9531, ootb@eircom.net, open 12:30–3 P.M. and 6:30–9:30 P.M. Thurs.–Sat. and Mon.–Tues., 6–8 P.M. Sun., closed Nov.–Feb., lunch €10–17, dinner €25–40), with an astonishingly extensive wine list, or the equally marvelous **Fenton's** (Green St., tel. 087/248-2487, open noon–2:30 P.M. and 6–10 P.M. Tues.–Sun., closed Dec.–Feb., 2/3-course dinner €23/28). At Fenton's there are lamb and chicken dishes as well as freshly caught fish, and as at all fine restaurants, the lone vegetarian option is well worth the lack of choice. Out of the Blue, on the other hand, sometimes doesn't open (or closes early) if there isn't fresh fish available.

For awesome Continental fare in a swanky-yet-cozy candlelit room, try **The Chart House** (Mail Rd., tel. 066/915-2255 or 085/122-1604, www.charthousedingle.com, open 6:30–10:30 P.M. daily, closed Mon.–Tues. in low season as well as Jan.–mid-Feb., mains €17–27, 3-course menu €35). The only downside is the staff; though mostly cordial, they can be borderline snooty at times. Make a reservation.

But of all the top-notch restaurants in Dingle, **◖ The Global Village** (Main St., tel. 066/915-2325, mains €17–25, 2/3-course early-bird menu €20/24 6–7 P.M.) is the least pretentious. The staff are lovely, the atmosphere relaxed, the internationally inspired

fare terrific—and the early-bird special is a great value.

Information

The ever-busy **tourist office** (Strand St., tel. 066/915-1188, www.dingle-peninsula.ie, open 9 A.M.–6 P.M. daily June–Sept., 9 A.M.–1 P.M. and 2–5 P.M. Mon.–Sat. Oct.–May) is located at the harbor. Before you go, check out both **DoDingle** (www.dodingle.com) and **GoDingle** (www.godingle.com) for more info on upcoming events.

Services

The **post office** and **O'Keefe's Pharmacy** (tel. 066/915-1310, open Sun.) as well as **AIB** and the **Bank of Ireland** (both with ATMs and bureaux de change) are all on Main Street.

The **Níolann an Daingin launderette** (Green St., tel. 066/915-1837) is open Monday, Wednesday, and Friday only November–April, and Monday–Saturday in high season.

The town **library** (Green St., tel. 066/915-1499) has free Internet access, but if it's closed, try the upstairs café at **Greany's** (Holy Ground, tel. 066/915-0924, open 10 A.M.–9 P.M. Fri.–Wed., 10 A.M.–7 P.M. Thurs., €4.50/hour). The **Dingle Internet Café** (Green St., tel. 066/915-1499, open 9 A.M.–10 P.M. Mon.–Sat. and noon–8 P.M. Sun. May–Sept., 10 A.M.–6 P.M. Mon.–Sat. and noon–5 P.M. Sun. Oct.–Apr., €5/hour) is another option.

Getting There

Dingle is 49 kilometers southwest of Tralee, 70 kilometers northwest of Killarney, and 346 kilometers southwest of Dublin. **Bus Éireann** (tel. 066/712-3566) can get you from Tralee to Dingle, dropping you off at the pier (#275, at least 4/day Mon.–Sat., 3/day Sun., 6/day Mon.–Sat. and 5/day Sun. in summer). A less frequent summer service links Killarney with Dingle via Inch and Castlemaine (#281, 1–2 buses a day June–Sept.). You could also ride **Irish Rail** (tel. 066/712-3522, 2/day Mon.–Sat. from Dublin Heuston, single/weekly return ticket €57/68) to Tralee and then transfer to Bus Éireann.

Getting Around

Dingle Town can be traversed end-to-end in under 15 minutes. Planning to cycle Slea Head Drive? Rent a cycle from **Paddy's Bike Hire** (Dykegate St., tel. 066/915-2311), **Mountain Man** (Strand St., tel. 066/915-2400), or **Foxy John's** (Main St., tel. 066/915-1316). Rates are generally €10–12 a day. **Kirrary B&B** (Grey's Ln., tel. 066/915-1606) also rents bikes for €8/day. Paddy's should be your first choice though—he may not be the cheapest, but he's a true professional and his bikes are always in tip-top shape.

Need a cab? **John Sheehy** (Spa Rd., tel. 087/239-9923, dinglecabs@eircom.net) will take you anywhere you need to go in his Mercedes. For 24-hour service, ring **Cooleen Cabs** (tel. 087/248-0008).

WEST OF DINGLE

Locals claim they breathe the freshest air in Europe, and that's no idle brag. You'll look back on a cycling tour of west Dingle, a still-vibrant Gaeltacht (Irish-speaking region) as one of the most—no, *the* most—exhilarating experience of your vacation.

◖ Slea Head Drive

Otherwise known as the R559, the Slea Head Drive loop takes you west from Dingle to the southern tip of the peninsula, Slea Head, and turns north, passing through several small villages before delivering you back to the hamlet of Milltown just over the bridge from Dingle Town. This route takes in some of the most incredibly beautiful scenery in Ireland.

Though it isn't signposted, Slea Head should be driven only in a clockwise direction, as the road clinging to the side of the cliff is too narrow for passing in several spots. Buses frequently get stuck on hairpin turns (one of which is crossed by a robust stream; prepare for soaked sneaks if cycling). The various sites and villages are listed in the order you will come upon them, the total distance from Dingle to Slea Head, Dunquin, Ballyferriter, and back to Dingle being just shy of 47 kilometers. To beat the tour buses, arrange to pick up your rental bike the evening before so you can make an early start.

It is also possible to reach the villages on the end of the peninsula via **Bus Éireann** (tel. 066/712-3566), which runs a Dingle–Dunquin service (stopping in Ventry and Ballyferriter) on Monday and Thursday only (#276, 2/day Mon., 3/day Thurs.). Clearly you're better off biking or hiring a taxi from town!

Ventry

The first village of substance on Slea Head Drive is Ventry (Ceann Trá, 7 km west of Dingle), with a pretty Blue Flag strand, an adjacent caravan park, and not much else. If that sounds like heaven, though, you can always spend the night here: try **Ceann Trá Heights** (signposted from the village, tel. 066/915-9866 or 087/683-6945, www.dingle-vacation. com, open mid-Mar.–mid-Nov., €30–33 pp, s €40–50, credit cards accepted), a bungalow overlooking Ventry Harbour offering sea and mountain views from bedrooms and a "sun lounge," Internet access, and a veggie-friendly breakfast menu.

West of Ventry

As you approach Slea Head you'll see signs for the Neolithic **Fahan beehive huts** and the Iron Age **Dunbeg Fort.** Admission fees are about €2.50 for each, provided someone is around to collect them. It's not that these ruins aren't worth seeing, but the cheekiness of these farmers' wives (sitting all day in a claustrophobic shed by the entry gates) in charging admission can dampen one's enthusiasm for the sight itself. Dunbeg isn't anywhere near the best example of a promontory fort, the cliff-side setting isn't as dramatic as it sounds, and even a careful visit will take you well under 10 minutes. The beehive huts are roofless, so it's their age (four millennia plus) more than their appearance that is noteworthy. In other words, these ruins would be worth seeing so long as you didn't have to pay for the privilege.

What is worth paying for, however, is a meal at the **Stone House** (directly across the R559 from Dunbeg Fort, tel. 066/915-9970, open

THE ARCHAEOLOGY OF THE DINGLE PENINSULA

The Irish name for the Dingle Peninsula, **Corca Dhuibhne,** means "The Seed of Duibhne" – Duibhne being a goddess worshipped by the Celtic settlers who arrived here a few centuries before Christ. Human habitation goes as far back as 4000 B.C., however. There are more than 2,000 extant archaeological sites on the peninsula, including Iron Age forts; the foundations of Bronze Age farmhouses, particularly in the **Loch a'Dúin Valley** near the village of Cloghane, on the northern end of the Conor Pass; Europe's most substantial collection of prehistoric *clocháin,* or beehive huts; early Christian monastic ruins at Gallarus and Riasc; and 60 **ogham stones** (OH-am), so named for their inscriptions using an old Celtic script with an alphabet of 25 characters, consisting of tick marks across (or above, or below) a continuous line.

Traveling Slea Head Drive will take you by the principal sights, though enthusiasts might want to sign up for a specialized tour. **Sciuird Archaeological Tours** (Holy Ground, tel. 066/915-1606 or 066/915-1937, archeo@eircom.net, tours at 10:30 A.M. and 2 P.M. daily, €15) jams 6,000 years' worth of information into a 2.5-hour minibus trip.

12:30–3:30 P.M. and 6:30–10 P.M. Wed.–Mon., lunch €9–14, dinner €17–25, dinner reservations required), in a striking building modeled after the Gallarus Oratory (and built with local stone). Enjoy your meal of fresh steak or seafood and local produce in the simple, cheery dining room, or at a picnic table out front.

Dunquin

The peninsula's westernmost village, Dunquin (Dún Chaoin) is scattered for a couple of kilo-meters along the R559. The village's much-ballyhooed pub, Kruger's (once a favorite haunt of bad-boy playwright Brendan Behan), isn't actually all that great: The grub is mediocre and the atmosphere provokes a vague and inexplicable sense of unease. The real reason to linger here, besides the view of course, is the Dúchas-run **Blasket Centre** (tel. 066/915-6444, open 10 A.M.–6 P.M. Easter–June and Sept.–Oct., 10 A.M.–7 P.M. July–Aug., admission €3.70), for an introduction to the culture and strife-strewn history of those islands in the distance. Be sure to visit before you hop the boat for Great Blasket (which departs from the village pier, signposted off the R559). Backpackers on their way to or from the Blaskets stay at the An Óige **Dunquin Hostel** (on the R559 on the northern end of the village, tel. 066/915-6121, www.anoige.ie, open Feb.–Nov., dorms €12–16, doubles €16–17 pp sharing, dinner €12, packed lunch €5).

Dunquin is 20 kilometers west of Dingle on the Slea Head road, and is served by **Bus Éireann** route #276 (2/day Mon., 3/day Thurs.).

The Blasket Islands

Europe's most westerly islands are the Blaskets (Na Blascaodaí), five kilometers off the Dingle coast. They are inhabited today only by the staff of a small café and visitors center on the largest of these seven lonesome isles, Great Blasket. All seven were once inhabited, and many bear archaeological evidence of Iron Age and early Christian settlements. In the early decades of the 20th century the savage weather conditions often prevented contact with the mainland—to the point of near-starvation—and the last inhabitants, native Irish speakers with a formidable literary tradition, finally quit these islands in 1953.

Great Blasket is only six kilometers long and just over a kilometer wide, but there is still plenty to see and do: Incredibly scenic walking routes take you by the melancholy ruins of many old cottages, opportunities for bird- and seal-watching abound, and there's a long lovely strand as well. There is no accommodation

KERRY

KERRY

on the island, though camping is possible and meals can be arranged at the café-cum-visitors center. You should plan on an open-ended visit, since the water is often too rough to sail. Boats depart the Dunquin pier every half hour 9:30 A.M.–7 P.M. April–October (last departure from Great Blasket at 6 P.M., return ticket €20), and the crossing lasts 20 minutes. And of course, don't forget to visit the Blasket Centre at Dunquin before you go.

Clogher

Along with more ordinary milk jugs and dinner plates, the potters at **Louis Mulcahy's** workshop (Clogher, 4 km west of Ballyferriter on the R559, tel. 066/915-6229, www.louis-mulcahy.com) produce huge (four- or five-foot) brightly glazed urns fit for an Etruscan funeral. Needless to say, Mulcahy ships worldwide.

Ballyferriter and Around

The pleasant, compact village of Ballyferriter (Baile an Fheirtearaigh) is 10 kilometers west of Dingle on the R553. From here you can continue north on a local road to scenic Smerwick Harbour with its small sandy strand and a few pubs with outdoor picnic tables overlooking the water.

It's worth seeking out **C Tig Bhric** (2 km east of Ballyferriter on the R559, tel. 066/915-6325, www.tigbhric.com, B&B open Easter–Oct., €35 pp, s €41, credit cards accepted). In addition to a small shop, petrol station, and B&B, this pub is an unusual but utterly delightful mix of traditional and bohemian: stained-glass panels depicting local ogham and decorated standing stones, a comfy sofa and armchairs before an open peat fire, and picnic tables in a verdant beer-cum-sculpture garden out back. Kick back with your pint in a slouchy chair and relax to the sounds of the Irish language spoken animatedly around the bar. Soup and sandwiches are served here during the day in the summer months, and you'll find traditional music on Friday nights. Tig Bhric is just west of the Riasc Monastic Settlement turnoff.

Another accommodation option is a spiffy (but tasteful) hotel, **Óstán Ceann Sibéal** (Main

The monks added a cross to the pagan carvings on this standing stone at Riasc.

© CAMILLE DEANGELIS

St., tel. 066/915-6433, www.ceannsibealhotel.com, open Mar.–Nov., €40–45 pp and s €50–60 Mar.–May and Sept.–Nov., high season €50–60 pp, s €70–80, bar food served 12:30–5:30 P.M. and 6–9 P.M. daily, until 9:30 P.M. weekends, mains €9–17), whose staff are very accommodating for those walking the Dingle Way.

Heading east from Ballyferriter, you'll find two of the most important archaeological sites on the peninsula: the Riasc Monastic Settlement and the Gallarus Oratory.

Riasc Monastic Settlement

About 1.5 kilometers east of Ballyferriter, look for the turnoff (an old-fashioned signpost) to the Riasc Monastic Settlement on your left; the site is about 300 meters down a narrow bumpy side-road. This 5th- and 6th-century monastic site includes the stone foundations of several *clocháin* (beehive huts) as well as an exquisitely carved standing stone dating somewhere around 500 B.C. (the cross at the top was added by the first monks). The location is splendid, a placid daisy-dappled enclo-

KERRY

© CAMILLE DEANGELIS

The Gallarus Oratory looks like an overturned boat, and it's just as watertight.

sure surrounded by sea and mountain vistas. If you've brought a picnic lunch, this just might be the spot for it. (And don't forget to have a pint in the beer garden at Tig Bhric in Ballyferriter afterward.)

Gallarus Oratory

It looks like an overturned boat made of stone, and the 8th-century Gallarus Oratory (signposted off the R559 3 km northeast of Ballyferriter, tel. 066/915-5333, gallarusoratory@hotmail.com, open 9:30 A.M.–8 P.M. daily Apr.–Oct.) is just as watertight. The walls of this tiny (8-by-5-meter) church are unmortared—and more than 1 meter thick—though there are remnants of plaster on the interior walls. The oratory was built on an east–west axis to allow morning light through the round window on the eastern wall.

A €2.50 admission fee gets you an informative 12-minute audiovisual on the peninsula's archaeology. But like Dunbeg Fort and the beehive huts, one gets the distinct impression this visitors center is more a business venture

than a conservation effort. You could keep walking up the lane (instead of making a left into the visitors center car park) to see the oratory on your own.

Nearby **Gallarus Castle** (tel. 066/915-6444, June–Aug., free admission) is Dúchas-run, however. Built by the Fitzgerald family sometime during the 15th century, this four-story tower house retains its original vaulted ceilings.

Ballydavid

Return to the R559 and head about 3.8 kilometers north toward Ballydavid (Baile na nGall, "Town of the Foreigner") for the 12th-century Hiberno-Romanesque **Kilmalkedar Church** (Cill Maolchédair, "Church of St. Maolcethair"). This four-hectare site is associated with St. Brendan, and the ruin of a two-story edifice—thought to have housed the clergy—bears his name. Kilmalkedar marks the start of the **Saint's Road,** the traditional pilgrimage route up Mt. Brendan.

The church has a typically decorated chancel doorway, and an alphabet stone bearing Latin script has been resurrected inside (in its broken state, it's just over 1.2 meters high). There's also a decorated sundial on the grounds, also 1.2 meters in height. Notice the hole at the top of the pre-Christian ogham stone (1.8 meters high) at the start of the lane, which was chiseled later on; when locals wanted to seal a deal or renew a marriage vow, they'd come here, stand on opposite sides of the stone, and touch fingers through the hole.

Ballydavid is another stop on the Dingle Way. Stay at the IHH **Tigh an Phóist** (An Bóthar Buí, beside the Carraig Church in Ballydavid, 12 km west of Dingle Town, tel. 066/915-5109, www.tighanphoist.com, open mid-Mar.–Oct., dorms €13–14, private rooms €16–20 pp, credit cards accepted), which has an adjoining grocery, bike rental, and bureau de change, as well as two spiffy new self-catering apartments (sleeping 4–5); the weekly rate starts at €150 and climbs to €550 in July and August.

NORTH OF DINGLE

The lush green fields east of Dingle give way to a stark and often surreal landscape as you head north out of town for **Conor Pass,** the highest in the country at 456 meters. Even in shoulder season there's often an ice cream truck at the car park near the summit, from where you can see Mount Brandon to the north, Dingle Bay to the south, and a lot of bleak and heathery slopes in between.

Castlegregory

The town itself isn't of much interest, but Castlegregory (Caislean an Ghraire) offers extraordinarily clear waters for scuba diving around the privately owned Maharees Islands. Divers (beginners included) can arrange accommodations, equipment, and boat hire through **Harbour House** (Scraggane Pier Rd., Kilshannig, 7 km north of town on the Fahamore road, tel. 066/713-9292, www.maharees.ie, €45 pp, s €60), which also sports an indoor pool, sauna, and deluxe exercise room as well as pilates and aqua aerobics lessons in high season. Weekend break packages include dinner in the adjoining restaurant (which is also open for lunch).

Surfers should contact **Jamie Knox Watersports** (Maharees, the Fahamore road, 4 km north of town, tel. 066/713-9411, www.jamieknox.com) for lessons and equipment rental.

A Friday-only **Bus Éireann** (tel. 066/712-3566) service links Tralee with Camp, Castlegregory, and Cloghane (#273, departs Tralee at 8:55 A.M. and 2 P.M., departs Cloghane at 10:05 A.M. and 3:10 P.M.).

Mount Brandon

Ireland's second-highest peak, Mount Brandon (Cnoc Bréanainn, 950 meters), was once a well-traveled pilgrimage, second only to Croagh Patrick in popularity. The ruins of St. Brendan's oratory top the summit; the seven-kilometer round-trip takes about 6–7 hours, and navigational skills are essential.

At the northern terminus of the Conor Pass, follow the signs for Brandon Point (12 km); you'll pass through the village of Cloghane and a couple of sandy beaches, Ballyquin and Brandon Bay, before the steep uphill road ends at the small Brandon Head car park. The worn grassy mountain path begins here.

EAST OF DINGLE

The second- and third-highest peaks on the peninsula, Caherconree (827 meters) and Baurtregaum (852 meters), are on the eastern side, and the Dingle Way walking route passes along their northern flanks. If you take the Caherconree Pass, from Camp south to Aughils Bridge, on your left you'll pass the turnoff for an Iron Age promontory fort that was supposedly built by an ancient king of Munster, Curaoi Mac Daire (The mountain's Irish name, Cathair Conraoi, means "Cú Roí's Stone Fort.") The views from the top of the pass are bleak but stunning, and seeing as fewer people know about this than about Conor Pass, there aren't nearly as many cars competing for road space.

Annascaul

When Antarctic explorer Tom Crean returned to his childhood home, Annascaul, to run a pub in his retirement, he put this sleepy one-street village on the map (he came home after World War I and opened the pub several years later, in 1927). Painted in predictable ice blue and white, the rough stone walls inside at **The South Pole Inn** (Main St., tel. 066/915-7388, food served €12:30–8 P.M. daily, mains €4–15) are covered in framed photos and news clippings. Not at all a tourist trap, it is certainly the coziest pub in town, with open fires, an amiable bartender, and hearty no-frills grub. Be sure to stop in for a pint if you're passing through; if you're spending the night, note there are trad sessions here Wednesday and Friday–Sunday nights.

There isn't much here otherwise, though Annascaul is on the 179-kilometer Dingle Way. Also, you might like to stop by the long-established **Annascaul Pottery** (Main St., tel. 066/915-7505, annascaulpottery@eircom.net). Niall Phelan's work is quietly whimsical, and definitely worth an extended browse.

For B&B, try **Four Winds** (Main St., tel. 066/915-7168, open Mar.–Nov., €30–33 pp, s €39–42), an unpretentious bungalow on the western edge of town with lovely mountain and bay views (but no TVs in the bedrooms, though there's a guest lounge). There are several townhouse B&Bs along Main Street as well.

Annascaul is 18 kilometers east of Dingle on the N86. The Tralee–Dingle **Bus Éireann** (tel. 066/712-3566) route stops in Annascaul (#275, at least 4/day Mon.–Sat. and 3/day Sun. year-round, 5–6/day daily in summer).

Inch

You'll find the best beach in County Kerry at Inch (Inse), a tiny hamlet 25 kilometers east of Dingle tucked beneath the Slieve Mish Mountains. The pale-golden sand here stretches for nearly five kilometers, and though popular with surfers there's no place to rent equipment. Pop by **Sammy's Store** (on the R561, tel. 066/915-8118) for tourist info, including camping.

Shanahill East

Aside from the lovely strand at Inch, there's not much along the south coastal road between Annascaul and Castlemaine—though no self-respecting vegetarian should pass **The Phoenix** (6 km west of Castlemaine on the R561, tel. 066/976-6284, www.thephoenixorganic.com, open Easter–Oct. and by arrangement, rooms €20–27 pp, s €35–40, camping €6 pp sharing, self-catering chalet for 2–4 people €490/week). It's a delightfully bohemian farmhouse B&B and organic vegetarian restaurant (breakfast €8, lunches under €10, dinner mains €10–14, 3-course dinner €25). The food is terrific, bountiful, and very reasonably priced; you'll enjoy your meal (be it a quinoa and spinach bake topped in pesto or a baked red pepper stuffed with sundried tomatoes, feta, and brown rice) on a rustic flagstoned patio with colored lights and all sorts of Eastern whirligigs suspended from the corrugated plastic roof. The restaurant opening times vary, so be sure to call ahead even if you aren't looking for accommodations. Credit cards are accepted.

In summer, **Bus Éireann** stops right outside The Phoenix on the Killarney–Dingle route (#281, 1–2/day daily June–Sept.).

The Iveragh Peninsula

One of Ireland's top three tourist destinations, the **Ring of Kerry**—the N70 on your road map—makes a 180-kilometer loop of the lovely Iveragh Peninsula, crowned in the west by the breathtaking Skellig Islands. Though it's possible to complete the ring in a single day, try to make a more leisurely two-day trip of it if your itinerary allows. You can also cycle it over three or so days, but it's wise not to attempt this in July or August. The 215-kilometer Kerry Way walking route also loops the peninsula (see the sidebar *The Kerry Way*).

Since you're driving on the left, it is best to start the Ring of Kerry at Kenmare and proceed in a clockwise direction to Killarney: This way there'll be no coach buses obscuring your view. Drive with great caution, as you'll be meeting those buses at blind curves instead!

The primary sights along the route are the late Iron Age Staigue Fort, Derrynane House (ancestral home of Daniel O'Connell), and the Skelligs (reachable by ferry from Portmagee, Caherdaniel, or Cahersiveen). If you're looking to dip out of the well-worn tourist track, make a detour off the N70 onto the scenic Skellig Ring, or Glencar and Caragh Lake in the Kerry highlands farther along the N70. Traffic is delightfully sparse along the narrow local roads skirting the mountains.

Avoid any roadside inn along the way that has parking spaces marked for tour buses. The only thing this kind of place usually has going for it is the view—but why stop when you can just pull off the road and savor it for free?

Bus Éireann (tel. 064/34777) runs a Ring of Kerry service. Route #279 goes from Waterville to Killarney via Cahersiveen (1/day Mon.–Sat., departing Waterville at 7:30 A.M., another bus originating at Cahersiveen departs at 12:15 P.M.). Summer-only route #280 makes the whole circuit, stopping in Cahersiveen, Waterville, and Caherdaniel (departing Killarney at 8:30 A.M. daily late June–early Sept., 1:45 P.M. daily early June–mid-Sept.).

KENMARE

Situated at the southern end of the Ring of Kerry and nestled on the shores of an eponymous bay, Kenmare (Neidín, "Little Nest," or Ceann Mara, "Head of the Sea") is a pleasantly bustling town, laid out in the 17th century, with a slew of great restaurants. The lovely shady park at the town square is a popular spot on sunny afternoons, with hardly any green visible between all the locals starved for some vitamin D! Kenmare makes a far nicer base than Killarney Town for the national park; while it's still a touristy location, Kenmare is never gaudily or overwhelmingly so. It's also a "gateway" to the Beara Peninsula, most of which belongs to County Cork—and so makes a feasible base for both Beara and Iveragh.

The town is compact and easy to get the hang of. A triangle of streets—Henry on the west side, Main to the northeast, and Shelbourne on the south leg—is crowned by the town square and park. Proceed past the park for Holy Cross Church (and free parking), or turn onto Market Street from the square to reach the Druid Stone Circle, Kenmare's primary sight.

Sights

You come to Kenmare more for the food and general atmosphere, though there are a few attractions of note. The first is the whimsically but inaccurately named **Druid Stone Circle,** a collection (15 meters in diameter) of 15 rocks around a small dolmen with a large boulder for a capstone. In peaceful suburban surroundings, this circle dates to the early Bronze Age (before 1000 B.C.) and may have been used to mark the solstices. The dolmen may cover a burial, though the site has not been excavated. To get here, walk from Main or Henry Street onto the square and turn left onto Market Street, and after five minutes or so you'll come to a fork in the road. Bear right and the site is straight ahead.

Erected in 1864, **Holy Cross Church** (Old

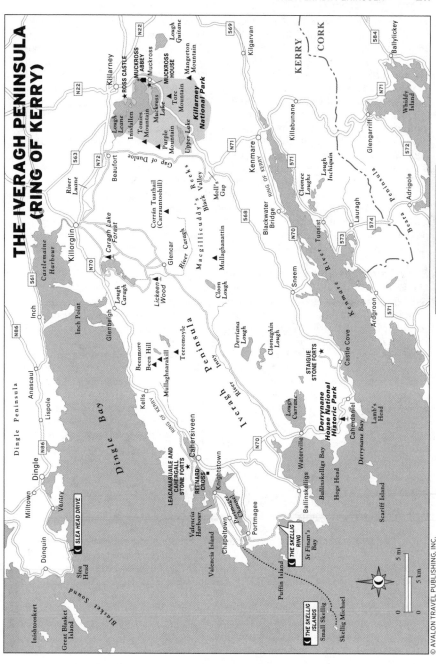

THE IVERAGH PENINSULA (RING OF KERRY)

KERRY

© AVALON TRAVEL PUBLISHING, INC.

Killarney Rd.) is well worth a visit for its exquisite angel spandrels carved out of wood from the Black Forest in Germany. Somewhat unusually, the altar window depicts the Crucifixion, and the Stations of the Cross were donated by the infamous Nun of Kenmare (presumably before she converted back to Protestantism).

On a rainy day, check out the **heritage center** (The Square, tel. 064/714-1233, open 9 A.M.–1 P.M. and 2–5:30 P.M. Mon.–Sat. May–June, 9 A.M.–6 P.M. Mon.–Sat., 10 A.M.–5 P.M. Sun. July–Oct., free admission), which includes exhibits on the local lace industry in the mid- to late 19th century as well as the woman who helped develop it: Margaret Anna Cusack, the "Nun of Kenmare," a renegade proto-feminist who converted from Protestantism to Catholicism and back again.

Entertainment and Events

Unlike those in Killarney, Kenmare's music pubs don't adhere to the frolicking-leprechaun kitsch-fest. You'll find trad at the small-but-jumpin' **Crowley's** (26 Henry St., tel. 064/714-1472) on Monday and Tuesday nights all year, and nearly nightly in high season. Other laid-back watering holes that have live music most nights in summertime are **Davitt's** (Henry St., tel. 064/714-2741, www.davitts-kenmare.com) and **Foley's** (Henry St., tel. 064/714-1379).

Shopping

You could spend the better part of a day shopping in Kenmare—and fortunately, there are proportionally fewer tourist traps here than in Killarney. Most shops are flush with swathes of crisp linen, sometimes finished off in intricate handmade lace or crochet. One shop to check out is **The White Room** (21 Henry St., tel. 064/714-0600), which has reasonably priced country-chic homewares on offer as well.

Cleo (2 Shelbourne St., tel. 064/714-1410) stocks Irish-made tweed, linen, and knitwear (some of which is produced locally). Most beautiful of all are the alpaca wool sweaters hand-knit on Inis Meáin. They're very expensive (more so than if you bought one on the

island), but considering the quality and work involved, they're worth every cent.

For local OS maps—or nearly any book ever written about Michael Collins—head to **Dolly McCarthy's** (22 Main St., tel. 064/714-1009) or the **Kenmare Bookshop** (Shelbourne St., tel. 064/714-1578).

There's also an outdoor **market** outside the park at the town square, with antiques and local produce on daily offer in the summer months.

Sports and Recreation

The 215-kilometer Kerry Way passes through Kenmare en route west to the southern side of the Ring of Kerry, and north to Killarney. Casual walkers can take to the trail at **Gleninchaquin Park** (signposted off the R571, 13 km west of Kenmare, tel. 064/84235, open daily year-round, admission €4.50), which culminates in a waterfall overlooking Kenmare Bay and the Caha Mountains on the Beara Peninsula. In fine weather you can swim in the rock pools beneath the cascade, so be sure to bring your suit.

Seafari River Cruises (Kenmare Pier, follow Henry St. south just out of town, tel. 064/83171, www.seafariireland.com, 2-hour cruise €16) can take you on a dolphin-, whale-, and seal-watching trip on Kenmare Bay; you can also rent water-sporting equipment. Or try the **Starsailing & Adventure Centre** (Dauros, 12 km west of Kenmare on the R571, tel. 064/714-1222, www.staroutdoors.ie), a five-minute drive west of town. (No wheels? No problem—the owners will pick you up and drop you off.) Here you can sign up for a sailing course, sea kayaking, canoeing, or a hill-walking excursion.

The **Ring of Kerry Golf & Country Club** (Templenoe, 6.5 km west of Kenmare on the N70, tel. 064/714-2000, www.ringofkerry-golf.com) offers a par-72 championship course in an exquisite location. **Kenmare Golf Club** (on the R569/Cork road just east of town, tel. 064/714-1291) is more convenient, though not as scenic.

To see it all on horseback, contact the

Hazelwood Riding Stables (Killaha, 3 km southwest of town on the R571/Lauragh road, tel. 064/714-1420, http://homepage.eircom. net/~hazelwood), which also provides B&B.

Accommodations

The owner of the IHH **Failte Hostel** (Shelbourne at Henry St., tel. 064/714-2333, failtefinn@eircom.net, open Apr.–Oct., dorms €15, private rooms €19–23 pp, credit cards accepted) prides herself on running a spotless-yet-comfortable establishment. The kitchen facilities are excellent, the sitting room is cozy, and the 1:30 A.M. curfew is pretty much a nonissue.

A restored period bungalow with gingerbread trim, **Whispering Pines** (Bell Height, Glengarriff Rd., tel. 064/714-1194, wpines@ eircom.net, open Mar.–Nov., €32–40 pp, s €42–45) is as cheerful as the exterior, with that increasingly rare traditional welcome of tea and fresh scones. It's only a three-minute walk south of town, yet this B&B (with only four rooms) is much quieter than those in the center.

The town center location isn't a plus if it's a bank holiday weekend, but **Virginia's Guesthouse** (Henry St., tel. 064/714-1021, www.virginias-guesthouse.com, €40–50 pp, s €65–75) is a good top-end choice for its incredible gourmet, organic, three-course breakfast menu (whiskey and fresh cream in your porridge, poached fruit with saffron and cardamom, that sort of thing), good showers, and extraordinarily helpful owners. It's pricey, but clearly a better value than the also-nice **Lansdowne Arms Hotel** (corner of Main St. and Shelbourne St., tel. 064/714-1114, www. lansdownearms.com, €75 pp, s €100). Off- and shoulder-season specials at the hotel are as low as €55 per person sharing, though.

There are larger, more upscale hotels on the outskirts of Kenmare, but you might consider staying at **Sallyport House** (Glengarriff Rd., tel. 064/714-2006, www.sallyporthouse.com, open mid-Mar.–Oct., €75–85 pp, s €100–110) instead, a tranquil country manor with extensive gardens and orchard. It's still owned by the Arthurs, the family who built the house in 1932. Many of the rooms boast four-poster queen- and king-size beds and other utterly gorgeous antiques, though the bathrooms all have modern bath-and-shower combos. The breakfast is as tasty as the rooms are luxurious. One caveat: Sallyport isn't kid- or dog-friendly (though children 13 and up are welcome).

Food

Kenmare lives up to its reputation for fine dining in every price range. Check out the **Kenmare Restaurant Guide** (www.kenmarerestaurants.com) before you go.

Small-town grocery meets organic whole foods at **The Pantry** (30 Henry St., tel. 064/714-2233, open 9 A.M.–6 P.M. Mon.–Sat.), the perfect place to stock up for a healthy picnic lunch. If it's just coffee and a snack you're after, try **Café Mocha** (The Square, tel. 064/714-2133, open 9 A.M.–5:30 P.M. weekdays, 10 A.M.–5:30 P.M. Sat., 10 A.M.–4 P.M. Sun., mains €4–8) or **Jam** (Henry St., tel. 064/714-2144, open 8 A.M.–5 P.M. Mon.–Sat., mains €4–8), which specializes in fresh baked goods.

"Pub grub" isn't quite the term—the food's too sophisticated for that—but stop by **P.J. McCarthy's** (14 Main St., tel. 064/714-1516, food served 10:30 A.M.–3 P.M. Mon.–Sat. and 5–9 P.M. Tues.–Sat, lunch mains €4–11, dinner €10–17) anyway for a terrific falafel pita, a hearty steak sandwich, or a "posh nosh nibble platter."

For a fantastic omelet or salad, eat at the **Purple Heather** (Henry St., tel. 064/714-1016, open 11 A.M.–6:30 P.M. Mon.–Sat., mains €6–18). This daytime eatery, a local favorite, is surprisingly publike in decor and atmosphere, and the food is super-fresh and creatively prepared. The only downside is the lackluster service. For great value at piggy-bank prices, try **Prego** (18 Henry St., tel. 064/42350, open 9:30 A.M.–3:30 P.M. and 6–10 P.M. daily, dinner mains €10–12), which has a warm, vaguely Mediterranean ambience and cordial staff. The evening menu offers top-notch gourmet pizzas and pasta. This smallish café is deservedly

© CAMILLE DEANGELIS

The Iron Age Staigue Fort was built without mortar.

popular, so be sure to pop in and make a reservation during the day.

Sample the inventive Continental fare at **Packie's** (Henry St., tel. 064/714-1508, open 6–10 P.M. Mon.–Sat. mid-Mar.–Oct., open weekends and the week before Christmas Nov.–Dec., closed late Dec.–mid-Mar., mains €17–33), a bustling bistro the owner converted from her (eponymous) uncle's old grocery. Or try the trendier, Asian-tinged **Mulcahy's** (36 Henry St., tel. 064/714-2383 or 087/236-4449, open 6–10 P.M. daily, closed Tues.–Wed. in low season, mains €18–30), whose owner is the brother of famous Dingle potter Louis Mulcahy. "Best restaurant" status is up for debate, of course, but lots of people would give the award to **The Lime Tree** (Shelbourne St., tel. 064/714-1225, www.limetreerestaurant.com, open 6:30–10 P.M. daily Apr.–Oct., mains €19–25). In a quaint stone cottage that was once part of the Lansdowne Estate, you'll find incredibly fresh, out-of-this-world seafood (or local lamb or beef) and lots of art on rough whitewashed walls.

Information
The **tourist office** (The Square, tel. 064/714-1233, www.kenmare.com or www.neidin.net, open 9 A.M.–6 P.M. Mon.–Sat. and 10 A.M.–5 P.M. Sun. May–Oct.) is closed in low season.

Services
The **Bank of Ireland** (on the square) and **AIB** (corner of Henry and Main) both have ATMs and bureaux de change.

Get your duds washed at **O'Shea's Cleaners and Launderette** (1 km north of town on the N71, tel. 064/714-1394, closed Sun.), which is located in the Kenmare Business Park. For a pharmacy, try **Brosnan's** (Henry St., tel. 064/714-1318).

Livewire (Rock St., just off Main St., tel. 064/714-2714, open 10 A.M.–1 P.M. and 2–6 P.M. Mon.–Fri. with extended summer hours, €4/hour) is an O2 store and high-speed Internet center. You can also check your email on the slower terminals at **WebPost** (Henry St., tel. 064/714-1490, kenmarepo@eircom.net, open 8:30 A.M.–1 P.M. and 2–8 P.M. Mon.–

Fri., 9:30 A.M.–1 P.M. Sat., €6/hour), which is part of the local post office.

Getting There
Kenmare is at the southeastern terminus of the Ring of Kerry, 32 kilometers south of Killarney on the N71. **Bus Éireann** (tel. 064/30011) services Kenmare on the Sneem–Killarney route (#270, at least 4/day daily June–Sept.). For buses to Dingle, Tralee, Cork, and Kinsale, you'll have to transfer in Killarney.

Getting Around
Driving in Kenmare's congested one-way traffic system can be a real nightmare. Park your rental car in the spacious free lot across the street from Holy Cross Church on the old Killarney road (and beside the public toilets).

Rent a cycle from **Finnegan's** (38 Henry St., at the corner of Shelbourne, tel. 064/714-1083, closed Sun., €15/day).

For a taxi, ring **Declan Finnegan** (tel. 064/714-1491) or **Denis Griffin** (tel. 087/614-7222, www.drivekenmare.com), both of whom also do day tours of Beara, Dingle, and the Ring of Kerry.

STAIGUE FORT
Sheep frolic in the heathery hills around Staigue Fort (4 km north of the N70, signposted from the village of Castle Cove), a remarkably well-preserved ring fort with a commanding view of Kenmare Bay. In the centuries before the advent of Christianity, a minor chieftain would have lived here (in long-gone wooden edifices within the fort) with his family and servants. Thirty meters in diameter, the fort features mortarless walls six meters high and four meters thick. The site is certainly worth a brief detour, though a cheeky notice at the entrance proclaims that "all visitors are to pay one euro land trespass charge."

CAHERDANIEL
The village of Caherdaniel is just large enough for a hostel, a couple of B&Bs, a petrol station, and a great pub, the Blind Piper.

Caherdaniel is on the Kerry Way walking route, though there are other recreational opportunities. Whether you need a lesson or just want to rent the equipment, **Derrynane SeaSports** (Derrynane Harbour, 3 km west of Caherdaniel, tel. 066/947-5266 or 087/908-1208, derrynaneseasports@eircom.net, open 10 A.M.–dusk June–Sept.) has the goods for canoeing, windsurfing, surfing, sailing, and waterskiing. **Eagle Rock Equestrian** (Caherdaniel, off the N70, tel. 066/947-5145) can set you up for a one- or two-hour beach, forest, or mountain trek.

Derrynane National Historic Park
Six kilometers west of the Staigue Fort turnoff is Derrynane National Historic Park, which includes the ancestral home of Daniel O'Connell, **Derrynane House** (2.5 km off the N70, turnoff signposted at the Blind Piper pub, tel. 066/947-5113, derrynanehouse@opw.ie, open 1–5 P.M. weekends Nov.–Mar., 1–5 P.M. Tues.–Sun. Apr. and Oct., 9 A.M.–6 P.M. Mon.–Sat. and 11 A.M.–7 P.M. Sun. May–Sept., admission €2.90). Built by O'Connell's uncle, Maurice "Hunting Cap" O'Connell, with the proceeds of a booming smuggling business, the house features ornate original furniture, family portraits, and plenty of personal effects, from snuff boxes to the pistols O'Connell used in his duel with John D'Estene in 1815; the tour is self-guided. In the coach house you'll find the gloriously restored chariot on which O'Connell rode through Dublin after his release from prison in 1844; unfortunately, the space is far too small to admire it properly. An excellent 20-minute audiovisual clearly explains the historical impact of O'Connell's law career.

Admission to the demesne is free of charge, with expansive, exotic gardens dotted with tiny moss-covered grottoes and wooded walking trails. Look out for the **summerhouse,** the ruin of a small tower house O'Connell used as a study. There's also beach access, and you can reach the small monastic ruin at **Abbey Island** at low tide.

Accommodations and Food

A charming and well-maintained hostel, the IHO **Traveller's Rest** (on the N70, tel. 066/947-5175, www.caherdanielhostel.com, dorms €14, double €17 pp) is popular with activity groups. There are only eight beds, so booking ahead is advisable. Inquire at the petrol station directly across the road if no one answers the door. The no-frills **Kerry Way** B&B (village center, just off the N70, tel. 066/947-5277, www.activity-ireland.com, €30 pp, s €45) is popular with walkers, and you can book water sports and other activities through the owners. Another option is **Derrynane Bay House** (1 km west of the village on the N70, tel. 066/947-5404, www.ringofkerry.net, €33–35 pp, s €45–55, credit cards accepted), a modern bungalow with splendid bay views (ask for a front room) and an outstanding breakfast array. There's also a hotel south of the village, **Derrynane Hotel** (4 km west of the village on the N70, tel. 066/947-5136, www.derrynane.com, two nights B&B and one dinner €199 pp, s €224), bereft of architectural virtue, whose selling points are the gorgeous ocean panorama and a leisure complex (with outdoor heated pool, steam room, sauna, and seaweed bath). The hotel attracts an older clientele, and as such is ideal for visitors looking for a quiet stay.

At the **Blind Piper** (just off the N70, 947-5126, food served noon–8 P.M. daily, until 10 P.M. June–Sept., mains €8–20), the service can be infuriatingly slow, but the grub is marvelous (with plenty of vegetarian options). Outside there's a picturesque riverside green where children frolic as their parents enjoy their pints at nearby picnic tables.

Getting There

Caherdaniel is on the N70 47 kilometers west of Kenmare, and is served by the Bus Éireann Ring of Kerry route (#280).

WATERVILLE

Waterville (An Coireán, "The Campion") is the Ring of Kerry's only real seaside resort—and like most other Irish resort towns, it has a distinctly worn-out air. Sure, the beach is nice and there are a couple of fine hotels, but consider staying in the smaller but far more cheerful villages of Caherdaniel, Ballinskelligs, or Portmagee.

That said, the championship **Waterville Golf Links** (signposted off the N70, tel. 066/947-4102, www.watervillegolfclub.ie) is one of the most scenic (and exclusive) courses in the country, and golfers generally stay at 18th-century **Waterville House** (same contact information, rooms €250–350, s €185). A bit more modest—just a bit!—is the family-run **Butler Arms Hotel** (Main St., tel. 066/947-4144, www.butlerarms.com, €90–150 pp) in the center of town, which is something of a celebrity hangout (check out the statue of regular Charlie Chaplin outside). The restaurant here has a local reputation for excellent seafood.

Tourist information is available at the **Waterville Craft Market** (on the N70 just north of town, tel. 066/947-4212, open 10 A.M.–late daily all year, open at 9 A.M. Apr.–Sept.), which also offers free shipping to the United States if your bill tops €300.

Waterville is on the N70 61 kilometers west of Kenmare, and is served by the **Bus Éireann** Ring of Kerry route (#279 or #280).

BALLINSKELLIGS

A scattered seaside hamlet at the start of the scenic but less-traveled Skellig Ring, Ballinskelligs (Baile na Sceilge, "Town of the Rocks") makes for a quiet stopover if you're doing the Ring of Kerry over more than one day. Overlooking the beach are the remains of the Augustinian **Ballinskelligs Priory** (signposted off the Skellig Ring 1 km north of the village, always accessible). It's said the monks of Skellig Michael moved here after quitting the island in the 12th century. What's left of the monastic buildings probably dates from the 15th century, and they have suffered the erosive effects of the sea. There's not much to see, but the windswept, somewhat melancholy locale is perfect for a contemplative stroll. Across the strand are the very scant remains of a tower house built by the MacCarthy clan in the 16th century.

No doubt the best gallery/café on the Ring of Kerry is **Siopa Cill Rialaig** (on the R566 just east of the village, tel. 066/947-9324, cillrialaig@esatclear.ie, open 10:30 A.M.–7 P.M. daily Easter–Sept., 11 A.M.–5 P.M. Thurs.–Sat. in low season), which is also an international artists' retreat of some renown (painters trade one or more of their works for food and board).

Like its sister hostel in Portmagee, the purpose-built, IHH **Ballinskelligs Hostel** (just north of the village on the Skellig Ring road, signposted on your left, tel. 066/947-9942 or 086/397-7834, www.skellighostel.com, twins €10–16.50 pp, doubles €13–22 pp, credit cards accepted) offers twin, double, and family rooms rather than the traditional big cramped dorms. Along with top-notch facilities (including two kitchens and two dining rooms), there are lovely views of Horse Island and Ballinskelligs Bay. There are surprisingly few B&B options in this area, the best being **Beach Cove** midway between Ballinskelligs and Portmagee on the Skellig Ring road (see *Portmagee*).

The 14-room, 19th-century **Ballinskelligs Inn** (on the R566, tel. 066/947-9106, www.ballinskelligsinn.com, B&B €40 pp, food served noon–9 P.M. daily, mains €8–16) won't cost you much more than a B&B. This no-frills hotel has a delightfully friendly and helpful staff—and the beach is just beyond the grounds. The hotel pub, **Cable O'Leary's,** is the locals' watering hole of choice.

In addition to trips to Skellig Michael, **Sean Feehan** (tel. 066/947-9182 or 086/417-6612, www.skelligsboats.com) also does sea fishing and diving excursions.

Ballinskelligs is 16 kilometers south of Cahersiveen (from the N70, turn right onto the R566) and just under 13 kilometers west of Waterville (turn left onto the R567 from the N70). There is no public transportation.

◖ THE SKELLIG RING

From Ballinskelligs, follow the signs for the Skellig Ring, a 19-kilometer loop (32 kilometers from Waterville) that takes you up a local road north through the Coomanaspig Pass before depositing you in Portmagee. From there,

you proceed east on the R565 to rejoin the Ring of Kerry south of Cahersiveen. There are plenty of layabouts along these narrow hill-hugging roads to provide panoramic views of the Skellig Islands and St. Finian's Bay. This detour provides a welcome break from the perennial Ring of Kerry madness, especially since the tour buses can't travel down these narrow lanes.

PORTMAGEE

Besides fishing, and lots of it, there's not a whole heck of a lot going on here in the tidy seaside hamlet of Portmagee (An Caladh, "The Ferry"). If you're determined to get to Skellig Michael (and you should be!), you may need to put down here for more than one night if the weather's too iffy to sail.

The Moorings (the pier, tel. 066/947-7108, www.moorings.ie, Mar.–Dec., standard room €38–40 pp, s €53–55, room with view €55–65 pp, s €70–80) is the village's top accommodation (with excellent dining), but there are other options. Budget travelers, look no further than the purpose-built, IHH **Portmagee Hostel** (on the Skellig Ring road just south of the village, tel. 066/948-0018 or 087/962-8100, www.portmageehostel.com, twins €10–13 pp, double and family rooms €12–22 pp, credit cards accepted), which offers family and en-suite rooms, twin rooms rather than dorms, and commodious facilities—two dining rooms, two kitchens, and a private garden. For B&B in an idyllic location right on the strand at St. Finian's Bay, make a reservation at **Beach Cove** (on the Ballinskelligs road 6.5 km south of Portmagee, tel. 066/947-9301 or 087/202-1820, www.stayatbeachcove.com, €30–32 pp, s €38). The very helpful owner will arrange your Skelligs trip for you (and there are views from the rooms of those two dramatic crags rising out of the sea). Ask for one of the upstairs bedrooms. A self-catering cottage nearby sleeps four.

Portmagee has one friendly bakery-café, **Skellig Mist** (on the main street, tel. 066/947-7250, 9:30 A.M.–6 P.M. daily, light meals under

€7), where you can pick up a sandwich for your picnic lunch on Skellig Michael. The desserts are tasty too, rhubarb pie and suchlike, and there's more seating on a terrace out back overlooking the harbor.

It's got a posh reputation, but the atmosphere at **The Moorings** guesthouse (restaurant open 6–10 P.M. Tues.–Sun., mains €18–35, reservations recommended) is actually quite relaxed. The seafood doesn't get any fresher (seeing as the harbor is all of two feet away), and you might describe the cuisine (fish and otherwise) as gourmet comfort food. The vegetarian lasagna is heavenly, and the service is friendly too. Slightly less expensive pub fare is available next door at the **Bridge Bar** (food served noon–8 P.M. daily, mains €12–18), under the same ownership. There's live trad here on Friday and Sunday nights. Or you could opt for the more traditional grub (no veggie options) at the **Fisherman's Bar** (on the pier, tel. 066/947-7103, food served 10 A.M.–9:30 P.M. daily, mains €10–17).

Portmagee is on the R565, 11 kilometers off the Ring of Kerry (the N70) and 15.5 kilometers west of Cahersiveen. Unfortunately, there is no public transportation to Portmagee. If you want to get to the Skelligs but don't have wheels, plan to leave from Cahersiveen.

VALENTIA ISLAND

The first transatlantic cable was run from Valentia Island ("vah-LEN-see-uh"), just off the Iveragh Peninsula, to New York in 1857. Another claim to fame transpired five years later, when the **Altazamuth Stone** in Knightstown, on the eastern side of the island, was used to determine the size of the world, along with its lines of longitude and latitude. Valentia also boasts Europe's westernmost harbor, which was established to export stone materials from the slate quarry on the northeastern side of the island.

The afternoon before your trip to Skellig Michael, visit the **Skellig Experience** (just over the bridge from Portmagee, tel. 066/947-6306, www.skelligexperience.com, open 10 A.M.–6 P.M. daily Apr.–May and Sept.–Nov., 10 A.M.–7 P.M. daily June–Aug., admission €5), a grass-roofed interpretive museum on everyday life for both the monks of Skellig Michael and the lighthouse keepers and their families who came long after them. The smallish exhibition also covers local bird- and waterlife, and includes model beehive huts and a 16-minute audiovisual. Since the guided tour of the island is extremely informative in itself, though, it's no biggie if you can't make it here. From here you can also book a two-hour cruise around the islands (tickets €25), an alternative for those not feeling up for that vertiginous climb to see the monastic ruins.

Valentia has yet another claim to fame: North of the slate quarry, off the road to the coast guard station at Reenadrolaun Point (the island's northernmost tip), the fossilized footprints of a primordial amphibian, a creature about one meter long, were discovered by a Swiss geology student (an undergrad, no less!) in 1992. Newly exposed by tidal erosion, the **Tetrapod Trackway** is by far the oldest set of footprints in Europe at 370 million years. The island is also dotted with holy wells, ogham stones, and souterrains, mostly on the island's northern and western sides. None of these sights are properly signposted, though, so it's worth asking at the **Valentia Heritage Centre** (Jane St., on the north side of Knightstown, tel. 066/947-6411, open daily Apr.–Sept., admission €2) for detailed directions. There's more information on the Valentia-U.S. transatlantic link here as well.

Christened after (and planned by) the local landlord, the "knight of Kerry," **Knightstown** is a delightful village with two bustling pubs, a diving center, and a ferry to Renard Point (5 km from Cahersiveen). The dearth of accommodations no doubt keeps the place relatively untouristy.

Valentia Island Sea Sports (on the pier, tel. 066/947-6204 or 087/242-0714, www.divevalentia.ie, open 9 A.M.–8 P.M. daily May–Aug., by appointment Sept.–Oct.) offers weeklong diving courses as well as full equipment and boat rental for experienced divers.

Accommodations and Food

A huge, rambling Victorian, the **Royal Pier Hostel and B&B** (on the pier, tel. 066/947-6144, www.royalpiervalentia.com, dorms €15, B&B €30 pp, s €40) is better maintained on the inside than the worn-looking facade might suggest. It's very convenient for divers and drinkers alike (as Knightstown's most popular pub is here too), though the midnight curfew puts the kibosh on a late-night moonlit stroll along the promenade, and there's no hostel kitchen. You'll get basic en-suite B&B at **Spring Acre** (on the west end of the village, tel. 066/947-6141, rforan@indigo.ie, open Mar.–Oct., €35 pp, s €38–45), which is right on the promenade (and just across the road from the car ferry to Renard Point). There are beautiful views of sea and peninsula from the front bedrooms, and the mattresses are comfortable.

The service might be on the slow side, but **Boston's** (Jane St., perpendicular to the pier, tel. 066/947-6140, food served noon–9:30 P.M. daily, mains €8–19) serves great pub grub. Notice the new irony in all those vintage tobacco ads on the walls.

Getting There

Valentia Island is off the Ring of Kerry via a bridge at Portmagee, and Knightstown is on the island's eastern end (7 km from the bridge); there is no public transportation. Taking the **car ferry** (runs 8:15 A.M.–10 P.M. Mon.–Sat. and 9 A.M.–10 P.M. Sun. Apr.–Sept., single/return tickets €5/8 cars, €2/3 cyclists, €1.50/2 pedestrians) from Knightstown to Renard Point will save you time and gas if you're headed to Cahersiveen and other points east; the passage is less than five minutes.

◖ THE SKELLIG ISLANDS

George Bernard Shaw described these islands—**Skellig Michael** (Sceilig Mhichíl, "Michael's Rock," after the archangel) and **Small Skellig** (Sceilig Beag), a UNESCO World Heritage site—as "an incredible, impossible, mad place. I tell you the thing does not belong to any world that you and I have lived and worked in; it is part of our dream world." No visit to Ireland is quite complete without experiencing the breathtaking precariousness of the 6th-century monastery on Skellig Michael, perched on a crag 180 meters above the waves, with a long ascent on true "stairway to heaven" rock steps that are more than 1,400 years old. The Skellig Islands have been inhabited mainly by birds since the last monks departed in the 12th century. Small Skellig is a designated bird sanctuary, and from the larger island it resembles the mother of all pillow fights.

Once ashore on Skellig Michael, you'll begin a long ascent of the island, climbing the same steps used by the monks for six centuries. (It's astonishing to remind oneself that none of this existed when the monks first arrived in the 6th century A.D. Talk about penitential works!) The monastery consists of six beehive huts used for sleeping and living quarters, an oratory, a high cross, and a very small graveyard. A dozen monks would have lived here at a time. While their life was arduous, it wasn't unbearable: They fished, gardened, and kept livestock. Rainwater was collected in cisterns under the courtyard; the cisterns are still there, though the water is definitely not potable!

The monastery survived many attacks over the centuries. The monks finally left in the 12th century, but not because the rough, secluded lifestyle became too difficult; the Normans were moving in, along with a more modern religious organization that had ever-lessening respect for ascetic ideals and the "spiritual warfare" the monks believed was necessary to preserve the souls of those on the mainland.

In the 19th century, lighthouse keepers and their families lived on Skellig Michael and used the oratory as their church, whitewashing its interior. At the turn of the 20th century it was decided that the structure should be conserved. Today a very smart and engaging guide lives on the island during the tourist season—a population of one.

All ferry operators let you have two hours on the island, which is enough time for an uphill hike, a lecture on the history of the monastery, a picnic lunch (there are no facilities on the island), and lots of picture-taking. Don't eat in

KERRY

© CAMILLE DEANGELIS

Ascend this vertiginous "stairway to heaven" to the monastery on Skellig Michael.

the monastery (you can eat anywhere outside it). Skellig Michael hosts around 15,000 annual visitors, so it's best to visit in April, early May, or late September.

Getting There

Skellig Michael is 12 kilometers off the coast of the Iveragh Peninsula; be forewarned that the 45-minute boat trip (as long as 90 minutes from Caherdaniel) can be somewhat rough, so bring your motion-sickness medicine. The round-trip ferry passage costs €35–40 across the board, and all operators run April–September.

If you're staying at Portmagee, try **Joe Roddy** (tel. 066/947-4268 or 087/120-9924, www.skelligstrips.com, departure from Portmagee Pier between 10 A.M. and 11 A.M. daily), who will also take you around Small Skellig afterward. **Sea Quest** (Valentia Island, tel. 066/947-6214 or 087/236-2344, www.skelligsrock.com, departs Valentia 10 A.M., Renard 10:05 A.M., and Portmagee 10:30 A.M.) is another option.

Another ferry operator leaves from Caher-

daniel: **John O'Shea** (tel. 087/689-8431 or 087/964-6325, departs Bunavalla Pier in Caherdaniel 11 A.M. daily), who also does fishing trips.

If you prefer to leave from Ballinskelligs, contact **Sean Feehan** (tel. 066/947-9182 or 086/417-6612, www.skelligsboats.com, departs Ballinskelligs Pier between 10 A.M. and noon daily, shoulder/high-season fare €35/45, credit cards accepted), who also runs weekend diving excursions.

CAHERSIVEEN

The "capital" of the Ring of Kerry, Cahersiveen (Cathair Saidhbhín, "Fort of Little Saidhbh," also spelled Cahirciveen, Cahirsiveen, or Caherciveen) is a small and surprisingly untouristy market town with an earthy, unselfconscious charm. Cahersiveen's claim to fame is "the Great Liberator" and uncrowned king of Ireland, Daniel O'Connell, who was born just outside town. This place is rich in history in other ways, too, with several Iron Age ring forts (only two of which have been reconstructed; the others are so ruinous you might not even notice them) and eerie Ballycarbery Castle on the far side of the River Fertha estuary, which is spanned by a 289-meter, late-19th-century railway bridge. For a generous helping of local history, don't miss the museum at the Old Barracks Heritage Centre.

Cahersiveen's primary street changes names several times, West Main (or New) to Main to Church to New Market to East End as you move west to east.

Sights

The Old Barracks Heritage Centre (Bridge St., tel. 066/947-2777, open 10 A.M.–5:30 P.M. Mon.–Sat. and 1–5:30 P.M. Sun. June–Sept., 10 A.M.–4:30 P.M. Mon.–Fri., 11 A.M.–4:30 P.M. Sat., 1–5 P.M. Sun. Oct.–May, admission €4) is housed in the erstwhile Royal Irish Constabulary barracks, which were built between 1869 and 1871, burned in 1922 by anti-treaty forces, and rebuilt in 1991. With its slender turrets and sickly hued facade, the building itself seems amusingly out of place in

© CAMILLE DEANGELIS

You can walk up the grassy rampart of the Cahergall ring fort.

this workaday town; the story goes, of course, that the British mixed up the building plans with those for another barracks on the northwest Indian frontier. The museum relies heavily on exhibition boards to tell the stories of Daniel O'Connell and many lesser-known local luminaries, like Monsignor Hugh O'Flaherty, a.k.a. "the Scarlet Pimpernel of the Vatican," and playwright Sigerson Clifford (whose exhibit includes a copy of his hilarious funeral instructions). This might not sound very exciting, but for a lover of history the sheer analysis and frank insight on these panels is entirely worth the price of admission. (The downside of this kind of presentation is that the museum isn't especially kid-friendly.)

It's so cold, cavernous, and gloomy, you might be forgiven for thinking the 19th-century **O'Connell Memorial Church** (Main St.) is *real* Gothic. As far as anyone knows, it's only one of three churches in the world named after a layperson.

Cahersiveen's most important historical sights are located over the River Fertha bridge

at a distance of about 2.5 kilometers; all are clearly signposted. There isn't much to see at the spooky, ivy-choked **Ballycarbery Castle,** and technically you aren't supposed to hop the fence to check it out. Built in the 15th century by the MacCarthy clan, the castle was later occupied by the O'Connells until the advent of Cromwell in 1652.

After the castle turnoff (about three kilometers from town) you'll pass a reconstructed Iron Age ring fort, **Cahergall,** and another called **Leacanabuaile** situated on a neighboring hill. Keep going until you reach the small car park, from where the separate paths to both forts begin. (The access road for Leacanabuaile is marked "private road—no cars.") Cahergall features an amphitheater-like interior with a grassy rampart about two meters wide, which you can walk all around, as well as the walls of a central beehive hut; this was excavated in 1991, the yield a small trove of metal tools in fragments.

To get to the castle and ring forts, turn onto Bridge Street, pass the barracks, and follow the signposts. On this same road, before you reach the forts, you'll come upon the ruinous **Abbey of the Holy Cross,** the final resting place of Daniel O'Connell's parents, Morgan and Catherine.

Entertainment and Events

If telling your life story to a bunch of crusty old Irishmen you've known for five minutes sounds like fun, head to **Mike Murt's** (East End, tel. 066/947-2396), which sells hardware and farming equipment on the side…or is a hardware store pulling pints on the side, depending on how you look at it. Same goes for **The Anchor** (Main St., tel. 066/947-2049), apart from the hoes and hayseed. This pub was once run by local playwright Pauline Maguire.

The best spot for music sessions is **The Shebeen** (East End, tel. 066/947-2361)—nightly in summer and Wednesday–Sunday in low season. Otherwise, the pool table and dartboard will keep you occupied. Other live trad venues include the **East End Bar** (East End, no phone), with music on Fridays, and the **Sceilig Rock** (New St., tel. 066/947-2305), with trad almost nightly.

The most happenin' time of the year is the weekend in August, when the **Cahersiveen Festival of Music & the Arts** (tel. 066/947-2589, www.celticmusicfestival.com) draws an international crowd for art and music workshops, free concerts, street performances, lectures, art exhibitions, and guided walks.

Shopping

In an erstwhile Anglican church, the **Old Oratory** (Main St., tel. 066/947-2996, open weekdays all year, daily July–Sept.) is now Cahersiveen's primary retail outlet, selling all manner of top-quality gifts and souvenirs. Also check out the selection at **G.T. Pottery** (New St., tel. 066/947-2444), whose potters have been hard at work here since the late 1970s.

Sports and Recreation

Walk or bike to the sights on the far side of the Fertha estuary, or to **White Strand** (5 km from town across the bridge, clearly signposted), a pretty beach with a view of Valen-

tia Island. Pick up a free list of short walking routes (3–5.5 km long) at the Old Barracks Heritage Centre.

For a half-day yacht charter, contact **Ten Degrees West** (tel. 066/947-2244 or 087/260-0748, www.YachtCharterKerry.com, charter €99, max. 6 people, no children under 16). Boats depart the Cahersiveen Marina at 10:30 A.M. (returning 2 P.M.) and 2:30 P.M. (returning 6 P.M.).

Accommodations

There aren't quite as many accommodations here as you might expect, being on the Ring of Kerry and all. Proprietors will generally be delighted to arrange a trip to the Skelligs for you.

Backpackers should head for the 30-bed IHO and IHH **Sive Hostel** (15 East End, tel. 066/947-2717, sivehostel@oceanfree.net, dorms €11–15, private rooms €15–20 pp), an immaculate townhouse with comfortable beds and a very helpful and informative owner. Also in the town center is **O'Shea's** (Church St., tel. 066/947-2402, www.osheasbnb.com, €28–33 pp, s €35–45), a spacious 18th-century home across the street from the bus stop. This should be your top choice if you're planning to spend the night in the pubs.

It means "Magic Nook" in Irish, and **Cúl Draíochta** (Points Cross, 1.5 km west of town on the N70, tel. 066/947-3141, www.esat-clear.ie/~culdraiochta, €28–35 pp, s €38–47) won't disappoint, what with sea and mountain views from the bedrooms in this cheerful, purpose-built, well-maintained bungalow set back from the main road. The welcome is a traditional one (with tea and fresh homemade scones), and a four-course dinner (€20) is served with advance notice. (Note that there's a guest lounge with television rather than sets in the rooms.)

Sure, the name's a bit cringe-worthy, but the **Ring of Kerry Hotel** (Valentia Rd., 1 km west of town on the N70, tel. 066/947-2543, www.ringofkerryhotel.ie, €50–55 pp), sister of the Ballinskelligs Inn, offers the same friendly, nothing's-too-much-trouble management style and smallish-but-comfortable rooms.

Food

There are a few cafés in town, but **Helen Shine** (Main St., tel. 066/947-2056, opening hours vary, meals under €8) is the cutest. For hearty, great-value pub grub with a few surprises (like a vegetarian cutlet!), try **O'Driscoll's** (8 New Market St., tel. 066/947-2531, food served 12:30–9 P.M. daily, mains €6–15), a delightfully unassuming "old man's pub."

If you're just passing through on your day trip, try to plan your arrival in Cahersiveen by half-two so you can have lunch at **QC's** (3 Main St., tel. 066/947-2244, www.qcbar.com, open noon–3 P.M. Mon.–Sat. and 6–9:30 P.M. daily May–Oct., open for dinner Fri.–Sun. Nov.–Apr., bar mains €11–16, restaurant mains €17–28), a classy but relaxed pub-cum-restaurant rightly renowned for its über-fresh seafood dishes. Everything is caught that morning by the owners' fishermen kin. The place itself is dimly lit, with a more formal elevated dining area in the rear, but you can get less pricey, fish-and-chips kind of bar food up front. Exposed stone walls back gorgeous landscape paintings by local artists (many of which are for sale). And as with all top Irish restaurants, the lone vegetarian option is an excellent one; in fact, the only downside is the lackluster service.

Information and Services

The Old Barracks Heritage Centre also dispenses **tourist information** (see *Sights*).

There's an ATM at the **Bank of Ireland** on Main Street beside the church. The **post office** is also on Main Street, and Internet access is available at the **public library** (Church St., tel. 066/947-2287).

Getting There and Around

Cahersiveen is 62 kilometers west of Killarney on the N70 (picking up the N72 from Killarney to Killorglin). **Bus Éireann** (tel. 064/34777) runs a Ring of Kerry service, stopping at Cahersiveen and other towns along the N70 (#279 and #280, 2/day Mon.–Sat. all year, 3–4/day Mon.–Sat. and 2/day Sun. June–Sept.).

You can reach Valentia Island by **car ferry** (runs 8:15 A.M.–10 P.M. Mon.–Sat. and 9 A.M.–10 P.M. Sun. Apr.–Sept., single/return tickets €5/8 cars, €2/3 cyclists, €1.50/2 pedestrians) from Knightstown to Renard Point (5 km west of Cahersiveen off the N70).

Bike rental is available from **Eamonn Casey** (New St., tel. 066/947-2474, €14/70 per day/week). For a taxi, ring **McCarthy's** (Church St., tel. 066/947-2249).

GLENCAR

The scattered and delightfully isolated region of Glencar lies at the western foot of Corrán Tuathail, and it's possible to base yourself here to scale it; the Kerry Way also meanders through. Even if you're just doing the regular Ring of Kerry route, take an hour or two to get off the N70 and dip into these Kerry highlands east of Glenbeigh. A local road encircles the placid Lough Caragh, ringed in gorse bushes and thick evergreen forests over hefty hills.

There are a few B&Bs here, all of which cater to long-distance walkers and mountain climbers. **The Climber's Inn** (18 km south of the N70 turnoff for Lough Caragh, signposted frequently on the local road, tel. 066/976-0101, www.climbersinn.com, open Apr.–Oct., B&B €35 pp sharing, dorms €14–19) is a shop, post office, pub (with bar food), B&B, *and* hostel. Unsurprisingly, this place gets buzzing on summer afternoons.

A spacious, charming old farmhouse in a truly lovely location overlooking the Caragh River, **Blackstones House** (15 km off the N70 on a local road just south of Lough Caragh, clearly signposted, tel. 066/976-0164, www.glencar-blackstones.com, open Apr.–Oct., €33 pp, s €45, credit cards accepted) offers four-course evening meals with advance notice (usually salmon or local lamb, and wine is included) and two self-catering cottages. After turning off the N70 for Caragh Lake (the turnoff is opposite the Bianconi Inn), just follow the signposts for the B&B.

◖ KILLARNEY NATIONAL PARK

Designated a UNESCO Biosphere Reserve in 1981, the glorious Killarney National Park

KERRY

comprises 102 square kilometers of lakes, mountains, and forest teeming with both indigenous and exotic plant- and wildlife. Killarney is also Ireland's oldest national park, established in 1932 with the bequest of Muckross Estate from the Bourn family and their son-in-law, Irish Senator Arthur Vincent. The adjacent lands of the former Kenmare Estate, most recently owned by an Irish-American businessman named John McShain, were added to the park in 1989.

Whether you just want a leisurely stroll, an afternoon biking excursion, a paddle to an uninhabited island, or a hardcore mountain-climb, Killarney has boundless opportunities for outdoor recreation. The park encompasses three lakes and four mountains—Torc (535 meters), Mangerton (840 meters), Purple (832 meters), and Shehy (570 meters)—as well as Muckross House and Gardens, Muckross Abbey, and Ross Castle.

The Lower Lake

Lough Leane (or Lower Lake) means "Lake of Learning," a reference to the 7th-century monastery founded by St. Finian the Leper on **Inisfallen Island.** The 11th- to 13th-century *Annals of Innisfallen* have provided much of what we know of early monastic Ireland; the manuscript is now in the Bodleian Library at Oxford (along with the *Book of Glendalough* and loads of other Irish biblio-treasures). You can rent a rowboat at the pier at **Ross Castle** (2.5 km west of the pedestrian entrance opposite the cathedral, on the lake's eastern shore, tel. 064/35851, open 9:30 A.M.–5:30 P.M. daily mid-Mar.–May and Sept.–mid-Oct., 9 A.M.–6:30 P.M. daily June–Aug., 9:30 A.M.–4:30 P.M. Tues.–Sun. mid-Oct.–mid-Nov., admission €5.30) to reach the ruins, which include a 12th-century oratory with a remarkable Romanesque doorway.

The castle itself was erected in the late 15th century by the O'Donoghue Ross chieftains, and in 1652 Cromwell's forces circumvented a prophecy that the castle would never be taken by land—by having a boat anchored in Castlemaine Harbour transported down the River Laune and set afloat on the Lower Lake. See-

THE KERRY WAY

At 215 kilometers, the Kerry Way is the republic's longest walking trail, and it's also the best way to experience the Kerry highlands – a region far less traveled than Killarney or the coastal Ring of Kerry but every bit as scenic. Beginning and ending in Killarney, the path winds along the eastern shores of the national park's famous three lakes, forking just south of the Upper Lake to form a great loop that mostly follows the coastline of the Iveragh Peninsula. Most hikers turn right at this fork to proceed in a counterclockwise direction: through the Black Valley, Macgillicuddy's Reeks (along the flank of Corrán Tuathail, Ireland's loftiest peak), and pretty wooded Glencar; Glenbeigh on the northeast of the peninsula; west to Cahersiveen; south through Waterville to Caherdaniel; then east to Kenmare before heading back north to Killarney. The whole route will take 10-12 days, though many travelers choose to walk only a portion of it and return to Killarney by bus. The three-day stretch from Killarney to Glenbeigh is the most challenging, and arguably the most visually rewarding.

For everything else you need to know – where to sleep, travel tips and caveats, what to expect along the trail – check out the helpful **Kerry Way.net** (www.kerry-way.net).

ing that the prophecy was about to be fulfilled, the castle's Irish defenders waved the white flag without further ado. Ross Castle is now furnished with 16th- and 17th-century furniture, and the 40-minute guided tour emphasizes the unhygienic conditions of medieval life. There isn't so much to see here that you should waste an hour inside on a sunny day, but if storm clouds are looming, it's worth a visit.

Another site of note on the eastern shore of the Lower Lake is the **copper mine** on a small peninsula just south of the castle (inaptly known as Ross Island), which dates to the early Bronze Age (c. 2000 B.C.).

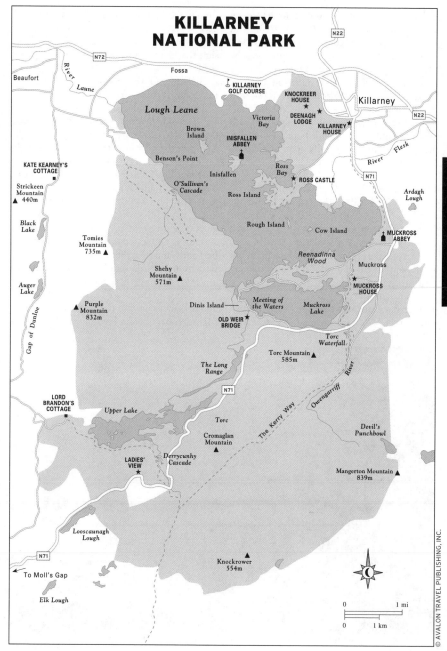

KILLARNEY NATIONAL PARK

N22

Beaufort

N72

River Laune

Fossa

KILLARNEY GOLF COURSE

KNOCKREER HOUSE ★

Killarney

N22

Lough Leane

Victoria Bay

DEENAGH LODGE ★

KILLARNEY HOUSE ★

Brown Island

INISFALLEN ABBEY

KATE KEARNEY'S COTTAGE ■

Benson's Point

Inisfallen

River Flesk

N71

Strickeen Mountain ▲ 440m

O'Sullivan's Cascade

Ross Bay

Ardagh Lough

Black Lake

Ross Island

★ ROSS CASTLE

Rough Island

Cow Island

† MUCKROSS ABBEY

Tomies Mountain 735m ▲

Reenadinna Wood

Muckross

Auger Lake

Shehy Mountain 571m ▲

★ MUCKROSS HOUSE

Purple Mountain 832m ▲

Dinis Island

Meeting of the Waters

Muckross Lake

Gap of Dunloe

OLD WEIR BRIDGE ★

Torc Waterfall

The Long Range

Torc Mountain 585m ▲

Owengarriff River

N71

LORD BRANDON'S COTTAGE ■

Upper Lake

Torc

Cromaglan Mountain ▲

The Kerry Way

Devil's Punchbowl

LADIES' VIEW ★

Derrycunhy Cascade

Mangerton Mountain ▲ 839m

Looscaunagh Lough

N71

← To Moll's Gap

Knockrower 554m ▲

Elk Lough

0   1 mi

0   1 km

KERRY

© AVALON TRAVEL PUBLISHING, INC.

KERRY

Near the park entrance is **Knockreer House and Gardens** (about half a kilometer west of the cathedral entrance, clearly signposted), former home of the last Earl of Kenmare. The original Victorian manor was destroyed in a fire, and the current edifice dates to the 1950s. It now serves as the **National Park Research and Education Centre** (tel. 064/35960, killarneynationalpark@ealga.ie), which puts on conservation and ecology workshops for students and groups. It isn't generally open to the public, though the gardens are.

Muckross

Killarney's Middle Lake is also known as Muckross Lake. "Muckross" derives from the Irish for "Pig Peninsula" (Muc Rois), so named for the area's former population of wild pigs. Muckross Lake is encircled by a bike path, but it is essential that you ride in a counterclockwise direction.

An ancient yew tree grows in the cloister of 15th-century **Muckross Abbey** (4 km south of town off the N71/Kenmare road, 7-minute walk from the parking lot and jaunting car depot, tel. 064/31440, open 10:30 A.M.–5 P.M. mid-June–Aug., free admission), a romantic sight. It's possible that the tree predates the monastery, and the cloister was built around it. The abbey has the nefarious Oliver Cromwell—who else?—to thank for its ruined state.

The most popular attraction in the park is the splendid Victorian **Muckross House and Gardens** (6 km south of town off the N71/Kenmare road, 15-minute walk from the parking lot and jaunting car depot, tel. 064/31440, www.muckross-house.ie, open 9 A.M.–5:30 P.M. daily Nov.–mid-March, 9 A.M.–6 P.M. daily mid-Mar.–June and Sept.–Oct., 9 A.M.–7 P.M. daily July–Aug., open for tourist info all year, admission €5.75, joint ticket to house and farms €8.65), country manor of the Herbert and Vincent families. In anticipation of a visit from Victoria in 1861—and hoping for a title—the Herberts spent most of their fortune doing up the house to impress the queen and her entourage, but the visit lasted only two nights, Albert died a few months later, Her-

© CAMILLE DEANGELIS

If the weather turns foul, pay a visit to Muckross House in Killarney National Park.

bert never got his title, and they went bankrupt soon afterward. The Vincent family donated the house and grounds to the state in 1932, and it's been impeccably restored and maintained with 70 percent of the house's original furniture. Every room is full of stunning art and antiques, with the requisite portraits of anemic white-wigged magistrates and elaborate silver tea services—not to mention the frighteningly vast collection of mounted deer heads (most of them in skeletal form). Admission is through an excellent 45-minute guided tour.

In addition to a deluxe craft emporium downstairs (there are potters, bookbinders, and weavers with workshops on the premises), there's also a rather posh restaurant with a wine license and views of Torc Mountain and the gardens.

And here's a fun time-warp experience for the kiddies: **Muckross Traditional Farms** (open 1–6 P.M. weekends mid-Mar.–Apr. and Oct., 1–6 P.M. daily May, 10 A.M.–7 P.M. daily June–Sept., admission €5.75, joint ticket €8.65) has three separate, fully functioning farms using technology (if you can call it that) from the 1930s.

West of here, the three lakes converge at the **Meeting of the Waters,** a popular spot with local anglers. **Dinis Cottage** (at the Meeting of the Waters, signposted, tel. 064/31954, open 9 A.M.–6 P.M. daily May–Sept.), a turn-of-the-19th-century hunting lodge, serves tea and light snacks.

Also clearly signposted across the N71 from Muckross Lake is **Torc Waterfall.** Tourists frequently brave these slippery rocks in questionable footwear for a snapshot.

The Upper Lake

Smallest of the three and dappled with "fairy islands," the Upper Lake lies just west of the Kenmare road (N71), and there is a small car park just south of **Ladies' View.** This lookout over Macgillicuddy's Reeks, Purple Mountain, and the lake below was so named because Victoria's ladies-in-waiting paused here during the queen's tour of Killarney in 1861. A walking trail west along the lake's south-ern shore leads to **Lord Brandon's Cottage,** another über-touristy 19th-century hunting lodge turned restaurant, which is also sign-posted just before the southern terminus of the Gap of Dunloe.

Information

The national park **visitors center** (tel. 064/31440 or 064/35960, www.heritage-ireland.ie, open 9 A.M.–6 P.M. daily mid-Mar.–June and Sept.–Oct., 9 A.M.–7 P.M. daily July–Aug., free admission) is located at Muckross House (see *Muckross*). There is also an information office at the **Torc Waterfall** near the eastern shore of Muckross Lake (open 9:30 A.M.–6:30 P.M. daily June–mid-Sept.).

For a guided walk, contact **Richard Clancy** (Currach, Aghadoe, tel. 064/33471 or 087/639-4362, www.killarneyguidedwalks.com, 2-hour walk €8), whose guided tours (mostly two-hour walks, but half- and full-day trips can be arranged) cover the history and botany of the park. Tours depart from the gas station opposite the cathedral at 11 A.M. daily all year.

Getting There and Around

There are two entrances to the park: one opposite St. Mary's Cathedral at the end of New Street and the other east of Muckross Lake on the Kenmare road. If you want to see Ross Castle, take the cathedral entrance; otherwise, head down the N71 (a distance of 5 km, certainly walkable, but get an early start if you want to get as far as the Torc Waterfall).

Cycling is the best way to see the park; rent a bike in Killarney Town. You can also hire a jaunting car with a crusty old local, though you'll cover far more ground hiking or biking. Frankly, this horse-drawn option is the lazy man's way to see the park, and walkers don't appreciate having to step around the horse dung all over the roads. Having said all this, it's actually the most practical option for families with small children; a one-hour tour will run you roughly €40. There's a depot at Kenmare Place in the center of town and another on the N71 at the Muckross entrance to the park (where you can also park your car).

WEST OF KILLARNEY NATIONAL PARK
The Gap of Dunloe

A marked contrast to the lushness of the national park, the glacier-carved Gap of Dunloe cuts south through a string of stark, ominously beautiful mountains: Macgillicuddy's Reeks to the west and the Tomies and Purple Mountains to the east.

Cars are forbidden in the gap in high season, and though it's possible to drive through in the off-season, this is not recommended—you'll get caught behind every jaunting car and hiking group on your way south (not to mention the scornful looks you might receive from said parties!). Walking and cycling are the best ways to see the gap; you can hire a jaunting car outside Kate Kearney's Cottage (a tourist-trap tearoom and restaurant), but the pony-trap route just dips into the mountains before returning you to the cottage, so you won't get to see more than a mile or two of dramatic scenery. A 1.5-hour ride will run you about €55.

To get to the Gap of Dunloe entrance from Killarney Town, take the Beaufort road (N72) and you'll see it clearly signposted on your left 10 kilometers west of town. If you follow the gap's full length, roughly 11 kilometers, you'll come to the junction of the R568 and the N71, also known as **Moll's Gap,** offering another stark and scenic panorama.

Those walking the Kerry Way—and/or tackling Corrán Tuathail, Ireland's highest peak—will probably need to pass the night at the An Óige **Black Valley Hostel** (13 km south of Beaufort Town along the Gap of Dunloe, also accessible from Moll's Gap on the Kenmare end of the N71, tel. 064/34712, open Mar.–Nov., dorms €14–15, 10 A.M.–5 P.M. lockout), but be forewarned that the mattresses are worn out and you've no hope of a hot shower.

◖ Macgillicuddy's Reeks

Ireland's highest mountain range, Macgillicuddy's Reeks (or Na Cruacha Dubha, "the black tops"), looms west of the national park. These glacier-carved, mist-shrouded sandstone peaks were named for a local landowning family and

are joined by ridges with colorful names like "Hag's Tooth" and "Devil's Ladder." King of the Reeks is Corrán Tuathail (sometimes anglicized "Carrauntoohill"), the country's tallest mountain at 1,040 meters. A trip to the summit takes at least four hours round trip, and most climbers leave in the late morning to avoid the early-morning cloud cover. Corrán Tuathail aside, "the Reeks" offer the only other two Irish peaks over 1,000 meters in their 20-kilometer stretch: 1,010-meter Beenkeragh (Binn Chaorach, "mountain of sheep") and 1,001-meter Caher.

Unless you're a seasoned climber, consider a guided hike (since there are no well-trod paths on Corrán Tuathail, orienteering experience is a must); try **Con Moriarty** (tel. 064/22844 or 087/258-1966, www.hiddenirelandtours.com), who provides tidbits of archaeology, folklore, flora, and fauna along with the requisite navigational skills.

KILLARNEY TOWN

You'd be smart to avoid Killarney, as it is garishly overcommercialized; it may not be as convenient, but Kenmare makes a much more pleasant base for exploring the national park. Most of Killarney's restaurants are mediocre and overpriced, many of the pubs push the old stage-Irish kitsch (some even charge a cover for their music sessions), and a sprawling indoor shopping mall adjoining the bus and rail stations dominates the eastern end of town. Droves of eager tourists keep on spilling out of those jumbo charter buses.

If you want to experience the national park but don't have wheels, though, you're going to have to spend a bit of time in town. Consider coming in the off-season; iffy weather for a blissful absence of charter buses is a worthwhile trade-off. (Whatever you do, don't come in July or August.)

Sights

National park aside, Killarney's primary sights are mostly ecclesiastical. The awe-inspiring **St. Mary's Cathedral** (Cathedral Pl. at the western end of Lower New St., tel. 064/31014) is

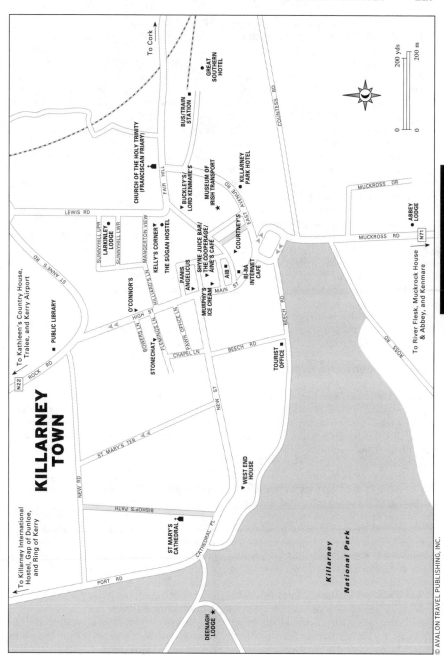

KERRY

KILLARNEY TOWN

To Cork

GREAT SOUTHERN HOTEL

BUS/TRAIN STATION ■

COUNTESS RD

200 yds
200 m

CHURCH OF THE HOLY TRINITY (FRANCISCAN FRIARY)

FAIR HILL

BUCKLEYS/ LORD KENMARE'S ▼

MUSEUM OF IRISH TRANSPORT ★

KILLARNEY PARK HOTEL ●

MUCKROSS DR

LEWIS RD

SUNNYHILL UPR

LARKINLEY LODGE ●

SUNNYHILL LWR

MANGERTON VIEW

EAST AVENUE RD

COURTNEY'S ▼

ABBEY LODGE ●

MUCKROSS RD

N71

ST ANNE'S RD

KELLY'S CORNER ▼

THE SÚGÁN HOSTEL ●

To Kathleen's Country House, Tralee, and Kerry Airport

HILLIARD'S LN

PANIS ANGELICUS ▼

SHYNE JUICE BAR/ THE COOPERAGE/ ÁINE'S CAFÉ ▼

AIB ▼

BI-RÁ INTERNET CAFÉ ■

O'CONNOR'S ▼

HIGH ST

MURPHY'S ICE CREAM ▼

MAIN ST

BOWERS LN

STONECHAT ▼

FLEMINGS LN

PAWN OFFICE LN

BEECH RD

● PUBLIC LIBRARY

ROCK RD

N22

CHAPEL LN

BEECH RD

TOURIST OFFICE ■

To River Flesk, Muckross House & Abbey, and Kenmare

MUCKROSS RD

NEW ST

ST MARY'S TER

To Killarney International Hostel, Gap of Dunloe, and Ring of Kerry

NEW RD

WEST END HOUSE ▼

BISHOP'S PATH

ST MARY'S CATHEDRAL ✝

CATHEDRAL PL

PORT RD

Killarney National Park

DEENAGH LODGE ★

© AVALON TRAVEL PUBLISHING, INC.

a cavernous neo-Gothic edifice built between 1842 and 1855. The unfinished church was used as a hospital during the famine, and victims often gathered on the lawn outside.

A highlight in Killarney is a typically superb five-lighted Harry Clarke window (designed by apprentice Richard King) that features the Seven Joys of the Blessed Virgin as well as St. Francis's stigmata; above these scenes are three rosettes, each depicting one element of the Holy Trinity. The window is above the organ gallery at the 19th-century **Church of the Holy Trinity** at the still-active **Franciscan Friary** (Fair Hill, tel. 064/31334), which also features an elaborate Flemish-style altarpiece.

Another rainy-day option is the **Museum of Irish Transport** (Scott's Gardens, East Ave. Rd., tel. 064/32638, open 10 A.M.–6 P.M. daily June–Aug., 11 A.M.–5 P.M. daily Apr.–May and Sept.–Oct., admission €5); though there isn't a whole lot here, you can check out a 1910 Wolseley Siddeley bicycle owned by Constance Markievicz (and once borrowed by her old pal W. B. Yeats) and other nifty vintage cars, bikes, motorcycles, and carriages.

Entertainment and Events

The least touristy music pub in town is **Buckley's** (College St., tel. 064/31037), with nightly sessions in high season; but the downside of a relatively unself-conscious place like this is that the musicians can be more lax in their performance—showing up a bit later and interspersing more chitchat with their buddies. Just give them an audience and they'll rise to the occasion. Cozier **Courtney's** (Plunkett St., tel. 064/32689) also offers live trad and folk in the upstairs bar, though not on a regular schedule as such. Courtney's is the only pub in the country licensed to serve Guinness in jam jars. More touristy, but still tolerable, is dim-and-dusty **O'Connor's** (High St., tel. 064/31115), which offers nightly sessions.

And if you're sick of fiddlin' and just want to have a quiet pint (quiet aside from the sports on the telly, that is) in a pub full of laid-back, youngish locals, try **Kelly's Corner** (Lewis Rd., tel. 064/35966), next door to the Súgán Hostel.

Shopping

Most of the gift shops in Killarney carry cringe-inducing Irish kitsch, but some nice stores are worth seeking out. Antiquers, look no further than **J. O'Leary** (Main St., no phone), who specializes in exquisite silverware; those who want cutting-edge Irish fashion and homewares should stop by the local branch of **Kilkenny Design** (3 New St., tel. 064/23309).

Looking for a souvenir for your little niece or nephew? **Ecotoys** (Kenmare Pl., tel. 064/38938) carries only battery-free playthings, with nifty marionette puppets bobbing in the front window.

And if you want to pick up some new underwear or something, you can always step inside the monstrous **Killarney Outlet Centre** (Fair Hill, tel. 064/36744, www.killarneyoutletcentre.com).

There are several bookstores in town, including the **Killarney Bookshop** (32 Main St., tel. 064/34108).

Sports and Recreation

What are you waiting for? Get thee to the park! (See *Killarney National Park*.)

There are plenty of golf courses in the area, chief of which is the **Killarney Golf and Fishing Club** (4 km west of town on the N72/Killorglin road, tel. 064/31034, www.killarney-golf.com) Founded in 1893, it offers a championship course on the Lower Lake with stupendous views of the national park and Macgillicuddy's Reeks.

It's possible to fish in the national park; stop by **O'Neill's** (6 Plunkett St., tel. 064/31970) for permit and equipment.

Equestrians should head over to the **Killarney Riding Stables** (Ballydowney, signposted on the N72 2 km west of town, tel. 064/31686, www.killarneyridingstables.com), which hosts 1–6-hour treks through the national park. Beginners are welcome.

Accommodations

Needless to say, there's no shortage of beds in this town—but it's still not wise to leave it to chance in summertime.

The best hostel in town, for "atmosphere" and otherwise, is ◖ **The Súgán** (Lewis Rd., tel. 064/33104, www.killarneysuganhostel. com, dorms €15–16, twins €17.50 pp, bike rental €12/day, credit card required for reservations, but payment is cash only), which has been attracting friendly backpackers for years. It's cramped but very cozy—there's nothing like coming back here to a crackling open fire after a night at the pubs. (Strictly no booze allowed in the hostel, however.) The Súgán's owner, Pa Sugrue, is a feisty guitar strummer who knows more about town and park than anyone at the tourist office, and Dave Sheehan, the manager, is similarly helpful. Despite less-than-ideal shower facilities, The Súgán is the best choice for those on a shoestring budget.

Outside of town is the An Oige **Killarney International Hostel** (5 km west of town on the N72, Aghadoe House, Fossa, tel. 064/31240, www.anoige.ie, open all year, dorms €14–18, twins €36–45, credit cards accepted), an immaculate converted 18th-century hunting lodge set in 75 acres of gardens. It's highly recommended for its clean and spacious kitchen facilities and common areas (often buzzing with school groups), but the location is majorly inconvenient if you're not driving. Note that though it's just outside the park, you can't actually access the park from anywhere nearby—you've got to walk, pedal, or drive to the entrance in town, opposite the cathedral. Amenities include coin-operated Internet kiosks.

Between seen-better-days B&Bs over pubs and guesthouses ostentatiously displaying their five-star AA ratings, quality "budget" B&Bs can seem a bit difficult to come by. Many undistinguished places are positively overpriced. An excellent choice is **Larkinley Lodge** (Lewis Rd., tel. 064/35142 or 087/238-9537, €25 pp, s €35)—unscramble the letters—an immaculately kept townhouse a couple minutes' walk from the College Street roundabout. The rooms are small but comfortable, with stylish bedspreads, a sprinkling of antiques, and real art on the walls. You'll find other townhouses along Lewis and St. Anne's Roads advertising

similarly low rates (just look for the shamrock seal of approval!).

Brick-and-stone, tastefully faux-Gothic **Abbey Lodge** (Muckross Rd., tel. 064/34193 www.abbey-lodge.com, €40–55 pp, s €55–95) is easily the most attractive guesthouse along the N71 south of town. It's every bit as nice on the inside, with comfortable rooms furnished with lovely antiques and excellent showers, not to mention the ultra-helpful proprietors, Mr. and Mrs. King. The whole house is a veritable art gallery. And with 15 rooms, it's also large enough to guarantee a greater degree of privacy. You can expect all the same on the other side of town at **Kathleen's Country House** (Tralee Rd., 1 km north of town, signposted on the N22, tel. 064/32810, www.kathleens. net, €50–70 pp, single rates vary): comfy rooms, helpful proprietors, an admirable art collection, more than a hectare of carefully manicured gardens, and greater anonymity (as there are 17 rooms). Kathleen's is ideally situated for golfers, as there are five courses within a five-minute drive (no children under five, though).

There are loads of hotels in and around Killarney, many of which are overwhelmingly ostentatious (and those with park views all too often rate poorly in every other respect). For the height of Victorian elegance with all mod cons, you've got to stay at the ivy-clad ◖ **Great Southern** (tel. 064/31642, www .greatsouthernhotels.com, rooms €100–400), gorgeous inside and out—and just as important, the staff are admirably efficient and courteous. If the gilt-and-marble lobby is too overwhelming, you can always kick back with a pint in a leather armchair by the (albeit gas-lit) fireplace in the classy-yet-atmospheric pub. Be sure to book a spa treatment while you're here.

Another establishment that won't disappoint is the five-star **Killarney Park Hotel** (Kenmare Pl., tel. 064/35555, www.killarneyparkhotel.ie, room €380, s €220), set back from the street for a bit of quiet in the heart of town. Deluxe pool and spa, complimentary DVD rental at reception for the big-screen television in your room (which you'll find to be the antithesis of anonymous corporate chic), fluffy slippers and bathrobes, wireless Internet, open fires in the elegant library and other sitting rooms, superb pub and restaurant food, refreshingly unpretentious staff—a room at this top-notch place is worth every euro.

Food

Nearly all the pubs do food at lunchtime, but you'll want to be off walking or pedaling around the park. Pick up fixings for a picnic lunch at the Tesco grocery store on Beech Street, or get fresh sandwiches for takeaway at ℂ **Shyne** (1 Old Market Ln., tel. 064/32686, www.shyne.ie, open 9:30 A.M.–6 P.M. Mon.–Sat. and 11:30 A.M.–6 P.M. Sun., later summer hours, light meals €4–8), a fantastic (and friendly) little juice bar serving fresh smoothies (also with vitamin supplements), Fair Trade coffee and tea, salads and sandwiches—even pro-biotic fro-yo! The takeaway prices are a bit lower. For two scoops of freshly made Bailey's ice cream or a cup of gourmet coffee, turn the corner for **Murphy's** (37 Main St., tel. 066/915-2644, www.murphysicecream.ie, open 11 A.M.–6:30 P.M. daily, desserts €4–8).

Easily the best café (and bakery) in town is **Panis Angelicus** (15 New St., tel. 064/39648, open 10 A.M.–5:30 P.M. daily all year, and until 9 P.M. Thurs.–Mon. May–Sept., mains €3–10), which doesn't need the bonus points for the clever name. Gourmet sandwiches, great coffee, scrummy desserts, plenty of veggie options: what more do you need?

Much more spacious than its Tralee counterpart, **Áine's Café and Winebar** (Market Ln., tel. 064/71489, www.ainescafeandwinebar.ie, open 9 A.M.–6 P.M. Mon.–Sat. and 11 A.M.–6 P.M. Sun. all year, open past 10 P.M. in summer, lunches under €7) is a fine spot for chilling out with a glass of Shiraz at the end of a long day of hiking, and the coffee and sandwiches are good as well. Next door is one of Killarney's hippest eateries, **The Cooperage** (Old Market Ln., tel. 064/37716, www.cooperagerestaurant.com, open 12:30–2:30 P.M. Mon.–Sat. and 6–10 P.M. daily, closed Mon. in winter, mains €14–25, 3-course early-bird menu €20 6–7:30 P.M. Sun.–Fri., mains on late-night menu €12), with swanky blue lighting and incongruous seating (high-backed leather office chairs at some tables, and cheap metal and plastic chairs at others). The food (standard Continental) is good—not great, but reliably good—and though the service is downright neglectful, the locals don't seem to mind. (Another tip: Don't order a cappuccino…unless you want a cupful of froth.) There's live jazz here on Saturday night.

Tucked down a quiet lane off High Street, **Stonechat** (Fleming's Ln., tel. 064/34295, open 10 A.M.–10 P.M. Mon.–Sat., 2/4-course early-bird menu €16/20 6–7:30 P.M., mains €12–20) is a romantic, low-key, good-value alternative to Killarney's plethora of pretentious eateries; though the menu is relatively unadventurous, vegetarians (and even vegans) are well catered to.

Serving delicious modern Irish fare to the strains of flamenco, ℂ **Lord Kenmare's** (College St., above Murphy's pub, tel. 064/37245, www.lordkenmares.com, open 6–10 P.M. daily, mains €15–26, 3-course early-bird special €25 6–7 P.M.) is refreshingly unpretentious. Some mains are better than others—the corn-fed chicken and the vegetarian pasta dish are safe bets—but it's the desserts that truly put the sparkle on your dining experience; the "real" Bailey's cheesecake is second to none. Reservations are recommended, as the place buzzes with locals any night of the week.

Another option for a deluxe meal is **West End House** (58 New St., tel. 064/32271, www.westendhouse.com, open 12:30–2 P.M. and 6–10 P.M. Tues.–Sun., most mains €17–30), a delightfully cozy ivy-covered restaurant opposite the cathedral with a reputation for reliably fine meat and seafood dishes. Go for broke with the €47 lobster. (Lord Kenmare's is a better option for vegetarians, though, as there may not be a single option on the West End House menu.)

Information

The **tourist office** (Beech Rd., tel. 064/31633, www.corkkerry.ie or www.killarney.ie, open

9 A.M.–6 P.M. Mon.–Sat. and 10 A.M.–6 P.M. Sun. June–Sept., 9:15 A.M.–5:30 P.M. Mon.–Sat. Oct.–May) is bustling yet efficient.

Services

You'll have no trouble finding an ATM in this town. The **AIB** (Main St.), **Bank of Ireland** (New St.), and **TSB** (New St.) all have cash machines as well as bureaux de change.

The **post office** is on New Street.

Drop off your dirty duds at **Gleeson's Launderette & Dry Cleaners** (Brewery Ln., College Sq., tel. 064/33877, closed Sun.). There are plenty of pharmacies in town, including **Shanahan's** (19 Plunkett St., tel. 064/32630).

You can get free Internet access at the **public library** (Rock Rd., tel. 064/32655), but if it's closed, try **Rí-Rá** (Plunkett St., tel. 064/38729, open 9 A.M.–11 P.M. Mon.–Sat. and noon–9 P.M. Sun. Mar.–Oct., 11 A.M.–9 P.M. daily Nov.–Feb., €3/hour), which has the best rates in town.

Getting There

Killarney is 33 kilometers south of Tralee and 87 kilometers northwest of Cork City on the N22, and 305 kilometers southwest of Dublin on the N7, picking up the N21 in Limerick and the N23 in Castleisland.

Bus Éireann (Park Rd., behind the outlet center, tel. 064/30011) can get you here from Dingle (#281, 1–2 early departures Mon.–Sat. June–mid-Sept., all other times via Tralee), Tralee (#14 or #40, at least 11/day daily), Cork (#40, at least 11/day daily), Kenmare (#270, at least 4/day daily June–Sept.), and most towns on the Ring of Kerry (#279 and #280, 2/day Mon.–Sat. all year, 3–4/day Mon.–Sat. June–Sept. and 2/day Sun.).

From here you can board a direct train service to Cork, Dublin, or Limerick via **Irish Rail** (off Park Rd., near East Ave. Rd. across from the Great Southern Hotel, tel. 064/31067, at least 4/day daily to each city, Dublin single/5-day return €57/60). There is no quick route from the bus depot to the train station; you have to walk around the outlet mall to get from one to the other.

You can also reach County Kerry by air. The tiny **Kerry Airport** (Farranfore, 15 km north of Killarney on the N22, tel. 066/976-4644, www.kerryairport.ie) has frequent flights from Dublin (4/day Mon.–Fri., 2/day Sat., 3/day Sun. on Aer Arann, tel. 081/821-0210, www.aerarann.com) and London Stansted (1–2/daily on Ryanair, tel. 081/830-3030, www.ryanair.com).

Getting Around

Killarney is eminently walkable; it'll take you less than 15 minutes to foot it from end to end, and most accommodations are within easy walking distance from the center. Rent a cycle from the Súgán Hostel (Lewis Rd., tel. 064/33104) or **David O'Sullivan's Bike Shop and Outdoor Store** (Bishop's Ln., tel. 064/31282, www.killarneyrentabike.com). The rate for both is €12/day and €70/week.

Free parking? No such luck (you can try the lot beside St. Mary's Cathedral at the western end of New St., but it's often filled to capacity). Ask when booking your room if you'll be able to park your car before you check in. There's a taxi rank on College Square, but you could also ring **John Burke** (tel. 064/32448 or 087/263-0323), who has a minibus.

KERRY

The Beara Peninsula

Though "the Beara" is often synonymous with West Cork, the north side of the peninsula is actually part of County Kerry. Of all Kerry's coastline it's the least traversed, a prime opportunity for a bit of peace and quiet just off the tourist merry-go-round. Glenmore Lake in particular is a haven of tranquility, though the lack of amenities necessitates a fair bit of advance planning.

For more on the Cork-side Beara, see the *Cork* chapter.

LAURAGH

A scattered hamlet 23 kilometers west of Kenmare, Lauragh (An Láithreach) is the starting point for the stunning, vaguely Alpine **Healy Pass** through the Caha Mountains south to the hamlet of Adrigole in County Cork, a journey of 11 kilometers. The views farther west along this peninsula are lovely, but not nearly so dramatic as this.

But before turning on to the Healy Pass, pause at **Derreen Gardens** (signposted on the R573, tel. 064/83588, open 10 A.M.–6 P.M. daily Apr.–Sept., admission €5), renowned for Tasmanian tree ferns, gargantuan rhododendrons, camellias, and red cedars. The garden was designed by the fifth Lord Lansdowne when he inherited his title in 1866, and work continued up until the 1950s; the house isn't open to the public.

There isn't much accommodation in the immediate area, and many people choose to see Derreen Gardens as an afternoon trip from Kenmare. A bungalow farmhouse on the northern end of the Healy Pass (translation: an awesome view from your bedroom window), **Mountain View** (on the R574, tel. 064/83143, mountainview@eircom.net, open Easter–mid-Oct., off-season by arrangement, €28–30 pp, s €30–40) offers evening meals (€20, bring your own bottle) often featuring fresh seafood, as well as high tea (€12).

tranquil Glenmore Lake

© CAMILLE DEANGELIS

And in terms of "nightlife," you'll often find live music and set dancing sessions at **An Sibin** (signposted from the R571, tel. 064/83941), a rather self-consciously rustic (and slightly twee) pub that's good fun nevertheless.

The summer-only Killarney–Castletownbere route on **Bus Éireann** (tel. 064/34777) passes through Lauragh (#282 from Castletownbere, #270 from Killarney, 2/day Mon.–Sat.) from late June to the beginning of September.

GLENMORE LAKE

A placid lake nestled in the low Caha Mountains south of Lauragh (and just west of the Healy Pass), Glenmore (also spelled Glanmore) is ringed with evergreens and splashes of purple rhododendrons in early summer. There's next to nothing out here—just a hostel and a restaurant—but that may be just the reason to go.

Old-school An Óige in the best way—and literally, since it's in the old Glenmore National Schoolhouse, built in 1880—the **Glenmore Lake Hostel** (signposted off the R571, 4 km south of Lauragh, tel. 064/83181, open end of May–Sept., dorms €15, sheet rental €2) has a

marvelous setting just above the lake (though the lake isn't visible from the back). Calling all backpackers looking to get off the well-worn tourist track: Arrive in late May or early June and you might even have the place to yourself. Note that there may be a 10:30 A.M.–5 P.M. lockout, because the kindly lady who runs the place (Eileen O'Shea, who lives directly across the road) is on her own. Bring provisions with you, as there isn't a grocery for miles.

For lunch, tea, or dinner, try the ideally situated **Josie's Lake View House & Restaurant** (clearly signposted off the R574, tel. 064/83155, opening hours vary, but generally 11 A.M.– 9 P.M. or later daily all year, mains €13–24), with a truly awesome vantage overlooking the lake and surrounding mountains. The bright, airy restaurant itself has a cordial staff and good food—good, not great, but it truly doesn't matter with a view like this!—and the vegetarian options are surprisingly bountiful. Make a reservation for a table with a view.

Those without wheels can take the Bus Éireann summer service to Lauragh and walk four kilometers south to Glenmore.

North Kerry

Most visitors just pass through inland Kerry, with its workaday towns and villages, en route to Dingle, Killarney, and the Ring of Kerry; its few attractions often don't justify a stop (like the 30-minute guided tour through Crag Cave, east of Tralee near Castleisland, which isn't worth the price of admission). That said, pleasant Listowel has a literary reputation, and Tralee makes a good stopover on the way to Dingle.

LISTOWEL

You might want to spend a night in the laid-back market town of Listowel ("liss-STOLE," Lios Tuathail, "Tuathal's Fort") just to decompress after the Dingle–Killarney–Ring of Kerry tourist circuit! It's also near enough to Shannon Airport that you can spend your

last night here, even if you're taking the bus. Granted, there isn't a whole lot to do most of the year (the annual Listowel Writers' Week in late May/early June being the exception), but if a quiet pint or three at a pub owned by one of Ireland's great modern dramatists sounds appealing, then Listowel's your place.

The River Feale bends around the town in a sideways C, with the main square tucked in the curve. St. Mary's Catholic Church and the bus stop are on the square's south end, and if you continue away from the square along Bridge Street you'll come to—what else?—the bridge to Tralee and other points south. The northern tip of the square becomes Main Street as it heads northeast, becoming Church Street after a block; William Street veers off to your left at this point.

KERRY

Sights

Overlooking the River Neale is the 12th-century, still-commanding **Listowel Castle** (The Square, behind the Kerry Literary and Cultural Centre, tel. 01/647-6593, open 9:30 A.M.–5:30 P.M. daily June–mid-Sept., free admission), which Dúchas has recently restored. This was the seat of the Fitzmaurices, the Anglo-Norman earls of Kerry, and it's the best example of Norman architecture in the county.

The lavish and splendidly detailed gold mosaics at the neo-Gothic **St. Mary's Catholic Church** (on the square) are also well worth seeing.

The **Kerry Literary and Cultural Centre** (24 The Square, tel. 068/22212, www.seanchai-klcc.com, open 10 A.M.–6 P.M. Apr.–Sept., admission €5.20) offers an exhibition on the lives and work of local writers. It also hosts film and ceilidh nights in July and August.

Entertainment and Events

Do your drinking at **John B. Keane** (37 William St., no phone), the bar the eponymous playwright worked behind all his life. His widow and son still own the place, and it's by far the most popular hangout for local literary types—especially during the annual **Listowel Writers' Week** (late May/early June, 24 The Square, tel. 068/21074, www.writersweek.ie), a busy festival of workshops and writing competitions that draws participants from all over the globe.

Sports and Recreation

There's a shady walk along the River Neale, but the view is marred by the ugly butter factory. Take a walk in **Childers Park** on the eastern end of town instead; the entrance is off Bridge Road, a block past the bus stop on the square.

Recreational pursuits include an afternoon at the **Listowel Races** (just west of the river, turnoff on the Ballybunion road opposite the hospital, tel. 068/21144, www.listowelraces.ie) or a round at the 9-hole, par-35 **Listowel Golf Club** (2 km west of town, signposted off the N69, tel. 068/21592). There are two more scenic courses at **Ballybunion** (Sandhill Rd.,

tel. 068/27146, bbgolfc@iol.ie), 14.5 kilometers northwest of Listowel on the R553, along with a Blue Flag beach.

Accommodations

Considering how untouristy it is, you might be surprised to find so many good B&Bs in and around Listowel. (There is one hostel, located above Lumberjacks Bar, but it is not recommended.)

An excellent choice for B&B is **◖ Whispering Pines** (Ballylongford Rd., Bedford, tel. 068/21503, t_keane@unison.ie, €26–33 pp, s €35–45), a 10-minute walk outside town. Proprietor Theresa Keane offers the kind of hospitality this country is known for. The breakfasts are generous (and mealtime is flexible, a significant plus), tea is served with style, and the Keanes bend over backward to ensure your comfort. Most of the bedrooms aren't en suite, but there are enough bathrooms that it feels like you have your own, and each bedroom does have a sink. The walk into town is a pleasant one, but the narrow road means you should ring for a taxi after a night at the pub.

The riverside **Ceol na hAbhann** (Tralee Rd., tel. 068/21345, knstack@eircom.net, €35 pp, s €50) also gets top marks for charm, comfort, and hospitality. A more upscale option is **◖ Mount Rivers** (less than 1 km south of town, over the bridge, on the R555/Abbyfeale road, tel. 068/21494, www.mountriverslistowel.com, €50–60 pp), run by the vivacious Liz O'Reilly. The three guest bedrooms in her ancestral home, erected in 1869, are brimming with Victorian elegance.

The ivy-covered **Listowel Arms Hotel** (The Square, tel. 068/21500, www.listowelarms.com, €65–85 pp, s €80–100) is grander than your average small-town hotel, the rooms are comfortable (just be sure to ask for one of the refurbished rooms), the staff are friendly, and the food is far better than the average hotel fare.

Food

Listowel isn't known for its restaurants, but you'll fare all right. Tasty pastries and full breakfasts are on offer at the friendly, no-frills **Lynch's**

Bakery (Main St., tel. 068/21099, open 8 A.M.–5 P.M. Mon.–Sat., mains under €6).

The fare at the **Listowel Arms Hotel** is above average, though the vegetarian option could disappoint. Perhaps a better choice is **Allo's** (41 Church St., tel. 068/22880, food served noon–9:15 P.M. daily, lunches €10–16, dinner mains €15–28), a Listowel mainstay. This is the best gastro-pub for miles, serving flavorful dishes like leg of venison in cider gravy. As usual at Irish bistros, lunch is a much better value.

Information and Services

The **tourist office** (tel. 068/22590, open 10 A.M.–1 P.M. and 2–6 P.M. Mon.–Sat. June–Sept. and Mon.–Fri. Oct.–Apr.) is located in the old Anglican St. John's Church at the center of the square. The **AIB** and **Bank of Ireland,** also on the square, have ATMs and bureaux de change. The **post office** is a five-minute walk up William Street.

Get your duds sudsed at **Moloney's Laundrette** (Bridge St., tel. 068/21263, closed Sun.) and pick up cough drops at **Trant's Pharmacy** (Listowel Shopping Centre, Convent St., tel. 068/24550). To get there, turn from Main onto William and make a quick left onto Market Street, which becomes Convent Street.

Getting There and Around

Listowel is 27 kilometers north of Tralee and 80 kilometers southwest of Limerick. To get here from Clare and other points north, consider taking the **Killimer-Tarbert Car Ferry** (Killimer, tel. 065/905-3124, www.shannonferries.com, single/return €15/25 with car, €4/6 pedestrians and cyclists) to Tarbert, 18 kilometers north of Listowel, to save considerable time and gas.

Bus Éireann (tel. 066/712-3566) provides frequent service from Tralee (#13, at least 8/day daily), Dublin and Limerick (#13, at least 11/day daily), Galway (#54, at least 3/day daily), and Athlone (#72, at least 3/day Mon.–Sat., 2/day Sun.).

There are several excellent taxi services in Listowel, including **D.J. Hannon** (tel. 087/254-2285 or 087/661-9676), good for late-night pickups, **P. J. Broderick** (42 Church St., tel. 068/21349 or 087/262-1797), and **Fitzpatrick Cabs** (55 Church St., tel. 068/21707).

TRALEE

Some folks seem to want to visit Tralee (Trá Lí, "Strand of the Lee") just because it's the location of the annual Rose of Tralee pageant, which is open to girls of Irish heritage as well as native lasses. Though it's a pleasant enough town—the largest in the county—there's little cause to linger here, what with all the dramatic landscapes of the Dingle Peninsula and Killarney National Park awaiting you. That said, public transportation connections might necessitate a stopover for the night.

The town is north of the slender River Lee, the main street being the Mall, Lower Castle Street, Upper Castle Street, and Boherboy as it proceeds west to east. On a south perpendicular is Denny Street, which culminates in the Kerry County Museum and entrance to the carefully manicured town park; from the main drag, turn north onto Edward Street for the post office and train and bus station. The town's square is one block south of the Mall.

Sights

Tralee's shortage of attractions is another reason to keep on driving west to Dingle.

Fans of sport and local Antarctic adventurer Tom Crean will find a fair bit of diversion at the **Kerry County Museum** (Ashe Memorial Hall, Denny St., tel. 066/712-7777, www.kerrymuseum.ie, open 10 A.M.–4:30 P.M. Tues.–Fri. Jan.–Mar., 9:30 A.M.–5:30 P.M. Tues.–Sat. Apr.–May and daily June–Aug., 9:30 A.M.–5 P.M. Tues.–Sat. Sept.–Dec., admission €8), but the admission price is downright ridiculous. Unless it's raining cats and dogs, you'll probably want to skip this one.

On your way out of town on the Dingle road, you'll spot the restored **Blennerville Windmill** (on the N86 1 km west of town, tel. 066/712-1064, open 9:30 A.M.–5:30 P.M. Apr.–Oct., admission €5), which is the largest

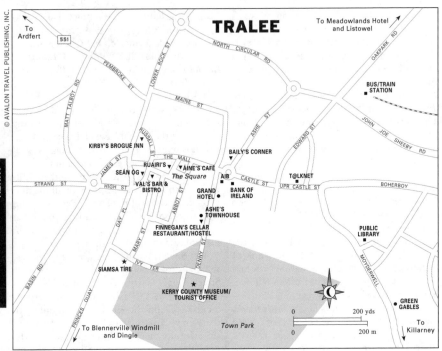

working windmill in Ireland or Britain. The price of admission gets you an eight-minute audiovisual, a one-room exhibition, and a half-hour guided tour of the windmill itself.

Entertainment and Events

Tralee's live trad scene isn't quite as hopping as Dingle's, but there are still a few pubs you can rely on for entertainment while you sup your pint. First stop by **Seán Óg** (41 Bridge St., tel. 066/712-8822), which has sessions pretty much every night of the week. **Baily's Corner** (Ashe St., tel. 066/712-6230) has trad on Tuesday, while local folk/rock bands are on the bill every Monday, Wednesday, Thursday, and Sunday.

With plenty of outdoor seating, **Ruairi's** (The Square, tel. 066/718-1289) is a good spot for a spell of people-watching in the afternoon. This one attracts a mostly 20-something crowd.

Siamsa Tíre ("SHAHM-sah TCHEE-reh,"

Ivy Terrace, west of the county museum and park, tel. 066/712-3055, www.siamsatire. com, tickets €8–25), Ireland's "national folk theater," hosts film screenings, comedy shows, drama, and concerts, but the primary draw is a series of dance-and-theater performances interpreting the finest tales in the canon of Irish folklore (starts at 8:30 P.M. Mon.–Sat. Apr.–Oct., tickets €18).

Shopping

There isn't too much in the way of retail therapy here. You've got the **Tralee Shopping Centre** on Russell Street, and there are several cute boutiques and shoe shops in the immediate vicinity, but that's about it.

Sports and Recreation

Tralee boasts an exquisitely designed and maintained **town park** that brims with roses in summertime.

Ireland's largest leisureland, **Aqua Dome** (tel. 066/712-8899 or 066/712-9150, open 10 A.M.–10 P.M. weekdays, 11 A.M.–8 P.M. weekends, admission €12, mini-golf €4.50 pp) features all the usual kid-friendly amusements under a huge plexi-dome, with an adjacent miniature golf park. Bring your own towels.

In a scenic location on Tralee Bay, the **Tralee Golf Club** (11 km west of town off the R558, signposted in the village of Spa, tel. 066/713-6379, www.traleegolfclub.com) was designed by none other than Arnold Palmer.

Feeling lucky? How about a day at the races? The action at the **Tralee Racecourse** (Ballybeggan Park, 2 km outside town on the N21/Limerick road, tel. 066/712-6490, www.tralee-horseracing.com, admission €15) hits its peak on the June bank holiday weekend.

You say you'd rather do the riding? Contact **Tralee Equestrian Centre** (Tonevane, off the N86/Dingle road, make a left immediately after Blennerville village and follow the signposts, tel. 066/711-7800, www.traleeequestriancentre.com) for hour-long lessons or two- or six-day holiday packages. You'll canter down backcountry roads in the shadows of the Slieve Mish Mountains west of town.

Accommodations

Backpackers stay at the pleasingly quirky, IHH **Finnegan's** (17 Denny St., tel. 066/712-7610, www.finneganshostel.com, dorms €16, private rooms €20 pp, credit cards accepted), a rambling Georgian townhouse in a central location. Though it's adequate in every other respect, this place is in dire need of new mattresses. If you aren't traveling with a sleeping bag you might want to spring for a B&B (no pun intended).

Where to spring? Two doors down is **Ashe's Townhouse** (15 Denny St., tel. 066/712-6475, www.accommodation-kerry.com, €30–40 pp, s €35–45), another Georgian townhouse with 12 bright, comfortable, freshly decorated rooms (two of which are family suites).

On the far side of Tralee's lovely town park is **Green Gables** (1 Clonmore Villas, Ballymullen Rd., tel. 066/712-3354, www.greengables-

tralee.com, open mid-Feb.–mid-Dec., €27–35 pp, s €37–45), a well-kept Victorian townhome painted a handsome olive. The rooms are smallish but full of genuine character (that's no euphemism), and the communal breakfast table is endowed with plenty of fresh fruit.

There are a few modern hotels in town, the one with the least offensive architecture being the **Meadowlands** (Oakpark Rd., 1 km from the town center, tel. 066/718-0444, www.meadowlands-hotel.com, €85–105 pp, s €105–125). Surrounded by more than a hectare of landscaped grounds, the Meadowlands has the best hotel food in town (with an emphasis on fresh seafood), and there's always someone at the piano in the classy restaurant with its stone walls, exposed pine beams, and open fires. The rooms are charmingly furnished as well—none of that anonymous corporate stuff.

Looking for a bit of old Victorian glamour? Look no further than the aptly named **Grand Hotel** (Denny St., tel. 066/712-1499, www.grandhoteltralee.com, €50–60 pp, s €60–70), though the bar and reception rooms are more old-fashioned than the rooms are. This is the most popular hotel with Irish weekenders, so be forewarned that the nightclub noise can seep up into some of the rooms on Friday and Saturday nights.

Food

You'll find a far greater restaurant selection—both in number and quality—in Dingle, but there are still a few nice places to eat here in Tralee.

Serving good gourmet coffee and fresh salads and sandwiches, **Áine's Café and Winebar** (The Square, tel. 066/718-5388, www.ainescafeandwinebar.ie, open 9 A.M.–6 P.M. Mon.–Sat. and 11 A.M.–6 P.M. Sun. all year, open later in summer, lunches under €7) is one of the most popular eateries in town day or night. It could certainly do with more space—ordering coffee for takeout can feel like being in a human logjam—but the service is excellent and you won't find a better cappuccino elsewhere.

For mostly traditional pub fare, head over to

Kirby's Brogue Inn (Rock St., tel. 066/712-3221, food served 4:30–9:30 P.M. daily, mains €6–12). To get here, head west down the Mall, bear right onto Russell Street, and you'll see Kirby's on your left.

By far the trendiest bar in town, **Val's Bar & Bistro** (Bridge St., tel. 066/718-1289, food served 6:30–10:30 P.M. daily, mains €16–26, tapas menu €3–8) serves up high-quality Continental fare and fantastically inventive cocktails in the downstairs bar, with its slouchy white leather armchairs, sleek wood paneling, and orange light fixtures. The upstairs restaurant is excessively formal, so you'll probably want to have your dinner down here. The portions are slightly stingy, however, and unfortunately there are no vegetarian main courses.

Located in the wine cellar of a Georgian townhouse that incorporated the ruins of Tralee Castle, **Finnegan's Cellar Restaurant** (17 Denny St., tel. 066/718-1400, open 6–11 P.M. daily, mains €14–25, 3-course early-bird menu €26 5:30–7:30 P.M. daily) serves up reliably good modern Irish (using local meat and seafood, with a couple of veggie options) in the most romantic ambience in town—checkered tablecloths, open fires, rough stone walls, candlelight, the whole shebang.

Information

The **tourist office** (Ashe Memorial Hall, tel. 066/712-1288, www.tralee.ie, open 9 A.M.–5:15 P.M. Mon.–Sat.) is around the corner at the Kerry County Museum, opposite the entrance to the town park on Denny Street.

Services

Two banks with ATMs and bureaux de change are **AIB** (Denny St. and Castle St.) and the **Bank of Ireland** (Castle St.). The **post office** is on Edward Street.

Take care of business at **Irwin's Pharmacy** (18 Upper Castle St., tel. 066/712-1287) and **Catherine's Launderette** (59A Boherboy, tel. 066/712-7173).

You can get free Internet access at the **public library** (Moyderwell, turn right at the east end of Upper Castle St., tel. 066/712-1200), but if it's closed, you can check your email on a speedy flatscreen at **T@lknet** (30 Castle St., tel. 066/718-5637, open 10 A.M.–10 P.M. daily, €3/hour).

Getting There

Tralee is 32 kilometers north of Killarney on the N22 and 104 kilometers southwest of Limerick on the N21. **Bus Éireann** (John Joe Sheehy Rd., tel. 066/712-3566) offers frequent service to Killarney (#14 or #40, at least 11/day daily), Cork (#40, at least 11/day daily), Galway and the Cliffs of Moher (#50, 2 direct services/day daily), and Dublin and Limerick (#13, 12/day daily).

You can also ride **Irish Rail** (John Joe Sheehy Rd., tel. 066/712-3522, at least 2/day Mon.–Sat. from Dublin Heuston, single/weekly return ticket €57/68).

Getting Around

Tralee is eminently walkable. Rent a bike from **Tralee Gas & Nursery** (Strand St., tel. 066/712-2018, €12/day).

There's a **taxi rank** on the Mall, or call **Radio Taxis** (tel. 066/712-5451) or **Jackie Power** (tel. 066/712-9444).

ARDFERT

In the sleepy village of Ardfert (Ard Fhearta, "The Height of the Burial Mounds") are the awe-inspiring remains of **Ardfert Cathedral** (signposted from the R551, in the village center, tel. 066/713-4711, open 9:30 A.M.–6 P.M. mid-Apr.–Sept., admission €2.10). The Dúchas-run site dates from the 6th century (and is associated with St. Brendan the Navigator, who supposedly reached the New World in a curragh at least 800 years before Columbus), though most of the present architecture dates from the 13th century onward. The cathedral itself is done in the English and Gothic styles, with a striking restored Romanesque west doorway made of sandstone (dating to the 12th century); it also boasts the tallest lancet windows in the country, a dozen in all. The round tower was destroyed in 1771, and the stones may have been used to build the site's low surrounding wall. There are two smaller churches on the site: the 15th-century **Temple na Griffin,** so named for an effigy of that mythical beast, and the late 12th-century **Templenahoe** ("Church of the Virgin"). Temple na Griffin was closed at time of writing; it may be reroofed and opened as a second exhibition center.

The old chancel (reroofed and used for Anglican services in the 17th century) has been converted into a visitors center with a small but informative exhibition that includes two late-13th-century effigies of local bishops anchored to the visitors center wall (one of which has been incorrectly identified as St. Brendan). Though there isn't much else of interest in the vicinity, those who enjoy wandering through monastic ruins will find the cathedral well worth a visit.

Ardfert is nine kilometers northwest of Tralee on the R551 (the Ballyheigue road). The Tralee–Ballybunion **Bus Éireann** (tel. 066/712-3566, #274) service passes through Ardfert, with at least four buses a day late June–early September. Service in the off-season is too infrequent to be of use.

KERRY

THE MIDLANDS

Used loosely to describe the landlocked counties of central Ireland, the "midlands" get short shrift where most tourists are concerned, and there *is* a grain of truth to the adage that Ireland is a pretty frame around a dull picture.

Yet amid these vast swaths of bog and farmland you'll find a fair bit to divert you, even if you're only passing through to Cork or Kerry; the magnificent monastic city of Clonmacnoise in County Offaly is a highlight, as is the neoclassical Emo Court in Laois. Longford (An Longphort, "The Fortress"), Westmeath (An Iarmhí), Offaly (Uibh Fhailí, "Descendants of Ros of the Rings"), and Laois (pronounced "leash," meaning "Church by the Oak") form the western half of the province of Leinster; Roscommon (Ros Comáin, "St.

Coman's Wood") is east of Mayo and Galway in the province of Connaught; Cavan (An Cabhán, "The Hollow") and Monaghan (Muineachán, "Place of Thickets"), along with Donegal, are the three Ulster counties that are not part of Northern Ireland. These border counties also offer opportunities to wander "off the beaten track": There's a fair bit to keep you here beyond those rather bleak-looking farmsteads, especially if you're an avid angler or hill-walker. Cavan's hills and lakes are some of the prettiest you'll see anywhere—so long as the sun is shining.

HISTORY

Many items on display in the National Museum in Dublin (wood carvings, clothing, even corpses) were uncovered in an eerily

© CAMILLE DEANGELIS

HIGHLIGHTS

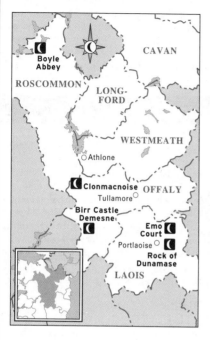

◖ Boyle Abbey: By far County Roscommon's most important monastic site, Boyle Abbey's Cistercian history and intriguing mix of architectural styles make it a worthwhile stop en route from Dublin to Sligo (page 248).

◖ Clonmacnoise: The country's most important monastic city was founded by St. Ciarán in the 6th century along the bank of the River Shannon (page 248).

◖ Birr Castle Demesne: Though the castle itself is not open to the public, Birr offers beautiful formal gardens along with the Great Telescope, built by the third Earl of Rosse in 1845 and the world's largest until 1915 (see page 250).

◖ Emo Court: This fine neoclassical manor has been sensitively restored by the Office of Public Works, and the picnic-perfect demesne is Ireland's, and Europe's, second-largest walled park (page 253).

◖ Rock of Dunamase: This hilltop stronghold offers a tremendous panoramic view of fertile green fields as far as the eye can see (page 254).

LOOK FOR ◖ TO FIND RECOMMENDED SIGHTS, ACTIVITIES, DINING, AND LODGING.

THE MIDLANDS

preserved condition in midland bogs. Some of these items—and people—go back as far as the Iron Age. One of the more recent discoveries was in January 2006, when a mangled yet well-preserved corpse was found on Croghan Hill in County Offaly; he was almost two meters (six feet, six inches) tall, in his early 20s, relatively wealthy judging by the softness of his hands—and he was very clearly tortured. This was not an unusual discovery, as many of the 150-odd corpses found in Irish bogs bear proof of a violent end. A far more cheerful find was made on the Offaly-Tipperary border in August 2006: a medieval

manuscript, the Book of Psalms, a discovery archaeologists say is on par with the Dead Sea Scrolls. Chances are it was dumped here more than a millennium ago by some dim-witted invader.

Literary buffs will note that County Longford has a distinguished history: Anglo-Irish novelist Maria Edgeworth *(Castle Rackrent)* spent most of her life here; Oliver Goldsmith *(She Stoops to Conquer)* and Gaelic revivalist Padraic Colum *(The Wild Earth)*, both novelist-poet-playwrights, were both born here, 150 years apart. (Longford has very little in terms of present-day attractions, however.)

PLANNING YOUR TIME

Most of the midlands' sights are "while we're in the area" side trips rather than peak-of-our-holiday destinations; Clonmacnoise is the lone exception, a common detour on the Dublin–Galway route. Frankly, though many of these sights are neat enough, they're ultimately worth seeing only if it's convenient.

As for Clonmacnoise, if you get an early enough start, there's no need to spend the night in the area; otherwise, plan to stay in Athlone (21 kilometers north), the best choice in the area in terms of amenities, nightlife, and quality eateries.

Westmeath and Roscommon

Ireland's geographical center is somewhere in Westmeath, though locals disagree as to where exactly. The county's name refers to its origin as part of County Meath (which was once Ireland's fifth province). Dotted with lakes and bogs, Westmeath is bordered on the west by the River Shannon, which empties into Lough Ree. The Shannon waterway is popular for boating holidays, and sailors regularly dock at the county capital, Athlone, which offers several great pubs and restaurants.

Bordered by the River Shannon to the east, Sligo and Leitrim to the north, and Mayo and Galway to the west, Roscommon offers little more than flat tracts of farmland; the casual visitor would probably not find its sprinkling of castle and abbey ruins worth seeking out, Boyle Abbey (near the Sligo border) being the exception.

ATHLONE

Most folks—natives and tourists both—know Athlone (Baile Átha Luain, "Town of the Ford of Luan") as the town midway between Dublin and Galway where the Bus Éireann bus makes a pit stop. Get off the bus, head into town, and you'll find it's actually a pretty cool place, mostly for its small but up-and-coming "Left Bank" quarter lined with neat little shops and cafés. There's not much to see in Athlone, but it's definitely the best place to base yourself when planning a visit to Clonmacnoise.

The town straddles the River Shannon, with the Catholic church and Athlone Castle just over the Town Bridge on the Left Bank.

From the castle, turn left onto Castle Street for Main Street and Fry Place, where you'll find the famous Sean's pub and delicious Left Bank Bistro. From there, turn left onto High Street (which becomes Bastion Street and then O'Connell Street) for more eats and shopping. Back on the right bank, the main drag (starting from the bridge) changes names from Custume Place to Church to Dublin Gate to Mardyke to Costello. Mostly everything you'll need is along this thoroughfare.

Sights

Athlone's sights pale in comparison to Clonmacnoise, Ireland's most important monastic site, 21 kilometers south over the Offaly border; if you're staying here in town, chances are that's what you've come to see. But if your itinerary allows, you might want to visit the massive early-13th-century **Athlone Castle** (St. Peter's Sq., tel. 090/644-2100, open 9:30 A.M.–5 P.M. daily May–mid-Oct., admission €5.50), built for the seemingly ubiquitous King John. The exhibition in the central keep includes a 40-minute audiovisual on the castle's history as well as a folklife and military museum. Though the castle is a national monument, it's not a Dúchas site, so admission isn't covered under the Heritage Card. You'll find Athlone's Saturday market on the square outside the castle.

Across the square from the castle is the Catholic **Church of Saints Peter and Paul,** clearly inspired by the Renaissance basilicas of Rome; inside you'll find admirable replicas of Michelangelo's *Pieta* and *Moses* sculptures.

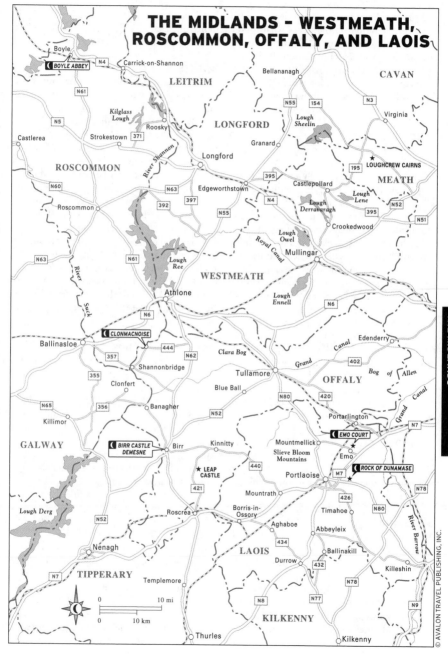

THE MIDLANDS - WESTMEATH, ROSCOMMON, OFFALY, AND LAOIS

THE MIDLANDS

The original Saint Peter's was built at the turn of the 19th century on the site of what is now the Dean Crowe Theatre on Chapel Street, and was replaced by this church in the late 1930s. Faux-Michelangelos aside, the church is worth a visit for its six stained-glass windows by Harry Clarke (four in the body of the church and two in the mortuary chapel).

Entertainment

Many pubs claim to be Ireland's oldest—there's the Brazen Head in Dublin, or Grace Neill's in County Down—but only **Sean's** (Main St., in the Left Bank section, tel. 090/649-2358) is listed in the *Guinness Book of Records*. Supposedly there's been a pub on this site since the beginning of the 10th century. Regardless of the authenticity of this claim, it's still the most happenin' spot in town, with live trad sessions in the front room on the weekends and a huge tented beer garden out back. Both spaces get packed to the rafters on a Saturday night, so be sure to get here early for a seat.

Gertie Browne's (Custume Pl., tel. 090/647-4848) might look ancient, but all the atmospheric miscellanea inside (including a rusty suit of armor apparently made for a dwarf) was assembled in the early '90s when the place last changed hands. This is one of Athlone's most charming pubs, always full of intriguing characters. You'll find trad here on summer weekends.

The **Dean Crowe Theatre** (Chapel St., off Bastion St. in the Left Bank, tel. 090/649-2129, www.deancrowetheatre.com) hosts jazz and pop concerts, theater workshops, and art exhibitions.

Shopping

Athlone's mega-shopping center, Golden Island, is on the south side of town, off Costello Street (beyond a series of car parks). But the town's best shops are mostly in the Left Bank neighborhood. The **Bastion Gallery** (tel. 090/649-4948), an atmospheric "Aladdin's cave" of exotic gifts and jewelry, and **Garbz,** a popular "alternative clothing" shop, are both on the ground floor of the excellent Bastion

B&B on—you guessed it!—Bastion Street. For more tips, pick up a free *Left Bank Walking & Shopping Guide* from the tourist office.

Sports and Recreation

As it's situated on the River Shannon, Athlone is popular with serious boaters and anglers; if you want to go fishing on Lough Ree, stop by the **Strand Tackle Shop** (The Strand, on the right bank south of the Town Bridge, tel. 090/647-9277) for equipment and a permit. Sailors can rent a self-drive cabin cruiser through **Athlone Cruisers** (Jolly Mariner Marina, 1 km north of town off Coosan Rd., tel. 090/647-2892, www.iol.ie/wmeathtc/acl, cruise tickets €15) or just go for a 90-minute cruise (no skills required!) on the MV *Ross*. Families and groups can try **Shannon Safaris** (36 Silverquay, off Northgate St. beside the Radisson Hotel, north of Custume Place, tel. 090/647-9558 or 086/284-9108, www.shannonsafari.ie), who'll plan a waterway excursion for you at any time of day for €20 per person per hour.

Accommodations

Located across the road from the Athlone Institute of Technology three kilometers east of town, **Lough Ree Lodge** (Kilmacuagh, Dublin Rd., tel. 090/647-6738, loughreelodge@eircom.net, open May–Aug., €16 pp) houses students during the year and budget travelers in the summer months. There are plenty of ensuite single and double rooms (as well as family rooms), all with television—though the location can be a pain if you don't have a car.

There aren't many B&Bs in Athlone, and most of them are either on the shabby side or were up for sale at time of writing. Just because ◖ **The Bastion** (2 Bastion St., tel. 090/649-4954, www.thebastion.net, €35–45 pp) has virtually no competition doesn't lessen its excellence. A labyrinthine townhouse filled with antiques, exotic knickknacks, and potted plants, it's a delightfully quirky, bohemian spot—and Anthony, the owner, is exceptionally friendly and helpful. Come morning there's a smorgasbord of fancy breads and cheeses along with fruit, cereal, and Fair Trade coffee and herbal tea—a nice change from the usual greasy fried breakfast.

A newly refurbished hotel on the main drag, the **Prince of Wales** (Church St., tel. 090/647-6666, www.theprinceofwales.ie, €60–85 pp, s €85–105) has business-class rooms with DVD/CD players (and a selection of DVDs), radio, wireless Internet, digital safes, and king-size beds in many of the rooms. There's also same-day laundry service. The four bars and nightclub downstairs attract a youngish local crowd.

It's not actually in town, but the **Wineport Lodge** (Athlone Relief Rd., 5 km north of town, just outside the village of Glasson off the N55, tel. 090/643-9010, www.wineport .ie, rooms €165–198, deluxe rooms €200–295, corporate rates available Sun.–Thurs., Sat. night supplement €35–75) is generally considered Athlone's best hotel-restaurant, in part for its great location right on Lough Ree. The carefully selected wine, champagne, and cocktail lists in the hotel lounge are worth the visit alone, but with spacious, swanky, lake-facing rooms (with balcony) and a top-notch room-service breakfast included in the price, this is *the* place to treat yourself when touring the midlands.

Food

Athlone has a small trove of great little places to eat, most of which are in the Left Bank. Take two of Athlone's nicest, most laid-back cafés, directly across the street from one another: **Slice of Life** (Bastion St., tel. 090/649-3970, open 8:30 A.M.–6 P.M. Mon.–Sat., mains €4–8) and **Foodie's** (Bastion St., tel. 090/649-8576, open 8:30 A.M.–6 P.M. Mon.–Sat., mains €4–8).

For traditional pub grub, try **O'Neill's** (47 Mardyke St., across from St. Mary's Church, tel. 090/647-1382, food served noon–8:30 P.M. Mon.–Sat., 12:30–4 P.M. Sun., mains €8–11), a large, comfortable, unassuming place where you'll find a load of regulars riveted to whatever sporting match or horse race is on the televisions above the bar.

No doubt it's the finest restaurant in town—with a bright, airy, minimalist dining room and an Asian- and Australian-inspired menu—but consider yourself warned that the service at the **Left Bank Bistro** (Fry Pl., off Main St. in the Left Bank, tel. 090/649-4446, www.leftbankbistro.com, open 10:30 A.M.–9:30 P.M. Tues.–Sat., lunch €8–11, 3-course early-bird special €25 5:30–7:30 P.M. Tues.–Fri., dinner mains €19–25) can be downright negligent. That said, you can have yourself an open-faced sandwich with exquisitely fresh goat cheese salad for lunch, or go all out for dinner with an Asian-marinated half-roast duck in apple-mint sauce.

The food isn't *quite* as delicious at the **Olive Grove** (Custume Pl., across the street from Gertie Browne's pub, tel. 090/647-1248, www. theolivegrove.ie, open noon–4 P.M. and 5:30–10 P.M. Tues.–Sun., lunch €8–11, €20/25 2/3-course early-bird menu 5:30–7:30 P.M., dinner mains €14–25), but it's just as popular with locals for its hearty, unpretentious modern Irish fare—and it's surprisingly vegetarian-friendly. In fact, this is the most popular lunch spot on the "Right Bank."

Information and Services

The **tourist office** (tel. 090/649-4630, open 9:30 A.M.–5:30 P.M. Mon.–Fri. Apr.–Oct., www.eastcoastmidlands.ie and www.athlone. ie) is at Athlone Castle. Just across the Town Bridge from the castle is a **Bank of Ireland** (31 Church St.) with ATM and bureau de change. You'll find the **post office** beside the Church of Saints Peter and Paul on Barrack Street (also opposite the castle).

Need a pharmacy on a Sunday? **Boots the Chemist** (tel. 090/647-6997) is in the Golden Island Shopping Centre. There's a **Laundromat** (27 Pearse St., tel. 090/649-2930) offering two-hour service in the Left Bank neighborhood; head west up Bastion Street and you'll see Pearse Street on your right. Check your email at the **Netc@fé** (Costello St., tel. 090/647-8888, www .thenetcafe.ie, open 11 A.M.–11 P.M. daily, €3.50/hour).

THE MIDLANDS

Getting There and Around

Athlone is roughly midway between Galway (93 km) and Dublin (123 km) on the N6. Get here from Dublin or Galway via **Irish Rail** (tel. 090/647-3300, www.irishrail.ie, 5/day Mon.–Sat., 4/day Sun., single/5-day return €19/32). The other option is the **Bus Éireann** (tel. 090/648-4406, www.buseireann.ie) Dublin–Galway route (#20, 15/day daily). Direct service is also available from Cork, Cashel, and Cahir (#71, 2/day Mon.–Sat., 1/day Sun.) and Limerick (#72, 4/day Mon.–Sat., 2/day Sun.).

The bus and train stations are on the east side of the Shannon, a 10-minute walk from the town center. From Station Road, head east and bear right onto Ballymahon Road, which becomes Gleeson Street. Then turn right onto Mardyke, the east section of Athlone's main drag.

Bike hire is available from **D.B. Cycles** (23 Connaught St., tel. 090/649-2280, €12/70 per day/week). Need a ride? Ring **Co-op Cabs** (tel. 090/649-3366) or **AA Taxis** (tel. 087/227-2731).

C BOYLE ABBEY

Stop in Boyle (Mainistir na Búille) en route to Sligo to visit one of the country's best-preserved Cistercian monasteries, Boyle Abbey (500 m east of the town center, signposted off the N4, tel. 071/966-2604, boyleabbey@opw.ie, open 10 A.M.–6 P.M. daily Easter–Oct., admission €2.10). Now run by Dúchas, the abbey was founded in 1161 as a "daughter" settlement of Mellifont in County Louth under the patronage of the MacDermott clan, and because of its prosperity it was targeted by Norman invaders on several occasions in the early 13th century. Most of the extant buildings date to the early 17th century, however. Given that Cromwell's troops bunked up here in 1659, it's surprising that so much of the abbey remains. The architecture is remarkable for its mix of Romanesque and English Gothic motifs, reflecting the shift in tastes between the founding of the abbey and the completion of the earliest buildings more than half a century later. Forty-minute guided tours begin on the hour from a restored 17th-century gatehouse that houses a small but thorough exhibition.

There's really no need to spend the night here—the abbey may be worthwhile, but the rest of the town is fairly drab. If you do want to stay over, **Abbey House** (tel. 071/966-2385, abbeyhouseboyle@eircom.net, open Mar.–Oct., €29–34 pp, s €40–45) is right next door, a large Victorian with mature gardens and neat little period details like stained-glass windows and the "Victoria Regina" postbox on the front step. There's Internet access available.

Boyle is 41 kilometers southeast of Sligo and 170 kilometers northwest of Dublin on the N4; the **Bus Éireann** Dublin–Sligo route (#23, 6/day Mon.–Sat., 5/day Sun.) stops here.

Offaly

Much of County Offaly is covered in bog, punctuated rather dramatically by the lovely, mostly unspoiled Slieve Bloom mountains. (They're really more like tall hills, though—the highest peak, Arderin, is only 529 meters.) The **Slieve Bloom Way**, a 35-kilometer loop, and the scenic driving route stretching east of Kinnitty (the R440) are both fine options for a road-less-traveled sort of experience. From the Glendine Gap (signposted off the R440), it's said you can see all four provinces. For more information on walking tours and local festivals, visit the Slieve Bloom Rural Development Society website (www.slievebloom.ie).

C CLONMACNOISE

Along with Glendalough in County Wicklow, Clonmacnoise (21 km south of Athlone, signposted off the N62, tel. 090/967-4195, open 10 A.M.–5:30 P.M. daily Nov.–mid-March, 10 A.M.–6 P.M. mid-Mar.–mid-May and Sept.–Oct., 9 A.M.–7 P.M. mid-May–Aug., admission

© CAMILLE DEANGELIS

The monastic city of Clonmacnoise features two round towers.

€5.30) is Ireland's most important monastic site, picturesquely situated right on the River Shannon. It's a strange irony that more than 100,000 visitors pass through this otherwise peaceful "monastic city" each year—then again, as William Bulfin noted sadly when he visited Cluain Mac Nois, these ruins attracted plenty of impious Victorian picnickers in his time, too. Get here first thing in the morning, before the advent of the coach buses, and you can almost hear echoes of laughter and tinkling teacups as you wander through the old graveyard.

The Irish name, meaning "retreat of the sons of the noble," probably refers to the monastic school's popularity with Gaelic princes. Founded by St. Ciarán in the 540s (less than a year before he died of yellow plague at the age of 33), Clonmacnoise flourished as a center of learning and scholarship for centuries, in part for its location at the crossroads of the island's two most popular travel routes: the River Shannon and the Eiscir Riada ("Highway of the Kings"), a ridge left by the ice age.

The monastery was plundered repeatedly (and finally by the English in 1552 under Henry VIII) for its trove of jewel-encrusted reliquaries, book covers, croziers, and so forth. Many of the world's most important medieval manuscripts were produced here, including the 12th-century *Leabhar na hUidhre,* the "Book of the Dun Cow," which contains the earliest extant version of that great Irish epic, the *Táin Bó Cuailnge.*

The ruins include three high crosses (all recently moved inside to the exhibition for preservation, but there are convincing replicas in their places), a cathedral, two round towers, and seven churches dating from the 10th to the 13th centuries. And on a small hill near the car park is the teetering remnant of an early-13th-century castle.

Trysting couples used to linger in the ornate doorway of **The Cathedral,** known as the **whispering arch** because a whisper carries from one side to the other. It is also said this acoustical marvel was used by priests to hear the confessions of lepers. This arch dates to the 14th or 15th century, and thus is not as old as the cathedral itself. You'll also find effigies of Saints Dominic, Patrick, and Francis above the doorway.

Another bit of folklore concerns the tiny **Temple Ciarán,** the saint's burial place: The earth from the church's interior is said to have miraculous properties, so for generations locals have been taking fistfuls to sprinkle on their fields for a successful crop, and on the floors of their homes to ward off sickness; this is why the church floor is on a much lower level than the surrounding ground. Temple Ciarán is the most sacred ruin at Clonmacnoise, but **Temple Finghin** (or Finian) near the Shannon's shore is the most attractive, with its restored 17-meter round tower and Romanesque carvings. The fully renovated **Temple Connor** nearby is used by the Church of Ireland.

Half a kilometer east of the main site, beyond the modern graveyard, is the **Nuns' Church,** built in 1180, which has an excellent example of a Hiberno-Romanesque doorway. This church was a gift to the monastery from

Dearbhforgaill (or Dervorgilla), the "Irish Helen of Troy," who ran off with the king of Leinster (MacMurrough, the same king who invited in the Normans) during a raid in 1152. This incident doubtless contributed to the Norman invasion, as Dervorgilla's husband was one of the chieftains who subsequently drove MacMurrough into exile. Afterward the princess came here to repent, and she died at Mellifont Abbey in Louth at the age of 85. Many people on the coach tours don't realize it's here, so if you find yourself in the midst of a noisy group outside the visitors center, you'll be relieved to find you have the Nuns' Church all to yourself.

The exhibition center offers a series of scenes illustrating the monastic city's history over time (including a scriptorium, a small wooden house where a monk would have copied and illuminated manuscripts). There's the usual 18-minute audiovisual, a collection of early Christian sandstone grave slabs, and the exquisitely carved high crosses brought indoors for preservation. The most famous of these, the Cros na Scraeptra (Cross of the Scriptures), has been hugged by thousands of superstitious visitors, as legend has it whoever can touch their fingertips on the far side will be blessed with healing powers.

Practicalities

Seeing as it's the closest town to Clonmacnoise, Shannonbridge (4 km southwest of the monastic site) might *seem* like the natural choice for a base. Not to malign the good people of Shannonbridge, but who wants to spend a night on vacation in the lee of the West Offaly Power Plant? You're best off staying in Athlone in County Westmeath, even if you don't have a car; Paddy Kavanagh, who ran tours in past years, is no longer active, but if you hook up with a few other tourists you can hire a taxi and negotiate a fee for the round-trip, allowing an hour and a half for your visit.

Or you could get here by boat from Athlone via **Viking Tours** (office at 7 St. Mary St., tel. 090/647-3383 or 086/262-1136, www. iol.ie/wmeathtc/viking, boats depart from the Strand at 9 A.M. Mon.–Fri. May–Sept., 4-hour trip €10–17 pp depending on size of party), but the one-hour stopover isn't nearly long enough to see Clonmacnoise properly. Seasoned cyclists might consider renting a bike from Athlone— but at 40 kilometers round-trip, this isn't a realistic option for the rest of us, and unfortunately, Bus Éireann only offers bus service to Clonmacnoise for school groups.

BIRR

Known for its rows of tidy Georgian houses and the gardens and telescope at Birr Castle Demesne, Birr (Biorra) still manages to feel workaday in the best possible sense. This is one of the best spots from which to base yourself when exploring Offaly and eastern Galway. Birr's Georgian layout is pretty straightforward; there are two squares, and Market Square is connected to Emmet Square one block south via Main Street; one block farther south is the shady, atmospheric Oxmantown Mall. Castle Street curves east from Market Square, passing the castle (and a free car park) before linking back with Oxmantown Mall.

◖ Birr Castle Demesne

Between the lovely formal gardens and Great Telescope, it's easy to see why Birr Castle Demesne (town center, tel. 057/912-0336, www. birrcastle.com, open 9 A.M.–6 P.M. daily all year, admission €9) is the town's primary attraction. The original castle, the medieval stronghold of the O'Carroll clan, was located 180 feet northwest of the present edifice, which is not open to the public. The British crown seized the castle and lands in 1619 and gave them the following year to Sir Laurence Parsons, nephew to Queen Elizabeth's secretary of state. Sir Laurence then took it upon himself to establish a new town layout (for "Parsonstown"), a glass factory, and public sanitation laws, in between enlarging the former home of the O'Carrolls for his own family. Most of the new castle's construction dates from this time, though extensive alterations were made in the early 1800s. Parsons' descendants were given the title of Earl of Rosse, and today the seventh earl still resides at the castle. (The hefty admission fees pay for his astronomical electricity bill…no pun intended.)

In 1845 William Parsons, the third Earl of Rosse, constructed a powerful telescope using local materials. For decades afterward astronomers from all over Europe came here to study the moon's surface, star clusters, and other heavenly bodies. This was the world's largest telescope until 1915, and demonstrations are held three times a day at the **Exhibition Pavilion** north of the castle. In a restored stable just inside the demesne's main entrance is **The Historic Science Centre** (open 9 A.M.–6 P.M. daily), which displays the various other inventions and scientific achievements of the Parsons family.

The Birr Castle gardens, 500 meters east of the castle itself, were laid out in the late 1770s, along with the creation of the artificial lake. All this was improved over successive generations by the green-thumbed earls and countesses of Rosse; the Millennium Garden, with its walkway of arched hedges, was designed by Anne Messel (the present earl's mother) to celebrate her marriage in 1935. The gardens feature at least 1,000 species of plants and shrubs from all over the world, and at 12 meters the box hedges (planted in the 1780s) are the tallest in the world.

Accommodations, Food, and Entertainment

Birr's top accommodation is **((Spinners Townhouse** (Castle St., tel. 057/912-1673, www.spinnerstownhouse.com, €40 pp, s €55), converted from four townhouses and a woolen mill (which is how the townhouse got its name). This place is a delight, with large, elegant, well-furnished, well-maintained rooms and top-notch modern Irish fare in the downstairs **((** **bistro** (food served 4–9 P.M. Mon. and Wed.–Thurs., 4–10 P.M. Fri.–Sat., 12:30–2:30 P.M. and 4–9 P.M. Sun., mains €17–25), which opens onto a new "Mediterranean-style" courtyard. Best of all are the genuinely friendly staff and owners: You have all the warmth and hospitality of a B&B with the class and privacy of a boutique hotel. You won't find a dirty corrugated roof outside your bedroom window, either—all rooms face either the pretty tree-dotted courtyard or the ivy- and wildflower-covered wall of the Birr Castle Demesne. Just be sure to ask for a real double bed when booking, because many of the bedrooms (though perfect in every other way) have two single beds pushed together.

If Spinners is booked, never fear: There are other nice places in town. Try **The Maltings** (Church St., tel. 057/912-1345, themaltingsbirr@eircom.net, €32–35 pp sharing), which is just a stone's throw farther from the castle gates. A converted hophouse built in 1810, this guesthouse has retained little atmosphere, but it's got all the mod cons; it also has Birr's second-most popular restaurant (food served 7:30 A.M.–9 P.M. daily, mains €11–20). There's no comparison with the food at Spinners, though; the menu is spaghetti-and-tomato-sauce kind of provincial. Another option is **The Stables** (Oxmantown Mall, tel. 057/912-0263, www.thestablesrestaurant.com, €40 pp, s €50)—another well-appointed Georgian, this one with an adjoining tearoom and upscale gift shop.

Birr's best watering holes are **Craughwell's** (Castle St., tel. 057/912-1839), with trad sessions on Friday night, and the classy, impeccably restored **Chestnut** (Green St., between Emmet Sq. and Castle St., tel. 057/912-0011), where the cappuccino is as good as the Guinness (albeit appealing to entirely different sets of tastebuds). The Chestnut also hosts the **Full Moon Market** on the third Saturday of the month in the courtyard out back.

You'll find the **Birr Theatre & Arts Centre** (tel. 057/912-2911, www.birrtheatre.com, tickets €5–16) on Oxmantown Mall.

Practicalities

Birr's **tourist office** (tel. 057/912-0110, www.midirelandtourism.ie, open 9:30 A.M.–1 P.M. and 2–5:30 P.M. Mon.–Sat. May–Sept.) is in the Small Business Centre (Brendan St., one block west of Market Sq.).

Birr is 144 kilometers west of Dublin (turning off the N7 to the N62 at Roscrea) and 34 kilometers south of Clonmacnoise (taking the R357 east from Shannonbridge to the N62 at Cloghan). **Bus Éireann** (tel. 090/648-4406) serves Birr on the Cork–Athlone route (#71, 2/day Mon.–Sat., 1/day Sun.) as well as Limerick–Athlone (#72, 4/day Mon.–Sat., 2/day Sun.).

KINNITTY

At the start of the 20th century, William Bulfin characterized the tiny village of Kinnitty (Ceann Eitigh) as "a sheltered Eden in the lap of the hills," and you'll happily find that not much has changed in the intervening century. The main reason to visit is to explore the mostly untouched, utterly enchanting Slieve Bloom Mountain range by car, bike, or on foot; or you can pick up the circular 35-kilometer **Slieve Bloom Way** 5 kilometers east of the village. You could also stay here but make the 20-minute drive west to Birr for dinner, drinks, trad, or maybe even a play at the arts center. Strangely enough, Kinnitty's Irish name means "Etech's Head"—Etech being a decapitated princess in some obscure Celtic legend. Stay at **Ardmore House** (The Walk, signposted off the R440 about 200 m east of the village, tel. 057/913-7009 or 086/278-9147, www.kinnitty.com, €37–40 pp, s €45–50), a beautifully restored farmhouse (built in 1840) with airy, immaculate rooms, home-baked goods, and an open turf fire in the sitting room, plus Internet access.

Other folks come here to relax in luxury at the Gothic revival **Kinnitty Castle** (3 km south on a local road, signposted from the village, tel. 057/913-7318, www.kinnittycastle.com, €110–185 pp, s €145–215). Despite the castle's popularity as a venue for minor celebrity weddings, it isn't particularly well maintained, and the restaurant food leaves much to be desired. Ghost hunters will be intrigued despite the shower mold, gristly steak, and overwhelming wedding parties, however. A long-dead monk who haunts the banquet hall is said to make (accurate) prophecies to one of the staff regarding her colleagues' personal lives, and you couldn't pay anyone who works here any sum of money to spend a night in the infamous "Geraldine Room."

Kinnitty is 14 kilometers east of Birr on the R440, and there is no public transportation.

LEAP CASTLE

As you'd expect in the most haunted spot in the country (if not all Europe), Leap Castle ("lep," Clareen, 16 km south of Kinnitty on the R421, tel. 057/913-1115 or 087/234-4064, seanfryan@oceanfree.net, open daily by request, admission €6) has a long and extremely violent history, starting with the priest murdered in the "Bloody Chapel" by his own brother in 1532. And then there's the spike-studded oubliette where people were said to have been pushed (and subsequently impaled).

What's that you say—you don't believe in all that hooey? Just *you* try to concoct a rational explanation for the horrible stench emanating from an uninhabited wing of the house (this odiferous brand of ghost is called an "elemental," and Leap's appears half-human, half-sheep) or the transparent old man sitting in a rocking chair by the fireplace. The owner, a musician by the name of Sean Ryan, knows there's no such thing as a rational explanation for the spectral parade he finds in his living room on a daily basis (ghost hunters say there are 20 of them in all)—though he likes to think his family's music calms the spirits. Mr. Ryan had to stop holding informal banquets at the castle when some busybody reported him to the taxman, but it's still possible to pop by during the day. Be sure to ring ahead, though.

Laois

Laois shares the lovely Slieve Blooms with Offaly. It also has the dubious distinction of being the only landlocked county surrounded by landlocked counties. Here there are some lovely, sleepy little places worth seeking out, as well as a few places best avoided: The county's administrative town, Portlaoise, is also home to Ireland's federal penitentiary (as well as a mental asylum). Even if you discount the prison, there's absolutely nothing to detain you there—though the Rock of Dunamase, the scant remains of a Norman fortress on a hill offering a wonderful view of the lush farmlands surrounding, is only six kilometers outside of town.

◖ EMO COURT

Run by Dúchas, the magnificent green-domed Emo Court (2.5 km from Emo village, signposted off the N7 7 km north of Portlaoise, tel. 057/862-6573, open 10:30 A.M.– 6:30 P.M. Tues.–Sat. June–mid-Sept., house admission €2.90, free admission to grounds) is unique as far as manor houses go; though the owner, Major Cholmeley Harrison, donated the manor to the Office of Public Works in 1994, he continues to live there. Emo was designed in 1790 in the neoclassical style by James Gandon for the first Earl of Portarlington, and was used as a Jesuit seminary in the early 20th century. Though the Jesuits tried to maintain the house and preserve its original features, when the major acquired the house in 1969 an extensive restoration was required. Access to the house is by 25-minute guided tour, taking you through the library, rotunda, and dining and sitting rooms, all wonderfully refurbished through the joint efforts of Cholmeley Harrison and the OPW. The grounds are an even greater delight, with 18th-century gardens, an ornamental lake, garden follies and mock towers, romantic Grecian statues, and sylvan lanes perfect for a long stroll. At 22 hectares, the Emo demesne is the second-largest walled park in Europe (after Phoenix Park in Dublin); it's open daily dawn to dusk. The giant sequoias lining the avenue are 150 years old, though they may live to be 3,000!

Emo Court is 78 kilometers southwest of Dublin just off the N7, and unfortunately there is no public transportation.

ABBEYLEIX

A tidy, pleasant 18th-century town unfortunately situated on the main Dublin–Cork road, Abbeyleix ("abbey-LEEKS," Mainistir Laoise) has a serious traffic back-up at any time of day. (Ah well, at least the parking's free.) There's not much to see, though it makes a pleasant lunch stop if you're driving from Dublin to Cashel (or even Kilkenny).

Abbeyleix boasts the best restaurant in Laois, the **Preston House Café** (Main St., the N8, tel. 0502/31432, open 12:30– 2:30 P.M. Tues.–Sat., 7–9 P.M. Thurs.–Sat., lunches €10–16, 3-course dinner €40, B&B €60 pp, s €70), a regal Georgian covered in thick clots of ivy (it looks like a manor house, but it used to be a school), where you can also spend the night in spacious, airy rooms sprinkled with antiques. The simple modern Irish fare here is generously portioned and exceptionally tasty, and the dining room is truly country-house pleasant (if a bit too pink, and slightly stodgy). If this isn't the kind of dining experience you're looking for, there's always the super-basic sandwich menu (under €4) at a delightfully unusual pub just up the main street, **Morrissey's** (tel. 0502/31233). This dark, high-ceilinged, incredibly atmospheric grocery, pub, and off-license (it used to be an undertaker's as well!) has been in the same family since the 1770s. You'll find random antiques throughout (meat scales, a sewing machine, even a bicycle with an old-fashioned delivery basket) and quasi-ancient cans of "coffee whitener" lining the dusty shelves behind the bar. When in Abbeyleix, a pint at Morrissey's is a must.

The tower at Timahoe has an unusual Romanesque doorway.

© CAMILLE DEANGELIS

Abbeyleix is 100 kilometers southwest of Dublin and 60 kilometers northeast of Cashel in Tipperary. **Bus Éireann** serves the town on the Dublin–Cork route via Cashel and Cahir (#8, 6/day daily).

TIMAHOE

If there were an award given out for the sleepiest Irish village, tiny Timahoe (Tigh Machua, "House of St. Machua") might well win it. Those interested in ecclesiastical architecture should make this detour for the sight of one of the most remarkable round towers in Ireland. Built in the 12th century, the **tower** stands about 30 meters tall and still has its (reconstructed) conical cap. Its most unusual feature is the Romanesque doorway positioned 4.5 meters above the ground, with concentric arches receding into the gloom of the interior. The faces carved around the doorway are particularly haunting, with long intertwining beards; each concentric arch is better preserved than the one before it, being more sheltered from the elements. The setting is lovely too—the

tower, the ruin of a church-turned-castle, and the adjacent Anglican church are surrounded by trees.

Timahoe is 12.5 kilometers northeast of Abbeyleix off the R430, and there is no public transportation.

⟨ ROCK OF DUNAMASE

There may be very little left of this hilltop castle, but the Rock of Dunamase (signposted off the N80 6 km east of Portlaoise, always accessible, free admission) affords a truly breathtaking pastoral panorama, hardly blighted at all by industry.

Doubtless the site held pre-Christian significance, as it's recorded on Ptolemy's famous map of A.D. 140. Later on, Dunamase served as the stronghold of Dermot MacMurrough—the king of Leinster who asked for the Normans' help in recovering his lands in 1169, thus setting the stage for nearly 800 years of English domination. Then the Rock passed into the Normans' hands through the marriage of MacMurrough's daughter Aoife to Richard de

Clare (alias Strongbow). The castle was later fully fortified in the mid-13th century and owes its present state to two of Cromwell's generals, who blew it up in the 1650s.

Dúchas was undertaking extensive conservation work at time of writing, and while they may eventually open a visitors center (and start charging admission), the site remains freely accessible for the foreseeable future. The view from the top of the hill is totally worthwhile even if you do someday have to pay for it, however.

Dunamase is six kilometers east of Portlaoise, about one kilometer off the N80; there is no public transportation, though you might take **Bus Éireann** (on the Dublin–Cahir–Cork route, #8, 6/day daily; or #12, Dublin–Limerick–Ennis, 13/day daily) to Portlaoise and hire a cab from there; try **Portlaoise Taxis** (tel. 057/866-2270). Be sure to get there early enough in the day to catch another bus out of town, though; you definitely don't want to spend the night in Portlaoise.

Cavan

Cavan's green hills and glassy lakes attract plenty of anglers, but not many others. Contrary to the old Irish stereotype, Cavan folk are no less generous than the people of any other county; you may find the opposite is true. Cavan's narrow "panhandle" extends west, hugging the Fermanagh border, and at the tip of it you'll find Blacklion—an unassuming village with a gourmet reputation, thanks to local celebrity chef Neven Maguire of MacNean's Bistro.

Bawnboy

Rural Cavan is pretty much the last place you'd ever expect to find a Tibetan Buddhist retreat center, yet here it is, in a fine old Georgian house: **Jampa Ling** (Owendoon House, 4 km south of Bawnboy village on a local road, tel. 049/952-3448, www.jampaling.org, dorms €32, private rooms €34–39 pp). The name means "Place of Loving Kindness," and that's exactly what you'll find: All the staff, regulars, and visitors are wonderfully friendly and welcoming, and you don't have to be a practicing Buddhist to stay—many folks just come with a sense of open-minded curiosity. A Panchen Lama—a "great scholar" in Tibetan Buddhism—by the name of the Venerable Panchen Ötrul Rinpoche lives and teaches here most of the year. Sit in on a meditation session or prayer service, take a more structured day or weekend course in Gelugpa Buddhism and

philosophy (generally €25–45), go for a walk through rolling fields to the nearby lake, or just relax with a copy of the Dalai Lama's latest treatise in the cozy library.

Only a small number of private rooms are available, and though the price of a dorm bed seems a bit steep, it's actually an awesome value when you consider you're being fed three healthy, hearty, delicious vegetarian meals as well (everyone here seems to have flawless culinary skills, and they're all really modest about it, too). It's essential to call ahead to reserve your room, because you'll need detailed directions to this out-of-the-way spot.

Bawnboy is 157 kilometers northwest of Dublin off the N3 (picking up the N87 at Kilconney). Though there's no bus service to the center itself, you can take the **Bus Éireann** Dublin–Donegal route (tel. 049/433-1353, #30, 4/day Mon.–Sat., 3/day Sun.) to Bawnboy village (be sure to remind the driver where you're going, as it's a request-only stop) and then ring the center; there's always someone around who'll happily pick you up.

Ballyconnell

There's something to be said for a posh hotel out in the middle of noplace special: All the perks would cost you twice as much (or more) at a hotel on St. Stephen's Green. The opulent yet refreshingly unsnobby ◖ **Slieve Russell Hotel** (Cranaghan, 2 km southeast of

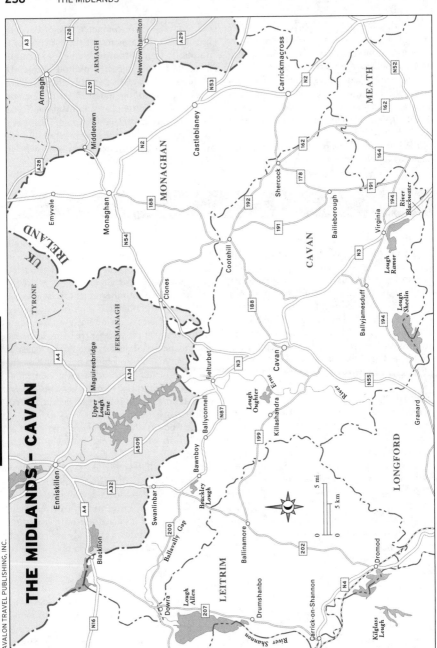

THE MIDLANDS

Ballyconnell, tel. 049/952-6444, www .quinnhotels.com, €105–215 pp) attracts golfers and wedding parties in equal measure, but the management does a fine job of keeping the latter from intruding on other guests. There's a deluxe spa, Ciúin (meaning "quiet"), along with a pool, steam room, and other exercise facilities, plus complimentary wireless Internet. A three-kilometer nature walk beside the championship golf course takes you into the woods, past a Neolithic wedge tomb and two of Cavan's countless small lakes. There are always special midweek and weekend packages available, whether you want a round of golf or an afternoon massage, and all packages include dinner in the excellent hotel restaurant.

Ballyconnell is 150 kilometers northwest of Dublin off the N3 (picking up the N87 in Kilconney), though you'll reach the hotel a couple of kilometers before the village.

Blacklion

Less than a kilometer south of the border with Northern Ireland, one-street Blacklion—named for an old coaching inn—is on the map for its gourmet, family-run restaurant-cum-B&B, **MacNean's** (Main St., tel. 071/985-3022, www.macneanrestaurant.com, open 6–9 p.m. Wed.–Sun., 1–3:30 p.m. Sun., closed Wed. in winter, lunch €27, 10-course dinner €55, B&B €40 pp sharing). MacNean's has developed a reputation as one of the finest restaurants in the country for its imaginative modern Irish fare. Vegetarians will be thrilled with the separate menu (the sign of a truly great restaurant)—and even better, the veggie menu is considerably less expensive. Try to save room for one of the exquisite desserts (but if you can't, at least have a petit four). Make a reservation well in advance, as this (albeit smallish) restaurant books up quickly even in the dead of winter.

The village itself has a mournful, run-down air about it, but out-of-towner foodies don't seem to notice. You come here for Mac-Nean's—and maybe a round at the nine-hole **Blacklion Golf Club** (Toam, 2 km south of the village on the R206, tel. 071/985-3024, www.blackliongolf.netfirms.com), a small but scenic course on the shores of Lough McNean. The 26-kilometer **Cavan Way** also begins here, signposted from the main street.

Blacklion is 48 kilometers east of Sligo on the N16 and 19 kilometers west of Enniskillen (in Fermanagh) on the A4; the **Bus Éireann** linking Sligo with Enniskillen stops in Blacklion (tel. 049/433-1353, #66, 4/day Mon.–Sat., 2/day Sun.).

TIPPERARY AND WATERFORD

The fertile rolling farmlands of Counties Tipperary (Tiobraid Árainn, "The House of the Well of Ara") and Waterford (Port Láirge, "Bank of the Haunch"; from the Danish Vadrefjord) are nourished by the River Suir and occasionally broken by mountain ranges—the Comeraghs and the Galtees, the Monavullaghs and the Knockmealdowns, the Slievefelim and the Silvermines. Natives of landlocked Tipperary can still go boating on Lough Derg at the county's western boundary, and Waterford's pretty coastline is nearly as sunny as Wexford's. Each county has its primary attraction—Tipperary the Rock of Cashel, a medieval ecclesiastical complex on the site of a pre-Christian fortress, and Waterford its world-renowned crystal factory. The Rock is indeed Tipperary's finest sight, but Waterford's is the hilltop St. Declan's Oratory and round tower, with its breathtaking position overlooking Ardmore Bay.

HISTORY

St. Declan was making converts in County Waterford in the mid-5th century, several years before Patrick's arrival. Originally a Celtic settlement, Waterford City was resettled by the Vikings in 853. They built the city walls around their new base and regularly traveled north into Tipperary to raid (and terrorize) smaller native farming settlements along the Suir. The Irish lived in fear of the Norsemen, yet they banded together to fight the Norman invaders in 1170. Their defeat was inevitable, and Waterford became the stronghold of Strongbow and his successors. Like the earlier invaders, they prized

HIGHLIGHTS

Rock of Cashel: This glorious hilltop stronghold was the seat of the kings of Munster, who later donated it to the church. With its spooky Romanesque chapel, ruined tower house, and soaring Gothic church, it's the perfect setting for a ghost story (page 260).

Cahir Castle: This imposing, seemingly impregnable fortress was conquered by Oliver Cromwell's troops only by means of a threatening missive (page 263).

Ormonde Castle: "Black Tom," the 10th Earl of Ormonde, built this lavish Elizabethan manor hoping his cousin (and rumored paramour), the Virgin Queen, would do him the honor of a visit (page 264).

Dunmore East: Escape the grittiness of nearby Waterford City in this delightful seaside village, which offers several fine restaurants and loads of *craic agus ceol* (fun and music) at the pubs (page 270).

St. Declan's Monastery and Cliff Walk: By far the loveliest spot in County Waterford is this elegant round tower and ruined church (with biblical scenes carved into western facade) overlooking Ardmore Bay. Go for an invigorating five-kilometer walk along the headland and come upon the remains of St. Declan's Well, where he baptized his first converts in the mid-5th century (page 273).

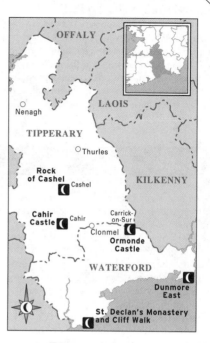

LOOK FOR **(** TO FIND RECOMMENDED SIGHTS, ACTIVITIES, DINING, AND LODGING.

Tipperary's rich farmlands, which were later carved into plantations for English colonists.

PLANNING YOUR TIME

The Rock of Cashel is Tipperary's crown jewel—and it should be at the top of your list when planning a tour of Ireland's southeast. Don't come in high season if you can help it; if the site is gorged with tour buses in April, May, and September, just think of how crowded it gets in July and August. If you must come in summer, spend the previous night in Cashel and arrive first thing in the morning. Tipperary's other sights, Cahir and Ormonde Castles, can be visited en route to Cork and Waterford, respectively.

Frankly, Waterford City would have few visitors without its famed crystal factory. It's an ordinary port town with a few charming medieval ruins saving it from downright dreariness. Don't linger here; the city's attractions can't begin to compare to the seaside loveliness of Ardmore and Dunmore East—and the former has a truly stunning monastic ruin along with a scenic cliffside walk.

Tipperary

Tipperary is the island's largest landlocked county, and one of its most fertile. In fact, the center of the county (within the basin of the River Suir) is called the "Golden Vale" for its high-yield farmlands, bounded by the Glen of Aherlow and the Galtee and Comeragh mountain ranges. From the lumpy Knockmealdowns to the aptly named Silvermines (which have the Shannon region's highest peak, the 694-meter Keeper's Hill), Tipperary's mountains and valleys provide plenty of hill-walking opportunities; see the sidebar *Tipperary and Waterford Walks* for more info. On the whole, the county's towns are refreshingly business-as-usual, even in Cashel. You'd do well to pass on through dreary Nenagh and Tipperary Town, though.

CASHEL

Aside from its magnificent hilltop fortress-cum-cathedral, there's not much going on in Cashel (Caiseal Mumhan, "Stone Fort of Munster"), though a few authentically traditional pubs, one excellent restaurant, and a touristy-but-fun ceilidh show warrant an overnight stay.

Most of what you'll need is located on or just off Cashel's Main Street, and it's easy to orient yourself since the Rock is visible from any place in town.

◖ Rock of Cashel

One of Ireland's most spectacular ruins, the hilltop Rock of Cashel (500 m from town center off the N8, tel. 06 2/61437, open 9 A.M.–7 P.M. June–mid-Sept., 9 A.M.–5:30 P.M. mid-Mar.–May and mid-Sept.–mid-Oct., 9 A.M.–4:30 P.M. mid-Oct.–mid-March, admission €5.30) dominates the surrounding landscape—so much so that the breath catches in your throat when you first spot it on your way into town. Walking through the ruins is just as overwhelming—not just because of the crowds, but because there's so much to see, so much medieval history to absorb. From the mid-4th century the Rock served as the seat of the kings of Munster, and Patrick baptized King Aengus here in 448 (why this place is often called "St. Patrick's Rock"). Much later, in 1101, another king donated the fortress to the church, and the 28-meter round tower, high cross, and Romanesque **Cormac's Chapel** all date from this early period.

The small, dark, spooky chapel is the Rock's most remarkable edifice. Carvings of individualized heads lining the walls are typical of the Romanesque style, but many of these faces belonged to real people: It's said the stoneworkers made likenesses of all the people who owed them money. The original wall frescoes were painted over in 1647 at Cromwell's command, and the remnants you see now were all that

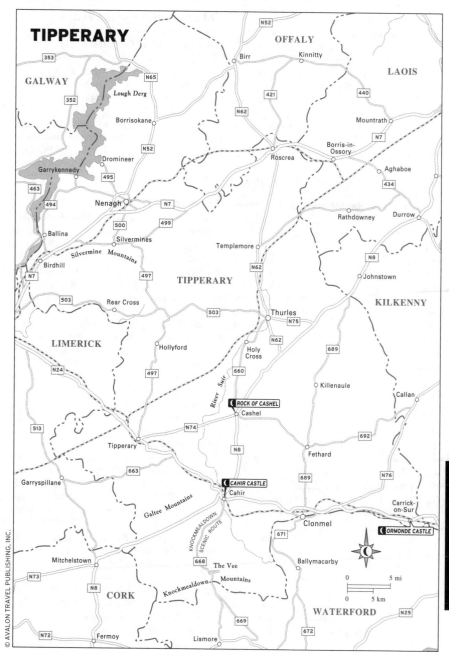

TIPPERARY

GALWAY

Lough Derg

OFFALY

LAOIS

Birr
Kinnitty

Mountrath

Borrisokane

Roscrea

Borris-in-Ossory

Aghaboe

Dromineer

Garrykennedy

Ballina

Nenagh

Silvermines

Silvermine Mountains

Birdhill

Rathdowney

Durrow

Templemore

TIPPERARY

Johnstown

Rear Cross

KILKENNY

LIMERICK

Thurles

Hollyford

Holy Cross

Killenaule

Callan

River Suir

ROCK OF CASHEL

Cashel

Tipperary

Garryspillane

Fethard

Galtee Mountains

CAHIR CASTLE

Cahir

Carrick-on-Sur

KNOCKMEALDOWN SCENIC ROUTE

Clonmel

ORMONDE CASTLE

Mitchelstown

The Vee

Ballymacarby

Knockmealdown Mountains

0   5 mi

0   5 km

CORK

WATERFORD

Fermoy

Lismore

© AVALON TRAVEL PUBLISHING, INC.

TIPPERARY AND WATERFORD

could be salvaged when the layers were carefully removed by modern technicians.

But the most dramatic building on the Rock is the 13th-century Gothic cathedral. At its western end is a 15th-century tower house built for the archbishop's residence, but it was so cold and damp that it wasn't used for long. A 19th-century lightning storm left a chunk of the castle wall on the grass outside, and it hasn't been moved since; you can gauge the wall thickness from the sheer size of this fragment. (By the way, "the Rock" refers to the whole medieval compound, not this particular "rock.")

The restored **Hall of the Vicars Choral** serves as the visitors center, where you can watch the 17-minute audiovisual and dutifully read the exhibition panels before the 45-minute guided tour begins. It's worth waiting for, as the guides have plenty of intriguing stories to tell. The most outrageous of these is about Miler McGrath, who served as Protestant archbishop here between 1571 and 1621—and simultaneously as a Catholic bishop near Belfast. At the time of his death no one had any idea that he'd embezzled from both churches *and* had two wives (one of each denomination) and several children by each. The truth came out only when they read his epitaph, in which he boasted he was able to exist in two places at once.

Other Sights

Across the street (and a dung-dotted pasture) from the Rock is **Hore Abbey** (always accessible, free admission), built by the Cistercians around the same time as the **Dominican Friary** you'll pass on the way up to the Rock. There may not be a whole lot to see among these ruins, but they can offer a bit of quiet should the crowds at the Rock overwhelm you.

Bibliophiles should make time for the 12,000-volume **Bolton Library** (John St., tel. 062/61944, open 10 A.M.–4 P.M. Mon.–Fri., admission €2), which houses the world's smallest book as well as a collection of priceless first editions of works by Dante, Machiavelli, Swift, Newton, and others.

Entertainment and Events

One of Cashel's best watering holes is the spacious, unassuming **Cantwell's** (Main St., tel. 062/61171): The crowd's local, the drinks are cheap, and the elderly bartender's a doll. Plus, there's live trad here Thursday. On Friday, catch the session at **Hannigan's** (Ladyswell St., tel. 062/61737).

Or for something more formal, catch the traditional song and step-dancing show at the **Brú Ború Cultural Centre** (tel. 062/61122, www.comhaltas.com, 9 P.M., tickets €15, reservations not necessary).

Accommodations

The IHH, family-run **Cashel Holiday Hostel** (6 John St., tel. 062/62330, www.cashelhostel. com, dorms €15–18, private rooms €20–25 pp, credit cards accepted) offers excellent facilities (including laundry, real hot showers, and bike hire) without sacrificing the building's Georgian character—there's even a piano in the common room.

Cashel has several friendly, atmospheric Georgian townhouse B&Bs. Just 50 meters from the Rock of Cashel is **Joy's Rockside House** (Rock Villas, tel. 062/63813, www.joyrockside.com, open mid-Feb–Oct., €33–40 pp sharing), where many of the homey rooms have a scenic view. The helpful proprietors of **Ashmore House** (John St., tel. 062/61286, www.ashmorehouse.com, €30–40 pp, s €40–60, credit cards accepted) do a great morning fry. Both Joy's and Ashmore have private parking. **Ladyswell House** (Ladyswell St., tel. 062/62985, www.ladyswellhouse.com, €29–33 pp, s €42–60) rents four neat but smallish rooms, and the owners offer their own "chauffeur" sightseeing tour.

If you've got wheels (but no kids), consider staying at **Carron House** (5 km south of Cashel off the N8, tel. 052/62142, www.carronhouse. com, open Apr.–Sept., €35 pp, s €55, credit cards accepted), on a working dairy farm. The owners are very kind and welcoming, but because of the emphasis on that elusive "peace and quiet," they have a no-children policy.

It could use some renovating, but the **Cashel**

Palace Hotel (Main St., tel. 062/62707, www. cashel-palace.ie, rooms €195–275, s €150–180, suites €300–370), built for a Protestant archbishop in the 1730s, is still the town's snazziest accommodation. It's worth paying a €30 supplement for stunning nighttime views of the floodlit Rock.

Food

Many of Cashel's pubs offer an all-day bar menu, but if you're looking for an extraordinary lunch you'll have to eat at ◖ **Café Hans** (Moor Ln., tel. 062/63660, open noon–5:30 p.m. Tues.–Sat., mains €10–17, no credit cards or reservations). Prepare to be astonished at the cosmopolitan feel of this always-crowded eatery, as well as the seemingly bottomless portions of fresh, inventively prepared pastas. Annoying as it is, it's worth waiting 15 or 20 minutes in the tiny vestibule beside the restrooms for food this good. **Chez Hans** (Moor Ln., up the street from the café and closer to the Rock, tel. 062/61177, open 6–10 p.m. Tues.–Sat., 3-course early-bird special €33 6–7:15 p.m., fixed-price dinner €45), Café Hans's sister restaurant, takes care of dinner—in a converted church with original stained glass, no less!—but it's quite a bit pricier. If you're trying to scrimp, do the café for lunch and have a simple bar meal for dinner.

Information and Services

Both the **tourist office** (tel. 062/61333, www .tipperary.ie and www.cashel.ie, open 9:15 A.M.–6 P.M. Mon.–Sat. May–Sept., daily July–Aug.) and **heritage center** (tel. 062/62511, open 9:30 A.M.–5:30 P.M. daily Mar.–Oct., Mon.–Fri. Nov.–Feb., free admission) are located in Cashel's Town Hall on Main Street.

For an ATM or bureau de change, visit the **AIB** or **Bank of Ireland,** both on Main Street, as are the **post office** and a couple of pharmacies, **Kennedy's** (tel. 062/61066) and the **Friary** (tel. 062/62120).

Cashel has one Internet café, **A.D. Weblink** (102A Main St., tel. 062/63304, open 10 A.M.–6 P.M. Mon.–Tues., 10 A.M.–9 P.M. Wed.–Sat., €3/hour).

© CAMILLE DEANGELIS

Cromwell seized Cahir Castle after its occupants quailed at his written threat.

Getting There and Around

Cashel is 160 kilometers southwest of Dublin and 97 kilometers northeast of Cork on the N8. **Bus Éireann** stops here on the Dublin–Cork (#8, 6/day daily) and Athlone–Cork (#71, 2/day Mon.–Sat., 1/day Sun.) routes. Rent a bike from **McInerney TV** (Main St., tel. 062/61225, €12/day), or ring **E. Cabs** (tel. 062/33399) for a taxi.

CAHIR

Overshadowed by the magnificent hilltop castle-cum-church at Cashel, the robust fortress at workaday Cahir (pronounced "care"; An Cathair, "The City") is a destination in its own right.

◖ Cahir Castle

The 15th-century Cahir Castle (Castle St., tel. 052/41011, open 9:30 A.M.–5:30 P.M. daily mid-Mar.–mid-June and mid-Sept.–mid-Oct., 9 A.M.–7 P.M. mid-June–mid-Sept., 9:30 A.M.–4:30 P.M. mid-Oct.–mid-Mar., admission €2.90) is on the site of a mid-12th-century stronghold belonging the O'Brien clan. The

TIPPERARY AND WATERFORD WALKS

You could pick up one of the country's shorter treks, the 70-kilometer **East Munster Way,** when you're done the South Leinster Way if you're feeling ambitious – the former begins where the latter ends, in Carrick-on-Suir, County Tipperary. You'll skirt the northern fringe of Comeragh Mountains on the East Munster Way, lots of heather-covered hills and eerily quiet evergreen forests. From Carrick-on-Suir, the route follows the River Suir, heading west through Clonmel and dipping into Waterford a couple of times before ending in the village of Clogheen (back in Tipperary). The route takes three days to walk. Then from Clogheen, the 185-kilometer **Blackwater Way**

extends farther southwest through the lumpy Knockmealdown Mountains and the Boggeraghs of northern Cork, ending at Muckross in Killarney National Park. The whole Blackwater route will take nine days to walk.

As with all long-distance walking routes, your first stop should be the nearest tourist office to the starting point, where you can pick up a detailed guidebook and Ordnance Survey Discovery Series maps (the East Munster Way requires numbers 74 and 75). Don't have time for a long-distance route? A much shorter walk – only an hour long – is the exhilarating cliff walk just outside the village of Ardmore on the Waterford coast.

Butlers acquired it during the 14th century and made extensive additions, including the great hall overlooking the River Suir, and at the time it was the largest castle in Ireland. An illustration from the turn of the 17th century shows the castle essentially as it appears today, thanks to the prompt surrendering of the Baron of Cahir to Cromwell's forces in February 1650. Though the castle was clearly built to be defended, it seems Cromwell's "letter of threat" left the guardian of the underaged baron quaking in his boots. Today you can wander through the feudal-style courtyard and ascend (with due caution) a narrow staircase to the old ramparts. The exhibition features an impressively detailed model of the castle and battle stages during the siege of 1599.

Swiss Cottage

Cahir's other attraction is the Swiss Cottage (Kilcommon, 1.5 km south of Cahir, signposted off the R670, tel. 052/41144, open 10 A.M.–1 P.M. and 2–6 P.M. Tues.–Sun. mid-Mar.–mid-Apr., 10 A.M.–6 P.M. daily mid-Apr.–mid-Oct., 10 A.M.–1 P.M. and 2–4:30 P.M. Tues.–Sun. mid-Oct.–mid-Nov., admission €2.90), reachable from the castle by a shady pathway through Cahir Park. This thatched-roof "cottage orné" was de-

signed by John Nash and built at the start of the 19th century for the first Earl of Glengall, Richard Butler. Access is by 40-minute guided tour only.

Practicalities

The **tourist office** (tel. 052/41453, open 9 A.M.–6 P.M. Mon.–Sat. Mar.–Oct., 11 A.M.–5 P.M. Nov.–Feb.) and the **AIB** (with ATM) are both on Castle Street.

Cahir itself is an uninteresting place, so you'll probably just want to stop here for an hour or two between Cashel (15 km north on the N8) and Cork (80 km south on the N8). **Bus Éireann** passes through on its Dublin–Cork (#8, 6/day daily), Athlone–Cork (#71, 2/day Mon.–Sat., 1/day Sun.), and Limerick–Waterford (#55, 6–7/day daily) routes.

CARRICK-ON-SUIR

The otherwise unremarkable riverside town of Carrick-on-Suir ("shoor") means "Rock of the Suir" in Irish, for the presence of Ormonde Castle.

◖ Ormonde Castle

Now Dúchas-run, Ormonde Castle (Castle Park, off Castle St. on the east end of town, tel. 051/640-787, tel. 056/24623 in winter, open

9:30 A.M.–6:30 P.M. daily mid-June–early Sept., free admission) is the best Irish example of an Elizabethan manor house, though it's unique for several other reasons: The manor, built in the 1560s, integrates the ruins of the original towers from the previous century, and it is also Ireland's only unfortified castle from the 16th century. The state rooms offer some of the best examples of decorative plasterwork—which might sound rather stuffy but is actually well worth a few minutes' study. "Black Tom," the 10th Earl of Ormonde, had Elizabeth's crown portrait done, flanked by figures representing Justice and Equity; there is another plasterwork portrait of the Virgin Queen beside one of the earl in the entrance passage, which is an inadvertent reference to the persistent rumor that Elizabeth bore him a child in 1554. As Brian de Breffny notes in his book on Irish castles, the earl spent many years at the English court and was "steadfastly devoted" to the queen, who reportedly referred to the "dark, amorous Irishman" as "my black husband." After all, Black Tom built this place hoping she'd someday honor her promise to visit him in Ireland. The 40-minute guided tour will provide you with plenty more interesting tidbits.

Getting There

Carrick-on-Suir is 27 kilometers northwest of Waterford City on the N24, and is served by **Bus Éireann** on the Dublin–Cork (#7, 6/day daily) and Limerick–Rosslare Harbour (#55, 6–7/day daily) routes.

Waterford

Wedged between Tipperary to the north and Wexford just east of the estuary, County Waterford features the fertile farmland of the former and the sunny coastline of the latter. Tramore may be Waterford's best-known resort town, but it's desperately overdeveloped—and though it's not as tacky a place as reputed, it's still far from the best the county has to offer. For pretty sea views, pristine beaches, and water-sporting opportunities, head for Ardmore or Dunmore East instead. The stretch between Tramore and Dungarvan is known as the Copper Coast—a name devised for tourism purposes, but fitting enough for its smattering of 19th-century copper mines. Awarded European Geopark status in 2001, the Copper Coast offers another Blue Flag strand at Bunmahon (Bún Machan).

WATERFORD CITY

A bustling commercial port on the River Suir, workaday Waterford was founded by the Vikings in 853, making it Ireland's oldest city. Its reputation for fine crystal began when the first factory opened in 1783. Stiff British taxes led to its closing in 1851, but it reopened in 1947, and the current factory dates to 1971. Frankly, were it not for the factory Waterford wouldn't see much in the way of tourist activity; it's downright depressing when the weather's gray.

Sights

Pert as a pepperpot, the fully restored **Reginald's Tower** (the Quay, tel. 051/304-220, open 10 A.M.–5 P.M. daily Easter–May and Oct., 10 A.M.–5 P.M. Wed.–Sun. Nov.–Easter, 10 A.M.–6 P.M. June–Sept., admission €2.10) was erected in the 12th century and is now run by Dúchas. Built by the Normans to defend their newly acquired city, it's said that Strongbow and Aoife held their wedding feast here. In later centuries the tower was used as a mint, prison, and arsenal. Today it houses a historical exhibit, charters and swords and whatnot—rather yawn-inducing compared to Waterford Treasures, but still worth a visit if you're a history buff. From the top floor of the tower you can spy the 13th-century **French Church** on Greyfriars Street. There are other medieval holdovers, scattered gates from the original city walls as well as the **Blackfriars**

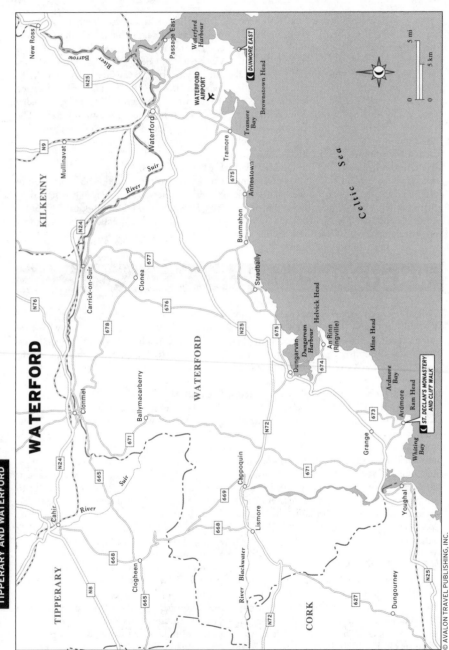

© AVALON TRAVEL PUBLISHING, INC.

Abbey from the same time period, covered in blooming weeds and tucked behind a tall iron fence on Conduit Lane, just off High Street.

It's best known for the gruesome 15th-century cadaver tomb (i.e., the effigy on the lid depicts the deceased in a decomposed state) of lord mayor James Rice, but the Anglican **Christ Church Cathedral** (Cathedral Sq., tel. 051/874-119, www.christchurchwaterford.com, open 10 A.M.–5 P.M. daily, tours at 11:30 A.M. and 3 P.M., admission €3), built on the site of a Viking church, has a few other things worth checking out. There is only one stained-glass window, but it's surely a masterpiece: A. E. Child's *Joy and Sorrow* from 1930, which depicts a line from the Revelations: "Sorrow may endure for a night, but joy cometh in the morning." The magnificent Elliott Organ, its rarity akin to the Stradivarius, was restored in 2003 at a cost of half a million euros. Notice that the intricate ceiling plasterwork in the antechamber and that in the church don't match—the former is done in the baroque style, the latter in rococo, owing to a fire in the organ loft in 1815. Also note the wall memorial for Susanna Mason, who opened the first girls' school in Ireland in the mid-1700s; unfortunately, the school building was demolished recently despite protests from local conservationists. There's a free summer concert series on Sunday mornings featuring top organists from all over Europe.

Waterford's Catholic cathedral, **Holy Trinity** (Barronstrand St., tel. 051/875-166, www.waterford-cathedral.com), was also designed by John Roberts. It was closed for renovation at time of writing.

Now for the reason you're here: the factory tour and showroom at the **Waterford Crystal Visitor Centre** (Cork Rd., Kilbarry, 2 km south of town on the N25, tel. 051/332-500, www.waterfordvisitorcentre.com, retail store open 9 A.M.–5 P.M. Nov.–Feb., 8:30 A.M.–6 P.M. Mar.–Oct., tours 8:30 A.M.–4 P.M. daily Mar.–Oct., 9 A.M.–3:15 P.M. Mon.–Fri. Nov.–Feb., tour €7.50). Guided tours of the factory floor start every 15 minutes, and it's best to ring ahead for a reservation in high season. Afterwards you can take a walk through the

© CAMILLE DEANGELIS

the lone and lovely stained glass window at Christ Church Cathedral

historical exhibition—and do some shopping! But buyer beware: Some Waterford crystal is now manufactured in Eastern Europe, some of which is for sale in the factory store, so before you buy, make sure your intended purchases were made on site.

If it's pouring out, peruse the archaeological exhibits and slick interpretive displays at **Waterford Treasures** (Merchants Quay, tel. 051/304-500, www.waterfordtreasures.com, open 9:30 A.M.–9 P.M. June–Aug., 9:30 A.M.–6 P.M. Sept., 10 A.M.–5 P.M. daily Oct.–Mar., admission €4), housed in an old granary. The exhibition features everything from Viking baubles to 18th-century crystal.

Tours

If you have only an hour to spare on your way to the coast, spend it on a **historical walking tour** (tel. 051/873-711 or 051/851-043 after 5 P.M., daily Mar.–Oct., one-hour tour €6). Tours depart the tourist office at 11:45 A.M. and 1:45 P.M.; amiable local guides breathe life into these old city gates and walls.

TIPPERARY AND WATERFORD

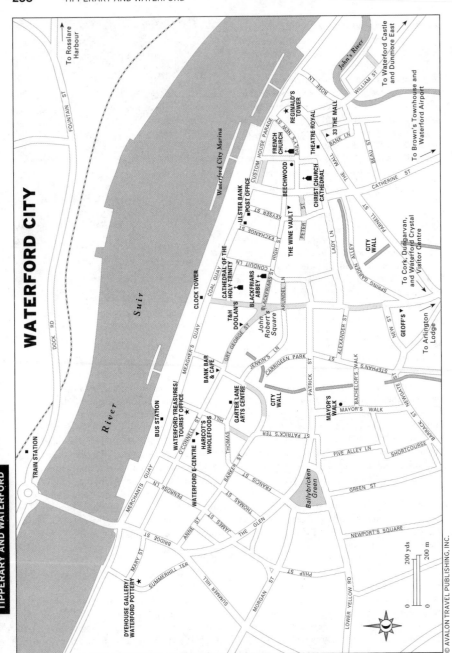

WATERFORD CITY

To Rosslare Harbour

FOUNTAIN ST

DOCK RD

River

Suir

TRAIN STATION

MERCHANTS QUAY

BRIDGE ST

MARY ST

SUMMERHILL TER

SUMMER HILL

MORGAN ST

PHIL ST

LOWER YELLOW RD

DYEHOUSE GALLERY/
WATERFORD POTTERY

PENROSE LN

THOMAS ST

JAMES ST

ANNE ST

THE GLEN

FRANCIS ST

BARKER ST

THOMAS HILL

BUS STATION

WATERFORD TREASURES/
TOURIST OFFICE

O'CONNELL ST

WATERFORD E-CENTRE

HARICOT'S
WHOLEFOODS

GARTER LANE
ARTS CENTRE

BANK BAR
& CAFÉ

MEAGHER'S QUAY

COAL QUAY

GRT GEORGE ST

CLOCK TOWER

T&H
DOOLAN'S

CATHEDRAL OF THE
HOLY TRINITY

BLACKFRIARS
ABBEY

John Robert's Square

JENKIN'S LN

CARRIGEEN PARK

CITY
WALL

ST PATRICK'S TER

Ballybricken
Green

GREEN ST

FIVE ALLEY LN

NEWPORT'S SQUARE

PATRICK ST

BLACKFRIARS ST

ARUNDEL

CONDUIT LN

HIGH ST

EXCHANGE ST

KEYSER ST

ULSTER BANK

POST OFFICE

CUSTOM HOUSE PARADE

Waterford City Marina

BAILY'S NEW ST

FRENCH
CHURCH

BEECHWOOD

THE WINE VAULT

PETER ST

CHRIST CHURCH
CATHEDRAL

LADY LN

SPRING GARDEN ALLEY

CITY
WALL

PARNELL ST

CATHERINE ST

REGINALD'S
TOWER

THEATRE ROYAL

ROSE LN

John's River

33 THE MALL

THE MALL

BANK LN

BEAU ST

WILLIAM ST

To Waterford Castle
and Dunmore East

To Brown's Townhouse and
Waterford Airport

To Cork, Dungarvan,
and Waterford Crystal
Visitor Centre

To Arlington
Lodge

GEOFF'S

NEW ST

ALEXANDER ST

STEPHEN'S ST

NEWGATE ST

BARRACK ST

BACHELOR'S WALK

MAYOR'S
WALK

MAYOR'S WALK

SHORTCOURSE

0   200 yds
0   200 m

© AVALON TRAVEL PUBLISHING, INC.

Shopping

Don't get too hyped up about Waterford crystal. Much of it isn't even made in the local factory anymore—it's being outsourced to Turkey. Instead, visit the smaller workshops of ex-Waterford craftspeople—they've got the skills, the prices are more reasonable, and you may even be able to meet the person who made your new purchase; try Criostal na Rinne on the Ring Peninsula (55 km southwest of Waterford) or Kinsale Crystal in Kinsale, County Cork.

For things noncrystal, a good place to start is **Dyehouse Gallery & Waterford Pottery** (Dyehouse Ln., tel. 051/844-770). There are two weekly markets, the **city market** on Jenkin's Lane (10 A.M.–4 P.M. Sat.) and the **country market** at St. Olaf's Hall (8:30–11:30 A.M. Fri.) across the street from Christ Church.

Accommodations

There was no hostel in Waterford at time of writing, so budget travelers will need to spring for a B&B. The most affordable is the homey **Mayor's Walk** (12 Mayor's Walk, tel. 051/855-427, mayorswalkbandb@eircom.net, €30 pp). Or try **Beechwood** (7 Cathedral Sq., tel. 051/876-677, bjoeryan@eircom.net, €35 pp, s €40), in a quiet section just across the street from Christ Church. One of the classiest guesthouses in the city center is the Victorian **Brown's Townhouse** (29 S. Parade, tel. 051/870-594, www.brownstownhouse.com, €40–55 pp, s €60), where you get complimentary Internet access and pancakes for breakfast at the communal dining table.

The city's top hotel is a restored boutique, **Arlington Lodge** (John's Hill, tel. 051/878-584, www.arlingtonlodge.com, rooms €170–270), once the home of the Catholic bishop of Waterford. The junior suites come with four-poster beds, robes, and slippers; all the individually decorated rooms have Internet access. Best of all is the service: All the staff have a sunny, nothing's-too-much-trouble attitude.

And of course, **Waterford Castle** (The Island, Ballinakill, 5 km east of town off the R683, tel. 051/878-203, www.waterford-castle.com, low/high season standard rooms

€195/335, superior €265/460, s €160/245) is one of the very finest accommodations in the country, in a restored 16th-century manor (incorporating a Norman keep built in 1190) on its own private island complete with golf course. The staff deliver on the king-and-queen-for-a-night promise, the food is tops, and the grounds are tranquil as can be. The only two things you can even begin to fault this place for are its slightly stodgy decor and that breakfast's not included in the room rate (continental €16, full Irish €20).

Food, Entertainment, and Events

Waterford has a good share of nonchain coffee shops. A more atmospheric spot in which to enjoy a cappuccino is the Deco-era **Bank Bar & Café** (Gladstone St. and O'Connell St., tel. 051/872-170, www.thebankbarcafe.com, food served 10 A.M.–5 P.M. daily, mains €6–12), which has a full lunch menu. You'll find good pub grub at salty **T&H Doolan's** (31 George's St., tel. 051/872-764, food served noon–9:30 P.M. daily, mains €10–19) or too-cool **Geoff's** (9 John St., tel. 051/874-787, food served 10 A.M.–4 P.M. daily, mains €7–14). Doolan's has the best trad in town—every night of the week.

Vegetarians, make a beeline for ◖ **Haricot's Wholefoods** (11 O'Connell St., tel. 051/841-299, open 9 A.M.–8 P.M. Mon.–Sat., 9 A.M.–6 P.M. Sun., mains €10), serving up hearty plates of baked potatoes and lentil loaf on rustic wooden tables and Marley on the stereo. You'll find a nice mix of boho students, savvy out-of-towners, and health-conscious ladies-who-lunch. Pause in the vestibule on your way out for plenty of info on upcoming concerts and other events in the city.

Quality eateries line the city's tiny, tucked-away High Street, one of which is **The Wine Vault** (High St., tel. 051/853-444, www.waterfordwinevault.com, open noon–10 P.M. Mon.–Sat., mains €15–25)—which offers, as you'd expect, a staggeringly long (and carefully chosen) wine list. The menu is fairly standard Continental, though there are a couple of imaginative vegetarian dishes.

Waterford's newest and hippest restaurant is the four-story, brasserie-style **33 The Mall** (33 The Mall, www.33.ie, open 5:30 P.M.– late Mon.–Sat., 11 A.M.–7 P.M. Sun., mains €17–25, Sun. brunch mains €12–18, no reservations), with an unpretentious menu and a fun selection of cocktails. This is the perfect spot for a pre-theater meal, as the 18th-century **Theatre Royal** (The Mall, tel. 051/874-402, www.theatreroyalwaterford.com, tickets €18–30) is just across the street. Take in an opera, musical, ballet, or slick Shakespeare production. The Theatre Royal also hosts the city's **Light Opera Festival** in late September and early October.

Or catch a film, concert, or whatever play's making the rounds at the **Garter Lane Arts Centre** (22A O'Connell St., tel. 051/855-038, tickets €10–20).

Information

The **tourist office** (41 The Quay, tel. 051/875-823, www.discoverwaterford.com, open 9 A.M.–5 P.M. Mon.–Sat., until 6 P.M. Apr.–Sept., 11 A.M.–5 P.M. Sun. July–Aug.) shares the old granary with the Waterford Treasures museum.

Services

There are plenty of banks with ATMs and currency exchange facilities in the city center, including **Ulster Bank** (97/98 Custom House Quay) and the **AIB** (72 The Quay). The main **post office** is on Parade Quay.

The local branch of **Boots the Chemist** (Barronstrand St., tel. 051/872-255) is on John Roberts Square. Do your laundry at **Suds 'n Duds** (6 Parnell St., tel. 051/841-168, closed Sun.).

Waterford's Internet cafés are surprisingly expensive. Try the **Waterford e-Centre** (10 O'Connell St., tel. 051/878-448, open 11 A.M.–11 P.M. daily, €5/hour); there are a couple other shops on the quay, but the rates are even higher.

Getting There

Waterford is 160 kilometers southwest of Dublin on the N9 and 122 kilometers east of Cork City on the N25. Plunkett Rail Station is on the far side of the Rice Bridge, north of the river; get here from Dublin (4–6/day daily) or Rosslare Harbour (2/day Mon.–Sat.) on **Irish Rail** (tel. 051/873-401); from Limerick, Ennis, Tralee, or Cork, change trains at Limerick Junction.

The **Bus Éireann** (tel. 051/879-000) station is on Merchants Quay, just east of the bridge. The Tralee–Cork–Rosslare Harbour route stops in Waterford (#40, 13/day Mon.–Sat., 10/day Sun.), and there is direct service from Dublin (#4 via Carlow, 10/day Mon.–Sat., 8/day Sun., #5 via Enniscorthy, 4/day daily) and Limerick (#55, 6–7/day daily).

You can also fly into **Waterford Airport** (Killowen, 7 km south of town on the R675, tel. 051/875-589, www.flywaterford.com) from London Luton, Manchester, or Lorient.

Getting Around

There are several parking lots on the Waterford quay, generally with a daily rate of €5.50; the city itself is easily walkable. **Rapid Cabs** (tel. 051/872-149) offers 24-hour service. Rent a bike from **Wright's Cycle Depot** (Henrietta St., tel. 051/874-411, €14/day).

PASSAGE EAST

The fastest way to get to County Wexford is on the **Passage East Ferry** (tel. 051/382-480, www.passageferry.com, frequent departures 7 A.M.–10 P.M. Mon.–Sat. and 9:30 A.M.–10 P.M. Sun. Apr.–Sept., until 8 P.M. Oct.–Mar., single/return fare €7/10 per car) across Waterford Harbour to Ballyhack. Passage East is 12 kilometers east of Waterford on the R683, and **Suirway** (tel. 051/382-209, www.suirway.com, 4/day Mon.–Sat., single fare €3) provides bus service from the city.

◖ DUNMORE EAST

Easily the loveliest part of eastern Waterford, Dunmore East (Dún Mór, "Big Fort") is a popular weekend getaway for city folk. Dunmore is spread out along a kilometer or so, from the strand (the lower village) to the harbor (the upper village), with the post office, grocery stores, and ATM located in the latter. Take a leisurely stroll past rows of immaculately maintained thatched-roof cottages, chat with friendly locals, and drink in the gorgeous view of the bay and Hook Head beyond.

Entertainment and Events
Locals flock to the Tuesday night trad-and-folk sessions at **Power's** (upper village, tel. 051/383-318), where you can socialize and watch the musicians in the front room (there could be two or 10, depending on the week), or have a more intimate conversation in the dimly lit snugs in the back. The walls here are covered with witty (mostly nautical) epigrams like "marriages performed by the captain are valid only for duration of voyage."

Sports and Recreation
You can tee off at the seaside **Dunmore East Golf & Country Club** (signposted from the lower village, tel. 051/383-151, www.dunmore-golf.com) or go sailboarding with the **Dunmore East Adventure Centre** (at the harbor, upper village, tel. 051/383-783, www.dunmoreadventure.com). The tennis court between the upper and lower villages has an awesome view of the Hook.

Accommodations and Food
For B&B, try **Church Villa** (tel. 051/383-390, http://homepage.eircom.net/~churchvilla, open mid-Feb.–mid-Nov., €29–34 pp, s €40–45), a charming townhouse across the road from picturesque St. Andrew's Anglican church. Red rosebushes sprout from between the flagstone patio outside Church Villa, and though the decor is excessively flowery, the showers are terrific and the coffee is brewed. Another option, **Springfield** (lower village, tel. 051/383-448, www.springfield-dunmore.com, open Mar.–Nov., €30–35 pp, s €45–60, credit cards accepted), is a stone's throw from the beach, and a delight in every respect.

Dunmore has two hotels, **The Ocean** (upper village, near the harbor, tel. 051/383-136, www.theoceanhotel.com, €50–60 pp sharing), a good choice if you plan to soak up the local nightlife, and **The Haven** (between the upper and lower villages, tel. 051/383-150, www.thehavenhotel.com, open Mar.–Oct., €55–75 pp sharing), older, grander, a bit on the quirky side, family-run, and child-friendly. Don't eat here, though.

The best eatery in town is a gastro-pub, ◖ **The Spinnaker** (lower village, tel. 051/383-133, food served noon–9:30 P.M. daily, mains €9–25), with a nautical theme (that somehow manages to feel elegant) and amiable staff. Top-notch steaks and fresh seafood are on the menu, along with a few superb vegetarian dishes—so good, in fact, that the desserts are a letdown! The food at **Ship** (Harbour Rd., opposite St. Andrew's, between the villages, tel. 051/383-141, open noon–2:30 P.M. daily June–Aug. and 6–10 P.M. daily Apr.–Oct., evenings Tues.–Sat. Nov.–Mar., mains €18–30) is equally high quality but offers comparatively poor value. It's also more posh, being popular with Waterford businesspeople here for golfing weekends.

Getting There
Dunmore East is 17 kilometers southeast of Waterford on the R684. **Suirway** (tel. 051/382-209, www.suirway.com, 4/day Mon.–Sat., single fare €3) offers bus service from the city.

DUNGARVAN
A pleasant-enough market and port town on the River Colligan, Dungarvan (Dún Garbhán, "Fort of Garvan," after a 7th-century saint) makes a good stopover between Cork and Waterford, as there are a couple of fine restaurants here. Have a nice lunch and keep on west to Ardmore, as Dungarvan's sights aren't terribly exciting. Access is by guided tour only to the squat 12th-century **Dungarvan Castle** (Castle St., tel. 058/48144, open 10 A.M.–6 P.M. daily June–Sept., free admission), built by order of King John. The adjacent barracks have been converted into a small military history museum. Another stop for history buffs: the **Dungarvan Museum** (St. Augustine St., tel. 058/45960, open 10 A.M.–5 P.M. Mon.–Fri., free admission), with small

© CAMILLE DEANGELIS

Installed in 1897, the Dungarvan bandstand is a superb example of Scottish ironwork.

exhibits on the Great Famine and the history of the town port.

You can have all three meals at **The Tannery** (10 Quay St., tel. 058/45420, www.tannery. ie, open 12:30–2:15 P.M. Tues.–Fri. and Sun., 6:30–9:30 P.M. Tues.–Sat., open 6–9 P.M. Sun. July–Aug., mains €16–28, 3-course early-bird menu €27 6:30–7:30 P.M. Tues.–Fri., B&B €50–70), the most popular eatery in town for its relentlessly inventive modern Irish fare. If you spend the night, a continental breakfast will be delivered to your room. The **Moorings** (Davitt's Quay, tel. 058/41461, www.moorings-dungarvan.com, food served noon–9:30 P.M. daily, mains €10–19, B&B €45 pp, s €60) does fine bar meals.

On the quay, the county's largest **library** (tel. 058/41231) provides free Internet access, and the **Bank of Ireland** has an ATM. The **tourist office** (Meagher St., tel. 058/41741, open 9 A.M.–6 P.M. Mon.–Sat.) is in the old courthouse beside the **post office.**

Dungarvan is 42 kilometers southwest of Waterford on the N25. **Bus Éireann** routes from Cork to Rosslare Harbour (#40, 13/day daily) and Cork to Waterford (#43, 11/day Mon.–Fri.) stop in Dungarvan.

AN RINN

The tourist board touts the Ring Peninsula (An Rinn) as an idyllic Gaeltacht region, but there's not much for the visitor—it's nearly all residential, and locals fear construction of new "luxury" harbor-view homes may somewhat diminish its charm. You can drive east to Helvick Head for a pretty (but not transcendent) view of Dungarvan across the bay. After admiring the individually designed pieces at the peninsula's small crystal showroom, **Criostal na Rinne** (signposted off the R674, tel. 058/46174), pause for a pint at the delightfully atmospheric **Mooney's** (on the R674, tel. 058/46204), where the walls are covered with rusty vintage tobacco ads and black-and-white photographs. Listen to the locals chatting in Irish in the front beer garden—and there's trad here Saturday nights.

The Ring Peninsula is south of Dungarvan, signposted off the Cork-bound N25.

© CAMILLE DEANGELIS

The exterior stone panels at St. Declan's Cathedral feature biblical scenes.

ARDMORE

The greatest delight in County Waterford is the seaside village of Ardmore (Áird Mhór), with its long sandy strand, spectacularly situated monastic ruins, and exhilarating clifftop walk. It may be a popular getaway for tourists and weekending Irish alike, yet Ardmore still manages to feel like a well-kept secret. No trip to Waterford is complete without at least one night here.

(St. Declan's Monastery and Cliff Walk

Ardmore boasts some of Ireland's most beautifully situated monastic ruins, St. Declan's Monastery (signposted from Main St., a 5-minute walk uphill, always accessible, free admission), founded in the 5th century. Surrounded by a modern cemetery, the ruins include an 8th-century oratory (or Beannchán, restored in the 18th century and said to mark Declan's grave), a complete 30-meter round tower built in the 12th century, and a Romanesque cathedral on the site of Declan's original church. Check out the stone carvings on the western wall exterior depicting both Old and New Testament scenes, which predate the building itself. Some of the scenes are still discernible: Adam and Eve, the Adoration of the Magi, and the Judgment of Solomon. There are two ogham stones inside the cathedral. The whole site overlooks Ardmore Bay, and there's no prettier place in Ireland when the sun's shining.

A five-kilometer, one-hour **cliff walk** begins at the monastery and loops around a pastoral headland, taking you past a couple of lookout posts, a rusted shipwreck from 1987, and **St. Declan's Well,** originally used to baptize the locals and later said to have curative properties. There's a church ruin nearby. From there it's a downhill walk back into town. Because most folks start from the cliff and walk clockwise, ending up at the monastery, you might want to walk it counterclockwise. Though you don't really need one, you can pick up a map at the tourist office or your B&B.

Ardmore Pottery

Something else the town is known for is Mary Lincoln's pretty, pastel Ardmore Pottery (The Cliff, at the start of the scenic walk, tel. 024/94152, ardmorepottery@eircom.net), which also sells locally made knitwear.

Accommodations and Food

A few B&Bs are just down the hill from the ruins of St. Declan's. A tranquil place teeming with flowerbeds, with a stream running beside the driveway, is (**Carraigdhoun** (Tower Hill, tel. 024/94436, €30–35 pp). The proprietors are very kind, and the bright and airy rooms are havens of comfort and simplicity: They come with radio, superlative mattresses and bedclothes, and garden view—but no television. A few minutes' drive from the village is the tranquil **Newtown Farm** (Grange, 6.5 km northwest of Ardmore off the N25, tel. 024/94143, www.newtownfarm.com, €40 pp, s €48). On a working dairy farm, all the immaculate, country-style rooms offer sea and pastoral views. There's a tennis court, too, so bring your racket. Or try the recently renovated,

12-room **Round Tower Hotel** (College Rd., a few minutes' walk down the Youghal road, tel. 024/94494, rth@eircom.net, food served until 9:30 P.M. daily, B&B €45–55 pp sharing). There's nothing fancy here, but the staff are affable and the seafood in the restaurant is worth writing home about.

You'd never know that Ardmore's one classy café-restaurant, **White Horses** (Main St., tel. 024/94040, open 11 A.M.–11 P.M. Tues.–Sun. May–Sept., 6–11 P.M. Fri., 11 A.M.–11 P.M. Sat., and noon–6 P.M. Sun. Oct.–Apr., mains €9–24, 3-course lunch €25), is in the old police barracks. Come here for tea and a pastry, or a full meal featuring fresh local produce and inventively prepared seafood.

Practicalities
There's a seasonal **tourist office** (tel. 024/94444, open 11 A.M.–4 P.M. daily May–Sept.) in a small, strange-looking glass building on the strand. There was no ATM in Ardmore at time of writing, so be sure to withdraw funds before leaving Waterford or Cork.

Ardmore is 21 kilometers west of Dungarvan and 71 kilometers west of Waterford via the N25 and R673. Get here via **Bus Éireann** (#260, 2/day Mon.–Sat., 1/day Sun.) from Cork or from Waterford (#362, 2/day July–Aug. only).

LISMORE
A pleasant spot tucked between the Knockmealdowns and the River Blackwater, Lismore (An Líos Mór, "The Great Enclosure") draws tour buses for the three-hectare Elizabethan gardens at **Lismore Castle** (tel. 058/54424, www.lismorecastle.com, open 1:45–4:45 P.M. daily Easter–Sept., admission €6), though the castle itself is not open to the public. Owned by Walter Raleigh, later the earls of Cork, and now the dukes of Devonshire, perhaps the castle's claim to fame is the discovery of the Lismore Crozier along with the 15th-century, so-called *Book of Lismore* during a renovation in 1814. Part hagiography, part chronicle of the voyages of Marco Polo, the manuscript's proper title is the *Book of Mac Cartach Riabhach*. Both treasures are now in the National Museum.

Accommodations and Food
There isn't a load of accommodations in the area, but you might try **Beechcroft** (Deerpark Rd., signposted off the east end of Main St., tel. 058/54273, www.beechcroftbandb.ie, open Apr.–Oct., €29–33 pp, s €40–45, credit cards accepted), which is within easy walking distance of Main Street and offers rooms with electric blankies and views of the carefully tended garden. Another option is **Pine Tree House** (signposted off the N72, tel. 058/53282, www.pinetreehouselismore.com, €29–35 pp, s €42–60, credit cards accepted), also just outside town. The welcome is warm, pets are permitted, and there's a discount for longer stays.

A traditional bar in front (see the pub's original name painted out over the doorway?) and a surprisingly stylish tapas and wine bar in the back, **Barça** (Main St., tel. 058/53810, food served 12:30–3 P.M. Tues.–Sat., 12:30–8 P.M. Sun., tapas and dinner 6–10 P.M. Thurs.–Sat., lunches €5–10, tapas €6–10, set dinner €30) does huge portions of terrific pasta dishes (though the bacon-happy chef is liable to throw some in with the supposedly vegetarian options, so be sure to ask for a meat-free version), and the service is quick and eager to please. Eating lunch here will keep you full to breakfast the next morning; it's a very good value. Come back for tapas in the evening, where you'll spend half an hour making a choice from the staggeringly long wine list. Otherwise, nearly all Lismore's pubs have all-day bar menus; the best grub's at **Eamonn's Place** (Main St., tel. 058/54025, food served noon–9:30 P.M., mains €8–16), with an outback beer garden.

Practicalities
You'll find both the **tourist office** (tel. 058/54975, www.discoverlismore.com, open 10 A.M.–4 P.M. daily Apr.–Oct.) and **heritage center** (tel. 058/54975, open 9:30 A.M.–6 P.M. Mon.–Sat., noon–6 P.M. Sun., admission €4)

© CAMILLE DEANGELIS

the gates of Ballysaggartmore, "the castle that never was"

in the old courthouse on Main Street. There's an ATM at the **Bank of Ireland** on West Street across the street from the public park.

Lismore is essentially one street, Main changing names to West Street. It's 68 kilometers west of Waterford via the N25 and N72. **Bus Éireann** provides infrequent service (#4/40, 1/day Mon.–Sat. leaving Waterford at 9 P.M.; #41, 1/day Fri. and Sun. only, no Sun. service July–Aug.).

Ballysaggartmore

Dubbed "the castle that never was," Ballysaggartmore (3 km west of Lismore on the N72, signposted "the towers" from the N72, always accessible, free admission) was planned by local landlord Arthur Keily as a splendid castle to please his wife, who wanted a manse even grander than that of her husband's brother and sister-in-law (just substitute "Keilys" for "Joneses" in that classic American expression). After building a turreted gateway fit for a fairy tale in 1850, the Keilys' funds were exhausted, and Mrs. Keily's castle of dreams was never built. (Note the date? As Lismore historians have pointed out, all that money could have gone toward famine relief.) The ornate stone gateway led only to a modest home where they continued to live, as Brian de Breffny writes, "perhaps regretful of their folly, or perhaps satisfied by the grandeur of their gate." The Keilys' home has since been demolished, but the gatehouses are still here, surrounded by an enchanting, eerily quiet forest park.

CLARE AND LIMERICK

Clare and Limerick are the northwestern counties in the province of Munster, demarcated from one another by the River Shannon on the south and east of County Clare. Many tourists head straight for County Clare (An Clár) to see the dramatic Cliffs of Moher, which are beseiged by coach buses year-round. Few of those visitors stick around to wander through Clare's wealth of monastic ruins, prehistoric sites, and castles, though some take part in pricey, kitschy-but-fun medieval banquets at Bunratty and Knappogue (where everyone's a lord or lady for an evening). There's also much to be said for the Burren's breathtaking, deceptively barren limestone peaks and plateaus, as well as the county's pretty coastline with its green cliffs and sandy beaches.

The terrain of County Limerick (Luimneach, "bare spot") is relatively featureless—mostly flat green farmland—until you reach the Galtee and Ballyhoura mountain chains slipping over the Tipperary and Cork borders. Situated on the River Shannon, Limerick City is still struggling to dispel a reputation for violence and poverty; when you say you've been there many Irish will ask you why. But 21st-century Limerick has a thriving arts scene, as exciting after dark as any other university town. (Many of the best fashion designers in Ireland honed their skills at the city's School of Art and Design.) Suffice it to say this is no longer the Limerick of Frank McCourt's memoirs, though you can still occasionally find him with a pint in hand at South's Pub on O'Connell Avenue, back from the States for a time.

© CAMILLE DEANGELIS

HIGHLIGHTS

◖ The Cliffs of Moher: No postcard can begin to convey the misty magnificence of this natural wonder, with dramatic cliffs standing sentinel over the waves (page 295).

◖ O'Connor's Pub: Kick back with a pint and savor a live trad session in Doolin, the mecca of Irish traditional music (page 297).

◖ The Burren Way: Hike 45 kilometers across a craggy limestone plateau dotted with fragrant wildflowers and prehistoric monuments (page 302).

◖ Dysert O'Dea: Examine the high crosses, round tower, and intricate Romanesque doorway at Clare's most important monastic site (page 309).

◖ St. Mary's Cathedral: This spooky 12th-century church contains medieval tombs behind the altar. Its black-oak misericords are unique in Ireland (page 312).

◖ Hunt Museum: Don't miss the finest collection of antiquities outside Dublin. Treasures include the 17th-century Galway Chalice and a da Vinci bronze (page 312).

◖ Lough Gur: Cycle around this picturesque lake and examine its Neolithic wedge tombs, stone circle, *crannóg*, and other remains (page 316).

LOOK FOR ◖ TO FIND RECOMMENDED SIGHTS, ACTIVITIES, DINING, AND LODGING.

HISTORY

The earliest evidence of human habitation in County Limerick dates to 3500 B.C., with the stone remains at Lough Gur dating 500 years later. Clare's megalithic tombs—Poulnabrone and 130 others—are all at least 5,000 years old, and archaeological digs in the Burren have revealed a Neolithic society nourished by the earliest hunters and fishermen, a society that eventually evolved into complex farming and animal husbandry. It's hard to imagine now, but the Burren's limestone plateaus were once covered in soil and light forest. It was those first farmers who cleared the trees for their fields, enabling the gradual soil erosion that resulted in this rocky landscape.

The first missionaries introduced Christianity in the 5th century, and the new religion spread as quickly in Clare and Limerick as it did elsewhere in Ireland. Evidence from early Christian and medieval ring forts shows many farmers lived and worked with their extended families in and around these ring forts, which may have functioned as a method of quarantine against the plague as much as for protection from invaders. Today there are remains of 2,300 stone and earthen forts in County Clare alone, as well as 150 early churches, eight

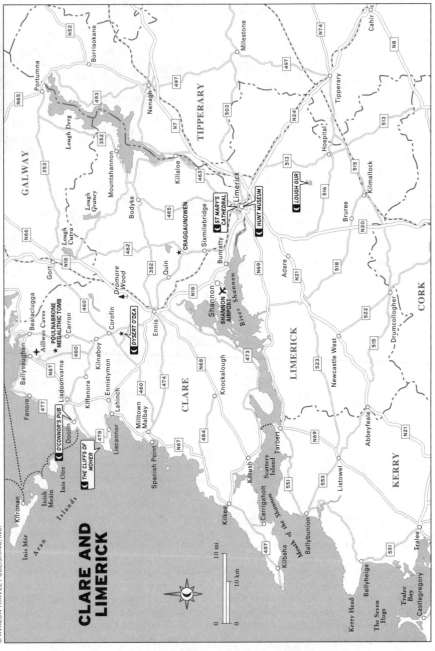

monasteries, three cathedrals, 10 stone crosses, five round towers, and 190 castles.

Though the county was divided into small baronies ruled by several prominent families (the O'Deas, the McNamaras, and others)—an arrangement dating back to the advent of the Celts around 400 B.C.—it was the O'Brien clan, the kings of Thomond (from "Tuath-Mumhan," meaning North Munster), that dominated Clare for centuries. The Danish Vikings raided the county many times over the 9th and 10th centuries, but Brian Boru, the most famous of the O'Briens, defeated them at the beginning of the 11th, and again at the Battle of Clontarf near Dublin in 1014.

Limerick City was founded on the site of an earlier Viking settlement dating to 922. In 1194 the death of Donal Mór O'Brien, the king of Munster—who had funded the establishment of dozens of monasteries in these counties—enabled the invading Normans to seize control of Limerick, and King John commanded a castle be built on the Shannon at the turn of the 13th century. The city enjoyed ongoing prosperity under Norman control.

Being a staunchly Catholic city, Limerick eagerly threw its support behind the Jacobite cause during the rebellion of 1691—known as Cogadh an Dá Rí, the War of the Two Kings. Defeat was inevitable, however, and the terms Jacobite general Patrick Sarsfield secured in the Treaty of Limerick were thrown out by the Irish Parliament. Hundreds of years of redoubled Catholic oppression were to follow.

PLANNING YOUR TIME

All told, you could easily spend your entire vacation in County Clare. With so much variety, several excellent child-friendly museums, and plenty of visitor amenities, Clare makes an especially good choice for families. The Burren can be done in a day, but hill-walkers and other nature-lovers should plan for a visit of at least three days. The sights of southeastern Clare—Ennis, Quin Friary, Dysert O'Dea, or Bunratty Castle—make a good last-day excursion, if you are flying out of Shannon. To do Clare thoroughly, from Hook Head to the Cliffs of Moher to the Burren to Killaloe, would take the better part of a week. Though a fine day in low season is the ideal time to visit the Cliffs of Moher (when there are fewer coach buses and visitors in general), keep in mind that many attractions (Ennis Friary, the Craggaunowen Project, Scattery Island, and so on) are closed between November and February, and in some cases October and March as well.

You can cover County Limerick's primary points of interest—Lough Gur, King John's Castle, the Hunt Museum—in under two days. Some visitors will want to pause in Limerick on the way to or from Killarney, the Dingle Peninsula, or County Cork.

Eastern Clare

ENNIS

If you plan to spend any time in the Burren or along the Clare coast, you'll likely pass through Ennis, the county capital, which straddles the River Fergus. Its medieval flavor is highlighted by the picturesque ruins of the 13th-century Ennis Friary, and there's some fine traditional music to be heard in and around town. This old market town can seem awfully drab when the sun's not shining, though. You may want to linger just long enough to take in the friary and the ruins at nearby Quin before you head out west to the wilder, rockier, more scenic parts of the county. That said, its proximity to the Shannon Airport makes Ennis a good place to spend your last night in Ireland.

Ennis's town square features an extremely tall pedestal topped by a statue of "the Great Liberator," Daniel O'Connell. The main streets—High, Abbey, O'Connell—extend from here. The tourist office is just east of the square, down Arthur's Row.

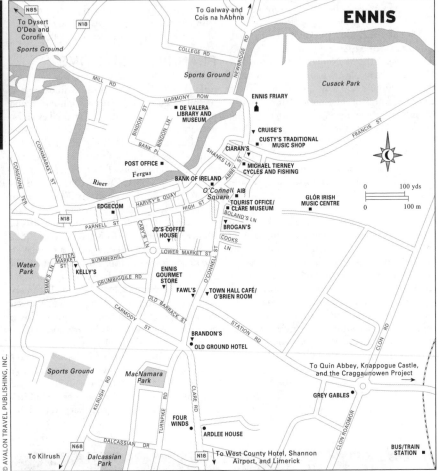

ENNIS

To Galway and
Cois na hAbhna

To Dysert
O'Dea and
Corofin

Sports Ground

N85

N18

MILL RD

COLLEGE RD

NEWBRIDGE RD

Sports Ground

Cusack Park

HARMONY ROW

ENNIS FRIARY

BINDON ST

BINDON LN

DE VALERA
LIBRARY AND
MUSEUM

CRUISE'S

CUSTY'S TRADITIONAL
MUSIC SHOP

FRANCIS ST.

BANK PL.

SHANKS LN

CIARAN'S

POST OFFICE

Fergus

MICHAEL TIERNEY
CYCLES AND FISHING

CORMARKET ST

River

BANK OF IRELAND

ABBEY ST

O'Connell AIB
Square

CONSIDINE TER.

HARVEY'S QUAY

EDGECOM

TOURIST OFFICE/
CLARE MUSEUM

GLÓR IRISH
MUSIC CENTRE

0   100 yds

N18

HIGH ST

BOLAND'S LN

0   100 m

PARNELL ST

JD'S COFFEE
HOUSE

BROGAN'S

CARY'S LN

COOKS
LN

O'CONNELL ST

LOWER MARKET ST

BUTTER
MARKET
ST

SUMMERHILL

ENNIS
GOURMET
STORE

Water
Park

SIMM'S LN

KELLY'S

DRUMBIGGILE RD

FAWL'S

TOWN HALL CAFÉ/
O'BRIEN ROOM

OLD BARRACK ST

CARMODY ST

STATION RD

BRANDON'S

OLD GROUND HOTEL

Sports Ground

MacNamara
Park

To Quin Abbey, Knappogue Castle,
and the Craggaunowen Project

KILRUSH RD

TURNPIKE RD

CLARE RD

GREY GABLES

CLON RD

CLON ROADMOR

FOUR
WINDS

N68

DALCASSIAN DR

ARDLEE HOUSE

BUS/TRAIN
STATION

To Kilrush

Dalcassian
Park

N18

To West County Hotel, Shannon
Airport, and Limerick

© AVALON TRAVEL PUBLISHING, INC.

Sights

Seven hundred years ago, a community of 1,000 men—400 friars and 600 pupils—lived a life of reflection and asceticism at the **Ennis Friary** (Francis St., tel. 065/682-9100, open 10 A.M.–5 P.M. daily Apr.–Oct., closed Nov.–Mar., admission €1.50). Now managed by Dúchas, the friary was established by Donough Cairbreach O'Brien for the Franciscans around 1240, though most of the ruins date from the 15th century (including most of the nave,

south wing, tower, and decorated windows). The lovely five-lighted east window in the choir was erected in the late 13th or early 14th century, however. The friary's most fascinating features are its old family tombs (particularly the MacMahons', which dates to 1460 and features alabaster panels carved with scenes from the Passion) and wall carvings, including one depicting St. Francis with the stigmata and another of the Crucifixion. The guided tour is optional, though highly recommended.

© CAMILLE DEANGELIS

Ennis Friary features several fascinating limestone carvings.

Housed in the tourist office, the **Clare Museum** (Arthur's Row, tel. 065/682-3382, www.clarelibrary.ie/eolas/claremuseum, open 9:30 A.M.–1 P.M. and 2–5:30 P.M. Mon.–Sat. and 2–5 P.M. Sun., closed Mon. Oct.–May, free admission) offers a perspective on 6,000 years of local history and is certainly worth a visit, especially on a rainy day.

Irish history buffs may want to visit the **De Valera Library and Museum** (Harmony Row, off Abbey St., tel. 065/682-1616, open 10 A.M.–5 P.M. Mon., Wed., and Thurs., 10 A.M.–8 P.M. Tues. and Fri., museum admission €4). Ennis's public library, housed in a renovated 19th-century Protestant church, also has a small museum containing many of de Valera's personal possessions and various other historical flotsam (literally, for one of the artifacts is a galleon door pulled out of the sea after the sinking of the Spanish Armada). The library also offers a gallery space for touring art and history exhibits.

One of Clare's most important monastic sites, Dysert O'Dea, is nine kilometers north of Ennis (see *Corofin* under *The Bureen*). Quin Abbey, Knappogue Castle, and the Craggaunowen Project are all within 16 kilometers.

Entertainment and Events

Many would say the best live trad in town is at **Cruise's** (Abbey St., tel. 065/684-1800), where nightly sessions commence at half-nine. There's also a "midday" session on Sunday. Other pubs with traditional music sessions include **Ciaran's** (Francis St., tel. 065/684-0180) Thursday–Sunday, **Kelly's** (Carmody St., tel. 065/682-8155) on Saturday night, and **Fawl's** (69 O'Connell St., tel. 065/682-4463) on Friday night.

You'll find more variety—jazz, blues, and rock—at **Brandon's** (tel. 065/682-8133, O'Connell St.), though the bar also offers an open trad session (all musicians welcome) on Wednesday night.

Fleadh Nua (tel. 065/684-0406 or 086/826-0300, fleadhnua.com), Ennis's annual music festival, takes place the last weekend in May; it features set and step dancing and storytelling events in addition to plenty of live trad. The festival organizers maintain a desk at the Ennis tourist office.

Cois na hAbhna ("CUSH nah HOW-nah," on the N18, 2 km north of Ennis, tel. 065/682-0996 or 086/826-0300, ceoltrad@iol.ie) is an Irish cultural center that offers two types of entertainments: a straight-up trad session and a *seisiún,* which also has plenty of singing and dancing (with audience participation all but mandatory), one Saturday a month. The center also houses a music archive and offers dancing and music lessons. Performances are at 8:30 P.M. Wednesday year-round and 8:30 P.M. Saturday June–September, tickets €3 for trad, €8 for the *seisiún.*

The **Glór Irish Music Centre** (Friar's Walk, tel. 065/684-3103, www.glor.ie, tickets €7–20) is primarily a folk, rock, and trad concert venue, but dramatic productions are also on the schedule. Performances usually take place at 8 P.M. Glór (Irish for "sound") is a safe option if you're looking for a more formal setting in which to enjoy good music.

Shopping

Ennis does have a shopping center on O'Connell Street, but it doesn't really have any shops of special interest to the visitor. If you're interested in traditional music, however, there's a shop you shouldn't miss: **Custy's Music** (Francis St., tel. 065/682-1727, www.custysmusic.com) has plenty of instruments (fiddles, tin whistles, bouzoukis, bodhrans, you name it), hard-to-find albums on independent labels, songbooks, and other goodies in its cozy little shop.

Sports and Recreation

Outdoor enthusiasts will want to continue through Ennis to the Burren region (Ballyvaughan, Corofin, Carron, and Doolin all make good bases from which to explore it). Alternatively, you can rent a bike, pack a picnic lunch, and pedal out to Quin Abbey (8 km), Knappogue Castle (10 km), and the Craggaunowen Project (14 km).

Accommodations

Old-world hotels outnumber budget accommodations in Ennis; note that the town's only hostel is not recommended.

One of the nicest B&Bs in Ennis is **Grey Gables** (Station Rd., tel. 065/682-4487, www.bed-n-breakfast-ireland.com, €32.50 pp, s €40), an elegant (but not too formal) place just down the street from the train station. There are also several B&Bs along Clare Road on the south end of town, two of which are **Four Winds** (Clare Rd., tel. 065/682-9831, fourwinds.ennis@eircom.net, €32 pp, s €45) and **Ardlea House** (Clare Road, tel. 065/682-0256, €40 pp, s €60), a five-minute walk from the center of town. Both are quiet and unpretentious, with friendly, helpful proprietors.

The ivy-covered 18th-century **Old Ground Hotel** (O'Connell St., tel. 065/682-8127, www.oldgroundhotel.ie, d €105–190, s €80–110) is as romantic on the inside, even post-renovation. Antique furnishings include a fireplace from Lemaneagh Castle (carved in 1553), so it's rather difficult to imagine that this building once served as the town jail!

Food

There isn't an astounding selection of great eateries in Ennis, but neither is a hearty meal hard to come by.

In addition to an impressive variety of gift baskets (wine, cheese, jam, chocolate, you name it), the **Ennis Gourmet Store** (1 Barrack St., tel. 065/684-3314, www.ennisgourmetstore.com, open 9 A.M.–7 P.M. Mon.–Sat., lunches under €8) does a brisk salad and sandwich business. Another good choice for an inexpensive lunch—or a huge Irish breakfast—is bright and airy **J.D.'s Coffee House** (15 Merchants Sq., tel. 065/684-1630, www.jdscoffeehouse.com, open 7:30 A.M.–6 P.M. Mon.–Sat., meals under €8).

The atmospheric Old Ground Hotel on O'Connell Street operates two eateries, the **O'Brien Room** (tel. 065/682-8127, open noon–2:30 P.M. and 6:30–9:15 P.M. daily, mains €14–22) and the less formal **Town Hall Café** (tel. 065/682-8127, open 10 A.M.–5 P.M. and 6–10 P.M. daily, lunches under €12, dinners €15–22). The former offers a gourmet menu with an emphasis on local meats and produce, and the latter is a solid choice for lunch or afternoon tea. A third option at the Old Ground is the pub grub at the **Poet's Corner,** served noon–9 P.M.

If you want it all—a juicy steak, a pint of stout, a rollicking-good trad session, and an authentic medieval atmosphere—then head to **Cruise's Pub and Restaurant** (Abbey St., tel. 065/684-1800, open 6–10:30 P.M. daily, mains €14–22). You might be surprised to learn that the building dates from 1658—it feels even older. The service isn't nearly as good as the food, however. **Brogan's** (24 O'Connell St., tel. 065/682-9859, open 10 A.M.–11:30 P.M. daily, lunches under €10, dinners €13–22) is another Ennis mainstay, offering hearty traditional Irish dishes.

Information

Before heading out to the Burren or the coast, stop by the Ennis **tourist office** (O'Connell Sq., tel. 065/28366, open 9 A.M.–9 P.M. daily June–Sept., 9 A.M.–6 P.M. Mon.–Sat. and

10 A.M.–6 P.M. Sun. Oct.–May) to pick up maps, walking guides, and other info.

Services

The Ennis **post office** is just off O'Connell Square (Bank Pl., tel. 065/682-1054, open 9 A.M.–5:30 P.M. Mon.–Fri., 9:30 A.M.–2:30 P.M. Sat.).

ATMs and bureaux de change are located at the **Bank of Ireland** (O'Connell Sq., tel. 065/682-8615) and **AIB** (Bank Pl., off O'Connell Sq., tel. 065/682-8089).

Internet access is available at **Edgecom** (Unit 3, River Ln., Woodquay, tel. 065/684-8642, www.edgecom.biz, open 9 A.M.–11 P.M. Mon.–Sat., 11 A.M.–11 P.M. Sun., €2/hour). Alternatively, the **public library** (Harmony Row, off Abbey St., tel. 065/682-1616, open 10 A.M.–5 P.M. Mon., Wed., and Thurs., 10 A.M.–8 P.M. Tues. and Fri.) allows one hour of free web-surfing.

Need a launderette? **White Knight** (Old Barrack St., tel. 065/682-3133, open 9 A.M.–6 P.M. Mon.–Sat.) is self-service.

The Dunnes Stores on O'Connell Street also houses a pharmacy, **Michael McLoughlin** (tel. 065/682-9511); another option is **Duffy's Pharmacy** (inside the Tesco Shopping Centre, Francis St., tel. 065/682-8833).

Getting There

Ennis is on the N18, which runs north to Galway (66 km) and southeast to Limerick (37 km). From Dublin, take the N7 to Limerick (198 km), then the N18 up to Ennis (235 km total).

Ennis is serviced by both **Bus Éireann** (tel. 065/682-4177) and **Irish Rail** (tel. 061/315-555, call the Limerick station for departure times). Buses depart for west Clare at least four times a day (the Liscannor–Cliffs of Moher-Doolin route is #337; Ballyvaughan requires a change of bus, usually at the cliffs); you can catch a direct bus to Ennis from the Shannon Airport, Limerick, Galway, and Cork (all on route #51, at least 14 buses/day). Change at Limerick for the Dublin bus (#12). Departure times are clearly posted outside the station office.

Eastbound trains run direct to Limerick (7–8/day daily), or you can change at Limerick Junction to get to Dublin (4–5/day Mon.–Sat., 3/day Sun.) and Waterford (2–3/day Mon.–Sat.).

Try to avoid a layover in Ennis if you can help it. The bus and train station waiting room is almost comically hellish—comical in retrospect, that is.

Getting Around

Ennis is a small town and can be traversed end to end on foot. Bike rental is available from **Michael Tierney Cycles and Fishing** (17 Abbey St., tel. 065/682-9433, tel. 065/682-1293 after 6 P.M., open 9:30 A.M.–6 P.M. Mon.–Sat., €20/day, €80/week).

Need a taxi? Ring **Joe Barry Taxicabs** (tel. 065/24759), **Michael Casey** (tel. 065/22230), or **Armstrong Kelleher** (tel. 088/256-3667).

QUIN AND VICINITY

Eight kilometers southeast of Ennis is a tiny village, Quin (Chuinche), renowned for its castle and monastic remains, as well as a preserved castle offering medieval banquets and an excellent outdoor museum of both reconstructed and original prehistoric architecture. In 1854 a trove of golden torcs and other ancient jewelry was discovered here during the Limerick–Ennis railway construction, though few pieces ever made it to the National Museum.

Quin Abbey (tel. 065/684-4084, open 10:30 A.M.–6 P.M. Mon.–Fri., 11:30 A.M.–5 P.M. Sat.–Sun. May–Oct., free admission) was erected in the 1430s on the ruins of a castle built in the late 1270s. The abbey ruins are not easily distinguishable from those of the earlier castle, and in this respect the friary is quite unique. There are several tombs of note within the church, the most interesting of which is the MacNamara tomb niche (dating to the mid-15th century) beside the altar stone. It was the MacNamaras who founded the abbey on the foundations of Richard de Clare's late 13th-century castle, and their tombs feature the family's leonine coat of arms. You can enter the old sacristy and look up the stairs that used

© CAMILLE DE ANGELIS

Vast Quin Abbey was extended from an existing castle in the 15th century.

to lead to one of the monks' dormitories. An arcade surrounds the well-preserved cloister on three sides, and you can climb the belfry for an aerial view.

Visible from the abbey across the stream is **St. Finghin's Church** (east of the R469, always accessible), a diminutive Gothic 13th-century nave-and-chancel edifice you can reach on foot from the primary ruin.

Knappogue Castle

Knappogue Castle (3 km southeast of Quin, signposted from the R469, tel. 061/368-103, open 9:30 A.M.–4 P.M. daily Apr.–Oct., admission €4), a three-story tower house, was erected by the MacNamara clan in 1467. Cromwell seized Knappogue to use as a base (which is why it's so well preserved), though it was returned to the MacNamaras after the Restoration. The castle was converted into an aristocratic residence in the 19th century and restored again in the 1960s. Rooms open to the public include the Dalcassian Room, which features a 15th-century carving of St. George,

and the 19th-century drawing and dining rooms with all their period furnishings.

Knappogue also does **medieval banquets** (tel. 061/360-788, sittings at 5:45 P.M. and 8:45 P.M. nightly Apr.–Oct., €46) in the banquet hall on the ground floor. The dinnertime theatrics here aren't quite so melodramatically silly as at Bunratty. You'll also be allowed to use cutlery rather than picking at the roasted chicken with your bare fingers.

Craggaunowen Project

The third sight in the Quin area is the Craggaunowen Project (6 km southeast of Quin, signposted off the R469, tel. 061/367-178, open 10 A.M.–6 P.M. May–Aug., admission €7), a fascinating outdoor museum established by John Hunt on the grounds of Craggaunowen Castle, another MacNamara tower house dating to the mid-16th century. The castle has been restored, and its ground floor houses medieval artifacts from the Hunt family's extensive collection.

Outside, you'll find a series of reconstructed

Iron Age and early Christian sites: a ring fort enclosing circular thatched huts, a souterrain (an underground passage used mainly for food storage), kilns, a prehistoric *crannóg* (or manmade island), and an open-air cooking site (or *fulacht fiadh*) where heated stones would have been used to boil water in a wooden trough. One original artifact is a *togher,* or wooden track, pulled from a bog and at least 2,000 years old.

Craggaunowen also houses "the Brendan Exhibition," which displays the leather curragh used successfully by explorers in 1976 to demonstrate the possibility that St. Brendan the Navigator could've beat Columbus to the New World by more than nine centuries.

Besides the reconstructions, there are walking trails through the surrounding forest and around nearby Lough Cullaun, and plenty of good spots for a picnic lunch. If it's raining, the café at Craggaunowen makes a good alternative. All in all, this is a must-see for archaeology enthusiasts as well as families with older children.

Getting There

Quin and its surrounding sights make an easy day trip from Ennis, though Bus Éireann doesn't stop here. Cyclists can rent a bike in town and head out on the R469, the road past the bus and train station.

BUNRATTY

Bunratty is often called a medieval Irish Disneyland, and it's true the place is tourist central in high season. The nightly medieval banquets at Bunratty Castle are the village's primary draw, and though they're extremely kitschy, they can be a lot of fun. The majority of attendees are on coach tours, and most of the crowd is older, along with a few families with small children. Those who would bypass Bunratty because of its crowds are encouraged to visit in the off-season, however, for Bunratty Castle is a delight in itself—not to mention its friendly tour guides, who turn the hefty admission price into a good value with their knowledge and genuine enthusiasm.

Bunratty Castle

From the Middle Ages onward the site of Bunratty Castle (tel. 061/361-511, www.shannonheritage.com, open 9 A.M.–4:45 P.M. daily June–Aug., 9:30 A.M.–4:15 P.M. daily Sept.–May, last admission to castle at 4 P.M., admission €12) offered a strategic position on the river, for its occupants could monitor the water traffic to and from the port of Limerick. The first stone castle on the site was built in the late 13th century by Sir Thomas de Clare, and a town populated by English settlers soon grew up around it. Clashes between the English gentry and the Irish rebels throughout the 14th century meant that the castle didn't remain in either side's hands for long, though by the mid-1400s the MacNamara clan was firmly established there. Through marriage the castle eventually passed to the O'Briens, one of whom surrendered it to Henry VIII in 1542. The castle was abandoned during the English Civil War, and afterward only a small portion of it was lived in by the next owners, the Studderts, who soon built a Georgian mansion on the far side of the demesne.

Bunratty Castle eventually fell into terrible disrepair, making it a popular mischief-making spot with the local hooligans. In 1956 it was purchased by Lord Gort, who set about carefully restoring it with the support of the Office of Public Works. The new timber roof was modeled after that of Dunsoghly Castle in County Dublin (the only castle in the country to retain its original medieval roof).

Today the castle houses an impressive collection of tapestries, sculpture, and furniture, including a series of bizarre horned-mermaid chandeliers called *leuchterweibchen.* (Needless to say, they are of German origin. The antlers predate the carved chandeliers by thousands of years, having been preserved in the bogs.)

The castle is best known, however, for its nightly **medieval banquets** (tel. 061/360-788, reservations@shannon-dev.ie, seatings at 5:30 P.M. and 8:45 P.M. nightly year-round, €50 pp), a kitsch-filled evening of songs, storytelling, and surprisingly good food for which you must forgo eating utensils. Mostly middle-aged tour groups greatly enjoy the songs and antics of several talented young performers in motheaten velvet garb. If you purchase banquet tickets, you are entitled to a discounted admission to the castle and folk park (€8).

A reconstructed village on the castle demesne, the **folk park** is much less interesting than the castle itself; it includes furnished one- and two-room cottages, a smithy and forge, a National Schoolhouse, and several gift shops offering woolen goods, hand-thrown pottery, and other quality stuff.

If you'd like to experience a medieval banquet at Bunratty but balk at the €50 price, an alternative is **traditional Irish night** (tel. 061/360-788, reservations@shannon-dev.ie, 7 P.M. nightly Apr.–Oct., €41.50 pp), held in the folk park. As you would expect, this version is meant to show you how the *peasants* ate and entertained themselves.

There's a cozy pub called Mac's located inside the folk park, offering live traditional music on Wednesdays and weekends during the summer, and weekends only in low season. It has a less touristy atmosphere than you would expect, making it one of the more popular spots with the locals once the folk park has closed for the night. (It's still accessible, and you don't have to pay to get in.) Mac's has a less touristy feel than **Durty Nelly's** (tel. 061/364-861), a pub dating to 1620 located right beside the castle. Locals still hang out there despite the hokey decor.

If you can, visit Bunratty in the off-season, as the castle and folk park are overwhelmed by charter buses all filled to capacity April–September. If you are actively interested in medieval castles and antiques, Bunratty is definitely worth a visit. Those who are not quite as enthusiastic about museums and drafty stone fortresses, however, will most likely pass on Bunratty in view of the steep admission price and touristy atmosphere.

Shopping

There's some fine shopping to be had in Bunratty (though you'll pay top dollar for

it). Just across the River Shannon from the castle and Durty Nelly's, on the same side of the road, is the **Avoca Handweavers** shop (tel. 061/364-029, www.avoca.ie, open 9:30 A.M.–5:30 P.M. daily, 9 A.M.–6 P.M. daily June–Aug.). Avoca mohair wool blankets are among the very nicest gifts you can bring home for family and friends.

There are several shops directly across the road from the castle (the complex is called Bunratty Village Mills), the largest of which is **Blarney Woolen Mills** (tel. 061/364-321, www.blarney.com, open 9:30 A.M.–6 P.M. Mon.–Sat., 10 A.M.–6 P.M. Sun.). This store has a huge inventory of crystal, sweaters, linens, porcelain, jewelry, and so forth.

Accommodations

Shoestring travelers should stay elsewhere (or splurge on B&B). The An Óige-affiliated **Jamaica Inn** (Mount Levers, Sixmilebridge, 13 km northwest of Bunratty on the R462, tel. 061/369-220, www.jamaicainn.ie, dorms €18, doubles €25–28) is your best bet.

There are many B&Bs along the main road (the N18) within a stone's throw of the castle, in addition to upscale hotels, the most established of which is **Bunratty Castle Hotel** (tel. 061/478-700, www.bunrattycastlehotel.com, €70–150 pp, €20–40 single supplement), on a hill right across the street from the castle (behind the shopping complex).

Perhaps the nicest B&B, **Headley Court** (tel. 061/369-768, www.headleycourt.net, €35 pp), is a five-minute drive outside Bunratty proper at Minister's Cross. Headley Court boasts exceptionally comfortable rooms, good breakfasts, brand-new bathrooms with spacious showers (a definite plus), and a sitting room with lovely Gothic-inspired pointed-arch windows and a crystal collection on display. The proprietor can be a bit temperamental at times, but that's only a minor downside.

Food

If you're opting out of the medieval banquet, Durty Nelly's is one dinner option, or you could try **Kathleen's Irish Pub** inside the

Bunratty Castle Hotel. Another possibility for lunch is the café inside the Blarney Woolen Mills (tel. 061/364-321, open 9:30 A.M.–6 P.M. Mon.–Sat., 10 A.M.–6 P.M. Sun., mains around €10–12). The **Avoca Handweavers** café also does good lunches in that price range.

Information and Services

A very helpful information office is located at **Bunratty Village Mills** (tel. 061/364-321, open 9 A.M.–5:30 P.M. Mon.–Fri. Oct.–mid-May, 9 A.M.–5:30 P.M. daily mid-May–Sept.), the small shopping complex across the road from the castle. There you'll find an ATM.

Getting There and Around

Bunratty is on the Newmarket road, the N18, between Ennis (24 km) and Limerick (13 km). The Shannon Airport is only 10 kilometers west of Bunratty, and it's the Shannon taxis you'll be calling should you need one (tel. 061/471-538). The fare from Shannon to Bunratty should be no more than €9.

Bus Éireann buses run between Shannon and Limerick, passing through Bunratty up to 17 times a day. There are also plenty of southbound buses from Ennis; check the times posted at the bus stop (in front of the Fitzpatrick Bunratty Shannon Shamrock Hotel, a couple minutes' walk from the castle), or call the Ennis (tel. 065/682-4177) or Limerick (tel. 061/313-333) station for bus times.

SHANNON AIRPORT

The republic's second-largest airport (tel. 061/712-000 for information) allows for a less stressful entry into Ireland than Dublin. Shannon was once an important refuelling stop on trans-Atlantic flights, and the Irish coffee (with whiskey and cream) was invented in the airport bar.

Since the town of Shannon exists only because of the airport (and the town center consists solely of a shopping center with no free parking or worthwhile dining options), it doesn't make much sense to spend your last night here. Galway is best. Ennis and Bunratty are other popular options for your last night

in Ireland, and if you're renting a car you have even more places to choose from (Corofin, 12 km north of Ennis, is recommended).

Accommodations

In case you are one of the unfortunate souls who have missed your flight, there are a couple of accommodation options. Since you'll have to take a taxi into town from the airport anyway, you might consider staying in Bunratty, which is less than 15 minutes away. The closest hostel to the airport is the **Jamaica Inn** (Mount Levers, Sixmilebridge, 14 km northeast of the airport on the R471, tel. 061/369-220, www.jamaicainn.ie, dorms €18, doubles €25–28 pp), spic-and-span in the An Óige tradition; it also offers a restaurant. There's a shuttle service to the airport and a Bus Éireann stop nearby.

The **Shannon Great Southern Hotel** (in front of the airport, tel. 061/471-122, €150 per room) offers comfort and convenience at a price (though discounts are often available, especially in the off-season).

Food and Services

The airport itself is quite small, but the duty-free shops offer plenty of last-minute gifts, and the upstairs **Estuary Café** does decent à la carte meals. The **Bank of Ireland** (tel. 061/471-100, open 6:30 A.M.–5:30 P.M. daily) is next to the information desk in the arrivals hall. There are ATMs outside. Shannon offers free wireless Internet access, and those without laptops can avail themselves of the flatscreens (€1.50 per 15 minutes) outside Hughes & Hughes bookshop between the check-in desks and the arrivals hall. Remember to drop the rest of your postcards in the mailbox outside the bookstore; you can purchase stamps from a kiosk at the adjacent convenience store.

Getting There and Around

The Citylink and Bus Éireann stop is just to the left of the arrivals hall as you exit the airport. The **Citylink** service (tel. 091/564-163, www.citylink.ie, 5/day daily, ticket €15) to or from Galway (the best alternative to staying near the airport) takes just over an hour and a half. The

Citylink buses are usually less crowded and more comfortable. Ennis is 20 minutes from Shannon Airport on Citylink. **Bus Éireann** buses leave frequently for Limerick (#51, 8/day Mon.–Sat., 10/day Sun.); Ennis and Galway (#17 or #51, up to 12/day daily); and Cork, Killarney, Waterford, and Dublin (#16, at least 12/day Mon.–Sat., at least 6/day Sun.). Destinations on the #16 route often require a transfer at Limerick. Purchase tickets on board, or stop by the ticket desk (tel. 061/474-311, open 7 A.M.–5 P.M. daily) in the arrivals hall.

The airport is at the end of the N19, which you can pick up from the N18 coming south from Galway and Ennis or northeast from Limerick. For information on airlines operating out of Shannon, see the *Getting There* section of the *Essentials* chapter.

KILLALOE

Hardcore anglers and boaters tend to dominate the Lough Derg area in eastern Clare, and most visitors bypass it entirely for the more dramatic scenery of the Burren. But the charms of Killaloe ("kill-ah-LOO," Cill Da Lúa), a small town nestled between the hills of Slieve Bernagh and the River Shannon on the Clare-Tipperary border, merit a day or two at least. Here the Shannon draws from Lough Deirgeirt, which in turn opens into the vast Lough Derg. There are lovely views of the lough as you drive north out of Killaloe; about four kilometers up the R463 is the **University of Limerick Activity Centre,** a great resource for anyone interested in water sports on the lake.

Killaloe and the village across the bridge in County Tipperary, **Ballina,** essentially function as one town. The Clare side is certainly more picturesque, not least of all for the medieval **Killaloe Cathedral** and the boats bobbing gently in the dark waters below. A scenic overlook at the end of Ballina's main street provides a fine opportunity for picture-taking.

Sights

At the bottom of Church Street stands the 12th-century, now-Anglican **Killaloe Cathedral,** whose finest feature is its Hi-

berno-Romanesque south doorway, a strange and ornate combination of chevrons, zigzags, and individualized human and animal heads. It's possible this doorway was moved here from another church. The cathedral is bisected by a wood-and-Plexiglas wall that separates the renovated church from the artifacts (a high cross taken from Kilfenora, an 11th-century ogham stone that also has a Scandinavian runic inscription, and the south doorway) in the cold, spooky, whitewashed antechamber. Among the gravestones outside is **St. Flannan's Oratory** with its steep pitched roof, also dating to the 12th century, which features a simpler Romanesque doorway on its western side.

On the opposite end of Church Street is the 10th-century **St. Molua's Oratory,** located beside St. Flannan's Catholic Church. What's so unusual about this oratory is that this is not its original location: It once stood on Friar's Island on the River Shannon, and was dissembled and reconstructed here in 1929 and 1930 after the damming of the river (at which point the island was submerged) as part of a new hydroelectric scheme. St. Flannan's has a rather creepy proliferation of painted plaster statues but is worth a peek for its three marvelous Harry Clarke windows, two flanking the altar and one on the southern wall.

Shopping

Both sides of the river have a few quaint little shops. Quaintest of all is the aptly named **An Siopa Beag** ("The Small Shop," Italian Warehouse, Main St., Killaloe, tel. 061/375-770, open Tues.–Sat. 10 A.M.–5 P.M.), a delightful hodgepodge of toys, colorful plant-dyed yarns, art supplies, eco-friendly clothing, and books on New Age and progressive topics.

Sports and Recreation

Killaloe is a great spot for water sports and horseback riding. For windsurfing, kayaking, sailing, and canoeing on Lough Derg, head up to the **University of Limerick Activity Centre** (Two Mile Gate, 4 km north of Killaloe on the R463, tel. 061/376-622, www.ulac.ie).

© CAMILLE DE ANGELIS

St. Molua's Oratory was moved from an island in the Shannon to this Killaloe church.

Those who'd like to fish for brown trout, pike, and bream on Lough Derg or along the Shannon should stop by **T.J.'s Angling Centre** (Main St., Ballina, tel. 061/376-009). The **Lough Derg Equestrian Centre** is on the Tipperary side (10 km south of Ballina, signposted on the R463, tel. 061/376-144 or 086/263-1361).

Two long-distance walking trails also pass through the town: the 180-kilometer circular **East Clare Way,** which passes through Mountshannon and other villages near Lough Derg's western shore, as well as the 65-kilometer **Lough Derg Way** from Limerick to Dromineer, of which Killaloe is the midway point. If a short leisurely stroll is more your thing, there are lovely paved paths along both sides of the river.

Accommodations

Killaloe is popular with weekenders as well as tourists, so it's wise to book ahead even in the off-season. The rooms at central **Lyons B&B** (Church St., Killaloe, tel. 061/376-652, €30 pp)

are immaculately clean without feeling at all antiseptic. You won't find a more pristine bed- and bathroom in a five-star hotel. It's a great value.

Another fine option nine kilometers north of Killaloe is **Lantern House** (Ogonnelloe, Killaloe, tel. 061/923-034, open mid-Feb.–Dec., €34 pp). Guests at this modern B&B can savor the idyllic location above Lough Derg and the excellent modern Irish cuisine in the adjacent restaurant (open 6–9 P.M. daily, mains €10–24).

Food and Entertainment

Dining options are surprisingly good for such a small place. Speedy service and plenty of vegetarian options make the airy, cheerful **Coffee Pot and Deli** (Derg House, Bridge St., Killaloe, tel. 061/375-599, open 8 A.M.–5 P.M. Mon.–Sat., 9 A.M.–4 P.M. Sun., breakfast €4–6, lunches €4–8.50) a fine spot for breakfast (served all day), lunch, or tea. On the Ballina side, another equally good lunch option is **Simply Delicious** (Main St., tel. 061/375-335, open 8:30 A.M.–6 P.M. daily, lunches under €8).

Most of the pubs in Killaloe and Ballina

serve good pub grub. Particularly popular with the locals are the thatched-roof, somewhat pricey **Gooser's** (Main St., Ballina, tel. 061/376-792, open 10:30 A.M.–10:30 P.M. daily, pub meals under €12, dinner mains €20–35) and **Molly's** (Main St., Ballina, tel. 061/376-632, food served noon–9 P.M., mains €10–20), which also has a nightclub downstairs on the weekends. **Crotty's** (Main St., Killaloe, tel. 061/376-965, mains €11–23) has an ivy-clad beer-garden entryway and a seafood-heavy menu. All three of these pubs offer live trad (usually on weekends), but they're not as formally scheduled as **The Anchor Inn** (tel. 061/376-108, Bridge St., Killaloe), which has a regular session on Wednesday night.

Information and Services

The **tourist office** (tel. 061/376-866, open 10 A.M.–6 P.M. daily mid-May–mid-Sept.), **Heritage Centre** (tel. 061/376-866, same hours, admission €2), and **public library** (tel. 061/376-062, open 10 A.M.–1:30 P.M. and 2:30–5:30 P.M. Mon., Tues., and Thurs., 10 A.M.–5:30 P.M. and 6:30–8 P.M. Wed. and Fri., 10 A.M.–2 P.M. Sat.) are all housed in the same building, The Lock House, on Bridge Street. The library offers free Internet access.

There's an ATM at the **AIB** (at the southern end of Church St., Killaloe, tel. 061/376-115). The **post office** (tel. 061/376-111) is on Church Street on the Killaloe side. **Collins' Pharmacy** (tel. 061/375-505) is on Ballina's Main Street.

Getting There and Around

Killaloe and Ballina are only 23 kilometers northeast of Limerick City on the R463. The Limerick–Birr **Bus Éireann** route (#323, tel. 061/313-333) passes through both towns, with at least four daily in each direction. It is necessary to take the bus back to Limerick for all other destinations.

If you need a taxi, ring **Margaret Coughlan** (tel. 087/264-4365).

MOUNTSHANNON

On the western shore of Lough Derg 26 kilometers north of Killaloe is the pleasant village of Mountshannon. The tourism here is geared toward serious boaters and anglers, and those whose interests lie elsewhere will feel pretty well out of the loop. Anglers should note the row of boat rental kiosks at the Mountshannon pier; if unattended, there will be a contact number posted on the door. Alternatively, you can contact **Michael Waterstone** (tel. 061/921-328), a local guide who also hires boats. Mountshannon does have one sight of general interest, however: **Holy Island,** two kilometers out on Lough Derg, on which lie the remains of a monastic settlement founded by yet another obscure saint, Cáimín, in the 7th century. Its ruined round tower, four churches, and medieval graveyard are worth a visit. If you're interested in making a day trip out to Holy Island, contact **Ireland Line Cruises** (Killaloe, tel. 061/375-011, late Apr.–Oct., tickets €7).

The Clare Coast

The Clare coastline is less haunting—but no less lovely—than the shores of Dingle or Connemara. Kilrush is an excellent spot for water sports, and Loop Head to the west affords tremendous views of both the Galway and Kerry coasts. Walking the periphery of Clare's westernmost tip is cold, windy, and truly exhilarating, especially since there aren't many others to have to share it with.

Driving north from Loop Head, you'll pass the super-touristy sea resort of Kilkee; the musical Miltown-Malbay and the sandy Spanish Point; another resort town, Lahinch, rather unappealing due to a proliferation of fast-food joints and identical pastel holiday homes, but a mecca for surfers; the fishing village of Liscannor; the famous Cliffs of Moher; and Doolin, whose three pubs offer great traditional music, still sublime for all its popularity. There isn't too much—people-wise, that is—when you get north of Doolin, but it's an awfully scenic drive through the tiny village of Fanore up to craggy Black Head on the R477 before turning southeast toward the pleasant harbor town of Ballyvaughan, "Gateway to the Burren."

KILRUSH

Situated on the Shannon estuary in southwestern Clare, Kilrush (Cill Rois) is a pleasant town whose scenic harbor fills with boaters and sailboarders in the summer months. People are friendly here, and resources for tourists are more than adequate, but its laid-back, workaday atmosphere makes Kilrush an especially appealing destination. The tourist office doesn't go overboard advertising the town's virtues, a refreshing change from the resort towns on Clare's west coast. Because water sports are its primary draw, Kilrush is actually something of a ghost town in the fall and winter months. Once you've dolphin-watched, windsurfed, and taken a stroll through the "lost" gardens on the old Vandeleur estate, you can use Kilrush as a base for exploring the delightfully remote Loop Head.

The town hub is Market Square, with a roundabout encircling the 19th-century Town Hall. From the west, the N67 drops you into Henry Street, which leads down to the square; broad Frances Street leads you from the bottom of the square out to the marina.

Sights

Two hundred years ago the Vandeleur family dominated every aspect of life in Kilrush. In the post-famine era, Hector Vandeleur treated his tenants without mercy, forcing 20,000 out of their homes onto boats bound for the New World. Today the late-18th-century **Vandeleur Walled Garden** (the Killimer road, 10 A.M.–6 P.M. daily Apr.–Oct., 10 A.M.–4 P.M. daily Nov.–Mar., admission €5), just over two acres, is newly restored and open to the public. Surrounded by 420 woodland acres, this garden with its high stone wall features tousled flowerbeds of white poppies and

purple daisies, a beech maze, and a new glasshouse for the nurturing of young specimens. If gardens and tearooms are your thing, you shouldn't miss this. And if you're interested in the garden's historic importance, check out the "Kilrush in Landlord Times" exhibit at the Heritage Centre.

Kilrush's Catholic church, **St. Senan's** (Toler St., off Frances St., tel. 065/905-1093), is known for its Harry Clarke windows.

Sports and Recreation

The **Kilrush Creek Adventure Centre** (on the marina, tel. 065/905-2855, www.kcac.nav.to, open 10 A.M.–4:30 P.M. daily, full/half day activities €60/35 pp) will equip you for all imaginable water sports (kayaking, sailing, windsurfing) as well as archery. To get here, follow Frances Street away from Market Square. You'll see the center just across the bridge at the end of the street.

April–October, you can go **dolphin-watching** (Scattery Island Ferries, Kilrush Creek Marina, tel. 065/905-1327, www.discoverdolphins.ie, 2-hour trip €18) on the Shannon Estuary, which is home to more than 100 of our lithe flippered friends. The boat is pretty high-tech—there's even a hydrophone through which you can hear the dolphins underwater, clucking their tongues at you. In high season there are four trips a day.

Kilrush Wood is just east of town on the Killimer road, surrounding the Vandeleur Walled Garden. It's a tranquil spot for short walk and a picnic lunch.

Accommodations

Budget travelers should stay at the IHH-affiliated **Katie O'Connor's Holiday Hostel** (Frances St., tel. 065/905-1133 or 065/908-0831, katieoconnors@eircom.net, open mid-Mar.–Oct., dorms €14.50–15.50, doubles €17–17.50), a central family-run townhouse with 28 beds. Quarters are close but cozy, and the owners provide thorough information on every imaginable activity in Kilrush.

Two superior guesthouses are ◀ **Hillcrest View** (Doonbeg Rd., tel. 065/905-1986, www.hillcrestview.com, €28–35 pp, s €40–50) and ◖ **Clarke's,** also known as **Bruach na Coille** (Killimer Rd., tel. 065/905-2250, www.clarkekilrush.com, €28–36 pp, s €35–50, credit cards accepted), a Georgian house directly opposite the Vandeleur Walled Garden. Both are a couple minutes' drive outside town and are open year-round (unlike many other B&Bs in the area). They are immaculate family homes, elegantly but comfortably furnished, with excellent breakfasts and all the little amenities you would expect at a hotel. Proprietors Ethna Hynes and Mary Clarke are kind and full of helpful information, including an introductory video on western Clare.

Food and Entertainment

There aren't a lot of great eating options in Kilrush, sadly. The coffee shop at the **Vandeleur Walled Garden** (Killimer Rd., tel. 065/905-1760, open 10 A.M.–6 P.M. daily Apr.–Oct., 10 A.M.–4 P.M. daily Nov.–Mar., lunches under €8) is a nice spot for tea or a light lunch, and **Coffey's Café and Pizzeria** (Market Sq., tel. 065/905-1170, open 12:30–9 P.M. daily, mains €3–12) does decent pizzas and sandwiches.

The best pub-cum-restaurant in town is **Kelly's Steak and Seafood House** (26 Henry St., tel. 065/905-1811, food served 11 A.M.–9:30 P.M. Mon.–Sat., 12:30–9:30 P.M. Sun., lunches under €10, dinners €10–24), with hearty, unpretentious fare and friendly service in a warm atmosphere. Despite the name, Kelly's does offer a few decent vegetarian options. There's live trad Saturday nights starting at 10 P.M.

Another option is the comparable pub grub a few doors down at the **Haven Arms** (Henry St., tel. 065/905-1267, food served noon–9:30 P.M., lunches €8–16, dinners €10–24).

Other pubs with live music on the weekends include **O'Looney's** (John St., tel. 065/905-1349) and **Percy French** (Moore St., tel. 065/905-1615).

The Saturday **farmers market** (Market Sq., 10 A.M.–2 P.M.) provides healthy snacks as well as atmosphere.

Information and Services

The Kilrush **tourist office** (tel. 065/905-1577, www.kilrush.ie, open 10 A.M.–1 P.M. and 2–6 P.M. Mon.–Sat. late May–Aug.) and the mildly interesting **Heritage Centre** (tel. 065/905-1596, open 10 A.M.–6 P.M. Mon.–Fri., noon–4 P.M. weekends June–Aug., admission €3) are both in the Market House. Two tourism websites, **Irish Heritage Towns** (www.heritagetowns.com/kilrush.html) and the **Kilrush Chamber of Commerce** (www.westclare.com), are loaded with useful information.

ATMs are available at the **Bank of Ireland** (corner of Francis St. and Toler St., tel. 065/905-1083) and **AIB** (Francis St., tel. 065/905-1012).

The **post office** (Frances St., tel. 065/905-1077) is located in a surprisingly spacious building. Internet access is available at the **public library** (O'Gorman St., around the corner from St. Senan's Church on Toler St., tel. 065/905-1504).

If you need a pharmacy, try **Malone's** (Frances St., tel. 065/905-2552).

Getting There and Around

Kilrush is on the N67, 44 kilometers southwest of Ennis. Bus Éireann routes #15 and #336 go from Limerick to Kilrush and Kilkee via Ennis (at least 7 daily). In summer, route #50 between Galway and Cork passes through Kilrush and other coastal towns (2 daily).

A handy shortcut, if you want to get from Clare to Kerry without driving back through Shannon and Limerick, is the **Killimer Car Ferry** (Killimer, tel. 065/905-3124, www.shannonferries.com, single/return €15/25 with car, €4/6 pedestrians and cyclists), which connects Killimer (8.5 km east of Kilrush) with Tarbert in northern Kerry. Sailings are hourly in wintertime and more frequent in high season, and the trip takes only 20 minutes (and saves you 137 km).

For a taxi, ring **Joe Cropera** (tel. 087/252-8888).

You can rent a bicycle from **Gleeson's** (Henry St., tel. 065/905-1127, €20/day, €80/week, €40 deposit).

SCATTERY ISLAND

Home to the remains of St. Senan's 6th-century monastery as well as a host of birds (at least 31 species have been counted), wildflowers, rabbits, goats, and gray seals, treeless Scattery—just a kilometer or so long—is an otherwise uninhabited island three kilometers out from the Kilrush pier. Legend has it that a sea serpent called the Cathach terrorized the locals until Senan banished it, miraculously, to a lake far north in County Mayo. The only trace left of the monster is the island's name, Inis Cathaigh, "Island of the Cathach" (sometimes mistranslated as "Island of the Battles," which is still accurate in light of the bloodthirsty Vikings' 9th-century raids). Today, Scattery makes a lovely afternoon trip from Kilrush and is a must-see for avid birdwatchers (the 31 species include oystercatchers and ringed plovers, both of which breed on the island) as well as those looking for a beautiful escape from the Cliffs of Moher–Doolin–Bunratty tourist circuit.

Ruins

The monastic ruins include five churches, an 24-meter round tower with conical stone roof intact (and, unusually, a ground-level doorway, which allows you to see all the way up to the roof). The most intriguing of the five churches is the Romanesque cathedral east of the round tower, which features antae projecting from the west wall. The other four are the part-early-Christian, part-medieval Church of the Hill of the Angel (southwest of the cathedral and round tower); the 14th- or 15th-century Church of the Dead, toward the eastern side of the island; Senan's Temple, medieval and much ruined; and a nameless smaller Romanesque nave-and-chancel oratory, just north of the round tower, mostly dating to the 1100s (though, as you can see, it was partially rebuilt in the 19th century).

There are also ruins of a Napoleonic-era battery, a holy well, and the village of the island's last inhabitants, who left Scattery for good in 1978.

Getting There

Passage is available only in summer through **Scattery Island Ferries** (tel. 065/905-1237,

tickets €12), which operates from the Kilrush Creek Marina. The trip out to Scattery takes only 20 minutes, but the sailing schedule is unfixed, so it's essential to ring ahead or at least stop by the ferry office at the marina.

Before you depart, check out the **Scattery Island Interpretive Centre** (Merchants Quay, Kilrush, tel. 065/905-2144, scatteryisland@ealga.ie, open 10 A.M.–1 P.M. and 2–6 P.M. daily June–Sept., free admission). The Dúchas-run interpretive center offers an informative exhibit on the island's ruins and wildlife.

THE LOOP HEAD PENINSULA

County Clare's westernmost tip makes a splendid afternoon drive, dotted with quiet hamlets and placid ocean panoramas, and punctuated by the lighthouse at Loop Head. "Loop" is actually a corruption of "Leap": One legend says the warrior Cuchulainn jumped from the cliff at the end of this peninsula to dodge Mal, the frightening and powerful beldam-goddess (who also inspired "Malbay" and "Hag's Head"); the other legend says it was Diarmuid and Gráinne who leaped while escaping her vengeful husband.

The nearest town is Kilkee, but unfortunately this resort town's old Victorian charms have given way to perpetual construction sites. Kilrush's tourism is more discreet, making it a nicer base.

Kilkee

Divers may want to visit Kilkee, 13 kilometers northwest of Kilrush on the N67, for its splendid sea caves. There are arches and stacks along this stretch of coast, and explorers will find plenty of geological interest beneath the waves as well. There's not a whole lot in terms of underwater life, however, though you may be able to spot a lobster or eel. **Kilkee Diving and Watersports Centre** (George's Head, tel. 065/905-6707, www.diveireland.com) can take you out to the caves on a rigid inflatable boat. Sailors, dolphin-watchers, and sea-anglers are also catered to.

Carrigaholt

The tiny village of Carrigaholt on the peninsula's southern side offers **dolphin-watching** excursions out at sea (Dolphinwatch, tel. 065/905-8156). There's also a swimmable strand just east of the village.

Kilbaha

The last village on the peninsula, Kilbaha, has a fascinating and unique piece of history within its small church: a "little ark" built by an intrepid priest named Michael Meehan in the mid-1850s to circumvent the Penal Laws (some Protestant landowners evidently paid no attention to the Catholic Emancipation Act of 1829). Celebration of the Mass was still forbidden by the local landlord, but when Father Meehan brought this tiny floating church just a few yards out at sea to say Mass for a few parishioners at a time, the landlord couldn't touch him. **The Church of the Little Ark,** clearly signposted from Keating's pub on the main Kilbaha street, has the floating ark on display in a side room. The altar and bible stand remain, and there's even a bit of patterned wallpaper still stuck to the back wall. If you're doing Loop Head Drive, you should definitely make a brief stop here.

Loop Head

Loop Head is crowned by a lighthouse that isn't open to the public. There is, however, an unpaved path from a car park beside the lighthouse around the edge of the peninsula that makes for a short but exhilarating walk of half an hour. You'll enjoy mist-swathed views of the Dingle Peninsula (the tallest peak is Mount Brandon) and the Blaskets to the south, and Connemara and the Aran Islands to the north. Approach the cliff edge with caution, as the winds can be gusty.

CENTRAL CLARE COAST
Miltown Malbay

Can't get enough of that trad? Miltown Malbay, an erstwhile Victorian resort town 32 kilometers south of Doolin (now with a slightly run-down air), hosts a tremendously popular **traditional music school and festival** (tel. 065/708-4148, early July, www.setdancingnews.net/wcss) in honor of

Willie Clancy, a native of the town and one of the country's best-ever uilleann pipers. There's good music and *craic* to be had in the pubs year-round, especially at **O'Friel's** (The Square, tel. 065/708-4275). This fine old-fashioned pub was once the home of Willie Clancy himself.

If you're passing through Miltown Malbay, a good spot for lunch is **The Old Bake House Restaurant** (Main St., tel. 065/708-4350, open noon–3 P.M. daily, 6–9 P.M. Tues.–Thurs., 6–10 P.M. Fri. and Sat., noon–8 P.M. Sun., lunches around €10, dinner mains €11–20). The walls at this laid-back eatery feature photography and oil paintings by local artists. The menu is diverse, the portions large, and the service excellent.

Spanish Point

Two kilometers west of Miltown Malbay is Spanish Point, which has a scenic beach. The waves there are rough, however, and swimming is not recommended if a lifeguard isn't on duty. The novelist Kate O'Brien, who spent her childhood summers at nearby Kilkee, wrote of nuns from convents all over the county spending their holiday at Spanish Point. O'Brien noted that they were often the only visitors brave enough to dive into those churning waves.

Lahinch

Twenty kilometers southeast of Doolin, Lahinch is Clare's most popular resort town. Like Kilkee, the place is extremely overdeveloped, far from the best the Clare coast has to offer. Surfers will disregard this advice, however, as the best waves are to be found here. Rent a surfboard and hire an instructor (if necessary) at the **Lahinch Surf Shop** (on the promenade, tel. 065/708-1543, www.lahinchsurfshop.com).

If you do want the resort experience, the best place to indulge yourself is the newly renovated, four-star **Lahinch Golf & Leisure Hotel** (Main St., tel. 065/708-1100, www.lahinchgolfandleisurehotel.com, €55–105 pp, s €75–125), which offers sleek, modern bedrooms and a 17-meter swimming pool and gymnasium on site—though contrary to the name, there isn't actually a golf course on site; it's a few minutes' drive out of town. Most surfers stay at the clean and sociable (read: noisy) **Lahinch Hostel** (Church St., tel. 065/708-1040, www. visitlahinch.com, dorms €15–17), within a few minutes' walk of the beach.

Liscannor

Liscannor (Lios Ceannúir) is a small fishing village just south of the Cliffs of Moher on the R478, at the end (or start) of the Burren Way. There are a couple of reasons to linger here for an afternoon in the summertime: the safe and sandy beach, Clahane, just west of the village, and, for equestrians, the **Cliffs of Moher Pony Trekking Center** (tel. 065/708-1283).

Backpackers will want to stay at the IHH-affiliated **Liscannor Hostel** (on the northern end of the village, tel. 065/708-1550, liscannorvillagehostel@eircom.net, open Apr.–Oct., dorms €12–16).

Aside from the hostel, another recommended accommodation is the **Moher Lodge Farmhouse** (tel. 065/708-1269, moherlodge@ eircom.net, open Apr.–Oct., €33 pp, s €40), three kilometers north of Liscannor on the road to the Cliffs of Moher; it offers the traditional Irish welcome along with amazing sea views.

The village itself is rather featureless, though it does boast an outstanding seafood restaurant, **Vaughan's Anchor Inn** (Main St., tel. 065/708-1548, www.vaughansanchorinn.com, food served noon–9:30 P.M. daily, lunch mains €9–13, dinners €18–23). There isn't even one vegetarian option, unfortunately.

On your way up to the cliffs from Liscannor, you'll see a tall stone pillar on the left side of the road. This marks St. Brigid's Well, a local pilgrimage site.

Ennistymon

Located at the junction of the N67 and the N85 in western Clare, Ennistymon (Inis Díomáin) is a pleasant enough place, but there's not much to keep you here. **The Cascades,** a small wa-

terfall on the River Inagh, are the town's prime diversion, reachable through an archway at the end of the town's main street. The surrounding construction sites have (albeit temporarily) marred its prettiness, however.

Because Doolin, Lisdoonvarna, and other popular destinations don't have banks, Ennistymon makes a good pit stop for a withdrawal from the ATM at the **AIB** (Main St., tel. 065/707-1018).

You might check your email at the **public library** (signposted off the square, tel. 065/707-1245), which offers free access.

◖ THE CLIFFS OF MOHER

This world-famous sight is a series of dramatic, mist-shrouded cliffs rising as high as 200 meters above the waves. This is one of Ireland's loveliest natural wonders. From the car park and visitor center a stone walkway leads out to the cliffs, where you can continue on a short walk pretty darn near the edge, looking south to the cliffs themselves and out at the glittering sea. It's not wise to hop the railings, as tourists have been blown off the edge. And expect crowds even in low season and foul weather—and in the fog and rain keep in mind that you may not be able to see anything. If the weather report is hopeless, consider driving to the Cliffs another day. Regardless of the time of year, you'll have fewer fellow tourists if you arrive before 9 A.M.

As you finish your walk up the main pathway toward the cliff edge, you'll spot **O'Brien's Castle** (open 9:30 A.M.–6 P.M. Mar.–Oct., admission €1) This small round tower may look medieval, but it was built in 1835. The view's just as good from the ground, so save that euro for that busker on the banjo braving the chilly winds.

Hag's Head Walk

From the Cliffs of Moher you can take the six-kilometer Hag's Head Walk south to the end of the Hag's Head peninsula, 134 meters above the waves at its pinnacle. It's a windy hike on an unpaved path, but the view of the cliffs and ocean is well worth the three-plus hours there

© CAMILLE DEANGELIS

Visitors take "living on the edge" literally at the Cliffs of Moher.

pin turns on the local roads. The tour buses start pulling in after 9 A.M., so try to arrive at least half an hour earlier to enjoy the view in peace and quasi-solitude. The first bus of the day leaves Doolin for the cliffs at 8 A.M. (arriving at 8:30). Those driving will pay €4 to park in the lot. On your way up to the cliffs you'll spot the 15th-century **Doonagore Castle,** built by the O'Briens and privately owned.

Not satisfied with the view from the summit? The **Cliffs of Moher Cruises** (The Pier, tel. 065/707-6060 or 087/245-3239, www.mohercruises.com, tickets €20) leave Doolin at least twice daily between Easter and September (and the village of Liscannor once daily), but departure times can vary. Try the office number for a recorded message the night before you wish to sail. Most sailings are round-trip, departing and arriving in Doolin (though the first and last trips of the day are one-way, with a shuttle bus returning you to the starting point).

DOOLIN

It might seem strange at first, flocking to a small village in rural County Clare to listen to world-class musicians, but once you've arrived you'll forget your skepticism. Music-makers from other countries often come to Doolin (Duláinn) with their guitars or fiddles in tow, spending every night in the pubs joining in the trad session. Even if you're not a musician, there's something exciting about watching a new friend you've just shared a pint with open her fiddle case and, after a warm invitation, start playing right alongside the regulars. Purpose-built B&Bs and holiday cottages have been sprouting like dandelions the last few years, yet Doolin seems to have retained most of its charm despite its burgeoning popularity. One can only hope the village remains as attractive through the ongoing construction.

Doolin comprises two villages: Fisherstreet, the lower village, and Roadford, the upper village. The lower village is closer to the harbor (about a kilometer and a half), and the upper village is across the Aille River bridge, on the way to Black Head and the village of Fanore. It

and back, especially since you'll meet very few people along the way. A ruined signal tower on the head was erected by the Brits in the early 19th century (fearing an attack by Napoleon); it lies on the site of a prehistoric promontory fort called **Mothar.** Now you know how the cliffs got their name.

Information and Services

The Cliffs of Moher **visitors center** (tel. 065/708-1171, open 9:30 A.M.–5:30 P.M. daily Mar.–Oct.) offers tourist info as well as the usual café and gift shop.

A new visitors center—a circular, ultramodern structure built into one of the hills so as to better integrate with the landscape—is due to open in 2007.

Getting There

Doolin makes the best base when visiting the Cliffs of Moher. From the village it's a brisk eight-kilometer uphill bike or walk, no more than a 10-minute drive, and nearly a half hour on the bus with all those hair-

takes 10–15 minutes to walk from one village to the other. Be sure to pack a flashlight—at night that road is darker than pitch. On a clear evening, though, all the constellations twinkle brilliantly.

Doolin is technically inside the Burren and is on the Burren Way, but the land is lush. Travel north or east, though, and you'll see that fissured limestone landscape—or is it moonscape?—tumbling out almost as far as the eye can see.

O'Connor's Pub

Hands down, O'Connor's (lower village, tel. 065/707-4168, www.oconnorspubdoolin.com) offers the best traditional music sessions in the county (and the best pub grub, too). Founded in 1832, it's also the oldest of Doolin's three watering holes. West Clare has always been especially known for its musical heritage—many of its natives, like whistler Micho Russell (from Doolin) and piper Willie Clancy (from Miltown Malbay), came from "musical families" and became internationally revered (and today, annual music festivals celebrate their legacies). The village is even home to its own trad record company.

At O'Connor's, the circle of musicians in the back of the pub can swell to over a dozen, and many of these music-makers have come here on vacation (because they've heard Doolin, and specifically O'Connor's, is the place to join in on a session). Other fiddlers and guitarists are well known among the regulars. With its low ceilings and open fires, the place still feels cozy and welcoming no matter how crowded it gets at night (and the owners have provided microphones for the performers so you can enjoy the music even if you can only find a table in the front room). Even in wintertime, you can find at least one talented guitar-strumming ballad singer every evening. In sum, you'll meet people from all over Europe, Australia, and the Americas while listening to some of the best live music Ireland has to offer.

Other Entertainment

The two other pubs in Doolin both offer food and nightly traditional music sessions in high season. In all the pubs, a main course at lunch will run you €12 or less, dinner €10–20.

McGann's (upper village, tel. 065/707-4133, www.esatclear.ie/~mcgannsdoolin) is good for a hearty meal—and note that if you are looking for a late dinner, McGann's is the safer bet, as it continues serving food a little past 9:30 P.M. (If you go to O'Connor's hoping for a meal at half-nine, they'll charge you an exorbitant amount for an undelectable toasted cheese sandwich.)

Many locals prefer the third pub, **McDermott's** (upper village, tel. 065/707-4328, www.mcdermottspubdoolin.com), which has more of a "corner bar" feel than the others. It also offers good pub grub, nightly trad sessions in high season, and weekend sessions in the winter months. McDermott's is the only pub of the three with a dartboard in the off-season, though it's only open weekends in winter.

Shopping

Doolin has an excellent crafts store and tearoom, the **Doolin Craft Gallery** (the Lisdoonvarna road, tel. 065/707-4688, www.doolincrafts.com, open 10 A.M.–6 P.M. Tues.–Sun., café open Easter–Christmas), filled with gorgeous sweaters, jewelry, and other fine souvenirs. The pottery selection is particularly noteworthy, and the owners are quite proud of the fact that Hillary Clinton shopped here as First Lady.

County Clare's first trad record company, **Magnetic Music** (Fisherstreet, tel. 065/707-4988, www.magnetic-music.com, open 10 A.M.–6 P.M. or later daily Easter–mid-Oct.), has a shop and café a few doors down from O'Connor's pub. The CD selection is sizable, as you would expect, and the cottage ("Ireland's most westerly coffee and music shop") is a popular concert venue, hosting Irish and international artists. Stop in for a list of what's on.

Sports and Recreation

Doolin is roughly midway along the 45-kilometer Burren Way (see the sidebar *The Burren Way* for more information).

Several hidden spots in the vicinity are suitable for diving and caving. The University of Bristol Speleological Society first explored the Doolin cave system in 1953, noting its length of 10.5 kilometers and network of rivers worn through the limestone. Access is via the **"Fisherstreet Potholes"** in an inconspicuous location near the Aille River Hostel; ask at your hostel or B&B for precise directions. Seawise, there's a network of undersea caves called the **Green Holes of Doolin,** beneath the rocks just to the north of the harbor. As there are no commercial caving or diving outfits in the area, the potholes and undersea caves should only be attempted by experienced spelunkers. There is, however, the **Doolin Activity Lodge** (nearer the Fisherstreet end, on the left side as you head toward the pier, tel. 065/707-4888, www.doolinlodge.com), which offers caving excursions in addition to horseback riding, guided walks and bike trips, kayaking, and deep-sea and lake angling. It's part of a brand-new tourist complex offering B&B and a substandard restaurant, however, so backpackers and other independent types might want to avoid it. It's a good choice for families, though.

Accommodations

There's no shortage of accommodations here. The vast majority of the purpose-built B&Bs along the main roads were erected very recently, and more are going up all the time.

The backpacking set's favorite place to crash is the **⟨ Aille River Hostel** (tel. 065/707-4260, www.esatclear.ie/~ailleriver, dorms €13–14, private room €33, camping €7, open mid-Mar.–Dec.), a converted 17th-century farmhouse that offers a cozy sitting room by the open turf fire (and plenty of board games and paperbacks), free laundry, Internet access (€1.50 per 15 minutes), bike rental, and decent beds.

Another highly recommended place is the cozy, family-run **⟨ Rainbow Hostel** (tel. 065/707-4415, rainbowhostel@eircom.net, dorms €13, no private rooms), on the Roadford side of the bridge (near McDermott's and McGann's). The Rainbow also offers bike rental, nice beds, and a cozy skylit sitting room with a turf fire. Another option is **Flanagan's Village Hostel** (tel. 065/707-4564, dorms €12.50–13.50, private rooms €15–17), an airy, family-run establishment farther removed from the upper village. It's farther from the pubs, but the owners are welcoming and the place is clean and comfortable.

Paddy's Doolin Hostel (tel. 065/707-4006, www.doolinhostel.com, open Feb.–Oct., dorms €14–15, private rooms €19–20), right across the street from the bus stop, is better than adequate (and so convenient), but the other hostels are cozier and more atmospheric (with turf fires and so forth).

The following B&Bs have all been around a while, so their atmospheres are quite homey.

⟨ The Rainbow's End (tel. 065/707-4415, rainbowhostel@eircom.net, €30–32 pp), next door to the Rainbow Hostel and owned by the same friendly couple, Carmel and Mattie, offers comfortable rooms (some with skylights) and gorgeous handcrafted woodwork designed and installed by the owner. Furthermore, Mattie offers a slide show for interested hostel and B&B guests. His photographs are outstanding, and his knowledge exceeds that of many professional tour guides. Mattie also does Burren walks free of charge in the summertime.

Also recommended is **Atlantic View** (tel. 065/707-4189 or 065/707-4980, atlanview@eircom.net, €35–45 pp), which is less than a 10-minute walk past the lower village down toward the pier. There's a lovely little library upstairs tucked into an alcove, and as you might imagine, the views from the bedrooms are incomparable. Atlantic View also accepts credit cards, a plus if you're running low on euros. The only downside is a sizable single supplement.

Another recommended B&B, for those on more of a budget, is **Doolin Cottage** (tel. 065/707-4762, €25 pp, open Mar.–Nov.), a cozy, unpretentious little place behind the Aille River Hostel between the upper and lower villages. The cottage's proprietor welcomes drop-ins for breakfast along with its own guests (a fine option for hostellers) and is very accommodating for vegetarians.

Book ahead at all these B&Bs, as they all offer only a half dozen or so rooms.

Food

Outside of the pubs (see *Entertainment*) there aren't many options for food, but two highly recommended eateries have been around for years. One is **Bruach na hAille** ("Bridge over the River Aille," Roadford, tel. 065/707-4120, doolinrestaurant.port5.com, open 6–10 P.M. Thurs.–Sat., 10 A.M.–4 P.M. Sun. mid-Mar.–Oct., mains €12–26, reservations recommended), which offers excellent Continental fare in a lace-tablecloth kind of atmosphere rescued from formality by a cheerful open fire. The other is ◖ **Doolin Café** (Roadford, near McDermott's and McGann's, tel. 065/707-4795, mains €15–22, posted hours noon–3 P.M. and 6–10 P.M., open Mar.–Dec., no credit cards), a relaxed little place offering organic veggies, fresh seafood, and other delights. This café is many locals' favorite spot, although the opening hours can be maddeningly inconsistent.

Information and Services

Doolin's only bureau de change is at Paddy's Doolin Hostel in the lower village. There is no bank (or tourist office) in Doolin, so hit the ATM in Ennis, Ennistymon, or Galway first. If you have any questions—about the Burren, the Cliffs of Moher, the pubs, or anything else—just remember that your B&B or hostel hosts are nearly always fonts of useful information.

Two spots for Internet access are the **Aille River Hostel** and an Internet café at the **Doolin Activity Lodge** (between Roadford and Fisherstreet, tel. 065/707-4888, www.doolinlodge.com, open 8 A.M.–10 P.M. daily).

Before you go, check out the helpful **Doolin Tourism** website (www.doolin-tourism.com).

Getting There and Around

Buses stop outside Paddy's Doolin Hostel in the lower village several times a day (the schedule is posted at the stop); most continue either to Ennis or Galway City. From Galway, the route #50 bus will take you directly to Doolin, and from Ennis and Limerick it's route #337.

Those coming from Dublin on the #12 bus will change at Limerick.

Beginning at 8 A.M., buses stop outside Paddy's Doolin Hostel before continuing on to the Cliffs of Moher. This is your best bet if you'd rather not hike, bike, or drive it. Do try to catch the first bus of the morning so as to beat the tour buses—you'll be glad you set your alarm.

You can rent a bike from Paddy's Doolin Hostel, **The Doolin Bike Store** (affiliated with, and adjacent to, the Aille River Hostel), or the Rainbow's End Hostel and B&B; the cost is €12 per day across the board. (Note that you may be out of luck if you want to rent a bike before the end of March.)

Doolin Ferries (The Pier, tel. 065/707-4455 or 065/707-4466, fax 065/707-4417, www.doolinferries.com, €25 return to Inis Oírr, €35 return to Inis Mór) can take you to the Aran Islands between Easter and September (though sailings are more subject to weather conditions than the ferries out of Rossaveal in County Galway). If the kiosk at the pier is closed, call or stop in at the nearby Atlantic View B&B (tel. 065/707-4189)—it's run by the same owners.

Another option is **Aran Islands Fast Ferries** (tel. 065/707-4550, www.aranislandsfastferries.com, €25/35 return to Inis Oírr/Inis Mór), which operates year-round. There are sailings to Inis Oírr every 90 minutes 9 A.M.–3 P.M. and departures to Inis Mór at 9 A.M. and 5 P.M. daily. Some ferries continue to Inis Meáin; ring for times.

In need of a cab in or around Doolin? Call **Dial-a-Cab** (tel. 087/290-2060 or 086/812-7049) or **Jimmy's Cab Service** (tel. 086/813-9090).

NORTH OF DOOLIN

The road north out of Doolin to the tiny village of **Fanore** offers a fabulous view of the sea on the left and the rocky Burren landscape on the right; it makes for an excellent bike ride, about 32 kilometers round-trip. On your way there, you'll spot privately owned 15th-century Ballinalacken Castle.

Black Head looms above sleepy Fanore, crowning the northwesternmost part of the county. Serious climbers will want to hike up the head to **Cathair Dhún Iorais,** an Iron Age fort. Needless to say, the view from the summit is incomparable, but note that there is no actual path up the hill. Tackle it only with the proper footwear and only if the weather is clear.

The Fanore area is also popular with sea anglers, as the shore teems with cod and sea bass, and the village's beach is the only safe one along the northern coast of Clare. For horseback riding on the beach, ring the **Burren Riding Centre** (tel. 065/707-6140, half-day excursions €25). From Black Head it's a short drive east to the town of Ballyvaughan. Bus Éireann operates a service to Fanore only two times a week, so you do need a set of wheels.

LISDOONVARNA

Renowned for its annual **matchmaking festival** (tel. 065/707-4405, late September), Lisdoonvarna is essentially a one-street town 16 kilometers southwest of Ballyvaughan on the N67 and 8 kilometers east of Doolin on the R478. The festival has traditionally drawn bachelor farmers from the county and beyond, but in recent years it's attracted fun-seeking gay men from all over Europe.

Lisdoonvarna's other attraction is the Victorian-era **Spa Wells Centre** (Kincora Rd., tel. 065/707-4023, open 10 A.M.–6 P.M. daily June–Sept., sulfur bath €25), which offers hot and cold mineral baths (doctor-recommended for those with arthritis and several other physical complaints), aromatherapy, and massage. This is the only true spa in Ireland.

You can use Lisdoonvarna as a base for visiting the Cliffs, but Doolin is much more scenic (and the pubs are more fun, too).

One recommended accommodation in "Lisdoon," as it's known among the locals, is **O'Neill's Town Home** (St. Brendan's Rd., tel. 065/707-4208, open May–Oct., €25–30 pp, s €32–37). O'Neill's is home to **The Burren Painting Centre** (www.burrenpaintingcentre.com), which offers two- to six-day painting courses between May and October. The O'Neills also cook an evening meal for €22 a couple of nights a week. Otherwise, the best bets for food in town are the **Irish Arms** (tel. 065/707-4207) and the **Royal Spa Hotel** (tel. 065/707-4288), both on Main Street, with good pub grub in the €8–15 range. There are two nice restaurants in the bright and airy **Imperial Hotel** (Main St., tel. 065/707-4042, www.whites-hotelsireland.com, mains €11–24).

Lisdoonvarna is on the #337 Bus Éireann route from Limerick through Ennis to Doolin (Mon.–Sat.) and the #50 or #423 route from Galway to Doolin (Mon.–Sat. in high season). Limerick- and Galway-bound buses stop four or more times a day.

The Burren

This rocky limestone plateau is Clare's true treasure, stretching for nearly 300 square kilometers in the northwestern part of the county. The land preserved within the Burren National Park is less than 17 square kilometers, however, centered around the limestone peak of Mullaghmore just north of Corofin. The Burren—from *boireann,* "a rocky place"—may seem a harsh and desolate region at first look, but these rain-carved crevices are teeming with strange and beautiful flora and fauna.

The Burren shelters a greater variety of plants than any other region in Ireland. Cross-pollination, the absence of trees and shrubs (any incipient growth is usually eaten by wild animals), and a unique soil composition of dried algae and rabbit dung allow Alpine, Arctic, and Mediterranean flowers to grow like little miracles in the soil between the limestone slabs. There are more than 30 varieties of orchids here, which serious botanists, photographers, and watercolor artists delight upon every summer. Wildlife abounds,

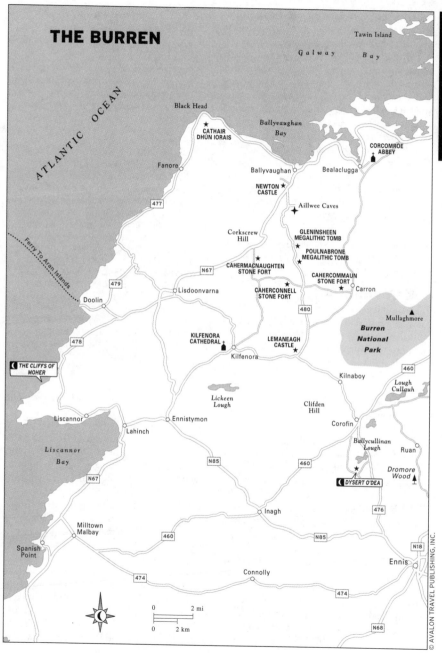

THE BURREN

Tawin Island

Galway Bay

ATLANTIC OCEAN

Black Head

★ CATHAIR
DHÚN IORAIS

Ballyvaughan
Bay

Fanore

CORCOMROE
ABBEY

Ballyvaughan   Bealaclugga

NEWTON ★
CASTLE

✦ Aillwee Caves

477

Corkscrew
Hill

Ferry To Aran Islands

GLENINSHEEN
MEGALITHIC TOMB

★ POULNABRONE
MEGALITHIC TOMB

N67

CAHERMACNAUGHTEN
STONE FORT ★

CAHERCOMMAUN
STONE FORT
★ Carron

479

Lisdoonvarna

CAHERCONNELL
STONE FORT ★

Doolin

480

Mullaghmore ▲

Burren
National
Park

478

KILFENORA
CATHEDRAL

LEMANEAGH
CASTLE

THE CLIFFS OF
MOHER

Kilfenora

Kilnaboy

460

Lough
Cullauh

Lickeen
Lough

Clifden
Hill

Liscannor

Corofin

Lahinch   Ennistymon

Ballycullinan
Lough   Ruan

Liscannor
Bay

N85

Dromore
Wood

460

N67

DYSERT O'DEA

476

Milltown
Malbay

Inagh

Spanish
Point

460

N85

N18

474

Connolly

N18

Ennis

474

0   2 mi

0   2 km

N68

© AVALON TRAVEL PUBLISHING, INC.

too: feral goats, rabbits, pine martens, stoats, badgers, foxes, birds galore, as well as seven bat species and 28 species of butterfly.

Nature lovers of all stripes will find much to inspire and intrigue. Though you can drive past the Burren's principal sights in a single day (or take a day tour on a coach bus out of Galway), it's well worth spending two or three days here on your own. Take part in a guided nature walk, bike part or all of the Burren Cycleway, or wander through the remains of several early Christian ring forts dotted around the area.

For more information before you go, visit **Burrenbeo** (www.burrenbeo.com), a great "one-stop information resource." Burrenbeo is far more substantive than the official Tourist Board sites because it's run by a journalist and an academic (Ann O'Connor and Brendan Dunford, respectively). Don't miss the excellent photo gallery.

BALLYVAUGHAN

A pleasant little harbor town situated between Galway Bay and the northern edge of the Burren, Ballyvaughan (Baile Uí Bheacháin) is home to the **Burren College of Art,** established in 1993, which uses the restored 16th-century **Newtown Castle** nearby as a gallery space. Many of the Burren's most important sights are within easy driving or cycling distance, including Poulnabrone, the Aillwee Caves, Dysert O'Dea, and several early Christian ring forts. A village eight kilometers east of Ballyvaughan on the N67, **Bealaclugga** (also known as **Bellharbour**), offers the substantial and picturesque ruins of the Cistercian Corcomroe Abbey. Guided Burren walks and other outdoor activities are readily available here, making Ballyvaughan an ideal base for exploring the lunar-limestone landscape. For more information, visit the helpful community website **Ballyvaughan Ireland** (www.ballyvaughanireland.com).

Sights

If Ballyvaughan is your entry into the Burren, you might want to visit **Burren Exposure** (in the village, tel. 065/707-7277, open 9 A.M.–

◧ THE BURREN WAY

Devoted hill-walkers shouldn't miss the Burren Way, a 45-kilometer signposted route from Ballyvaughan southwest to Liscannor (or vice versa) that takes you across the limestone plateau and down along the coast. The walk is designed to be self-guided, though you can join a group walk with a local guide through **Burren Walking Holidays** at the Carrigann Hotel (Lisdoonvarna, tel. 065/707-4036, www.gateway-to-the-burren.com). **Walk Ireland** (www.walkireland.ie), part of the Irish Sports Council, recommends you break it down into four half-day segments; check out the website for detailed info on the terrain and recommended maps, which are available for purchase at **The Burren Centre** in Kilfenora (on the R476, tel. 065/708-8030, open mid-Mar.-May and Sept.-Oct. 10 A.M.-5 P.M. daily, 9:30 A.M.-6 P.M. daily June-Aug.) or the tourist office in Ennis (O'Connell Sq., tel. 065/28366, open 9 A.M.-9 P.M. daily June-Sept., 9 A.M.-6 P.M. Mon.-Sat. and 10 A.M.-6 P.M. Sun. Oct.-May).

6 P.M. daily Mar.–Nov.), which offers an outstanding audiovisual introduction to the area's botany and geology.

Founded by Donal Mór O'Brien in 1194, most of what remains of **Corcomroe Abbey** (1.5 km southeast of Bealaclugga, signposted from the N67, free admission) dates to the early 13th century. The church's transverse wall was erected in the 15th century, just after the Black Plague; the lay brothers had fled the monastery, and apparently the remaining monks wanted a smaller house of worship to suit their diminished community.

There's a second morbid tale attached to this monastery. In 1317, two branches of the O'Brien clan (led by Dermot and Donough) were about to do battle near the abbey for dominion of the county. The evening before the battle, Donough O'Brien encountered a specter doing her washing among a mess of bloody limbs and severed heads in a stream near the abbey—one of which was Donough's. The Morrigan (a Celtic war goddess who often appeared in this form) told the chieftain that this would be his fate if he went ahead into battle. Donough ignored her warning, and by the following night he and all his warriors were lying lifeless in the abbey.

The abbey is in a secluded spot, surrounded by farmlands, and like other monastic ruins, its land serves as a modern graveyard (which the local farmers' dogs have been known to desecrate on occasion). The Office of Public Works was undertaking a restoration effort at time of writing, though the abbey remains open.

Shopping

There's a worthwhile **craft market** at Ballyvaughan Village Hall (tel. 065/707-8955 or 086/811-1511, open 10 A.M.–6 P.M. Sun. Easter–Oct.). Look out for watercolors by talented botanical artist **Leueen Hill** (tel. 065/707-8955 or 086/811-1511). Otherwise, have a look inside **Quinn's Craft Shop** (Main St., tel. 065/707-7052).

Sports and Recreation

The 69-kilometer signposted **Burren Cycleway** connects Ballyvaughan with Doolin and Lisdoonvarna. For travel tips and detailed information on the terrain, visit the tourist office in the village center. The 45-kilometer **Burren Way** also begins here (see the sidebar *The Burren Way*). Moderately ambitious walkers can ascend **Corkscrew Hill** (180 meters high); most others will probably want to drive it. It offers amazing panoramic views. It's signposted from the N67, about six kilometers south of Ballyvaughan.

For a guided walk with a knowledgable local, you have a few choices. **Burren Hill Walks** (Corkscrew Hill, Ballyvaughan, tel. 065/707-7168, http://homepage.eircom.net/~burrenhillwalks, half-day walks €15 pp) offers guided nature walks year-round (twice daily in high season). You can also arrange sunrise and sunset walks, weekend and weeklong trips.

Another equally reputable company is **Burren Wild Guided Walking Tours** (Oughtmama, Bealaclugga, tel. 087/877-9565, www.burrenwalks.com, 3-hour walks €20 pp). An option for those traveling in a group is **The Burren Outdoor Education Centre** (Turlough, Bealaclugga, tel. 065/78033, www.oec.ie/burren, dorm accommodation €16 pp), which does hill-walking along with a smorgasbord of other activities—rock climbing, caving, sailing, you name it.

River Ocean Kayak (2 Muckinish W., Ballyvaughan, tel. 065/707-7043, www.riverocean.com, half-day beginning course €25, full-day advanced €45) offers excursions for all experience levels.

As for "strands," there are a few fine beaches in the area: Popular with locals, **Flaggy Shore** is at the tip of the small Finavarra Peninsula, which opens up north of Bealaclugga. Flaggy Shore and nearby New Quay village are signposted from the N67. There are also sandy beaches at Fanore and Bishop's Quarter, which is about three kilometers east of Ballyvaughan off the Kinvara road.

Accommodations

Though Ballyvaughan is a natural base for Burren exploration, budget travelers should probably stay in Carron or Doolin, as there are no hostels in the vicinity.

Rusheen Lodge (on the N67, just south of Ballyvaughan, tel. 065/707-7092, www.rusheenlodge.com, s €52–68, d €76–96) may be on the pricey side for a B&B, but it receives consistently rave reviews for its elegant-but-comfortable rooms, hospitable proprietors, and outstanding breakfasts. Another recommended place is the more modest but just as welcoming **Stonepark House** (2 km east on the N67, Bishop's Quarter, tel. 065/707-7056, €27 s, €40 d, en-suite d €46), located on the Kinvara side of Ballyvaughan. Most of the rooms aren't en suite.

Those with a car—and a New Age bent—should consider staying in Fanore, at the **Rocky View Farmhouse** (14 km west of Ballyvaughan, signposted off the R477, tel.

065/707-6103, www.rockyviewfarmhouse. com, €28 pp, s €36). Not only are vegetarian, vegan, and other special diets catered for to a far greater extent than at the average B&B, but also there's a holistic healing center on the premises.

Food

Burren Exposure has a nice café attached, good for a light lunch. Another option is the **Tea Junction** (Main St., tel. 065/707-7289, open 9 A.M.–5 P.M. daily mid-Mar.–Oct., Wed.–Sun. Nov.–mid-Mar., meals under €6), a cozy, laid-back spot for breakfast, soup and sandwiches, or afternoon tea.

There's fine seafood to be found at **Monk's** (The Old Pier, tel. 065/707-7059, food served noon–8 P.M., mains €10–20), a light, airy, spacious pub with a large open fireplace. Monk's also has a decent selection of meat and vegetarian dishes, lasagna and suchlike. You'll find traditional music here Saturday night year-round and Tuesday June–August.

But perhaps the best choice for eating out around Ballyvaughan is the **Holywell Italian Café** (off the N67, 3 km south of Ballyvaughan, tel. 065/707-7322, www.holywell.net, open 11 A.M.–11 P.M. daily, mains €8–12), adjacent to the Burren College campus. The restaurant at Holywell (which is actually an English language school) serves excellent (and excellent-value) pasta and pizza, all made from scratch.

Information and Services

Ballyvaughan has no bank or ATM, so make your withdrawal before leaving Ennis, Galway, or Ennistymon. The **tourist office** (tel. 065/707-7077, www.ballyvaughantourism. com, open 9 A.M.–5 P.M. Mon.–Sat.) is inside **Linnane's Village Stores** in the center of town.

The **post office** (tel. 065/707-7079) and the **Burren Pharmacy** (tel. 065/707-7029) are both on Main Street.

Getting There and Around

Ballyvaughan is at the intersection of the N67 and R477 in northern Clare, 38 kilometers northwest of Ennis and 49 kilometers south of Galway. Bus Éireann routes #50 and #423 go from Galway to the Cliffs of Moher, stopping in Ballyvaughan (at least 3/day Mon.–Sat., 1/day Sun. year-round, at least 8/day Mon.–Sat., 2/day Sun. June–Sept.). The bus stop is right outside Linnane's Village Stores.

Rent a bicycle from **Burren Bike** (The Launderette, tel. 065/707-7061, www.burren-bike.com, €13/day, €50/week), just across the street from the gas station. For a taxi, ring **Mary McNamara** (tel. 065/707-7084).

SOUTH OF BALLYVAUGHAN
Newtown Castle

Like so many other castles in Clare, Newtown Castle (3 km south of Ballyvaughan, signposted off the N67, tel. 065/707-7200, www.burren-college.ie, open 10 A.M.–6 P.M. daily, free admission) was built by a branch of the O'Brien clan, and it has quite a unique shape—"a cylinder impaled upon a pyramid." It later belonged to the O'Loughlin family, who proclaimed themselves "princes of the Burren." The last of the O'Loughlins lived there in the late 19th century, and the tower house had fallen into ruin before the newly established Burren College of Art restored it in the early 1990s. The castle has five floors, the top of which serves as an exhibition space—quite dramatic with the new conical oak roof overhead. This room was originally a bedchamber.

Outside the castle, a 1.3-kilometer **nature trail** will lead you through the northern Burren.

Aillwee Caves

Few Irish tourist attractions are as thoroughly advertised as the Aillwee Caves (signposted from the N67 3.5 km south of Ballyvaughan, tel. 065/707-7036, www.aillweecave.ie, open 10 A.M.–5:30 P.M. daily Nov., 10 A.M.–6:30 P.M. July and Aug., €9 admission)—there are billboards dotted all over the county. Retreating glaciers at the end of the Ice Age carved these caves from the same limestone that covers the Burren, and you can see stalagmites that are thousands of years old along the 1.3-kilometer floodlit pathway. The visitors' experience of the caves is as touristy as the advertising would suggest, and it's by no means a must-see if you've been inside other caves. Admission is by 40-minute guided tour only.

Poulnabrone

Keep heading south for Ireland's best-known (and most-photographed) Neolithic portal tomb, Poulnabrone (signposted and visible from the R480 between Ballyvaughan and Corofin, 8 km south of Aillwee, always open). It's usually called a dolmen, but this is inaccurate—a dolmen consists of two standing stones and a capstone, but Poulnabrone has three standing stones, and its capstone weighs five tons. Picture this 5,400-year-old monument filled in with smaller stones and soil, as it would have been originally. Archaeologists found 22 skeletons buried underneath the stones in 1986. Six were children, none were over the age of 30, and all suffered from severe malnutrition.

It's best to visit early or late in the day, at sunrise or sunset ideally; the site will be deserted, and in the changing light, your view of the portal tomb will be rather dramatic.

Historic Forts

One kilometer south of Poulnabrone on the R480 is the early Christian **Caherconnell Stone Fort** (signposted and visible from the road, tel. 065/708-9999, www.burrenforts.ie, open 10 A.M.–5 P.M. Mar.–Oct., 9:30 A.M.–6 P.M. July–Aug., €3 admission, €5 for both fort and visitors center). This ring fort probably dates to the 5th century and protected a prosperous farmer and his family. Archaeological evidence says it may have been inhabited as late as the 17th century.

Another fort with even greater historical significance is **Cahermacnaughten** (12 km south of Ballyvaughan, signposted from the N67 and visible from the minor road to Kilfenora, free admission), the site of a Brehon law school that flourished here until the end of the 17th century. This fort is 30 meters in diameter, and at its west end are the foundations of another building most likely used by the school. Be-

cause the fort was occupied for so long, the interior ground level is nearly flush with the surrounding wall.

CARRON

The delightfully remote village of Carron (An Carn) may best be known for the **Burren Perfumery and Floral Centre** (Carron, tel. 065/708-9102, www.burrenperfumery.com, open 9 A.M.–5 P.M. Mon.–Fri., open until 7 P.M. June–Sept., free admission). The only handicraft perfumery in the country distills the scents of Burren wildflowers. There's also a lovely tearoom, an organic herb garden, and a short movie on the local botany. Looking for the perfect souvenir for your mother? Look no further.

Three kilometers south of Carron is the cliff-facing **Cahercommaun Hill Fort,** one of 45,000 medieval Irish ring forts that archaeologists believe may have been designed to prevent the plague from afflicting its inhabitants. Others think the fort may date to the Iron Age. Either way, the fort was last occupied in the 9th century. Note the triple-walled construction and the souterrain leading from the interior to the outer face of the rampart. The uphill path to the fort is steep and rocky, but the climb is well worth the effort for breathtaking panoramic views of the rocky Burren landscape.

Accommodation and food options in Carron are very slim, but of good quality. Popular with families and groups, **Clare's Rock Hostel** (Carron, tel. 065/708-9129, www.claresrock.com, dorms €14, en-suite doubles–quads €15–19 pp, bike rental €10, open May–Sept., only group bookings in off-season) enjoys a scenic location in the mountains overlooking the largest disappearing lake (or *turlough*) in western Europe. The hostel also rents out bikes. The pub next door, **Cassidy's** (Carron, tel. 065/708-9109, open Apr.–Oct., food served noon–9 P.M. Mon.–Sat., noon–6 P.M. Sun., mains €7–10) is a pleasant, slightly quirky place (alluding, in decor and dish names, to the building's former uses as a British Royal Irish Constabulary station and subsequently a police barracks). Cassidy's has trad sessions on Friday and Saturday nights, with set dancing on Friday.

Note that Carron is not served by Bus Éireann or any private buses, so unfortunately it's not a viable destination if you don't have a car.

KILFENORA

A sleepy little place between Lisdoonvarna and Corofin on the R476, Kilfenora (Cill Fhionnúrach) offers both a Burren information center and the remains of an important cathedral. Despite its remote location, the parish prospered so much during the medieval period that it was made its own diocese in 1152. Because Kilfenora currently has no bishop, the title officially belongs to the pope. Driving south from Lisdoonvarna, you'll pass through a lovely evergreen forest, leading you to forget you're in the Burren. Kilfenora is best done as a day trip, since there's a greater choice of accommodations in Doolin, Ballyvaughan, or even Corofin.

St. Fachnan's

Kilfenora's modest 12th-century cathedral, St. Fachnan's, is renowned for its high crosses. The cathedral stands on the site of St. Fachnan's 6th-century monastery. Though the nave is still used (for Protestant services) and is closed during the week, the ruined chancel is always open. It features a triple sedilia on the north wall, a delightfully creepy effigy of a medieval bishop opposite, and a dramatic three-lighted east window.

In the adjacent room, fitted with a new pitched glass roof, are two 12th-century high crosses. The most famous, the Doorty Cross, was "re-used" to mark the Doorty family grave in the 18th century, subsequently broken in two, and finally restored in 1955. It depicts a bishop, perhaps St. Fachnan, with mitre and crozier and four birds perched on his shoulders. The opposite face is carved with the Crucifixion. The North Cross, shorter and better preserved, features abstract Celtic designs. An unnamed ringed cross from the same period

This 12th-century Kilfenora high cross depicts the crucified Christ.

© CAMILLE DE ANGELIS

stands tall in the adjacent field, clearly visible from the gravel track that leads to the cathedral itself. This last cross is also carved with the Crucifixion, along with intricate interlacing.

Other Sights

The Burren Centre (Kilfenora, tel. 065/708-8030, www.theburrencentre.ie, open mid-Mar.–May and Sept.–Oct. 10 A.M.–5 P.M. daily, 9:30 A.M.–6 P.M. daily June–Aug., admission €5.50) offers a detailed topographical model of the Burren as well as a short audiovisual and a 15-minute lecture on the region's geology, botany, archaeology, and history. Those planning to explore the Burren in depth should definitely stop here first. The usual tearooms and craft shop are here, too.

On the way south from Kilfenora to Kilnaboy and Corofin on the R476, you will pass the 15th-century, O'Brien-built **Lemaneagh Castle.** It is privately owned and not open to the public, but it bears mentioning for its intriguing history. Conor O'Brien, who built the mid-17th-century mansion facade with the

© CAMILLE DEANGELIS

At Lemaneagh Castle, look for the murder hole above the east entrance.

mullioned windows, married the wild Máire Rua. After Conor died in battle, she refused to allow his corpse back into the castle, and later on she even married one of Cromwell's soldiers in order to retain the estate.

Food

For a traditional pub lunch, try **Vaughan's** (tel. 065/708-8157) or **Linnane's** (tel. 065/708-8157), both on Main Street. Vaughan's does more elaborate dishes and so is a bit pricier (mains under €12).

COROFIN

An utterly peaceful village less than 20 minutes from Ennis, Corofin's rolling green farmlands give way to a few rocky peaks on the northern horizon, reminding the visitor that they're still on the fringes of the Burren. Corofin (Cora Finne) is relatively quiet even in July and August, since visitors often make only a brief stop before heading out to Doolin or other points along the coast. There are enough worthwhile sights within a few kilometers to keep you here

for at least a day and night, however, and Corofin's tranquil setting may convince you to dally even longer.

Entertainment and Events

The cozy, unpretentious **Bofey Quinn's** (Main St., tel. 065/683-7321, open noon–11 P.M. or later daily) hosts trad sessions on Wednesday and Saturday nights in winter and on Monday, Wednesday, and Friday in high season (unscheduled sessions often happen other days of the week). The food's good, too. There's music almost 24/7 here during the **Corofin Traditional Music Festival** in early March.

Shopping

Corofin can boast one of the finest potteries in Ireland, **The Pottery Shop** (Church St., tel. 065/683-7020, open 9:30 A.M.–6 P.M. daily). Yvonne McEnnis's work is lighter and more elegant than most of what comes out of the larger workshops, though her prices are comparable. Being able to meet the potter herself is a great experience, especially since Yvonne is so friendly, kind, and helpful. Once you've stepped inside this wonderful little shop, you'll never again be tempted to buy Nicholas Mosse or any other assembly-line pottery.

Sports and Recreation

The nearby loughs (Inchiquin, Atedaun, Ballycullinan, and others) and the River Fergus are very popular with anglers, and there is boat hire available in season. The Wood Road around Lough Inchiquin is a nice place for a quiet ramble on a sunny afternoon. The lake and road, just west of Corofin, are signposted from the village.

Those with proper footwear can tackle the Burren's southern peaks, **Clifden Hill** (west of the village, off the Ennistymon road) or **Mullaghmore,** north of Kilnaboy, reachable by the road beside the old church (where the Kilnaboy church and school are signposted). The path is about four kilometers down on the right side of the road.

If you are visiting Dysert O'Dea, you may want to bring a picnic lunch to pretty **Dromore Wood** (Ruan, 8 km southeast of Corofin on the R476 to a regional road, tel. 065/683-7166, open daylight hours, free admission). This Dúchas-run nature reserve encompasses several medieval ruins, including two ring forts and a castle built by the O'Brien clan.

If it's raining buckets, though, there's another way to get some exercise: the **Power 2 Fitness Gym** (Baunkyle, Corofin, tel. 065/682-7833, open 9:30 A.M.–noon Mon.–Tues. and Thurs.–Fri., 5–9:30 P.M. Mon.–Fri., noon–3 P.M. Sat., €5 per use). In addition to the usual exercise machines and free weights, there's a Swedish sauna and Turkish steam room. At five euros a pop, it's quite a deal.

Accommodations

One outstanding B&B in the area is (**Fergus View** (3 km outside town in Kilnaboy, across the street from the church, tel. 065/683-7606, www.fergusview.com, €36 pp, €48–52 single), with a peaceful, bucolic view from every window. The Kellehers' gorgeous family home was built at the turn of last century as a teacher's

residence for none other than Declan Kelleher's grandfather. (Fittingly enough, Mr. Kelleher now serves as principal of the Corofin school.) The welcome is a warm one, with tea (brewed the old-fashioned way, from loose leaves) and homemade raisin bread. Mary's breakfasts are absolutely out of this world. The firm, comfortable beds also come with electric blankets!

Another recommended B&B, the **Corofin Country House** (Ennistymon Rd., tel. 065/683-7791, €27–30 pp, s €39–43), is run by Mary Kelleher's sister-in-law, Mary Shannon. The elegant landscaping and decor of this modern home will make the place seem like more of a splurge than it actually is. It has only four bedrooms, and Fergus View six, so be sure to book ahead in high season. Corofin may be a remote spot, but both B&Bs are flourishing with repeat business.

Food

In addition to fine trad, **Bofey Quinn's** (Main St., tel. 065/683-7321, open noon–11 P.M. or later daily, mains €8–18, full Irish breakfast €8.50) is good for hearty traditional dishes, pizza, or an old-fashioned ice cream sundae.

When the locals want to treat themselves to a special meal, they go to **Restaurant Le Catelinais** (on the Kilnaboy end of Main St., tel. 065/683-7425, open 5:30 P.M.–late Tues.–Thurs., mains €18–24). Here is a story that, fortunately for us, occurs with increasing frequency nowadays: Irish girl goes abroad, meets talented French chef, brings him home, and opens a restaurant! The €25 three-course early-bird menu (5–7 P.M.) is a tremendous value.

Information

Housed in a deconsecrated Protestant church, the **Clare Heritage Centre** (Church St., tel. 065/683-7955, clareheritage@eircom.net, open 10 A.M.–6 P.M. daily mid-May–Oct., admission €4) offers a trove of historical information. There are scale models and artifacts illustrating everyday life in the 19th-century, as well as exhibits on the famine, emigration, and traditional music. The center's Dr. George McNamara Gallery holds a collection of Neolithic stone ax heads, 17th-century chalices, and other treasures. The **Genealogical Centre** (tel. 065/683-7955, www.clareroots.com, open 9 A.M.–5:30 P.M. Mon.–Fri.), catercorner across Church St., is the place to visit if you're tracing your roots in County Clare.

Services

There is no bank or ATM in Corofin, so make your withdrawal before leaving Ennis or Galway. Corofin has one pharmacy, **Rochford's** (Main St., tel. 065/682-7932).

The **post office** (Main St., tel. 065/683-7681) is inside the Spar supermarket. The **public library** (behind the Geneaological Centre on Church St., tel. 065/683-7219, open 1–5 P.M. and 6–8 P.M. Mon. and Wed., 10 A.M.–2 P.M. and 6–8 P.M. Fri.) offers one hour of free Internet access.

Getting There and Around

Mid-May–September, a Bus Éireann service (tel. 065/682-4177, #337) to Corofin departs from Ennis once a day (Mon.–Sat. at 2:25 P.M., arriving at 2:45 P.M.; on Sun., it departs at 12:20 P.M.). That bus continues to Doolin and Lisdoonvarna. Returning to Ennis, the #333 bus passes through Corofin at 9:20 A.M. Monday–Friday, and the #337 bus comes by at 6:55 P.M. daily.

Corofin is only 12 kilometers northwest of Ennis, so even if you aren't renting a car, you could easily take a taxi from the principal town.

◖ Dysert O'Dea

Corofin is the closest town to one of Clare's most important monastic sites, Dysert O'Dea ("desert oh-DEE," 1.5 km west of the R476, just south of Corofin, open year-round), which includes a ruined church, round tower, and high cross. The church is a 17th-century reconstruction of a 12th- or 13th-century edifice and features a remarkable Romanesque doorway with voussoirs of eerily individualized human and animal heads. What makes it even more noteworthy is that this doorway is a composite of the original arch and one from another unidentified site. The famous high cross here, east of

the spooky Romanesque doorway at Dysert O'Dea
© CAMILLE DEANGELIS

the church (in the pasture beyond the enclosure wall), has the figure of a bishop carved on the east face, which is surmounted by a smaller effigy of the crucified Christ. The remains of the 12th-century round tower are about 15 meters high. A three-kilometer footpath takes you past dozens of ancient and medieval remains—ring forts, more high crosses, and so forth.

The very worthwhile **Archaeology Centre** (connected to the monastic site by footpath, tel. 065/683-7401, open 10 A.M.–6 P.M. daily May–Sept., admission €4) is within a four-story tower house that was built by the O'Deas in the late 15th century and trashed by the nefarious Cromwell in 1651. The collection includes Neolithic stone ax heads, Bronze Age spear and javelin heads, medieval and 18th-century swords, and IRA weapons used during the Civil War. A half-hour movie describes the local archaeology.

Kilnaboy

About four kilometers north of Corofin on the R476 is the tiny village of Kilnaboy. Its ruined church is known for the **sheila-na-gig** above the doorway. Carved in stone, this is a female effigy with exaggerated genitalia (the phrase literally means "Sheila of the teats"). Sadly, the stone is so worn that the figure is barely distin-guishable, but the church is still worth a peek. Its haunting serenity has generations of roman-tic poets yet to inspire. The church is always open, accessible from a set of steep stone steps from the main road.

Limerick City

Limerick is no longer the crime-ridden "Stab City" out-of-towners made a point to avoid be-fore the advent of the Celtic Tiger. On sunless days it can still be a vaguely drab place, but its fairly good arts scene and a prominent art and design school do much to counteract that sour vibe of yesteryear. What crimes do happen are almost always drug-related and do not affect upstanding citizens or visitors (who exercise caution when out late at night, as in any city). Today, the republic's third-largest city is truly a working study in urban renewal.

The brilliant novelist Kate O'Brien was born here in 1897, and despite her eloquent distaste for her native city (it has "the grave, grey look of Commerce," a place "corrective of literary fancies"), she set some of her best-known nov-els here. In O'Brien's fictive universe, it goes by the name of Mellick.

You've no doubt heard of another Limerick luminary, Frank McCourt, whose Pulitzer-winning memoir *Angela's Ashes* has garnered mixed reviews from locals. Even if McCourt's account of a poverty-stricken childhood in 1930s Limerick is somewhat exaggerated (as some protest), his story illustrates the economic polarities prevalent in any city in any age. After all, actor Richard Harris was growing up about the same time in a manor house filled with ser-vants just down the Ennis Road.

Limerick doesn't have to be just a stopover on your way south to Killarney or west to rural Clare. King John's Castle and the spooky St. Mary's Cathedral are emblematic of the city's rich history and render the city worthy of an overnight visit. Limerick's Georgian architec-tural heritage is exemplified in landmarks like the Old Customs House and in the doorways of townhouses all over the city. And not only are the late Neolithic remains at nearby Lough Gur of tremendous archaeological importance, but the lakeside is splendid for a bike ride and picnic lunch.

Downtown Limerick is laid out in a simple grid system, quite easy to navigate. O'Connell Street is the main drag, running parallel to the River Shannon, and becomes Patrick Street, then Rutland Street as it continues north to the Abbey River. Cross the Abbey River and you'll find the castle and cathedral. Colbert Bus and Train Station, the People's Park, and the municipal art gallery are on the south side of the city center. Everything you need is on the eastern shore of the River Shannon.

SIGHTS

There are enough worthwhile stops to keep you in Limerick for at least a full day.

King John's Castle and Vicinity

The keepless King John's Castle (Nicholas St., tel. 061/411-201, open 9:30 A.M.–5:30 P.M. daily May–Oct., 9:30 A.M.–4:30 P.M. daily Nov.–Feb., 9:30 A.M.–5 P.M. daily Mar.–Apr., admission €7) was erected on the banks of the Shannon between 1200 and 1207 at the command of the castle's namesake. It is one of Ireland's oldest intact examples of medieval architecture, though the expensive restoration effort of the 1990s had mixed results: The in-terpretive center looming out of the castle's cen-ter is downright hideous, but on the upside, visitors can now descend into archaeological excavations dating to the Hiberno-Norse pe-riod (the 9th and 10th centuries), a truly fasci-nating experience.

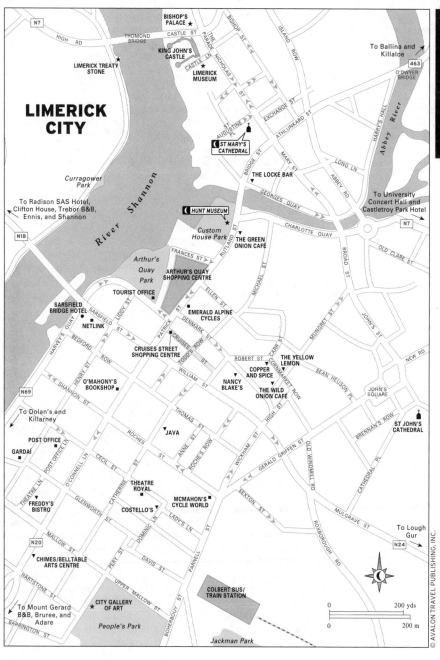

LIMERICK CITY

© AVALON TRAVEL PUBLISHING, INC.

There isn't much in the adjacent **Limerick Museum** (Castle Ln., Nicholas St., tel. 061/417-826, open 10 A.M.–1 P.M. and 2:15–5 P.M. Tues.–Sat., free admission) to occupy you for more than half an hour, but it's still worth a look. Items include Bronze and Stone Age artifacts, antique silver and lace from the city's workshops, a few paintings, and official documents under glass.

There are a couple of landmarks across the road from the castle. The **Bishop's Palace,** originally part of Cromwell's 1649 settlement, served as the grand residence of Limerick's Protestant bishops until 1784. After two centuries of neglect, the Limerick Civic Trust rescued the palace from demolition, and now, fully restored, it serves as Trust headquarters. Also directly across the street from the castle is a "Gothic folly" **toll house,** erected in 1840 by the architects of the Thomond Bridge.

Across the bridge from the castle and museum is the **Limerick Treaty Stone,** on which the Treaty of 1691, the surrender of Jacobite Patrick Sarsfield to the troops of William of Orange, is believed to have been signed. The treaty was also meant to provide protection for Irish Catholics, but it should come as no surprise that this particular clause was forgotten almost as soon as the treaty was signed.

◖ St. Mary's Cathedral

It is ancient, dank, and cavernous—in other words, the perfect setting for one of Sheridan Le Fanu's scariest short stories. As Limerick's oldest edifice, St. Mary's Cathedral (Bridge St., tel. 061/416-238, open 9 A.M.–5 P.M. daily Oct.–May, 9 A.M.–1 P.M. June–Sept., admission €2) is a must-see even if your taste doesn't veer toward the Gothic.

Parts of the original late-12th-century building survive in the nave, chancel, and restored Romanesque west doorway (visible from the outside). Items of interest include black-oak misericords (cheat-seats for standing choristers)—dating to 1489, they are unique in Ireland and are intricately carved with animal figures—and a stone reredos (an ornamental partition in front of the altar) carved by the

father of patriot Patrick Pearse and installed in 1907. Also contributing to the sense that one has wandered into a Gothic tale are the medieval tombs behind the altar. One of these belongs to Donal Mór O'Brien, king of Munster, who donated the land to the church in 1180.

St. Mary's is now under the Church of Ireland. Be sure to pick up the brochure as you enter—the counterclockwise self-guided tour is full of strange historical tidbits.

St. John's Cathedral

The neo-Gothic Catholic cathedral, St. John's (Cathedral Place, tel. 061/414-624), was designed by the English architect Philip Charles Hardwick and built in the late 1850s. The cathedral is crowned with an ornate 85-meter spire, one of the three tallest in Ireland. The austerity of its facade isn't continued inside—it's certainly worth a look, though this church is inevitably less intriguing than St. Mary's.

◖ Hunt Museum

No visit to Limerick would be complete without an afternoon at the marvelous Hunt Museum (The Old Custom House, Rutland St., tel. 061/312-833, www.huntmuseum.com, open 10 A.M.–5 P.M. Mon.–Sat., 2–5 P.M. Sun., admission €7.20), which offers the greatest collection of ancient and medieval artifacts outside of the National Museum in Dublin (though not all its treasures are of Irish origin). John and Gertrude Hunt, a couple of philanthropic art historians, donated their vast private collection to the state in 1974, though the museum was only opened in 1997 (the collection was housed at the University of Limerick in the interim); the oldest pieces are Neolithic tools as well as Bronze Age jewelry, funerary pottery, and cooking utensils. Religious artifacts include 8th- and 9th-century bronze monastic bells, a reliquary cross that belonged to Mary, Queen of Scots, and the 17th-century Galway Chalice. The prize of the small painting collection is a self-portrait of the neoclassicist Italophile Robert Fagan and his wife *à la grecque,* and in the same room you'll see a small bronze horse cast by Leonardo da Vinci.

The building itself is of interest, too, for the 1769 facade is an (albeit smaller) reproduction of the Petit Trianon at the palace of Versailles, and the museum restaurant is a great choice for lunch. If you have time for only one diversion in Limerick, make it the Hunt.

Limerick City Gallery of Art

If the Hunt hasn't quite satisfied your love of fine art, head for the Limerick City Gallery of Art (Pery Sq., tel. 061/310-633, open 10 A.M.–1 P.M. and 2–6 P.M. Mon.–Wed. and Fri., 10 A.M.–1 P.M. and 2–7 P.M. Thurs., 10 A.M.–1 P.M. Sat., free admission), in the neo-Romanesque Carnegie Building (built at the turn of the 20th century). As is the case with many municipal art galleries, this one has many small treasures (landscapes and portraits mostly) but not enough space for them. The upper floor feels more airy and hosts rotating exhibitions that can be surprisingly postmodern.

Tours

Fans of Frank McCourt's memoirs can take a two-hour *Angela's Ashes* walking tour, which commences at the tourist office at Arthur's Quay at 2:30 P.M. daily and costs €8. A general historical walking tour is also available through **St. Mary's Action Centre** (tel. 061/318-106, 44 Nicholas St., tours at 11 A.M. and 2:30 P.M. Mon.–Fri., departure point by arrangement, tickets €8).

ENTERTAINMENT

Limerick isn't exactly a clubber's dream city, but the live music venues are nothing to shake a stick at, and there's a watering hole to suit every taste.

The best pubs in Limerick City for live trad include **The Locke Bar** (3 Georges Quay, tel. 061/413-733, www.lockebar.com), established in 1724, with sessions Tuesday, Thursday, and Sunday nights; **Nancy Blake's** (19 Upper Denmark St., tel. 061/416-443) Sunday–Wednesday; and **Costello's** (4 Dominic St., tel. 061/418-520) for trad on the weekends. The Locke and Nancy Blake's offer a charming old-world ambience and popular outdoor beer

---

---

gardens, and Costello's offers (relatively) cheap drinks and a somewhat arty crowd.

For rock shows, the place to go is **Dolan's Warehouse** (Dock Rd., tel. 061/314-483, www.dolanspub.com, tickets €7–20), adjoining the more traditional Dolan's Pub (which also has excellent live trad nightly). Featured bands at the warehouse run the gamut from indie pop/rock to "Irish metal," and Wednesday night is reserved for stand-up comedy.

Limerick's prime concert and theater venue is the **Belltable Arts Centre** (69 O'Connell St., tel. 061/319-866, www.belltable.ie, tickets €8–30), which also has a gallery for contemporary art exhibitions and occasional film screenings.

The University of Limerick's **University**

Concert Hall (University of Limerick campus, tel. 061/331-549, www.uch.ie, tickets €8–30) is the place to go if you enjoy classical and choral music. More convenient than the UCH box office is the City Centre Ticket Desk, located at the Limerick tourist office at Arthur's Quay (tel. 061/314-314, open 9:30 A.M.–1 P.M. Mon.–Sat.). You can also book online, though a €1 service charge applies. (Take a taxi to the campus, which is about 5 km east of the city off the R503.)

Another option is the dinner recital series at the **Hunt Museum** (The Old Custom House, Rutland St., tel. 061/312-960, friends@hunt-museum.com, tickets €50). On Sunday evenings, an intimate concert featuring top-notch classical artists is followed by a candlelit dinner in the museum restaurant.

SHOPPING

Limerick has two shopping malls, the **Arthur's Quay Shopping Centre** (Arthur's Quay, tel. 061/419-888, open 9 A.M.–7 P.M. Mon.–Thurs., 9 A.M.–9 P.M. Fri.–Sat., 9 A.M.–6 P.M. Sun.), which offers the usual women's boutiques and other chain stores, and the outdoor **Cruises Street Shopping Centre** (Cruises St., off Patrick St.). Though Cruises Street is rather atmospheric, its charm is dampened by all the chain stores lining the pedestrian street. You'll be hard-pressed to find any shops that sell quality souvenirs in this town; you're better off heading to Bunratty.

Limerick boasts the country's largest indie bookstore, **O'Mahony's** (120 O'Connell St., tel. 061/418-155)—it's more spacious than the Eason's on Cruises Street and offers a fine selection of Irish history and literature.

SPORTS AND RECREATION

Serious walkers will want to check out at least part of the 65-kilometer **Lough Derg Way,** which begins in Limerick City, heads up to Killaloe in eastern Clare, and continues north through the shale-flecked Arra Mountains to Dromineer in northern Tipperary, a pleasant resort town. Most walkers begin at Killaloe and walk either south to Limerick or

north to Dromineer, though the way can be traversed in either direction, and lush countryside, lovely Shannon and lake views, and wildlife-watching opportunities abound along both sections. The signposted route begins at the Arthur's Quay tourist office, where you can pick up maps and guides on local flora and fauna.

Lough Gur is a popular cycling destination since it's only 20 kilometers southeast of the city (on the R512). For more information, see the *Lough Gur* section in this chapter.

Limerick's nearest golf course is **Rathbane** (3.2 km south of town, signposted off the R512, tel. 061/313-655, www.rathbanegolf.com, open daily); advance booking is recommended.

ACCOMMODATIONS

Unfortunately, at time of writing there were no hostels left in the city.

Several B&Bs dot the Ennis Road on the far side of the Sarsfield Bridge. One of the best on that end of town is **Trebor** (Ennis Rd., tel. 061/454-632, open Apr.–Oct., €29–33 pp sharing, s €34), which is popular with cyclists and other outdoorsy types (in part, perhaps, for the above-average vegetarian breakfast options). Rooms are smallish but immaculate.

Alternatively, O'Connell Avenue has a couple of B&Bs (O'Connell St. turns into the avenue south of the city center). Recommended in particular is **Mount Gerard** (O'Connell Ave., at the end of Alexandra Terrace, tel. 061/314-981 or 061/411-886, s €35–40, d €50), a homey Victorian with a lovely dining room and wireless Internet access for a few extra euros. Mount Gerard is also a good choice for vegetarians, and the rooms are simply appointed but comfortable. The kindness and hospitality of proprietors John and Nora Coyne knows no equal.

With 16 rooms, **Clifton House** (Ennis Rd., tel. 061/451-166, €40–45 pp, s €50–60) is more a guesthouse than a B&B, though the owners are just as welcoming as if you were staying in their lone spare room. You'll find tea, coffee, and cookies in the guest lounge at all hours.

The rooms are void of any personal touches, but its central location and helpful reception recommend the **Sarsfield Bridge Hotel** (Sarsfield Bridge, at Harvey's Quay, tel. 061/317-179, www.tsbh.ie, €55–70 pp), across the street from Dunnes Stores. It may be antiseptic, but this hotel is your best bet if you aren't driving—it's within a couple minutes' walk of all the city sights. Or if you'd rather splurge (and have a rental car), try the **Castletroy Park Hotel** (Dublin Rd., 5 km east of town, tel. 061/335-566, www.castletroy-park.ie, €80–230 pp, s €145–195), directly across the road from the University of Limerick main entrance—it's a four-star hotel with five-star service. There's a 20-meter pool and gymnasium as well as a salon and spa; WiFi is complimentary. Castletroy Park is arguably the best hotel in town, though another option is the **Radisson SAS Hotel & Spa** (Ennis Rd., 3 km west of town, tel. 061/456-200, www.limerick.radissonsas.com, rooms €115–180), which is set on 20 acres of landscaped grounds and offers similar facilities to Castletroy Park (plus a special wing for female business travelers with rooms featuring extra girly comforts like lavender-scented cushions and deluxe bath products). WiFi is complimentary.

FOOD

As with any city on the upswing, fine new restaurants and cafés are opening in Limerick all the time. The pub grub at **The Locke Bar and Bistro** (3 Georges Quay, tel. 061/413-733, www.lockebar.com, meals served noon–10:30 P.M., lunches €8–12, dinners €17–26) is recommended in particular, since you can access wireless Internet (€3 per half hour) while chowing down on your fancy sandwich.

Growing tired of fried tomatoes and beans from a can? **The Wild Onion Café** (Cornmarket Row, on High St. at the top of Denmark St., tel. 061/440-055, www.wildonioncafe.com, open 8 A.M.–4 P.M. Tues.–Fri., 9 A.M.–3 P.M. Sat., lunches under €10) does hearty American-style breakfasts and lunches (as well as baked goods), from French toast to barbecue.

A hip spot for coffee, snacks, or meals is **Java's** (5 Catherine St., tel. 061/418-077, www.javas.ie, open 9 A.M.–8 P.M. Mon.–Sat., 11 A.M.–8 P.M. Sun., mains under €8, Internet access €3/hour), popular with students and backpackers.

Two recommended lunch spots are **DuCartes,** the Hunt Museum restaurant (The Old Custom House, Rutland St., tel. 061/312-662, www.huntmuseum.com, open 10 A.M.–5 P.M. Mon.–Sat., 2–5 P.M. Sun., lunches under €12), serving up heaping salads (using local produce) and hearty plates of meat and veggies, and **Chimes** (69 O'Connell St., tel. 061/319-866, open 8:30 A.M.–5 P.M. Mon.–Fri., breakfast €4, mains under €10), in the basement of the Belltable Arts Centre, for soups, sandwiches, and Fair Trade coffee and tea.

It used to be a straight-up, upscale Continental eatery, but the reincarnation of **The Yellow Lemon** (Cornmarket Sq., Denmark St., tel. 061/312-333, www.theyellowlemon.com, open daily 12:30–3 P.M. lunch, 5:30 P.M.–late for dinner, mains €8–13) into a Tandoori restaurant has augmented its popularity—which illustrates how fine dining in Limerick has, quite possibly, evolved farther from the "modern Irish," so-sophisticated-it-can-be-boring cuisine to a more global palate. Vegetarians and meat-eaters will be equally enthused. Visit the website before you go, because The Yellow Lemon offers a one-time 10 percent discount to those who sign up to their "friends" group.

Another good spot for Indian (and Thai) is **Copper and Spice** (2 Cornmarket Row, tel. 061/313-620, www.copperandspice.com, open Tues.–Sun. 5–10:30 P.M., mains €10–18). The three-course early bird menu (€22.50, 5–7 P.M.), which includes a glass of beer or wine, is a great value.

Good for tea, lunch, or dinner, the trendy **Green Onion Café** (Old Town Hall, Rutland St., tel. 061/400-710, open noon–11 P.M. Mon.–Sat., mains €13–22), off Patrick's Street across from the Arthur's Quay Shopping Centre, does scrumptious modern Irish fare.

For a special night out, make a reservation at

cozy, family-run **((** **Freddy's Bistro** (Theatre Ln., Lower Glentworth St., tel. 061/418-749, open 6:30–10:30 P.M. Tues.–Sat., mains €19–27), which recently won the Best Restaurant in Limerick award from the Epicurean World Master Chefs. Regular joes think this Irish-Italian fusion eatery is the greatest, too.

INFORMATION

For guided walking tours, UCH concert tickets, and general sightseeing advice, visit the Limerick **tourist office** (Limerick Tourism Centre, Arthur's Quay, tel. 061/317-522, www.shannonregiontourism.ie, open 9 A.M.–7 P.M. Mon.–Fri. and 9 A.M.–6 P.M. Sat.–Sun. July–Aug.; 9:30 A.M.–1 P.M. and 2–5:30 P.M. Mon.–Sat. May–June and Sept.–Oct.; 9:30 A.M.–1 P.M. and 2–5:30 P.M. Mon.–Fri. and 9:30 A.M.–1 P.M. Sat. Nov.–Apr.). The Shannon regional tourism website (www.shannonregiontourism.ie) is a very helpful pretrip planning resource.

SERVICES

The **General Post Office** (Cecil St., tel. 061/313-825) is between Henry and O'Connell Streets.

ATMs and bureaux de change are available at the **Bank of Ireland** (O'Connell St., tel. 061/415-055) and **AIB** (O'Connell St., tel. 061/414-388).

The city has several Internet cafés, most of which are rather dodgy. **Netlink** (Sarsfield St., across the street from Dunnes Stores, no phone, €4/hour) is one option. **Java's** (5 Catherine St., tel. 061/418-077, www.javas.ie, €3/hour) has three computers on the second floor—not as speedy, but the price and atmosphere are the best in town.

Got a suitcase full of dirty duds? Take it to **Suds Laundrette and Dry Cleaners** (51 Henry St., tel. 061/411-860). If you need a drugstore, try **Charlotte Quay Pharmacy** (Charlotte Quay, tel. 061/400-722). There's also a pharmacy at the Arthur's Quay Shopping Centre.

Limerick's **Garda Síochána headquarters** (Henry St., tel. 061/212-400) are on the southwestern end of town, one block west of O'Connell Street.

GETTING THERE

Limerick is 25 kilometers southeast of the Shannon Airport on the N18, also the road to take if you're coming from Galway (103 km). Take the N24 from Waterford (126 km), the N20 from Cork (100 km), the N21 from Tralee (105 km), and the N7 from Dublin (232 km).

Colbert Bus and Train Station (Parnell St., tel. 061/315-555) is catty-corner to the People's Park on the southern side of the city. You can reach Limerick by **Bus Éireann** (tel. 061/313-333) from Dublin (route #12, 10/day); Galway, Ennis, Cork (all #51, 13/day); the Shannon Airport (#343, 2/hour); Tralee (#14, 9/day); Athlone (#72, 10/day), or Waterford (#55, 8/day).

Direct **Irish Rail** service is available from Ennis (7–8/day). Other destinations are via Limerick Junction: Dublin (6/day), Waterford (3/day), and Cork (7/day). Ring the station for train times.

GETTING AROUND

Though Bus Éireann offers local service, Limerick is small enough that you can walk everywhere you need to go. Taxis line up outside Colbert Station and on two side streets off O'Connell Street (Thomas and Cecil); to ring for one, try **Gerry O'Connell** (tel. 087/279-3354 or 061/313-325), **Top Cabs** (Wickam St., tel. 061/417-417), **Economy Taxis** (tel. 061/411-422), or **Fixed Price Taxis** (tel. 061/417-777).

Both Limerick's bicycle shops offer one-way rental for an additional fee: **Emerald Alpine Cycles** (1 Patrick St., tel. 061/416-983, www.irelandrentabike.com, open 9:15 A.M.–5:30 P.M. Mon.–Sat., €20/day, €80/week, €25 one-way fee), which offers free luggage storage, and **McMahon's Cycle World** (30 Roches St., tel. 061/415-202, open 9 A.M.–6 P.M. Mon.–Sat., €15/day, €80/week, €25 one-way fee). Given the city's size, you won't need a bike unless you're planning to explore the outlying countryside.

((LOUGH GUR

The remains of a series of settlements between 3000 B.C. (the late Neolithic period) and the

Grange Stone Circle, near Lough Gur

Middle Ages surround the small, picturesque Lough Gur, only 11 kilometers southeast of Limerick City. The **Lough Gur Interpretive Centre** (on the R514, tel. 061/361-511, open 10 A.M.–6 P.M. daily mid-May–Sept., admission €4.50) is unique in that it's housed in a pair of replica Bronze Age thatched huts, the result of an archaeological dig led by John Hunt (of Hunt Museum renown). The admission fee is somewhat excessive for the amount of insight it contains, however. You may want to skip the center and explore the sites on your own.

Looking south from the interpretive center, you will see **Bolin Island,** which was originally a Bronze Age *crannóg* (man-made from rocks and other natural materials). From here you can spot the ruins of 15th-century Bourchier's Castle (to your left) and the 13th-century Black Castle on the far side of the lake; the former is inaccessible, but you can reach the latter by heading east on the lakeside path.

The Lough Gur periphery is dotted with standing stones, the ruins of millennium-old cottages, and burial mounds. The two most important sites, Grange Stone Circle and Giant's Grave, are slightly farther away.

Grange Stone Circle

The Grange Stone Circle (signposted on the left-hand side of the R512 from Limerick, just past the village of Grange, 3 km west of the interpretive center, €2 suggested donation) is at least 4,000 years old, putting it within the early Bronze Age. The circle—sometimes referred to as Ireland's Stonehenge—is 45 meters in diameter and comprises 113 boulders and cut stones, the tallest of which is 2.4 meters high. New Agey types flock here for the summer solstice, when a beam of light cuts through the circle's center at sunrise. Timothy Casey, the kindly farmer who owns the land, lets his newborn calves test their legs in the circle every spring. There's a smaller stone circle and a huge standing stone also on his land, both visible from the Grange.

Giant's Grave

The second monument is the Giant's Grave (signposted on the R512, 1.5 km southwest of the interpretive center), a Bronze Age wedge tomb at least 2,500 years old. Its double stone walls, in-filled with rubble, are topped with several capstones and bisected by a perpendicular slab, forming a low dual-chambered gallery about 3 meters wide and over 15 meters long. This was most likely a communal tomb, but "giant's grave" is certainly more poetic.

Getting There

Bus Éireann does offer a service through the village of Bruff near Lough Gur, but it's so limited that busing it just isn't a viable option. Driving or cycling out of Limerick City, take the Waterford-bound N24, and then pick up the R512 just outside of town.

ADARE

Sixteen kilometers southwest of Limerick City on the River Maigue, Adare is popular with the coach-bus set for its picture-perfection—the town's tourism promoters actually hype it as a "storybook village." Thatched-roof gift shops line the main thoroughfare, and accommodations are disproportionately expensive. Some might say that Adare's charm is unabashedly contrived, but others will find reason to linger for a few hours. The town's exclusive golf course (the Adare Manor Golf Club, tel. 061/396-204) includes the splendid ruins of **Desmond Castle** and a **Franciscan Friary.** Obtain permission from the club before visiting them.

If churches are your thing, you shouldn't miss the **Trinitarian Friary Church** (Main St., beside the Heritage Centre), which now serves as Adare's Catholic parish church. The Trinitarian Friary was founded in the 13th century and is the only surviving church of this religious order in the country. There's also the 14th-century **Augustinian Friary** (on the Limerick road, on the right side as you enter Adare), founded by the first Earl of Kildare, which now serves as the Church of Ireland.

Take a peek at the cloister and the restored domestic buildings, as well as the lovely switchline tracery on the Gothic windows inside the church. In fine weather you can take the picturesque riverside walk originating at the friary gates.

For more information on medieval Adare, check out the **Adare Heritage Centre** (Main St., tel. 061/396-666, www.adareheritagecentre.com, open 9 A.M.–6 P.M. daily, admission €5), which offers an audiovisual presentation along with a model of the town at the turn of the 16th century. Walking tours depart here July–September.

You can reach Adare from Limerick City on the N20, and Bus Éireann services Adare on the #13 or #14 route between Limerick and Tralee (at least 8/day out of Limerick).

BRUREE

If you have a keen interest in Irish history, you may want to make a side trip to the **De Valera Museum and Bruree Heritage Centre** (Water St., tel. 063/90900, open 10 A.M.–5 P.M. Tues.–Fri., 2–5 P.M. Sat.–Sun., admission €5), which is in the National Schoolhouse that Ireland's first Taoiseach (and co-founder of the Fianna Fail party) attended long ago. The exhibit includes de Valera–related memorabilia and other historical tidbits.

De Valera's childhood home nearby (where he lived with his uncle) is also open to the public; it's filled with period furnishings, though there isn't much to distinguish it as "deV's." Follow the signpost on the eastern (Kilmallock) end of the village, about a kilometer down the road. The key is available from the neighboring house.

Bruree is 35 kilometers south of Limerick City, accessible by the N20 to the R518. Bus Éireann services Bruree on the Limerick–Charleville route (#320), with at least two buses per day out of Limerick Monday–Saturday.

GALWAY

Ireland's second-largest county, Galway (Gaillimh) is the west at its best: a vibrant, quasi-bohemian capital city; wild, boggy, mountainous Connemara, dotted with lakes that look black in fog but shimmer brilliantly when the sun shines, bordered on the east by Lough Corrib, the republic's largest; and islands crisscrossed in ancient stone walls, rich in pre-Christian and monastic heritage as well as traditional Gaelic language and culture. Galway is a deservedly popular tourism base, since you can visit Connemara and the Burren in County Clare on easy day trips, but it's a bit easier to hop off the merry-go-round here than it is in County Kerry. Once you get outside Roundstone and Clifden, Connemara feels almost as lonely and remote as it would have a hundred years ago.

In contrast, the plains of eastern Galway offer little in the way of interesting scenery or tourist attractions, though there are a few sights worth a detour en route to Galway City from points east.

HISTORY

No one quite knows the origin of "Gaillimh"; some people say it was named for the daughter of an Iron Age chieftain who drowned in the River Corrib, which was originally known as the River Galway. At any rate, archaeological evidence indicates that the first settlement of Galway dates to Neolithic times, and there may have been an earthen fort erected in what would later become the city's Claddagh section. Though the Vikings pillaged the native Irish settlements here several centuries before

© CAMILLE DEANGELIS

HIGHLIGHTS

◖ **Galway City's Saturday Market:** It's not just farm stands at the city's Saturday market outside St. Nicholas' Collegiate Church; shop for whimsical souvenirs and treat yourself to anything from vegetarian Indian grub to deluxe crepes, fresh bagels and doughnuts, chocolate-covered strawberries, and gourmet coffee (page 328).

◖ **Dún Aengus:** Surrounded by *cheveaux de frise,* this 2,000-year-old semicircular fort is stunningly situated atop a 90-meter sea cliff (page 336).

◖ **Dún Dúbhchathair:** Just as breathtaking as Dún Aengus, but as quiet as Aengus is touristy, the scant remains of this cliffside fort are the perfect spot for a picnic (page 337).

◖ **Connemara National Park:** These 1,300 boggy, beautiful hectares include three of the Twelve Bens (page 353).

◖ **Leenane and Killary Harbour:** The hills bordering Ireland's only fjord have a haunting, almost supernatural atmosphere, and the village of Leenane makes a lovely base for exploring northern Connemara (page 355).

◖ **Kilmacduagh:** The highlight of this off-the-beaten-track monastic ruin is a 34-meter round tower leaning 60 centimeters off-center, a truly arresting sight (page 360).

LOOK FOR ◖ TO FIND RECOMMENDED SIGHTS, ACTIVITIES, DINING, AND LODGING.

the advent of the Normans, they did not found their own city here as they'd done in Wexford, Waterford, Dublin, and other places.

Galway is often called the "City of the Tribes" for the 14 Norman families who established themselves here from the 13th century on; the native Irish were forced to move to the Claddagh, a fishing village outside the city walls. The Normans had erected these walls to defend themselves against the O'Flaherty clan, from whom they had usurped the land. The Normans were loyal to the English crown,

of course, and in the 15th and 16th centuries the port of Galway flourished with trade from Spain and Portugal. It's even said that Columbus stopped here for Mass at the Anglican Cathedral sometime in 1477; others say the city was his last stop before departing for the New World 15 years later. The city never regained its medieval power and prestige after Cromwell's nine-month siege in 1652 and its ill-fated backing of the Catholic king James against William of Orange in 1691; its bohemian vitality may feel deep-rooted, but this is truly more

GALWAY

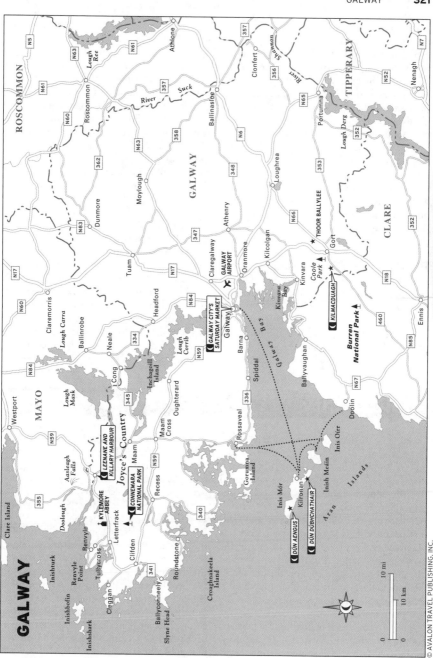

GALWAY

a development of the "Celtic Tiger" boom of the 1990s.

The demise of the Claddagh came in 1934, when the Galway Corporation claimed the area was a threat to health and hygiene. The cobblestoned streets were tarred over and the thatched-roof cottages demolished; the village's inhabitants were forced to move into charmless new buildings erected by the city council.

West of Galway, the region of Connemara was mostly isolated from the county's principal settlement throughout the centuries; the farming life on these rock- and heather-strewn hills was extremely difficult even during relatively prosperous periods. As H. V. Morton wrote of Connemara in the 1920s, "I know now where the world ends."

PLANNING YOUR TIME

In Galway City there's really no such thing as "planning," mainly because the city is short on sights and so rich in atmosphere. Traverse Shop Street, maybe pop into a few stores, wander through the market outside the cathedral and down to the Spanish Arch on the River Corrib, and wind up at a streetside table at Neachtain's

pub, savoring a pint—that's a full day's sightseeing by Galway standards.

Connemara does require a strategy, however. Most visitors drive it in a clockwise direction over a day or two, but frankly southern Connemara is pretty bleak, and not attractively so, even in summertime. You might want to hightail it west to Clifden and loop around north from there, perhaps venturing into County Mayo. Then savor a drive back through the gorgeous Lough Inagh Valley. Meanwhile, backpackers will want to get straight to the heart of the action in Letterfrack (for the national park) or Leenane (on Killary Harbour, where there's an outstanding adventure center).

The sights of southern Galway—Kinvara, Coole Park, Kilmacduagh, and so forth—are best taken in en route to Galway City after your tour of the Burren in County Clare.

As for the Aran Islands, most folks just visit Inis Mór, the largest of the three, as a day trip out of Galway—yet to see everything worthwhile requires at least a one-night stay, ideally two. The sights on the two smaller islands, Inis Oírr and Inis Meáin, can each be scoured in a single day.

Galway City

"It must be difficult to arrive in Galway and not feel glad," wrote Kate O'Brien in 1962, and all the millions of visitors to this sparkling medieval city before and since would heartily concur. Some folks even call it Ireland's San Francisco. Its west-coast setting; popularity with artists, musicians, and writers; friendly, laid-back vibe; and fresh sea air make this a viable comparison, and the presence of a national university enriches an already vibrant nightlife and theater scene. Though Galway is the republic's fourth-largest city, it still feels as accessible and friendly as a small town.

The city's medieval main drag, Shop Street, is always buzzing with buskers and other enterprising entertainers—puppeteers, flame-throw-

ers, even the occasional didgeridoo. From the recently refurbished Eyre Square (where the bus and train station is), walk south, passing Eglinton Street on your right, and venture down the cobblestoned pedestrian thoroughfare: Like most Irish main streets, Shop Street starts out as William, then becomes Shop, then High Street, before splitting into Quay Street (on the left) and Mainguard (later Bridge) Street on your right. At the end of Quay Street you'll find the Spanish Arch, a popular hangout for the city's bohemian population in fine weather (while Eyre Square tends to attract all the terminally bored teenagers). Cross the Wolfe Tone Bridge and you're in the old Claddagh section of the city, which now offers some of Galway's best pubs and cafés.

GALWAY

© CAMILLE DEANGELIS

the atmospheric quadrangle at the National University of Ireland, Galway

SIGHTS

Noteworthy architecture can be spotted on the northwestern side of Eyre Square, at the 17th-century **Browne's Doorway** (as you can see, the doorway itself is all that remains of Browne's townhouse); at the 16th-century **Lynch's Castle** on Shop Street at Abbeygate Street, which has housed the main Galway branch of the Allied Irish Bank since the 1960s (look for the original stone carvings high on the exterior walls); and at the solid, 16th-century **Spanish Arch** at the bottom of Quay Street on the River Corrib, so named for the Spanish ships that sailed through the no-longer-extant city wall carrying cargoes of exotic spirits.

Cathedrals

Galway's two cathedrals, one Catholic and one Anglican, are both named for Santa Claus (who was also the patron saint of sailors) and thus are easily confused. In the center of town, just off Shop Street, the Protestant **St. Nicholas' Collegiate Church** (Lombard St.,

tel. 091/564-648, generally open 9 A.M.–6 P.M. Mon.–Sat. and 1–6 P.M. Sun. in high season, 10 A.M.–4 P.M. Mon.–Sat. and 1–5 P.M. Sun. Oct.–Mar., free admission but donation appreciated) dates to the early 14th century. There are several medieval tombs and 19th-century stained-glass windows worth a short visit.

On the western side of the Protestant Cathedral churchyard is the **Lynch Memorial Window,** whose horrible history is well documented. In 1493 the mayor of the city, James Lynch FitzStephen, invited a Spaniard into his home. A spat of jealousy between the visitor and FitzStephen's son Walter ended in murder, and the mayor found his son guilty of the crime. When all the usual hangmen (understandably) refused to tighten the noose around the neck of the mayor's own son, legend states that the just-to-a-fault FitzStephen did the deed himself, from the window of his house on Market Street. Now you know the probable origin of the word "lynch."

Built in the mid-1960s on the site of the old city jail, the cavernous, green-domed

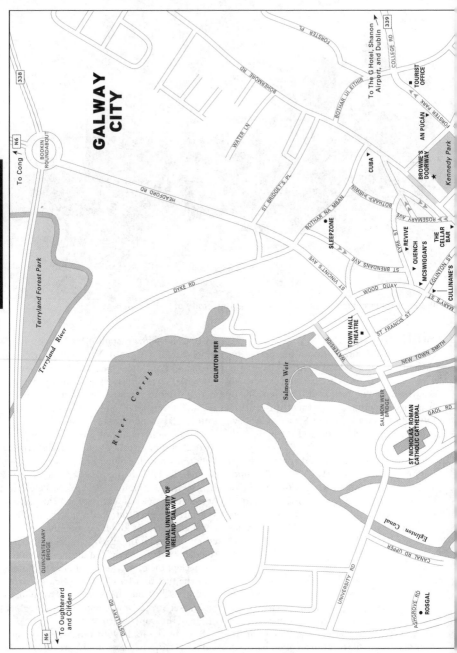

GALWAY

GALWAY CITY

To Cong N6

338

BODKIN ROUNDABOUT

N6

HEADFORD RD

BOHERMORE RD

WATER LN

FORSTER PL

BOTHAR UI EITHIR

To The G Hotel, Shanon Airport, and Dublin

COLLEGE RD 339

TOURIST OFFICE

FORSTER PARK

AN PÚCÁN

BROWNE'S DOORWAY

Kennedy Park

ROSEMARY AVE

CUBA

ST BRIDGET'S PL

BOTHAR NA MBAN

SLEEPZONE

ST BRENDANS AVE

ST VINCENT'S AVE

EYRE ST

BOTHAR IRWIN

REVIVE

QUENCH

MCSWIGGAN'S

EGLINTON ST

CULLINANE'S

MARY'S ST

THE CELLAR BAR

WOOD QUAY

DYKE RD

Terryland Forest Park

Terryland River

River Corrib

EGLINTON PIER

Salmon Weir

TOWN HALL THEATRE

ST FRANCIS ST

WATERSIDE

NEW TOWN SMITH

SALMON WEIR BRIDGE

ST NICHOLAS' ROMAN CATHOLIC CATHEDRAL

GAOL RD

QUINCENTENARY BRIDGE

NATIONAL UNIVERSITY OF IRELAND-GALWAY

DISTILLERY RD

UNIVERSITY RD

CANAL RD UPPER

Eglinton Canal

ASHGROVE RD

ROSGAL

To Oughterard and Clifden

N6

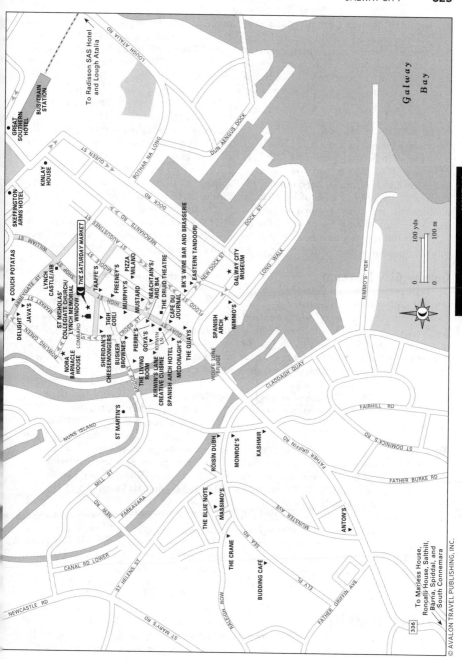

GALWAY

Galway Bay

To Radisson SAS Hotel and Lough Atalia

GREAT SOUTHERN HOTEL
BUS/TRAIN STATION

SKEFFINGTON ARMS HOTEL
KINLAY HOUSE
QUEEN ST
BOTHAR NA LONG
DUN AENGUS DOCK
LOUGH ATALIA RD
DOCK RD
DOCK ST
MERCHANT'S RD
NIMMO'S PIER
LONG WALK

COUCH POTATAS
WILLIAM ST
LYNCH CASTLE/AIB
JAVA'S
SHOP ST
ST AUGUSTINE'S ST
MIDDLE ST
ABBEYGATE ST
MARKET ST
DELIGHT
ST NICHOLAS' COLLEGIATE CHURCH/ LYNCH MEMORIAL WINDOW
THE SATURDAY MARKET
TAAFFE'S
FREENEY'S
PIZZA MILANO
MUSTARD
NEACHTAIN'S/ ARD BIA
EASTERN TANDOORI
BK'S WINE BAR AND BRASSERIE
NEW DOCK ST
GALWAY CITY MUSEUM
HIGH ST
MURPHY'S
TIGH COILI
CROSS ST
PIERRE'S
GOYA'S
KIRWIN LN
CAFÉ DU JOURNAL
THE DRUID THEATRE
FLOOD ST
SPANISH ARCH
NIMMO'S
NORA BARNACLE HOUSE
BOWLING GREEN
LOMBARD ST
SHERIDAN'S CHEESEMONGERS
BUSKER BROWNES
BRIDGE ST
THE LIVING ROOM
KIRWIN'S LANE CREATIVE CUISINE
SPANISH ARCH HOTEL
McDONAGH'S
THE QUAYS
WOLFE TONE BRIDGE
CLADDAGH QUAY
FAIRHILL RD
ST DOMINICK'S RD

ST MARTIN'S
NUNS ISLAND
MILL ST
NEW RD
PARKAVARA
FATHER GRIFFIN RD
FATHER BURKE RD

ROISIN DUBH
MONROE'S
KASHMIR
MUNSTER AVE

THE BLUE NOTE
MASSIMO'S
ANTON'S

THE CRANE
SEA RD
BUDDING CAFÉ
ELY PL
FATHER GRIFFIN AVE

CANAL RD LOWER
ST HELENS ST
ST MARY'S RD
RALEIGH ROW
NEWCASTLE RD

To Marless House, Roncalli House, Salthill, Barna, Spiddal, and South Connemara

336

0   100 yds
0   100 m

© AVALON TRAVEL PUBLISHING, INC.

St. Nicholas' Roman Catholic Cathedral

(University Rd. and Gaol Rd., tel. 091/564-648, free admission) features a mosaic portrait (in a side chapel) of John F. Kennedy, whom the Irish have all but canonized. This cathedral is on the west shore of the Corrib, just over the Salmon Weir Bridge.

Nora Barnacle House

Of primary interest to Joyce buffs, Nora Barnacle House (8 Bowling Green, tel. 091/564-743, open 10 A.M.–1 P.M. and 2–5 P.M. daily mid-May–mid-Sept. and by appointment, admission €2.50) offers a trove of love letters, photographs, and other memorabilia on display in the childhood home of James Joyce's wife. This 19th-century townhouse is also the smallest museum in the country!

Galway City Museum

The Galway City Museum (Spanish Arch, tel. 091/532-460, open 10 A.M.–5 P.M. Tues.–Sat., 2–5 P.M. Sun., free admission), which reopened with temporary exhibitions in June 2006, is in a sleek new building behind the quaint old museum. The temporary exhibitions complement a small permanent collection of art, photographs, and local artifacts, which is set to officially reopen in 2007. Admission was free at time of writing, though there may be a small entrance fee in the future.

Tours

Galway makes a good base for exploring both Connemara and the Burren. If time is tight, try a day tour with **Lally's** (tel. 091/562-905, www.lallytours.com, €22) or **Healy's** (tel. 091/770-066 or 087/259-0160, www.healytours.ie, €22), both of which have coaches departing Merchants Road just off Eyre Square at 10 A.M. daily (returning around 6 P.M.) for both regions. You can purchase your ticket at the tourist office, online, or on the bus, but be sure to get there by 9:30 A.M. at the latest, especially in high season.

ENTERTAINMENT

Galway entertainment offers something for everyone—good plays, live rock and traditional music, and a choice of nightclubs (though most of them are teeming with rowdy teenagers).

The **Town Hall Theatre** (Courthouse Sq., tel. 091/569-777, www.townhalltheatregalway.com, tickets €8–20) is the city's primary venue for traveling dramatic and musical productions. Some plays are better than others, but the congenial atmosphere in the upstairs bar makes for a worthwhile evening even if the play is mediocre (though fortunately most of the plays are very good). Town Hall also hosts a foreign film series on Sunday night in the spring and fall, as well as most of the readings during the Cúirt literary festival.

The **Druid Theatre** (Courthouse Ln., tel. 091/568-617, www.druidtheatre.com, tickets €15–20) is more avant-garde than Town Hall and showcases contemporary Irish playwrights.

Galway also boasts plenty of live trad, though **Monroe's** (Upper Dominick St., tel. 091/583-397) is the only pub in the city with set dancing sessions (on Tuesday night). It has traditional music sessions every night of the week and decent pizzas in the adjoining shop—recommended for the late-night munchies. Other spots for traditional music nightly include **The Crane** (2 Sea Rd., tel. 091/587-419), **Taaffe's** (19 Shop St., tel. 091/564-066), and **An Púcán** (11 Forster St., tel. 091/561-528). **Tigh Coili** (Mainguard St., tel. 091/561-294) has a rollickin' Wednesday-night (and occasional Saturday-night) session.

Two labyrinthine, multilevel pubs with fairly good food are the **Quays Pub** (Quay St., tel. 091/568-347) and **McSwiggan's** (3 Eyre St., Woodquay, tel. 091/568-917). The Quays is the more ancient and cavernous of the two, offering live music (trad on Mon.–Thurs. nights and Fri.–Sun. at 5 P.M., pop/rock on weekend nights) and a hearty, good-value buffet lunch upstairs on the weekends.

If you're looking for a change of pace—an unpretentious pub frequented by garrulous old Irishmen instead of busloads of tourists—try **Freeney's** (19 High St., tel. 091/562-609) or **Murphy's** (9 High St., tel. 091/564-589), across the pedestrian street from one another;

FESTIVALS AND EVENTS IN GALWAY CITY

Galway's busy festival calendar underscores the city's popularity with artists, poets, and dramatists. The biggest event is the **Galway Arts Festival** (tel. 091/566-577, www.galwayartsfestival.com, tickets €7-35), which keeps the city humming with a marvelous smorgasbord of concerts, plays, avant-garde exhibits, and street performances during the last two weeks of July. The drama lineup has been short on local talent in recent years, so Galwegians have started a fringe festival with plays, concerts, and readings that are often more enjoyable than the main events (the tickets are a lot less pricey, too). The name of the fringe fest changes by the year; in 2006 it was called Project '06. (Just keep your eyes peeled for posters and program booklets at cafés, pubs, and the tourist office.) **Cúirt International Festival of Literature** is the city's literary festival, bringing together an international assortment of distinguished and emerging writers around Eastertime, generally mid- to late April. The likes of Seamus Heaney, J. M. Coetzee, Maxine Hong Kingston, Rick Moody, and Chuck Palahniuk have given readings in the last few years; most readings take place at the Town Hall Theatre. For more information, contact the **Galway Arts Centre** (47 Dominick St., tel. 091/565-886, www.galwayartscentre.ie). And as you'd expect, the weeklong **Galway Film Fleadh** (tel. 091/751-655, www.galwayfilmfleadh.com) in mid-July offers a busy schedule of international film screenings.

As for music events, the **Jazz Festival** (contact the Town Hall, tel. 091/569-777, www.galwayjazzfestival.com) takes place over four days in mid-October, showcasing both local and American talent. Another four-day fest in early November is the **Spirit of Voice** (contact Mulligan Records, 5 Middle St., tel. 091/564-961, www.spiritofvoice.com), a reincarnation of the Galway City Festival of World Music. Proceeds benefit the Cystic Fibrosis Foundation.

None of that artsy-fartsy stuff for you? There's the **International Oyster Festival** (tel. 091/522-066, www.galwayoysterfest.com), a four-day event at the end of September featuring lots of live music. Here's your chance to sample that ambrosial combination of oysters and Guinness. And no self-respecting horse-racing fan should miss the **Galway Races** (tel. 091/753-870, www.galwayraces.com), which often overlap with the Galway Arts Festival in late July. You can take a special Bus Éireann shuttle service (single/return €5/7) from Eyre Square East to the Ballybrit Racecourse five kilometers east of town. (Needless to say, you've got to book accommodations many months in advance if you'll be in the city around this time.) It also goes without saying that both these events are characterized by staggering amounts of drink!

---

or **Cullinane's** (Eglinton St., tel. 091/562-242), which has a more mixed crowd and plenty of cozy snugs.

A perennial favorite with hip young Galwegians is **Neachtain's** (17 Cross St., entrance on Quay St., tel. 091/568-820), an exceedingly old-fashioned pub with outdoor seating in the summer (but good luck finding a table).

Róisín Dubh ("raw-SHEEN DOVE," "Black Rose," Upper Dominick St., tel. 091/586-540, tel. 091/589-202 for concert info, www.roisindubh.net, cover €7–15, sometimes free) is by far the best live music venue in Galway—and certainly one of the top venues nationwide. Artists like Warren Zevon, Christy Moore, Andy Irvine, Luka Bloom, and Karen Casey (formerly of Solas) have played there over the years, as have bands like Doves and The Frames—and plenty more fine musicians who may never be household names. A recent renovation has purged the ground floor of its quaint bookshelves and open fire, but a neat new roof deck is a decent compensation. Another solid venue for live rock is **Massimo's** (10 William St. W., tel. 091/582-239), or try **The Blue Note** (3 William St. W., tel. 091/589-116) for live jazz. All of these pubs are top picks even if you aren't interested in what's going on in the back room; Massimo's is trendy yet cozy, The Blue Note is dimly lighted and slightly seedy (in a basement

GAY GALWAY

While Galway has a very open-minded atmosphere, it doesn't offer as many resources or meeting spots as Dublin or Cork. There's no resource center as such, though there are a couple of switchboards: the **OutWest Gay Helpline** (tel. 094/937-2479, 8–10 P.M. Wed.) or **Gay Galway** (tel. 091/566-134, www.queergalway.com, 8–10 P.M. Tues. and Thurs.). The Gay Galway website is also a decent source of entertainment info.

It's the city's most established gay bar, but due to run-ins with the police for serving underage drinkers, **Strano's** (1 William St. W., tel. 091/588-219, www.stranos.ie) may not be open while you're around (it depends on whether or not they've paid their latest fine). Galway's other watering hole is **The Stage Door** (Wood Quay, tel. 091/563-418), one block north of the Town Hall Theatre, a spacious, dimly lighted pub that tends to attract an older crowd. There's really only one club, **Eden** (Forster St., no phone, www.edenexperience.com), which takes place on Friday nights at the Junction Nite Club (just up the street from the tourist office). Eden clubbers are a more eclectic group – girls and guys, young and not-quite-so-young.

jazz club kind of way), and Róisín Dubh is the most crowded of the three in the evenings.

For bigger concerts, there may be something on at the **Radisson SAS Hotel** (Lough Atalia Rd., tel. 091/538-300, www.radissonhotelgalway.com); the likes of Mary Black, Martin Hayes, Beth Orton, and the Tiger Lillies have all played here in the last few years.

The best nightclub in town is **Cuba** (Eyre Sq., tel. 091/565-991, www.cuba.ie, admission usually €6), playing both live and spin jazzy pop and hip-hop on three floors well into the wee hours. Three spacious pubs that also serve good food in the daytime but are better for students and young professional types at night, are **The Cellar Bar** (Eglinton St., tel.

091/563-966), **The Living Room** (Bridge St., tel. 091/56804, www.thelivingroom.ie), and **Busker Brownes** (Cross St., tel. 091/563-377, www.buskerbrownes.com).

SHOPPING
◖ The Saturday Market

The Saturday market along Churchyard Street outside St. Nicholas' Collegiate Church (10 A.M.–6 P.M., daily in summer) is perfect for leisurely browsing: You'll find handmade silver and beaded jewelry, pottery, incense, artsy photos of the Connemara landscape, and plenty more. Great lunch and snacking options also abound at the market (see *Food*).

Other Shopping

Poke around at **The Bridge Mills** (O'Brien Bridge, Mill St.), where the **Tús Craft Design Shop** (tel. 091/532-500, www.tuscraft.net) sells hand-painted silk scarves, stained-glass pieces, stone lamps, colorful fairy dolls, glassware, and more of the same pottery and photography available at the market. This quaint little mall also houses several specialty shops (yarn, vintage clothing, custom-made purses and accessories) and a nice café for lunch or tea.

The Treasure Chest (31-33 William St., tel. 091/563-862, www.treasurechest.ie) stocks classy gifts (Avoca blankets, Galway crystal, and the like) along with the kitschy stuff. There's a choice of sweater stores along Shop Street, but most of the inventory is machine-knit.

The best bookshop in Galway is **Charlie Byrne's** (The Cornstore, Middle St., tel. 091/561-766, www.charliebyrne.com), which specializes in secondhand and overstock books. Charlie Byrne's is a Galway institution, so it's hard to believe it only opened in 1989. Helpful, laid-back staff, plenty of bargains on quality titles, the occasional reading and signing with a local author: For the bibliophile it's like Christmas every time you step inside.

SPORTS AND RECREATION

Locals' favorite way to burn a few calories is walking the promenade in **Salthill,** with its surprisingly clean strand, diving platform, and small amusement park overlooking Galway Bay. On Salthill's western end is the **Galway Golf Club** (Blackrock, Upper Salthill, less than 5 km west of the city center, tel. 091/522-033 or 091/522-169, www.galwaygolf.com).

Eight kilometers west of the city center on the R336, under an hour's walk past the end of Salthill promenade, is **Barna Wood.** This lovely park with its huge, gnarled, ancient moss-clad trees is Galway's closest thing to an enchanted forest. There's also a clean and far more secluded strand at Barna as well, signposted from the R336. On the way to Barna Wood is the **Rusheen Riding Centre** (signposted on the R336, tel. 091/521-285 or 087/681-1837, www.galwayhorseriding.com), which offers afternoon treks on the beach.

Corrib Canoe Courses (tel. 087/743-5644, www.nuigkc.com/corribcanoe, weeklong course €85) offers a five-day (two sessions per day) canoe course for all ages and experience levels. Just looking to rent a boat for the afternoon? Try **Corrib Boat Hire** (17 Corrib Terrace, Waterside, Woodquay, tel. 091/564-743, ring for rates).

ACCOMMODATIONS
Hostels
There's no shortage of budget accommodations in Galway, but a few places are sketchy, and others are downright cramped. The city has two excellent hostels, my favorite being the relatively new **Sleepzone** (Bothar Na mBán, Woodquay, tel. 091/566-999, www.sleepzone.ie, dorms €13–22, s €30–50, credit cards accepted). The kitchens are spacious enough to accommodate everyone at mealtimes, the free wireless Internet access is a major plus (though you have to wonder why so many tourists web-surf for hours on sunny afternoons!), and the spotless en-suite rooms range from singles to four-, six-, and eight-bed dorms to long-term self-catering apartments. There's also a regular shuttle service to Sleepzone Connemara (5 km outside Leenane, 50 km from Galway City; ask at reception). No wonder Sleepzone was rated the seventh best hostel on earth in a Hostelworld.com survey.

The other recommended hostel, **Kinlay House Galway** (Merchants Rd., Eyre Sq.,

www.kinlayhouse.ie, tel. 091/565-244, fax 091/565-245, dorms €15–22, s €33–45, credit cards accepted), offers a convenient city center location, though it can be mobbed with school groups in high season. You can buy tickets to the Aran Islands at a kiosk on the ground floor, and the shuttle bus departs right outside the door. Very nice kitchen and common areas, and a light breakfast is included in the room price. Note that reception is on the fourth floor—and there is no elevator.

Bed-and-Breakfasts
One of the best B&Bs, **St. Martin's** (2 Nun's Island Rd., tel. 091/568-286, €35 pp sharing) is a whitewashed townhouse with a lovely little garden facing the River Corrib, visible as you cross the O'Brien Bridge heading out to the west side of town. Along with the unbeatable location, the fine breakfasts and hospitable owners put this place at the top of the list.

A quiet, homey B&B near National University of Ireland Galway, a five-minute walk from the cathedral, is **Rosgal** (Ashgrove Rd., off Newcastle Ave., tel. 091/524-723, €35 pp), a small, clean, unpretentious place with hearty traditional breakfasts run by the kind-hearted Nancy O'Neill. Rosgal is a great value, too, as it is becoming increasingly difficult to find B&B in Galway for less than €40 a night.

Or you might prefer to stay in Salthill—after all, nothing beats a seaside stroll first thing in the morning. (The promenade is a great place to watch sunrise and sunset, if the weather is clear.) A B&B just up from the waterfront on the west end of town is **Marless House** (Threadneedle Rd., tel. 091/523-931, www.marlesshouse.com, €33–36 pp, s €45–50), which also serves very good breakfasts. Closer to town is light and airy **Roncalli House** (24 Whitestrand Ave. at Lower Salthill Rd., tel. 091/584-159, www.roncallihouse.com, €30–33 pp, s €40–45), whose breakfasts fall into the near-legendary category. Chelsea Clinton stayed here in 1997.

Hotels
Galway offers a variety of fine hotels, the most posh being **The g Hotel** (Wellpark, on the

GALWAY

northeast fringe of town, tel. 091/865-200, www.theghotel.ie, rooms €280–400), a brand-new, five-star establishment with interior design by celebrated British accessory designer Philip Treacy and €19 cocktails in the unbelievably swanky hotel bar. The view isn't so posh, though—it overlooks the parking lot of the new Eye Cinema.

But before The g Hotel opened, the Victorian **Great Southern** (Eyre Sq., tel. 091/564-041, www.greatsouthernhotels.com, d €180–280, off-season specials as low as €89) was the grandest in town; it has a pool, sauna, and steam room. A less opulent and slightly more relaxed choice on the square is the **Skeffington Arms** (south side of Eyre Sq., tel. 091/563-173, www.skeffington.ie, d €118–150, weekday corporate rate €65). Special rates abound, so be sure to check the website. The televisions in the hotel pub, "the Skeff," are often tuned to American sporting events. Another atmospheric hotel with an excellent pub is the **(Spanish Arch** (Quay St., tel. 091/569-600, www.spanisharchhotel.ie, s €75–85, d €99–145). Erected in 1584, the building first served as a Carmelite convent.

It may be ugly as sin on the outside, but the four-star **Radisson SAS** (Lough Atalia Rd., tel. 091/538-300, www.radissonhotelgalway.com, rooms €240, s €220) boasts a ritzy spa and leisure center, and the ballroom is a popular concert venue.

FOOD

Downtown Galway holds many fine eateries; just walk down Shop Street, the old medieval main drag, until it turns into Quay Street. There are so many excellent restaurants along here that you'll have a difficult time choosing between them. Seafood is the highlight of most menus, unsurprisingly, but there are restaurants here to suit every taste.

Cafés

The best people-watching spot, aside from Neachtain's pub up the street, is **Café du Journale** (Quay St., tel. 091/568-426, open 10 A.M.–6 P.M. daily, until 10 P.M. in summer,

mains €6–18). The café does an excellent cup of cappuccino, though the food is definitely hit-and-miss. The walls are decorated with the first lines of classic novels; try to remember which books they belong to as you sip your coffee.

It seems like new cafés are opening all the time on Eyre Street, near the Corrib Shopping Centre, one of which is **Revive** (35 Eyre St., tel. 091/533-779, open 8 A.M.–5:30 P.M. Mon.–Sat., mains €7–11). Killer gourmet coffee and huge, super-fresh salads and sandwiches are on the menu here; the place is always bustling with loyal regulars, and there's outdoor seating out back on fine days.

Pick up lunch for a riverside picnic at the aptly named **(Delight** (29 Upper Abbeygate St., tel. 091/567-823, open 9 A.M.–6 P.M. Mon.–Fri., lunches €6–10), which offers a long list of mostly organic gourmet sandwich options, many of which are vegetarian, vegan, or gluten-free. The coffee and brownies are awesome.

Java's (Upper Abbeygate St., tel. 091/567-400, open 11 A.M.–3 A.M. or later daily, sandwiches under €8), now billing itself rather amusingly as a "Paris-Galway café," is good for a late-night snack after the pubs close.

Brought to you by one of Ireland's premiere wedding cake designers, **Goya's** (2/3 Kirwan's Ln., tel. 091/567-010, www.goyas.ie, open 10 A.M.–6 P.M. Mon.–Sat., lunch served 12:30–3 P.M., mains €5–10) is the ideal spot for tea and a slice of freshly baked pear tart. You'll have a hard time deciding on a dessert—they're all scrumptious.

A short walk off the tourist circuit, **Anton's** (Father Griffin Rd., tel. 091/582-067, open 8 A.M.–6 P.M. Mon.–Fri., mains €6–9) has that laid-back arthouse vibe about it. This one isn't as busy as the city center cafés, but the sandwiches are amazing and the coffee's some of the best anywhere.

A hidden gem, the **(Budding Café** (Sea Rd., tel. 091/588-821, fax 091/753-357, open 10 A.M.–5 P.M. Mon.–Sat., lunch entrées €7–9) is at the rear of Heneghan's Florists. Relax with a cup of infused tea as you watch the florist arrange a bouquet of exotic flowers while the rain falls on the pitched glass roof above. The lunch menu is all-vegetarian, and though the choices are few, everything is fresh and scrumptious.

Casual Restaurants

McDonagh's (22 Quay St., tel. 091/565-001, noon–10 P.M. Mon.–Sat., 5–10 P.M. Sun., mains €5–10) is a Galway institution, serving up fresh battered fish and chips for four generations. There are three shops in one here: the chipper on the left with its long wooden tables, the full restaurant on the right (reservations accepted only in the off-season), and a fishmarket around the back. Salmon, trout, cod, turbot, prawns, sole, silver hake, lobster—you name it, they've got it, and you can be certain it came off a local fishing boat that very morning. Too bad the chips are sold separately.

Don't miss ⓒ **Mustard** (Middle St., tel. 091/566-400, open noon–10 P.M. daily, mains €7–14) for its long and mouthwatering menu of delightfully inventive gourmet burgers, salads, and pizzas. There are plenty of meat dishes, but the wealth of veggie options makes Mustard a must if you're a vegetarian (try the goat cheese or pumpkin couscous burgers). The ambience is relaxed and the service is top-notch.

If you're in the mood for spuds (and who isn't?), check out ⓒ **Couch Potatas** (40 Upper Abbeygate St., tel. 091/568-427, open noon–10 P.M. daily, mains €7–9), always bustling because locals (mostly students) know what a terrific value it is. Not only are the stuffed potatoes to die for, but the desserts are delicious as well, and the friendly waitstaff never hurry you from your table.

Yes, it's a chain, but **Pizza Milano** (Middle St., tel. 091/568-488, open 11:30 A.M.–11:30 P.M. daily, mains €8–14) does delicious, good-value pizzas and pastas and excellent desserts. It may look swanky from the outside, but this place isn't at all formal.

For exotic eats, try **Kashmir** (Father Griffin Rd. opposite the fire station, tel. 091/589-900, open noon–2:30 P.M. and 5:30–10:30 P.M. or later Mon.–Fri., open 2:30–11 P.M. weekends, mains €9–15), which does some of the best Indian anywhere in Ireland. **Eastern Tandoori** (2/3 Spanish Parade, tel. 091/564-819, open 12:30–2:30 P.M. and 6–11:30 P.M. Mon.–Sat., 1–4 P.M. and 6–11:30 P.M. Sun., mains €11–17) can also boast good-value Indian fare with impeccable service in a classy dining room. Next door, **BK's Wine Bar and Brasserie** (Spanish Parade, tel. 091/568-450, cartebrasserie@aol.com, open 6 P.M.–1 A.M. daily, mains €11–23) is a darling little French place with delicious desserts, an extensive wine selection, and service so slow you should plan to spend the evening here.

Another recommended French restaurant is **Pierre's** (8 Quay St., tel. 091/566-066, www.pierresrestaurant.com, open 6–10:30 P.M. Mon.–Sat., 6–10 P.M. Sun., mains €13–25, 3-course early-bird special €24), a Galway pre-theater mainstay.

The upstairs wine bar at **Sheridan's Cheesemongers** (14-16 Churchyard St., tel. 091/564-829, open 2–9 P.M. Tues.–Sat., gourmet snacks under €12) is delightfully relaxed, with wine crates stacked in the corners and delicious nibble platters with fresh bread, cheese, olives, and tapenades.

Fine Dining

Numerous upscale restaurants in downtown Galway offer sophisticated modern Irish fare. Try the airy, upstairs **Ard Bia** ("High Food," 2 Quay St., www.ardbia.com, tel. 091/539-897 or 087/236-8648, open 10 A.M.–5 P.M. Mon.–Sat. and noon–6 P.M. Sun., 6:30–10:30 P.M. daily, lunch €10–14, dinner €16–25), with an exciting menu and distinctly arty ambience (it's also a gallery space). The food is also top-notch (well, it should be, for the price) at **Kirwan's Lane Creative Cuisine** (Kirwan's Ln., off Quay St., tel. 091/568-266, open 12:30–2:30 P.M. and 6–10:30 P.M. Mon.–Sat. Sept.–June, daily July–Aug., lunch €12–23, dinner €22–35), though the atmosphere isn't nearly as relaxed as Ard Bia's. Both have awesome vegetarian options, and both are fine choices for a special evening out. Note that "formal" is indicative of price rather than atmosphere—don't worry about what you're wearing!

GALWAY

© CAMILLE DEANGELIS

Galway's Saturday market is the highlight of the week.

Located a stone's throw from the Galway City Museum on the River Corrib, **(Nimmo's** (Long Walk, Spanish Arch, tel. 091/561-114, info@nimmos.ie, mains €13–24) is widely considered the best eatery in Galway. The food's so fresh there's little sense printing a menu, so your waiter greets you with a large blackboard detailing the evening specials. The steaks and seafood dishes are well worth the price, and the pastas melt in your mouth. Nimmo's has a warm, romantic ambience that's perfect for a date or a celebratory meal. Reservations are essential on weekends and in the summertime: The only bad thing about this place is that it's often so heavily booked you might have to give up your table before you're ready for your coffee.

The Saturday Market

On Saturdays, don't miss the outdoor market (10 A.M.–6 P.M.) along Churchyard Street outside the Protestant Cathedral. There are also a few stalls open on Sundays year round, and there are loads of food and gift merchants open every day of the week in high season. You'll find plenty of terrific lunch and snacking options, including the pricey-but-worth-every-cent Mediterranean stand, a popular crêperie, and a doughnut stand with a strong-lunged owner you can hear across the O'Brien Bridge. Best of all is **(Govinda's** (open 10 A.M.–6 P.M. Sat., noon–6 P.M. Sun., lunches under €5), whose vegetarian Indian dishes and whole-wheat samosas are truly sublime.

INFORMATION

The **tourist office** (Forster St., tel. 091/537-700, www.irelandwest.ie, open 9 A.M.–5:45 P.M. daily June–Sept., 9 A.M.–5:45 P.M. weekdays and 9 A.M.–12:45 P.M. Sat. Oct.–May) is one block east of the bus and train station. Read up on city news and events in the *Galway Advertiser* (www.galwayadvertiser.ie, a free weekly) and on **Galway.Net** (www.galway.net) before you go.

SERVICES

Banks with ATMs and bureaux de change include **AIB** (Shop St.), **Bank of Ireland** (Eyre

Sq.), and **Ulster Bank** (33 Eyre Sq.). The main **post office** is on Eglinton Street.

Need a pharmacy? **Boots** (35 Shop St., tel. 091/561-022) is open daily. Get your duds sudsed, or do it yourself, at the **Prospect Hill Launderette** (44 Prospect Hill, tel. 091/568-343, closed Sun.) just north of Eyre Square.

Galway's cheapest Internet access is at a copy center across the street from National University of Ireland Galway, **DigiCopy Express** (Newcastle Rd., no phone, open 9 A.M.–6 P.M. weekdays, €3/hour). Second-best is **Quench** (27 Eyre St., tel. 091/562-013, www.quench. ie, open 8 A.M.–5:30 P.M. daily, €3.60/hour), which also offers wireless access and tasty eats and smoothies. There are several cafés in the center of town, but expect to pay upward of €4.50/hour. As in Dublin, wireless Internet in the pubs isn't free, but if you buy a drink, ask for a free 20-minute voucher (The Living Room on Bridge Street is your best bet).

GETTING THERE

Galway is 217 kilometers west of Dublin on the N6, 105 kilometers north of Limerick on the N18, and 217 kilometers north of Killarney on the N23, N21, and N18.

You can get here from Dublin Heuston via **Irish Rail** (Eyre Sq., tel. 091/561-444, www. irishrail.ie, 5 trains/day daily, single/5-day return fare €29/41) or **Bus Éireann** (Eyre Sq., tel. 091/562-000, www.buseireann.ie), which offers services from Dublin and Athlone (#20, 15/day daily), Killarney and Tralee (#54, 3/day daily, transfer at Limerick), Cork and Limerick (#51, 12/day daily), Belfast (#65, 4/day daily,

transfers at Sligo and Enniskillen), Derry (#64, 5/day daily), and many other towns.

Citylink (tel. 091/564-163, www.citylink. ie, at least 14/day daily to Dublin, 5/day daily to Shannon) offers frequent service to Dublin (city and airport, single/return €14/18) as well as Shannon airport (€16/23). You can purchase your ticket at the Citylink desk at the tourist office on Forster Street, or on board; the bus stop is also on Forster Street, adjacent to the main bus station. Bus Éireann also offers a service (#51) to Shannon Airport, with at least 10 departures per day daily; the first bus leaves at 7:05 A.M. (single fare €14.50). The Citylink service is faster, and the buses are newer and more comfortable, however.

The **Galway City Airport** is six kilometers from the city center (Carnmore, tel. 091/755-569, www.galwayairport.com). Fly here from Dublin (4/day weekdays, 3/day Sat.–Sun.), Belfast, and other locations in the United Kingdom.

GETTING AROUND

Downtown Galway is easily walkable, though you might want to take the local bus (#1, 3/hour, fare €1.20) to Salthill. All local buses depart from the northern side of Eyre Square.

Rent a bike from **Europa Cycles** (Hunters Building, Earls Island, signposted opposite the Catholic cathedral, tel. 091/563-355, €10/50 per day/week).

Taxi ranks are at Eyre Square and Bridge Street, or you can ring **Abby Taxis** (11A Eyre St., tel. 091/533-333) or **City Taxis** (tel. 091/525-252).

GALWAY

The Aran Islands

These three rocky islands seem far removed from the Burren region of County Clare, yet the sea has carved them out of the same limestone reef lurking beneath Galway Bay. The ubiquitous stone walls demarcating the farmers' fields on the largest island alone run 4,800 kilometers in total. There are more pubs on

this island than there are schools or churches (six pubs, three primary schools, one secondary school, and three Catholic churches, to be exact), and the butcher pays a visit from the mainland two days a week. The local priest is a very busy man: He performs Mass on all three islands.

The largest island, Inis Mór, also offers some of the most important archaeological sites in the country, the crown jewel of which is Dún Aengus. You will spend your first night on Inis Mór reworking your itinerary so you can stay twice as long as you'd planned—and if you can't, you'll be thinking well ahead to your next trip.

Though you'll be hard-pressed to find an islander in traditional garb, and only a couple of homes still have thatched roofs, much of the old lifestyle remains. The denizens of the Aran Islands speak English only in the presence of strangers. If you can, spend a few days before you arrive learning a few Irish words and phrases. It's the surest way to see a native smile, and you'll quickly distinguish yourself from the hordes of stereotypical vacationers.

GETTING THERE AND AROUND
By Ferry from Galway (Rossaveal)

Island Ferries (4 Forster St., Galway, tel. 091/568-903 or 091/561-767, tel. 091/572-273 after hours, fax 091/568-538, www.aranisland-ferries.com, €25 return plus €6 for the bus) sails to all three islands year-round, operating a double-decker shuttle service from Kinlay House off Eyre Square in Galway to the port at Rossaveal. Bus and ferry tickets may be purchased at the Kinlay House lobby or at any of the Island Ferries offices sprinkled throughout downtown Galway.

April–October, ferries leave for Inis Mór at 10:30 A.M., noon, 1 P.M., and 6:30 P.M. More sailings are added in July and August, so call or drop in for the high summer schedule. April–October, ferries leave Inis Mór for Rossaveal at 8:30 A.M., noon, 4 P.M., and 5 P.M. (and 7:30 P.M. June–September). November–March, ferries depart Rossaveal for Inis Mór at 10:30 A.M. and 6 P.M., departing Inis Mór at 9 A.M. and 5 P.M.

The Inis Meáin/Inis Oírr ferry departs from Rossaveal at 10:30 A.M. and 6 P.M., leaving the islands at 8:15 A.M. and 4:30 P.M. Departure times are subject to change, especially

the early sailings, so be sure to ring ahead for confirmation.

The Galway–Rossaveal bus departs one hour before sailing time. Allow yourself an extra half hour to purchase your tickets and use the restroom at Kinlay House—even in the early spring the shuttle bus is filled to capacity.

Those driving from Galway should take the R336 west to Rossaveal and park in the €4-per-day lot beside the dock. You can purchase ferry tickets at the office there.

By Ferry from County Clare

If you want to reach the Aran Islands from County Clare, **Doolin Ferries** (The Pier, Doolin, tel. 065/707-4455 or 065/707-4466, fax 065/707-4417, www.doolinferries.com, €25 return to Inis Oírr, €35 return to Inis Mór) is an option, though the service isn't as reliable as the ferry out of Rossaveal. The ride is about 10 minutes shorter, however, as Inis Oírr is only eight kilometers off the Clare coast. Boats leave Doolin for Inis Oírr daily April–September (June–August at 10 A.M., 11 A.M., noon, 1 P.M., and 3:30 P.M., plus 4:30 P.M. on Fri.; in spring and autumn, at 10 A.M., 11:30 A.M., 1 P.M., and 3:30 P.M.). The ferry leaves Inis Oírr for Doolin at 9 A.M., 12:30 P.M., 3 P.M., and 5 P.M. in summer, and at 9:30 A.M., 12:30 P.M., and 5 P.M. during off-peak months. In summer, the boat to Inis Mór departs Doolin at 9 A.M., noon (July 15–September 1), 1 P.M., 4 P.M., and 5:30 P.M. Off-peak, ferries leave for Inis Mór at 10 A.M. and 1 P.M.; the ferry departs Inis Mór at 11:30 A.M. and 4 P.M. April–September. Call the Doolin Ferries office for Inis Meáin departure times.

The other ferry option out of Doolin is **Aran Islands Fast Ferries** (tel. 065/707-4550, www.aranislandsfastferries.com, single/return fares €20/35 Inis Mór, €18/30 Inis Meáin, €15/25 Inis Oírr), which operates year-round. Ferries depart for Inis Oírr every 90 minutes 9 A.M.–3 P.M. daily, and to Inis Mór at 9 A.M. and 5 P.M., with occasional "lunchtime" sailings. Ring office for Inis Meáin schedule.

GALWAY

© CAMILLE DEANGELIS

Na Seacht dTeampaill on Inis Mór sometimes floods in the springtime.

By Air

The faint of stomach can fly to the islands via **Aer Arann** (tel. 091/593-034, fax 091/593-238, www.aerarannislands.ie, €45/37 adult/student return, €37 group rate of four or more, €23 one-way), also via shuttle bus from Galway City. Flights depart the Connemara airport at Minna (35 km west of Galway) and last 10 minutes. Reserve your seats by phone or email well in advance during high season, as the planes carry only nine passengers.

Flights depart Minna for Inis Mór at 10 A.M. and 11:30 A.M. year-round, as well as at 8:30 A.M. February–November, 3:30 P.M. November–January, and 5:30 P.M. April–October. The flights return to Connemara at 10:15 A.M. and 11:45 A.M. year-round, plus 8:45 A.M. February–November, 3:45 P.M. November–January, and 5:45 P.M. April–October. The airstrip overlooks Killeany Bay, two kilometers southeast of Kilronan.

Flights leave for the two smaller islands at 9 A.M. and 10:30 A.M. year-round, as well as 3 P.M. November–January and 5 P.M.

April–October; island departure times are at 9:15 A.M. and 10:45 A.M. year-round, plus 3:15 P.M. November–January) and 5:15 P.M. April–October). (Double-check this schedule on the website before you make a reservation, as times are subject to change from year to year.) The Inis Meáin airstrip is on the northeastern end of the island a good two kilometers from the pier, and the Inis Oírr strip is more conveniently situated just east of the strand.

Getting Around

To get from Inis Mór to one of the other islands the old-fashioned way, you can hire a curragh from **Aran Watersports** (Kilronan, tel. 099/75073).

INIS MÓR

Inis Mór (Inishmore), the "Great Island," is 14.5 kilometers long and 4 kilometers at its widest point. Though the largest of the Aran Islands is also the most frequently visited, Inis Mór has a way of accommodating tourists without feeling the slightest bit commercial. Much has inevitably changed since the days of Aran fishermen going to work in their curraghs and rerooffing their thatched cottages every six years, yet you'll be pleasantly surprised at how remote and romantic this place still seems, especially at night. Even in Kilronan, the island's heavily touristed port town, the moon lends a preternatural aura as it illuminates the low stone walls and shimmers over the dark sea beyond.

Most visitors only spend the day here—they take the early ferry in, rent a bike or board a minibus just before noon, travel to the more prominent sights before a late lunch, and return to Galway on the last ferry at 5 P.M. Ideally, however, you should allow yourself at least two days to see everything in between Dún Dúbhchathair ("The Black Fort") on the eastern side of the island to the quieter villages beyond Dún Aengus and Na Seacht dTeampaill ("The Seven Churches"), all of which are among Ireland's greatest archaeological treasures. It's best to spend the day of your arrival seeing the less touristy sights around Killeany, like the Black Fort, then rising early the following morning to beat the rush of day-tourists to Dún Aengus and the Seven Churches. Being able to walk through these ruins in relative peace and solitude is well worth the extra planning.

If you're especially interested in the islands' archaeology, geology, flora, and fauna, make your first stop at Ionad Árann, the Aran Islands Heritage Centre.

Ionad Árann

Ionad Árann, the Aran Heritage Centre in Kilronan (tel. 099/61355, www.visitaranislands .com, open 10 A.M.–7 P.M. daily June–Aug., 11 A.M.–4 P.M. daily Apr.–May and Sept.–Oct., admission €3.17, €5.08 for film and exhibition combination ticket), offers a worthwhile introduction on the history, culture, geology, and wildlife of the Aran Islands. The cost of admission used to include a screening of Robert Flaherty's 1934 film *Man of Aran,* but these days you'll have to purchase a combo ticket if you'd like to see it. Use your time wisely, however, and visit Ionad Árann on a foul-weather day. There's also a small coffee shop and bureau de change here.

◖ Dún Aengus

Dún Aonghasa, or Dún Aengus, is a magnificent semicircular hill fort perched 90 meters above the ocean and flanked on the remaining sides by *cheveaux de frise,* which are stone spikes arranged to deter invaders. The site is about 2,000 years old, and despite the spikes and defensive walls (5.5 meters high and 4 meters thick), archaeologists are still unsure as to its precise function. Dúchas operates a small exhibition at the base of the rocky uphill path to the fortress (tel. 099/61008, open 10 A.M.–6 P.M. Mar.–Oct., 10 A.M.–4 P.M. Nov.–Feb., admission €2.10). Dún Aengus is the Aran Islands' prime tourist attraction, and with good reason: There are precious few thrills in the world as heady as this one. Pop your head over the stony brink to feel the spray from the water crashing on the rocks hundreds of feet beneath you.

Na Seacht dTeampaill

Na Seacht dTeampaill ("The Seven Churches") is an early Christian monastic site comprising two churches and the ruins of several other domestic buildings dating from the 8th century, with 19- and 20th-century gravesites covering the ground between them. Look closely and you can also spot what's left of a few penitential beds *(leapacha)* and 11th-century inscribed high crosses. St. Brendan the Navigator, the intrepid holy man who supposedly crossed the Atlantic in a curragh, is said to be buried here as well. To get to the Seven Churches, take the main road past the Dún Aengus turnoff; the Seven Churches signpost is down less than a kilometer on the right.

The Seven Churches are a popular stop on the tourist circuit, so if you're cycling try to visit before the first ferry arrives (around 11:30 A.M.) or after the last one leaves at 5. If you go during the day, wait for a pause between the minivans—this place is best savored in relative solitude. (Both Dún Aengus and the

Seven Churches can flood in the springtime, so be sure to bring a pair of waterproof boots. Some determined travelers have braved the cold waters in the Dún Aengus entryway with waterproof sandals or even barefoot, but needless to say this isn't the best option.)

◀ Dún Dúbhchathair

Dún Dúbhchathair ("The Black Fort") is a gem: utterly breathtaking cliffs, and very few tourists with whom to share them. The actual fort is older and not as well-preserved as Dún Aengus is, but you can still spot some of the *cheveaux de frise,* and what's left of the spiraling dead-end corridors are well worth an extended visit. The fort and the cliffs surrounding it make the ideal spot for a picnic lunch. If you want to keep well away from the tourist track, the Black Fort is your new haven—just be careful not to walk too close to the edge. On the eastern end of the island, the Black Fort isn't an easy hike from the Killeany road (which is too rocky for cycling in some parts), but it's worth the time and effort.

Other Sights

Near the Seven Churches, **Dún Eoghanachta** is an inland ring fort housing the ruins of several *clocháin,* or beehive dry-stone huts. You can see another better-preserved *clochán* (known as **Clochan na Carraige**) on the north side of the main road, just before the Seven Churches turnoff. If you take a peek inside the little round hut you'll notice that the interior is actually rectangular.

Another ring fort with impressive walls and terraces near the highest point on the island, **Dún Eochla** offers a splendid panoramic view of the eastern side of the island. It's about 400 meters south of the main road about a kilometer outside Kilronan, a gentle uphill walk of 15 or 20 minutes.

Other less prominent sites south of the main road between Kilronan and Dún Aengus include the **Leaba Diarmuda agus Ghráinne** ("Bed of Diarmuid and Gráinne," a pair of doomed lovers in Irish mythology), a megalithic wedge tomb dating back to the time of Dún Aengus, and the probable burial site of several early farmers; and the **Teampall an Cheathrair Áileann,** the 15th-century "Church of Four Beautiful Saints" who were supposedly laid to rest beneath four nearby flagstones. Near these church ruins is a holy well that inspired John Millington Synge's play *The Well of the Saints.* Near the village of Gort na gCapall, off the walking route on the southern side of the island, is the **Poll na bPéist,** the "Serpent Hole." A rectangular pool in the old stone nourished by the ocean through an underground channel, it makes for an eerie but worthwhile detour.

There is more to see on the eastern end of the island. The Killeany road is dotted with queer vertical tombs, mostly from the early 19th century, which are dedicated to those fishermen whose bodies were never found. It's a tricky path up to **Teampall Bheanáin,** a tiny 6th-century church set on the north–south axis rather than the customary east–west. Just remember that there's no need to hop any stone walls—there is a set path uphill, so if you don't spot any weathered markers see if you can flag a passing local to ask for directions. Going the right way, you'll spot the remains of a round tower on your walk up, along with what's left of the 5th-century **monastery of St. Enda,** patron saint of the Aran Islands. Benin's church is a creepy site with a fine view over Killeany and the harbor, but it's not a must-see unless you're a pilgrim or archaeological enthusiast. The humbleness of this site belies its importance, for St. Benin succeeded St. Patrick at his monastery in Armagh, and in its heyday St. Enda's was an important center of learning. Historian Peter Harbison has called this place "a veritable nursery of saints."

On the northern coast road outside Kilronan are the ruins of **Teampall Chiaráin,** named for the St. Ciarán who later founded the magnificent monastery at Clonmacnoise in County Offaly. It's mostly notable for the high Celtic cross in the churchyard and is worth a peek if you're biking back from Dún Aengus on the quieter coast road.

Tours

Of all the tour operators clamoring for your attention as you disembark at the Kilronan pier at 11 A.M., **Noel Mahon** (tel. 087/778-2775, €10 for a 3-hour tour) is by far the least obnoxious, and arguably the most knowledgeable. After stops at Dún Aengus and the Seven Churches, he'll take you through the village of Bun Gowla at the far end of the island and back to Kilronan, offering plenty of interesting tidbits about life on the island as he drives. If you're lucky you'll sight a few seals bobbing in the waves off the north shore at **Port Chorrúch** on the return trip. Just ask if you'd like to be dropped off at the entrance to either the Black Fort or Dún Eochla, both of which are well worth the uphill hikes (though the latter is the only viable option if you're leaving on the evening ferry). If you don't feel up to biking the island, this is your best option for seeing the most in the least amount of time.

Entertainment and Events

Finding live traditional music in the pubs of the Aran Islands is often a matter of luck, since there doesn't seem to be any sort of fixed performance schedule. Sometimes you'll find just two or three musicians playing as if for themselves, and other times you'll find something totally unexpected, like a troupe of Spanish bagpipers. For something more structured, try **Ragús** (Kilronan, tel. 099/61515 or 087/237-1642, tickets €15), a one-hour music and step-dance performance at the Halla Rónain community center (on the road to Killeany, within a five-minute walk of the pier). Shows are offered in summer only (June–Aug.) at 2:45 P.M., 5 P.M., and 9 P.M., and you can purchase tickets either at the Aran Fisherman restaurant or at the door.

Despite the Kilronan Hostel just up the stairs, the cozy **Tí Joe Mac's** (tel. 099/61248) seems to attract more weekending Irish than it does foreigners. Basic pub grub (soup and sandwiches), a crackling fire, and live "trad" (short for traditional music) most nights make it a fine place to pass a rainy evening. A few yards up the main Kilronan road on the right side is

The American Bar (Kilronan, tel. 099/61130), so named for the pool table in the back room and the '90s rock tunes on the speakers. This pub seems to be generally less popular than Joe Watty's or Tí Joe Mac's.

The brightly painted facade has no doubt caught your eye, but gaining entrance to **The Lucky Star Bar** (tel. 099/61219) is as mysterious an achievement as becoming a Freemason. Feel free to knock, but don't hold your breath. Farther up the road is the cozy **Joe Watty's** (tel. 099/61155), surprisingly swanky after its recent renovation. You can find live music here most nights, and this pub has the friendliest ambience of all those in Kilronan.

There are two more pubs on Inis Mór. **Tigh Fitz** in Killeany (tel. 099/61213, www.tighfitz.com, info@tighfitz.com) also offers pub food, set dancing, and live music in high season, and accommodations year-round. **Tigh Chreig** in Kilmurvey (tel. 099/61366, creggs@hotmail.com) is just a stone's throw from the Blue Flag beach.

Shopping

You're probably in the market for an authentic Aran sweater for yourself or a loved one back home, but don't waste your time inside the first shop you see. Local rumor has it that the Carraig Donn sweaters (at the Kilronan pier) are actually machine-knit in Guatemala. Whether or not they're made in Ireland, you can tell on sight they aren't made by hand. Same goes for the merchandise at the Aran Sweater Market next door.

The best place to pick up a sweater is **Sarah Flaherty's Aran Knitwear** (Bungowla, by the Dún Aengus entrance, tel. 099/61233, open 9 A.M.–5 P.M. Mon.–Sat.). Mrs. Flaherty hand-knits gorgeous sweaters, hats, and scarves in richly colored yarns, chatting animatedly with her customers as her needles work their magic between her hands. She'll even whip up a pullover or cardigan especially for you if you call ahead with your chest and underarm-to-waist measurements. You'll pay upward of €90 for one of these sweaters, but it goes without saying they're worth it. There

ARAN SWEATERS

In John Millington Synge's heart-wrenching one-act play set on the Aran Islands, *Riders to the Sea*, a young woman realizes that the clothes of a drowned fisherman (found on the shores of Donegal, and buried there) are those of her missing brother when she notices the stitch she herself dropped while knitting his socks. Art imitates life on these islands, for each family used a unique pattern when knitting pullovers (called *báinín*, "baw-NEEN") for their fishermen in the all-too-likely event that one should be lost at sea.

You probably won't see any shawls, *crios* (woolen belts), *mairtíní* (stockings sans feet), or other traditional garb outside the Aran museum, though the scarves and gloves sold in the shops are no less cozy for their lack of authenticity. Of course, the most popular seller remains the fisherman's sweater, knit in the traditional unbleached wool or a variety of jewel-toned yarns, but you have to wonder if the sweater pattern used by Sarah Flaherty and other speedy native knitters is one designed specially for the tourists.

Otherwise, as Pat Boran wryly notes, Aran jerseys are "now worn almost exclusively by German hippies, University College Dublin science students, and on RTE soap operas."

---

are several other shops by the Dún Aengus entrance selling jewelry, handkerchiefs, and other souvenirs.

Sports and Recreation

At Ionad Árann you can pick up a map detailing the various **walking routes** around the island. You can spend three full days sightseeing on foot without seeing everything, though, so you might want to hire a **bicycle** for at least a day. Wear waterproof boots and clothing, unless by some freak chance you're visiting on a brilliant cloudless day (they do happen every once in a while), and pick up sandwich fixings at the Spar before you leave. Except for the government-handled Dún Aengus, several of the other ruins make great spots for a picnic lunch if the weather holds.

Plenty of cyclists brave the minibus-clogged main road—it is the most direct route to Dún Aengus—but to avoid most of the traffic on the way back, take the coast road on the north side of the island.

There's a terrific Blue Flag beach at **Kilmurvey,** though it's rarely warm enough to go for a swim. If you're not visiting in July or August and still want to go for a dip, come prepared with a wet suit. **Aran Watersports** (Kilronan, tel. 099/75073) can accommodate fisherfolk and kayakers alike, and those interested in chartering a fishing boat can call **Aran Deep Sea Angling** (tel. 091/68903).

Equestrians can inquire about **pony-trekking tours** (tel. 099/61371) in the afternoons during high season.

Accommodations

Most hostels and B&Bs do not accept credit cards, so pay a visit to the ATM at the Spar in Kilronan before you check in.

The **Kilronan Hostel** (tel. 099/61255, www.kilronanhostel.com, info@kilronan.com, four- and six-bed dorms €14–16), on the pier, is above Tí Joe Mac's, which is either convenient or noisy depending on your priorities. It's clean and otherwise adequate, and a continental breakfast is included in the price, but you may not receive as warm a welcome here as you would at other hostels on the island (probably because this is the hostel of choice for the vast majority of backpackers arriving off the ferries, thus overwhelming the receptionist).

The great thing about **Mainistir House Hostel** (tel. 099/61169, www.mainistirhouse-aran.com, four-bed dorms €15, d €27 pp, s €36) is its nightly vegetarian buffet, so if you're interested in eating here it makes sense to stay here, too. The room prices include continental breakfast with freshly baked bread. It's a bit of a hike from the pier; the owners claim it's only a 10-minute walk, but you should expect to walk about 20. It's up the main road, past Joe Watty's, on the left-hand side. You may be able to get a ride from one of the hostel owners if you call. At least there are bikes to rent once you arrive.

Kilronan has a fair number of modest B&Bs. **Claí Bán** (tel. 099/61111, €28–35 pp, s €40–60) is perhaps the nicest in town, tucked down a path just beyond the Bank of Ireland. On your way up the main Kilronan road, you'll see a sign for Claí Bán on your left. You could also try the new **Pier House** (tel. 099/61417, €30–35, s €45–55), even closer to the dock, which is pricier for the convenience but offers a downstairs restaurant.

Like Mainistir House, the **Man of Aran Cottage** (Kilmurvey, tel. 099/61301, manofaran@eircom.net, €35 pp, s €45) is convenient because the owners also serve a terrific dinner. If you visit Ionad Árann, the island's heritage center, you'll see this old thatched cottage in the 1934 film of the same name, for which it was built. Man of Aran is six kilometers outside Kilronan, near Kilmurvey Beach (on the main road, it's on your right), so you should probably take a taxi when you get off the ferry, but it's worth the fare for the peaceful setting.

Another atmospheric option is **Kilmurvey House** (tel. 099/61218, www.kilmurveyhouse. com, €35 pp), an 18th-century stone home near Dún Aengus, with the Blue Flag beach a stone's throw away. A fixed-price dinner menu featuring fresh seafood and lamb is available for €22 (though the vegetarian option is not worth the price).

Food

As you would expect, seafood dominates the menus at the island's restaurants, and its small cafés offer simple but hearty fare. Unless noted, restaurants deal in cash only.

Excellent service, a nifty book-trading practice, and hearty, reasonably priced sandwiches, soups, and stuffed Rooster potatoes make ◖ **Lios Aengus** (Kilronan, tel. 099/61030, open 9:30 A.M.–5 P.M. daily, mains €3–7) the ideal place for breakfast before a day of biking,

or for an early supper afterward. The desserts are scrumptious, too (try a slice of banoffee pie or chocolate cake). This is probably the best bet for vegetarians in Kilronan. Take the main road up from the pier about 150 meters and you'll see it on your right. Lios Aengus is next door to the **Spar** supermarket (open 9 A.M.–8 P.M. Mon.–Sat., 10 A.M.–5 P.M. Sun.), site of the island's lone ATM. There's a good selection of frozen dinners and baked goods for hostellers, but beware the produce section, the contents of which hail from far-off lands and consequently may not be fresh.

Another good café option just across the road from the Spar is the whitewashed **An tSein Ceibh** ("The Old Pier," tel. 099/61228, open 11 A.M.–8 P.M. daily Apr.–Oct., mains under €12), popular for its fish-and-chip meals. Takeout is an option, but ask for "takeaway" instead.

If you find yourself at Dún Aengus around lunchtime, and it's more than likely you will, you have a couple of options: **Teach Nan Phaidt** (tel. 099/61330), closer to the main road, and **An Sunda Cáoch** ("The Blind Sound," tel. 099/61218 or 099/61983), closer to the Dún Aengus turnoff. Teach Nan Phaidt is usually the more crowded of the two due to its heartier, less cafeteria-like fare, but An Sunda Cáoch is the better choice if you're in the mood for a cappuccino at a quiet table by an open fire. Both cafés are open 11 A.M. to 5 P.M. daily April–October.

A seat at the all-you-can-eat vegetarian buffet at the **Mainistir House Hostel** (tel. 099/61169) will set you back €15, a humble price considering that dessert is included (and the rave reviews it's received in *The Irish Times*). Dinner is served at 8 P.M. in summer and 7 P.M. in wintertime. Do call ahead to reserve a spot, especially in summertime. Alternatively, the **Man of Aran Cottage** (Kilmurvey, tel. 099/61301, €25–30) offers soup and sandwiches during the day, and a much-praised dinner featuring homegrown organic vegetables and fresh seafood.

If it's seafood you're after, **The Aran Fisherman** (Kilronan, tel. 099/61104, open

11 A.M.–9 P.M., mains €10–20) will gladly accommodate, though it offers one or two pasta and pizza dishes as well. Follow the pier road past Carraig Donn; the restaurant is down a few meters on your right.

In the evenings there's a fast food stand just down the main road from Joe Watty's on the north side of the street, handy for those with a case of the late-night munchies.

Information and Services

The wee tourist office, or **Oifig Fáilte** (tel. 099/61263 or 099/61420, open 10 A.M.–1 P.M. and 2–5 P.M. daily Apr.–mid-Sept.), on the Kilronan pier can provide you with maps, B&B accommodations, and the like.

The **Bank of Ireland** (tel. 099/61178) on the main road is open on Wednesday only, so the best place to get cash is at the Spar supermarket ATM. You'll find the **Oifig an Phoist,** the post office, on the main road in Kilronan, next to the Lucky Star Bar.

If you need medical assistance, call the island's doctor (tel. 099/61171) or one of two nurses (tel. 099/61165). (There is no hospital on any of the islands, so emergency cases must be airlifted.) There is a lone *garda* (police officer) assigned to all three islands (tel. 099/61102).

Getting Around

There's no doubt that biking this island is the best way to go, and hiring one at the Kilronan pier is the easiest thing you'll ever do; the universal rate is €10 a day plus a deposit. There are plenty of bikes for all, but if you want to call ahead, you could try **Aran Cycle Hire** (tel. 099/61132); **Mullin's Bicycle Hire** (tel. 099/61132), which offers a group discount; or **B&M Bicycle Hire** (tel. 099/61402), which also has baby carriers and children's bikes.

A **public minibus** serves the whole island. Ask for the schedule at the tourist office, but if that's closed, there's also one posted at the Lios Aengus café.

You could travel to Dún Aengus in a **pony trap,** which will run you about €40 for up to four people. There are plenty for hire down at the Kilronan pier.

INIS MEÁIN

The 225 natives of Inis Meáin (or Inishmaan), the "Middle Island," have garnered a reputation for unfriendliness that may in small part explain why most tourists choose not to visit it. For every smileless islander there are plenty who'll welcome you, however. The landscape is somehow bleak and breathtaking at the same time, the stones of the endless dividing walls culled from the limestone beneath the shallow soil. Honeysuckle and orchids bloom all over the island, and the pollen of hundreds of other exotic flowers has been transported across the ocean from places as far off as the Mediterranean and the Arctic Circle. If the thought of elbowing your way through the summer crowds on Inis Mór doesn't appeal, take the ferry here instead. You'll be happy you did.

The middle island also offers plenty of activity for bird-watchers and other nature enthusiasts. There's a wealth of prehistoric and early monastic ruins, the most important of which is Dún Chonchúir, "Conor's Fort"—Conor being the brother of Aengus (as in Dún Aengus on Inis Mór).

Inis Meáin is only five kilometers wide and two and a half kilometers long, so you could certainly visit it on a day trip from Inis Mór or Inis Oírr (both of which offer more amenities for tourists). You'll have enough time to visit the principal ruins and enjoy a leisurely pint at Teach Ósta before heading back to the pier. Two main roads head west from the pier, a high road on your left (leading to the pub, church, and Conor's Fort) and a low road on your right that leads to the knitwear factory.

Dún Chonchúir

Though its three outer walls have crumbled, the fortress wall of the oval-shaped Dún Chonchúir remains almost completely intact, and it affords a tremendous view over the whole island: church and houses to the south, newfangled windmills to the north, and Gregory's Sound to the east. As with many other ruins on these islands, the age of this fort falls within a wide range of centuries—the 1st through the 7th A.D., that is.

Other Sights

John Millington Synge, whose dramatic works dominated the calendar at the Abbey Theatre in Dublin during the Gaelic Literary Revival of the early 20th century, gleaned much of his inspiration from the Aran Islanders. *Riders to the Sea* is set on Inis Meáin, in fact. Synge spent his summers here between 1898 and 1902, and you can visit **Teach Synge** (open noon–2 P.M. and 3–4 P.M. Mon.–Sat. June–Sept., admission €3), the small thatched cottage where he stayed, just across the road from the entrance to Dún Chonchúir. **Cathaoir Synge** ("Synge's Chair"), the playwright's favorite thinking spot, is just a rocky limestone promontory overlooking Gregory's Sound; you can even see the cliffs of the Black Fort on Inis Mór. Synge's Chair is marked on your right up the main road after the Dún Chonchúir turnoff.

On Inis Meáin there's another Neolithic wedge tomb known as **Leaba Diarmuda agus Ghráinne,** signposted from the low road (as you've no doubt surmised, the story of Diarmuid and Gráinne is one of the more lascivious in Irish mythology). This one has collapsed, however, so there's not too much to see.

Another stone fort on the eastern side of the island, **Dún Fearbhaí** (signposted off the high road, just up from the Tigh Chonghaille B&B) could be as old as the 1st century or as "new" as the 8th, and its square layout makes it peculiar. Climb onto the ramparts for an excellent view of the northern side of the island.

Though little remains of the **Teampall na Seacht Mac Rí** ("Church of the Seven Sons") near Conor's Fort, the nearby freshwater spring and holy well, **Tobar Chinndeirge,** is said to have restorative properties. The well is named for St. Cinndearg, who is supposedly buried by the south door of the *teampall.* In bygone centuries the Church of the Seven Sons was a popular pilgrimage site, and faithful islanders still flock here for the Stations on the ides of August.

It seems St. Gregory spent much time in lonesome contemplation on this island, as several sites in addition to the sound on the west side of the island bear his name. Near Dún Fearbhaí on the eastern side of the island is the 8th-century **Cill Cean Fhionnaigh** ("Church of the Fairheaded One," an epithet for St. Gregory), which is one of the most perfectly preserved of the early Aran churches (though there is still not much to see). The people of Inis Meáin buried their dead here up until the mid-1950s, and there's another holy well nearby. On the opposite side of the island is **Uamhain Ghríora** (Gregory's Cave), on the strand facing Gregory's Sound.

Ready to visit a church with roof intact? The **Seipeal Eoin agus Naomh Mhuire gan Smal** ("Chapel of Saint John and Immaculate Mary"), built in 1939, features typically exquisite stained-glass windows by Harry Clarke: a three-lighted altar window of the Madonna and Child flanked by Saints Peter and John the Baptist, as well as four smaller windows on the north and south walls, the most striking of which depicts Mary Magdalene. Most churches in rural Ireland are painfully austere, so this *seipeal* is a real gem.

Shopping

In the factory showroom at the Inis Meáin Knitting Company, **Cniotáil Inis Meáin** (on the low road about 1 km west of the pier, tel. 099/73009, fax 099/73045, www.inismeain.ie), you'll find hand-knit Aran sweaters at below-retail prices. (They're still considerably more expensive than Sarah Flaherty's on Inis Mór, though, so just think how much they cost at those exclusive shops in Paris, Tokyo, and New York!)

Sports and Recreation

It may be too cold for a swim, but you can at least doff your boots and socks for a walk down the sand at **Trá Leirtreach,** a sheltered strand 500 meters north of the small pier. There's another beach on the far side of the island, facing Gregory's Sound, where you can see the cliffs on Inis Mór's southeast side.

Food and Entertainment
Teach Ósta Inis Meáin (high road, 3-minute walk west of the church, tel. 099/73003, food served noon–7 P.M. daily, mains €8–15) is the island's sole pub, and it's every bit as rustically charming as you pictured it on the ferry ride over: stone floors, thatched roof, brilliantly colored flowers exploding out of the window-boxes. This is your best bet for lunch or dinner on the middle island, with seafood dominating the menu along with the customary soup and sandwiches. If you've picked up any Irish, now's the time to use it. You can also find traditional music sessions here on summer evenings.

Most bed-and-breakfasts also serve evening meals, since there aren't any other restaurants on the island. A full dinner using organic homegrown produce will cost you about €20.

Accommodations
B&Bs offer a handful of basic rooms with a shared bath. **Ard Alainn** (tel. 099/73027, open May–Sept., €25 pp), run by the most hospitable Mrs. Faherty, serves the heartiest breakfasts on the island, but alas, doesn't provide dinner. Looking at it on the map, it seems quite far from the pier, but it's actually only two kilometers. Take the main road (making a left at the fork up from the pier) and you'll see Ard Alainn on the left.

Two sound B&B-cum-restaurants are **Tigh Chonghaille** (tel. 099/73085, €25 pp, s €35), a cheerful yellow edifice just up from the pier at the fork in the road, and **An Dún** (tel. 099/73047, €33 pp, s €40), which is up the main road about a kilometer and a half on the right-hand side, directly opposite Dún Chonchúir; this one also has a shop where you can throw together an impromptu picnic to bring up to the fort. With a sauna and Jacuzzi, An Dún is the ritziest accommodation on the island.

Information and Services
There is no bank or ATM on the island, so be sure to make your withdrawal before leaving Galway. The **post office** is next door to the **Inis Meáin Island Cooperative** (tel. 099/73010, open 9 A.M.–4 P.M. Mon.–Sat.), which also serves as a tourist information point in high season. Take the low road from the pier to get here, and you'll see it past the knitwear factory on your left, on a side road that brings you up to the high road.

INIS OÍRR
The "Eastern Island," anglicized as "Inisheer," is just over three by three kilometers. Its population is greater than that of Inis Meáin, however. The rocky shore on the western side of the island makes for an awesome spot to watch the sun set, since the road back to the pier is perfectly safe to traverse in the twilight. Its three pubs are some of the warmest, friendliest spots anywhere in Ireland. Trad performances are on a rather spotty schedule in the off-season, but during the summer months you're guaranteed live music at all three. There may only be enough on this island to occupy you for the day, but Inis Oírr's charming cottages, lonely ruins, and sandy lanes make for quite a serene afternoon.

Sights
The O'Briens were one of two ruling families on the Aran Islands until the late 16th century, and their three-story tower house (better known as **Caislean Uí Bhriain** or "O'Brien's Castle") was built in the 1400s within the ruins of another 1st-century ring fort, **Dún Fhormna.** The castle overlooks the pier on the north side of the island, and from that vantage you can spot the **wreck of the Plassey** off the eastern shore. A storm in 1960 threw that freighter onto the reef of **Carraig ná Finnise,** where it remains to this day.

On the western end of the harbor, past Tigh Ned and the Fisherman's Cottage restaurant, **Inis Oírr Heritage House** (tel. 099/75021, open 2–4 P.M. July–Aug., admission €1) offers a small museum, café, and craft shop. It's one of the few buildings left with a traditional thatched roof.

Also on the northwestern side of the island, a short walk from the Inis Oírr Heritage House, the 8th- or 9th-century **Cill Ghobnait** ("St. Gobnait's Church") was dedicated to a Cork-born nun-on-the-run who apparently had more than one enemy in County Clare (legend has it that she kept an army of bees with which to defend herself). Back then Gobnait was the only woman allowed on these islands. Continue two kilometers down that road on the western edge of the island and come to the holy well of St. Enda, **Tobar Éinne,** which is still as sacred to the islanders today as it was a millennium and a half ago. Enda is said to have lived for a time in a *clochán* near this well, though very little remains of it now.

Enda may be the patron of Aran, but Kevin is the patron saint of Inis Oírr. The 10th-century **Teampall Chaoimháin** ("St. Kevin's Church"), just southeast of the airstrip, seems to be drowning in the ever-shifting sands, but the denizens of Inis Oírr clear it out every year on St. Kevin's feast day, June 14. Note the more recent gravestones, the Gothic chancel, and the shells and other remnants of a medieval kitchen dump.

The lower level of **Cnoc Raithni,** a two-level burial mound, dates from the Bronze Age, making it the oldest ruin on the island by far. It was serendipitously uncovered after a storm in 1885 blew away the tons of sand hiding it. The tumulus is situated beside the campground overlooking the harbor.

Accommodations and Food

The **Brú Radharc Na Mara** hostel (at the pier, tel. 099/75024, radharcnamara@hotmail.com, open mid-Mar.–Oct. dorms €15, private rooms €20 pp, credit cards accepted) is exceptionally cozy, clean, and comfortable, so much so that to stay at the nearby hotel might even seem like a waste of money. There's a spacious self-catering kitchen, though the small grocery store beside the hotel doesn't offer much of a selection. There are nearly 40 beds, so it's not necessary to book ahead in spring or autumn; there are only two private rooms, though, so reserve one in advance if that's your preference.

For B&B, look no further than **Radharc an Chláir** (near O'Brien's Castle, tel. 099/75019, bridpoil@eircom.net, €30–35 pp, s €35–40, evening meals €20). Bríd Poil provides a traditional welcome of tea and scones fresh out

of the oven (with homemade jams) in a warm and tranquil atmosphere. Be sure to book in advance, as this one deservedly draws loads of return visitors.

You can drink, sleep, and eat three meals a day at the island's sole hotel, the friendly, family-run **Óstán Inis Oírr** (tel. 099/75020, www.ostaninisoirr.com, €33 pp, s €40, credit cards accepted), where the price of a room includes a hearty breakfast. The restaurant is open daily in July and August and on weekends April–June and September. If the restaurant is closed, there's always decent grub to be had on the pub side, where there's live trad every night during the summer months.

The **Fisherman's Cottage** (tel. 099/75073, open Apr.–Oct., mains €12–22), which serves exceptionally good seafood and organic vegetables, is near the pier just past Tigh Ned and the bike-rental shop.

Entertainment

There are two pubs in addition to the bar at Óstán Inis Oírr: **Tigh Ruairí** (tel. 099/75020) and **Tigh Ned** (tel. 099/75004), both of which are fun places to pass an evening. The walls of Tigh Ruairí are peppered with rusted American license plates and other fun tchotchkes, and the live music is spirited even when only a couple of musicians show up. Tigh Ned is just as cozy but attracts a younger, rowdier crowd of dart-throwers, so unless you're backpacking it you might want to stick with Tigh Ruairí or the hotel pub. All three are very close to the Inis Oírr pier; when standing at the pier with your back to the island, the hotel lies straight ahead, with Tigh Ruairí just beyond it and Tigh Ned to your right.

Inquire at the Heritage House or tourist kiosk about the island's boat-racing festival, which is usually held in August. There's also **ceilidh dancing** in high season; ask for the particulars if you're visiting in summer.

Sports and Recreation

An Trá, "The Strand," makes for a pleasant stroll east of the harbor. The signposted **Inis Oírr Way,** 10.5 kilometers long, leads you through the uninhabited part of the island, where farmers have long demarcated their rolling fields. You'll meet more cows and horses than people there, however. An uninhabited **lighthouse** stands at the island's southern tip, and though visitors aren't allowed, the path that leads there (down the eastern side of the island) is more popular with tourists than the western road. You can rent a bike at **Rothair Inis Oírr,** by the pier.

Information and Services

There's a small stand right at the pier offering tourist information 10 A.M.–6 P.M. daily in July and August, but in the off-season call the **Island Cooperative** (tel. 099/75008) should you need assistance. The **post office** is inland, past O'Brien's Castle, and while you can change money there it makes more sense to take out as much as you'll need from the Spar ATM on Inis Mór.

Before you go, check out the official **Inis Oírr website** (www.inisoirr-island.com).

Getting Around

Rothair Inis Oírr (tel. 099/75033, €10/day plus deposit) rents bicycles, as do many B&Bs, but the island is so small you can definitely see everything in one afternoon on foot.

Connemara

Wild, wet, boggy, and mountainous, Connemara (Conmhaicne Mara, "Descendants of Con Mhac of the Sea") is still seen as a remote stronghold of traditional Irish culture despite ongoing development and exorbitant real estate prices in many parts. The name "Connemara" is generally used to describe the region west of Lough Corrib, with the Atlantic forming a border on the north, west, and south (between northern Connemara and southern Mayo is Ireland's only fjord, the starkly beautiful, salmon-dotted Killary Harbour). The region is also known for its production of whitish-green marble and strong-and-sturdy ponies.

Much of Connemara lies within the Gaeltacht, or Irish-speaking area, and many visitors come to learn the Connaught dialect at local summer schools. Others want to trample through the relatively small but utterly lovely Connemara National Park, and the most adventurous (not to mention experienced) of them all come to trek through the Maumturks and the Twelve Bens (also called the "Twelve Pins"). The valley formed by these two mountain ranges shelters the loveliest of Connemara's many lakes, Lough Inagh, and many consider this scenic drive the finest in the region.

Most visitors experience Connemara in a whirlwind coach tour from Galway, but ideally you should spend at least two nights out here. Connemara's "capital," Clifden, may seem like the natural choice for a base, but keep in mind that this town was all but established for tourists, making it high on amenities but lacking "authenticity." The hamlets of Leenane and Letterfrack are much quieter, offering picturesque scenery and a sense of quotidian life in Connemara without all the harp-and-shamrock foolishness.

Regarding the stretch of Connemara west of Galway City, the novelist Kate O'Brien put it best when she wrote: "There are stretches of South Connemara that are terrifying, grey and as if denying life." This description is apt even in the summertime. Eventually the inevitable suburban sprawl around Spiddal, depressing in itself, gives way to rock-and-heather-strewn desolation. You might want to skip this area altogether, cutting through Connemara via the N59 and heading north from Recess or Clifden into far lovelier parts, particularly the Lough Inagh Valley (the R334 from Recess north to Lough Fee, just east of Connemara National Park). Here you'll find the shimmering black lakes and evergreen-swathed mountains you've heard so much about.

© CAMILLE DEANGELIS

What could be as pretty as a Connemara sunset?

GETTING THERE

All roads lead from Galway City: The N59 takes you west to Clifden and loops around for Letterfrack and Leenane before passing into County Mayo. The R336 will take you west from Galway into southern Connemara. Plan on two and a half hours to reach Clifden or Letterfrack, longer if you're driving through south Connemara. Drive with especial caution, as the Connemara roads are narrow and full of dangerous hairpin curves.

You have a choice when it comes to bus transportation, though **Bus Éireann** service (tel. 091/562-000, #61 or #419, 3–4/day Mon.–Sat., 1–2/day Sun.) in Connemara is disappointingly spotty. Route #61 links Galway City with Oughterard, Maam Cross, Recess, Roundstone, and Clifden between late June and early September (5/day Mon.–Sat., 3/day Sun.). September–June, route #419 leaves Galway for Oughterard, Maam Cross, Leenane, Kylemore, Letterfrack, Cleggan, Recess, Roundstone, and Clifden (3/day Mon.–Sat., 2/day Sun.).

A less expensive, more comfortable alternative is **Michael Nee Coaches** (tel. 095/34682, www.michaelneecoaches.com, single/return ticket €10/13), which serves Maam Cross, Recess, Cashel, Clifden, Letterfrack, Tullycross, and Cleggan. Buses depart Forster Street in Galway (between the train station and tourist office) at noon and 5:30 P.M. daily, and there's an additional 9:30 P.M. bus on Friday and Sunday. Return service is somewhat less convenient: Buses pass through Letterfrack at 8:40 A.M. Monday–Saturday and at 2:35 P.M. on Monday, Friday, and Sunday; departures from Clifden are at 9:15 A.M. and 3:15 P.M. daily, with an additional 7 P.M. service on Friday and Sunday. Visit the website for a full timetable.

SOUTHERN CONNEMARA
Spiddal

Overdeveloped Spiddal (An Spidéal) has two reasons to linger for an hour or so: a lovely beach (which gets far too crowded in summertime) and a large gift shop, **Standún** (on the R336, tel. 091/553-108), known for its quality

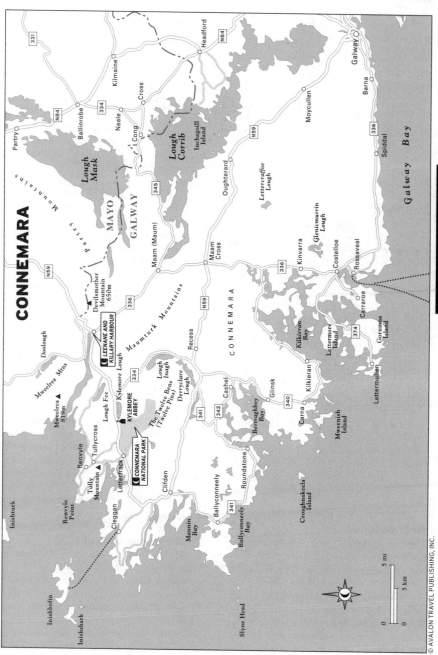

GALWAY

CONNEMARA

© AVALON TRAVEL PUBLISHING, INC.

souvenirs and airy bay-facing tearoom. Be warned, however, that this is the first stop on the Connemara day tours out of Galway, so you would do well to keep on driving.

Rossaveal

Thirty-nine kilometers west of Galway City off the R336, the pier at Rossaveal is the departure point for the Aran Islands. There is a ticket office and car park here for those who don't need the shuttle bus from outside Kinlay House off Eyre Square. See *The Aran Islands* for more information.

Pearse's Cottage

History buffs might want to pause in Carraroe to visit Pearse's Cottage, or **Teach an Phiarsaigh** (Inbhear, just west of Gortmore on the R340, signposted, tel. 091/574-292, open 10 A.M.–6 P.M. daily June–mid-Sept., weekends late Sept., admission €1.60), the restored summer home of Gaelic revivalist, poet, playwright, and Easter patriot Patrick Pearse (also spelled Pádraic or Pádraig). Born in Dublin in 1879 to an Irish mother and an English father, he began learning Irish as a young teen and became a devoted teacher of the language, establishing St. Enda's School in Dublin. It was to this cottage he brought his city pupils for summer classes. Pearse and his brother Willie were two of the 15 rebel leaders executed by the British after the Easter Rising of 1916, and the house was burned during the War of Independence. Fully restored, the house features a small exhibition and collection of personal memorabilia. A half-hour guided tour is available on request.

Roundstone

Dubbed "Galway 4" for its holiday-home popularity with well-heeled Galwegians (Dublin 4 is a swanky residential section), Roundstone (Cloch na Rón, "Stone of the Seals") is still a pretty low-key fishing village, drawing visitors for its proximity to pristine beaches: **Gurteen Bay** and **Dog's Bay** are two kilometers west of town. There are two more lovely strands at **Trá Mhóir** and **Mannin Bay** near the hamlet of Ballyconneely, 14 kilometers farther west on the R341. And even the most casual hikers can take a walk up **Errisbeg** (300 meters), which affords a postcard-perfect view of Bertraghboy Bay. A side road (beside O'Dowd's pub) heading west out of town will get you there.

Though Roundstone's shopping can't compare with Clifden's, a few shops are definitely worth stopping for. The **Starraic Gallery** (Main St., tel. 095/35977) also serves as the community arts center, and **Roundstone Musical Instruments** (signposted from Main St., tel. 095/35808, www.bodhran.com, open Mon.–Sat. all year, daily July–Aug.), located in an old Franciscan monastery, specializes in the goatskin drum used in every proper traditional music session: the bodhrán.

Roundstone's most popular B&B is **St. Joseph's** (Main St., tel. 095/35930 or 095/35865, www.connemara.net/stjosephs, €33–36 pp, s €42–46), a cheerful 19th-century townhouse with comfortable rooms and ample breakfasts (and vegetarians are catered to). A spiffy guesthouse featuring locally made bedroom furniture and a cozy library/sitting room, **Eldon's** (tel. 095/35933, www.eldons. ie, open Mar.–Oct., bar food served noon– 9 P.M. daily, mains €10–20, €35–45 pp, superior rooms €60) has a fine adjoining restaurant, **Beola** (tel. 095/35871, open 6–9 P.M. daily Mar.–Oct., mains €15–25), where seafood is a specialty. Also on Main Street is the small, friendly, family-run **Roundstone House Hotel** (tel. 095/35864, www.roundstonehousehotel. com, open Apr.–Oct., bar food served noon– 7 P.M. daily, €55–60 pp sharing), which offers excellent fish dishes in the restaurant and bay views from the front bedrooms.

A third dining option is the praiseworthy pub grub at **O'Dowd's** (Main St., tel. 095/35809, food served noon–9 P.M. daily, mains €10–22), a local favorite. You'll find live trad in Roundstone's three pubs nightly in high season, or you might want to time your visit for the two-part **Roundstone Arts Week** (tel. 095/35871, www.roundstoneartsweek. com), which hosts a music-and-art weekend in late June and a theater-and-literature weekend in late July. **Summerfest** (www.roundstone-summerfest.com) is a music festival and charity fundraiser for the Irish Lifeboats Service over four days in mid- to late August.

There is no tourist office here (the closest is in Clifden), but you can always visit the **community website** (www.roundstone.ie) before you go for more information.

Roundstone is 23 kilometers south of Clifden on the R341 and 77 kilometers west of Galway, and is served by Bus Éireann routes #61 and #419.

CLIFDEN

The "capital of Connemara," Clifden (An Clochán, "Beehive Hut") was laid out by local landlord John D'Arcy in 1819, and its long broad streets and tall church spires evoke a Victorian flavor. The area is historic for other reasons: Guglielmo Marconi chose Clifden for his first transatlantic wireless telegraphy station in 1907 (linking Clifden with Nova Scotia), and in June of 1919 John Alcock and Arthur Brown completed the first nonstop transatlantic flight when they crash-landed into a bog just six kilometers outside town.

The River Owenglen passes through the southern part of town before it empties into narrow Clifden Bay. Though the town isn't unpleasant, per se, its charming situation is significantly marred by tacky tourism, and ongoing development on the fringes of town promises a new crop of hideous concrete hotels and apartment complexes. It's got the banks, shopping, and lunch options, but you're best off just passing through Clifden for such necessities en route to Renvyle or Leenane. There isn't much in the way of "sights" in Clifden, though you could use it as a base for Kylemore Abbey and the national park.

The central Market Square forms the west base of a triangle of streets, with Market on the south side, Main on the west, and Bridge on the east. Most of what you'll need is on these three streets. Church Street rises north from the square toward the Anglican Christ Church, and the Galway-bound N59 empties into the town center at the corner of Main and Bridge.

Entertainment and Events

Trad sessions take place at **Mannion's** every night in the summer starting at 10 P.M., and on weekends in the off-season. It's a nice spot for a pint despite all the televisions. **D'Arcy Inn** (Main St., tel. 095/21146) offers traditional music as well as open-mic guitar and poetry nights. **Lowry's** (Market St., tel. 095/21347) has ceilidh sessions almost nightly in high season.

Shopping

Clifden offers the usual cheesy souvenir stores, but fortunately it's not hard to find unique gifts elsewhere in town. For guilt-free shopping, check out the small but delightful **Insaaf Fair Trade Shop** (Bridge St., no phone), which sells jewelry, picture frames, shoulder bags, and incense along with African drums and hand-painted didgeridoos and the usual tea, coffee, and chocolate. *"Insaaf"* means "justice" in Hindi, by the way. Just next door is **Clifden Secondhand Books** (tel. 087/947-1773).

The courtyard at **The Clifden Station House** (on the southern end of town, at the end of Bridge St., tel. 1850/377-000, www.clifden-stationhouse.com) offers serious retail therapy, be it super-chic women's clothing, 19th-century antiques, or Connemara landscapes. Much of the inventory at **Whistlestop** (tel. 095/21532, whistlestop@eircom.net) is kitchen- and home-related, but there's a gorgeous selection of jewelry, soaps, and other gifts, and the wall clocks inspired by French vintage advertisements are particularly delightful. The shopping courtyard is part of a larger complex converted from the town's old train depot, which includes a hotel, bar, and restaurant.

Sports and Recreation

Cycle down the wonderfully scenic **Sky Road** stretching west from town, which is signposted at the Market Square. Or go for a half-day walking tour with **Walking on Eire** (tel. 095/22804 or 087/281-7478, www.walking-on-eire.com) or the **Connemara Walking Centre** (Island House, Market St., tel. 095/21379, www.walkingireland.com), whose tours focus on the region's archaeology and botany.

Windsurfing and sailing lessons and equipment rental are available through the **Clifden Boat Club** (Coast Rd., tel. 095/21711 or 087/241-8569). Or go deep-sea angling with **Blue Water Fishing** (Sharamore House, Streamstown, tel. 095/21073, www.seafishingireland.com), which welcomes beginners.

Equestrians should contact the **Cleggan Beach Riding Centre** (tel. 095/44746 or 086/875-7333, www.clegganridingcentre.com) or the **Errislannan Riding Centre** (Ballyconneely Rd., 3.5 km south of town on the R341, tel. 095/21134), which also offers beach treks.

Designed by Eddie Hackett, **Connemara Championship Golf Links** (Aillebrack, Ballyconneely, tel. 095/23502, www.connemaragolflinks.com) is the finest course in the region.

Accommodations

Clifden has two solid IHH hostels, the spiffier **Clifden Town Hostel** (Market St., tel. 095/21076, www.clifdentownhostel.com, dorms €13–16, private rooms €17–19, credit cards accepted) and the more bohemian **Brookside Hostel** (Fairgreen, tel. 095/21812, www.brookside-hostel.com, open Mar.–Oct., dorms €13–14, private rooms €18–20, credit cards accepted).

Many of the guesthouses in and around Clifden are pretty posh (aside from the multitude of rather worn B&Bs in the center of town). For something more rustic, stay at **Faul House** (signposted off the Ballyconneely road 1 km south of Clifden, 2 km down a winding road on the right, tel. 095/21239, www.faulhouse.com, open Mar.–Oct., €35 pp, s €40). Connemara ponies are bred on this working farm in a serene, bucolic setting. Sure, the decor could use a bit of freshening, but the beds are supremely comfortable, and the owners are delightfully warm and welcoming. On that same road, before you reach Faul House, is the more upscale **Mallmore House** (Ballyconneely Rd., tel. 095/21460, www.mallmore.com, open Mar.–Oct., €32–35 pp sharing), a

restored Georgian manor with spacious, comfy rooms sprinkled with antiques and a highly lauded breakfast menu that includes pancakes and smoked salmon.

Nearer to the town center is **Joyce's Waterloo Guesthouse** (1 km east of Clifden on the Galway road, tel. 095/21688, www.joyces-waterloo.com, €37–45 pp sharing), a large modern B&B offering queen- and king-size beds, a deluxe breakfast menu, bike rental, and an outdoor hot tub. The very accommodating owners also pack picnic baskets and serve evening meals with advance notice. Price- and atmosphere-wise, Joyce's is more for couples and families than single travelers.

The pick of the town-center hotels is the uniquely situated **Clifden Station House** (in the station courtyard off Hulk St. on the east side of town, tel. 095/21699, www.clifdenstationhouse.com, rooms €210, s €125, two nights B&B plus dinner €140–200 pp sharing). This swanky-yet-atmospheric complex incorporates the old Clifden Railway Station, which stopped running in the 1940s, and offers a leisure center with pool and all other facilities, friendly and professional staff, and better-than-average bar and restaurant fare. Deluxe, modern self-catering apartments are available as well, and they include leisure center privileges.

A four-star option one kilometer west of town is the **Abbeyglen Castle Hotel** (Sky Rd., tel. 095/21201, www.abbeyglen.ie, €119–176 pp, s €169–226, 12.5 percent service charge). Built in 1832 by John d'Arcy, the local landlord (and founder of Clifden), this incomparably situated neo-Gothic hotel is small, fully renovated, family-run, and even has a resident parrot. In the off-season you can often snag a killer rate, like one night's B&B and a three-course meal (of Connemara lamb or locally caught fish) for €69.

Food

The two popular cafés in town are both great spots for lunch or coffee. The friendly ◖ **Two Dog Café** (1 Church St., tel. 095/22186, www.twodogcafe.ie, open 10:30 A.M.–6:30 P.M. Mon.–Sat., 12:30–4 P.M. Sun. June–Oct., 10:30 A.M.–

5 P.M. Tues.–Sat. Nov.–May, mains about €8) serves gourmet paninis and imaginative soups (like courgette and almond) along with scrumptious desserts and the best cappuccino in Connemara. In fact, the only less-than-excellent thing about this café is the totally ridiculous price for Internet access (€7.70/hour).

The bright and comfortable second-floor seating area at **Upstairs/Downstairs** (Main St., tel. 095/22809, open 9 A.M.–6 P.M. weekdays, 10 A.M.–6 P.M. Sat., 11 A.M.–4 P.M. Sun., sandwiches €3–5) is a perfect vantage for people-watching. It's a great spot for a simple, hearty, inexpensive sandwich. The baked goods are delish, though the coffee isn't quite as good as Two Dog's.

Pretty much all the Clifden pubs do bar food, but **Mannion's** (Market St., tel. 095/21780, food served 12:30–8:30 P.M. daily, mains €3–13) offers the best value. The soups and paninis at **Lowry's** (Market St., tel. 095/21347, meals €3–8) are also popular with the locals.

It's a bit self-consciously elegant, which is why **Mitchell's** (Market St., tel. 095/21867, open noon–10 P.M. daily Mar.–Oct., lunch €10–12, dinner €16–25, 3-course early-bird menu €25 5–7 P.M.), the best restaurant in town, attracts such a well-heeled crowd for lunch and dinner. The menu emphasizes local seafood, of course, though there are gourmet takes on traditional dishes and a veggie-dish-of-the-day as well.

A less pretentious option is **Fogerty's** (Market St., tel. 095/21427, open 5–10 P.M. Wed.–Sun., mains €9–22). The country-cottage decor has a more authentic feel, perhaps because of the dusty antiques suspended from the ceiling (a birdcage, a rocking horse—even a baby carriage!). The food (seafood, by and large) won't send you to a whole new dimension, but it's reliably good and the portions are generous.

Information

The **tourist office** (Galway road, tel. 095/21163, www.clifden.ie, open 10 A.M.–5 P.M. daily July–Aug. and Mon.–Sat. Sept.–June) is on the N59, directly across the street from the Connemara coach bus stop.

Services

You'll find ATMs and bureaux de change at the **AIB** (on Market Sq.) and at the **Bank of Ireland** (Beach Rd., west of the Market Sq.). The **post office** is on Main Street.

Do what you gotta at **Moran's Pharmacy** (Main St., tel. 095/21273) and **Shamrock Dry Cleaners & Washeteria** (Market Sq., tel. 095/21348), which offers same-day and delivery service.

Your best bet for Internet access is the **Video Vault** (Main St., tel. 095/22033, open 11 A.M.–11 P.M. daily, €3.50/30 minutes, €6/hour). Even more absurdly priced are the flatscreens upstairs at the **Two Dog Café** (1 Church St., tel. 095/22186, www.twodogcafe.ie, open 10:30 A.M.–6:30 P.M. Mon.–Sat., 12:30–4 P.M. Sun. June–Oct., 10:30 A.M.–5 P.M. Tues.–Sat. Nov.–May, €7.70/hour). In the off-season it may be possible to snag one of the three computers at the **public library** (Market St., tel. 095/21092) for about €3/hour, though access is officially for library members only.

Getting There

Clifden is 78 kilometers northwest of Galway City and 64 kilometers southwest of Westport on the N59. **Michael Nee Coaches** (tel. 095/34682, single/return ticket €10/13) passes through Clifden twice a day (3/day on Fri. and Sun.) in either direction on the Galway–Cleggan route. This service is faster, less expensive, and more comfortable than **Bus Éireann** (tel. 091/562-000, #61 or #419, 3–4/day Mon.–Sat., 1–2/day Sun.).

Getting Around

Parking in the town center is pay-and-display April–September (€1.20/hour). Bike hire is available from **John Mannion & Son** (Bridge St., tel. 095/21160, €10/day). For a taxi or tour of Connemara, ring **O'Neill Cabs** (tel. 095/21444 or 086/859-3939).

NORTHERN CONNEMARA

The **Connemara Loop** (www.goconnemara .com), which can be cycled or driven, takes in all the highlights of northern Connemara:

starting at Maam Cross, you're on the westward N59 before turning off for the scenic Lough Inagh valley drive (R334), getting back onto the N59 for Letterfrack and turning off again for the Renvyle Point loop. Back on the N59, Leenane is the next stop before taking the R336 south for a view of the Maumturks from their eastern sides, finishing back in Maam Cross 85 kilometers later. Ask in the tourist office in Galway for more info and a free map.

Inishbofin Island

Ten kilometers off Connemara's northwest coast, flat and low-lying Inishbofin Island (Inis Bó Finne, "Island of the White Cow") was the place to which Oliver Cromwell banished a group of Catholic priests in 1652. Actually, he went as far as to build a prison—on an island!—and even chained a bishop to a lowlying rock, leaving him to drown when the tide came in (hence a stone known as "Bishop's Rock" near the harbor). Long before this, however, St. Colman founded a monastery here in the 7th century, and the ruins of a 13th-century church are northeast of the harbor; in the 16th century the piratess Grace O'Malley used "Bofin" for her own strategic purposes. Because of the island's size (6 km by 3.5 km), Inishbofin's pristine beaches and seal- and bird-watching opportunities may only keep you occupied for a day, but it will be a day well spent. And when it's over, head to Day's pub (which serves grub all day) to mingle with the genuinely friendly locals.

You can rent a bike from a kiosk on the pier, but the island's small enough that you don't really need one. Once disembarked, most of the ferry traffic heads down the road to your right, which is where you'll find the newly refurbished **Day's Hotel and Spa** (tel. 095/45809, www.dayshotel.ie, B&B plus evening meal midweek/weekend €95/110 pp June–Aug., €85/95 in May and Sept.). Also in this direction is the IHH **Inishbofin Island Hostel** (700 m up from the pier, tel. 095/45855, www.inishbofin-hostel.ie, open mid-Apr.–Sept., dorms €12–14, private rooms €16–18 pp, credit cards accepted), in a charming and well-run converted farmhouse.

Turn left from the pier for the unpretentious, somewhat less popular **Doonmore Hotel** (near the harbor, tel. 095/45804, www.doonmorehotel.com, open Apr.–Oct., low/high season €45/60 pp, s €60/70, lunch €15, dinner €30). This hotel has few en-suite rooms, leading you to feel a little bit like you're staying in a boarding house. Nevertheless, the views from the bedrooms are the best on the island (better than Day's), and the seafood in the restaurant is über-fresh.

Ferries to Inishbofin depart the Cleggan pier, 11 kilometers north of Clifden off the N59. Make a reservation on the **Island Discovery** (tel. 095/45819 or 095/45894, Cleggan ticket office 095/44878, www.inishbofin.com, 30-minute ride, return fare €15). Ferries depart from Cleggan at 11:30 A.M. and 2 P.M. daily, and 6:45 P.M. daily except Tuesday and Friday, when the late ferry leaves at 7:30 P.M.; departure times from Inishbofin are 1 P.M. and 5 P.M. daily, and 9 A.M. daily except Tuesday, Friday, and Saturday, when the early departure is at 8:15 A.M. All times are valid May–September; ring for low-season sailing times.

Letterfrack

The village of Letterfrack (Leitir Fraic, "Frac's Hillside"), founded by Quakers, is the obvious base for visiting the national park; it's no more than a crossroads with a couple of pubs and shops, but it's a quiet and picturesque spot to spend the night.

You can't miss the Letterfrack Furniture College as you pull in on the N59; the new campus was designed by illustrious Dublin architects O'Donnell & Tuomey and was completed in 2002. The school's prestige is growing so rapidly that it's now easy to forget its humble origins: Out of economic necessity, the college opened in 1987 on the site of a Catholic boys' reform school, infamous for the horrific child abuse that transpired there.

On a happier note, there's a great hostel here, the **⦗** **Old Monastery** (signposted at the Letterfrack crossroads, less than 500 m from the main road, tel. 095/41132, www.oldmonastery-hostel.com, dorms €13, private rooms €16–20 pp, credit cards accepted), whose name reveals the charming building's former function. Built in the 1840s, the Old Monastery is cozy in a bohemian way, if a bit dusty, and the kindly owner serves mighty tasty oatmeal and scones for breakfast (included in the price). It's a popular spot for campers, and the national park is literally in the backyard. Pick up groceries at the general store across the street from the hostel turnoff.

Another excellent budget choice is **Letterfrack Lodge** (200 m off the N59, signposted on the Clifden end of the village, tel. 095/41222, www.letterfracklodge.com, open mid-May–mid-Sept., dorms €15–17, private rooms €20–40 pp), a purpose-built hostel clad in handsome stone, super clean and with a tremendously friendly and helpful staff and great facilities (including three kitchens, two dining rooms, and Internet access).

Run by the very kind and easygoing Patrick Connolly, **Dooneen Lodge** (signposted off the N59 2 km west of Letterfrack, tel. 095/41060, padconn2@eircom.net, open May–Oct., €35–40 pp) is a purpose-built B&B situated on more than two hectares of wooded grounds on Barnaderg Bay. The excellent breakfast menu features pancakes, smoked salmon, fresh-squeezed O.J., and homemade jams.

You'll find a dizzying array of seafood dishes on offer at **The Bard's Den** (Main St., tel. 095/41042, www.bardsden.com, food served noon–9 P.M. in summer, until 6 P.M. in low season, mains €8–20) and a more eclectic menu at **Veldon's**, a.k.a. **Molly's** (Main St., tel. 095/41042, food served noon–9 P.M., until 7 P.M. in low season, mains €5–12). There's live music at both pubs at the weekend: trad at the Bard's and often folk/rock (think Van Morrison) at Veldon's. Though the fare at these two pubs is pretty good, Letterfrack's culinary gem is 【 **Pangur Bán** (on the Clifden end of the N59, tel. 095/41243, www.pangurban.com, open noon–3 P.M. and 6–10 P.M. daily Easter–Oct., closed Mon. in spring and fall, mains €15–25). Savor an inventively prepared steak or Guinness-and-venison stew in this quaint and intimate 300-year-old cottage. (Vegetarians are catered for as well.)

The Connemara Environmental Education & Cultural Centre gets up its annual **Bog Week** in late May and **Sea Week** in late October (tel. 095/41034 or 095/43443, lfrack@eircom.net for both festivals), both of which feature conservation talks, sporting events, and loads of great trad.

Letterfrack is 14 kilometers north of Clifden on the N59, served by both Bus Éireann and Michael Nee Coaches.

【 Connemara National Park

You may be surprised to find that this national park, while full of beautiful vistas and well worth a visit, can be traversed in a single afternoon: Though it encompasses three of the Twelve Bens, the park is only 13 kilometers square. Three easy walking trails, none over an hour in duration, cover bog-and-heathered hills where you can often watch Connemara ponies grazing on the slopes; you might be surprised to find the ruins of 19th-century homes and outhouses that predate the park itself (most of this land once belonged to the Kylemore Abbey estate). A few scattered megalithic court tombs on the park grounds date as far back as 2000 B.C.

With time and patience, you might be able to spot a stoat, shrew, badger, fox, or pine marten. Park birdlife includes skylarks, chaffinches, wrens, meadow pipits, kestrels, and peregrine falcons. The native red deer population was rendered extinct in the mid-19th century, though park officials have recently introduced a new herd from elsewhere in Ireland.

The mountain and blanket bogs give life to a surprising variety of flora. Orchids and purple moorgrass color the heathery slopes. The largely temperate plantlife includes insectivorous species like butterworts and sundews, though some Arctic plants (like mountain sorrel, roseroot, and purple and starry saxifrages) can also be found at higher altitudes.

The **visitors center** (signposted on the

N59 just east of Letterfrack, tel. 095/41054 or 095/41006, open 10 A.M.–5:30 P.M. daily mid-Mar.–Oct., 10 A.M.–6:30 P.M. June, 9:30 A.M.–6:30 P.M. July–Aug., grounds open all year, admission €2.90) offers the usual exhibition on local botany and geology and 15-minute audiovisual. Guided nature walks (2–3 hours long, included in admission price) depart the visitors center at 10:30 A.M. on Monday, Wednesday, and Friday in June, and every weekday in July and August.

Kylemore Abbey

One of Connemara's prime attractions is Kylemore Abbey (signposted on the N59 3 km east of Letterfrack, tel. 095/41146, www.kylemore-abbey.ie, open 9 A.M.–5:30 P.M. daily, admission €10), a neo-Gothic manor erected on the shores of Lough Kylemore in the 1860s. Originally known as Kylemore Castle, it was built by an English businessman, Mitchell Henry for his wife, Margaret, who died in Cairo just a few years after its completion. Henry erected a lovely neo-Gothic chapel (with exquisite stained-glass windows) down a lakeside path to honor his wife's memory, and both are buried in a small brick mausoleum a little farther along the path.

Just after the First World War, the manor was converted into an abbey by an order of Benedictine nuns (known in Belgium, their erstwhile home, as De Iersche Damen, "The Irish Dames"). The nuns of Kylemore Abbey now run it as a prestigious international boarding school for girls, though it came as a shock to parents all over Europe in early 2006 when they announced the school's impending closure in 2010 due to the order's dwindling numbers. Those who remain are shrewd businesswomen, however, exploiting (however tactfully) tourists' interest in their abbey on the lake with a café, an incredibly posh gift shop, and a steep entry fee to the manor (three downstairs rooms, only interesting enough for a quick peek), the Victorian gardens, and the lakeside walk leading to the neo-Gothic chapel.

Kylemore Abbey is a three-minute drive east of Letterfrack and the national park on the N59. **Bus Éireann** (#61 or #419, 3–4/day Mon.–Sat., 1–2/day Sun.) can drop you off at the Kylemore post office.

Tullycross

There's not much going on in this wee hamlet 4.5 kilometers north of Letterfrack on a local road, but Tullycross (Tulach Na Criose, "Cross on the Hill") is well worth pointing out for **Paddy Coyne's** (tel. 095/43499). Established in 1811, this is quite possibly the coziest pub in all Connemara. It's a crime to pass through on your way to the beach without stopping for a pint here (not to mention the legendary Wednesday night trad sessions).

Just next door is the **Maol Reidh Hotel** (tel. 095/43844, www.maolreidhhotel.com, €45–65 pp, s €70–90). This is quite a nice establishment, with views of the Twelve Bens and the sea from many of the rooms—but as with all too many Irish hotels, the restaurant fare is a disappointment (especially considering the prices). The pub grub is also substandard and overpriced. Drive to the excellent Pangur Bán in Letterfrack for dinner instead.

Also, those with an appreciation for stained-glass windows should check out **Christ the King Church,** which features three pieces by the brilliant Harry Clarke.

Renvyle

Remote Renvyle (Rinn Mhaol, "Bare Headland") is on a local road looping a peninsula of the same name, which makes for an excellent walk or bike ride (11 kilometers round-trip from Letterfrack); you can see Inishbofin and Inishturk islands from Renvyle Point.

A fair number of the guests at the **Renvyle House Hotel** (signposted off the N59, on a local road 17 km north of Clifden, tel. 095/43511 or 095/43444, www.renvyle.com, open Mar.–Nov., €55 pp low season, €85 shoulder season, €120 July–Aug.) are returning customers. The former home of surgeon, writer, and wit Oliver St. John Gogarty, Renvyle House boasts a heated outdoor pool, private lake for trout fishing, and nine-hole golf course. The hotel has a lovely seaside setting,

80 hectares of landscaped grounds, and top-notch restaurant fare, but don't be surprised to find that the building itself is in considerable need of remodeling.

Go diving in Killary Fjord with **Scuba Dive West** (tel. 095/43922, www.scubadivewest. com), on pristine white **Glassilaun Beach.**

Renvyle is three kilometers north of Letter-frack (the N59) on a local road. There is no public transportation.

◖ Leenane and Killary Harbour

Ireland's only fjord is the hauntingly lovely Killary, 16 kilometers long and 45 meters deep, which separates northern Connemara from the mountains of southern Mayo (the tallest of which is 814-meter Mweelrea, the "Bald King"); just east of the tip of the fjord is another bleakly intimidating peak, the 650-meter Devil's Mother (the original Irish name meant "devil's testicle," but the Brits declined to use the literal translation when they rejigged their maps).

In the 2005 novel *Notes from a Coma,* Mike McCormack captured Killary's mood to perfection: "What no tourist bumf will tell you is that this inlet is suffused with an atmosphere of ineffable sadness. Partly a trick of the light and climactic factors, partly also the lingering residue of an historical tragedy which still resonates through rock and water…think of grey shading toward gunmetal across an achromatic spectrum; think also of turbid cumulus clouds pouring down five centimetres of rainfall above the national average and you have some idea of the light reflected within the walls of this inlet." This is a land- and seascape both melancholy and enchanting, the sort of remote locale where you can still imagine wailing banshees and changelings wandering through the heather.

Base yourself near tiny Leenane (An Líonán, "The Fill") on the lip of the fjord, best known as the setting of Jim Sheridan's 1989 film *The Field,* starring John Hurt, Richard Harris, and Brenda Fricker. The village itself offers three pubs, a shop, a tourist office, and not much else (not even an ATM, though the post office has a bureau de change), but there are plenty of colorful characters in its two cozy Main Street pubs, **Hamilton's** (tel. 095/42234) and **Gaynor's** (tel. 095/42271), on any given evening (and both do no-frills soup and sandwiches during the day).

Killary Harbour is ideal for water sports, and there's an outstanding adventure center here to satisfy your thirst for action. **Killary Adventure Company** (signposted off the N59 5 km south of Leenane, tel. 095/43411, www.killary.com), established in 1981, offers sea kayaking, canoeing, windsurfing, water-skiing, sailing, archery, clay-pigeon shooting, mountain biking, rock climbing, and plenty more. Congenial owner Jamie Young has rounded Cape Horn in a kayak (and that's only one on the Youngs' long list of feats), so you know you're in good hands! Accommodation (both hostel and B&B-style) is provided at "K2," a sleek new building across the N59 from the center. The 84-kilometer **Connemara Way** (part of the longer Western Way walking route) also converges briefly with the N59 at this point.

If you'd rather just kick back and enjoy the scenery, board a ship on **Killary Cruises** (tel. 091/566-736, www.killarycruises.com, 5/day daily July–Aug., 4/day daily Apr.–June and Sept., 2/day daily Oct., 90-minute cruise €18, cruise and bus from Galway City €34) for a tour of the fjord.

ACCOMMODATIONS AND FOOD

There's not a load of accommodations in the Leenane area, but you won't have much trouble finding a room. Like its sister hostel in Galway City, **Sleepzone Connemara** (6 km south of Leenane off the N59, tel. 095/42929, www. sleepzone.ie, open weekends only Nov.–Mar., dorms €15–22, twin/double €25–30 pp, s €35–50, campsites €10 plus €7 per extra person, credit cards accepted) offers wireless Internet access, friendly staff, and plenty of opportunities for socializing. No car? No worries: You can take a shuttle bus from the hostel in Galway (single/return ticket €5/8, €10/15 for non-guests), and there's usually someone around who can give you a lift down to the pubs. In fact, the only less-than-stellar thing about this hostel is that it often attracts large school groups. To get here, head south out of the village on the N59 (toward Letterfrack), and after five kilometers you'll see the hostel clearly signposted. Make that right, and it's another kilometer down a horribly potholed road.

Just a bit farther down the N59 is the turnoff for **Glen Valley** (www.glenvalleyhouse.com, €35 pp, s €50), a secluded farmhouse B&B with a kind reception and fabulous views from the bedroom windows. If you don't have a car, there are a few places within a few minutes' walk of the village, including **The Convent** (Leenane Hill, just outside the village on the Westport-bound N59, tel. 095/42240, www.connemara.net/convent, €30 pp sharing)—which, despite the name, has been a B&B for quite a few years now and is far more comfortable than you might expect. The chapel-turned-dining room features original brilliantly colored stained-glass windows.

A 19th-century coaching inn overlooking the water, the **Leenane Hotel** (just south of the village, tel. 095/42249, www.leenanehotel.com, open mid-Apr.–Oct., €55 pp, s €75) is delightfully old-fashioned, with claw-footed tubs in the bathrooms and open turf fires in the sitting rooms and bar; the restaurant menu features local meat, seafood, and produce, and it's as good as the grub available in town. Though there is a single supplement for double rooms, if you book ahead you should be able to get a single room (with a harbor view) for €55.

PRACTICALITIES

Be sure to withdraw funds before leaving Westport or Galway. For tourist information, head to the **Leenane Cultural Centre** (village center, tel. 095/42323, open 10 A.M.–6 P.M. daily Apr.–Sept.), which includes a small exhibit on the local wool industry (not really worth the admission price) as well as a gift shop and café.

Leenane is 32 kilometers south of Westport, 19.5 kilometers east of Letterfrack, and 34 kilometers northeast of Clifden on the N59. From Galway (64.5 km), take the N59 to Maam Cross and make a right onto the R336 (or continue on the N59 to Recess and take the R334 north through the Lough Inagh Valley).

Need a lift to or from the pub? There's a Leenane-based **24-hour taxi and minibus service** (tel. 087/204-8929).

Recess

Near the southern end of the lovely Lough Inagh Valley, Recess (Sraith Salach, "Dirty Line") is a popular stopover for anglers and hikers alike (though the village itself consists of a pub, shop, and gas station). The former stay at the stately Victorian **Lough Inagh Lodge** (7 km north of Recess on the R334, tel. 091/34706, www.lough-inaghlodgehotel.ie, €115 pp, s €135) and spend a few days fishing in Lough Inagh or Lough Derryclare; the latter crash early at the old-school, idyllically situated An Óige **Ben Lettery Hostel** (8 km west of Recess on the N59, tel. 091/51136, www.anoige.ie, open Mar.–Nov., dorms €13–15.50) and set off to conquer one of the Twelve Bens first thing in the morning.

Or what if you're looking for a fairy-tale getaway? Look no further than the Victorian **Ballynahinch Castle** (signposted off the N59 6 km west of Recess, tel. 095/31006, www.ballynahinch-castle.com, €120–200 pp sharing May–Sept., €105–170 pp sharing Oct.–Apr., s €150–230/135–200, 10 percent service charge), where even the "standard" rooms offer lavish extras like fluffy bathrobes and slippers. The 180-hectare estate, with its wealth of small lakes and the Ballynahinch River, is also a haven for serious anglers, but you could easily pass the afternoon in the terraced gardens or on wooded walking trails. The restaurant fare—using only local fish, meats, and produce—is certainly worth writing home about.

Backpackers can take **Michael Nee Coaches** (tel. 095/34682, www.michael-neecoaches.com) to get to the An Óige hostel, or **Bus Éireann** (tel. 091/562-000, www.buseireann.ie) in high season.

Oughterard

A small, pleasant-enough town on the west shore of Lough Corrib, Oughterard ("OOK-ter-ard," Uachtar Ard, "High Top") is a popular stop for angling enthusiasts, as the lake is rich in sea and brown trout as well as salmon. Just south of town are the ruins of a six-story tower house overlooking the Corrib, **Aughanure Castle** ("The Field of the Yews," 3 km east of town, signposted off the N59, tel. 091/552-214, open 9:30 A.M.–6 P.M. daily Apr.–Oct., admission €2.90). Now run by Dúchas, this 16th-century O'Flaherty fortress was built on a series of natural caves through which lake water still flows. The tower has a modern roof, and there's a detached banquet hall in an advanced state of ruin.

Farther south is a fine stop for families, **Brigit's Garden** (Pollagh, Roscahill, 9 km south of Oughterard off the N59, tel. 091/550-905, www.galwaygarden.com, open 10 A.M.–5:30 P.M. daily mid-Apr.–Sept., admission €6.75), with a series of themed gardens and nature trails, plus a calendar of cooking, weaving, and wine appreciation courses.

A three-star guesthouse with evening meals (with advance notice) and wine license, **Corrib**

Wave (Portacarron, 3 km east of Oughterard, signposted off the N59, tel. 091/552-147, www.corribwave.com, open Feb.–Nov., €35–45 pp, s €50–55, dinner €24) hires boats and fishing equipment. Another B&B that caters to anglers, this one just outside the town center, is the stately Victorian **Waterfall Lodge** (Glann Rd., signposted from the town center, tel. 091/552-168, www.waterfalllodge.net, €40 pp, s €50), with mature gardens and an excellent breakfast menu.

The town's best eatery is **Le Blason** (Bridge St., tel. 091/557-111, http://homepage.eircom.net/-leblason, open 7–10 P.M. Tues.–Sun., mains €15–35), giving all that fresh Corrib-caught seafood the royal French treatment in a comfortable, unpretentious atmosphere.

Oughterard is 27 kilometers northwest of Galway on the N59. **Bus Éireann** will get you here from Galway (tel. 091/562-000, summer-only #61 runs late June–early Sept., 5/day Mon.–Sat., 3/day Sun.; route #419 runs Sept.–May, 3/day Mon.–Sat., 2/day Sun.).

Southern and Eastern Galway

KINVARA

A pretty little fishing village on the Burren's northern fringe, Kinvara (Cinn Mhara, "Headland of the Sea") offers small-town charm and plenty of peace and quiet despite its location on the busy N67. There isn't a whole lot to do here, but Kinvara makes a good base for exploring the Burren and sights of southern Galway—Kilmacduagh, Coole Park, and Thoor Ballylee.

Sights

The name of restored 16th-century **Dunguaire Castle** (half a kilometer north of the village on the N86, tel. 091/637-108, open 9:30 A.M.–5 P.M. daily Apr.–Sept., admission €4.75) is anglicized as "Dungory," and though you'll never see it spelled that way now, it sure helps with the pronunciation! Perched atmospherically on the lip of Kinvara Bay, the castle demesne har-

bors freshwater springs. This was the royal seat of the king of Connaught in the 7th century, a ruler renowned for his hospitality. (His name was Guaire Aidhneach, hence Dún Guaire, "Fort of Guaire.") The present structure once belonged to the surgeon and wit Oliver St. John Gogarty, who purchased Dunguaire for its proximity to other literati of the Irish renaissance, Edward Martyn (of Tullira Castle), Yeats, and Lady Gregory.

During the day you can check out the historical exhibition and admire the view, but most visitors experience the castle as the setting for a **medieval banquet** (tel. 1800/269-811 for reservations, 5:30 P.M. and 8:30 P.M. nightly May–Oct., tickets €48), on a smaller scale than the entertainment at Bunratty—fewer diners and entertainers, but the four-course meal (with silverware) and format are the same.

© CAMILLE DEANGELIS

Lunch is self-serve at low tide on the shores of Kinvara Bay.

Entertainment and Events

If the medieval banquet isn't your thing, there are a few good pubs in the village to occupy you for the evening. Try **Tigh Uí Chonghaile** (The Quay, tel. 091/637-131) with its "real" beer garden (albeit made of potted plants); inside, an open fire burns in the grate. There's often traditional music here, though it isn't scheduled as such. **Keogh's** (The Square, tel. 091/637-145) has live trad on Monday and Thursday nights, and visiting musicians are always welcome to join in.

Annual festivals include **Fleadh na gCuach,** "The Cuckoo Festival," which offers a load of traditional music sessions over the May bank holiday weekend, and **Cruinniú na mBad,** the "Gathering of the Boats," when sails are raised in homage to the traditional Galway hooker every August.

Shopping

Kinvara has a few really nice little gift shops. **Burrenbeo** (Main St., tel. 091/638-096, www.burrenbeo.com) sells soaps from the Burren

purfumery, funky knitwear, toys, and nature books, and **Murphy Store** (The Quay, tel. 091/637-760, www.murphystore.com) does locally made soaps, jewelry, pottery, and the like. Both shops have pleasant cafés.

Sports and Recreation

Kinvara's Blue Flag strand is at **Trácht,** 6.5 kilometers west of the village (and signposted from the N67). Contact **Burren Adventures** in Ballyvaughan (Main St., tel. 065/707-8914 or 087/202-0880, www.burrenadventures.com) for information on scuba-diving courses for every experience level.

Or you might like a weekend yoga retreat at the **Burren Yoga & Meditation Centre** (Lig do Scith, Cappaghmore, 8 km southwest of Kinvara on a local road, tel. 091/637-680, www.burrenyoga.com).

Accommodations

In an old Burren-facing manor house built by the Count de Basterot in 1866, the An Óige **Doorus Hostel** (6 km northwest of Kinvara, signposted off the N67 at Doorus Cross, tel. 091/637-512, www.kinvara.com/doorushouse, dorms €16, laundry €5/load, credit cards accepted) was the veritable birthplace of the Irish National Theatre, since it was here that Yeats, Gregory, and Martyn congregated to discuss the possibility in 1897. In keeping with its literary heritage, the hostel now offers weekend and weeklong workshops in painting, writing, music, and set dancing. Evening meals are available for groups only, so backpackers should arrive with provisions. Bus transport is a bit inconvenient but still doable: the Doolin/Cliffs of Moher Bus Éireann service (#50 or #423, 5–6/day Mon.–Sat., 1–2/day Sun.) goes through Doorus Cross, and be sure to request the stop. It's a three-kilometer walk to the hostel from there.

The best B&B in town, for location and comfort, is **Cois Cuain** (The Quay, tel. 091/637-119, €36 pp) is an adorable little white house set back from the harbor. Otherwise there's not too much choice in the village proper; most B&Bs are a few kilometers outside.

You won't find any fancy extras at the **Merriman Hotel** (Main St., tel. 091/638-222, www.merrimanhotel.com, €55–65 pp, €80 pp July–Aug.), with its rather ridiculous-looking thatched roof, but the staff are friendly and the breakfast menu superb.

Food

Kinvara is in need of a really good restaurant, but you certainly won't go hungry. The nicest café in town is upstairs at **Burrenbeo** (Main St., tel. 091/638-096, open 10 A.M.–7 P.M. Wed.–Sun., lunches €4–8), full of sunlight and animated chitchat. The waiters are cheerful and the cappuccino is more than decent.

Your best bet for a full meal is **Keogh's** (The Square, tel. 091/637-145, food served 10 A.M.–10 P.M. daily, mains €8–18), renowned for its hearty seafood dishes and old-fashioned atmosphere. It's also the only place in town open for breakfast. The grub's good at the fluorescent-yellow **Pier Head** (on the harbor, tel. 091/638-188, food served 5–10 P.M. Mon.–Sat., noon–8 P.M. Sun. June–Oct., 5–8 P.M.

daily Nov.–May, mains €15–27), where you can order steak, duck, quail, or lamb if you're not in the mood for seafood; tables at the upstairs restaurant offer a better view of the bay. The Pier Head also has a "vegetarian dish of the day," making it the (de facto) top choice for veggie lovers. **M'Asal Beag Dubh** ("My Little Black Donkey," tel. 091/638-222, food served 12:30–8 P.M., mains €8–16) also does bar food, but it's not as good as Keogh's or the Pier Head.

It may look like a lovely place to eat, but the colorful facade and the view are unfortunately the only good things about the Café on the Quay. The atmosphere is nondescript, the food just a little better than mediocre, and the service can be downright neglectful.

Information and Services

Kinvara does not have a tourist office, though there's plenty of info to be found at **Kinvara Online** (www.kinvara.com) before you go.

Kinvara's two supermarkets, Londis and McMahon's, have ATMs, and there's a bureau de change at Merriman's Hotel—all of which are on Main Street.

The **Kinvara Pharmacy** (tel. 091/637-397) is also on Main Street, and the **post office** is tucked just off it, on the Gort road. Internet access is available at **Postscript** (Main St., tel. 091/637-657, open 9 A.M.–7 P.M. daily, €2.50/15 minutes), a book and gift shop, but the computer is pokey and the price exorbitant.

Getting There and Around

Kinvara is 30 kilometers south of Galway on the N18, picking up the N67 in Kilcolgan. **Bus Éireann** (tel. 091/562-000) can get you there on the summer-only route from Cork and Tralee to Galway via the Burren and Cliffs of Moher (#50, 2–4/day daily June–Sept., 1–2/day Sun.). Route #423 from Galway to the Cliffs of Moher via Kinvara operates all year (3/day Mon.–Sat.).

For a taxi, ring **Jacko's** (tel. 086/161-5707 or 086/843-7676) or **Shay Davern** (tel. 087/980-6152).

GALWAY

C KILMACDUAGH

One of Ireland's most stunning monastic ruins is little-known even among many natives. The old churches may not offer much out of the ordinary, but the round tower at Kilmacduagh (5.5 km west of Gort, site always open, free admission) is Ireland's equivalent of the Leaning Tower of Pisa. Complete with conical roof, the tower—perhaps the tallest in the country at 34 meters—slants a full 60 centimeters to the south, and the visual effect is extraordinary (and strangely unsettling). Though the other buildings (mostly dating to the 14th century) are generally locked, you can wander around them and poke your head through the gates for a peek at the interiors.

The monastery was founded by St. Colman MacDuagh (the name means "Church of MacDuagh") in the 7th century and patronized by the king of Connaught, Guaire Aidhne, who lent his name to Dunguaire Castle in Kinvara. Kilmacduagh was another important center of learning in medieval times and eventually received its own diocese, though it never quite attained the power or influence of Clonmacnoise or Glendalough.

Getting to Kilmacduagh can be downright tricky. Though it is possible to reach the site from Kinvara, there are no signposts on these backcountry roads (what is signposted is often inaccurately so), and one can all too easily lose the way. It's easiest to approach Kilmacduagh from Gort, 37.5 kilometers south of Galway City. From the town square, follow the sign for Corofin. About a block off the square, make a right onto the road directly opposite the SuperValu (you'll see Kilmacduagh signposted there). Then it's a straightforward trip, just two minutes by car. There's no public transportation to the monastic site, though it's possible to ride **Bus Éireann** to Gort (tel. 091/562-000, route #51 or #55, 14/day daily) and walk or bike (if you've brought your own).

COOLE PARK

Lady Augusta Gregory, friend and patron of William Butler Yeats and cofounder of the Abbey Theatre, entertained most of Ireland's greatest writers at her estate at Coole Park from the 1890s until her death in 1932. In 1880 she had married William Gregory, member of Parliament and former governor of Ceylon, and made her home here; after his death in 1892—he was 35 years her senior—she devoted herself to literary pursuits, recording the folktales of the native Irish and writing several plays of her own. The house no longer exists, but Coole Park (3 km north of Gort, signposted off the N18, tel. 091/631-804, www.coolepark. ie, open 10 A.M.–5 P.M. Apr.–May and Sept., 10 A.M.–6 P.M. June–Aug., park free and open all year, visitors center admission €2.90) now offers a historical exhibit, tearoom, and audiovisual along with a nature reserve with wooded lakeside walking trails. Don't miss the "autograph tree," carved by many of the turn-of-the-century literati: the Yeats brothers, Synge, George Bernard Shaw, George Russell ("Æ"), Augustus John, Sean O'Casey, and Lady Gregory herself.

Coole Park is 35 kilometers south of Galway off the N18. The park is easiest to reach by car, though you can take **Bus Éireann** (#51 or #55, 14/day daily on the Galway–Shannon–Cork route) and ask to be dropped off at the Coole turnoff.

THOOR BALLYLEE

A tower house built by the de Burgo clan in the 16th century, Islandmore Castle is far better known as Thoor Ballylee ("Ballylee Tower," Peterswell, tel. 091/631-436, open 9:30 A.M.– 5 P.M. Mon.–Sat. late May–Sept., admission €6). It was purchased by William Butler Yeats for a whopping £35 in 1916, the bargain-basement price due to the castle's neglected state. The poet had chosen the tower for its romantic situation as well as its proximity to the home of his great friend and patron, Lady Gregory. After a period of restoration work funded by his lecture tours, Yeats moved there in 1919 with his wife and daughter, and the modest tower served as their summer home for the dozen years that followed. Yeats's new home inspired many of the poems in his aptly named collection, *The Tower*.

A witty inscription appears on a stone installed by the Abbey Theatre board outside:

I, the poet William Yeats,
With old mill boards and sea-green slates,
And smithy work from the Gort forge,
Restored this tower for my wife George;
And may these characters remain
When all is ruin once again.

The Yeats family stopped coming here in the late 1920s, and the poet retreated there only sporadically during the 1930s. After another period of disuse, the Irish Tourist Board purchased and renovated the castle in 1965, turning it into a small Yeats museum with original furniture and the usual gift shop and tearoom. There's also a short audiovisual, but it (like the rest of the exhibition) covers only the tower's 20th-century history.

Thoor Ballylee is 47 kilometers south of Galway and is signposted off the N18 south of the village of Ardrahan (the tower is 1 km farther down a local road). There is no public transportation.

PORTUMNA

Located on the fringes of an otherwise unremarkable market town on the north shore of Lough Derg, **Portumna Castle and Gardens** (tel. 090/974-1658, portumnacastle@opw.ie, open 10 A.M.–6 P.M. daily Apr.–Oct., admission €2.10) was the seat of the de Burgo family for more than two centuries. This 17th-century stronghouse was one of the first Irish castles to incorporate the architectural refinements of the Italian Renaissance. Many aristocratic visitors prior to the fire that gutted the building in 1826 claimed its opulence was unrivaled anywhere in Ireland, though today only small remnants of the old decorative plasterwork remain. The ground floor of the restored castle is now open to the public, and guided tours are available on request. The adjacent Portumna Forest Park makes a good spot for a ramble and picnic.

Portumna is 67 kilometers southeast of Galway on the N6 (picking up the N65 in Loughrea) and 25 kilometers west of Birr in County Offaly on the R489. Unfortunately, bus service from either town is too infrequent to be of use.

CLONFERT CATHEDRAL

Near the Galway-Offaly border, the sleepy hamlet of Clonfert is on the map for its small, 12th-century St. Brendan's Church of Ireland, better known as Clonfert Cathedral. Its six-arched, pedimented Romanesque doorway features limestone carvings of eerily individualized human and animal heads and plant motifs; it is absolutely exquisite and well worth a detour (despite a botched restoration attempt sometime in the 19th century).

The church itself was founded by St. Brendan the Navigator in the 6th century (before his epic voyage to the New World in a small curragh), and he is supposedly buried here (the site of Na Seacht dTeampaill on Inis Mór claims the same distinction, however). Though the building is generally locked except for Sunday services, what's inside pales in comparison anyway (if you do really want to get inside, knock at the house next door and ask for the key). Otherwise, just spend a while staring up at those faces carved above the doorway, wondering what they might tell you of the last 900 years if only they could speak.

Clonfert is 82 kilometers east of Galway City. It's most efficient to visit en route to Galway from Athlone, since the nearest town to Clonfert, Ballinasloe, is on the N6 between those two cities. From Ballinasloe, take the R355 south for Laurencetown; once there, you'll see Clonfert signposted on your left. The church is another 8 kilometers or so down a local road. The journey from Ballinasloe is 20 kilometers altogether. Unfortunately, there is no bus service to Clonfert.

THE NORTHWEST

You hear a lot about Ireland's west—its dramatic landscapes, its stubborn adherence to tradition, its blissfully slow pace—and this notion is most accurate in the counties of Mayo (Maigh Eo, "Plain of Yews"), Sligo (Sligeach, "Place of Shells"), and Leitrim (Liatroim or Liath Druim, "Gray Ridge"). Gorgeous (if sometimes bleak) sea and mountain landscapes are thoroughly worth the extra effort in getting up here, especially considering that your fellow travelers are more often weekending locals than stereotypical tourists. Lovely as Galway is, you can't say this of Connemara. And if you need a bit of nightlife along with your surfing or hillwalking, you'll find plenty of *craic* in Westport and Sligo Town.

There's a certain element of Bord Fáilte spindoctoring to the pervasive "Sligo is Yeats country" catchphrase, since the poet never spent much time here after those childhood summers with his maternal grandparents; nevertheless, Irish literary buffs won't be disappointed with what there is to see at Drumcliffe, Lissadell, and the Sligo County Museum. Located between Sligo and Donegal and the source of the River Shannon, tiny Leitrim isn't a tourist destination as such. Like nearby Counties Cavan and Fermanagh, Leitrim is dotted with lakes, and it's a local joke that land here is sold not by the acre, but by the gallon; with Sligo the county shares Lough Gill, on whose shore is located Leitrim's most important sight, Parke's Castle.

HISTORY

Sligo abounds in prehistoric monuments; dating before the turn of the third millennium

HIGHLIGHTS

(Doolough Valley: Take a long quiet drive up this lonely road, which winds through the Mweelrea Mountains south of Westport (page 369).

(Croagh Patrick: Generations of pilgrims and casual hikers alike have journeyed to the summit of "Ireland's Sinai," which offers stunningly beautiful vistas on a clear day (page 373).

(Knocknarea: This unexcavated megalithic tomb tops another hill, this one in Sligo, with an awesome panorama of sea and countryside (page 391).

(Kilcullen's Seaweed Baths: Relax in a hot porcelain tub of saltwater and freshly gathered seaweed – which eases sore joints and gets your skin soft and glowing – in this delightfully authentic Edwardian bathhouse overlooking Killala Bay (page 397).

(Carrowkeel Passage Tomb Cemetery: This prehistoric necropolis in the Bricklieve Mountains of southern Sligo is perhaps the spookiest spot in the country (page 398).

LOOK FOR **(** TO FIND RECOMMENDED SIGHTS, ACTIVITIES, DINING, AND LODGING.

THE NORTHWEST

B.C., the megalithic tombs at Carrowmore and Knocknarea are probably as old as Newgrange, and the lesser-known Carrowkeel and Creevykeel sites date from somewhere in the third millennium. There was plenty going on in Mayo in the Stone Age, too, as the subterranean remains of a substantial farming settlement at Céide Fields attests. Local history in early Christian times centers around St. Patrick's sojourn on the summit of the mountain that bears his name, somewhere around A.D. 441. The snake-banishing bit may be more legend than truth, but his 40-day fast atop Croagh Patrick is probably based in fact.

In 1588, the ill-fated Spanish Armada (on its way to England with the rather optimistic hope of deposing the Virgin Queen, a Protestant) was wrecked off these shores; Broadhaven and Blacksod Bays in northern Mayo swallowed thousands of sailors, and the beaches north of Sligo Town were covered in casualties of the sea. Those who survived were slain by the English garrison. One Spanish survivor was harbored for a time at Parke's Castle in Leitrim, though his host was ultimately hanged for his hospitality.

The consequence of so much starkly beautiful scenery is a dearth of arable land, and the people of Mayo, Sligo, and Leitrim had a more difficult time of it even before the Great Hunger. The Great Famine of 1845–1846 exacted a disproportionate number of casualties in these

THE NORTHWEST

Benwee
Head

Downpatrick
Head

Erris
Head

Eagle
Island

Broadhaven
Bay

Ross Port

Belderg

★ CÉIDE
FIELDS

Ballycastle

Pollatomish

Belmullet

314

Barnatra

Killala

Inishglora
Inishkeeragh

Trawmore
Bay

Carrowmore
Lake

315

MOYNE ★
FRIARY

313

313

Bangor
Erris

314

Tiraun
Point

Owenmore River

N59

Ballina

Inishkea
North

Owenmore River

Crossmolina

Inishkea
South

Blacksod
Point

N59

MAYO

312

Duvillaun
More

Duvillaun
Beg

Blacksod
Bay

Dugort

Nephin Beg Mountains

316

Lough
Conn

Achill
Island

Lough
Cullin

Achill
Head

Keem

Dooagh

Keel

Achill
Sound

319

Lough Feeagh

317

Dooega

Achill
Sound

Mallaranny

Furnace Lough

312

Newport
Bay

Newport

311

Achillbeg
Island

Clew Bay

Castlebar

N5

Clare
Island

Westport
Bay

Westport

N84

Roonagh
Quay

Kilsallagh

335

ATLANTIC

Emlagh
Point

Louisburgh

Murrisk

330

Ballintober

OCEAN

Caher
Island

⟨ CROAGH PATRICK

Killeen

335

Bunowen River

N59

Inishturk

Killadoon

⟨ DOOLOUGH VALLEY

River

Lough
Carra

Doolough
Valley

Ballinrobe

Inishbofin

Mweelrea

Doolough

Ertiff

Partry Mountains

Aasleagh
Falls

Lough
Mask

0   10 mi

Killary
Harbour

Neale

0   10 km

Leenane

Cong

N59

334

336

GALWAY

Lough
Inagh

Lough Corrib

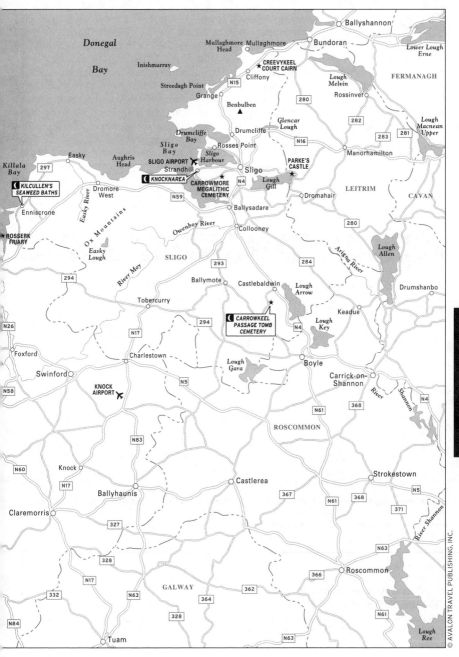

counties; there were 100,000 dead in County Mayo, and another 100,000 emigrated. In Sligo, a young man who would become the most famous of the Anglo-Irish Gothic writers witnessed a man, mistaken for dead, struggling to lift himself out of a mass grave. No doubt this sight made a terrible impression on Bram Stoker, who later penned one of the most influential novels of all time: *Dracula.*

PLANNING YOUR TIME

County Sligo's small size means you can take in the principal sights—Drumcliffe, Knocknarea and a handful of other megalithic monuments, and the cultural attractions of Sligo Town—in a matter of two days. Westport is the tourist hub of County Mayo, a natural base for taking in Croagh Patrick, Achill Island, and the islands of Clew Bay. Northern Mayo is far more remote, though hill-walkers will find two or three days' diversion here. If you're planning to spend most of your time in Mayo, Sligo, and/or Donegal, it makes more sense to fly into Knock Airport. Owing to its location between Counties Sligo and Donegal and its relative dearth of attractions, Leitrim is generally considered a county one sees while en route to Donegal Town. Parke's Castle, on the eastern shore of Lough Gill, is commonly visited as a day trip from Sligo Town.

Mayo

County Mayo is Ireland at its wildest and most remote, particularly on Achill Island, the Nephin Beg mountains, and the Mullet Peninsula. Even the most isolated reaches of Donegal won't give you the almost frightening sense that you've arrived at the end of the world. Thanks to the Celtic Tiger, myriad other locales across the country can no longer offer such enchantment; though the forces of capitalist progress move at a slower pace up here, it's still only a matter of time.

That said, Mayo's largest towns, Castlebar and Ballina, are workaday places with very little to deter the visitor. You'll probably want to base yourself in or near the pleasantly bustling Westport; from here you can scale Croagh Patrick, the greatest pilgrimage in Irish Catholicism, or catch a ferry to Clare Island from nearby Roonagh Quay. If driving, approach Westport from Connemara via the Doolough Valley, which affords some of the most stunningly isolated mountain scenery in the west. The **Clew Bay Archaeological Trail** (www.clewbaytrail.com) is liberally signposted in this southwestern section of the county and includes both monastic sites and prehistoric tombs of lesser importance.

Another route into Mayo from points south runs through Cong, a kitschy-yet-charming town just over the border from Galway, renowned for the filming of John Ford's film *The Quiet Man* in the summer of 1951.

CONG

A tidy little town between the northern shore of Lough Corrib and the southern shore of Lough Mask, just over the Galway-Mayo border, Cong (Conga Feichin, "Feichin's Narrows") draws visitors for one reason: Much of *The Quiet Man,* the 1951 film starring John Wayne and Maureen O'Hara, was shot in and around it. The movie was considered a technicolor marvel at the time—and the tourist trade is still selling the decades-old excitement over the arrival of a Hollywood crew. Movie aside, the lovely Cong Abbey and a walk along the Cong River will keep you occupied for an hour or so, and you can even sign up for a falconry lesson at the swanky Ashford Castle on the outskirts of town.

Cong is a snap to navigate: Main Street runs north–south; Abbey Street on the southern end loops north, following the River Corrib as the Circular Road, and meets Main Street again at O'Connor's grocery and gas station.

© CAMILLE DEANGELIS

the Cong Abbey monks' fishing hut on the Cong River

Sights

Forget all the *Quiet Man* hubbub. No, really. Many small businesses are still trying to cash in on the kitsch more than 50 years after the movie was made, and their tackiness is a blight on this otherwise charming riverside village. A tour of the original film locations is a disappointment: Many places no longer exist, and others aren't in or near Cong at all. Most tourists come to the **Quiet Man Heritage Cottage** (at the end of Abbey St., tel. 094/954-6089, open 10 A.M.–5 P.M. daily, €6) believing that the movie was actually filmed here, but it wasn't; this small building has no connection to the film whatsoever. The building features a wall of photocopied newspaper clippings from the summer of 1951, when *The Quiet Man* was being filmed in the area, as well as a bedroom furnished to look like that of the main character. The only authentic thing in it is a horse saddle, though, and who in their right mind would pay €6 to look at a saddle? Don't waste your time or money here.

No, the best reason to visit is **Cong Abbey** (always accessible, free admission), refounded in the 12th century on the site of an earlier monastery established by St. Feichin, along with the marvelous Harry Clarke altar window at the adjacent **St. Mary's Church.** That this 1933 masterpiece could exist within such an architectural monstrosity is sadly amusing (more sad though, seeing as the window is now artificially lighted). The Virgin Mary of the left panel looks more like a flapper than the mother of God. (If you do end up watching *The Quiet Man* while you're here, look for this window in the early church scene.)

The abbey is a delight to wander through, with a late-Romanesque doorway, the substantial remains of a cloister, and an upstairs dormitory. (The magnificent gold Cross of Cong, which supposedly contained a splinter from the True Cross, is now in the National Museum in Dublin.) Follow the path west toward the stream, cross the small bridge, and you'll alight upon a striking pointed archway with the noseless face of Rory O'Connor, the last high king of Ireland, who spent his last days here at the abbey once he'd seen the proverbial writing on the wall. Through the archway, a path leads to the **monks' fishing hut** perched over the river, where a bell (attached to the net dropped through the slot in the floor) would ring every time a fish was caught. If you continue over the Cong River bridge, you'll find another regal countenance carved above a pointed archway: This is the face of Turlough O'Connor, father of Rory and patron of the abbey, which he reestablished in 1120. Continue through this arch on a tranquil stroll through the woods.

Shopping

You won't find anything too far out of the ordinary at the **Cong Art Gallery** (Main St., tel. 094/954-5675 or 086/358-3468 for off-season inquiries, www.congartgallery.com), but there are plenty of oil paintings of local landscapes. The other shops in town are mostly of the cheap-and-cheesy variety.

Sports and Recreation

You can make a half-hour visit to Inchagoill Island, which has monastic ruins dating to the 5th and 12th centuries, with **Corrib Cruises** (tel. 087/679-6470, www.corribcruises.com, departs Lisloughrey Pier at Ashford Castle, 1 km south of town, at 11:15 A.M. and 3 P.M. daily Apr.–Oct., tickets €15). A night cruise with live folk music departs at 6:15 P.M. daily June–September. Anglers are well catered to in Cong; ring Frank at **Ashford Bay Boat Hire** (tel. 094/954-6348 or 087/252-4253, ashfordbay@hotmail.com).

The highly regarded **Ashford Equestrian Centre** (tel. 094/954-6507, www.rideatashford.com) is on grounds adjacent to Ashford Castle (but no longer part of the estate). No prior experience is necessary for a lesson at **Ireland's School of Falconry** (Ashford Castle, tel. 094/954-6820, www.falconry.ie).

Accommodations

Affiliated with both An Óige and IHH, the **Cong Hostel** (Lisloughrey, Quay Rd., turn left at the Ashford Castle gates onto the R345 and make the next right at the signpost, tel. 094/954-6089, www.quietman-cong.com,

dorms €15–18, private rooms €20 pp, credit cards accepted) offers small dorms with comfy beds and clean facilities.

In the center of town, you can expect comfortable, no-frills bedrooms at **Lydon's Lodge** (Circular Rd., tel. 094/954-6053, open Mar.–Oct., €50 pp), which also arranges boat hire, and at **Ryan's Hotel** (Main St., tel. 094/954-6243, www.ryanshotelcong.ie, open Feb.–Dec., €40–60 pp, s €45–65). Both hotel pubs have live trad almost nightly in the summer months. The **White House** (Abbey St., tel. 094/954-6358, open Mar.–Oct., €30 pp, s €35)—a cozy, homey B&B—is a better value.

Considering the lengthy list of politicians, entertainers, and royalty who have stayed here over the years, it should come as no surprise that both grounds and hotel at the sprawling, fairy-tale **Ashford Castle** (signposted from the southern end of town, tel. 094/954-6003, www.ashford.ie, room €220–400), erstwhile home of the Guinness clan, are as exclusive as exclusive gets (if you're not staying here, prepare to be shooed out of the lobby without further ado). In summertime, though, you can pay €5 to walk the grounds (open to nonguests 9 A.M.–5 P.M. daily), and there are often special room deals available in low season. The original castle was erected in the early 13th century by the O'Connors (the last Irish kings), and successive owners added a French chateau and two Victorian wings.

Food

There isn't a huge selection of dining options here, but you'll have no trouble finding a decent meal. Better than decent, in fact—the sandwiches and salads at the super-cheerful **Hungry Monk Café** (Abbey St., tel. 094/954-6866, open 10 A.M.–6 P.M. daily July–Aug., 10 A.M.–6 P.M. Tues.–Sun. mid-Mar.–June and Sept.–Oct., meals under €10) are the tastiest in town. This should be your first choice for lunch. Otherwise, the **Crowe's Nest** pub at Ryan's Hotel (Main St., tel. 094/954-6243, www.ryanshotelcong.ie, food served 9 A.M.–7 P.M. daily, bar meals €5–15) does good paninis, and for a more formal dinner there's the hotel restaurant, the **Fennel Seed** (open 7–9:30 P.M. daily, mains €14–25).

You can also find hearty (if unadventurous) pub grub at **Danagher's** (Abbey St., tel. 094/954-6028, meals served noon–9:15 P.M. daily, mains €10–20). These two pubs are also sure bets for live trad in the summertime.

Far and away the best restaurant in town is the small, family-run **Echoes** (Main St., tel. 094/954-6059, open 7–10 P.M. daily Apr.–Sept., hours vary in low season, mains €15–25), whose steak, lamb, and seafood dishes are all top-notch. Finish off with a bowl of awesome homemade ice cream.

Information

The very helpful **tourist office** (Abbey St., tel. 094/954-6542, open 10 A.M.–6 P.M. Apr.–May and Sept.–Nov., 9:30 A.M.–7 P.M. July–Aug., sometimes closed 1–2 P.M. for lunch in low season) is in Cong's comically tiny old courthouse.

Services

Cong doesn't have a bank, but there's an **ATM** at O'Connor's, the shop-cum-gas station on Main Street, and a bureau de change at the **post office** (Main St., tel. 094/954-6001). Cong has a pharmacy, **Mary Daly** (Abbey St., tel. 094/954-6119), and Internet access at the **Hungry Monk Café** (Abbey St., tel. 094/954-6866, open 10 A.M.–6 P.M. daily July–Aug., 10 A.M.–6 P.M. Tues.–Sun. mid-Mar.–June and Sept.–Oct., €5/hour).

Getting There and Around

Cong is 42 kilometers north of Galway City on the N84. The **Bus Éireann** (tel. 091/562-000) route from Galway passes through Cong en route to Ballina (#420, 4/day Mon.–Sat. June–Sept., additional Galway–Cong weekday service on route #432).

Rent a bike from the local gas station, **O'Connor's** (Main St., 954-6008, daily/weekly €20/80). For a taxi, ring **Marty Holian** (tel. 094/954-6403 or 087/238-6820) or **Mike's Hackney Cabs** (tel. 087/926-0040).

◖ DOOLOUGH VALLEY

The road from Leenane in northern Connemara up to Louisburgh and Westport winds around the end of Killary Harbour (the N59 to the R335 at Aasleagh); once you've passed the waterfall, a left turn onto the R335 will take you through the splendidly remote Doolough Valley—so named for Lough Doo, on your left as you traverse the narrow road that winds through heathered peaks and the occasional swathe of evergreens. These are the Mweelrea Mountains (Maol Réidh, "Bald King" very loosely translated); the highest (eponymously named) peak overlooking the Killary fjord is also the tallest in the province of Connaught (814 meters).

A place called Delphi, on this road just over the Galway-Mayo border, was christened by Lord Sligo after a trip to the infamous Grecian oracle. It was to his grand Georgian fishing lodge that 400 local people journeyed on foot in 1847 to beg for assistance, a futile death march that turned into one of the very darkest chapters of Mayo history.

WESTPORT

A tidy 18th-century planned town on the River Carrowbeg, Westport (Cathair na Mairt, "City of Cows") offers more visitor amenities than any other town in the county. Not only is it a handy (if touristy) base, but the pub scene in itself is worth a few nights' stay. Westport Quay, two kilometers west of town, features some fine upscale shopping opportunities.

It's easy to orient yourself from the central octagon, marked by a diminutive clock tower; from here, head down James Street and you'll pass the tourist office and plenty of accommodations to reach the tree-lined North and South Malls, the river running beneath them. Continue down the South Mall and you'll reach the Altamount Street train station after half a kilometer. Or turn onto Shop Street from the octagon and make a quick left onto Bridge Street, where most of the action is.

Sights

Westport's primary attraction is the shamelessly touristy **Westport House & Country Park** (tel. 098/25430, www.westporthouse. ie, open 11:30 A.M.–5 P.M. daily Mar.–Oct.,

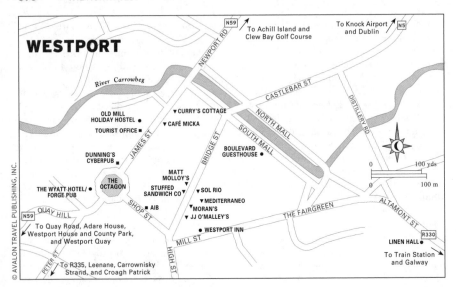

weekends only in Nov., house and gardens €9.50, including fun park €18). The owners of this 18th-century manor house, who claim to be direct descendants of Grace O'Malley (the wife of the original owner, John Browne, was supposedly her great-granddaughter), have turned the grounds of their ancestral home into a kiddie amusement and caravan park. The house itself is only worthwhile if you don't have time to visit another restored Irish manor (for, tackiness aside, any work of neoclassical architects Richard Cassels and James Wyatt is worth a visit).

The **Westport Historical Society** hosts guided town walks departing from the clock at the center of the octagon (8 P.M. Tues. and Wed. July–Aug., admission €5).

Entertainment and Events

You'll find no shortage of unself-consciously old-school pubs in this town. A grocery in front and pub in the back, **Moran's** (15 Bridge St., tel. 098/26320) exudes a pleasantly old-fashioned atmosphere, with colorful football scarves festooned from the ceiling. Sports television aside, it's a nice spot for a quiet pint.

It may be a fire hazard by night (you can

barely breathe, with all the trad lovers craning their necks for a view of the musicians), but during the afternoon there's no better spot than **Matt Molloy's** (Bridge St., tel. 098/26655) for a Bailey's coffee with cream by a crackling open fire. Matt Molloy's the flutist for the celebrated trad-orchestral group The Chieftains (having previously performed with Planxty and the Bothy Band), so it's no surprise the walls are covered with framed photos of some of Ireland's most illustrious musicians. Somewhat less crowded near-nightly trad venues include **Conway's** (Bridge St., tel. 098/26145), **J.J. O'Malley's** (Bridge St., tel. 098/27307), and **The Forge** (Wyatt Hotel, The Octagon, tel. 098/25027). Pretty much every pub in Westport has live music in the summertime, though, so if all else fails just follow your ears.

If you're here around the end of September, see what's on the lineup for the **Westport Arts Festival** (1 James St., tel. 098/27375 or 087/054-8544, www.westportartsfestival. com, tickets €5–12); generally there's a healthy dose of contemporary theater and opera, film screenings, art exhibitions, and jazz and trad sessions. Most performances take place in hotels and pubs around town. There should be a mobile box office on or around James Street (open noon–2:30 P.M. and 4:30–6:30 P.M. during the festival).

And in the "touristy but fun" category, we have **Teach Ceol** ("Music House," Mill St., tel. 098/29200, performances 8 P.M. Wed., tickets €8), a quasi-traditional ceilidh (music, song, and step dancing).

Shopping

Westport should be proud of its delightful little shops. The tomes at **Young's Interesting Books** (James St., tel. 098/29914, youngsbooks@eircom.net) are expensive for secondhand—but then again, you won't find half these books in Eason. Fabulous (and reasonably priced) vintage costume jewelry, prints, and other treasures are in stock at **The Bar of Gold** (Shop St., tel. 098/24803). Another antiques shop chock-full of deals is **The Long Acre** (in the courtyard off Bridge St. behind Gavin's Coffee Shop, tel. 087/206-6341, www.thelongacre.com). It's a true hodgepodge.

Sports and Recreation

There's a lovely Blue Flag beach, **Carramore,** within easy driving distance (28 km west on the R335, following the signs for Carramore from Louisburgh), though the strand at **Carrownisky** near Louisburgh is most popular with surfers. You can rent surfboards and other water-sport equipment from the **Portwest Outdoor Shop** (Bridge St., tel. 098/25177, open 9:30 A.M.–6 P.M. Mon.–Sat.); alternatively, lessons and boards are available from **Surf Mayo** (on Carrownisky Strand, Louisburgh, tel. 087/283-4420).

The **Drummindoo Stud & Equitation Centre** (1.5 km east of Westport, follow signs for Knockranny village, tel. 098/25616, www.anu.ie/drummindoo, open Mon.–Sat. Easter–Sept., only Sat. in low season) offers bay and backcountry rides as well as a foul-weather indoor arena. And of course, you can't beat the vistas on the nine-hole **Clew Bay Golf Course** (Claggan, Kilmeena, signposted 6 km north of Westport on the N59 and a further 3 km

west, tel. 098/41730 or 098/41739, www.clewbaygolf.com).

See also the *Croagh Patrick* section.

Accommodations

Westport accommodations can be overpriced; it seems like you have to look a bit harder to find good-value rooms.

The **Old Mill Holiday Hostel** (James St., beside the tourist office, tel. 098/27045, www.oldmill-hostel.com, dorms €16.50–17.50, private rooms €20 pp) is the only hostel in Westport open year-round. Being along Westport's main drag, it's not quite as charming as the name suggests, though the kitchen facilities are good, the beds are comfortable, and the brisk but efficient management takes pains to prevent rowdiness.

There are several relatively modest B&Bs on Altamount Street, which leads to the train station—still only a five-minute walk from the center of town. The cream of these is **Linden Hall** (Altamount St., tel. 098/27005, www.lindenhallwestport.com, €30–35 pp, s €35–45), a beautifully maintained townhouse with exceptionally friendly and accommodating owners. You can expect the same at **Boulevard Guesthouse** (South Mall, tel. 098/25138 or 087/284-4018, www.boulevard-guesthouse.com, €30–35 pp, no single rooms), another immaculate townhouse (this one on the River Carrowbeg, on the quiet end of town); the breakfasts are well above average, the mattresses quality, the five rooms colorful yet tastefully decorated, and the cozy, light-filled upstairs sitting room is the perfect spot to decompress. There's even a game room (complete with snooker table) out back.

On the other end of town, the back bedrooms and dining room at **Adare House** (Quay Rd., tel. 098/26102, adarehouse@eircom.net, €29–33 pp, s €35–45, credit cards accepted) offer splendid views of Croagh Patrick. This and other B&Bs on Quay Road are within a seven-minute walk of Westport proper and Westport Quay.

Of the hotels in town, the **Westport Inn** (Mill St., tel. 098/29200, www.westportinn.ie,

€50 pp weekdays, €70 pp weekends) offers great value (especially on weekdays!) without sacrificing luxuries like canopy beds. Though the rooms have somewhat standard corporate furnishings, the **Wyatt Hotel** (The Octagon, tel. 098/25027, www.wyatthotel.com, €50–75 pp, s €70–95, €80–100 pp and s €100–120 July–Aug. and bank holidays) still comes recommended—with rollickin'-good trad and folk sessions in the Forge pub and surprisingly good bar and restaurant fare, you might not end up leaving the hotel at all.

Food

Considering all its well-heeled visitors, Westport's eateries are rather disappointing. There are no charming cafés down quiet side streets, and even the town's most popular restaurants won't quite send you over the moon. In general, the pub grub is disappointing.

Scrambled eggs meet Irish cottage kitsch at **Curry's Cottage** (Lower James St., tel. 098/25297, open 10 A.M.–6 P.M. Tues.–Sat., meals under €6), where you can enjoy breakfast, a light lunch, or a frosted cupcake beside the open peat fire. For a light breakfast or a panini or quiche for lunch, try the French-owned **Café Micka** (James St., tel. 098/26538, open 9 A.M.–5:30 P.M. Mon.–Sat., mains €5–9). It may look like any of the other super-ordinary cafés scattered about town, but the food and (Fair Trade) coffee are far better. The owner is a pastry chef, so save some room for dessert. Sure, it's a chain, but **The Stuffed Sandwich Company** (Bridge St., tel. 098/27611, open 9 A.M.–6:30 P.M. Mon.–Sat., daily in summer, mains €4–8) does the best gourmet sandwiches in town (and they, too, serve Fair Trade brew).

It's certainly difficult to find a good Italian restaurant in this country, which makes ◖ **Mediterraneo** (1 Brewery Ln., off Bridge St. opposite Matt Molloy's, tel. 098/26730, open 6–10:30 P.M. Wed.–Mon., mains €11–22) even more of a gem. Once you've found this delightfully romantic little spot, with Leonardo prints on the walls and candles in the wall sconces, you won't be surprised to learn it's owned by a pair of Italians (Sardinian and Sicilian, to be specific). The wine list is impressive, the fresh pasta divine, and the service impeccable. Mediterraneo's tucked-away location means many locals haven't yet discovered it—and most tourists never do.

Climb the stairs to **Sol Rio** (Bridge St., across from Matt Molloy's, tel. 098/28944, open noon–3 P.M. and 6–10 P.M. Wed.–Mon., mains €8–17) for decent (and reasonably priced) Continental fare in a warm ambience.

Information

If you're planning to head farther north, stop for advice before leaving town at the **tourist office** (James St., tel. 098/25711, www.irelandwest.ie and www.sligotourism.ie, open 9 A.M.–6 P.M. Mon.–Sat. and 10 A.M.–6 P.M. Sun. July–Aug., 9 A.M.–5:30 P.M. Mon.–Sat. Apr.–June and Sept., 9 A.M.–12:45 P.M. and 2–5 P.M. weekdays Oct.–Mar.).

Services

You'll find ATMs and bureaux de change at the **Bank of Ireland** (North Mall, tel. 098/25522) and the **AIB** (Shop St., tel. 098/25466).

The **Washeteria** (Mill St., tel. 098/25261) is self-service. One pharmacy is **O'Donnell's** (Bridge St., tel. 098/25163, tel. 098/27347 after hours). The **post office** (tel. 098/25475) is on the North Mall.

One thing this town lacks is reasonably priced Internet access; your only option is the **Dunning's Cyberpub** (James St., on the octagon, tel. 098/25161, open 11 A.M.–9 P.M. daily, €5/hour), since the public library doesn't offer access to nonmembers.

Getting There

Westport is 270 kilometers northwest of Dublin on the N5 and 80 kilometers north of Galway on the N84 (picking up the N5 in Castlebar). A longer (108-km) but far more scenic alternative from Galway is via northern Connemara: Take the N59 west to Maam Cross, picking up the R336 there and heading north to Leenane. Get back on the N59 briefly, and once in County Mayo, turn left for the R335, the Doolough Valley route. It's well worth the extra mileage.

The **Bus Éireann** (tel. 091/562-000) stop is on the octagon. Direct routes to Westport include Galway (#52, 4/day daily), Dublin and Athlone (#21, 2/day daily at 2 P.M. and 5 P.M. Mon.–Sat., 8 A.M. and 8 P.M. Sun.), and Sligo (#66, 3/day Mon.–Sat., 2/day Sun.). **Irish Rail** (Altamount St., tel. 098/25253, 3/day daily, ticket €29) can get you here from Dublin Heuston.

Getting Around

Westport is small enough that you can walk everywhere. For a taxi (or minibus), ring **Ollie's Cabs** (tel. 087/777-0812), **Michael O'Toole** (tel. 087/243-2600 or 098/25305), or **Austin McNeely** (tel. 087/294-1357).

Rent a bicycle from **Seán Sammon** (James St., tel. 098/25471, €10/56 day/week).

MURRISK

A tiny hamlet in the shadow of Croagh Patrick, Murrisk (Muir Riasc, "Marsh by the Sea," or Muir Iasc, the name of a Celtic sea monster) is well worth an overnight stay for its utterly picturesque setting on Clew Bay, an outstanding pub-cum-restaurant, and a couple of lovely B&Bs. Have a memorable meal, get to bed early, and tackle "the reek" first thing in the morning.

There isn't much left of the Augustinian **Murrisk Abbey** (signposted on the R335 opposite the Croagh Patrick car park, always accessible, free admission), founded in 1457, but it's still worth the short stroll from the main road—provided you have any energy left over after your climb! The **National Famine Monument,** a metal sculpture of a "coffin ship" installed in 1997, is also directly across the road from the Croagh Patrick car park.

For B&B, you can do no better than **Béal an tSáile** ("Mouth of the Sea," on the R335 in Murrisk, tel. 098/64012, waltbrencole@ eircom.net, €30 pp, s €40). The charming 18th-century-style decor is a welcome change from flowered bedspreads and bland watercolors. Walter and Brenda Coleman's four com-

fortable rooms offer lovely views of Clew Bay from triangular gable windows, and there are even jumbo-size bathtubs instead of the usual cramped shower stall. The fantastic breakfast (with fresh home fries!) is an added bonus. You could also try **Ben Gorm Lodge** (signposted off the R335, tel. 098/64791 or 087/655-1752, www.bengormlodge.com, €30–34 pp, s €45), which also offers a hearty breakfast and splendid views from the bedrooms. Stay three or more nights for a discount.

You'll have an utterly divine meal at **(The Tavern** (on the R335, tel. 098/64060, www. tavernmurrisk.com, food served noon–10 P.M. or later, lunches €4–10, mains €10–25, 3-course early-bird menu €23 6:30–7:30 P.M. Mon.–Fri.). Owner, chef, and bartender extraordinaire Myles O'Brien has put a lot of sweat, love, and savings into this place—and it shows. The Tavern is so popular with locals you'd be forgiven for thinking this place has been around for decades, but it only opened in 2001. Halfway decent modern Irish would have ensured the Tavern's popularity (seeing as you used to have to drive into Westport for any meal at all), so it's a delightful surprise to find it's good-value (a €48 dinner for two on Wednesday night includes a bottle of wine!), top-notch gourmet. Live trad plays on the weekends—and menus are posted inside the bathroom stalls.

Murrisk is just 10 kilometers west of Westport on the R335; drive north from Connemara through the Doolough Valley and you'll reach the village before you hit Westport. **Bus Éireann** can get you here from Westport (ring the Galway office, tel. 091/562-000, #450, 2/day Mon., Wed., and Fri., 3/day Tues. and Sat., 4/day Thurs., no Sun. service). If you need to get to Westport (or elsewhere), ring **Carrowkeel Cabs** (tel. 087/988-2267).

(CROAGH PATRICK

A starkly beautiful mountain rising over Clew Bay, Croagh Patrick ("Patrick's Hill," 762 meters) was rightly described by H. V. Morton as "Ireland's Sinai." It's said that St. Patrick rang a bell on the summit, at which point all the snakes in Ireland threw themselves into the Atlantic—and the mountain, also referred to as "the reek," has been the ultimate pilgrimage destination ever since. As many as 40,000 people have climbed it in a single day, and the most devout of all do it sans shoes (when you climb it yourself in a pair of sturdy boots, you'll see why this act in itself merits beatification). Even the most bitter of lapsed Catholics should consider a climb, though, as the views from every point on the way up are utterly incomparable on a clear day. In an admirable display of religious devotion, local men schlepped eight-pound bags of cement mix up the mountain to build a chapel at the summit in 1905; this edifice is typically hideous and creepy in the tradition of provincial Irish Catholic churches.

The climb is a challenging one, and the precarious scree-strewn path just below the peak will make you glad you brought a walking stick (you can borrow one from the owner of your B&B or purchase one at the visitors center). Even with frequent pauses for breath-catching and picture-taking, it should take you no more than two hours to reach the summit, and the descent takes a little less than an hour and a half. As always, bring raingear and a big water bottle, and wear at least a good set of running shoes.

There is a **visitors center** (signposted on the R335, tel. 098/64114, www.croagh-patrick.com, open 10 A.M.–6 P.M. daily Apr.–May, 10 A.M.–7 P.M. daily June–Aug., 11 A.M.–5 P.M. daily Sept.–Oct., irregular winter hours) at the foot of the mountain with the usual facilities—an information desk that organizes guided tours of the mountain, gift shop, and a tearoom that also sells packed lunches. Lockers and shower facilities cost a couple of euros. For transportation info, see *Murrisk*.

CLARE ISLAND

At only 16 kilometers square, Clare Island (Oileán Chliara) is still the largest of the 365 islands in Clew Bay. Most foreigners never make it out here—there aren't many "sights" as such, and it's more of a local getaway—but Clare is the perfect place to kick back and take

it easy, going for long walks across Mayo's "green pearl" with a pair of binoculars strung around your neck (for birdlife abounds—gannets, red-beaked choughs, and the like). And there are three routes to the isle's highest point, **Knockmore** (461 meters), on the western side, between 90 minutes and four hours in length. (Your ferry passage includes a map of the island's walking trails.)

The locals place an emphasis on environmental responsibility (organic farming, solar energy, and New Agey pursuits like yoga and reiki are popular) and are very proud of their Blue Flag beaches.

Irish history buffs will note that the pirate queen Grace O'Malley is buried in the churchyard of the 13th-century, Cistercian **Clare Island Abbey** (3 km down the south road from the pier, always accessible), and her eponymous **castle** still guards the harbor.

Frequent ferry service makes Clare an easy day trip from Westport, but there are a few accommodations on the island: the **Bay View Hotel** (on the north side of the harbor, tel. 098/26307, clareislhotel@hotmail.com, open June–Sept., food served 1–9 P.M. daily, €35–45 pp) hosts guided island walks, and reception serves as a de facto information office. The hotel also offers a self-catering hostel annex.

Or, if your eyes light up at the mention of the words "organic vegetarian" and you never ever turn on the television in your room, contact Ciara at the **Ballytoughey Retreat Centre** (on the lighthouse road, 2.5 km from the pier, tel. 098/25412 or 087/250-4845, cliara@eircom.net, B&B €35 pp, s €40, veggie dinner €20, self-catering cottages €100–125/day, minimum stay 2 nights, or €250/week, €400/week June, Sept., and low-season holidays, €500/week July–Aug.). Log on to the **Clare Island Community Co-op** website (www.anu.ie/clareisland) for a year-round schedule of yoga and meditation retreats at the center. The island's "official" website is another fine resource when planning your trip (www.clareisland.org).

From Roonagh Quay, 28 kilometers west of Westport (take the R335 to Louisburgh and turn off onto the local road, pier signposted), you can board the **Clare Island Ferry** (tel. 098/28288, 098/26307, or 087/241-4653, www.clareislandferry.com, 4/day May, June, and Sept., 8/day July and Aug., return ticket €15). The passage takes about 15 minutes (the island's only 5.5 km from the mainland); once on the island, you can rent a bicycle from the ferry operator. Unfortunately, there is no public transport to Roonagh Quay. You can purchase tickets at the quay or at the **Westport tourist office** (James St., tel. 098/25711).

INISHTURK ISLAND

Home to not even a hundred souls, Inishturk (Inis Toirc, "Wild Boar Island") is a delightfully unspoiled island on Clew Bay between Clare Island and Inishbofin off the coast of Galway. At only five kilometers long, the island is short on "sights" but rich in opportunities for bird-watching and long rambling walks in the hills or on two lovely sheltered strands (**Tranaun** and **Curraun,** both on the eastern coast). Inishturk is an even better opportunity for "getting away from it all."

The three B&Bs on the island all serve evening meals featuring locally caught seafood and organic produce: **Ocean View House** (half a km north of the harbor, tel. 098/45520), **Teach Abhainn** (1.5 km west of the harbor, tel. 098/45110), and the **Harbour Lodge** (on the harbor, tel. 098/45610). B&B will run you €30 per person (s €35), with dinner an additional €20–25.

Inishturk is 14.5 kilometers off the coast of south Mayo. The island's sole ferry service is **John V. Heanue** (tel. 098/45541 or 086/202-9670), which operates two 12-passenger ferries: one from Roonagh Quay (departures at 11 A.M. and 6:30 P.M. Fri.–Mon.) and the other from Cleggan in County Galway (departures at 11 A.M. and 6 P.M. Tues.–Thurs.) There's no tourist office on the island, so stop by the office in Westport before you go.

CASTLEBAR

A workaday town 18 kilometers east of Westport—a revolutionary "hotbed" once upon a time in 1798—Castlebar (Caisleán an Bharraigh) has an uncanny way of appearing in your front windshield whether or not you were intending to drive there. Check the road map, and you'll find that Castlebar (Mayo's administrative town) is basically a gateway for all points north and west in the county. It's not a very pleasant town, but there are a few reasons to make a brief stop on your way to Westport, Achill, or anyplace else: First, **McHale's** (Lower Chapel St., tel. 094/902-1849) pours the best pint in the west. Second, note the **Imperial Hotel** on the mall: Mailman-turned-rebel Michael Davitt founded the Land League here in 1879, an organization that agitated for the rights of impoverished tenant farmers (a cause later championed by MP Charles Stewart Parnell).

Need lunch? It may be lacking in atmosphere, but you can rely on **The Stuffed Sandwich Company** (Linenhall St., tel. 094/902-9044, open 9 A.M.–6:30 P.M. Mon.–Sat., daily in summer, mains €5–8) for a gourmet baguette at a reasonable price.

NEWPORT

The starting point for the 48-kilometer **Bangor Trail,** Newport (Baile Uí Fhiacháin) is popular with anglers for its proximity to Clew Bay, Loughs Furnace, Beltra, and Feeagh, as well as the River Newport bisecting the town. You'll pass through on your way to Achill Island. The place itself has a distinctly run-down feel, and as such is only worth a pause for the truly magnificent Clarke window inside the neo-Romanesque **St. Patrick's Church** (signposted from Main St., a two-minute walk uphill), erected in 1918. These three windows over the high altar feature an almost excruciatingly vivid Last Judgment scene, complete with damned grotesques lurking at the bottom of the right panel. It was Harry Clarke's last work—and could very well be his greatest.

Two sites west of Newport, en route to Achill Island, are worth a brief detour: the scant remains of the 15th-century Dominican **Burrishoole Abbey** (signposted 2.5 km north of town on the N59, and another 1 km down a local road, always accessible, free admission), with a tranquil riverside setting; and a simple

© CAMILLE DEANGELIS

Grace O'Malley's Rockfleet Castle, outside Newport

16th-century tower-house set on a Clew Bay inlet, **Rockfleet Castle** (signposted from the N59, 5 km west of Newport). This tower house was the primary residence of the pirate queen Grace O'Malley after the death of her second husband in 1583. (Back then it was called Carraig an Chabhlaigh, or Carrigahowley, meaning "rockfleet" in Irish.) The sign on the castle door states the key is available from the neighboring garage, but seeing as there *is* no neighboring garage you'll just have to survey the castle on the outside.

Those finishing or starting the Bangor Trail should stay at the An Óige **Traenlaur Lodge** (tel. 098/41358, www.anoige.ie, open June–Sept., dorms €15, 10 A.M.–5 P.M. lock-out), built in the 1830s as a fishing lodge for Lord Sligo. This secluded hostel overlooking Lough Feeagh (with its own pier, no less) is signposted five kilometers west of town on the N59 (and it's three kilometers farther up a road winding through the hills over the lake). The hostel serves breakfast (€4–6.50) and evening meals (€9–11) as well as packed lunches (€5.50). You can ring **Kilroy's Taxis** (tel. 098/41900) to get you there from town.

Newport also has a genteel, ivy-clad Georgian hotel, **Newport House** (Main St., tel. 098/41222, www.newporthouse.ie, open Mar.–Sept., €108–162 pp, s €134–188), popular with golfers and anglers. The renowned hotel restaurant emphasizes local seafood and produce. All the commodious rooms are filled with gorgeous antiques, though there's a €22 supplement for rooms with four-poster beds.

For a lunch break, try **Kelly's Kitchen** (Main St., tel. 098/41647, open 11 A.M.–9:30 P.M. Mon.–Sat., 12:30–9:30 P.M. Sun., mains €8–11), which does hearty, no-frills meat and pasta dishes in a cheerful spot that's humming with locals. The owners claim it's the oldest building in Newport.

Newport is 13 kilometers north of Westport on the N59. From Galway and Westport, take **Bus Éireann** (tel. 091/562-000) route #441 (or #440 from Westport only), which passes through town en route to Achill Island (2/day Mon.–Sat., 1/day Sun.).

WALKING ROUTES IN COUNTY MAYO

Mayo walking routes are more frequently traveled by local hill-walking groups than international walkers, which can be a great way to meet a few like-minded natives.

The 48-kilometer **Bangor Trail** begins in Newport, stretching north to Bangor Erris through the extremely remote and boggy Nephin Beg mountain range. While the trail can be done in two days, there aren't any accommodations available at the midway point, so bring your camping gear and grub. In Newport, most folks stay at the An Óige hostel five kilometers north of town, **Traenlaur Lodge** (see the *Newport* section), and in Bangor Erris at **Hillcrest House** (see the *North Mayo* section), a friendly B&B where an evening meal can be arranged. As with all walking routes, pick up the applicable Ordnance Survey Discovery Series maps – in this case, you'll need more than one (numbers 23 and 31, available at tourist offices and bookstores).

A longer walking route that spans Mayo as well as Connemara is the 193-kilometer **Western Way,** which begins in Oughterard on the southern shore of Lough Corrib, heading through the Maamturk Mountains in northern Connemara and passing through Westport and Newport en route to Killala and Ballycastle on Mayo's north coast, near the Céide Fields site, and terminating at the Sligo border near Ballina. The Galway section of this route is 84 kilometers long and is often called the "Connemara Way," though it's more accurately known as "the Connemara section of the Western Way." Most folks walk only a portion of this route (which would take 10–12 days total), though the diversity of the landscape is remarkable – from lush forests to desolate boglands, the rocky southern flank of Croagh Patrick to the heathery hills near Downpatrick Head, and vistas studded with lakes of all sizes, their surfaces black and shimmering when the sun shines.

In addition to the OS Discovery Series maps, other materials for both walking routes are available from the tourist offices in Galway, Oughterard, and Westport.

ACHILL ISLAND

At 147 kilometers square, Achill Island (Oileán Acla) is the largest island off the Irish coast, joined to the mainland by a 200-meter swing bridge named after 19th-century patriot and Land League founder Michael Davitt. Artists have found plenty of inspiration in this bleak and boggy landscape (87 percent of the island is blanketed in peat bog), among them the painter Paul Henry and the Nobel laureate Heinrich Böll, whose Achill Island passages are among the most poignant in his travelogue, *Irish Diary* ("Everything not made of stone eaten away by wind, sun, rain, and time, neatly laid out along the somber slope as if for an anatomy lesson, the skeleton of a village").

Roughly 24 kilometers long by 17 kilometers wide, the island looks like an inverted boot, with the R319 connecting its main villages—Dooagh and Keel on the western end and Achill Sound on the east, just beyond the mainland bridge (with Cashel in between, though there's nothing to note here besides the gas station and tourist office).

Frankly, you do not want to visit Achill in the fall or winter months; grim landscape and weather aside (and it's pretty grim), there's next to nothing open.

Sights

Achill doesn't have any tourist attractions, per se. There isn't much to see at the **Slievemore Deserted Village,** in the shadow of the island's highest mountain—just the mortarless remains of a group of cottages carpeted in sheep pellets, a sad and lonely reminder of the famine. It's an all too appropriate spot for some quiet reflection. To get here from Keel, take the road for McDowell's Hotel (it's signposted), between the Achill Cliff House Hotel and the Minaun View pub. The deserted village, beside a modern graveyard, is just over two kilometers down that road.

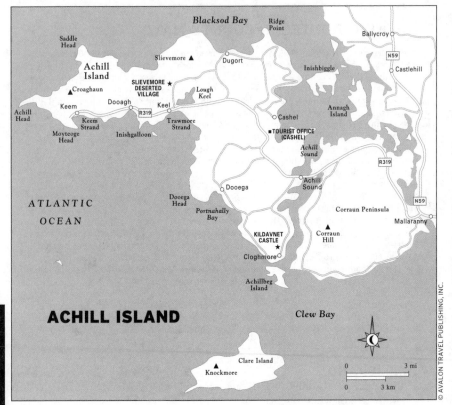

ACHILL ISLAND

Blacksod Bay

ATLANTIC OCEAN

Clew Bay

© AVALON TRAVEL PUBLISHING, INC.

On the island's eastern coast, 6.5 kilometers south of the village of Achill Sound, is **Kildavnet Castle,** a tower house probably built by the O'Malley clan in the 15th century; in any case, it was frequented by the infamous Grace, the pirate queen. Follow the local coast road south from Achill Sound to get here.

Entertainment and Events

Many of the island's pubs host live trad, generally only on Saturday in low season and nearnightly in July and August. Try **The Annexe** (Keel, tel. 098/43268), **Gielty's** (Dooagh, tel. 098/43119, www.gieltys.com), or **The Pub** (Dooagh, tel. 098/43120), all of which are along the R319. The best time to be in Achill is in late July or early August, when the an-

nual weeklong summer school for language and music, **Scoil Acla** (tel. 098/43414, www. scoilacla.com), gets the island hopping with traditional sounds. Aspiring fiddlers and pipers flock here from all over the world to join in on the pub sessions.

Shopping

Achill is home to several potteries, one of which is the simply named **Achill Pottery** (Keel, tel. 098/43145, open daily May–Sept., ring for appointment in low season). The **Beehive** (Keel, tel. 098/43134, open daily Easter–Oct.) stocks a wide range of locally made crafts.

Sports and Recreation

With a coastline of 127 kilometers, Achill

THE NORTHWEST

© CAMILLE DEANGELIS

Achill's most haunting sight is the Slievemore Deserted Village.

has plenty of beaches, quiet and pristine. All five are Blue Flag: **Trawmore Strand** at Keel; **Keem Bay,** at the western terminus of the R319; **Dooega** on the southern side; and there are two strands at **Dugort,** on the island's northeastern edge. Rent a boat (or bike) from **O'Malley's Island Sports** (Keel, signposted off the R319, tel. 098/43125); divers should contact **Dol-fin Divers** (Achill Sound, tel. 098/45473), which provides lessons as well as equipment rental. The **Achill Outdoor Educational Centre** (Keel, tel. 098/47253 or 098/47304, www.achilloutdoor.com) offers courses in windsurfing and mountaineering.

Achill's tallest peak, **Slievemore** (671 meters), makes for a very strenuous all-day hike (figure on 12 hours round-trip); the trail begins at the deserted village. A shorter option (about 6 hours round-trip) is second-tallest **Croaghaun** (668 meters) on the island's western edge; its northeast face is a nearly perpendicular sea cliff (600 meters), and along its slopes there are five corrie lakes (i.e., small glacier-carved dips in the mountainside). Begin the Croaghaun hike at the Keem Bay car park. An OS map (pick up Discovery Series #30 at any Mayo tourist office) and all the usual gear (rainwear, boots, compass, etc.) are essential for both hikes.

Accommodations

The island offers several good hostels. Shay at the cozy, clean, 16-bed **Rich View Hostel** (Keel, tel. 098/43462, richviewhostel@hotmail.com, dorms €12, private rooms €15 pp) is the ideal owner: friendly, ultra-informative, eager to help, and of a musical persuasion (he's in a trad band that performs in the pubs). Rich View is the only place open year-round. The IHO, family-run **Valley House Hostel** (Dugort, turnoff signposted at the village of Bunacurry on the R319, and a further 4 km to the hostel, tel. 098/47204, www.valley-house. com, open mid-Mar.–Oct., dorms €15, private rooms €15 pp, credit cards accepted) has comfy beds, good showers, and—best of all—a pub with an open turf fire that's popular with locals and backpackers alike. It's also within spitting distance of the strand at Dugort.

Granted, nearly all B&Bs are family homes, but many of those on Achill can feel a bit *too* homey; in other words, you might feel like you're just staying in somebody's spare room (which, come to think of it, you are!). One to recommend for its sea views, helpful owner, and adorable resident dalmatian is **Hy Breasal** (St. Fionan's Rd., Achill Sound, signposted off the R319, tel. 098/45114, hybreasalmayo@hotmail.com, €30 pp, s €35). ("Hy Breasal," by the way, is a legend about a lost island and a preternatural stallion that comes galloping out of the sea.)

One of the most established B&Bs on the island is **Joyce's Marian Villa** (Keel, on the R319, tel. 098/43134, www.joycesachill.com, €45–60 pp), a spacious, immaculately kept place with a helpful proprietor, hearty breakfasts with homemade jam and other trimmings, and beach and cliff views (though rooms with sea views cost more than those without). Another option in Keel is **Atlantic Breeze** (Pollagh, Keel, tel. 098/43189, atlanticbreeze01@hotmail.com, €30 pp, s €35), which offers bike hire, babysitting, and a conservatory with a sea view in which to savor your rashers.

Achill's hotels are all of the slightly stodgy, small-town variety. You'll receive a warmer reception at the **Ostan Ghob A'Choire,** a.k.a. the **Achill Sound Hotel** (Achill Sound, on the R319, tel. 098/45245, www.achillsoundhotel.com, €45–50 pp, s €55), which also rents bikes, but the 10-room, three-star **Achill Cliff House Hotel** (Keel, on the R319, tel. 098/43400, www.achillcliff.com, €35–45 pp, s €45–55, and in July–Aug. €60–70 pp, s €85–95) is a bit more posh, with bathtubs in all rooms (though there's an extra fee for use of the sauna). Outdoorsy types may want to stay at **McDowell's Hotel** (Slievemore Rd., Dugort, signposted from the R319, tel. 098/43148, www.mcdowellshotel.com, €50 pp), since you can rent surfboards, canoes, and pedal-boats, or join in on a guided hill walk.

Food

Follow the old adage of the pessimist when it comes to dining on Achill: Don't expect much, and you won't be disappointed. The **Beehive** (Keel, on the R319, tel. 098/43134, open 10:30 A.M.–6 P.M. daily Easter–Oct., mains under €10), a café and craft gallery, does the tastiest cakes and scones on the island; if that's not open, try friendly **The Last Drop Coffee Shop** (Dooagh, on the R319, tel. 098/43119, open 10 A.M.–7 P.M. daily, lunches €3–6), adjoining Gielty's pub, which does basic soup and sandwiches.

You'll find decent, good-value grub at the **Achill Sound Hotel** (Achill Sound, tel. 098/45245, food served noon–8 P.M. daily, bar meals under €12), and the **Annexe** pub does burgers-and-chips kind of meals in high season. The relatively fancy fare at the **Achill Cliff House Hotel** (Keel, tel. 098/43400, food served 7–9 P.M. daily, 1–3 P.M. Sun., 3-course dinner €25, mains €12–22) follows the general standard of Irish hotels—mediocre and overpriced—but if you're here in low season it's pretty much your only dinner option.

Hostellers should stock up at the **supermarket** (Achill Sound, tel. 098/45243) just over the bridge from the mainland.

Information and Services

The community-run **tourist office** (Cashel, tel. 098/47353, www.achilltourism.com, open 9 A.M.–6 P.M. weekdays July–Aug., 9 A.M.–5 P.M. weekdays Sept.–June) is in a trailer beside the Esso station.

In addition to two "mobile banks" that pass through Keel, Achill Sound, and all points in between, there is an **ATM** and bureau de change at **Sweeney's Spar and Craft Shop** (Achill Sound, tel. 098/45243).

Getting There

Achill Island is midway along Mayo's west coast, south of the Mullet Peninsula and Blacksod Bay, and north of Murrisk and Clew Bay. The gateway village, Achill Sound, is 43 kilometers northwest of Westport, and the primary villages of Dooagh and Keel are 18.5 kilometers and 14.5 kilometers west of Achill Sound along the R319. From Westport, you can take **Bus Éireann** (tel. 096/78100) to Achill (#440 or #441, 2/day Mon.–Sat., 1/day Sun., departure times vary daily); the bus stops in each village along the main road.

Getting Around

For a taxi on Achill, ring **K. O'Riordan** (tel. 086/190-1259) or **Paul McLoughlin** (tel. 098/45652 or 087/239-0408), who offers 24-hour service.

O'Malley's Island Sports (Keel, signposted off the R319, tel. 098/43125, ring for rates) can rent you a cycle.

NORTH MAYO

You want off the tourist merry-go-round—far, far off? You got it.

Driving north toward the Mullet Peninsula, where heaping piles of turf are drying on the side of the road, is a strange experience in itself. The bog-and-heathered landscape has a placid, color-bleached, on-and-on bleakness that—were it not for the smudgy hills of the Nephin Beg mountain range—would nearly remind one of Wyoming. The haze lingering on the horizon gives you a queer sensation, like a portal has opened to that ominous fairy world of Irish folklore.

There's another reason for that ominous feeling. This region (particularly the villages of Rossport and Ballinaboy along the Broadhaven Bay inlet) has attracted attention in recent years for its battle against Shell, the oil conglomerate, which plans to open a gas pipeline on land owned by local farmers (five of whom have gone to prison for their protests): a classic David-and-Goliath tale with profound environmental consequences. Now you know the reason behind all those "Shell Out!" and "(S)HELL" signs tacked to telephone poles all over the country.

If traveling the R314, which follows Mayo's north coast, you may notice signposts for **Tír Sáile**, the North Mayo Sculpture Trail (tel. 098/45107 for more information). A group of native artists, along with several from the U.K., the U.S., Japan, and Denmark, installed 15 sculptures in 1993 that were intended to celebrate "the integral vitality of the landscape"—

and as a consequence you might hardly notice some of them without the brown signpost pointing them out!

Needless to say, public transport is scarce. If you don't have a car, frankly, you're better off sticking to Westport; while the renowned archaeological site at Céide Fields is worth a visit, most people wouldn't consider it a must-see. Furthermore, ATMs are still something of a rarity in these parts (though there are a couple of banks in Belmullet), so be sure to get to the bank before leaving Westport.

Bangor Erris

The barely there hamlet of Bangor Erris (Beannchar Iorrais or Beann Géar, "Sharp Peak")—Bangor for short—warrants a mention because it's the start- or end-point of the 48-kilometer Bangor Trail, which ends (or begins) in Newport.

Not that you've much choice, but the most popular accommodation—whether you're finishing the trail, going fishing, or just passing through—is **Hillcrest House** (Main St., tel. 097/83494, http://homepage.eircom.net/~hillcresthouse, €25 pp, s €35). Mrs. Cosgrove will bring you a proper tea tray in her comfortable sitting room, and she also serves evening meals in high season. Anglers are well cared for here as well, with fishing permits, equipment, boat hire, and packed lunches all taken care of. Another option for B&B is **Faye Carey** (signposted off Church Rd., turnoff at the West End Bar on Main St., tel. 097/83532, atimes@eircom.net, €21–26 pp), another bungalow with a friendly reception—but this one has prettier views from the bedroom windows.

There are no respectable dining options in Bangor, just fast food. If you aren't planning on an evening meal at your B&B, drive 20 kilometers north to An Chéibh or the Broadhaven Bay Hotel in Belmullet. There's a Spar supermarket on Main Street with an ATM.

Bangor Erris is 62 kilometers north of Westport on the N59 and 49 kilometers north of Newport. In July and August only, **Bus Éireann** (#446, 1/day Sun.–Thurs., 2/day Fri.–Sat.) offers a service between Ballina and

THE NORTHWEST

Blacksod Point on the Belmullet Peninsula, stopping in Bangor along the way.

The Mullet Peninsula

This Gaeltacht region, roughly 30 kilometers long, is possibly the least traveled of any place on the Auld Sod. The town of **Belmullet** (Béal an Mhuirthead, "Mouth of the Isthmus") is more substantial than you'd expect, but there's little to interest the visitor. The town's principal streets shoot out from the central Carter Square, where at the **Bank of Ireland** (tel. 097/81311) you can pad your wallet at the ATM. Then stop by the seasonal **tourist office** (Barrack St., tel. 097/81500, open 9:30 A.M.– 4:30 P.M. weekdays Easter–Sept.) for help in getting your bearings in the area.

Continue on the R313 south another 20 kilometers to **Blacksod Point,** which affords a starkly beautiful view over the eponymous bay to Slievemore and Croaghaun, Achill Island's highest peaks. There are two splendid, oft-deserted strands along the peninsula's eastern edge, **Elly Bay** and **Mullaghroe Beach** a bit farther south.

Belmullet has a reputable pub-cum-seafood restaurant, **An Chéibh** (Barrack St., tel. 097/81007, open 12:30–7:50 P.M. Mon.– Thurs., 12:30–9:30 P.M. Fri.–Sat., 12:30– 7:30 P.M. Sun., mains €10–24), which offers a few chicken and meat dishes as well. Your alternative is the above-average pub fare at the **Broadhaven Bay Hotel** (on the R313, tel. 097/20600, www.broadhavenbay.com, €50–65 pp, s €70 Sun.–Thurs., €65–75 pp and s €80 Fri.–Sat., food served 12:30–8:30 P.M. daily, mains €10–18), an unoffensively modern establishment with panoramic sea views from the platform seating area. The spacious, candlelit ambience, friendly barstaff, generous portions and reasonable prices make this hotel the best dining option in the area.

Belmullet is 20 kilometers northwest of Bangor Erris on the R313. In July and August, **Bus Éireann** (tel. 096/71800) offers a service between Ballina and Blacksod Point via Belmullet (#446, 1/day Sun.–Thurs., 2/ day Fri.–Sat.).

Pollatomish

A scattered and delightfully remote village on Broadhaven Bay, Pollatomish (Poll an tSómais, "Hollow of Comfort") is completely untouched by the Celtic Tiger: There are no restaurants, gift shops, nightclubs, or housing estates to be found. You can go for a long walk along the water to Benwee Head without meeting a soul for miles. In other words, it's heaven on earth for outdoorsy travelers looking to get well off the beaten track.

The area's sole accommodation is the IHH **Kilcommon Lodge** (signposted off the R314, Pollatomish, tel. 097/84621, www. kilcommonlodge.net, dorms €12, private rooms €15 pp, laundry service €4), easily the best hostel in County Mayo. This clean, cozy, 25-bed hostel has been around for nearly 30 years; four out of five guests are repeat visitors, and aging backpackers often return with their own children. The kind and helpful owners, Betty and Fritz Schult, cook both breakfast (€4–5) and dinner (€10) by prior arrangement. They can also make a reservation for you on one of the ferries to the **Inishkea Islands,** which you can spot from the large windows in the common room with its open peat fire, multitude of books and classic board games, and broadband Internet access. Contrary to reports, this hostel does *not* have a curfew or lockout—in fact, Betty is quite laid-back about the checkout time (and laid-back in general). If it's a private room you're after, ask for #8—it's the coziest. And be sure to ask for a free copy of *A Guide to Walking in the Barony of Erris,* which details two dozen walking routes in the area.

There are two pubs in Pollatomish, **McGrath's** (by the pier) and **McGuire's** (signposted off the local Pollatomish road), which is the more popular, especially with the younger crowd. Neither pub serves food, but McGuire's does offer the occasional trad session. The village's lone grocery is sparsely stocked and rather pricey, so you're better off stocking up before leaving Belmullet, Ballina, or even Bangor.

Pollatomish is 16 kilometers east of Belmullet, signposted off the R314 and 6 kilometers farther down a local road. From that turnoff, it's 21 kilometers east to Céide Fields and 29 kilometers to Ballycastle. There is no public transportation.

Céide Fields

You may have heard that Céide Fields ("KAY-juh," on the R314 8 km west of Ballycastle, tel. 096/43325, ceidefields@opw.ie, open 10 A.M.–5 P.M. daily mid-Feb.–mid-Oct., admission €3.70) is one of Ireland's most important Stone Age sites, but don't expect anything dramatic and you won't be disappointed. Most of the evidence of an early Neolithic farming community remains beneath the bog, and only small white posts indicate the presence of ancient stone walls deep under the heather. The interpretive center (a sleek but acutely out of place glass-and-steel pyramidal structure poking up out of the hill) is certainly worth a visit—so long as you're in the mood for an archaeology lesson.

Admission to this Dúchas site includes a 20-minute audiovisual (very informative, but with some weirdly ominous background music) and a guided tour of the site. The center is dominated by a pillar-like pine tree trunk, thousands of years old, that was fished out of a nearby bog.

Céide Fields is eight kilometers west of Ballycastle on the R314, and there is no public transport.

Ballycastle

A one-street village along the R314, Ballycastle (Baile an Chaisil, "Townland of the Ring Fort") is a common stopover for visitors heading to or from Céide Fields, and the dramatic Downpatrick Head is only six kilometers away. Ballycastle's sole eatery is **Mary's Cottage Kitchen** (Main St., tel. 096/43361, open 10 A.M.–4 P.M. Mon.–Fri., 11 A.M.–3 P.M. Sat., until 6 P.M. Mon.–Sat. Apr.–Oct., light meals €3–6), a lovely old-fashioned café with a cheerful fire and seating in the open loft beneath a pitched wood roof. You can also take your tea and tasty rhubarb pie in the garden out back when the weather's fine.

If you're spending the night in Ballycastle,

either have an early meal at Mary's or drive to The Golden Acres pub in Killala for dinner. Sadly, there really aren't any other options here besides the overpriced hotel fare at the Stella Maris, which is three kilometers outside town on the Belmullet road.

The rooms at the delightfully homey **Keadyville** (Carrowcubbic, the first right outside the village off the Killala road, tel. 096/43288, €25–30 pp, s €30–35), a working farm, feature window seats with views of Downpatrick Head and comfy beds with real quilts and electric heating pads. Continue to admire the sea view with an excellent, carefully prepared breakfast in the conservatory. Barbara Kelly, the nicest proprietor you'll find anywhere, also serves evening meals in high season. Another good choice is **Suantraí** (on the Killala-bound R314 just before the Keadyville turnoff, tel. 096/43040, open June–Aug., €30 pp), but Keadyville is open year-round.

Ballycastle is 53 kilometers northeast of Bangor Erris via the N59 (picking up the R315 in Crossmolina). **Bus Éireann** operates a local Ballina–Killala–Ballycastle service on weekdays only (#445, 2/day Mon.–Thurs., 3/day Fri.); to get to Ballina, take route #52 from Galway and Westport (5/day daily) or #22 from Dublin (6/day daily). For a taxi, ring **Ballycastle Cabs** (tel. 086/847-7845 or 086/285-8359).

Downpatrick Head

Don't pass through Ballycastle without making a detour for Downpatrick Head. The first sight you'll come to is the **Poll na Seantoine,** an eerie cavity beneath the cliff that's claimed dozens of lives over the centuries. No wonder there's a high fence around the circumference now. Beyond the blowhole is a statue of St. Patrick erected in 1993, and an ugly cement lookout station dates from World War II. Finally you come to the edge and a rock stack known as **Dun Briste** ("Broken Fort"). Even if you aren't a geology buff, you'll appreciate the 350 million years' worth of rock formations in this birds' haven separated from the mainland in the shifting of the continents. On

the rock stack at Downpatrick Head

© CAMILLE DEANGELIS

the northwestern horizon you can see the Inishkea Islands.

Someday far in the future, the earth above the blowhole will collapse into the sea—and so will Dun Briste. The view seems even more dramatic when you consider this.

To get here, take the coast road turnoff opposite MacNamee's grocery on the Killala end of Ballycastle and proceed for about six kilometers. This quiet winding road makes for a pleasant walk or cycle, especially since the road after the final turnoff for Downpatrick is hideously potholed. If you're driving, you might want to park before the gravel gives way to trenches and walk the rest of the way.

If you turn left at the final Downpatrick turnoff instead of back toward Ballycastle, you'll eventually reach **Lacken Strand,** a golden, gorgeously expansive and sheltered beach.

Killala

The distinguishing feature of the small and slightly dreary town of Killala (Cill Ála) is a 25-meter **round tower;** if it seems a bit too well-preserved to be authentic, that's because the roof was replaced in 1841. Dining and accommodation options are sparse all over this part of the county, but you'll find both at **The Golden Acres** (Upper Market St., tel. 096/32183, food served noon–9 P.M., mains €6–10, B&B €33 pp, s €35), a spacious, comfortable bar with amiable bartenders and good-value, mostly traditional pub grub (though there are no veggie options on the menu, the staff will cheerfully accommodate any special requests). Hanging from the ceiling are teapots and cups, copper kettles, dirty socks, boots, and hats—even a lobster claw the size of an oven mitt. Short on character, this place is not.

Killala is 14 kilometers southeast of Ballycastle on the R314. **Bus Éireann** operates a weekday service (#445, 2/day Mon.–Thurs., 3/day Fri.) between Ballina and Ballycastle, stopping at Killala along the way.

Ballina

Mayo's biggest town, Ballina (Béal an Átha, "bah-lih-NAH," 56 km northeast of Westport and 60 km southwest of Sligo) offers little to interest the visitor; where's the sense in wasting your vacation in a place that's gray and depressing even on a sunny day? That said, there are two fine monastic ruins several kilometers northwest of Ballina—Moyne Abbey and Rosserk Friary—that are well worth seeking out, should you find yourself passing through en route to Sligo.

Driving east from Killala on the R314, you'll see **Moyne Abbey** clearly signposted. Turn left and left again at the second signpost, and you'll find a third pointing to a farm gate on which is posted a "beware of the bull" notice. The gate should be open, so mosey on down the muddy lane—the abbey is straight ahead, just a couple minutes' walk. Moyne Abbey is a substantial, labyrinthine ruin, consecrated in 1462 by MacWilliam de Burgo. The English governor of Connaught, Sir Richard Bingham, burned the abbey (and tortured its inhabitants) in 1590, though the stalwart friars had returned here sometime before 1606. The abbey was still in use until the 18th century, and is most notable for the completeness of its cloister, a rarity in Ireland. Water drips a slow rhythm from the mold along the vaulted stone ceilings, and a gurgling stream passes beneath the dark rooms on the western side. The church holds several glorious mullioned windows and a complete holy water font, though you will certainly not be tempted to dip your finger. You can even walk upstairs to what were once the dormitories.

There's also an open staircase at **Rosserk Friary,** though the dormitory is much smaller. To get here, make a left out of the Moyne driveway, and Rosserk is signposted after three kilometers. Make a left and another left at the Y junction; the abbey is 1.4 kilometers from the main road. This abbey was also founded around 1460, and was also set fire to by the nefarious Bingham in 1590. In a tranquil setting on the western shore of Killala Bay, Rosserk is particularly interesting considering those who lived and worked here; it was founded for the Third Order of St. Francis, a group of laypeople who wished to emulate that most venerated of saints, but who could not become monks or nuns because they had already married. There isn't quite as much to explore here, though the abbey's mullioned windows are even more beautiful than Moyne's, and the bell tower makes a dramatic impression from the road. Note the double piscina to the right of the altar (for draining water used during the Mass) and the well-preserved angel carvings above the right bowl.

The local **Bus Éireann** Ballina–Killala–Ballycastle service (#445) is infrequent enough (only 3/day Mon.–Fri.) to make getting to these sites by public transport logistically infeasible. You could ask to be dropped off at the Moyne Abbey turnoff, but then it's still a few kilometers' walk. Or you could ring for a taxi in Ballina: **P.J. Reilly** (tel. 096/22222) or **Abbey Cabs** (tel. 087/261-6024).

To get to those remote places in northwestern Mayo via Bus Éireann, you'll first have to switch buses in Ballina. Direct services to Ballina include Galway and Westport (#52, 5/day daily) or Dublin (#22, 6/day daily).

KNOCK

As many as 1.5 million people per year visit the little town of Knock (Cnoc Mhuire, "Hill of Mary") to pray at the **National Shrine of Our Lady of Knock** (tel. 094/938-8100, www. knock-shrine.ie). One night in August 1879, 15 people claimed to have seen a trio of apparitions—the Virgin Mary, St. Joseph, and St. John the Evangelist—in the south gable of the parish church.

Today you'll find a sprawling religious complex on the site of the apparition, replete with larger-than-life statues, "confessions, this way" signs, and some of the most hideous ecclesiastical architecture on God's green earth. Knock, its churches, and the **folk museum** (tel. 094/938-8100, open 10 A.M.–6 P.M. daily May–Oct., until 7 P.M. July–Aug., noon–4 P.M. daily Nov.–Apr., admission €4) will appeal only to devout Catholics.

Accommodations and Food

There is accommodation available on the shrine grounds at the three-star **Knock House**

Hotel (Ballyhaunis Rd., tel. 094/938-8088, www.knockhousehotel.ie, open May–Dec., restaurant open 7:30 A.M.–10 P.M. daily, hotel rates €61 pp, s €80 May–June; €73 pp, s €93 July–Sept.; €53 pp, s €63 Oct.–Dec.), which has 68 standard business-class rooms. A more economical option is the comfortable, immaculately maintained B&B **Ashford Manor** (Claremorris Rd., tel. 094/938-8514, omgreal@oceanfree.net, open Feb.–Nov., €30 pp). The town doesn't have much in the way of proper dining options, so the Four Seasons restaurant at the Knock House Hotel is your best bet.

Getting There

Knock is signposted off the N17, 72 kilometers north of Galway and 71 kilometers southwest of Sligo, and 225 kilometers northwest of Dublin off the N5. **Bus Éireann** (tel. 096/71800) provides direct service from Dublin and Athlone (#21, at least 2/day daily), Galway (#52 or #64, at least 4/day daily), Westport (#21, 3/day Mon.–Sat., 1/day Sun.), and Sligo and Derry (#64, at least 2/day daily). The **Irish Rail** station at Claremorris (tel. 094/71011, 3/day Sat.–Thurs. from Dublin Heuston, 4/day Fri.) is 9.5

kilometers southwest of Knock, and you can ring **Brennan's** (tel. 094/938-8325) for a taxi.

Locals regard **Knock Airport** (tel. 094/936-7222, www.knockairport.com) as their *other* miracle. From here you can fly to Dublin (Aer Arann, www.aerarann.ie, 1/day daily), London Stansted (Ryanair, www.ryanair.com, 1/day daily), London Luton (Ryanair, 1/day daily), London Gatwick (Ryanair and easyJet, www.easyjet.com, 2/day daily), and there's at least one flight a day to/from Manchester, Birmingham, and Durham Tees Valley (all on bmibaby, www.bmibaby.com). Seeing as Knock and Shannon are nearly equidistant from Galway, you might want to consider leaving from here if you're heading for England. It's a tiny airport, though, so expect bare-bones amenities along with a €10 "development fee."

Knock Airport is 13 kilometers north of Knock and 89 kilometers north of Galway off the N17, and 63 kilometers east of Westport on the N5. There is only local bus service to the airport (not from the town of Knock, though, inexplicably), so if you don't have a rental car to return, it is much easier to catch a flight from Shannon or Dublin.

Sligo

Bordered by Mayo to the west, Roscommon to the south, Leitrim to the east, and the Atlantic to the north, County Sligo has the richest trove of prehistoric sites on the island. Sligo is popular with local golfers, and surfers will find some of Europe's best waves at Enniscrone and Easky along the county's western coast. The northern landscape is dominated by a limestone "table mountain" called **Benbulben** (530 meters), which appears in several Irish legends, including those of Fionn mac Cumhaill (who discovers his long-lost son wandering along the mountain's lonely plateau) and Diarmuid and Gráinne (though these star-crossed lovers have supposedly jumped off every cliff in the country).

But more than anything else, Sligo is synonymous with the nation's most beloved poet,

William Butler Yeats. Though Yeats didn't actually spend much time here (he was born in Dublin, educated in London, bought a tower house in Galway, and spent his last years in France), his mother's home was obviously dear to his heart: He asked to be reburied 7.5 kilometers north of town in the Drumcliffe churchyard, where his great-grandfather once served as rector.

SLIGO TOWN

It may seem a bit gritty around the edges now, but word on the street is that developers are hoping Sligo (Sligeach) will become the "new Galway" within the next few years. While that's on the optimistic side, it's certainly true that Sligo's nightlife and arts scene is on the

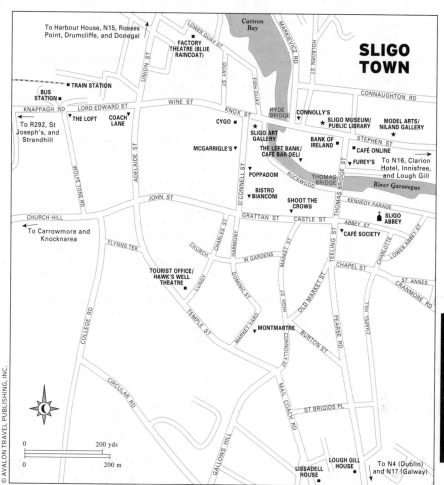

To Harbour House, N15, Rosses Point, Drumcliffe, and Donegal

LOWER QUAY ST

Cartron Bay

MARKIEVICZ RD

HOLBORN ST

SLIGO TOWN

FACTORY THEATRE (BLUE RAINCOAT)

UNION ST

QUAY ST

FISH QUAY

CONNAUGHTON RD

■ TRAIN STATION

BUS STATION ■

KNAPPAGH RD

LORD EDWARD ST

WINE ST

KNOX ST

HYDE BRIDGE

CONNOLLY'S

SLIGO MUSEUM/ PUBLIC LIBRARY

MODEL ARTS/ NILAND GALLERY

To R292, St Joseph's, and Strandhill

THE LOFT ▼

COACH LANE

CYGO ■

SLIGO ART GALLERY ★

STEPHEN ST

CAFÉ ONLINE ■

ADELAIDE ST

McGARRIGLE'S ▼

THE LEFT BANK/ CAFÉ BAR DELI

BANK OF IRELAND ■

To N16, Clarion Hotel, Innisfree, and Lough Gill

WOLFE TONE RD

O'CONNELL ST

POPPADOM ▼

ROCKWOOD

THOMAS BRIDGE

FUREY'S ▼

THOMAS BRIDGE ST

River Garavogue

JOHN ST

BISTRO ▼ BIANCONI

SHOOT THE CROWS

KENNEDY PARADE

CHURCH HILL

GRATTAN ST

CASTLE ST

ABBEY ST

SLIGO ▲ ABBEY

To Carrowmore and Knocknarea

FLYNNS TER

CHARLES ST

HARMONY

TEELING ST

CAFÉ SOCIETY ▼

CHARLOTTE

LOWER ABBEY ST

CHURCH ST

W GARDENS

MARKET ST

CHAPEL ST

COLLEGE RD

LUNGI

DOMINIC ST

IS HIGH

OLD MARKET ST

CHAPEL HILL

ST ANNES CRANMORE RD

TOURIST OFFICE/ HAWK'S WELL THEATRE ■

TEMPLE ST

MARKET YARD

▼ MONTMARTRE

BURTON ST

PEARSE RD

CONNOLLY'S

CIRCULAR RD

MAIL COACH RD

ST BRIGIDS PL

GALLOWS HILL

LISSADELL HOUSE ●

LOUGH GILL HOUSE ●

To N4 (Dublin) and N17 (Galway)

0 — 200 yds
0 — 200 m

© AVALON TRAVEL PUBLISHING, INC.

upswing. Put it this way: if you want an (albeit small) taste of urban bohemia without all those fanny-packed, ballcap-wearing tourists gorging Galway's Shop Street, then Sligo's the spot for you.

The town straddles the River Garavogue, with an L-shaped bend at Rockwood Parade; the main drag, O'Connell Street, is one block west. Head south on O'Connell and you'll hit one of those streets that keeps changing names; this one from John to Grattan to Cas-tle to Abbey Street (from west to east), and there are plenty of shops and pubs along this road. The bus and train stations are on the southwest of town.

Sligo's coolest attractions—namely, Knocknarea and Carrowmore—are a pleasant bike ride out of town.

Sights

Locals will tell you of the days when **Sligo Abbey** (Abbey St., tel. 071/914-6406, open 10 A.M.–6 P.M. daily mid-Mar.–Oct., 9:30 A.M.–4:30 P.M. Fri.–Sun. in winter, admission €2.10) lay weed-choked and derelict. Fortunately, Dúchas has conserved this 13th-century Dominican friary in recent years, and though it won't knock your socks off if you've already been to other monastic ruins, it's worth checking out for the carvings on the 15th-century high altar, the only one of its kind extant in the country.

Art lovers should head for the **Model Arts and Niland Gallery** (The Mall, tel. 071/914-1405, www.modelart.ie, open 10 A.M.–5:30 P.M. Tues.–Sat., 11 A.M.–4 P.M. Sun., free admission) for its permanent collection of the works of Sean Keating and Jack B. Yeats, along with major traveling exhibitions. If you dig the contemporary stuff (and might even want to take it home), stop by the **Sligo Art Gallery** (Yeats Memorial Building, Hyde Bridge, tel. 071/914-5847, www.sligoartgallery.com, open 10 A.M.–5 P.M. Mon.–Sat.), which usually has an exhibition on offer.

With the personal effects of the Yeats brothers and Easter rebel Constance Markievicz on display, the **Sligo Museum** (Stephen St., tel. 071/914-1623, www.sligolibrary.ie, open 10 A.M.–noon and 2–4:50 P.M. Tues.–Sat. June–Sept., 2–4:50 P.M. Tues.–Sat. Apr.–May and Oct., free admission) should be another item on your rainy-day backup plan.

Entertainment

Sligo's nightlife is getting livelier all the time. There are enough great pubs to keep you entertained for a full week.

Without a doubt, the trendiest bar in town is **The Left Bank** (15/16 Rear Stephen St., tel. 071/914-0100, www.leftbank.ie)—formerly known as The Garavogue—which offers live rock music, open mic nights (usually on Monday), and an atmosphere abuzz. (The new name is a misnomer; as the river flows, the Left Bank is actually on the right bank.) The barstaff are notoriously lazy (so if it takes you a full 15 minutes to catch the bartender's eye, don't wonder fumingly if it's just you). The crowd is mixed during the day, but at night

it's just college students and 20-somethings. Another popular spot day or night—worth checking out for the chandelier and medieval decor alone—is **The Belfry** (Thomas St., tel. 071/916-1250, lunch noon–2:30 P.M., bar food served 3–9 P.M.).

But you'll find the best *craic* by far at **Shoot the Crows** (Castle St., tel. 071/916-2554, www.shootthecrows.ie). "Shoots" is snug and dimly lighted, with creepy wood sculptures hanging above the bar. All this character attracts an arty, laid-back crowd, and there's live trad (and sometimes blues) here on Tuesday and Thursday nights. **Furey's** (Bridge St., tel. 071/914-3825), owned by the Irish trad band Dervish, also does great sessions nightly (three or four nights a week in winter).

It was closed at time of writing, but hopefully **Hargadon's** (4 O'Connell St.) will be reopening in the not-so-distant future. It was a wonderful traditional pub with cozy snugs galore, and with any luck the new owners will bring this Sligo institution back soon. In the meantime, take your black stuff at **McGarrigle's** (O'Connell St., tel. 071/914-1667), whose traditional atmosphere is rather deceptive—there's free broadband access (you need your own ethernet cable, however) and an alternative/rock bar upstairs. Even better is **Connolly's** (Markiewicz Rd., tel. 071/914-3340), a pleasantly dingy old man's pub. Nothing's changed here since Jesus walked on water. Notice the neat poster in the window listing pint prices from 1900 to 1995—€3.90 sure seems like highway robbery, doesn't it?

The **Model Arts and Niland Gallery** (The Mall, tel. 071/914-1405, www.modelart.ie, event tickets €7–15) often has film screenings, concerts, and comedy shows. For mainstream theater, check out the **Hawk's Well Theatre** (Temple St., tel. 071/916-1518, www.hawkswell.com, most tickets €10–20).

Sligo's true dramatic gem, however, is **Blue Raincoat** (The Factory, Lower Quay St., tel. 071/917-0431, www.blueraincoat.com, tickets €10–15). Everyone thought artistic director Niall Henry was touched in the head for opening a mime-based theater company in little old

FESTIVALS AND EVENTS IN SLIGO TOWN

The old Sligo Arts Festival has disappeared from the roster under somewhat mysterious circumstances, but there are several smaller festivals to occupy you until the local arts council gets its act together. The **Sligo Jazz Project** (www.sligojazzproject.com, tel. 071/917-0431) is a newly established music school and jazz festival – it was in mid-August in 2006 and mid-October in 2005 – featuring teacher-performers from all over Europe and a couple from the United States. There are free gigs in pubs all over town, including Shoot the Crows and the Left Bank. Most of the events in the **International Choral Festival** (November, tel. 071/917-0733 or 086/259-2290, www.sligochoralfest.org), a four-day blitz of competitions and concerts, take place at the Aula Maxima at the Sligo Institute of Technology (entrance on Ash Ln., on the northern side of the city). The **Model Arts and Niland Gallery** (tel. 071/914-1405, www.modelart.ie) hosts several international musical events, including the **Festival of Baroque Music** (late October) and the **New Music Festival** (late March).

Sligo Town—in an erstwhile slaughterhouse, no less—but since its inception in 1990 the troupe is flourishing. Blue Raincoat isn't for everyone, but if you enjoy experimental drama you'll find their plays an immensely satisfying way to pass an evening. Note that they often take their shows to Westport, Galway, and a few other towns.

Shopping

Sligo has a couple of shopping centers full of chains, including the new Quayside Centre off Wine Street, but the best shops are along O'Connell Street and the other main drag, Grattan-Castle-Abbey Street. The nicest sweater shop in town is **P.F. Dooney** (36 O'Connell St., tel. 071/914-2274), with a wide selection of warm and colorful pullovers. **The Cat & the Moon** (4 Castle St., tel. 071/914-3686, www.thecatandthemoon.com) does beautiful jewelry, crafts, and framed art.

Several small bookshops have particularly good Irish-interest (i.e., Yeats) sections: **Keohane's** (Castle St., tel. 071/42597), **The Winding Stair** (Lower Knox St., tel. 071/914-1244), which has a nice café, and **The Book Nest** (Rockwood Parade, on the river, tel. 071/914-6949, www.booknest.ie).

Sports and Recreation

With so many great sporting opportunities just outside town, you'll barely notice that Sligo doesn't have a park of its own. Don't leave without climbing **Knocknarea:** It's a 45-minute walk to the summit (becoming moderately difficult only at the end), and the views from the cairn are awesome. **Dooney Rock,** a scenic viewpoint seven kilometers east of town overlooking the famous Innisfree on Lough Gill, incorporates a nature reserve and a brief but tranquil walk through the woods.

For long walks on sandy shores, drive north to **Rosses Point, Streedagh,** and **Mullaghmore,** or west to **Strandhill.**

Excellent golf courses in the vicinity include the **County Sligo Golf Club** (Rosses Point, tel. 071/917-7134, countysligogolfclub. ie) and the club at Strandhill (see *South and West of Sligo Town*).

Equestrians should contact **Island View** (Grange, 16 km north of Sligo on the N15, tel. 071/916-6156, islandviewridingstables.com), which offers rides on the beach, or the **Sligo Riding Centre** (Carrowmore, tel. 087/230-4828, irelandonhorseback.com).

Go Skydive Ireland (tel. 087/279-2014, www.goskydive.ie, training course and first dive €320) operates out of Sligo Airport.

Accommodations

The private rooms at the spotless IHH **Harbour House** (Finisklin Rd., tel. 071/917-1547, www. harbourhousehostel.com, dorms €18, d €20 pp, s €25, credit cards accepted) are B&B quality

(TVs and towels included), and the whole place has a homey atmosphere few other hostels can match. Free Internet access and DVD rental and a comfortable, character-filled common room make it an excellent choice, despite a less-than-ideal location in an industrial area. (Note that the coffee shop two doors down is not recommended.)

Pearse and Mail Coach Roads on the south end of town are lined with B&Bs, one of which is ivy-covered **Lough Gill House** (Pearse Rd., tel. 071/915-0045, www.loughgillhouse. com, €30 pp, s €40). Here you'll find electric blankets, friendly owners, and tasty breakfasts. **Lissadell House** (Mail Coach Rd., tel. 071/916-1937, €32–35 pp, s €45–48) around the corner is another safe bet: comfortable, friendly, with no frills. Since there are only three rooms you're more likely to get a good night's sleep. Another really nice B&B is **St. Joseph's** (Strandhill Rd., tel. 071/917-0655, gemma35@gmail.com, €35 pp, s €40), with a gorgeous, stained-glass entryway that will catch your eye from the road. Pem O'Dowd is a jovial and very helpful and informative host. Each of these B&Bs is a 10-minute walk from the center of town.

Frankly, there are no outstanding hotels to be found in Sligo; the occasional maintenance glitches and management slip-ups can plague even the newly renovated ones like the regal **Clarion Hotel** (Clarion Rd. on the northern edge of town, off Enniskillen Rd., signposted from the N4, tel. 071/911-9000, www.clarionhotelsligo.com, rooms €200–275). The leisure center here is second to none, with a pool, sauna, Jacuzzi, exercise room, the works (though the facilities can get crowded in the evenings). Looking at this place now, you'd never in a million years believe it was once the town's asylum!

Food

Much more casual than the name suggests, **Café Society** (3 Teeling St., tel. 071/914-2712, open 8:30 A.M.–9:30 P.M. Mon.–Sat., mains €6–10) does very tasty (and healthy) pastas, salads, and sandwiches, along with a full breakfast until 11:30 A.M. A more upscale option for pasta and pizza is **Café Bar Deli** (15/16 Stephen St., tel. 071/914-0100, www. cafebardeli.ie, open 6–10 P.M. Wed.–Sun., mains €10–15). Similar fare is available downstairs at **The Left Bank** for €8–10 (bar food served noon–8 P.M. daily, Sun. brunch noon–4 P.M.). The Left Bank may be too trendy for some folks, but the coffee is quite good.

Swanky, minimalist **Poppadom** (34 O'Connell St., tel. 071/914-7171, poppadomireland@hotmail.com, open 5:30–11 P.M. Sun.–Thurs., 5:30 P.M.–midnight Fri.–Sat., mains €10–16) does the best Indian fare you're likely to find in this country, and the service is excellent. Or if you're in the mood for French, try the highly regarded **Montmartre** (Market Yard, tel. 071/916-9901, open 5–11 P.M. Tues.–Sun., mains €15–25).

Other above-average restaurants include **The Loft** (17/19 Lord Edward St., tel. 071/914-6770, bar food served noon–9:30 P.M., restaurant open 6–10 P.M. daily, mains €10–20). For upscale surf-and-turf, free-range waterfowl, and chicken à la everything, the place to go is **Coach Lane** (1-2 Lord Edward St., tel. 071/916-2417, www. coachlane.com, bar food 3:30–10 P.M., restaurant open 5:30–10 P.M. daily, mains €14–25), near the bus and train station.

◖ Bistro Bianconi (44 O'Connell St., tel. 071/914-1744, www.bistrobianconi. ie, open 12:30–2:30 P.M. and 5:30–10 P.M. Tues.–Sat. year-round, daily June–Aug., mains €13–25) is Sligo's best restaurant—the gourmet pizzas are truly to die for. (Actually, so is everything else on the menu; the sticky toffee pudding is amazing.) This isn't a formal eatery by any means, but reservations are essential on the weekends.

Information

The **North-West Regional Tourist Office** (Temple St., tel. 071/916-1201, www.irelandnorthwest.ie, open 9 A.M.–6 P.M. weekdays and 10 A.M.–6 P.M. weekends June–Sept., 9 A.M.–5 P.M. weekdays Oct.–May) is on the south side of town, in the same building as the Hawk's Well Theatre.

Cyberside, the **Unofficial Tourist Guide** website (www.sligotown.net) is definitely worth a browse before you go, especially if you're planning to be out after dark.

Services

The **public library** (Stephen St., tel. 071/914-2212, open 10 A.M.–5 P.M. Tues.–Fri., 10 A.M.–1 P.M. and 2–5 P.M. Sat.), housed in a deconsecrated church, has free Internet access. Directly across the street is **Café Online** (1 Calry Ct., Stephen St., beside the Bank of Ireland, tel. 071/914-4892, www.cafeonline.ie, open 10 A.M.–11 P.M. Mon.–Sat., noon–11 P.M. Sun., €3.50/hour). Another option is **Cygo** (19 O'Connell St., tel. 071/914-0082, www.cygo.ie, open 10 A.M.–10 P.M. Mon.–Sat., 11 A.M.–10 P.M. Sun., €3.50/hour, €2.50/hour Sun. and after 7 P.M.).

Getting There

Sligo Town is 210 kilometers northwest of Dublin on the N4 and 138 kilometers north of Galway on the N17. **Bus Éireann** (Lord Edward St., tel. 071/916-9888) has direct services to Sligo from Dublin (#23, 5/day daily), Galway (#53 or #64, 5/day daily), Belfast (#65 or #66, 5/day Mon.–Sat., 2/day Sun.), Donegal and Derry (#64 or #480, 5/day daily), and Westport (#66, 2/day Sat.–Thurs., 3/day Fri.).

There are at least five **Irish Rail** (tel. 071/916-9888) departures per day Monday–Saturday, from Dublin Connolly to Sligo via Boyle, Carrick-on-Shannon, and Mullingar (7/day Fri., 4/day Sun.).

You can fly from Dublin on **Aer Arann** (tel. 01/844-7700, www.aerarann.ie, one-way tickets €40–52, web rates available on airport website, 2/day at 7:45 A.M. and 5:05 P.M. weekdays, 10:20 A.M. and 4:30 P.M. weekends); the **Sligo Airport** (tel. 071/916-8280, www.sligoairport.com) is near Strandhill, and you can take Bus Éireann into town (#472). A taxi will run you about €15.

Getting Around

Sligo Town is totally walkable. Board buses to Strandhill (#472), Rosses Point (#473), or Drumcliff (#64, #474, #480, or #483) at the bus station on Lord Edward Street.

Rent a bicycle from **Flanagan's** (Market Yard, tel. 071/914-4477, €15/60 day/week). Need a taxi? Ring **Budget Cabs** (tel. 071/916-9000, "€5 local day or night"), **Ace Cabs** (tel. 071/914-4444), or **Feehily's** (tel. 071/914-3000).

SOUTH AND WEST OF SLIGO TOWN
Carrowmore Megalithic Cemetery

Carrowmore Megalithic Cemetery (Ceathrú Mór, "Great Quarter," 5 km south of town, signposted off Strandhill Rd. on the western end of Sligo, tel. 071/916-1534, open 10 A.M.–6 P.M. mid-Apr.–Oct., admission €2.10) is Ireland's largest, with more than 60 tombs—dolmens, cairns, and stone circles—scattered in the fields on either side of the road, within a diameter of only a kilometer or so. This is also one of the oldest funerary complexes in Ireland; archaeologists date the oldest tombs at Carrowmore to 700 years before Newgrange, somewhere around 4370 B.C. The primary monument is a huge cairn/passage tomb in the field beyond the small visitors center, which has been excavated and refitted with wire screens to keep the stones in place. If you're visiting in the off-season, it's still possible to jump the fence and pop inside the passage tomb. Frankly, though, if you only have time for one megalithic monument, get thee to Knocknarea instead.

◖ Knocknarea

A 45-minute hike up Knocknarea (Cnoc na Rí, "Sacred Hill," 6.5 km southwest of town off the R292, always accessible, free admission), at an elevation of 329 meters, brings you to an enormous cairn known as Queen Maeve's Tomb. Maeve, of course, was the legendary ruler of Connaught, a notorious troublemaker and Cuchulainn's perennial nemesis. The cairn is 55 meters wide and 10 meters high, and most likely dates to the beginning of the third millennium B.C. It has never been excavated, despite widespread speculation that a passage tomb on par with Newgrange lies beneath those 40,000 tons of stone. William Bulfin, who cycled all over the country at the turn of the last century, wrote of Knocknarea that "there is an epic suggestiveness which you cannot miss if you climb the mountain. You cannot keep your hold upon the present while you are up there." These words still ring true despite the modern structures dotting the valleys below.

The climb is easy at first, but the path gets steep the last 5–10 minutes; the panoramic pastoral and sea views are well worth the exertion, however. Many visitors climb the cairn once they've reached the summit, but seeing as this is a Neolithic monument it's in rather poor taste to do so. At any rate, don't leave Sligo without having climbed up to Medbh's Grave. To get there, take the Strandhill road out of the center of town and turn left at the signposts for Knocknarea and Carrowmore. This makes for a nice afternoon of cycling if the weather's fine.

Strandhill

It may be the locals' beach of choice, but the resort town of Strandhill (8 km west of Sligo on the R292) has a vaguely run-down feel. There are prettier (and less crowded) beaches at Streedagh and Mullaghmore farther north, though Strandhill does have the best surfing. For lessons, rentals, or whatever else you need, try **Perfect Day Surf Shop & School** (on the promenade, tel. 071/912-8488, www.perfectdaysurfing.com). Strandhill also has its own **golf club** (tel. 071/916-8188, www.strandhillgc.com).

The best reason to visit Strandhill is the **Celtic Seaweed Baths** (on the promenade, tel. 071/916-8686, www.celticseaweedbaths.com, open 10 A.M.–9:30 P.M. Mon.–Fri. and 10 A.M.–8:30 P.M. Sat.–Sun. May–Oct., 11 A.M.–9 P.M. Mon.–Fri. and 10 A.M.–6:30 P.M. Sat.–Sun. Nov.–Apr., 50-minute steam and bath €22, shared bath €29). After 45 minutes in a hot tub full of seaweed plucked from the shore that very morning, you'll feel like a brand-new person. The center also does Swedish and aromatherapy massage.

There's not much in the way of accommodations here, but you might try the small, friendly, family-run **Ocean View Hotel** (Strandhill Rd., tel. 071/916-8115, http://homepage.eircom.net/~oceanview, oceanviewhotel@eircom.net, open Mar.–mid-Dec., €45–68 pp, s €60–93, email for special rates, food served noon–3 P.M. and 6–9 P.M. daily). The hotel's 13 rooms are airy and spacious, with pleasingly no-nonsense decor.

Strandhill is eight kilometers west of Sligo Town on the R292. Provided it's not a Sunday, **Bus Éireann** (tel. 071/916-0066) can get you there from Sligo (#472, 7/day Mon.–Fri., 5/day Sat.). The Strandhill bus departs outside the Spar across from the station on Lord Edward Street.

NORTH OF SLIGO TOWN
Drumcliffe

A picturesque early-19th-century Anglican church and monastic site a quick journey north of Sligo Town, Drumcliffe (Droim Chliabh, "Back of the Baskets," 7.5 km north of Sligo Town on the N15, tel. 071/914-4956, open 9 A.M.–5 P.M. Mon.–Sat. and 1–5 P.M. Sun., free admission) was founded by St. Colmcille in the year 575—and of course, it is also the final resting place of Ireland's most beloved poet, chosen because his great-grandfather served as rector here between 1811 and 1846. The epitaph on **Yeats's grave** is taken from the poem "Under Ben Bulben," in which he details the circumstances of his own burial, finishing with:

Cast a cold eye
On life, on death.
Horseman, pass by!

These last three lines are inscribed on his headstone, which draws thousands of visitors every year. It's easily County Sligo's greatest tourist attraction. Yeats's wife, Georgie Hyde-Lee, is buried nearby.

For most, Yeats entirely eclipses the historical importance of Colmcille's monastery (see the sidebar *The Battle of the Books*). All that remains is an exquisite 11th-century **high cross** (see if you can discern Adam and Eve, Cain and Abel, the Crucifixion, and other scenes) and a **round tower** across the road, reduced to a 16-meter stump after a lightning storm in 1396. Legend states that what's left of the tower will crumble on the wisest person to stand beside it; by all means, hop the wall and see if you're as sagacious as you think.

There's a **visitors center** (same contact info, admission €2.50); a ticket will allow you a 15-minute audiovisual on Yeats and Colmcille as well as admission to the church. Frankly, though, the AV is dumbed-down, and the church's interior is mostly unremarkable. There's also a gift shop and tearoom across the lane (always crowded, but worth elbowing your way to a table for some surprisingly good desserts and snacky things).

You would expect **Davis's Restaurant** and **The Yeats Tavern** (Drumcliff Bridge, tel. 071/916-3117, www.yeatstavernrestaurant. com, mains €12–21) to be something of a tourist trap, but it's not. It's a cozy spot, popular with locals and visitors alike, and the menu is surprisingly eclectic. You'll find it on your left just after you've passed Drumcliffe churchyard on the way out of Sligo.

Drumcliffe is a five-minute drive north out of Sligo Town on the N15. **Bus Éireann** (tel. 071/916-0066) offers service from the station on Lord Edward Street (#64, 6/day Mon.– Thurs. and Sat., 7/day Fri., 3/day Sun.) en route to Derry, but be sure to request a stop in Drumcliffe.

Rosses Point

A small but happenin' resort town on Drumcliffe Bay (especially on sunny weekend afternoons), Rosses Point (An Ros) boasts a gorgeous Blue Flag strand and bountiful sea fishing; contact **Jim Ewing** (tel. 086/857-7579) or **Tommy McCallion** (tel. 087/239-7789) for a charter. The grassy slopes above the strand are a good spot for a picnic lunch; you have a vantage of Coney Island, namesake of the Brooklyn amusement mecca, and beyond it Sligo's sprawl glittering across the water.

THE BATTLE OF THE BOOKS

While abbot of Drumcliffe, in A.D. 561, St. Colmcille (also known as Columba, meaning "dove" in Latin) borrowed an Italian manuscript during a visit to his friend Finian; when Finian discovered that Colmcille had secretly copied his book, he brought his case to the high king, Diarmuid. Finian claimed that the copy belonged to him, and Diarmuid agreed (though some say a prior grievance between Diarmuid and Colmcille influenced the king's decision). Colmcille refused to accept his verdict, raised an army, and defeated Diarmuid's forces on the slopes of Benbulben (supposedly aided by an angel, though why both Finian and Colmcille were canonized after such a devastating squabble is more or less inscrutable). The blood of thousands of men on his hands, Colmcille departed Drumcliffe for Iona off the Scottish coast, where he vowed to convert at least as many people to Christianity as had died on the battlefield that day.

If you have a car, you might want to stay at **Serenity** (Doonierin, Kintogher, signposted off the R291 just east of Rosses Point, tel. 071/914-3351, serenitysligo@eircom.net, open Mar.–Oct., €33–40 pp sharing) even if you plan to spend much of your time in Sligo proper; it's a lovely B&B in a restful setting, a far better value than the B&Bs in town for its sea views, excellent breakfasts, handmade quilts on the beds, and very helpful and knowledgable proprietors.

Though it's something of a landmark in the village, note that the Yeats Country Hotel—both restaurant and lodging—is not recommended. Have your meal—what else but fresh seafood?—at the cozy, quasi-rustic **Moorings** (Main St., tel. 071/917-7112, open 5:30– 10 P.M. Mon.–Sat., daily June–Aug., mains €15–30). Vegetarians are also well served here, thankfully.

Rosses Point is only 9.5 kilometers northwest

of Sligo Town on the R291, accessible by a local **Bus Éireann** route (#473, 7/day weekdays, 5/day Sat.) departing the Lord Edward Street bus station.

Lissadell

The new owners of the stern, Greek Revival Lissadell (7 km north of Sligo, signposted off the N15, tel. 071/916-3150, www.lissadell-house.com, gardens open 10:30 A.M.–4 P.M. daily June–Sept., house open 10:30 A.M.–6 P.M. daily mid-Mar.–Sept., admission to garden/house €5/6), home to the Gore-Booth family from 1834 to 2003, have set about restoring the old gardens to their former glory. A two-hour guided demesne walk takes place at 2:30 P.M. Sunday (admission €10).

This was the childhood home of Easter rebel Constance Markievicz (the wife of a Ukrainian count) and her beloved sister, the poet Eva Gore-Booth. The sisters devoted their lives to charity work in the slums of Dublin and Manchester, and Constance was the first woman elected to the British Parliament (though she refused to take her seat, being vehemently anti-treaty). Yeats spent a fair bit of time here at Lissadell in the sisters' company, and the Yeats Study and his usual guest room are preserved much as he left them (though, in truth, he only visited four times). No student of Irish history should pass up an opportunity to tour the house and demesne. It's a snap to get here from Sligo Town by car; the house is clearly signposted from the N15, though the busy road makes cycling a less than ideal transport method.

Mullaghmore

A tiny fishing village beautifully situated over Donegal Bay, Mullaghmore (An Mullach Mór, "The Great Summit") is an angler's heaven on earth (or sea, to be more accurate)—and there's a lovely sheltered strand to boot. There are half a dozen charter boat operators, including **Liam Carey** (tel. 087/257-4497), who does evening trips to Killybegs in Donegal, and **Rodney Lomax** (tel. 071/916-6124), who can also take you to Inishmurray Island if the weather's right. On your way out here you'll spot 19th-century **Classiebawn Castle** on a cliff to the west, like something straight out of a fairy tale; the castle's original owner, the third Viscount Palmerston, was twice elected English prime minister. You'll pass another fine strand at **Streedagh,** where a Spanish Armada shipwreck in 1588 left 1,100 lifeless sailors on the sand.

Once you've arrived at the **Beach Hotel** (on the harbor, tel. 071/916-6103, www.beachhotelmullaghmore.com, pub food served noon–9 P.M. daily, restaurant open 6–9 P.M. daily and 12:30–3:15 P.M. Sun., €45–65 pp, s €70–90, 15 percent surcharge on bank holiday weekends), you won't find much reason to leave, what with the ample leisure facilities (gym, pool, sauna, Jacuzzi), seafood pub and restaurant, and self-catering apartments—heck, they even host the occasional Murder Mystery weekend. And of course, you can't beat the view from many of the bedrooms—though the management is cheeky enough to charge you an extra €10 for it! (Be that as it may, it's nearly the only accommodation in the area.)

If you're spending the night here, though, eat at **Eithna's Seafood Restaurant** (on the harbor, tel. 071/916-6407, open 6:30–9:30 P.M. daily Easter–Sept., opening hours vary in low season, mains €18–38), which also does a smattering of satisfying meat and veggie dishes using organic produce where possible. Unless you've ordered the deluxe seafood platter, try to save some room for a scrummy dessert.

Mullaghmore is 28 kilometers north of Sligo Town off the N15, clearly signposted on the left from the village of Cliffoney (3 km). There's no public transport to Mullaghmore, though Cliffoney is a request stop on the **Bus Éireann** (tel. 071/916-0066) route from Sligo to Derry (#64, 6/day Mon.–Thurs. and Sat., 7/day Fri., 3/day Sun.).

Inishmurray Island

Yet another obscure Irish saint, Molaise, founded a monastery on the flat, low-lying island of Inishmurray (Inis Muirígh or Inismuireadhaigh), 22 meters above sea level and

THE NORTHWEST

© CAMILLE DEANGELIS

The Creevykeel Court Cairn is one of Sligo's many megalithic treasures.

six kilometers off the Sligo coast, around A.D. 520. Several ruins lie within a cashel, or ring fort: *clocháin,* or beehive huts, several outdoor altars, and three small churches, which were partially "restored" at the end of the 19th century. There was also a separate church and burial ground for the island's nuns. This place is steeped in superstitions and spooky rituals, one of which is the "cursing stones": If you wanted to lay a curse, you would perform the Stations of the Cross in reverse order, turning over the stones beside each devotional station as you went along. Another story said the Leac na Teine inside the Teach na Teine (the "Stone of the Fire" in the "House of the Fire") was said to ignite a brick of turf laid upon it, should every other fire on Inishmurray have been extinguished.

As far as local historians can make out, the monastic community persevered here continuously into the 20th century, making a living selling fish, seaweed, and poteen on the mainland (the last item being, of course, illegal, though due to the remote location law enforcement could never actually catch those mischievous monks distilling it). The last monks, a community of 100, finally left the island in 1948.

Unfortunately, passage to Inishmurray is dependent on the mood of the morning tides. Compounding foul-weather concerns is the fact that boat operators don't find a group of less than six worth their while. On a nice day in high season, though, you might be able to join up with another small group. Ring **Joe McGowan** (tel. 071/916-6267 or 087/667-4522), **Rodney Lomax** (tel. 071/916-6124), or **Keith Clarke** (tel. 087/254-0190), all of whom operate out of Mullaghmore. Return passage will run you about €15.

Creevykeel Court Cairn

It won't inspire awe on the scale of Knocknarea or the great passage tomb at Carrowmore, but the Creevykeel Court Cairn (30 km north of Sligo on the N15, clearly signposted just east of Cliffoney, always accessible, free admission) is still the most remarkable memorial of its type. Dating to the third millennium B.C., Creevykeel consists of an open oval-shaped central court, with a pair of passage graves and a primary burial chamber at opposite ends.

In 1935 the site was excavated by a team of Harvard archaeologists, who brought to light a collection of decorated and undecorated Neolithic pottery, arrowheads and axes, and four cremation burials (all of which is now in the National Museum). The cairn was "restored" after the excavations, which might account for why it's still so *neat*-looking.

This site is worth a stop if you happen to be traveling north to Donegal—but if you're sticking to Sligo Town, a visit to Carrowmore is enough to satisfy most people's interest in megalithic monuments.

EAST OF SLIGO TOWN
Lough Gill

William Butler Yeats's most famous poem, "The Lake Isle of Innisfree" ("I will arise and go now, and go to Innisfree . . ."), was inspired by the ruins of a tiny monastic settlement on **Innisfree Island** (Inis Fraoigh, "Grouse Island") on Lough Gill, which is supposedly hiding a lake monster of its own. You'll find the best vantage of the island at **Dooney Rock,** a small but tranquil nature reserve seven kilometers west of Sligo on the R286 (Yeats wrote a poem about this place, too: "The Fiddler of Dooney"). There are several short wooded walks to enjoy here. To get to the lake, keep cycling or driving the R286 past the Dooney Rock car park, and the lakeshore turnoff is another three kilometers down the road.

It's touristy, all right, but an hour-long lake cruise on the *Rose of Innisfree* (Lough Gill, Kilmore, Fivemilebourne, 11 km west of Sligo on the R286/Dromahair road, tel. 071/916-4266, www.roseofinnisfree.com, tickets €12) is the closest you can get to the fabled island. Cruises depart from Parke's Castle in County Leitrim (11 A.M., 12:30 P.M., 1:30 P.M., 3:30 P.M., and 4:30 P.M. daily Easter–Oct.; ring for a shuttle bus from Sligo).

Ruins on Innisfree Island inspired Yeats's most famous poem.

© CAMILLE DEANGELIS

Glencar Lough

Nestled in the Dartry Mountains 11 kilometers northeast of Sligo, Glencar Lough straddles the Sligo-Leitrim border. Along with opportunities for a leisurely walk by the lake or down the backcountry lanes nearby, a pretty (but not terribly remarkable) **waterfall** draws plenty of visitors (especially families with small children) on sunny weekend afternoons. To get here, take the N16 north out of Sligo and you'll see Glencar Lough clearly signposted on your left. There's a car park and small visitors center across the road from the waterfall.

ENNISCRONE

Enniscrone (Innis Crabhann, also spelled "Inniscrone") is a pleasant seaside town despite the smattering of garish amusement arcades. The primary draw here is a lovely five-kilometer sheltered strand known as "The Hollow," a surfers' haven; it runs parallel to the main street and is easily accessible from there (it's just behind the houses).

C Kilcullen's Seaweed Baths

Surfboards aside, don't leave Enniscrone without taking a soak at Kilcullen's Seaweed Baths (Cliff Rd., signposted from Main St., tel. 096/36238, www.kilcullenseaweedbaths.com, open 10 A.M.–9 P.M. daily May–Sept., noon–8 P.M. weekdays and 10 A.M.–8 P.M. weekends Oct.–Apr., steam and soak €20, twin room €35/30 with/without steam). The therapeutic properties of seaweed and hot water are well known, especially for those suffering from arthritis. There are several reasons why these baths are even better than those in Strandhill: Established in 1912, Kilcullen's is still family-run, and retains its original porcelain bathtubs and other charming Edwardian features; the staff are genuinely friendly; and best of all, there's no time limit! You can soak as long as you like. When you're ready to get out, you pull the handle on the ancient shower above the bathtub and douse yourself in cold seawater, emerging pink-cheeked and fresh as a newborn baby. Massage therapy is also available by appointment (€25/half hour).

Sports and Recreation

Strangely enough, there's no place to rent surf equipment in town; you can purchase a surfboard and other goods at the small shop at Kilcullen's, or drive 13 kilometers south to Ballina in County Mayo for a shop called **Faoin Tuath** (Market Ln., Tone St., take the R297 from Enniscrone and pick up the N59, tel. 096/77594, ballina@faointuath.com). In the village of Easky (13 km northeast on R297) you'll find a **Surf and Information Centre** (tel. 096/49020, open 9:30 A.M.–5 P.M. daily July–Aug., 10 A.M.–2 P.M. Mon.–Fri. Sept.–May). The **Enniscrone Golf Club** (Enniscrone, tel. 096/36657, www.enniscronegolf.com) is another draw, especially with Irish weekenders.

Accommodations

There isn't as much in the way of accommodations as there should be here; several small hotels have closed in recent years (and their dust-filmed windows add an unsightly element to an otherwise pleasant main street). The rear bedrooms at **Ceol na Mara** ("Music of the Sea," Main St., tel. 096/36351, www.ceol-na-mara.com, €30–38 pp, s €35–45) offer expansive ocean views. The rooms are modern-minimalist yet comfortable (with excellent showers), and you're welcome to use the owners' sitting room, where there's often a fire burning in the grate. Mr. and Mrs. O'Regan also offer self-catering holiday homes nearby (€375–700/week, highest rates July–Sept.). Another option is **Enniscrone Lodge** (Pier Rd., tel. 096/36181, http://homepage.tinet.ie/~ennislodge, €32 pp), which offers special packages for golf groups.

Most surfers stay at the **Atlantic Caravan & Camping Park** (on the beach, tel. 096/36132, open Apr.–Oct., tent sites €10), or at the **Atlantic 'n Riverside Caravan & Camping Park** in Easky (behind the surf info center, tel. 096/49001, open Apr.–mid-Sept., tent site €11).

Food and Entertainment

Enniscrone's kind of short in the eats department, too, but the following two spots do great meals. **The Tea Clipper** (just off Main St., turnoff at the Pilot's Bar, no phone, open 10 A.M.–4 P.M. Tues.–Fri., 10 A.M.–5 P.M. weekends, mains €5–11) is a small, friendly café serving up fresh salads, soup, quiches, and pastries. You'll find the best pub grub in town at ⬛ **The Pilot's Bar** (Main St., tel. 096/36131, food served 5–9 P.M. weekdays, 1–9 P.M. weekends, mains €7–12)—it does fabulous gourmet pizzas as well as more traditional fare, steak sandwiches and the like. This watering hole is an appealing amalgam of old and new: There's a load of nautical junk on the walls and strung from the ceilings, yet the indie music on the stereo system is playing off an iPod behind the bar.

Information and Services

There's no bank in Enniscrone, but you'll find an ATM at the **Spar supermarket** (Main St., tel. 096/36417, open 8 A.M.–10 P.M. or later daily).

Enniscrone's **tourist office** (Main St., tel. 096/36760, enniscronetourism@eircom.net, open noon–8 P.M. Mon.–Sat. July–Sept.) is community-run, and the town's website (www.enniscroneonline.com) is a good planning resource. Internet access is available at the **public library** (Pier Rd., signposted off Main St., tel. 096/37199, open 6–8 P.M. Mon. and Wed., 3–5 P.M. Tues. and Thurs., 1–5 P.M. Fri., 10 A.M.–1 P.M. and 2–5 P.M. Sat.), though as there are only two computers you may have to wait a bit.

Getting There and Around

Enniscrone is 54 kilometers west of Sligo Town on the R297 (from Sligo, take the N4 south, pick up the N59 at Collooney, and then turn off onto the R297 at Dromore West). **Bus Éireann** (tel. 071/916-0066) has a Sligo–Ballina service that stops in Enniscrone (#66 or #458, 5/day Mon.–Sat., 1/day Sun. at 3:30 P.M., additional departure at 7:10 P.M. Fri.), though you may have to change buses at Dromore West. The Dublin–Ballina bus (#22, 3/day daily) also stops here.

For a lift, ring **Tuffy Taxis** (tel. 087/251-3107) or **Queenan Cabs** (tel. 096/36515).

⬛ CARROWKEEL PASSAGE TOMB CEMETERY

Owing in part to the remote location in the Bricklieve Mountains, Carrowkeel Passage Tomb Cemetery (6 km off the N4, 33 km south of Sligo Town, always accessible, free admission) is one of the creepiest megalithic sites in the country—especially in the rain and fog. This Neolithic necropolis of dolmens and cairns was constructed sometime in the third millennium B.C., which means it's not as old as Newgrange or Carrowmore. For dramatic location and spooky atmosphere, though, Carrowkeel beats both those sites, hands down. There are 14 cairns, though the entryways of even the largest tombs are too small for more than a peek inside. There are also about 50 circular stone foundations that indicate a Neolithic settlement, perhaps only inhabited while the tombs were being constructed. Even if you find all these archaeological wonders only of mild interest, it's worth venturing out here for the gorgeous panoramic view of Benbulben, Lough Arrow, and plenty of lush countryside. In foul weather it's easy to lose your orientation, so bring a compass if the sky looks threatening.

To get here, take the N4 south from Sligo Town or north from Boyle in County Roscommon (18 km) and follow the signs for Carrowkeel beginning in the hamlet of Castlebaldwin (coming from Sligo, the turnoff is on your right). After a few kilometers you'll come to a cattle fence; open, pass through, and close, and once you reach a large sign with a map of the area, make an immediate left and it's only a kilometer more (down some really narrow and horribly bumpy unpaved roads). You'll know you've arrived when you spot a couple of rusted sign-holders to your left (which, at time of writing, had no signs at all) beside some space for a few cars to park. Unfortunately, public transportation isn't a viable option.

Leitrim

Most visitors just pass through Leitrim (Liatroim) from Sligo to Donegal—it has the shortest coastline of any nonlandlocked county, rather comical when you look at it on the road map—but there are a couple reasons to pause here. Leitrim shares picturesque Lough Gill with County Sligo, and the lakeside Parke's Castle is one of the highlights of the 45-kilometer Lough Gill scenic loop from Sligo Town. And Carrick-on-Shannon, a busy market town to the southeast, has a couple good pubs and restaurants worth stopping for if you're cruising the Shannon waterway. Like other less-traveled counties, Leitrim offers an opportunity to observe an unpackaged, modern yet authentically Irish way of life.

PARKE'S CASTLE

A 17th-century fortified manor on the shores of Lough Gill, Dúchas-run Parke's Castle (Fivemile Bourne, on the R286 just south of Leckaun village, tel. 071/916-4149, open 10 A.M.–6 P.M. daily mid-Mar.–Oct., admission €2.90) has been fully restored using traditional craftsmanship. The original castle belonged to the Irish rebel Brian O'Rorke, who entertained an officer rescued from the Spanish Armada shipwreck in the castle. O'Rorke was hanged for high treason in London in 1591, and his lands were given to Robert Parke. Clearly the new landlord feared an Irish uprising, as the castle features high bawn walls and turrets. The exhibit includes a 20-minute audiovisual on the castle and other ruins in the area, and you may be able to get a guided tour if there are enough visitors around. The castle is 11 kilometers west of Sligo R286, and there is no public transport.

CARRICK-ON-SHANNON

Straddling the River Shannon on the Leitrim-Roscommon border, Carrick-on-Shannon (Cora Droma Rúisc, "The Weir of Drumrusk")

is a popular stopover for holiday boaters. River cruises are available with **Moon River** (The Quay, tel. 071/962-1777, www.moon-river.net, departures in summer at 3:15 P.M. and 4:30 P.M., plus 2 P.M. Sat.–Sun., 90-minute trip €12), or you can rent a fishing boat from **Carrick Craft** (at the marina, tel. 071/962-0236, www.carrickcraft.com).

If you want to spend the night, try the modern **Hartley Lodge** (Hartley, 800 m north of town off the Leitrim road/R209, tel. 071/965-0883, www.hartleylodge.com, €35 pp, s €45, dinner €20, credit cards accepted), a friendly but fairly standard B&B a five-minute walk from the town center. The more upscale **Hollywell Country House** (signposted from the N4 in the town center, tel. 071/962-1124, hollywell@esatbiz.com, open Mar.–Oct., €50–70 pp, s €90–100), a Georgian home overlooking the Shannon, offers comfy rooms full of antiques and just about the best, most original breakfast menu in Connaught. Almost as classy is the four-star **Landmark Hotel** (on the N4 by the quay, tel. 071/962-2222, www.thelandmarkhotel.com, €65–80 pp).

The best eatery in Carrick is a gastro-pub, **The Oarsman** (Bridge St., tel. 071/962-1733, www.theoarsman.com, food served noon–2:30 P.M. Mon.–Sat., until 3:30 P.M. Mon.–Wed., 6:45–9:45 P.M. Thurs.–Sat., lunch €12–17, dinner mains €18–30); the modern Irish here is Dublin-grade, with a dessert menu to make a grown man cry. There's live trad here Friday and Sunday nights.

Carrick is 53 kilometers southeast of Sligo on the N4. **Bus Éireann** provides regular service on the Dublin-Sligo route (#23, 5–6/day daily). It's also on the **Irish Rail** line from Dublin to Sligo (tel. 071/962-0036, 3–4/day daily, single/return fare €22/31). Buses stop in the town center, but the train station is one kilometer south of town on the Elphin road (R368).

DONEGAL

An extended visit to the republic's northernmost county, wonderfully remote Donegal (Dún na nGall, "Fort of the Foreigner"), is an excellent way to get off the beaten tourist track. There are more weekending Northern Irish than international tourists at any time of year, but the relative lack of tourism is due to simple geography, not a lack of gorgeous landscapes: Most people just don't have enough vacation time to do Dublin, Kerry, Clare, *and* Galway, *then* drive another six or more hours to reach Donegal. The county doesn't have many "sights" as such, another factor keeping the coach tours to a minimum.

The Donegal accent (or *accents,* as there are supposedly 20) is lilting and melodic, so distinctive that after a couple days up here you'll recognize it anywhere. A third of the county is in the Gaeltacht, the Irish-speaking region, and there are more native speakers of the Donegal (or Ulster) dialect than there are Connaught (Mayo and Galway) or Munster (Kerry and Cork). The natives have earned a reputation for genuine friendliness no matter which tongue they're using.

For more info (without the Tourist Board spin), visit **County Donegal on the Net** (www.dun-na-ngall.com).

HISTORY

The "foreigner" of the county's Irish name far predates the English or even the Normans—it refers to the Celts, though oddly enough it was the English who initiated use of the name in the late 16th century (and the change became permanent after the native Irish

© CAMILLE DEANGELIS

HIGHLIGHTS

◖ Rossnowlagh Beach: There may be no such thing as Donegal's finest strand – many are worthy of the title, after all – but Rossnowlagh is certainly one of them, popular with surfers yet far quieter than the tacky resort of Bundoran (page 406).

◖ Slieve League: The muddy track along the ridge of Europe's tallest sea cliffs makes for a tough but very rewarding five-hour hike (page 411).

◖ Glenveagh National Park: Take a walk through the "Poisoned Glen," climb the quartzite-capped Mount Errigal, tour the Victorian Glenveagh Castle, and watch for the golden eagle in the country's northernmost national park (page 413).

◖ Grianán of Aileách: This superbly situated Iron Age ring fort near the Donegal-Derry border offers a view of five counties as well as Loughs Swilly and Foyle (page 420).

◖ Malin Head: Savor the dramatic vistas of the Inishowen Peninsula in northeastern Donegal, culminating in a rocky foreland punctuated by blowholes (page 421).

LOOK FOR ◖ TO FIND RECOMMENDED SIGHTS, ACTIVITIES, DINING, AND LODGING.

---

chieftains were forced to flee their lands in the early 1600s). Before this, the county was divided into smaller kingdoms, each with a ruling family. If the name of one of these kingdoms, the O'Donnell-ruled Tir Conaill, seems ubiquitous, it's because native Irish speakers understandably prefer it over Dun na nGall.

County Donegal is dotted with Neolithic remains, and archaeological evidence says human habitation in the area goes back as far as 7000 B.C. Donegal's most dramatic ruin, a hilltop ring fort known as Grianán of Aileách, isn't nearly that old; the original fort was said to have been built in 1700 B.C. by Dagda, king of the mythical Tuatha De Danann, and what still exists today was built circa A.D. 1000. In early Christian times, Grianán was the home of the O'Neills and later the O'Donnells.

In the early 1590s the leaders of both these local ruling families, "Red" Hugh O'Donnell and Hugh O'Neill, joined forces in an attempt to purge the English; they achieved initial victories in 1595 and 1598, but their disastrous defeat at Kinsale in 1601, O'Donnell's hasty departure for Spain (whose waylaid Armada was not able to help them in battle at Kinsale), and O'Neill's eventual surrender and self-imposed exile allowed the subsequent English Plantation. The departure of O'Neill and O'Donnell and their families became known as the "Flight of the Earls" or "Flight of the

DONEGAL

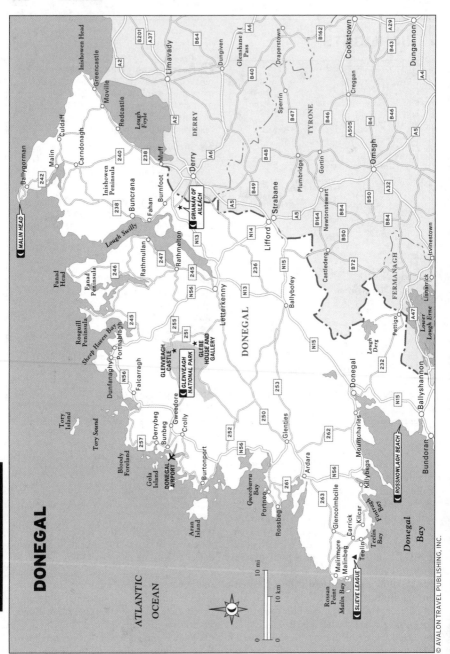

DONEGAL

Wild Geese," and their lands became forfeit to the English crown.

PLANNING YOUR TIME

Some visitors "do" Donegal while touring Northern Ireland, since it's easy to dip into the Inishowen Peninsula as a day trip out of Derry City. But Donegal's refreshing remoteness can be addictive, and those looking to veer off the beaten track should plan to spend the greater part of their vacation here. You can easily while away a full week, spending a couple days each in Glencolmcille, Gweedore, Glenveagh National Park, and Inishowen. If the long bus or car ride from the Shannon, Knock, or Belfast airport sounds too tiring, consider flying into Donegal Airport, near Gweedore, via Dublin. It takes an extra effort to get here no matter how you come, but you'll be rewarded with otherworldly landscapes and few other visitors with whom to share them.

Getting around Donegal without a rental car can be a real headache; those without wheels are best off choosing just one region to visit, since public transport within the county is downright poor. If you can, bring your own bicycle to cover more ground.

Banking facilities are very limited outside Donegal's larger towns, so be sure to withdraw enough cash before leaving Donegal Town, Ardara, or Letterkenny; there's also an ATM at Bunbeg in Gweedore.

Southern Donegal

DONEGAL TOWN

Donegal is far more pleasant than most other county towns, and there are enough sights to keep you here for an afternoon. With so much otherworldly scenery awaiting you farther north and west, though, why linger much longer? Pad your wallet at the ATM, have a pint at the Scotsman pub, get a good night's sleep, and get an early start.

The center of Donegal Town is marked by "the diamond" (really a triangle), where you'll find nearly all the shops, banks, pubs, and eateries. The Quay runs south from the diamond, leading to the pier, tourist office, and car park (€0.60/hour); Main Street runs east from the diamond; and Castle Street runs north, passing Donegal Castle before crossing the River Eske.

Sights

Built in 1505 by the first "Red Hugh" O'Donnell, Dúchas-run **Donegal Castle** (Castle St., just off the diamond, tel. 074/972-2405, open 10 A.M.–6 P.M. daily mid-Mar.–Oct., winter opening hours usually 9:30 A.M.–4:30 P.M. Fri.–Sun., admission €3.70) fell into English hands after the Flight of the Earls in 1607. (His descendant, also known as Red Hugh, lost the O'Donnell ancestral home after the English won the Battle of Kinsale in 1601.) The castle's new owner, Captain Basil Brooke, was also made governor of Donegal, and he added an English manor-style banquet hall to the original tower house. There isn't a whole lot to see, although the historical exhibit on the tower's top floor is very informative. If you have any interest in Irish history, especially the Flight of the Earls, then take the tour; otherwise just snap a photo from the front gate. In past winters the castle has been open Friday–Sunday, but these hours are subject to change; ask at the tourist office if the gate is closed.

Past the waterbus pier (by the tourist office) are the scant remains of Franciscan **Donegal Abbey,** also built by the first Red Hugh and his wife, Nuala, in 1474. The abbey is pleasantly situated on the mouth of Donegal Bay, but only a few abbey walls are standing, thanks to Rory O'Donnell, who mistakenly dropped a cannonball here during his war with the English (Rory was one of the earls who departed Ireland for good after the disastrous Battle of Kinsale).

DONEGAL

DONEGAL

© CAMILLE DEANGELIS

Donegal Castle passed into English hands after the Flight of the Earls.

Entertainment and Events

Donegal pubs are the good old-fashioned kind. Most folks, visitors and locals alike, pass the evening at **The Scotsman** (Bridge St., no phone), which has live music nightly year-round. Visiting musicians are encouraged to bring their instruments. You'll also find trad sessions on the weekends at the **Schooner Inn** (Upper Main St., tel. 074/972-1671).

The last weekend in June brings the **Donegal Town Summer Festival** (contact the tourist office for info, tel. 074/972-1148), with street entertainment and more formal traditional music and dance performances featuring musicians from as far afield as Roscommon and Galway. Scarce funding has prevented the festival from running every year, but if you're here in late June or early July keep your eyes peeled for announcements.

Shopping

Most visitors head straight for **John Molloy's** (The Diamond, tel. 074/972-2882, www.john-molloy.com), an excellent shop stocked with lo-cally made tweeds and sweaters. You can also purchase tweed by the yard.

Souvenir hunters shouldn't miss the **Donegal Craft Village** (Ballyshannon Rd., 1.5 km west of town, tel. 074/972-2225, open 9 A.M.–6 P.M. Mon.–Sat., 11 A.M.–6 P.M. Sun.) for its selection of jewelry, tweed, paintings, glassware—even sculptures made of bog wood! Claire O'Presco's handmade tweed scarves, handbags, and bean-bag frogs make particularly nice gifts, and check out her century-old loom. You'll find every artisan at work inside their individual shops, and because you're buying direct the prices are truly reasonable. There's also a **café and bakery** (tel. 074/972-3222, open 9:30 A.M.–5:30 P.M. Mon.–Sat.) that does terrific vegetarian lunches.

Sports and Recreation

The 117-kilometer **Bluestack Way** begins in Donegal, heading north past Lough Eske ("Lake of the Fish") and west along the Bluestack foothills to Ardara. You could take a shorter walk (or cycle) along a path encircling the lake before returning to town. You'll pass through some utterly charming pastoral scenery along the way. Fishing permits are available from **Doherty's** (Main St., tel. 074/972-1119, open 9 A.M.–6 P.M. Thurs.–Tues.).

In fine weather you can take an informative boat trip across Donegal Bay on the **waterbus** (at the pier by the tourist office, tel. 074/972-3666, www.donegalbaywaterbus.com, 5/day daily in summer, 1/day the rest of the year, €8). The 70-minute tour takes in a seal colony, oyster farm, various castle and monastic ruins, and other points of historical import.

The 18-hole, 73-par course at the **Donegal Golf Club** (Murvagh, Laghey, 10 km south of town on the N18, tel. 073/34054, www.donegalgolfclub.ie) is beautifully situated on the Murvagh Peninsula with a backdrop of the Bluestack Mountains.

Accommodations

The IHH and IHO **Donegal Town Independent Hostel** (Killybegs Rd., Doonan, tel. 074/972-2805, dorms €14–15, doubles €17–19 pp, credit cards accepted) gets top marks for friendly reception, clean facilities, comfy beds and common room, and an all-around great vibe. It's one kilometer west of town, but the walk will only take you 10 minutes, and the distance makes for a quiet night.

You'll find a wide selection of B&Bs on and signposted from the Killybegs and Ballyshannon roads. Situated on a small hill five minutes' walk from town, **Drumholm** (Killybegs Rd., tel. 074/972-3126 or 087/648-5734, €30–40 pp) is decidedly not your average, hohum B&B. Dramatic cherrywood staircases, decorative plasterwork, bathtubs, and fluffy, expensive comforters: You'd be hard-pressed to find other such elegant accommodation in this price range. Drumholm is best for early risers, however, as Mrs. Browne seems to relish making wakeup calls.

Another excellent choice is aptly named **Belle View House** (Ballyshannon Rd., tel. 074/972-2167, open Apr.–Nov., €27 pp, s €33), whose virtues include lovely views of bay and

Bluestacks, an open fire in the sitting room, and a very hospitable proprietor.

One of many reasons to stay at **Ard na Breatha** (Drumrooske Middle, a 20-minute walk or 3-minute drive from town, tel. 074/972-2288, www.ardnabreatha.com, closed mid-Jan.–mid-Feb., €35–50 pp, s €50–65) is the excellent bar and restaurant, which is open only to guests during the week (by arrangement). Each of the six rooms in this small and very atmospheric guesthouse features pine furniture, big comfy wrought-iron beds, and Bluestack views. Breakfast is a delight, with a buffet of fruit, cheeses, and homemade breads and smoked salmon with your scrambled eggs. To get here from town, take the Killybegs road and you'll see the restaurant signposted 200 meters down on your right.

If you're looking for a splurge, forgo the ordinary hotels at the center of town for the early-19th-century **St. Ernan's House Hotel** (off the R267/Ballyshannon road, 3 km west of town, tel. 074/972-1065, www.sainternans.com, €115–175 pp sharing, dinner €26–50). Built by a nephew of the Duke of Wellington in the 1830s, St. Ernan's is situated on its own little island at the end of a causeway. The dinners here are legendary, and every bedroom offers a view of Donegal Bay. If you want to treat yourselves, here's certainly the place.

Food

Donegal has far more lunch than dinner options, unfortunately. The cozy **Blueberry Tea Room** (Castle St., tel. 074/972-2933, open 9 A.M.–7 P.M. Mon.–Sat., mains under €10) is easily the best eatery in town, serving delicious sandwiches, quiches, cakes, and pies. No wonder it's packed with locals at any time of day. (You can also snag a computer upstairs for €4 an hour.)

Another excellent lunch option is **Aroma** (Ballyshannon Rd., tel. 074/972-3222, open 9:30 A.M.–5:30 P.M. Tues.–Sat., daily in summer, mains under €12), an unassuming café/bakery at the Donegal Craft Village renowned for its melt-in-your-mouth asparagus risotto.

DONEGAL

Otherwise, the **Deli Coffee House** (The Diamond, tel. 074/972-1014, mains under €7, open 9 A.M.–6 P.M. daily) does simple, quick meals, and the bus stops right outside.

Hostellers and picnickers might stop by **Simple Simon's** (The Diamond, tel. 074/972-2687), a small whole-foods store with prepared meals (quiche, tortillas, and the like) ready for reheating, and plenty of fruit and snacks.

For dinner, **Dom Breslin's** (Pier 1, Quay St., tel. 074/972-2719, food served noon–9:30 P.M. daily, mains €13–20) does reliably good seafood, meat, and pasta dishes in a comfortable (if slightly generic-feeling) atmosphere. If sophisticated modern Irish fare using fresh local produce is what you're after, try **Ard na Breatha** (Drumrooske Middle, a 20-minute walk or 3-minute drive from town, tel. 074/972-2288, www.ardnabreatha.com, open 6:30–9:30 P.M. Fri.–Sun. for nonresidents, nightly for guests, 5-course dinner €38, à la carte also available), where reservations are essential for nonguests. You might want to stay in the adjoining guesthouse, one of Donegal Town's top accommodations.

Information

The staff at Donegal's **tourist office** (The Quay, just south of the diamond, tel. 074/972-1148, www.irelandnorthwest.ie, www.donegal.ie, or www.donegaltown.ie, open 9 A.M.–6 P.M. Mon.–Sat. and noon–4 P.M. Sun. July–Aug., 9 A.M.–5 P.M. Mon.–Sat. Sept.–June) are exceptionally helpful.

Services

ATMs and bureaux de change are available at the **AIB** (tel. 074/972-1016), **Ulster Bank** (tel. 074/972-1064), and the **Bank of Ireland** (tel. 074/972-1079), all on the diamond.

The **post office** (Tirchonaill St.) is up Castle Street, over the bridge and on the left.

For Internet access, the only spot in town is the **Blueberry Cybercafé** (Castle St., tel. 074/972-2933, open 9 A.M.–7 P.M. Mon.–Sat., €4/hour), above the popular tearoom.

Begley's Pharmacy (tel. 074/972-1232) is also on the diamond.

Getting There and Around

Donegal Town is 65 kilometers north of Sligo on the N15, 203 kilometers north of Galway on the N15/N17, and 73 kilometers southwest of Derry City on the N15/A5. **Bus Éireann** service (tel. 074/972-1101, www.buseireann.ie, #30 from Dublin via Enniskillen, 7/day Mon.–Sat., 4/day Sun.; #64 from Derry or Galway via Sligo, 5/day Mon.–Sat., 3/day Sun.) in County Donegal is fairly spotty, but private bus companies are picking up the slack. **Feda O'Donnell** (tel. 074/954-8114 or 091/761-656, www.fedaodonnell.com, buses depart Galway at 9 A.M. and 4 P.M. Mon.–Sat., plus 1:30 P.M. and 5:30 P.M. Fri., 3 P.M. and 8 P.M. Sun., return €25) can get you here from Galway City via Sligo.

Hire a cycle from the **Bike Shop** (Waterloo Pl., tel. 074/972-2515, €10/60 per day/week). To get to Waterloo Place, take Bridge Street past the castle, cross the bridge, and turn right.

For a taxi, ring **Quinn's** (tel. 087/262-0670 or 074/913-2000) or **Brendan McBrearty** (tel. 074/972-3420).

◖ ROSSNOWLAGH BEACH

Rightfully known as "The Heavenly Cove" in Irish, the utterly pristine beach at Rossnowlagh (Ros Neamhlach, "ross-NOW-lah") extends for nearly five kilometers. Surf-wise, it's a fine alternative to cheesy Bundoran farther south on Donegal Bay. The village also has the dubious distinction of hosting the only Orange Order parade in the republic (on the weekend before July 12, the anniversary of the Battle of the Boyne). There's not much going on here otherwise; just make it your business to chill out (literally, if you try to go for a dip; wearing a wet suit would be smart even if you're not riding any waves).

For lunch, try the **Smuggler's Creek Inn** (tel. 071/985-2366, food served 12:30–8:30 P.M. daily, closed Mon.–Tues. Oct.–Easter, mains €14–24), which offers hefty seafood platters and terrace seating overlooking the beach. This place also offers B&B, though you're better off at the lovely **Ard na Mara** (tel. 071/985-1141, €35–45 pp), under new ownership, whose beach views (it's on a small cliff overlooking the strand) are every bit as nice (and the rooms are better maintained and more comfortable).

The area's nicest accommodation is the four-star, family-run **Sand House Hotel** (on the beach, tel. 071/985-1777, www.sandhouse-hotel.ie, €90–160 pp, 10 percent service charge), however, with individually designed rooms (some with four-poster beds, many with sea views), a rooftop garden, and a spa offering a full range of exotic newfangled treatments (balneotherapy, anyone?).

Rossnowlagh is 18 kilometers south of Donegal Town off the N15, and there is no public transportation.

BUNDORAN

An overdeveloped resort town just over the Leitrim-Donegal border, Bundoran holds little appeal unless you're a surfer. Rows upon rows of identical holiday homes conjure unpleasant thoughts of an Irish seaside Stepford. That said, wave-riders can contact **Fitzgerald's Surfworld** (Main St., tel. 071/984-1223) for equipment rental, or the **Donegal Adventure Centre & Surf School** (Bay View Ave., Dinglei Cush, tel. 071/984-2418, www.donegal-holidays.com) if in need of lessons. The center also hosts sea kayaking, canoeing, and snorkeling excursions as well as a long list of non-water sports. All others, keep on driving north.

The Glen Head Peninsula

KILLYBEGS

With Ireland's deepest port, Killybegs (Na Cealla Beaga, "The Little Churches") has a huge fleet of fishing boats and a fishmeal processing plant on the outskirts of town. Visitors tend to plug their noses at the fishy stink, but the smell isn't nearly as strong as reputed. There isn't much to see in Killybegs (outside the seafood festival in mid-August, which brings fireworks and clowns on stilts), but it's a pleasant enough town that makes a nice stopover if you're driving west from Donegal. And don't miss the gorgeous sandy strand at **Fintragh Bay** (signposted on the R263 3 km west of town).

Take your tea at one of the harbor-side hotels—the **Bay View** (Main St., tel. 074/973-1950, www.bayviewhotel.ie, rooms €120–150) or the **Tara** (on the harbor, tel. 074/974-1700, www.tarahotel.ie, bar food served 3–9 P.M. daily, mains €7–10, dinner and two nights B&B €145 pp sharing)—and watch the fishing boats bobbing on the pier and the seabirds wheeling overhead. These are also your best bets for accommodations if you decide to spend the night; the Tara has a sauna, Jacuzzi, and steam room, and ironically, the executive

suites at the Bayview are far homelier than the standard rooms. Both hotels offer wireless Internet. The **Harbour Bar** (on the harbor, tel. 074/973-1049) is a bit of a dive, but the trad's the best in town; **Hughie's** (22 Main St., tel. 074/973-1095) has live trad on Tuesday and an open mic on Wednesday.

See porpoises, birds, seals, even a dolphin or two on the **Donegal Bay Safari** (tel. 087/777-5755, www.donegalbayseafari.com, departing at noon, 2 P.M., and 4 P.M. in high season, 90-minute trip €25), on a 12-seater rigid inflatable boat. It's essential to prebook by phone.

Don't forget to hit one of the ATMs before you go: the **AIB, Ulster Bank,** and the **Bank of Ireland** are all on Main Street.

Killybegs is 27 kilometers west of Donegal Town off the N56. Now affiliated with Bus Éireann, **McGeehan Coaches** (tel. 074/954-6150, www.mgbus.com) offers regular service between Dublin, Donegal Town, Killybegs, and Glencolmcille (#490, 2–4/day daily).

KILCAR

A sleepy village between Killybegs and Glencolmcille, Kilcar (Cill Charthaigh, "Church of St. Cartha") makes a good base if you're

DONEGAL

© CAMILLE DEANGELIS

Locals teach their kids to swim at Kilcar Strand, the country's most sheltered beach.

taking a scenic boat trip from nearby Teelin Pier. In addition to a small tweed factory that welcomes visitors, **Studio Donegal** (west end of Main St., tel. 074/973-8194), there are two highly recommended accommodations outside the village: a hostel and a hotel, both atmospheric in their own way.

The IHH and IHO **☾ Derrylahan Hostel** (3 km past the village, signposted from the west end of Main St. and thereafter, tel. 074/973-8079, derrylahan@eircom.net, dorms €12–16, d €16–21 pp, s €24, credit cards accepted) is among the county's best. Shaun McCloskey will greet you with tea and biscuits—he's the sweetest hostel owner you'll ever meet. Derrylahan is a working farm, and fresh eggs are available for 20 cents each. There's a warm, well-stocked kitchen, cozy common rooms, and en-suite rooms in the adjacent building suitable for families. An extension to house a restaurant-grade kitchen is in the works; Shaun is a chef-in-training and will someday offer gourmet dinners for tired hill-walkers.

Note that there are two other hostels posted on the road out of Kilcar. Keep driving past the Dun Ulun Hostel/B&B and Cara's Hostel—both have shady reputations. Eventually you will find the Derrylahan turnoff on the left. If you don't have wheels, ring Shaun and he'll gladly pick you up. Or if taking the bus, ask the driver to drop you off at "The Rock, Kilcar," which means you'll only have to walk half a kilometer to get there. A 20-minute walk downhill from the hostel leads to the wonderfully sheltered, utterly pristine **Kilcar Strand** (also known as Portahowley).

Just over five kilometers east of Kilcar is the **Blue Haven Hotel** (Killybegs Rd., Largymore, tel. 074/973-8090, www.bluehaven.ie, €45–50 pp, s €45–55), modern yet not at all institutional. The open, airy "dome" lounge is a great spot for an aperitif, and you'll hear mainly Irish spoken at the neighboring tables. The food here is just adequate, but at least the prices are reasonable, and the service is cordial and unpretentious. Next door, the elegant **Inishduff House** (tel. 074/973-8542, www.inishduffhouse.com, closed Jan., €40 pp sharing) offers a warm traditional welcome along with the amazing sea views you simply can't find at the few B&Bs in town.

Your dining options are scant even in summer, but fortunately Kilcar offers a world-class seafood restaurant, **Teach Barnaí** (Main St., tel. 074/973-8160, 6–10 P.M. daily and noon–3 P.M. Sun. in summer, low season opening hours vary, mains €12–22). (And the quality of the meat and vegetarian dishes more than makes up for a lack of choice.) If Teach Barnaí isn't open, the **Blue Haven** hotel restaurant (food served 12:30–9:30 P.M. Mon.–Sat., 3–9 P.M. Sun., mains €8–22) is your best bet.

Kilcar is 12 kilometers west of Killybegs on the R263; make a withdrawal there before you get here, though there's a bureau de change at the newsagent on Main Street if you need it. **Bus Éireann** (#420, 2–4/day Mon.–Sat., 1–2 Sun.) can get you here from Donegal Town.

TEELIN

Boat trips depart from the pier at Teelin (Teileann) west of Kilcar. **An Shannen Álainn** (tel. 074/973-8495, www.bluefin.ie) offers cruises along Slieve League, angling charters, and bird-, dolphin-, and whale-watching excursions. **Nuala Star Teelin** (tel. 074/973-9365 or 087/628-4688, www.nwcsa.com/nualastar) offers the same activities, plus diving. Those who wish to walk Slieve League can also arrange a drop-off in Malinbeg after taking the cruise. To get to the Teelin Pier from Killybegs or Kilcar, take the R263 to Carrick, turn left just before the Óstán Sliabh Liag (it's signposted), and proceed five kilometers to the pier. On the way, you'll pass the **Slieve League Cultural Centre** (tel. 074/973-9077 or 087/770-6334, www.sliabhleague.com, open 10 A.M.–7 P.M. daily in summer), which dispenses tourist information and organizes hill-walking and archaeology tours. There's also a craft shop and tearoom with homebaked goods.

GLENCOLMCILLE

Dotted with Neolithic and early Christian tomb markers, rolling moorland punctuated by the occasional glade, lovely Glencolmcille (Gleann Cholm Cille, "Glen of Columba's Church") is within the Donegal Gaeltacht. This is a parish on the western end of the Glen Head Peninsula (also known as the Slieve League Peninsula) comprising five villages; Cashel, the easternmost, has most of the pubs and shops (not that there are many of either!). Sights and accommodations are spread out along the R263 west to the hamlets of Malinmore and Malinbeg.

Glencolmcille is connected to the tweed center of Ardara via the wild and heathery **Glengesh Pass** between the Glengesh and Mulmosog Mountains. The view from the summit, 275 meters above sea level, is as exhilarating in fine weather as it is desolate in the rain.

Sights

An Cláchan, the **Glencolmcille Folk Village** (on the R263 1.5 km west of Cashel, tel. 074/973-0017, www.glenfolkvillage.com, open 10 A.M.–6 P.M. Mon.–Sat., noon–6 P.M. Sun. Easter–Sept., admission €2) features a series of three cottages furnished to look like authentic 18th, 19th-, and early-20th-century homes along with a barn and schoolhouse, the idea being that you can see firsthand how your ancestors lived. "Rustic" doesn't quite capture the scene, especially regarding the oldest cottage! The museum was opened in 1967 by Father James McDyer, who opened a cooperative here in the 1950s in an effort to curb emigration. It's the biggest tourist draw in the area, no less worth seeing for its popularity with coach tours. A craft shop, tearoom, and bakery are also on the premises, and there are traditional music sessions in the evenings in high season.

Entertainment and Events

Three pubs stand along Cashel's main street—the Glen Head Tavern, Roarty's, and Biddy's. Of these, **Biddy's** (at the Cashel crossroads, tel. 074/973-0016) has the best *craic*—live trad most summer nights, two open fires, and cheeky barstaff to match the plaques on the walls ("dirty old men need love too").

Glencolmcille is home to one of Ireland's

DONEGAL

most outstanding Irish language schools, **Oideas Gael** (on the R263, tel. 074/973-0248, www.oideas-gael.com), which offers weekend and weeklong language immersion, music, and art courses April–August.

Shopping

Several tweed and knitwear shops dot the main road west of Cashel. The uncrowned king of tweed, **John Molloy** (on the R263, tel. 074/973-0282, www.johnmolloy.com) has a factory shop here, as does the family-owned **Glencolmcille Woolen Mill Shop** (on the R263, The Lace House, tel. 074/973-0016). The larger factory shop (tel. 074/973-0070) is clearly signposted on the local road to Malinmore. It may be a popular coach bus stop, but the tweeds and sweaters made on the premises are well worth a browse.

Sports and Recreation

Part of the Gaeltacht Way, **Slí Cholmcille** (St. Columba's Way) links Glencolmcille with Ardara, 70 kilometers to the north. A far less strenuous alternative is **Trabane Strand** in Malinbeg, a long strand tucked beneath a cliff and accessible by a vertiginous concrete staircase; there's another sandy beach just across the road from the Glencolmcille Folk Village.

Formerly known as the Malinmore Adventure Centre, the newly refurbished **Áras Ghleann Cholm Cille** (on the R263 in Malinmore, tel. 074/973-0077, www.arasgcc.com) offers the gamut of water-sporting activities as well as accommodation. It's affiliated with the Glencolmcille Hotel, which runs the 9-hole **Glencolmcille Golf Club** (tel. 074/973-0003, www.glengolf.com), so Áras participants get priority booking over non-hotel guests.

Accommodations

As you'll find elsewhere in Donegal, hostels are a popular option even for those not on a budget. There aren't as many B&Bs in this area as you'd expect, and most of them are open only in the height of summer.

The **Dooey Hostel** (Cashel, signposted off the R263 at the Glenhead Tavern, 1.5 km up a bumpy road, tel. 074/973-0130, dorms €12.50, private rooms €13.50 pp), flagship property of the IHO, is one of Ireland's most individual hostels. It's built into the mountainside, so when you open the front door you'll find a sloping rocky wall covered in ivy on your left and paper lanterns overhead (a vaguely tropical effect, were it not for the temperature). Delightful "Mad Mary" O'Donnell serves tea, biscuits, and a generous dose of wry pessimism on your arrival. Each eight-bed dorm has its own kitchen and bathroom, and there are six kitchens in all. The beds aren't terribly comfy, however, and the hostel is nonsmoking in name only. If you need creature comforts (like real mattresses and new en-suite showers) and don't mind the relative lack of character, stay at the purpose-built **Malinbeg Hostel** (Malinbeg, 9 km west of Cashel at the end of the R263, www.malinbeghostel.com, tel. 074/973-0006, dorms €12–15, private rooms €15 pp), which offers family and private rooms as well as dorms. There's a small grocery directly across the street. Both hostels have amazing sea views.

The best B&B in the area is the **Corner House** (Cashel village center, tel. 074/973-0021, open June–Sept., €30 pp, s €38). The two double and two twin en-suite rooms are spotless but fairly basic (no televisions in the rooms, sorry!), and smoking is permitted indoors. For a modern en-suite room, decent bar food, and live trad nightly, drive two kilometers past Cashel to the canary-yellow Glencolmcille Hotel, **Óstán Ghleann Cholm Cille** (on the R263, tel. 074/973-0003, www.glenhotel.com, €40–60 pp, s €55–75). There's a golf course right out back.

Food

Dining options are paltry indeed. Your two choices in high season are on the road west of Cashel, **The Lace House** (tel. 074/973-0444, open 9:30 A.M.–9 P.M. daily, mains €6–9), a shop-cum-café specializing in fresh fish and chips; and **An Chistin** ("The Kitchen," tel. 074/973-0213, open 12:30–9:30 P.M. weekdays, 9:30 A.M.–9:30 P.M. weekends, mains €6–9), a delightful spot where Irish language students at Oideas Gael come for a sandwich or snack. In low season you are limited to the pub grub at the Glencolmcille Hotel, however.

Information and Services

Be sure to withdraw money in Killybegs, as there is no ATM in this remote locale. The Cashel post office does change money, however. There is no tourist office, but the best source of info is the reception at the **Folk Village** three kilometers west of Cashel.

Getting There and Around

The village of Cashel in the parish of Glencolmcille is 26 kilometers west of Killybegs and 53 kilometers west of Donegal on the R263. Now affiliated with Bus Éireann, **McGeehan Coaches** (tel. 074/954-6150, www.mgbus.com) offers regular service between Dublin, Donegal Town, Killybegs, and Glencolmcille (#490, 2–4/day daily).

For a taxi, ring **William O'Brien** (tel. 087/293-9466), who serves all of southwest Donegal in his sturdy red minivan. He also does minitours of the Slieve League Peninsula for up to seven people and can take you back to your accommodation after you've completed the eight-kilometer walk.

◖ SLIEVE LEAGUE

One of Donegal's most exhilarating experiences is the eight-kilometer trek along the Slieve League (Sliabh Liag) cliffs—at 300–600 meters, these are the highest sea cliffs in Europe. The cliffs start at Bunglás (6 km west of Teelin) and end at Trabane Strand (An Trá Bán) near Malinbeg. Coming from Killybegs, take a left at Hegarty's/The Slieve League Bar (which welcomes tourist inquiries, incidentally). After a few kilometers, a fork in the road appears: Make a left for Bunglás or go right for the Slieve League walking trail. If you take a left, you'll come to a gate fastened with rope; open the gate, drive through, close the gate again, and drive past the car park on the left. A winding road continues for 1.5 kilometers before terminating in a smaller car park, where you can view the eastern cliffs. This is also where

you begin the four- to five-hour hike. Be extremely careful when walking the often-muddy track, as gale-force winds have been known to blow hikers over the edge. And be sure follow the ridge to avoid slipping in the mud.

Driving yourself to Bunglás presents its own logistical challenge, of course, since you'll have to ring for a taxi to return you to your vehicle afterward. You could ring for a taxi to drop you off at Bunglás and pick you up at Trabane Strand later in the day, or the taxi could just drop you off and you could walk back to Glencolmcille from Trabane afterward. However you choose to do it, **William O'Brien** (tel. 087/293-9466) is your man.

ARDARA

A pleasant town with a long handweaving tradition, Ardara (ar-DRAH, Ard an Rátha, "Height of the Circular Fort") straddles the trickley River Owentocker at the mouth of Loughros Bay. Other than shopping for tweeds and admiring the **Eas A' Ranca waterfall** (8 km west of town), there isn't a lot to occupy you in the town itself—but it's a good place to spend the night before heading up to Gweedore. Further afield, the **Kilclooney dolmen** (6.1 km north of Ardara, 400 m east off the R261) reportedly dates from 3500 B.C. and probably has the country's second-largest capstone (after Browne's Hill in Carlow).

Shopping

Tweed-stocked gift shops line the main drag, the largest of which is **Kennedy's** (Front St., tel. 074/954-1106). Another big shop on the Donegal end of town, **Tríona Design** (tel. 074/954-1422, www.trionadesign.com), which specializes in classy tweed jackets and trousers, also has a café. Farther along the Donegal road is another **John Molloy** (tel. 074/954-1133, www.johnmolloy.com) outpost.

Purists will want to patronize the handweavers, however. **Eddie Doherty** (Front St., tel. 074/954-1304) does comfy throws, ponchos, and shearling-lined slippers; call in to Doherty's pub next door if there's no one in the shop.

DONEGAL

Sports and Recreation

Ardara is on the **Slí Cholmcille** portion of the Gaeltacht Way, which links the town with Glencolmcille (a distance of 70 kilometers).

Bicycle nine kilometers west of town to Loughros Head (on a local road, signposted at the western edge of town). For pony treks along the beaches of Loughros Bay, contact **Castle View Horses** (Kilcashel, Ardara, 4 km outside town, tel. 074/954-1212), which also provides B&B accommodation. To get here, follow the sign for Loughros Point from the western end of town, proceed for two kilometers, and you'll see the Castle View turnoff signposted on your left.

It's possible to fish on the River Owentocker; stop by **McGill's** on Main Street for tackle.

Accommodations

The IHO **Drumbarron Hostel** (tel. 074/954-1200, dorms €12–13) is beside Ulster Bank on the diamond, but it was closed for repairs at time of writing. Just across the way is an excellent guesthouse, **Drumbarron B&B** (The Diamond, tel. 074/954-1200, €30 pp). Mrs. Feeney will greet you with tea, freshly made scones, and blackberry jam. The decor is stylishly eclectic; you'll find a cheerful fire, a selection of classic books, and comfy leather armchairs in the sitting room, and the beds have down comforters *and* electric heating pads. Breakfast is lovingly prepared and cheerfully served.

Set on a hill overlooking the lush highland countryside, the Georgian **Woodhill House** (about 1 km outside Ardara, tel. 074/954-1112, www.woodhillhouse.com, open Jan.–Oct., restaurant open Mar.–Oct., €48–75 pp, credit cards accepted) was once the home of the Nesbits, Ireland's last commercial whalers. This outstanding guesthouse features a French-inspired restaurant using local produce and fish from Killybegs, a small, cozy bar, and a delightful garden through an old stone archway. Nancy and John Yates are genuinely friendly—the ideal hosts (and Nancy is the granddaughter and namesake of Ardara's still-favorite publican). To get here, go straight through the diamond (rather than following Main Street as it curves left toward the bridge), and you'll see Woodhill signposted at the fork in the road (take a right). If you're driving up from Donegal, you can also get here off the N56; it's signposted about a kilometer outside town. (Also consider Woodhill as an alternative to the Nesbitt Arms Hotel in town, which is mediocre at best.)

Food and Entertainment

Your dining options are slim. **Charlie's West Side Café** (Main St., tel. 074/954-1656, open 9:30 A.M.–10 P.M. daily, mains under €8) is a relatively classy "chipper" known for its fresh fish. This café also does sandwiches, lasagna, and suchlike. It gets quite packed with locals in the evenings.

The best pub in town is **Nancy's** (Front St., tel. 074/954-1187, food served noon–9 P.M. daily), which attracts an eccentric older crowd. It feels a bit like having a pint in your grandmother's living room, especially with the collection of porcelain mugs and milk saucers hanging above the tiny bar. There's basic pub grub for under €10 (and, humorously enough, only one menu to go around).

Nancy's often has live music, but the town's best venue is **The Corner House** (The Diamond, tel. 074/954-1736). Ardara's *other* best pub has live trad nightly in summer and weekends in the winter. Visiting musicians are welcome to join in alongside the owner, Peter Oliver, who plays a slew of instruments (though only one at a time).

Sadly, most of the other pubs in town have been renovated out of their traditional charm.

Information and Services

Whether or not you're interested in the history of the local tweed industry, the **Ardara Heritage Centre** (Main St., tel. 074/954-1704, open 10 A.M.–6 P.M. Mon.–Sat. and 2–6 P.M. Sun. Easter–Sept., free admission) is a good place to ask questions. **Tríona Design** (tel. 074/954-1422) on the west end of town offers visitor information as well.

Hit the ATM at the **Ulster Bank** on the diamond. The Ardara **post office** is on the west side of Main Street.

The **Ardara Pharmacy** (tel. 074/954-1120) is also on Main Street, just before the bridge.

Getting There and Around

Ardara is 37 kilometers northwest of Donegal Town and 16 kilometers north of Killybegs on the N56. Getting here by public transport is tricky: **Bus Éireann** (tel. 074/912-1309) route #492 links Donegal Town with Ardara, leaving at 9:30 A.M. and arriving in Killybegs at 10:15 A.M., with a layover until noon (Mon.–Fri., runs end June to end Aug.); there's an-other bus at 4:05 P.M. that gets to Killybegs at 4:50 P.M. (Mon.–Fri. all year); the connection departs 10 minutes later. The return times are also infrequent. **Feda O'Donnell** (tel. 091/761-656 or 074/954-8144, www.fedaodonnell.com, return €25) offers a Friday-only service from Galway City at 4 P.M. (during the school year only) and 5:30 P.M., departing Ardara at 3:30 P.M. Sunday and 8:50 A.M. Monday.

Don Byrne (the west end of Main St., tel. 074/954-1658, €15/60 per day/week, €12.50 for multiple days), a Raleigh agent, will rent you a bike. Ring **O'Donnell's** (tel. 087/266-5500) for a cab.

Northwestern Donegal

◖ GLENVEAGH NATIONAL PARK

Like Killarney National Park in County Kerry, the centerpiece of Glenveagh National Park (Gleann Bheatha, "Glen of the Birches") is a Victorian manor house, the fanciful-looking Glenveagh Castle. Covering 160 square kilometers, the park is best known for its proliferation of red deer and rhododendrons, both of which were introduced by Adelia Adair, mistress of the castle. Early summer is the best time of year to visit the park, when the rhododendrons are in full bloom. Other park wildlife includes badgers, hares, stoats, foxes, and the golden eagle, reintroduced in 2000 after a 100-year absence caused by over-hunting.

On the park's western side is Mount Errigal, the county's highest peak. The park also encompasses Lakes Dunlewey, Beagh, and Gartan, and the romantic-sounding Poisoned Glen, whose name is the result of a simple misspelling (the Irish name was An Gleann Neamhe, "The Heavenly Glen," which an English cartographer transcribed as An Gleann Neimhe—you can guess what that means).

The national park **visitors center** (entrance off the R251 10 km east of Dunlewey, tel. 074/913-7090, open 10 A.M.–6 P.M. Feb.–Nov., admission €2.50, free admission to the park) offers a 20-minute audiovisual covering the usual botany and fauna, as well as the sins of tyrannical landlord John Adair, who built Glenveagh Castle.

Eight kilometers south of the visitors center is the **Glebe House and Gallery** (on Lough Gartan, off the 251, tel. 074/913-7071, open 11 A.M.–6:30 P.M. daily Easter week and July–Aug., open Sat.–Thurs. June and Sept.–mid-Oct., admission €2.90), which features works by Picasso and Jack B. Yeats—though access is by guided tour only.

There are five signposted walks in Glenveagh National Park, the shortest being 5 kilometers, the longest 22 kilometers. Rule #1: Always wear your bug spray. Pick up a can before you get here, because the midges will bite you something fearsome if you don't.

Glenveagh Castle

Dúchas-run Glenveagh Castle (tel. 074/913-7090, open 10 A.M.–6:30 P.M. daily Feb.–Nov., admission €3, plus €2 shuttle bus fare), built of granite by John Adair in 1870, is nestled between the Derryveagh and Glendowan Mountains on the southern shore of Lough Beagh. The beauty of Adair's estate belies a tragic history:

DONEGAL

He was a cruel landlord who in April 1861 ruthlessly evicted 244 of his tenants—simply because their presence was spoiling his view!

Professor Arthur Kingsley Porter, an art historian from Harvard University, purchased the castle in 1929 and lived there with his wife until his mysterious disappearance on Inishbofin Island (in County Galway) four years later. An American guest of the Porters, Henry McIlhenny, purchased it from Mrs. Porter in 1938, redecorated the mansion, and restored the gardens with great care and attention. Both Porter and McIlhenny entertained a parade of writers, artists, academics, and aristocrats at Glenveagh; as Brian de Breffny writes of this place, "Few are not enchanted by the blaze of rhododendron in June, by the statue-garden, the rose-garden, the mysterious moss-garden on the mountainside and the shimmering lake, and by the atmosphere of the house and the beauty of the furnishings."

Having said all this, if you aren't that interested in examining the china, hunting trophies, and fancy furniture of country manor houses, then you should skip the tour and just enjoy the grounds. Admission is free to the visitors center (same phone and hours), and there's a restaurant open from mid-April through September and a tearoom open daily in high season and weekends in wintertime.

Mount Errigal

Almost perfectly conical, Mount Errigal (An tEargail) is visually striking for its cap of white quartzite. At 752 meters, Errigal sounds more formidable than it really is; the reasonably fit can scale it on the 5-kilometer "tourist route" in two hours or less. The 3.5-kilometer alternative walk along the scree-covered northwestern ridge is more difficult and is a popular training route for hardcore climbers with loftier ambitions (pun intended). The popular route approaches from the south, beginning at a ruined gateway on the R251 by a bridge just west of Dunlewey village.

Stop in at the national park visitors center or Dunlewey Lakeside Centre for more detailed information before attempting either route. For either hike, be sure to pick up OS map #1.

Dunlewey

You could barely call it a village, but Dunlewey (Dún Lúiche, "Fort of Lú") attracts plenty of backpackers in summertime for its location under Donegal's highest peak. There are two long-established hostels here, **Lakeside Backpackers** (on the R251, tel. 074/953-2133, open mid-Mar.–Oct., dorms €10) and the An Óige **Errigal Hostel** (on the R251, tel. 074/953-1180, www.errigalhostel.com), the latter of which was closed for extensive renovations at time of writing and due to reopen in early summer 2007. Lakeside has seen better days (it used to be the Dunlewey Hotel), but it's still an adequate place to bunk up while the An Óige hostel is closed. Hostellers can stock up at Dunlewey's small grocery-cum-petrol station.

Unfortunately, public transportation is so limited in this part of the county that shoestring travelers often end up hitching to get to Dunlewey. There are much livelier places from which to base yourself—Bunbeg, Dunfanaghy, or even Letterkenny—but those who aren't all that into the pub culture will find Dunlewey's tranquility a welcome change.

B&Bs aren't at all plentiful along this stretch, but one to recommend is **Glen Heights** (tel. 074/956-0844 or 087/218-8632, www.glenheightsbb.com, €35 pp sharing), a lovely dormer with a breakfast conservatory and front patio overlooking Lough Dunlewey. It's signposted from the R251 two kilometers east of the village; make a right at the Poisoned Glen turnoff and continue for about one kilometer. You'll see another sign for the B&B on your left, up a steep driveway.

Mostly of interest to families is **Ionad Cois Locha,** the Dunlewey Lakeside Centre (turnoff at Lakeside Backpackers, tel. 074/953-1699, www.dunleweycentre.com, open 10:30 A.M.– 6 P.M. Mon.–Sat. and 11 A.M.–6 P.M. Sun. mid-Mar.–Oct., admission €5.50), in the restored home of local handweaver Manus Ferry, who died in 1975. There are weaving demonstra-

LONG-DISTANCE WALKS IN COUNTY DONEGAL

A 111-kilometer stretch of the 900-kilometer **Ulster Way** is located in County Donegal. Beginning in tiny Pettigo on the border, this stretch hugs Lough Derg through the Bluestack and Derryveagh Mountains and into Falcarragh. If basing yourself in Gweedore, you might want to walk part of this route, which forks off the Poison Glen Horseshoe Trail inside Glenveagh National Park.

Another option is the 117-kilometer **Bluestack Way,** which begins just east of Donegal Town, winding around Lough Eske before meandering through the Bluestack Mountains northwest to Ardara. From there, you can join the 70-kilometer **Slí Cholmcille** (St. Colmcille's Way), which loops around Glencolmcille on the Glen Head Peninsula, passing through Carrick, Kilcar, and the Glengesh Pass. This is one of a series of circular walks in Donegal known as the **Bealach na Gaeltachta,** with 290 kilometers of walking trails in all.

Far less traveled is the eerie **Tullaghobegley Walk** ("tull-o-BEG-lee") from Gweedore to Falcarragh, a route used for carrying corpses to the nearest consecrated ground dating back to the 13th century. The 5-6-hour, 11-kilometer walk begins at **Loch na Cuinge,** or Lough Nacung, just east of the village of Gweedore. The route takes you over a mountain called **Taobh an Leithid** (430 meters), with superb panoramic views despite a crop of windmills; local hikers pause for rest at the summit, where you'll find seven cairns. It's tradition to add a rock to the cairns as you pass. Tullaghobegley is not waymarked, so an Ordnance Survey Discovery Series map (#1) is even more essential; **Údarás na Gaeltachta** in Derrybeg (Páirc Ghnó Ghaoth Dobhair, tel. 074/956-0100, www.udaras.ie) has maps on offer as well. Do not attempt to walk alone, as the weather's inconstancy can pose navigational dilemmas no matter how trusty your compass.

For more information on all walking routes, stop first at the Donegal Town tourist office. The hosts of your B&B can also be a great source of information.

---

tions and an audiovisual as well as a boat trip on Lake Dunlewey, narrated with area history and folklore. It's worth stopping by for the cozy café with open turf fire.

Dunlewey is 11 kilometers east of Bunbeg on the R251 and 40 kilometers west of Letterkenny. There is no public transport.

GWEEDORE

Tucked between the Atlantic and the Derryveagh Mountain range in northwestern Donegal, the parish of Gweedore (Gaoth Dobhair, "Inlet of the Water"; pronounced "ghee DOH-wer," with a hard "g") is a visual feast of boggy hills, glens, lakes, and shimmering sea beyond an undulating coastline. You'll also find Ireland's largest community of native Irish speakers.

In Gweedore you'll hear some of the best traditional music sessions on the island; the region has produced many outstanding musicians and groups, among them Clannad on the "first wave" of traditionally influenced Irish "supergroups" in the 1970s, Altan singer Mairéad Ní Mhaonaigh, and Enya. Writing of Altan for *Hot Press,* writer Bill Graham called Gweedore a "slippery and elastic concept and state of mind," but this is often the case when an outsider confuses "village" and "parish." There may be a point labeled Gweedore on your road map, but the name actually applies to the whole region.

It isn't as remote as you may have heard, though—not anymore. Ongoing development (cute little holiday homes especially) has scattered the villages of Bunbeg (Bun Beag, "Little Root") and Derrybeg (Doirí Beaga, "Little Oaks") for several kilometers along the R257. Since Gweedore is so spread out, getting around can be a pain without a rental car, but it can be done. If you need a taxi in the area, try **Paddy McGee** (tel. 087/254-3666, 7-seater minibus), **Sean Mac** (tel. 087/280-2011, 14-seater bus), **Charlie Mac** (tel. 087/260-3757), or **Cronan Mac** (tel. 087/237-8888). You'll find most of the action in and around the village of Bunbeg; the ATM and bureau de change are there, too, at the **AIB** on Main Street (the R257, tel. 074/953-1077). The nearest tourist office is in Letterkenny, but the locals here are some of the friendliest, most eager-to-help folks on the planet. Check out the **Visit Gweedore** website (www.visitgweedore.com) before you go.

Patrick Gallagher (tel. 074/953-1107 or 087/233-0888, www.gallagherscoaches.com, ring for fares) provides a one-a-day bus service (two on Friday during the school year) from Belfast to Gweedore (at the Bunbeg crossroads) via Derry, Letterkenny, and Dunfanaghy. The bus leaves Jury's Hotel in Belfast (at 5:30 P.M. Mon.–Sat. and 9:15 P.M. Sun., arriving in Bunbeg at 8:45 P.M. and 12:30 A.M., respectively).

The **Lough Swilly Bus** (tel. 074/912-2863, or tel. 028/7126-2017 from N.I. for the Foyle St. Station office, 4/day Mon.–Fri., 2/day Sat., single/return from Derry to Gweedore £10.20/12.80) links Derry City with Bunbeg. Ring for timetable, or visit the unofficial Lough Swilly website (www.sjp.clara.net/nibus/lstt.htm).

Bunbeg

Six kilometers west of the village of Gweedore is Bunbeg, still laid-back and delightful despite ongoing development. The quaint, tiny Bunbeg Harbour is signposted on the southern end of the village, and from here you can board ferries to Gola or Tory Islands via **Donegal Coastal Cruises** (tel. 074/953-1320, www.toryisland-ferry.com, daily service Apr.–Oct., weekdays only Nov.–Mar., return fare €20).

One of the best B&Bs in the area is **Teach Champbell** (Bunbeg village, signposted on the left on the R257 a few houses past the AIB, tel. 074/953-1545, teaccam@eircom.net, €30 pp, s €35–42, evening meals €16 in summer), a cheerful, deceptively spacious home clad in ivy. The Campbells are lovely people, and you'll feel like you're staying with an old family friend. The back bedrooms have views of Gweebarra Bay. This is a great place to practice your *Gaeilge bhriste* (broken Irish). Another great accommodation, **Bunbeg House** (signposted off the R257, tel. 074/953-1305, www.bunbeghouse.com, €35–40 pp, s €40–45), has a quaint location right on the Bunbeg pier, two kilometers south of the village center—though perhaps the best reason to stay here is the tiny pub downstairs.

Gweedore's best hotel is the Óstán Radharc na Mara, the **Sea View Hotel** (on the R257 in the village center, tel. 074/953-1159, www.seaviewhotel.ie, €55–70 pp sharing). Rooms are comfortable but no-frills (unless you count the trouser press); it's the surprisingly good restaurant (with an open turf fire) and the pub, **Hughie Tim's,** that make the Sea View special. Hughie Tim's is one of the locals' favorite watering holes. The only caveat is the nightclub noise on the weekends; if you aren't planning to dance the night away (no cover for hotel guests), be sure to request a room on the far side of the hotel. The breakfast is outstanding.

A five-minute walk south on the R575 brings you to **Teach Hudí Beag** (tel. 074/953-1016), an unself-consciously traditional pub offering Gweedore's biggest (up to a dozen musicians!) and best trad session on Monday nights. Whatever you do, don't miss this one.

The Bloody Foreland

Named for the crimson-hued sunset over the Atlantic, the Bloody Foreland (Cnoc Fola) at the northwest tip of Gweedore is arguably the singlemost breathtaking vista in the county. Just keep driving north on the R257 from Derrybeg. Proving the old real estate maxim ("location, location, location") is the family-run **Foreland Heights** hotel (on the R257, about 10 km north of Bunbeg, tel. 074/953-1785, forelandheights@hotmail.com, B&B €40 pp sharing, bar food served noon–10 P.M., restaurant open 5–10 P.M. daily and noon–4 P.M. Sun., bar meals under €15). No amount of gushing can prepare you for the view from every bedroom. It would otherwise impress you as a pleasant and rather ordinary (albeit attractively priced) hotel, but the clifftop setting puts this place somewhere darn near close to heaven (perhaps literally). You'll find live trad and set-dancing sessions here nightly in high season, too.

Crolly

Tourists and locals alike flock to Leo's Tavern, **Tábhairne Leo** (Meenalick, Crolly, on the R259, signposted from the N56 south of Bunbeg, turnoff right after Paidi Og's pub in Crolly, tel. 074/954-8143, food served 5–8:30 P.M. Mon.–Fri. and 1–8:30 P.M. weekends, mains €10–20), because Leo is the father of Enya, that eerily ageless goddess of New Age. This isn't one of those crusty old man's pubs where you can kick back with a pint and a feeling of relative anonymity; it's quite modern on the inside, with too-bright lighting and loud-mouthed American college students often taking up half the tables. That said, the bar food is decent, and there's live music most nights. Plus, you never know which famous Irish songbird you might spot here.

Falcarragh

The real reason to mention workaday Falcarragh (An Fál Carrach, "The Rocky Fence"), 22 kilometers northeast of Bunbeg on the R258 and N56—which is not actually in Gweedore, but just outside it—is the historic **Tullaghobegley Walk,** which starts near the village of Gweedore and ends here. (For more information, see the sidebar *Long-Distance Walks in County Donegal.*)

For a lift back to Bunbeg, ring or stop by **Joe's Taxis** (Main St., tel. 074/916-5017) or **Manus McGee** (tel. 087/244-6198).

If you want to spend the night here, try **Cuan-na-Mara** (Ballyness, 1 km north of town on the local road to Ballyness Bay, turnoff signposted on the western end of town, tel. 074/913-5327, crisscannon@hotmail.com, open June–Sept., €26–33 pp, s €39–45), a cheerful bungalow with electric blankets on the beds.

From Falcarragh, if driving, you can take **Muckish Drive** south through the Derryveagh Mountains, eventually hitting the R251, the northern border of the national park, between Dunlewey and the park entrance. You'll pass plenty of rock- and heather-strewn hills on melancholy Muckish Drive, but you won't see anyone for miles. There are no houses or any other kind of development along this stretch.

Getting There and Around

To cut down on travel time, consider flying directly from Dublin into Aerfort Dhún na nGall, the **Donegal Airport** (Carrickfinn, Kincasslagh, 14 km south of Bunbeg on the R266, signposted turnoff at Crolly on the N56, tel. 074/954-8284, www.donegalairport.ie). **Aer Arann** (tel. 0818/210-210 or 061/704-428, www.aerarann.ie) offers two daily flights to/from Dublin (40 minutes), and there's a flight from Glasgow Prestwick on Sunday, Wednesday, and Friday. Once here, you can rent a car with **Avis** (tel. 074/954-8469, www.avis.ie), though you probably won't be able to get one with automatic transmission.

DUNFANAGHY

A delightfully understated resort town of Presbyterian origins, Dunfanaghy ("done-FAN-a-hee," Dún Fionnachaidh, "Fort of the Fair-Haired Tribe") is a popular vacation spot for Northern families—yet it's never too crowded, even in peak season. The range of accommodations and variety of exhilarating walks nearby (out to Horn Head, or the wonderfully secluded Tramore Strand), plus its proximity (23 kilometers) to Glenveagh National Park, make Dunfanaghy a fine place to base yourself for a few days.

Sights

If you're feeling even an ounce of self-pity for whatever reason, a visit to **The Workhouse Museum** (just outside town on the N56/Falcarragh Rd., tel. 074/913-6540, open 10 A.M.–5 P.M. Mon.–Sat., noon–5 P.M. Sun. mid-Mar.–Sept., admission €4.25) is a surefire way to snap out of it. The exhibit, using mannequins inside life-size dioramas, tells the life story of "Wee Hannah" Herritty, a local woman who spent years wasting away in the

DONEGAL

19th-century workhouse on this site. You walk from room to room and listen to "Hannah" speak matter-of-factly of the various horrors she endured in this very building, and the ground-floor rooms give more straightforward information about the workhouse using old photographs and a brief audiovisual. The "wee Hannah" bit might sound like a weird combination of the macabre and the cheesy, but it's a real eye-opener for those who know little about this horrible aspect of Irish history (which is nearly all of us). Fortunately, Hannah eventually found a way out of here and lived to the ripe old age of 90.

The museum has a pleasant tearoom and a gift shop, and the staff are a good source for tourist info.

Entertainment

Not that there's a whole lot of competition for the title, but the best pub in town is **Danny Collins** (Main St., tel. 074/913-6205), with live trad most nights in summer. Because of its jukebox and television above the bar, **McColgan's** (Main St., tel. 074/910-0947) tends to attract a younger crowd for live blues and rock music several nights a week in high season.

Shopping

McAuliffe's (Main St., tel. 074/913-6135) stocks the gamut of souvenirs, from Aran sweaters to locally made greeting cards and Sex-on-the-Beach-scented incense. On a more prosaic note, Ordnance Survey maps are also for sale.

But if it's pottery you're looking for, skip the assembly-line mugs and plates at McAuliffe's for the goods at **Muck 'n Muffins** (The Square, tel. 074/913-6780, www.mucknmuffins.com). You can watch the girls at their wheels in the open workshop area.

The inventory at **Pauline's Country Quilts** (Main St.) is mainly for those who sew, of course, but with a little luck you can find a beautiful locally made quilt here for an incredible price.

For quality antiques as well as oil and wa-

tercolor paintings, visit **The Gallery** (just outside town on the N56/Falcarragh Rd., tel. 074/913-6224).

Sports and Recreation

Whatever you do, don't leave Dunfanaghy without walking or driving out to **Horn Head** (clearly signposted from the Falcarragh end of town). It's an exhilarating hour-long walk up a few steep, quiet residential lanes out to a heather-covered headland with dazzling clifftop (just under 200 meters high) views of the sea and Tramore Strand to the west.

If there's time, make a detour to the pristine **Tramore Strand** on your way back to town. Turn left immediately after crossing the Horn Head Bridge (or before, if you're coming back from the Head), where you'll find three stone steps down to a small wooden gate. Pastures lie beyond it (as well as a football pitch), but you'll see a path worn through the short grass. It'll take roughly half an hour to get from bridge to strand.

Another Blue Flag strand, **Marble Hill Beach,** lies three kilometers east of Dunfanaghy in the village of Portnablagh.

Fancy a canter along the strand? **Dunfanaghy Stables** (Arnold's Hotel, Main St., tel. 074/913-6208, www.dunfanaghystables.com) can accommodate. The **Dunfanaghy Golf Club** (just east of town off the N59, tel. 074/913-6335, www.dunfanaghygolfclub.com) has one of the most scenic courses you'll ever play.

Accommodations

Another of Donegal's best hostels is the IHH **Corcreggan Mill** (3 km southwest of Dunfanaghy on the N56, tel. 074/913-6409, www.corcreggan.com, dorms €12–15, private rooms €20–40 pp, credit cards accepted). Army man Brendan Rohan spent years lovingly fixing up the place, converting a 120-year-old railway carriage into a row of five private rooms using other recycled materials. The kitchen and dining facilities are excellent, and the sitting room with its open fire, comfy armchairs, and spare guitar is second to none. Those not driving should note the hostel's distance from town—

it's a 40-minute walk by day along the busy road, but at night you'll need to ring a taxi. And for those who don't fancy spending the night in a sometimes-drafty railway car, Corcreggan Mill also offers en-suite B&B accommodations in another restored building on the premises.

On the Falcarragh end of Dunfanaghy's Main Street is a good B&B, **The Willows** (tel. 074/913-6446, mcfaddenwillows@hotmail.com, €30 per person). Electric heating pads, small refrigerators to keep the milk for your tea (no plastic-cup creamers here!), and the convenient location make it a safe bet. For a thoughtfully decorated room with a view, try **The Whins** (less than 1 km east of town on the N56, tel. 074/913-6481, www.thewhins.com, open mid-Feb.–mid-Nov., €31–33, s €42–50), which overlooks the golf course and bay, or **Rosman House** (signposted off the Falcarragh side of the N59 just outside town, tel. 074/913-6273 or 074/913-6393, www.rosmanhouse.ie, closed Dec., €30–33 pp, s €40–50), a working farm with outstanding views of Horn Head. Both these B&Bs have lovely gardens and accept credit cards.

Besides having a fine gourmet restaurant, **The Mill House** (signposted on the Falcarragh Rd., tel. 074/913-6985, www.themillrestaurant.com, €45 pp, s €60) is also the one of the classiest places to stay in Dunfanaghy. The great thing about **Arnold's Hotel** (Main St., tel. 074/913-6208, www.arnoldshotel.com, open Apr.–Nov., €69–79 pp, s €99–129, superior rooms €99–109 pp), besides the above-average restaurant fare, is that you can arrange bird-watching, horseback riding, or painting excursions with reception. Arnold's is the favored accommodation of all those well-heeled Protestant ladies who spend their summer holidays walking the beach at Portnablagh.

Food

Don't leave town without stopping at **Muck 'n Muffins** (The Square, tel. 074/913-6780, www.mucknmuffins.com, open 9:30 A.M.–6 P.M. Mon.–Sat. and 10 A.M.–6 P.M. Sun. Mar.–Nov., 9:30 A.M.–5 P.M. Mon.–Sat. Dec.–Feb.,

lunches under €7) for a cappuccino. There's a pottery and gift shop on the ground floor and a delightful, friendly café upstairs. You can have a basic-but-tasty lunch (and fabulous desserts) overlooking the garden center next door, teeming with herbs and flowers, and Sheephaven Bay beyond. On Friday night in high season (Saturday too, if the town is jumpin') and holiday weekends in winter, the café transforms into a wine bar serving up antipasto platters and plenty of atmosphere.

For pub grub, **Danny Collins** (Main St., tel. 074/913-6205, food served noon–8 P.M. daily, mains under €12) is pretty much the only option in town. The menu at **Arnold's Hotel** (Main St., tel. 074/913-6208, food served noon–9 P.M. daily, mains €8–20) is far tastier and more creative than your average hotel fare.

But the area's finest restaurant is **The Mill** (signposted on the Falcarragh Rd./N56 just outside town, tel. 074/913-6985, www.themillrestaurant.com, open 7–9 P.M. Tues.–Sun., set dinner €38, reservations required). You're guaranteed an otherworldly gourmet meal here from chef and owner Derek Alcorn, be it lamb, lobster, or slow-roast duck.

Information and Services

Dunfanaghy has no tourist office, so your best source of info is the **heritage center** (just north of town on the N56, tel. 074/913-6540) at The Workhouse Museum just outside town. The ladies behind the desk are very helpful.

The **AIB** next to Arnold's Hotel has a bureau de change but no ATM. The **post office** is on the Falcarragh end of Main Street.

Getting There and Around

Dunfanaghy is on the N56, 36 kilometers northwest of Letterkenny. **Feda O'Donnell** (tel. 091/761-656 or 074/954-8144, www.fedaodonnell.com, 4.5-hour trip with a pit stop in Sligo, return €25) serves Dunfanaghy from Galway, departing the Catholic cathedral of St. Nicholas (9 A.M. and 4 P.M. Mon.–Sat., with additional Fri. buses at 1:30 P.M. and 5:30 P.M., Sun. departures at 3 P.M. and 8 P.M.). The bus stops at the square in Dunfanaghy.

DONEGAL

Patrick Gallagher (tel. 074/953-1107 or 087/233-0888, www.gallagherscoaches.com, ring for fares) provides a one-a-day bus service (two on Friday during the school year) from Belfast to Gweedore, passing through Dunfanaghy en route. The bus leaves Jury's Hotel in Belfast (5:30 P.M. Mon.–Sat. and 9:15 P.M. Sun., arriving in Dunfanaghy at 8:05 P.M. and 11:50 P.M., respectively).

The **Lough Swilly Bus** (tel. 074/912-2863, or 028/7126-2017 from N.I. for the Foyle St. Station office, 4/day Mon.–Fri., 2 Sat., single/return from Derry £10/12.50) also serves Dunfanaghy on a route between Derry City and Gweedore. Ring for timetables.

Unfortunately there is no bike rental available in Dunfanaghy. For a taxi, ring **McBride Cabs** (tel. 074/913-6370, tel. 086/831-0482, or 086/601-0844).

Northeastern Donegal

LETTERKENNY

Between the ugly industrial sites, a lack of attractions, and the nightmarish traffic bottleneck, frankly Letterkenny (Leitir Ceanainn) is not worth lingering in. You'll surely pass through Donegal's largest town at some point, however, and if it's getting hungry out you might want to make a stop. Make a withdrawal at one of the ATMs on Main Street, which is said to be the longest in the country, before heading north into Inishowen.

A whole-foods store-cum-café, **Simple Simon's** (Oliver Plunkett St., just off Main St., tel. 074/912-2382, open 8 A.M.–5:30 P.M. Mon.–Sat., mains under €8) is a vegetarian's paradise, with an inventive and ever-changing menu of soups, sandwiches, and quiches using fresh produce from The Organic Centre in Rossinver (in County Leitrim), as well as a dizzying array of herbal teas.

Another good choice for lunch is **The Quiet Moment** (95 Lower Main St., tel. 074/912-7401, www.quietmoment.ie, open 8:30 A.M.–6 P.M. Mon.–Sat., open Sun. during festival times, mains under €10), an atmospheric tea-room with a specialty of humongous "doorstep sandwiches." There's B&B and self-catering accommodation available under the same ownership at 94-96 Upper Main Street (tel. 074/912-8382, €32 pp sharing).

Before leaving town, you might want to stop at the **tourist office** (1.5 km east of town on the N13, tel. 074/912-1160, www.ireland-northwest.ie, open 9 A.M.–5 P.M. Mon.–Sat., noon–3 P.M. Sun. June–Aug., 9 A.M.–5 P.M. Mon.–Fri. Sept.–May).

The **Lough Swilly Bus** (tel. 074/912-2863, or 028/7126-2017 from Northern Ireland for the Foyle St. Station office, 9/day Mon.–Sat., single/return from Derry £5/6.50) links Letterkenny with Derry City. If Donegal is the last leg of your trip, you can take a **Bus Éireann** (tel. 074/912-1309, 3–4/day Mon.–Sat., 2/day Sun.) express route from Letterkenny back to Dublin Airport. The bus station is at the Port Road roundabout east of Main Street.

◖ GRIANÁN OF AILEÁCH

A superbly situated Iron Age ring fort 29 kilometers east of Letterkenny, Grianán of Aileách (Grianán Ailigh, "The Solarium of Aileách" or "Fortress of the Sun," signposted off the N13 and a further 2 km uphill, always open, free admission), served as the royal seat of the northern O'Neills from the 5th century, though the site certainly held pre-Celtic significance. In 1101 the fort was sacked by the king of Munster, Muirchertach O'Brien, as retribution for the destruction of his own seat in Clare. Legend has it that he ordered each of his men to pull a stone from the fort and carry it away. The structure was improperly restored by an amateur archaeologist in the 1870s, and no drawings of the original structure remain. The fort has three walls; the innermost is four meters thick and contains

Grianán of Aileách boasts a panoramic view of five counties.

chambers of unknown function. The enclosure, 23.5 meters in diameter, will bring to mind a classical amphitheater. What really sends this ruin into the breathtaking category is the panoramic view over five counties as well as Loughs Foyle and Swilly; it's well worth seeking out. Though there are "official" opening hours posted at the gate, it's possible to view the site at any time.

History buffs should stop by the **visitors center** (Burt, on the N13 near the site turnoff, tel. 074/936-8512, www.griananailigh.ie, open 10 A.M.–6 P.M. daily June–Aug., noon–6 P.M. daily Sept.–May, admission €5) before visiting the site. The admission price includes a shuttle bus up to the site.

Those without wheels are best off doing the Grianán as a day trip out of Derry City. You can take the **Bus Éireann** (tel. 074/912-1160) Derry–Letterkenny route (#64, 6/day Mon.–Sat., 3/day Sun., 7 return buses/day Mon.–Sat., 3/day Sun.) and ask to be dropped off at the visitors center; then it's another couple kilometers uphill by foot.

THE INISHOWEN PENINSULA

Ask a well-traveled Irishman what his favorite part of Donegal is, and he may very well answer Inishowen. Tourism seems like even less of a priority here, and though there may be a shortage of accommodations and other amenities, you'll be too intoxicated by the view to care. The road up the western side of the peninsula, the R238, is sparsely populated and very dramatic; narrow roads wind through pristine hills and mountains (Slieve Snaght is Inishowen's highest at 615 meters) swathed in heather and evergreens. Follow signs for the "Inis Eoghain 100," a 100-mile scenic drive around the peninsula. For more info, check out **Inishowen On-Line** (www.inishowenon-line.com).

Be sure to withdraw funds before leaving Derry or Letterkenny.

◖ Malin and Malin Head

There's not much going on in Malin (Málainn), 14 kilometers south of Malin Head on the R242, but you should definitely stock up on gas and groceries at the village shop before going any farther.

Ireland's most northerly point, Malin Head is marred a bit by a couple of ugly concrete WWII lookout posts (as well as an older tower dating from the Napoleonic period). A steep rocky path from the car park leads down to a blowhole with the hyperbolic name of **Hell's Hole.** The eight-kilometer Malin Head loop starts at the end of the R242, just north of the hostels, and it's perfect for walking or cycling. If you take the loop clockwise, you'll see the turnoff for the **Wee House of Malin,** a hermit's cave turned Marian shrine (it's more a niche than a cave, so the hermit thing is probably just a legend). Nearby are the ruins of a church used during Penal times.

The immaculate IHH ◖ **Malin Head Hostel** (on the R242, tel. 074/937-0309, http://homepage.eircom.net/~malinheadhostel, open Mar.–Dec., dorms €13, twins €18 pp, s €24, sheet rental €2, bike rental €10/day) is a delight, with an open fire in the homey sitting room, homegrown organic vegetables and farm

DONEGAL

eggs for sale in the kitchen, a cozy loft for reading and other quiet pursuits, and a refreshingly anti-technology attitude (guests are discouraged from using cell phones, radios, or laptops in common areas). Owner Mary is also a licensed reflexologist, and you can book a reflexology (€35) or aromatherapy (€45) session in high season. If this one's fully booked, try the also-good IHH **Sandrock Holiday Hostel** (Malin Head, signposted off the R242, tel. 077/937-0289, sandrockhostel@eircom.net, dorms €10, sheet rental €1.25), overlooking a small slipway on Trawbreaga Bay a bit farther up the road.

Now affiliated with Bus Éireann, the **Lough Swilly Bus** (tel. 074/912-2863, or tel. 028/7126-2017 from N.I. for the Foyle St. Station office, 2/day Mon., Wed., Fri., 3/day Sat., single/return from Derry to Malin £6/8) links Derry City with Malin and other towns on the peninsula.

Culdaff

With its sandy beach and excellent pub-cum-guesthouse, quiet Culdaff (Cúil Dabhcha, "Back of the Sandhills") makes a good base for exploring the peninsula. No visit to Inishowen is complete without at least one night at (**McGrory's** (town center, tel. 077/937-9104, www.mcgrorys.ie, €55–60 pp, s €70–75, food served 12:30–8:30 P.M. daily, restaurant mains €15–22, bar meals €8–17), an all-in-one complex that admirably manages to feel completely untouristy—perhaps because it's so beloved by locals. McGrory's is best-known as Ireland's most northerly concert venue (having hosted Altan, Sharon Shannon, Damien Dempsey, Ron Sexsmith, and Peter Green from Fleetwood Mac), but it also has a guesthouse and a wonderfully cozy pub with friendly waitstaff and sophisticated (not to mention thoroughly delicious) bar food. There's traditional music here on Tuesday and Friday nights all

year starting at 10 P.M., and it's worth timing your visit to catch one of these sessions. And of course, there's something going on in Mac's Backroom Bar several nights a week all year long, every night in high season.

Culdaff is 6.5 kilometers east of Malin on the R238, and there is no public transport. Should you need a taxi, ring **Carn Cabs** (tel. 077/937-4580).

Doagh

Opened in 1997 and added to continually since then, the **Doagh Famine Village** (Doagh, on the R238, tel. 074/937-8078 or 086/846-4749, www.doaghvisitorscenter.com, open 10 A.M.–5:30 P.M. daily Easter–Oct., admission €6) is more than a Great Famine museum. This interpretive center offers a series of cottages and other buildings featuring scenes from everyday rural life in the 19th century, from a wake scene in one cottage to a "sod house" used as a refuge for unwed mothers. There's also a "Mass rock," where Catholics would have gathered to meet their priest for Mass during Penal times (this particular Mass rock has been labeled "interdenominational," which doesn't make much sense—but such is the legacy of political correctness). The center makes an admirable effort to connect the 19th-century tragedy in Ireland with the ongoing problem of starvation worldwide. "If you can walk up to your fridge and find food in it," the center says, "if you have clothes on your back, a roof over your head and a bed to sleep on, then you are richer than 75 percent of the world's population today." They're aiming to provide much more than a history lesson here—and they succeed. The admission price includes a guided tour and a cup of tea afterward.

Doagh is 21 kilometers west of Culdaff on the R238 and is on the Lough Swilly bus route (tel. 074/912-2863 for timetable).

BELFAST, ANTRIM, AND DERRY

Counties Antrim (Aontroim, "Solitary Farm") and Derry (Doire, "Oak Grove") have most of Northern Ireland's biggest tourist attractions, including Giant's Causeway, the Carrick-a-Rede rope bridge, the Downhill Estate, the early 17th-century Derry City walls, and the Nine Glens. Antrim in particular is renowned for its coast and glens; its beauty has often been likened to that of County Kerry, and like Kerry it is by far the most visited of Northern Ireland's six counties.

The political history of these counties is as infamous as their pretty landscapes, and during the Troubles era (the summer of 1969 through the 1994 ceasefire) their capital cities were hotbeds of guerrilla fighting between republican and loyalist paramilitary groups. Up North, Belfast in particular, is tradition-ally where looking like a tourist is a good thing. That's not to say early-21st-century Belfast still deserves its reputation for sectarian violence; the shadow of the Troubles still looms in the city's working-class neighborhoods (chiefly in the form of supposedly temporary "peace walls" erected during the Troubles to separate Catholic and Protestant neighborhoods), but unless you take a Black Taxi tour you won't notice much of it. Belfast is a truly cosmopolitan city, boasting some of the island's best pubs and eateries, and its crowded festival roster offers something for everyone at any time of year. You'll find Northern Ireland's recent tourism blitz isn't all (or even mostly) skillful spin-doctoring. Derry City has also geared itself for tourism in recent years, and ironically it's those reminders of the city's bloody history

© CAMILLE DEANGELIS

HIGHLIGHTS

◖ **Black Taxi Tour:** Providing an extended glimpse of working-class, sectarian Belfast and a running commentary on the city's political history, this two-hour excursion is a real eye-opener (page 430).

◖ **Layde Old Church:** This centuries-old graveyard and ivy-clad church ruin has a wonderful situation overlooking the North Channel, making it an ideal spot for some quiet reflection (page 440).

◖ **Carrick-a-Rede Rope Bridge:** Not for the faint-hearted, this 65-foot suspension bridge sways 80 feet above a sea gorge, still linking a once salmon-rich seastack to the mainland (page 445).

◖ **Dunluce Castle:** Famous for a tragedy in 1639 in which the castle kitchen dropped into the sea (taking many servants along with it), this stronghold was built precipitously on a basalt cliff, its stability compromised by the caves beneath (page 446).

◖ **Derry City Walls:** Built in the 17th century, these are Ireland's only intact city walls, and you can make the 1.25-mile circuit for neat views of both the old city and the Bogside neighborhood to the west, which features a series of often-poignant peace murals (page 449).

◖ **Downhill Estate:** The gutted ruin of Bishop Hervey's 18th-century manor is a profoundly unsettling sight, yet the neo-Grecian Mussenden Temple (which housed the bishop's library) is a lovely sight, perched on a cliff overlooking a pristine strand (page 457).

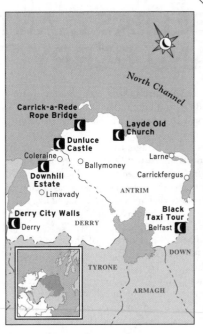

LOOK FOR ◖ TO FIND RECOMMENDED SIGHTS, ACTIVITIES, DINING, AND LODGING.

that are most attractive to visitors—the Bogside murals in particular, most of which are visible from the southwestern portion of the city walls. Derry's eateries and nightlife may not measure up to Belfast's, but its sights are arguably more affecting.

HISTORY

These counties are known as Protestant (or loyalist) strongholds, with origins in the widespread Plantation of Ulster, or recolonization, starting in the early 17th century. These lands were confiscated from the native Irish after the Flight of the Earls in 1607. Though loyal British soldiers and other subjects were given estates all over the island, more English settled in Antrim and "Londonderry" by virtue of simple geographical proximity. This is why the partition of Ireland in 1921 would reserve for Britain the six counties closest to it.

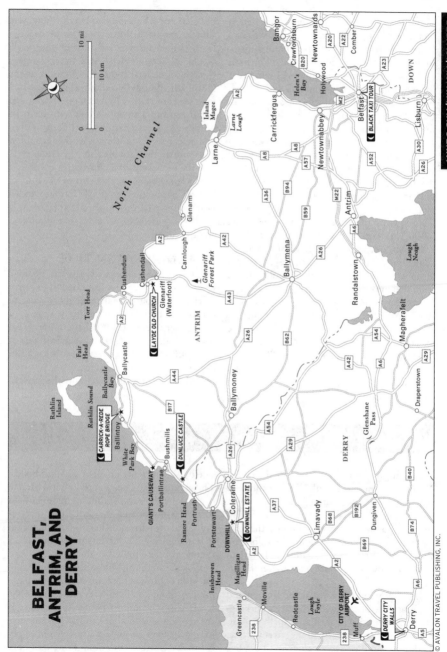

BELFAST, ANTRIM, AND DERRY

North Channel

Rathlin Island

Rathlin Sound

Ballycastle Bay

Fair Head

Torr Head

Island Magee

Larne Lough

Lough Neagh

0   10 mi
0   10 km

CARRICK-A-REDE ROPE BRIDGE
GIANT'S CAUSEWAY
DUNLUCE CASTLE
DOWNHILL ESTATE
LAYDE OLD CHURCH
BLACK TAXI TOUR
DERRY CITY WALLS

Inishowen Head
Greencastle
Moville
Redcastle
Magilligan Head
Muff
Derry
CITY OF DERRY AIRPORT
Lough Foyle

White Park Bay
Ballintoy
Ramore Head
Portrush
Portstewart
DOWNHILL
Portballintrae
Bushmills
Coleraine
Limavady
Dungiven

Ballycastle
Cushendun
Cushendall
Glenariff (Waterfoot)
Glenariff Forest Park
Carnlough
Glenarm

Larne
Carrickfergus
Newtownabbey
Antrim
Ballymena
Randalstown
Magherafelt
Draperstown
Glenshane Pass

Ballymoney

ANTRIM
DERRY
DOWN

Belfast
Lisburn
Comber
Newtownards
Bangor
Crawfordsburn
Helen's Bay
Holywood

A2
A22
A20
B20
A23
A2
A8
A6
A57
A52
A30
A26
M2
A36
B94
B59
M22
A6
A54
A29
A42
A6
B62
A26
A43
A42
A2
A44
B17
A26
A54
A29
A37
B68
B192
B40
B74
B69
A6
A5
238
236
A2

© AVALON TRAVEL PUBLISHING, INC.

In the 19th century both Derry and Belfast had flourishing linen industries (and it's said Northern Irish factories provided uniforms for both sides on the American Civil War); the cities were also common points of departure for many emigrants to America and Australia. The *Titanic* was built in the shipyards of Belfast, a connection the tourist board milks for all it's worth.

Nearly three centuries separate the two most vivid chapters in the history of Derry City, and both feature the number 14. During the 105-day Jacobite siege, which began on December 7, 1688, 14 "apprentice boys" had the presence of mind to swipe the keys to lock the Ferryquay Gate against the invaders. The siege killed 7,000 residents and decimated everything within the city walls (apart from St. Columb's Cathedral), but the loyalists managed to hold on to what was known as the "Maiden City" from then on.

And on January 30, 1972, "Bloody Sunday," 14 Catholic demonstrators, among the 20,000 protesting the then-commonplace practice of internment without trial, were massacred by British troops, the 1st Battalion of the Parachute Regiment, to be exact (13 people were killed on Bloody Sunday; the 14th victim, John Johnston, died of his injuries four and a half months later). Many were shot in the back. More than three decades later, this chapter is still not closed; none of the soldiers involved have been charged, though an official inquiry is ongoing at the Guildhall. Bloody Sunday was one day in a long series of clashes between republican and loyalist groups, an epoch rife with terrorist bombings, assassinations, police brutality, and street-fighting known as the Troubles. For more on the Troubles, see the *History* section in the *Background* chapter.

In a lesser-known and far happier chapter of Derry County history, Amelia Earhart landed near Culmore (at the Donegal border) on May 21, 1932, thus completing her first solo transatlantic flight.

PLANNING YOUR TIME

The Glens and Causeway Coast can be done in a rigorous one-day arc from Belfast to Derry or vice versa, but it makes far more sense to stop over in Ballycastle or Ballintoy if you want to experience everything on the route. (Two days will suffice, even if you plan to linger at the Giant's Causeway.) Derry warrants a full day's sightseeing, Belfast at least two days. You should spend three nights or more there just to sample all the wonderful eateries!

Belfast

Welcome to the new Belfast (Beál Feirste, "Mouth of the Sandbank"), the capital of Northern Ireland, a former industrial town with a population on the rise at 275,000. Whether you want chic or traditional, the city's vibrant pubs and gourmet restaurants alone are worth lingering for a week, and you'll have to go out of your way to observe any reminders of the Troubles.

It's important to note that the friction and segregation are exclusive to the city's working-class communities in west and north Belfast, the same locations of most of the street warfare. Catholics and Protestants, then and now, live side by side in more affluent neighborhoods. The working-class neighborhoods are back to back, along the parallel thoroughfares of Falls Road (Catholic) and Shankill Road (Protestant), and the barricades between them, meant to be temporary, date to the summer of 1969—the start of the Troubles.

Violence since the 1994 ceasefire has been in the form of isolated flare-ups between the paramilitary groups on both sides (the IRA and the UVF, Ulster Volunteer Force); today, though the tension is sometimes subtly but unnervingly palpable—in, say, the woodpiles in empty car parks, collected by young Protestant boys in anticipation of the marching season celebrations, which mark William of Orange's victory over the Catholic James II at the Battle of the Boyne—Belfast is a perfectly safe city, every bit as cosmopolitan and fast-paced as Dublin.

Belfast is situated on the River Lagan at the mouth of an eponymous Lough, which is a bay rather than a lake. The city center is marked by Donegall Square, which encloses the imposing Edwardian Belfast City Hall; north of here, along Royal Avenue, you'll find the prime shopping district, as well as the Cathedral Quarter around St. Anne's (Anglican), which has emerged (through copious redevelopment funding) as Belfast's "Left Bank." Great Victoria Street, home to the infamous Hotel Europa (bombed 40 times in all) is the start of the Golden Mile, a thoroughfare with an exaggerated moniker lined with some of Belfast's best pubs and eateries; the street changes names to Bradbury Place, Shaftesbury Square, and Botanic Avenue, where you'll find Queen's University and the lovely Botanic Gardens. On Donegall Quay, in the northeastern section, is the Lagan Lookout, a weir-cum-pedestrian bridge that's another product of multimillion-pound urban renewal. Sightseeing boats depart here.

SIGHTS

Belfast offers enough attractions to keep you busy for two full days. If this is a fly-by-night visit, at least take the Black Taxi tour for a crash introduction to the city's sectarian politics. You'll learn more in two hours than you might in a semester-long university course.

City Center

If you've got more time, take a guided 45-minute tour of the magnificent **Belfast City Hall** (Donegall Sq., tel. 028/9027-0456, tours depart 11 A.M., 2 P.M., and 3 P.M. weekdays and 2 P.M. and 3 P.M. Sat. Feb.–Dec., free admission) with its 173-foot copper dome, built between 1898 and 1906. Admire the classical Renaissance architectural details during your introduction to Belfast civic history. Even if you don't have time for a tour, pop in to admire

the lobby and see what's posted in the "What's On" room near the entrance.

Across the street is the **Linen Hall Library** (17 Donegall Sq. N., entrance on Fountain St., tel. 028/9032-1707, www.linenhall.com, open 9:30 A.M.–5:30 P.M. weekdays, 9:30 A.M.–4 P.M. Sun.), the city's oldest, which has a substantial collection of art, political posters, and photographs on the Troubles and the sectarian conflict in general. Linen Hall makes a point of advertising itself as a neutral space in which to ponder the collection. Get a free visitor's pass on your way in.

The great thing about the cavernous, Anglican **St. Anne's Cathedral** (Donegall St., tel. 028/9032-8332, www.belfastcathedral.org, free admission, but £2 donation appreciated) is the warm reception you receive at the door. Volunteers jump to answer any questions you might have—and the answers might turn into a minitour. This Hiberno-Romanesque edifice was built at the turn of the 20th century and features gorgeous gold ceiling mosaics in its Chapel of the Holy Spirit and Baptistery on either side of the entrance. On Sunday at 11 A.M. and 3:30 P.M. (excluding July and Aug.) you can hear the Cathedral Choir sing.

The purpose of the 143-foot **Albert Memorial Clock** on Queens Square, built in 1865, is pretty self-explanatory. It stands four feet off center, so locals like to call it Belfast's own Leaning Tower.

The Golden Mile

Fresh off a £9 million renovation, the late-19th-century **Grand Opera House** (Great Victoria St., tel. 028/9024-0411, www.goh.co.uk) has more than opera on the calendar: Stop in anytime for a drink at the bar and take a look at what's on in the exhibition space.

Unfortunately, the **Ulster Museum** (tel. 028/9038-3000, www.ulstermuseum.org.uk, open 10 A.M.–5 P.M. weekdays, 1–5 P.M. Sat., 2–5 P.M. Sun., free admission) closed in October 2006 for a major renovation, expected to last two and a half years. At least the adjacent **Botanic Gardens** (entrances at Stranmillis Rd. and Botanic Ave., open daily until

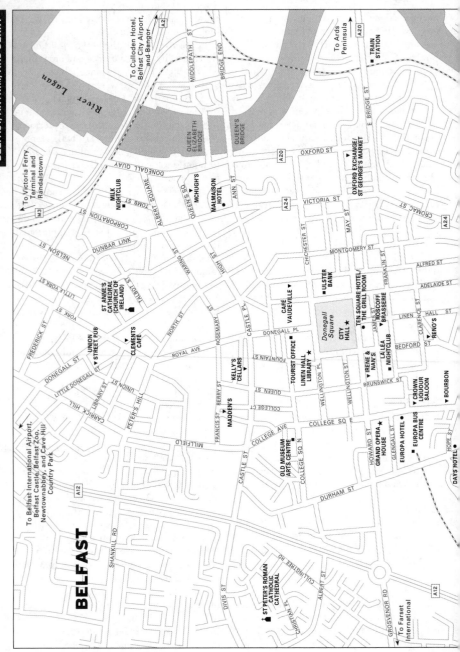

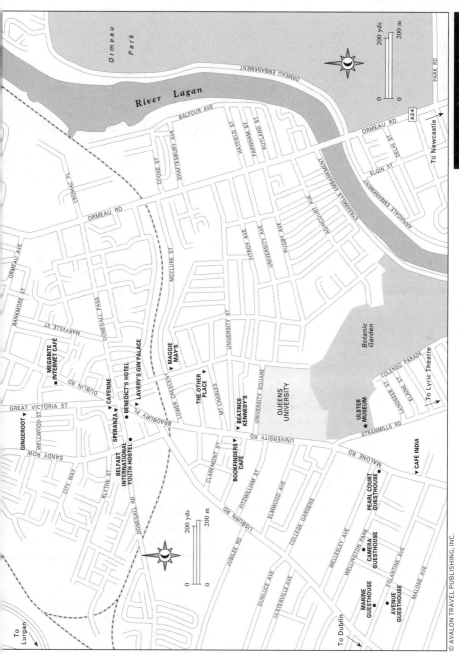

© AVALON TRAVEL PUBLISHING, INC.

dusk) are still open. The restored **Palm House** (tel. 028/9032-4902, open 10 A.M.–noon and 1–5 P.M. weekdays, 1–5 P.M. weekends, shorter hours in winter, free admission) dates to 1852, and the **Tropical Ravine** features a fishpond with mutant waterlilies (and enough steam to unwrinkle your button-down shirt). These delightful gardens, perfect for a long stroll or jog, are basically the backyard of **Queen's University.** The original college, the ornate English-Gothic **Lanyon Building,** is named for its architect, Charles Lanyon, and was opened in 1849. The Lanyon Building houses the **Naughton Gallery** (tel. 028/9097-3580, www.naughtongallery.org, open 11 A.M.–4 P.M. Mon.–Sat., free admission), which showcases local and international artists in an exciting variety of media.

West and North Belfast

It's older (1860s) than St. Anne's, and with its neo-Gothic twin spires it's just as grand, but the interior of **St. Peter's Cathedral** (St. Peter's Sq., off Falls Rd., tel. 028/9032-7573, www.stpeterscathedralbelfast.com) isn't of much interest for non-Catholics. The cathedral is a 15-minute walk west of the city center in the Falls Road neighborhood.

Brian de Breffny offers a few colorful words to describe the 19th-century **Belfast Castle** (off Antrim Rd./A6, 3.5 mi/5.6 km north of the city, tel. 028/9077-6925, www.belfastcastle.co.uk, reception open 9 A.M.–10 P.M. Mon.–Sat. and 9 A.M.–6 P.M. Sun., private rooms open 9 A.M.– 1 P.M. daily by arrangement, free admission), overlooking Belfast Lough, and the attitudes that shaped its design: "Intellectual and aesthetic values were subordinated to a romantic nostalgia, producing a showy mixture of gables and turrets with strangely contrived proportions…massive six-storey tower, crow-stepped gables, conical turrets and restless skyline…the porch is an uneasy combination of Doric columns and bogus-looking strapwork; two gaunt bow-windows sit spuriously on curved courses of corbelling heavily carved with foliage and flowers." Unsurprising given this description, the refurbished sandstone castle is now one of

the city's most popular wedding venues, though you can visit as part of a trip to Cave Hill Country Park. Downstairs, **The Cellar** restaurant (open for lunch and snacks 11 A.M.–5 P.M. daily, 5–9 P.M. Tues.–Sun., lunch £7–13, dinner £10– 15), brimming with Victorian atmosphere, is a fine choice for lunch.

The **Belfast Zoo** (off the Antrim road/A6 4 mi/6.4 km north of the city, tel. 028/9077-6277, www.belfastzoo.co.uk, open 10 A.M.– 5 P.M. daily Apr.–Sept. and 10 A.M.–2:30 P.M. daily Oct.–Mar., admission £7.50, £6 Oct.– Mar.) houses more than 160 exotic and endangered species.

◖ Black Taxi Tour

Most folks come to Belfast without a solid grasp of the Northern Ireland conflict, but a Black Taxi tour will remedy that in two hours or less. The black taxi dates to the Troubles era in the late 1960s, when renegades on both sides would hijack buses to use as barricades in street fights. So law-abiding citizens needed a safer and more reliable means of transport.

An experienced and articulate driver will take you to the murals and memorial gardens in the **Falls Road** and **Shankill Road** neighborhoods, home to Belfast's Catholic and Protestant working class populations, respectively, and provide you with a thorough background of the Troubles. Frankly, some of the murals are downright frightening—the loyalist ones invariably feature ski-masked men with machine guns, and not even skillfully rendered at that—but you can't say you've truly seen Belfast without them. At the end your driver will take you to a "peace wall" where tourists have been scribbling pacifist messages for years.

There isn't one "Black Taxi" company; there are several with very similar names, and more than one claims to be the "original." Try **Black Taxi Tours** (tel. 028/9064-2264 or 078/1003-3831, freephone tel. 0800/052-3914, www.belfasttours.com) or the **Original Black Taxi Tours** (tel. 028/9058-6996 or 077/5156-5359, www.tobbtt.com). The tour lasts 1.5–2 hours and generally costs £7–8 per person (for a 3–6-person tour; 1–2 people might be £10 per person or more). If you're traveling alone, ask at your accommodation to see if you can join in with a group. Or just ask one of the drivers at the taxi rank outside the Europa Hotel.

Independent taxi operators include **Ian's Cab Service** (tel. 078/5094-4223 or 028/9071-4168 at night), from whom you can expect the same frank but unbiased info in easy-to-understand terms.

Other Tours

Belfast Safaris (tel. 028/9022-2925, www.belfastsafaris.com, ticket £8) does themed walking tours like "Scholars, Skills & Skulls" and "Pawn Shops & Public Baths" between April and September. Reservations are required, and you can book your place at the tourist office (where many of the tours depart).

ENTERTAINMENT

Quaint period watering holes abound in Belfast, and the best way to sample them all is on the **Bailey's Historical Pub Tour** (tel. 028/9268-3665, www.belfastpubtours.com, tickets £6, includes free Bailey's shot). The tour commences from the upstairs dining room at the king of them all, the **Crown Liquor Saloon** (46 Great Victoria St., tel. 028/9027-9901, www.crownbar.com), on Thursday at 7 P.M. and Saturday at 4 P.M. Book ahead at the tourist office. Another old-school, über-British grog-house is **Lavery's Gin Palace** (12-16 Bradbury Pl., tel. 028/9087-1106), run by the same family for more than 100 years. There's live music nightly—reggae, rock, and blues—in two of the Lavery's four bars.

You'll find Belfast's best traditional music sessions at **Madden's** (74 Berry St., tel. 028/9024-4114) on Monday, Friday, and Saturday nights; a minute's walk away is the crustier **Kelly's Cellars** (30 Bank St., tel. 028/9024-6058, www.kellyscellars.com), established in 1720, with sessions on Saturday afternoons. There's also a Thursday-night session at **McHugh's** (29-31 Queen's St., tel. 028/9050-9990, www.mchughsbar.com) and live bands in the basement bar on Friday and Saturday.

FESTIVALS AND EVENTS IN BELFAST

Unfortunately, the revelry during the annual **St. Patrick's Carnival** has resulted in sectarian brawls in the past, prompting the city council's decision (pending appeal) not to fund the event in the future. The week after Paddy's Day brings the **Belfast Film Festival** (tel. 028/9032-5913, www.belfastfilmfestival.org).

The **Belfast Marathon** (tel. 028/9032-0202, www.belfastcitymarathon.com) takes place in early May – the race begins from Belfast City Hall at 9 A.M. You don't have to settle for watching, though; there's a recreational run-walk as well.

Between May and September, **Summer in the City** (www.belfastcity.gov.uk/events) offers an eclectic calendar of entertainments: classical concerts, guided tours, and art exhibitions. You'll find more art, street theater, and concerts on offer through the **Cathedral Quarter Arts Festival** (tel. 028/9023-2403, www.cqaf.com) in late April and early May, and the **Féile an Phobail** (tel. 028/9031-3440, www.feilebelfast.com) in August. In late October and early November, the **Belfast Festival at Queen's** (tel. 028/9097-1034, www.belfastfestival.com) also offers concerts, plays, and art exhibitions at venues all over the city. The **Halloween Carnival** is a five-day event featuring ghost tours and fireworks along with a parade on the 31st.

The **Ulster Orchestra** (Elmwood Hall at Queen's, 89 University Rd., tel. 028/9066-8798, www.ulster-orchestra.org.co.uk, tickets £8–24) hosts Europe's most distinguished conductors and guest performers. Several concerts are held at Waterfront Hall (2 Lanyon Pl., tel. 028/9033-4455).

It's not all *Figaro* at the **Grand Opera House** (2-4 Great Victoria St., tel. 028/9024-1919, www.goh.co.uk, tickets £5–30). There are

© CAMILLE DEANGELIS

The Crown Liquor Saloon is the best known of Belfast's Victorian gin palaces.

plenty of American-style musicals and cheesy children's pantomimes along with traditional opera and ballet. For something more experimental, check out the bill at the **Old Museum Arts Centre** (7 College Sq. N., tel. 028/9023-3332, www.oldmuseumartscentre.org, tickets £6–10). There's always something out of the ordinary going on here, be it an interactive play, indie vocalists reinterpreting work from other genres, or off-beat visual art exhibitions.

Northern Ireland's only full-time professional theater, the **Lyric Theatre** (55 Ridgeway St., tel. 028/9038-1081, www.lyrictheatre.co.uk, tickets £10–17) stages both specially commissioned and classic works from an international list of playwrights.

Fueled by a burgeoning Queen's University enrollment, Belfast's club scene is hopping. The city's two best nightclubs are **Milk** (10 Tomb St., tel. 028/9027-8876, www.club-milk.com, open nightly, cover £3–10, ladies free Wed.), in an old brick warehouse admirably converted into a chic dance floor and downstairs lounge where you're guaranteed not to hear a single top 40 track. More upscale is **La Lea** (43 Franklin St., tel. 028/9023-0200, www.lalea.com, closed Sun.–Tues., cover £3–7), with a classy design that aspires to the title of Ireland's poshest nightclub (were there such an award). Fashionistas will find it worth enduring the bouncer's discerning gaze for the elegant lounge rooms inside. Clubs are generally open 9 P.M.–3 A.M. and don't admit anyone after 1 A.M.

SHOPPING

As the name suggests, the **Spires Shopping Centre** (Wellington St., tel. 028/9032-2284) is in a converted, ornate early-20th-century church, and while it looks amazing from the street, the shops inside are mostly disappointing. One exception is **Fairtrade in-Spires** (tel. 028/9024-3056, www.fairtrade-inspires.org.uk), which rightly bills itself as an "Aladdin's cave" of exotic gifts, all fairly traded from the developing world: wood carvings, silver jewelry, greeting cards, handwoven cotton garments, and the like.

There are several other shopping centers in Belfast, but most of them offer nothing but the usual chain stores. Check out the small-ish **Donegall Arcade** (5-7 Castle Pl., www.donegallarcade.com), which offers an even mix of chains and independent shops. For chic boutiques, galleries, and home-goods shops, the street to walk is Lisburn Road (forking off Bradbury Place on the southwestern part of town).

Fine yet affordable artwork can be tricky to find, especially in the city. Take a look around the **Belfast Print Workshop and Gallery** (Cotton Ct., 30-42 Waring St., tel. 028/9023-1323, www.belfastprintworkshop.org.uk), which features the work of local artists—be it silkscreen, lithograph, etching, or woodcut.

For Irish-language books (for all levels) and locally made T-shirts, glassware, pottery, and jewelry, stop by the **An Ceathrú Póilí Book & Craft Shop** (216 Falls Rd., tel. 028/9032-2811, www.an4poili.com), part of a larger Irish cultural center, Cultúrlann Mc Adam Ó Fiaich (www.culturlann.ie).

GAY BELFAST

Northern Ireland's capital isn't quite as gay-friendly as Dublin is, but you'll find several fun nightspots in the Cathedral Quarter. The city's primary resource center is **Rainbow Project N.I.** (33 Church St., tel. 028/9031-9030, open 10 A.M.-4 P.M. Mon.-Fri.).

No trip to the Belfast is complete without a night at **The Kremlin** (96 Donegall St., tel. 028/9031-6061, www.kremlin-belfast. com, open 9 P.M.-2 A.M. Tues., 9 P.M.-3 A.M. Thurs.-Sun.), the biggest (not to mention kitschiest) gay nightclub in Northern Ireland. The theme is all things Soviet, as you'd expect from the name – all but the music, which is mostly techno. Another option is Monday night, "Forbidden Fruit" at **Milk** (10 Tomb St., tel. 028/9027-8876, www.clubmilk.com, open 9 P.M.-3 A.M.). Both clubs are good bets if you enjoy the company of drag queens. Or if you're just looking for a pint and a chat, try **The Nest** (22-28 Skipper St., tel. 028/9024-5558), the city's oldest gay bar.

Also in the Cathedral Quarter, **Union Street** (8-14 Union St., tel. 028/9031-6060) is a gay-friendly gastro-pub definitely worth checking out.

The island's oldest continually open marketplace is the delightful 230-stall **St. George's Market** (May St. and Oxford St., tel. 028/9043-5704), always open Friday and Saturday, and sometimes other days for special craft fairs, art exhibitions, and concerts. Along with 23 seafood stalls (it's also the largest fish-market), you'll find plenty more ready-to-eat nibbles and the occasional stall of gifty things. The gourmet **Oxford Exchange** restaurant is just upstairs.

SPORTS AND RECREATION

For a bit of fresh air, there's no better place to frolic than **Cave Hill Country Park** (3.1 mi/5 km north of the city center off the A6, tel. 028/9077-6925, open dawn–dusk daily), with marked trails ranging from short and easy strolls to a strenuous walk up Cave Hill (1,182 feet/360 meters). The **visitors center** at Belfast Castle can provide you with a free map. To get there, take Metro bus #1 from Donegall Place (at least 4/hour, fare £1).

Boat trips on the River Lagan are a popular excursion. The **Lagan Boat Company** (tel. 028/9033-0844 or 077/1891-0423, www.lag-anboatcompany.com, 2–3 trips daily, 75-minute trip £7) departs Donegall Quay beside the Lagan Lookout. A *Titanic*-themed tour takes place three times a day on weekends May–September. Another, more adventurous option is **Belfast Boat Charters** (tel. 077/0692-4123, www.belfastboatcharters.co.uk, departure times vary, 5-hour tour including lunch and drinks £95), also departing the Lagan Lookout. Zoom up Belfast Lough in a Stormforce Rigid Inflatable! You can book any of these tours through the tourist office.

Golfers are well served with the 300-acre, 27-hole **Malone Golf Club** (240 Upper Malone Rd., Dunmurry, 5 mi/8 km south of the city off the M1, tel. 028/9061-2758, www.malone-golfclub.co.uk), a championship course, and the **Royal Belfast Golf Club** (Station Rd., Craigavad, 7 mi/11 km north of the city on the A2/Bangor road, tel. 028/9042-8165, www. royalbelfast.com), established in 1881.

Here on a Sunday afternoon? Catch a **hurling** or **Gaelic football** match at **Casement Park** (Andersontown, West Belfast, tel. 028/9038-3815, www.gaa.ie).

ACCOMMODATIONS
Hostels

Belfast has plenty of borderline-sketchy hostels, many of which advertise the cheapest beds in town—a classic case of getting what you pay for. Unfortunately, even the respectable places don't fall into the "excellent" category. The HINI **Belfast International Youth Hostel** (22-32 Donegall Rd., just off Shaftesbury Sq., tel. 028/9032-4733, www.hini.org.uk, dorms £8–12) comes the closest—clean dorms and above-par facilities all around—but it's huge and can be rather noisy. A good budget option—for friends traveling together, anyway—is **Farset International** (466 Springfield Rd., tel. 028/9089-9833, www.farsetinternational.co.uk, £24 pp, s £34). Located beside a wildfowl reserve, Farset offers 38 spotless ensuite twin rooms with television and hostess tray, and a full breakfast in the rather antiseptic restaurant is included in the room price. (There's also a self-catering kitchen.)

Bed-and-Breakfasts

For B&B, try a tidy brick townhouse just south of the university—it's a quiet, tree-lined neighborhood with ample on-street parking if you need it, and you're only a couple minutes' walk from the Botanic Gardens. One of the best is the ◖ **Avenue Guesthouse** (23 Eglantine Ave., tel. 028/9066-5904, www.avenueguesthouse.com, £25 pp, s £40), which offers free Internet access (wireless as well), DVD players and flatscreen TVs in all four rooms, and a gorgeous little garden out back. An equally great value is the **Pearl Court Guesthouse** (11 Malone Rd., tel. 028/9066-6145, www.pearlcourt.com, £25–30 pp, s £28–40, ask about weekend discounts), which also offers free Internet (wireless as well as a terminal for those traveling sans laptop). The 11 rooms are spacious.

Other B&B options include the three-star **Marine Guesthouse** (30 Eglantine Ave., tel. 028/9066-2828, www.marineguesthouse3star.com, £25–28 pp, s £40) and the **Camera Guesthouse** (44 Wellington Park, tel. 028/9066-0026, camera_gh@hotmail.com, £28–32 pp, s £34–47, ask about weekend discounts) in the same quiet, shady tree-lined neighborhood.

Hotels

City hotel room rates generally do not include breakfast. It may be an impersonal chain, but the **Days Hotel** (40 Hope St., tel. 028/9024-2494, www.dayshotelbelfast.co.uk, rooms £65–75) offers wireless Internet, laundry service, free parking, a central-but-not-too-central location, and weekend discounts.

The three-star **Benedict's** (7-21 Bradbury Pl., Shaftesbury Sq., tel. 028/9059-1999, www.benedictshotel.co.uk, standard/executive £35/40 pp, s £60/80) boasts a great location on the Golden Mile, luxurious bedroom fittings, wireless Internet, and an atmospheric neo-Gothic bar and restaurant, converted from an old church, where you can often catch a rock concert at the weekend. This is definitely a hotel for those wanting to sample the Belfast nightlife; early-risers, stay elsewhere.

The newest hotel in town is the four-star, beyond-swanky **Ten Square** (10 Donegall Sq. S., tel. 028/9024-1001, www.tensquare.co.uk, rooms £165–210, suites £250), in a former bank building. You'll find all the trimmings here (wireless Internet, fancy toiletries and bathrobes, lush linen sheets on king-size beds, in-room safes, and wet-bars), and there's top-notch pub grub downstairs at The Grill. Two things to note: Breakfast is included in the rate, and the weekend rate is higher than midweek.

Another four-star establishment is the Italianate **Malmaison Hotel** (34-38 Victoria St., tel. 028/9022-0200, www.malmaison.com, midweek/weekend room rate £99/135), with über-chic, individually designed rooms featuring wireless Internet, plasma television and DVD, and a smallish gymnasium. Check out the website for a sweet meal/room/Ulster Orchestra package; a three-course dinner at the Brasserie restaurant, concert ticket, and B&B will run you £120 per person. Two caveats: Reception can be a bit spotty, and there's no parking available.

The four-star **Europa Hotel** (Great Victoria St., tel. 028/9027-1066, www.hastingshotels.com, midweek/weekend £65/45, s £90/70, breakfast not included) has the unfortunate distinction of being the most bombed hotel on the planet. Those days are long since past, thankfully, and this business-class hotel is even more a Belfast institution than it ever was. There's a special orchestra combo rate here, too: a three-course dinner, Ulster Orchestra concert ticket, and one night's accommodation is only £75 per person. Another Hastings company establishment is the five-star **Culloden Hotel** (Bangor Rd., 5 mi/8 km east of the city, tel. 028/9042-1066, www.hastingshotels.com, rooms £210–230, suites £350–600, s £170–190), with a motto of "built for a bishop, fit for a king." The location overlooking Belfast Lough is truly superb, as are the facilities: a deluxe spa and fitness suite with pool, steam room, Jacuzzi, sauna, and gym, and comfortable rooms (more homey than chic) appointed with fruit baskets and bathrobes. Breakfast is an additional £14–18. The same combo rate (dinner, concert, and room) will run you £95 per person sharing.

FOOD

Belfast offers loads of upscale restaurants and gastro-pubs, many of which will give you a free glass of wine or a discount on your food bill if you're headed to the Ulster Orchestra or Grand Opera House after your meal.

Cafés

There are comparatively few hip or comfy cafés; the university neighborhood is your best bet if you're just looking for a cup of coffee and a place to chill. Beloved student haunts include the musty secondhand **Bookfinders Café** (47 University Rd., tel. 028/9032-8269, open 10 A.M.–5:30 P.M. Mon.–Sat., mains £2–4); **Maggie May's** (50 Botanic Ave., tel. 028/9032-2662, open 8 A.M.–10:30 P.M. Mon.–Sat., 10 A.M.–10:30 P.M. Sun., mains £3–5), famous for its wall murals and huge fried breakfasts; and the **Other Place** (79 Botanic Ave., tel. 028/9020-7200, open 8 A.M.–11 P.M. daily, mains £6–7) for burgers, lasagna, and other hearty grub.

Hankering for a *good* cup of (Fair Trade) coffee? In the Cathedral Quarter, **Clements** (131-133 Royal Ave., tel. 028/9024-6016, open 8 A.M.–5 P.M. weekdays, 10 A.M.–5 P.M. Sat., lunches £3–5), with the likes of Portishead coming through the speakers, can boast cheerful, efficient staff (this may look like a British Starbucks, but there's table service) and an array of tasty gourmet sandwiches and desserts. There are six more branches throughout the city (including at Donegall Sq. W. and 66-68 Botanic Ave.).

Casual Restaurants

Student hangouts not your thing? The perfect place for afternoon tea and pastries, **Café Vaudeville** (25-39 Arthur St., tel. 028/9043-9160, www.cafevaudeville.com, food served noon–3 P.M. Mon.–Thurs. and Sat., noon–5 P.M. Fri., and 5–8 P.M. Mon.–Sat., lunches £7–9, dinners £8–12) boasts a truly stunning art nouveau interior with a champagne bar on the mezzanine level. The dessert and cocktail menus are as fantastic as the atmosphere.

Popular with Queen's students for its delicious, good-value gourmet pizzas and pastas, spacious ◖ **Speranza** (16-19 Shaftesbury Sq., tel. 028/9023-0213, www.thinkitalian.co.uk, open 5–11:30 P.M. Mon.–Sat., 3–10 P.M. Sun., mains £6–16) has a relaxed ambience featuring great pop/rock tunes on the stereo that you may not have heard in a while, and decidedly non-Italian decor.

If you're in the mood for Indian, there are a bunch of restaurants to choose from. **Café India** (42-46 Malone Rd., tel. 028/9066-6955, www.cafeindiabelfast.com, open noon–2:30 P.M. Mon.–Sat., 5–11:30 P.M. weekdays, 5 P.M.–midnight Sat., 1–11:30 P.M. Sun., mains £5–8) has an atmospheric upstairs dining room, though the family-run **Gingeroot** (75 Great Victoria St., tel. 028/9031-3124, www.gingeroot.com, open noon–2:30 P.M. and 5–11:30 P.M. Mon.–Sat., 5–10:30 P.M. Sun., mains £5–10) is a much better option for vegetarians. The weekday buffet lunch (£6) is a really good value, and there's a surprisingly decent wine selection.

Don't feel like eating in a swanky restaurant? Belfast has plenty of top-notch gastro-pubs too. Try gay-friendly **Union Street** (8-14 Union St., tel. 028/9031-6060, www.unionstreetpub.com, food served noon–3:30 P.M. Mon.–Thurs. and 5–9 P.M. Thurs., noon–9 P.M. Fri.–Sat., 1–5 P.M. Sun., lunches £6–7, dinner £8–11) in a 19th-century converted shoe factory, where you can get 10 percent off your food bill when you show your Grand Opera House tickets; the **Grill Room** (Donegall Sq. at Linenhall St., food served noon–10 P.M. daily, bar meals £6–15), downstairs at the Ten

Square Hotel, which offers up huge portions of chicken, salmon, duck, steak, and fresh salads, as well as a terrific homemade veggie burger; or **McHugh's** (29-31 Queen's St., tel. 028/9050-9990, www.mchughsbar.com, food served 5–10 P.M. Mon.–Sat., 5–9 P.M. Sun., lunch £6–8, dinner £8–12), a city mainstay and one of Belfast's oldest pubs (there was a brothel upstairs in days gone by). Save room for the banana and amaretto cheesecake.

It may *sound* old-fashioned, but **☾ Irene & Nan's** (12 Brunswick St., tel. 028/9023-9123, www.ireneandnans.com, food served noon–9 P.M. daily, 2/3-course early-bird menu £12/14 5–7 P.M., mains £6–13) is actually quite a stylish '50s-retro bar and bistro, with a classic cocktail list and popular pre-theater menu (get a free glass of wine with your Ulster Orchestra ticket). Or, with that same ticket, get 10 percent off your total bill at the excellent **Oxford Exchange** (upstairs at St. George's Market, Oxford St., tel. 028/9024-0014, www.oxfordexchange.co.uk, food served noon–9 P.M. Mon.–Thurs., noon–3 P.M. and 5–10 P.M. Fri.–Sat., mains £7–15), on the mezzanine level of Belfast's bustling Victorian marketplace. The produce on your plate's come straight from the stalls downstairs.

Fine Dining

Get 10 percent off your food bill with an Ulster Orchestra concert ticket at both of celebrity chef Paul Rankin's restaurants, **Roscoff Brasserie** (7-11 Linenhall St., tel. 028/9031-1150, www.rankingroup.co.uk, open noon–2:30 P.M. weekdays, 6–10:30 P.M. Mon.–Sat., mains £15–22) and **Cayenne** (7 Ascot House, Shaftesbury Sq., tel. 028/9033-1532, open noon–2:15 P.M. weekdays, 6–10:30 P.M. Mon.–Thurs., 6–11:15 P.M. Fri.–Sat., 5–8:45 P.M. Sun., mains £11–18). Both of these restaurants are excellent and deservedly popular.

For a thoroughly divine meal along with impeccable (yet friendly) service and a classy yet relaxed atmosphere, the place to go is **☾ Beatrice Kennedy's** (44 University Rd., tel. 01/2322-2290, www.beatricekennedy.co.uk, open 5–10:30 P.M. Tues.–Sat., 12:30–2:30 P.M. and 5–8:30 P.M. Sun., mains £10–16). It's been described as "refreshingly unfashionable," but that just means you girls'll wish you'd worn red lipstick and seamed stockings to go along with the vintage decor and music. Reservations are recommended at peak periods—especially at graduation time, when all the Queen's students are enjoying a fabulous three-course meal on Mum and Dad. There's a separate vegetarian menu.

With live music nightly (blues, jazz, and swing), **Reno's** (34-36 Bedford St., tel. 028/9031-1026, www.renosbelfast.com, open noon–2:30 P.M. and 5–10 P.M. Mon.–Sat., 2/3-course pre-theater menu £12/14, mains £7–15) is another excellent dining choice before heading off to the opera or orchestra, with high-class takes on traditional comfort food (try the roast beef with chestnut stuffing and horseradish potato cakes). Opposite the Europa Hotel, **Bourbon** (60 Great Victoria St., tel. 028/9033-2121, www.bourbonrestaurant.com, open noon–10 P.M. Mon.–Thurs., noon–11 P.M. Fri.–Sat., noon–9 P.M. Sun., mains £7–23) has decadent New Orleans decor (couldn't you tell by the name?) and offers gourmet pizzas, seafood, and steaks. Flash your Ulster Orchestra concert ticket and get a glass of wine on the house.

INFORMATION

The city's large but efficient **tourist office** (47 Donegall Pl., tel. 028/9024-6609, www.belfastvisitor.com or www.gotobelfast.com) also provides a left luggage service (£5/bag, not overnight though) and bureau de change. Hours vary seasonally (9 A.M.–7 P.M. weekdays, 9 A.M.–5:15 P.M. Sat., 10 A.M.–4 P.M. Sun. June–Sept., 9 A.M.–5:30 P.M. Mon.–Sat. Oct.–May).

The **Queen's Visitors' Centre** (Lanyon Building, Queen's University, University Rd., tel. 028/9097-5252, www.qub.ac.uk/vcentre, open 10 A.M.–4 P.M. weekdays and Sat. May–Sept.) also dispenses tourist info, in addition to a full calendar of art exhibitions.

For information on the republic (including accommodation bookings), stop by **Fáilte Ireland** (53 Castle St., tel. 028/9032-7888, open 9 A.M.–5 P.M. weekdays all year, 9 A.M.–12:30 P.M. Sat. July–Aug.).

While you're at the tourist office, pick up a free copy of *WhatAbout?,* a monthly magazine with exhaustive event listings as well as shopping, accommodation, dining, and transportation info. *GoBelfast* is another free monthly, but it also prints local-interest articles, fashion spreads, and lots more ads.

SERVICES

You'll have no trouble finding an ATM. Banks in Belfast include **Ulster Bank** (11-16 Donegall Sq. E.) and **Bank of Ireland** (1 Donegall Sq. S.). **Thomas Cooke** (11 Donegall Pl., tel. 028/9088-3900), the Belfast **tourist office,** and the main **post office** on Castle Place all have bureaux de change. Post office branches are at 16-22 Bedford Street and 1-5 Botanic Avenue.

The **U.S. Embassy** (Danesfort House, 233 Stranmillis Rd., tel. 028/9038-6100, www. usembassy.org.uk, open 8:30 A.M.–5 P.M. weekdays) is a 15- to 45-minute bus ride from the city center (route #8a, frequent departures from Donegall Sq. E. and across the street from the Europa Hotel on Great Victoria St., get off at the Richmond Park stop on Stranmillis Rd.).

Need a pharmacy? You won't have trouble finding one along Belfast's main drags, but head to **Boots** (35-47 Donegall Pl., tel. 028/9024-2332) on a Sunday, or if you need a better selection. For medical advice, ring **Health Information Service** (tel. 0800/665-544). Belfast's most centrally located hospital is the **City Hospital** (tel. 028/9032-9241) on Lisburn Road.

For laundry service, try **Laundry Duds 'n Suds** (37 Botanic Ave., tel. 028/9024-3956), which is convenient if you're staying in the university neighborhood.

You'll find no bargains for Internet access in this city. Try **Megabite** (77 Dublin Rd., just north of Shaftesbury Sq., 9032-2272, www. mega-bite.biz, open 9 A.M.–10 P.M. weekdays, noon–10 P.M. Sat.–Sun., £2.50/hour), which

has the lowest rate you're likely to find. Or try the **Linen Hall Library** (Donegall Sq. at Fountain St., tel. 028/9032-1707, open 9:30 A.M.–5:30 P.M. weekdays, 9:30 A.M.–4:30 P.M. Sat., £0.75/15 minutes).

GETTING THERE

Belfast is 104 miles (167 km) north of Dublin on the M1 motorway and 72 miles (116 km) southeast of Derry City on the A6. **Ulsterbus** pulls into the **Europa Bus Centre** (adjacent to Europa Hotel, entrance on Glengall St. off Great Victoria St., tel. 028/9066-6630).

If you happen to be coming from Derry City, **Northern Ireland Railways** (www.translink. co.uk) will get you to **Belfast Central Station** (E. Bridge St., tel. 028/9066-6630, travel time 2 hours 10 minutes, 9/day Mon.–Sat., 3/day Sun., single/daily return £9.80/14).

From the republic, take **Irish Rail** (tel. 01/836-6222, www.irishrail.ie, 8/day Mon.–Sat., 5/day Sun., single/weekly return from Dublin €35/50) or **Bus Éireann** (tel. 01/836-6111, www.buseireann.ie, single/5-day return from Dublin €35/50, route #1).

From New York (Newark, change required in Manchester from JFK), Orlando, and Toronto you can fly direct to **Belfast International Airport** (18 mi/29 km west of Belfast on the A57, tel. 028/9448-4848, www.belfastairport. com); nonstop flights are also available to Paris, Amsterdam, Geneva, Prague, Berlin, Rome, and many smaller European destinations. To get to the city center, take the **AirBus** (#300) to the Europa Bus Centre off Great Victoria Street (departures at 5 past the hour every 20 minutes, single/return fare £6/9). Otherwise, a taxi will cost you nearly £25.

There are direct flights from Cork (on Aer Arann), London Stansted, Edinburgh, Glasgow, and other U.K. cities into the **Belfast City Airport** (4 mi/6.4 km east of the city on the A2, tel. 029/9093-9093, www.belfastcityairport.com). Most U.K. flights are on **FlyBE** (tel. 087/1700-0123, www.flybe.com); you can also fly **bmi** (tel. 087/0607-0555, www.flybmi.com) into London Heathrow. **AirLink** (#600) can get you to the Europa Bus Centre (runs on the hour every 20 minutes, single/return fare £2.50/5). A taxi will run you £6–7.

It's also possible to get to Belfast by ferry from Liverpool via the **Norfolk Line** (tel. 01/819-2999, www.norfolkline.com, 2/day at 10:30 A.M. and 10:30 P.M., no Mon. morning sailing, travel time 8 hours, day sailings: car and 2 passengers £95–160, additional passengers £10–15, pedestrians £20–30, night sailings: car and 2 passengers £155–240, additional passengers £15–20, pedestrians £40–50). Ferries depart the Victoria Terminal (3 mi/4.8 km northeast of town), reachable by the M2 motorway.

GETTING AROUND

Provided you plan your sightseeing with efficiency, Belfast is walkable from end to end, though you will want to take a Black Taxi to visit the murals in the Falls and Shankill neighborhoods. You can take **Ulsterbus** (tel. 028/9066-6630, www.ulsterbus.co.uk) route #8 from Donegall Square East south to the Queen's University/Botanic Gardens area, where most of the city's B&Bs are located. During the months of July and August you can avail of a £7 Day Tracker pass (£5 on Sun.) that's perfect for day excursions. An unlimited bus-and-rail combo ticket (£14/34/50 for 1/3/7 days' travel) is available year-round (www.translink.co.uk).

Bike rental is available from **McConvey Cycles** (183 Ormeau Rd., tel. 028/9033-0322, www.mcconveycycles.com, open 9 A.M.–6 P.M. Mon.–Sat., until 8 P.M. Thurs., day/week rental £10/40).

Ring **fonaCAB** (tel. 028/9033-3333) from a landline and a nifty automated system sends a taxi to the address you're calling from; or try **Value Cabs** (tel. 028/9080-9080).

Antrim

CARRICKFERGUS

A rather bland commuter suburb 20 minutes north of Belfast, on the north shore of Belfast Lough, Carrickfergus (Carraig Fhearghais, "Rock of Fergus") is known for the island's most complete medieval castle. **Carrickfergus Castle** (Marine Hwy., tel. 028/9335-1273, open 10 A.M.–6 P.M. Mon.–Sat. and 2–6 P.M. Sun. Apr.–Sept. plus noon–6 P.M. Sun. June–Aug., 10 A.M.–4 P.M. Mon.–Sat. and 2–4 P.M. Sun. Oct.–Mar., admission £3) was Ireland's first Norman fortress. Anglo-Norman adventurer John de Courcy began its construction in the 1180s after a successful invasion, and the building continued after de Courcy was vanquished in 1204 by Hugh de Lacy, Earl of Ulster. King John, worried that de Lacy was becoming too powerful, beseiged the yet-to-be-completed Carrickfergus and took it over in 1210. And that was only the beginning of a long and checkered history. One of its darkest episodes occurred when the Scottish Bruces attacked the castle in 1315; the English garrison survived the yearlong siege by eating their Scottish prisoners (who were already dead, at least).

Considering its dramatic setting and fascinating history, you would think Carrickfergus would be a must-see. Kid-friendly exhibits are one thing, but the National Trust has gone over the top here with melodramatic audiovisuals, amateurish wall murals, and half-size fiberglass statues representing soldiers, archers, John de Courcy and his wife, and so forth. You'll even see one of these creepy figures perched on the throne—the *other* throne.

The castle must have been a far more worthwhile excursion in past years, when it housed the city's military museum (it was used as an armory before 1928). Those artifacts have been transferred to the new **Carrickfergus Museum and Civic Centre** (11 Antrim St., tel. 028/9335-8049, www.carrickfergus.org, open 9 A.M.–5 P.M. weekdays, 10 A.M.–5 P.M. Sat., free admission), however—and here you'll also find the town's **tourist office** (tel. 028/9335-8000, open 10 A.M.–6 P.M. Mon.–Sat. and 1–6 P.M. Sun. Apr.–Sept., 10 A.M.–5 P.M. Mon.–Sat. and 1–5 P.M. Sun. Oct.–Mar.). As it is, the castle is of primary interest to middle-schoolers and military history buffs.

Accommodations and Food

If you're spending the night in Carrick (as the locals know it), the best guesthouse in town is **The Keep** (93 Irish Quarter S., tel. 028/9336-7007 or 079/8120-2169, £25 pp, s £30), a three-minute walk from the castle on the Belfast end of the main drag. The en-suite rooms are capacious and much more stylish than at your average B&B, and Heather and Raymond are very kind and accommodating hosts. Note that many of Carrick's long-established B&Bs have closed or been converted to halfway houses in recent years, so The Keep or the authentically old-fashioned, unpretentious (it's a two-star) **Dobbin's Inn Hotel** (6-8 High St., tel. 028/9335-1905, www.dobbinshotel.co.uk, £35 pp, s £40–45) is your best option.

You can take your chances with the hotel food, but a better choice for lunch or dinner is the **Joymount Arms** (16-18 Joymount, on the same street as the public library, catty-corner to the castle, tel. 028/9335-1850, joymountarms@aol.com, open noon–2:30 P.M. and 5–8:30 P.M. Mon.–Thurs., noon–3 P.M. and 5–9 P.M. Fri.–Sat., 12:30–8 P.M. Sun., lunch £3–8, dinner £7–13), a cozy, dimly lighted pub and restaurant with a beer garden and very friendly and accommodating staff. Kids eat free every weekday 5–7 P.M. and during the day on Saturday.

Getting There

Carrickfergus is 10 miles (16 km) northeast of Belfast on the A2. Get here via **Ulsterbus** (tel. 028/9066-6630, www.ulsterbus.co.uk, route #163 or #263, 2–3/hour, 45–60-minute trip, departs Bridge St. in Belfast, single/return £2.60/4.70) or **N.I. Railways** (tel. 028/9066-6630, www.ulsterbus.co.uk, 2–4 Larne-bound trains/hour, 43-minute trip, single/day return £2.70/4.90) from Belfast's central station.

THE GLENS OF ANTRIM

The Northern Ireland Tourist Board may wax poetical on the beauteous Nine Glens of Antrim, but frankly the base towns from which one might explore them—Glenarm, Waterfoot, and Carnlough—are strangely run-down, not particularly friendly, and noticeably lacking in tourist amenities (especially the first two). Cushendall and Cushendun at the northern edge of the Glens are by far the most pleasant, and even they can be sleepy-in-a-bad-way. Furthermore, most of these nine glens are home to a few fortunate locals and aren't tourist attractions as such, the exception being Glenariff Forest Park. Having said all this, the coastal drive north from Belfast on the A2, with the glens on your left, is downright lovely. Take this ride as part of your Causeway Coast tour, and allow two days to do it right.

Glenariff

One of the few glens you can actually traipse through, **Glenariff Forest Park** (signposted on the A43, 8 mi/13 km south of Cushendall on the B14, tel. 028/2175-8232, open 10 A.M.–dusk all year, cars/pedestrians £4/2) also happens to be the prettiest of them all (Gleann Airimh means "Fertile Glen"). The whole park is remarkably quiet and peaceful. There are plenty of walking trails (from 30 minutes to three hours' duration), but the gem of the park is the substantial **Ess-na-Larach waterfall** ("The Mare's Fall"). Eyeing it from the bridge will give you the distinct feeling you've entered an enchanted forest. Maybe you have.

Cushendall

The glens' largest town, Cushendall ("The Foot of the River Dall") is pleasant enough, though it doesn't come near Cushendun's charm. Everything you need—grub and Northern Bank ATM, at least—is within spitting distance of the distinctive sandstone **Turnley's Tower** on Main Street, built in 1817 by the local landlord for double duty, as both curfew lookout and prison for "troublesome citizens." You will probably just want to stop for a meal, as the nightlife is nothing to write home about.

THE ULSTER WAY

With approximately 900 kilometers (560 miles) of trails, the Ulster Way is the island's longest walking route, winding through all six Northern counties as well as central Donegal. Trekking all of it would take about five weeks, though most travelers walk the coastal stretch between the Giant's Causeway and the Glens of Antrim (from Portrush to Ballycastle, or vice versa) known as the **Causeway Coast Way;** there are plenty of accommodations along the way, but be sure to book well advance even in shoulder season. The Ulster Way begins in the suburbs of northern Belfast, by far the least attractive part of the route, before you come to the most popular segment in northern Antrim. Other sections are broken down into regional walking routes, like the **Central Sperrins Way,** in the mountains of Tyrone and southern Derry, and the **Mourne Trail,** in the mountains of County Down.

As with all signposted walking routes, there are detailed guides with maps available at the local tourist office and bookstore. Websites like the **Ramblers Association** (www.ramblers.org.uk) and **WalkingWorld** (www.walkingworld.com) are helpful planning resources.

A café without much atmosphere to speak of, **Arthur's** (1 Shore St., tel. 028/2177-1627, open 9 A.M.–4 P.M. Wed.–Mon., 9 A.M.–2 P.M. Tues., mains under £4) will nevertheless get the job done whether you're after breakfast, lunch, or tea. For dinner, **Harry's** (10 Mill St., tel. 028/2177-2022, food served noon–9:30 P.M. daily, mains £8–14), a gastro-pub serving hearty no-frills dishes along with a few vegetarian options, is pretty much your only option.

If you do want to spend the night, try **Riverside** (14 Mill St., tel. 028/2177-1655, £20 pp, s £25), a small sliver of tranquility in the town center, or the cheerful **Glendale** (46 Coast Rd., tel. 028/2177-1495 or 078/2105-

2597, glendaleguesthouse@lineone.net, £18 pp, s £20, credit cards accepted), which is a great value.

If you're driving north to Cushendun, try following the signs for the Glendun Scenic Route instead of continuing up the A2. It may take you 12 or so miles (19 km) out of the way (leaving you back to the A2 about 3.5 mi/5.6 km farther up), but the vistas are worth the extra gas: Glendun is the boggiest of the nine, with moorlands cloaking the mountain peaks and hazel copses dotting the lower slopes. Glendun is dazzlingly remote (despite the sawmill). This is a great option for a long cycle if you're basing yourself in Cushendun (though you've got to bring your own bike).

Cushendall is 48 miles (78 km) north of Belfast on the A2. **Ulsterbus** (tel. 028/9066-6630, route #252 or #150/162, 8/day Mon.–Sat., 3/day Sun., single/return fare £7.40/13.50) has a couple of services to Cushendun and Cushendall from Belfast, but a change in Ballymena is usually required. The journey takes 2–2.5 hours.

◖ Layde Old Church

Signposted from Cushendall (0.6 mi/1 km outside town) is the absolutely lovely Layde Old Church, overlooking the North Channel, an island popularly known as "Paddy's Milestone," and the Scottish coast beyond. Owing much to a babbling brook rushing toward that phenomenal ocean view, these are undoubtedly the most romantic monastic ruins in the north. Once you've admired the McDonnell family monuments, including an exquisite 19th-century high cross—it may not be "authentic," but its lack of age means you can clearly discern the carvings—follow the unpaved path to the right of the ruins for a short coastal walk.

Cushendun

Rather unusually, most of seaside Cushendun ("The Foot of the River Dun") is owned by the National Trust—which is why those cute Cornish cottages in the village center, built in the 1920s, are still in pristine condition. Locals still grumble about the row of blank-faced flats built on the far side of the small harbor, and they're the first thing you see when driving into town on the Torr Road, but other than the new apartments and the Mace convenience store on Main Street, Cushendun feels blissfully untouched by modernity. Adding a touch of melancholy to the postcard-prettiness are the two old hotels on the harbor beside the flats, both of them long since closed and inching toward dereliction. But when the sun rises over the water (a sight well worth dragging yourself out of bed for), you can almost imagine you're here in Cushendun circa 1928. There may not be much to do besides hanging out on the sandy white strand, but does it really matter?

The village pub, **Mary McBride's** (2 Main St., tel. 028/2176-1511), supposedly has the smallest bar on the island (though the pub itself has several rooms, as well as an upstairs restaurant). It's a pleasant enough spot for a pint (despite the TVs tuned to the latest sporting event), but the overpriced food is best avoided. You're far better off heading to Harry's in Cushendall for dinner.

Thankfully, an excellent lunch spot is just across the street: **Theresa's Tearoom** (1 Main St., tel. 028/2176-1506, open 11 A.M.–7 P.M. Mon.–Sat. and 11 A.M.–8 P.M. Sun. Easter–Sept., 11 A.M.–6 P.M. weekends Oct.–Mar., mains £3–5) does heavenly homemade desserts as well as soups, quiches, and salads. Save room for the lemon meringue, served straight out of the oven.

Cushendun has one of the best B&Bs in Northern Ireland. Delightful nonagenarian Catherine Scally has run **C The Villa Farmhouse** (185 Torr Rd., tel. 028/2176-1252, maggiescally@amserve.net, £20 pp, s £30, evening meals £12) for well over four decades (and she's lived in this atmospheric 19th-century farmhouse since 1936). There's also a self-catering cottage available, the Coach House, with a private garden. Mrs. Scally's daughter Maggie cooks up scrumptious dinners in the summer months—a great option, considering the slim dining options in the village. Drop-ins (cyclists, usually) as well as those staying in the Coach House can have a full breakfast

(with fresh fruit) for £5. The bedrooms feature gorgeous antique furniture and real quilts on the beds, and the front rooms have expansive sea views. There are only six rooms and repeat business is considerable, so advance booking is essential from May onward. Coming from points south, turn left at the crossroads on the southern edge of town, and the Villa Farmhouse is one mile (1.6 km) down the road on the left. If you're driving the scenic route south from Ballycastle, you'll spot the farmhouse clearly signposted on the right-hand side.

Another option, this one just a bit more out of the ordinary, is **Mullarts** (114 Tromra Rd., on the Cushendall road 1.5 mi/2.5 km south of the village, tel. 028/2176-1221, www.mullarts. fsnet.co.uk, £140/375 d/5-person apartment), three well-appointed self-catering apartments converted out of a whitewashed church built in 1849. Private gardens, patio, an outdoor play area for the kids, and barbecue facilities complete a perfect picture—in fine weather, anyway. Two doubles and one five-person apartment are all available for short-term let (i.e., just for the weekend).

Cushendun is 53 miles (85 km) north of Belfast off the A2. **Ulsterbus** (tel. 028/9066-6630, route #252 or #150/162, 8/day Mon.–Sat., 3/day Sun., single/return fare £7.80/14) can get you to Cushendun from Belfast.

THE CAUSEWAY COAST

County Antrim's biggest attraction is its north coast, from pleasant seaside Ballycastle with its haunted priory ruins to gorgeous Whitepark Bay and the vertiginous Carrick-a-Rede rope bridge, to Bushmills and its infamous distillery, to the natural wonder of Giant's Causeway, and finally the bustling seaside resort and surfers' mecca of Portrush. You could drive it in either direction; most visitors start in Belfast, drive north past the Glens and begin in Ballycastle, and wind up in Derry City after a two- or three-day tour. There is also something to be said for driving it west–east, however, since that way you'll have an uninhibited view of the coast from the road.

Got time—and a sturdy pair of kicks? Go for the 10-mile (16 km) **Causeway Coast Way**

© CAMILLE DEANGELIS

The ruins of Bonamargy Friary feature lovely tracery windows.

between Ballintoy and the Giant's Causeway, which will take you about five hours. Without a doubt, this is the best way to experience the Causeway Coast, studded with funky rock formations and breathtaking vistas all around. Stop by the Causeway tourist office for more information before you head off, and plan to spend the night in Ballintoy.

The **Ulsterbus** (tel. 028/9066-6630, www. ulsterbus.co.uk) Portrush–Ballycastle route (#172) serves Bushmills, Giant's Causeway, and Ballintoy, and you can request other stops along the way (5/day Mon.–Sat., 3/day Sun.).

For visitor information without the usual Tourist Board spin, check out the nonprofit **North Antrim info site** (www.northantrim. com) before you go. You might also want to visit the slick-yet-informative **Causeway Coast and Glens tourism website** (www.causeway-coastandglens.com).

Torr Head

The 11-mile (18-km) scenic route from Ballycastle to Cushendun, **Torr Road,** takes you through some of the most blissfully unspoiled bucolic countryside in Northern Ireland, made even more stunning by panoramic sea views. This winding road is so narrow in places that the dotted line down the center seems a quintessential example of Irish humor. At Torr Head, signposted a short distance off the main road, you'll spot a coast guard building abandoned in the 1920s (to reach it, you can hike up a rocky path from the small car park) and an ice house (used for packing fish) left to ruin around the same time. The hill holds a couple of passage tombs as well, though there isn't much to see. This is Ireland's closest point to Scotland, which is 12 miles (19 km) away.

The downside of such an unspoiled area is, of course, that there are no accommodations to be found until the route's end.

Ballycastle

At the eastern end of the Causeway Coast, Ballycastle (Baile an Chaistil) has a lovely Blue Flag beach and a wonderfully friendly vibe. The castle for which the town was named, built by the first Earl of Antrim in the 16th century, is long gone. The town is best known for its annual **Ould Lammas Fair** over the last weekend in August, which features plenty of market stalls and street entertainment. Here you can also sample two local delicacies: **dulse,** a dried seaweed, and **yellow man,** hard toffee made from a top-secret recipe. Not here for the fair? You can usually pick up both quirky snacks at **The Fruit Shop** (The Diamond, tel. 028/2076-3348, closed Sun.). To get there, walk up Quay Road away from the harbor and after a few minutes you'll see the tiny shop on your left.

Founded in 1485 by Rory McQuillan (of the same family who built Dunluce Castle), the buildings of the Franciscan **Bonamargy Friary** were built of handsome red sandstone, dark basalt, and granite. On the eastern end of town, these ruins (always accessible) contain the family tomb of the McDonnell clan. But the friary graveyard's most famous inhabitant is Rory's descendant, Julia McQuillan, the "Black Nun" who is said to haunt the grounds…missing her head. Centuries-old headstones mossed over and tipped askew, inscriptions long since worn away: The scene is romantic despite the friary's location beside the 18-hole **Ballycastle Golf Club** (Cushendall Rd., tel. 028/2076-2536, www.ballycastlegolfclub.com). Actually, the golf course surrounds the ruins and graveyard on all sides! To get to the ruins, make a left onto the road just after the big, white, modern golf clubhouse (Cushendall Rd.), and the abbey is signposted on the right, a couple minutes' walk.

Lookin' for live music? Look no further than the locals' favorite watering hole, established in 1766: the **House of McDonnell** (71 Castle St., west of the diamond, tel. 028/2076-2975). Fridays are trad and Saturdays are folk.

ACCOMMODATIONS AND FOOD

The garish yellow-and-red facade might well burn your retinas, but the family-run, IHH **Castle Hostel** (62 Quay Rd., tel. 028/2076-2337, www.castlehostel.com, dorms £9, private rooms £10–12 pp) is a good choice for budget travelers. It's clean (if a bit threadbare), with two kitchens and a fire in the common room. The staff are friendly and helpful, the place just small enough to attract solo travelers instead of noisy school groups. With colorful, comfortable rooms and a ground-floor tearoom serving lunch and coffee, **Glenluce** (42 Quay Rd., tel. 028/2076-2194, www.glenluceguesthouse.com, £30 pp, but as low as £18 in off-season, credit cards accepted) is a fine choice a few doors up.

The relatively new **Glenmore House** (4.5 km west of Ballycastle on the B15, 94 White Park Rd., tel. 028/2076-3584, www.glenmore.biz, low/high season £20/25 pp, Jacuzzi rooms 27/32, s £30/35, credit cards accepted) features Jacuzzis in two of its seven rooms, a private two-acre fishing lake, an outstanding breakfast menu, and simple-but-hearty fare in the downstairs restaurant. This is a great choice for families and anglers alike.

The modern, three-star **Marine Hotel** (1-3 North St., tel. 028/2076-2222, www.marinehotel.net, rooms £90–110, family rooms £120–140) offers harbor views from many of the bedrooms. While there's no leisure center on-site, guests can use the facilities at the Marine Country Club (including large pool, sauna, steam room, Jacuzzi, and gym). This not a good choice for singles, however: Though the rate is per room, there is a ludicrous "single occupancy charge" of £15.

Ballycastle doesn't have much in the way of dining options. The food's very basic, but the cafeteria-style **Beach House Café** (13 Ann St., on the water, tel. 028/2076-2262, open 10 A.M.–7 P.M. daily in summer, 9 A.M.–5 P.M. Sun. only in off-season, mains under £4) is a nice spot to sit with a cup of tea and watch the boats bobbing in the harbor. For a proper meal, try **Wysner's** (16 Ann St., tel. 028/2076-2372, open 8 A.M.–9 P.M. Mon.–Sat. July–Aug., 8 A.M.–5 P.M. Mon.–Tues. and Thurs. and 8 A.M.–5 P.M. and 7–9 P.M. Fri.–Sat. Sept.–June, mains £6–12), which has an emphasis on fresh seafood (the Carrick-a-Rede salmon is a specialty). The pub menu at **The Strand** (9 North St., tel. 028/2076-2349, food served noon–9 P.M. daily, mains £6–12) also offers a choice of fresh fish.

PRACTICALITIES

For more information about the fair, stop by the local **tourist office** (7 Mary St., on the eastern side of town, straight through the roundabout by the harbor, tel. 028/2076-2024, open 9:30 A.M.–5 P.M. weekdays, until 7 P.M. July–Aug.), located in the Moyle District Council building on the way to the golf club and priory ruins.

Ballycastle is 56 miles (90 km) north of Belfast via the A2, A26, and A44. From the capital, take **Ulsterbus** route #131 (change usually required at Ballymena or Larne, 6/day Mon.–Sat., no Sun. service, single/return £8.20/14), or from points west on the Causeway Coast take #172 (5/day Mon.–Sat., 3/day Sun.).

Rathlin Island

Eight miles (13 km) out over Rathlin Sound, legend has it that L-shaped Rathlin Island (Reachlainn) was cast into the sea by Fionn mac Cumhaill's mother as a stepping-stone between Ireland and Scotland (she was headed there to pick up some whiskey). In fact, Rathlin—Northern Ireland's only inhabited offshore island—did serve as hideaway for Robert the Bruce at the beginning of the 14th century (before he returned to Britain to whup the English good). There isn't anything in terms of megalithic or monastic ruins here, so most of the out-of-towners heading to Rathlin on the ferry are devoted seal- and bird-watchers (who focus their binoculars at the **Kebble National Nature Reserve** on the island's western end)—or those just looking to get off the beaten track.

The IHO **Soerneog View Hostel** ("Kiln," Ouig, a 10-minute walk from the pier, tel. 028/2076-3954, www.n-irelandholidays.co.uk/rathlin, open Apr.–Oct., dorms £10) sleeps only six people (in three private rooms), which means booking ahead is absolutely essential. While making your reservation, mention if you'd like to rent a bike. There's a shop near the pier where you can stock up for dinner, though it's only open 10 A.M.–4 P.M. seasonally.

It may sound posh, but the tariffs at the **Manor House** (Church Quarter, on the northside of the harbor, tel. 028/2076-3964, uravfm@smtp.ntrust.org.uk, £23 pp, £27 en suite, s £25–30) don't match the name (perhaps in part because it's owned by the National Trust). This wonderfully atmospheric Georgian (with its own walled garden providing fresh herbs for the tearoom/restaurant) is your best bet for an evening meal, though if you aren't staying here reservations are required. Or for a meal-in-a-glass, stop by the island's lone pub, **McCuaig's** (tel. 028/2076-3974), by the pier.

Caledonian MacBrayne operates the Rathlin Island ferry (tel. 028/2076-9299, www.calmac.co.uk, 45-minute crossing from the Ballycastle pier, £9 return, £11 with bike). Ferries depart daily from Ballycastle (10 A.M., noon, 4:30 P.M., and 6:30 P.M.) and Rathlin (8:30 A.M., 11 A.M., 3:30 P.M., and 5:30 P.M.) April–September (2/day daily until Oct. 20). The **Boat House Visitor Centre** (near the pier, tel. 028/2076-3951, open 11 A.M.–4 P.M. daily May–Aug.) dispenses tourist info and historical tidbits.

Ballintoy

Next stop on the Causeway Coast tour is sleepy Ballintoy (Baile an Tuaighe, "Town of the Ax"), with fantastic sea and pastoral vistas but not much else to detain you, save the touristy-but-really-fun Carrick-a-Rede Rope Bridge just east of the village. Walk down to the harbor at Whitepark Bay, a favorite spot for landscape painters, and if you continue along a westward footpath you'll come to the hamlet of Portbraddan and Ireland's (supposedly) smallest church, **St. Gobnan's.** It's only 6 by 10 feet—yet there are ruins of an even tinier church, **St. Lasseragh's,** perched on a cliff above.

Backpackers have two options. The IHH **Sheep Island View Hostel** (42a Main St., tel. 028/2076-9391, www.sheepislandview.com, dorms £11, private rooms £12 pp, credit cards accepted) is clean and offers good facilities, but it's a magnet for school groups. The quieter option is **Whitepark Bay** (157 Whitepark Rd., signposted off the A2, 3 mi/4.8 km west of the village, tel. 028/2073-1745, www.hini.org.uk, open Mar.–Oct., dorms £11.50, twins £13 pp, credit cards accepted), in a totally idyllic beachside location. It's a two-minute walk from the main road; if you're taking the bus, ask to be dropped off at the turnoff.

For B&B, try the homey, 18th-century **Ballintoy House** (9 Main St., tel. 028/2076-2317 or 077/5180-8120, £17 pp, s £20), on the eastern end of the village. It's the closest B&B to the rope bridge, and you can walk there in less than 10 minutes.

As you would expect in a place like this, the three-star **Fullerton Arms** (22-24 Main St., tel. 028/2076-9613, www.fullertonarms.co.uk, food served 12:30–9 P.M. daily, mains £5–15, £30 pp, s £34–38) is a bit on the stodgy side. Christened after Ballintoy's teetotaling 18th-century landlord, the guesthouse rather ironically features a pub with backyard beer garden, live folk and ballad sessions in summer (Mon. and Thurs. starting at 7 P.M.), pool table, and dartboard. This is your best bet for lunch or dinner in Ballintoy (and the pub and restaurant menus thankfully provide veggie lovers with several options). There's also traditional music at the **Carrick-a-Rede** pub (tel. 028/2076-2241) on Tuesday, Friday, and Sunday nights.

To get to Ballintoy, turn off the A2 in Ballycastle and follow the B15 for about 5.5 miles (8.9 km). You'll pick up the A2 again a couple miles west of the village. **Ulsterbus** (tel. 028/9066-6630, www.ulsterbus.co.uk) route #172 can get you here from Belfast (one or two changes required) or all points along the Causeway Coast route.

C Carrick-a-Rede Rope Bridge

One of the most exhilarating experiences in the north is a walk across the 65-foot Carrick-a-Rede Rope Bridge (signposted off the B15, tel. 028/2073-1582, open 10 A.M.–5:15 P.M. daily early Mar.–May and Sept.–Oct., 10 A.M.–6:15 P.M. daily June–Aug., admission £2.50), suspended 80 feet above a dramatic sea gorge and swaying in the blustery winds. *Do* look down to drink in the whole effect! There's nothing on the wee island on the far side (which is called Carrick-a-Rede) but pretty ocean views, but most folks take their time snapping photos and watching the birds. Local fishermen used to reassemble the bridge every spring to catch salmon on the far side of this little island, and today it's one of the National Trust's most popular attractions. Needless to say, those with a fear of heights should avoid this one, and opening is always subject to weather conditions; it's wise to call ahead if the forecast is anything less than perfect.

Giant's Causeway

According to legend, this UNESCO World Heritage Site was a footbridge between Ireland and Scotland, destroyed by the warrior Fionn mac Cumhaill to prevent the giant Finn Gall from following him back to Ireland. Under an undulating series of cliffs are towering walls and a seaward staircase fashioned by nature out

© CAMILLE DEANGELIS

Carrick-a-Rede Rope Bridge

of gray basalt, some 37,000 hexagonal columns in all. Frankly, while the causeway is genuinely beautiful and well worth a visit, don't expect anything fantastic to look at and you won't be disappointed. Photographers hired by the Tourist Board have a knack for taking dramatic snapshots with impossible hues. Lovely as this place is, it is not the eighth wonder of the world.

On arrival you can either take the cliff route (part of the 10-mi/16-km Causeway Coast Way) to the right or head down a paved road straight to the sea and rock formations. This is, of course, where all the other tourists go (many of them on a shuttle bus called the "Causeway Coaster"; it's only a five-minute walk from visitors center to causeway, and most of those on the bus aren't handicapped or elderly—for whom the shuttle was no doubt intended). The gorse-lined cliff path is easy, dramatic, but far less popular. After a mile or so a rather precipitous wooden staircase will bring you down to the paved shore path, or you could keep walking and turn back later.

Notice all the cars parked along the main road? That's because it costs £5 to park in the visitors center parking lot. It seems even the National Trust can't resist price-gouging on occasion. And don't waste your money at the visitors center tearoom; get thee to **The Nook,** a fantastic schoolhouse-turned-restaurant just up the road.

The **visitors center** (2 mi/3.2 km north of Bushmills on the B146, tel. 028/2073-1855, www.giantscausewaycentre.com, admission to audiovisual £1) also serves as a tourist information point. Hours vary seasonally (10 A.M.–6 P.M. daily July–Aug., 10 A.M.–5 P.M. daily Mar.–June and Sept.–Oct., 10 A.M.–4:30 P.M. daily Nov.–Feb.).

The nearest B&B to the causeway is **Kal-Mar** (64A Causeway Rd., tel. 028/2073-1101 or 077/4611-5396, £22.50 pp, s £25). None of the three rooms are en-suite, but this unpretentious little bungalow still has much to recommend it. Besides the convenient location, proprietor Maud Mitchell is a sweet and hospitable lady who serves hearty breakfasts with plenty of grandmotherly panache. Hand-knitted scarves for sale are on display by the front door. Best of all, you can leave your car here and walk to the causeway in the morning (avoiding the ludicrous £5 fee at the visitors' center, or the risk in parking on the main road). To get here from the road leading to the causeway, turn right at The Nook restaurant and you'll see the B&B just up the road on your left.

As you would expect, the **Causeway Hotel** (40 Causeway Rd., tel. 028/2073-1226, www.giants-causeway-hotel.com, B&B £35 pp, s £50, lunch £6–11, dinner £8–15) offers unbeatable views of ocean and causeway. The atmosphere may be downright stodgy and the staff not particularly welcoming, but the location is reason enough to stay here. Even if you're staying at the hotel, though, you should take your lunch, tea, and dinner at ◖ **The Nook** (48 Causeway Rd., tel. 028/2073-2993, food served 10:30 A.M.–8:30 P.M. daily, lunches £4–7, dinners £8–14), an excellent pub-cum-restaurant in a converted schoolhouse just across

the road from the hotel and Giant's Causeway visitors center. The menu offers both creative and traditional dishes using only local produce, and the barstaff are pleasant and attentive. You can eat on the original slanted desks beside an open fire (but be careful your dishes don't slide off); the back room, brightened with white Christmas lights, has glass-fronted cupboards filled with vintage toys. You can get a cup of gourmet coffee here, too, sipping it as you muse over whatever memories are brought to mind by the '80s and '90s pop tunes playing on the stereo.

◖ Dunluce Castle

If there were an award for a castle ruin with the most dramatic situation, Dunluce Castle (87 Dunluce Rd., signposted off the A2 5 mi/8 km west of Giant's Causeway and 3 mi/4.8 km east of Portrush, tel. 028/2073-1938, open 10 A.M.–5:30 P.M. daily Apr.–Sept., 10 A.M.–4:30 P.M. daily Oct.–Mar., admission £2) would surely win the distinction. The castle perches precipitously on a cliff over a cave (called Mermaid's Cave, reachable by a steep path down from the castle), and the basalt rock beneath is slowly crumbling away: In 1639 part of the castle tumbled into the sea during a reception, taking most of the servants along with it. Though nothing so tragic has transpired in the intervening centuries, it's only a matter of time before the rest of the castle is lost to the waves.

The earliest extant structures (towers and walls) date from the mid-13th century, though archaeological excavations indicate the land was inhabited as early as the 9th century. Dunluce was home to the McQuillans, the ruling family of north Antrim in the 16th century, and was later owned by Scottish rogue Sorley Boy McDonnell (whose brother married a McQuillan), who added a highly incongruous sandstone loggia (some of which remains).

Even if you haven't budgeted the time for an extended visit, do take a few minutes to admire the view from the grassy hill down from the car park. The Ulsterbus Causeway route makes frequent stops at Dunluce (5/day between Coleraine and the Giant's Causeway Hotel). You

© CAMILLE DEANGELIS

Dunluce Castle perches precipitously on a cliff over a cave.

could easily walk or bike here from Portrush or Bushmills (though due caution is required on the busy A2), or walk via the Causeway Coast Way.

Bushmills

If you aren't a whiskey-drinker, then chances are you'll find Bushmills a rather dull little town. That said, you can certainly base yourself here when visiting Giant's Causeway, which is only a few miles down the road.

The **Old Bushmills Distillery** (Distillery Rd., signposted on the B66, www.bushmills. com, tel. 028/2073-1521, open 9:30 A.M.– 5:30 P.M. Mon.–Sat. and noon–5:30 P.M. Sun. Apr.–Oct., 10:30 A.M.–3:30 P.M. weekdays and 1:30–3:30 P.M. weekends Nov.–Mar., admission £5) is, of course, the prime attraction. It's been licensed to distill since 1608 (making this the oldest licensed distillery on the planet), and on the tour you'll learn everything you ever wanted to know about the making of *uisce beatha*. Naturally, a shot or two is included in the price of admission.

The new, purpose-built **Mill Rest Hostel** (49 Main St., tel. 028/2073-1222, www.hini. org.uk, dorms £12, twins/doubles £15 pp, credit cards accepted) is popular with tour groups, but it's the place to stay if you're on a shoestring. For B&B, try the homey, unpretentious **Portcaman House** (11 Priestland Rd., tel. 028/2073-2057, www.portcamanhouse. com, £25 pp, s £35); Mr. and Mrs. Robinson are very accommodating and helpful hosts. The Priestland Road turnoff is opposite the railway entrance on Dunluce Road.

The **Bushmills Inn** (9 Dunluce Rd., tel. 028/2073-3000, www.bushmillsinn.com, rooms £88–228, s £58–198, food served noon– 6 P.M. and 7–9:30 P.M. Mon.–Sat., noon– 9 P.M. Sun., lunch £10–14, dinner £13–20) is a gorgeously authentic 17th-century hotel where you'll still find gas lamps burning in the downstairs sitting rooms. The rooms in the new wing are relatively characterless (and much more expensive), so you may want to request one of the smaller rooms in the original building. These "budget" rooms overlook the main street rather than the river, but they're absolutely charming. Kill the time before your dinner reservation poking through the spooky old hallways in search of secret passages.

Bushmills is 58 miles (93 km) north of Belfast on the A26 (picking up the B66 in Ballymoney), 13 miles (21 km) west of Ballycastle and 39 miles (63 km) northeast of Derry City on the A2. Bushmills is served by the Ulsterbus Causeway route.

The niftiest way to reach Giant's Causeway from Bushmills (only a 2-mi/3.2-km trip) is via a narrow-gauge **steam locomotive** (Ballaghmore Rd., signposted from the A2, tel. 028/2073-2844, www.giantscausewayrailway. org, departures on the half hour 11:30 A.M.– 5:30 P.M. daily June–Sept., single/return ticket £3.50/5).

Portrush

Popular with surfers and Northern families on holiday, Portrush (Port Rois, "Port of the Promontory") frankly has that tacky resort-town feel, with the requisite amusement arcades, neon signs, and chippers lining its primary streets. Unless you're a surfing enthusiast there's not much to linger for, especially since the town's family-focused amenities can make others feel out of the loop. Stop by **Troggs** (88 Main St., tel. 028/7082-5476, www.troggs. com, open 9 A.M.–5:30 P.M. Tues.–Sun.) for equipment rental; it also offers two-hour lessons. Another attraction is the **Royal Portrush Golf Club** (Dunluce Rd., tel. 028/7082-2311, www.royalportrushgolfclub.com).

MaCool's (35 Causeway St., tel. 028/7082-4845, www.portrush-hostel.com, dorms £10, twin/double £12/14 pp) is a small (18-bed) hostel within a stone's throw of the beach, with friendly owners and continental breakfast included in the price. You can rent a bike for £5 per day even if you aren't staying here.

For B&B, try **Pier View** (53 Kerr St., tel. 028/7082-3234 or 077/5128-7995, www. pierview.com, £23–25 pp, s £28–30), which boasts a breakfast room overlooking the harbor, or the **Belvedere** (15 Lansdowne Crescent. tel. 028/7082-2771, open Jan.–Nov., £20 pp, s £25), a quiet Victorian townhouse with a cheerful peat fire in the sitting room. This is the best-value B&B in town.

Now part of the Best Western chain, the newly renovated three-star **Magherabuoy House Hotel** (41 Magheraboy Rd., 1 mi/1.6 km south of town, tel. 028/7082-3507, www. magherabuoy.co.uk, B&B and dinner £85– 165 pp) is still family-run, and still the top accommodation in the area. All rooms have king-size beds and complimentary wireless Internet.

The best restaurant in town is the **Harbour Bistro** (at the harbor, tel. 028/7082-2430, open 12:30–2:30 P.M. and 5:30–10 P.M. Mon.–Sat., 12:30–3 P.M. and 5:30–9 P.M. Sun., lunches £6–8, mains £8–16), a comfortable spot to dig in with a hearty, top-notch meal of steak or fresh seafood. You'll find a similar menu at the atmospheric **Ramore Winebar** (at the harbor, tel. 028/7082-4313, same hours), run by the same folks.

Portrush has a seasonal **tourist office** (Dunluce Centre, 10 Sandhill Dr., tel. 028/7082-3333, open 9 A.M.–7 P.M. daily mid-June–Aug., 9 A.M.–5 P.M. weekdays and noon–5 P.M. weekends Apr.–mid-June and Sept., noon–5 P.M. weekends March and Oct.).

Reach Portrush by **Northern Ireland Railways** (tel. 028/9066-6630, www.translink.co.uk), with frequent daily service from Belfast (9/day Mon.–Sat., 3/day Sun., single fare £8.20) and Derry (7/day Mon.–Sat., 4/ day Sun., single fare £7.60). Portrush is on the western end of the Causeway Coast bus route (#172, 5/day Mon.–Sat., 3/day Sun.).

Derry

DERRY CITY/LONDONDERRY

Vibrant Derry, known to British loyalists as Londonderry, is the island's fourth-largest city. During the war between the Protestant William of Orange and the deposed Catholic James II, Derry got the moniker "Maiden City" because the inhabitants of its walled city were able to withstand a siege that lasted more than a year. To this day, you'll still see the words "never give up—never surrender!" painted on brick walls in unionist sections of town—which leads you to wonder which century these people think they're living in.

A note on the Derry/Londonderry dilemma: Derry is the city's original name, preferred by a majority of its inhabitants (the city is roughly 75 percent Catholic and 25 percent Protestant), so henceforth in this chapter "the Maiden City" is referred to as Derry. (Besides, even if you're not a hardcore republican, you've got to admit that "Londonderry" stinks of imperialism.)

There's enough to keep you here for two full days—if nothing else, take a leisurely walk along the early-17th-century city walls, the only ones intact in all Ireland—but don't bank on spending more than three nights here. By your third morning, as in Belfast, all that lingering sectarianism is no longer a sad-yet-fascinating novelty.

On opposite sides of the River Foyle are the **old city walls,** dating to the early 17th century, and the traditionally Protestant **Waterside** section (though in fact the Catholic/Protestant population is nearly 50/50). West of the old city is the **Bogside,** the traditionally Catholic working-class neighborhood that saw so much violence and bloodshed in the late '60s and early '70s, but which is now completely rebuilt. Waterside and Bogside are connected via the double-deck Craigavon Bridge.

☾ Derry City Walls

Constructed between 1614 and 1619, these are the only intact city walls in all Ireland, though the four original gates were rebuilt in the 18th and 19th centuries along with three new entrances. No visit to Derry is complete without making the circuit around the walls to observe the city within and without; it may sound perilous, but these walls are sturdy enough at 30 feet thick and up to 26 feet high. The circumference is about a mile and a quarter (nine furlongs, to be precise), and staircases are located at many points along the inner walls. It'll take you half an hour to make a complete circuit, but you'll want to walk it more than once. They're always open and admission is free. You can view many of the peace murals from the southwestern section of the city wall, including *The Death of Innocence,* but take the time to exit the old city and view them from the street.

Guildhall

Step inside the neo-Gothic Guildhall (Guildhall Sq., tel. 028/7137-7335, www.derrycity.gov.uk, open 9 A.M.–5 P.M. weekdays, free admission), which houses the Derry City Council headquarters as well as the greatest number of stained-glass windows of any building on the island. The Guildhall was built in 1887, destroyed by fire on Easter Sunday 1908, and rebuilt and reopened in 1912. Its clock face is the largest in Ireland, and at 13 feet and one-quarter inch, its pendulum is one-quarter inch longer than Big Ben's. In the foyer is a larger-than-life (six-foot 10-inch) statue of Queen Victoria at her dowdiest. Fashioned out of Sicilian marble, the statue weighs in at a staggering 2.5 tons—and the pedestal is another three! You can take your time wandering through the building looking at all the windows—though the Main Hall, with its California redwood ceiling panels and grand pipe organ, is particularly atmospheric. The organ was built in 1914 and was restored by the same firm 68 years later, after the 1972 IRA bombing.

Tower Museum

The Tower Museum (Union Hall Pl., tel. 028/7137-2411, www.derrycity.gov.uk/museums, open 10 A.M.–5 P.M. Tues.–Sat., plus

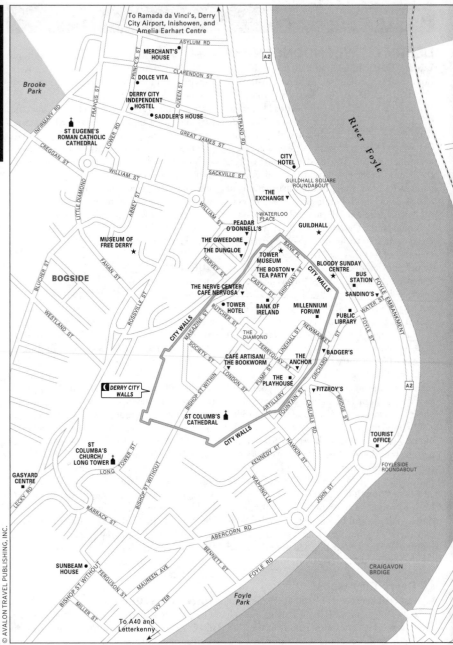

To Ramada da Vinci's, Derry
City Airport, Inishowen, and
Amelia Earhart Centre

ASYLUM RD

MERCHANT'S
HOUSE

DOLCE VITA

Brooke
Park

DERRY CITY
INDEPENDENT
HOSTEL

SADDLER'S HOUSE

ST EUGENE'S
ROMAN CATHOLIC
CATHEDRAL

CLARENDON ST

A2

CITY
HOTEL

River Foyle

WILLIAM ST

SACKVILLE ST

GUILDHALL SQUARE
ROUNDABOUT

THE
EXCHANGE ▼

WATERLOO
PLACE

GUILDHALL ★

MUSEUM OF
FREE DERRY ★

PEADAR
O'DONNELL'S

THE GWEEDORE ▼

THE DUNGLOE ▼

BOGSIDE

TOWER
MUSEUM

THE BOSTON
TEA PARTY ▼

CITY WALLS

BLOODY SUNDAY
CENTRE

BUS
STATION

THE NERVE CENTER/
CAFÉ NERVOSA ▼

TOWER
HOTEL

BANK OF
IRELAND

MILLENNIUM
FORUM

SANDINO'S

PUBLIC
LIBRARY

CITY WALLS

THE
DIAMOND

CAFÉ ARTISAN/
THE BOOKWORM

THE
ANCHOR

BADGER'S ▼

DERRY CITY
WALLS

THE
PLAYHOUSE

FITZROY'S ▼

A2

ST COLUMB'S
CATHEDRAL

CITY WALLS

TOURIST
OFFICE

ST
COLUMBA'S
CHURCH/
LONG TOWER

FOYLESIDE
ROUNDABOUT

GASYARD
CENTRE

SUNBEAM
HOUSE

ABERCORN RD

CRAIGAVON
BRDIGE

Foyle
Park

To A40 and
Letterkenny

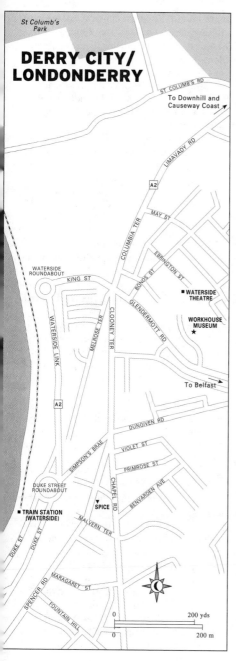

St Columb's Park

DERRY CITY/ LONDONDERRY

ST COLUMB'S RD

To Downhill and
Causeway Coast

LIMAVADY RD

A2

MAY ST

COLUMBIA TER

EBRINGTON ST

WATERSIDE
ROUNDABOUT

KING ST

BONDS ST

■ **WATERSIDE
THEATRE**

GLENDERMOTT RD

**WORKHOUSE
MUSEUM**
★

MELROSE TER

CLOONEY TER

WATERSIDE LINK

A2

To Belfast

DUNGIVEN RD

SIMPSON'S BRAE

VIOLET ST

PRIMROSE ST

DUKE STREET
ROUNDABOUT

CHAPEL RD

BENVARDEN AVE

▼ **SPICE**

■ **TRAIN STATION
(WATERSIDE)**

MALVERN TER

DUKE ST

DUKE ST

MARAGARET ST

SPENCER RD

FOUNTAIN HILL

0   200 yds

0   200 m

bank holiday Mon. in summer, admission £3) has two permanent exhibitions, one a thorough history of the city and the other with various treasures dredged up from a Spanish Armada ship that sank in Kinnegoe Bay, Donegal, in 1588. The shipwreck was discovered by members of the Derry Sub-Aqua Club in 1971 and subsequently excavated by a team of underwater archaeologists.

St. Columb's Cathedral

The oldest parts of St. Columb's Cathedral (London St., tel. 028/7126-7313, www.st-columbscathedral.org, open 9 A.M.–5 P.M. Mon.–Sat., 9 A.M.–1 P.M. and 2–4 P.M. in low season, admission £2) date to 1633, and the whole place is a monument to the loyalist triumph against the Jacobites during the siege of 1688–1689—for the relics inside (including a cast-iron cannonball weighing 280 pounds) as well as the fact that the cathedral was the only building still standing afterward. The chancel has a stained-glass window depicting the Ascension along with a series of mosaics of the four Evangelists along with Patrick and Columba. Some of the dust-laden flags above your head are more than two centuries old. To the rear of the church is the chapter house, containing aforesaid historical artifacts, along with the choristers' vestry, featuring a triad of windows glorifying the Williamites' victory. Note that if you take the guided city tour through the tourist office, your admission to the cathedral is covered under the same ticket—and you'll get more out of your visit.

The Bogside

Head to the Bogside, Derry's traditionally Catholic blue-collar neighborhood, for better views of the **peace murals** as well as the **Bloody Sunday Memorial,** all of which are located along on Rossville Street and its side roads. These 10 murals are the work of only three local artists (William Kelly, Tom Kelly, and Kevin Hasson), along with a rainbow-hued 2004 addition that features the work of Derry schoolchildren from both sides. The murals depict Bernadette Devlin, a republican activist

THE DERRY CITY COAT OF ARMS

You might be wondering what the deal is with that smiling yellow skeleton on Derry City's coat of arms. William de Burgo, the "Brown Earl" of Ulster and ruler of the city of Derry, was having a castle, called Greencastle, built on the east coast of the Inishowen Peninsula in County Donegal. William bricked his cousin Walter de Burgo, an Anglo-Norman knight, into a dungeon in said castle in 1332, where Walter starved to death. Why do this, you ask? William suspected Walter of having an affair with his wife. So that yellow skeleton represents the murdered Walter de Burgo – though no one's sure what he had reason to grin about...

elected a mid-Ulster MP at the age of 21; Bobby Sands, shown long-haired and bearded, during the last phase of his fatal hunger strike; and a kaleidoscope of smiling faces, the 14 demonstrators massacred by British troops on Bloody Sunday.

Another mural shows the figure of 14-year-old Annette McGavigan, who was murdered in 1971 by a sniper perched on the city wall; she was carrying a towel on her way to the pool, which the soldier suspected hid a bomb. The oldest mural declares "You are now entering Free Derry" at the intersection of Rossville and Fahan Streets; it was painted in 1969 after the "Battle of the Bogside" of August 12–14, when republicans managed to cut their neighborhood off from all British police and paramilitary activity (a period that lasted nearly a year). This wall is all that remains of the old Bogside; all the flats and townhouses you see now are new construction, and the rest of the murals date from 1994 onward. You might be surprised to see how quiet and workaday the Bogside is; it's a perfectly safe place nowadays. You can view all the murals on **The Bogside Artists** website (http://cain.ulst.ac.uk/bogsideartists).

Developed by the Bloody Sunday Trust, the

Museum of Free Derry (55-61 Glenfada Park, off Rossville St., tel. 028/7136-0880, www.museumoffreederry.org, open 9:30 A.M.–4:30 P.M. Mon.–Thurs., 9:30 A.M.–3 P.M. Fri., 1–4 P.M. Sat.–Sun., admission by donation) chronicles the Catholic struggle for civil rights, including background on individual Bogside neighborhoods and emphasizing the personal experiences of local residents.

Construction of the Catholic cathedral, the neo-Gothic **St. Eugene's** (Great James St., tel. 028/7126-2894), was begun after the Great Famine and dedicated in 1873. There isn't nearly as much here in terms of history as at St. Columb's, but many will find this church's soaring ceiling and quiet austerity reason for a slight detour.

While in Bogside, check out the wonderfully ornate Catholic **St. Columba's Church, Long Tower** (Long Tower St., off Barrack St., tel. 028/7126-7284), which features several excellent reproductions of masterpieces by Raphael, Leonardo, and others (a full-size *Last Supper* is painted above the altar). The church opened in 1786 (partly through the generosity of Derry's left-leaning Protestant bishop, the infamous Frederick Augustus Hervey), though construction continued for many decades afterward.

Other Sights

Featuring exhibits peopled with the usual creepy mannequins in period dress, the **Workhouse Museum** (23 Glendermott Rd., Waterside, 0.9 mile north of the Craigavon Bridge, tel. 028/7131-8328, www.derrycity.gov.uk/museums, open 10 A.M.–4:30 P.M. Mon.–Thurs. and Sat., free admission) is housed in the same building as the Waterside public library. This workhouse was opened in 1840 and only closed in 1948, at which time it was converted into a hospital; the hospital closed in 1991, and the building reopened as a museum in 1997. Along with material on the Great Famine and 19th-century poverty in general, there are rotating historical exhibitions that don't necessarily have much to do with the Workhouse itself.

A guide at the **Amelia Earhart Centre** (Ballyarnett Country Park, 3 miles north of

FESTIVALS AND EVENTS IN DERRY CITY

Derry's festival calendar rivals Belfast's in scope and excitement. More than just an arts festival, **Blathanna** ("Flowers," tel. 028/7126-4132, www.blathanna.org) seeks to celebrate and promote the Irish language through bilingual workshops, art and music classes, storytelling, trad sessions, and film screenings. The festival runs for two weeks in early-mid-March.

Derry offers a music fest to suit every taste. In mid- to late April, the **Feis Doire Cholmcille** is the largest festival of Irish traditional music in Derry or Donegal. For more information, contact the **Millennium Forum** (Newmarket St., tel. 028/7126-4455, www.millenniumforum.co.uk), which hosts most of the events. Alternatively, Derry's annual **jazz festival** (tel. 028/7137-6545, www.cityofderryjazzfestival.com) is usually the

last weekend in April. And for something you can dance to, there's the **Celtronic Festival** (tel. 078/1491-8452, www.celtronic.co.uk) in late June and early July.

August brings competing cultural events (music, readings, exhibitions, and suchlike) in the form of the Bogside **Gasyard Wall Féile** (tel. 028/7126-2812, www.freederry.org/feile) and the **Maiden City Festival** (tel. 028/7134-9250) for "Prods."

Autumn brings more entertainments. The culmination of the city's weeklong **Halloween Carnival** (tel. 028/7137-6545, www.derrycity.gov.uk) is fireworks on the night itself. The **Seagate Foyle Film Festival** (tel. 028/7126-7432, www.foylefilmfestival.com), the largest in Northern Ireland, generally takes place in mid-November and features both Irish and international flicks.

the city on the A2, tel. 028/7135-4040, www.derrycity.gov.uk/museums, open 9 A.M.–4 P.M. Mon.–Thurs., 9 A.M.–1 P.M. Fri., ring for an appointment, free admission) will take you to the very spot where the famous American aviator made her unexpected landing on May 21, 1932.

Tours

Politically correct, nonsectarian city tours (including a circuit of the city walls) start at the **tourist office** (44 Foyle St., tel. 028/7126-7284)—they're a bit more expensive than other tours but last nearly two hours (tours depart 2:30 P.M. Mon.–Fri. Sept.–June, 11:15 A.M. and 3:15 P.M. Mon.–Fri. July–Aug., tickets £5).

Alternatively, ring Martin McCrossan at **City Tours** (11 Carlisle Rd., tel. 028/7127-1996 or 077/1293-7997, www.irishtourguides.com, hour-long tour £4), which depart the office on Carlisle Road at 10 A.M., noon, and 2 P.M. year-round.

Those interested in the republican perspective should contact Ruairi at **Free Derry Tours** (tel. 028/7126-2812 or 077/9328-5972, www

.freederry.net, £4). Tours last 60–90 minutes and depart at 10 A.M. and 2 P.M. almost daily from the Museum of Free Derry (55-61 Glenfada Park, off Rossville St.).

Entertainment

No trip to Derry would be complete without a pint (or five) at one of the pubs along Waterloo Street, especially **Peadar O'Donnell's** (59-63 Waterloo St., tel. 028/7126-7295, peadars@tiscali.co.uk), named for the Donegal-born IRA rebel-turned-novelist. Peadar's has the best trad in town, with different fiddlers, strummers, and singers on every evening at 11 P.M. onward—not to mention the quaintly unsettling decor, mounted boar and ram heads and taxidermied birds of prey. The squeamish should avoid looking above the bar, where you'll find dried pork (including a pig's head decked out in sunglasses) strung from the ceiling. Fortunately, Peadar's attracts mostly locals despite its reputation for great trad. The other two pubs of note along this street are **The Gweedore,** which has a couple of long-haired strummers singing bluesy rock every night, and is attached to Peadar's by a door at the rear of the pub; and **The Dungloe** (41-43 Waterloo St., tel. 028/7126-7716), which offers trad on Thursday, rock on Friday and Saturday, and karaoke on Sunday. **The Anchor** (38 Ferryquay St., tel. 028/7136-8601, www.anchorbar.co.uk), still family-run, is another excellent spot for live blues most nights of the week.

If you're looking for a trendier spot, the hands-down favorite of 20-something locals is **Sandino's** (1 Water St., tel. 028/7130-9297, www.sandinos.com)—named after the Nicaraguan guerrilla (makes sense, considering the occasional political events held here). There's always something going on Thursday–Sunday, be it live rock or trad, DJs, or film screenings.

Besides classical, folk, and pop concerts, dramatic offerings at the **Millennium Forum** (Newmarket St., tel. 028/7126-4455, www.millenniumforum.co.uk, tickets £8–20) run the gamut from Shakespeare and Brontë adaptations to classic American musicals. The **Waterside Theatre** (The Ebrington Centre, Glendermott Rd., tel. 028/7131-4000, www.watersidetheatre.com, tickets £5–11) hosts both local and international dance and theater companies, with a few tribute bands and children's plays thrown in for variety's sake. The **Playhouse** (5-7 Artillery St., tel. 028/7126-8027, www.derryplayhouse.co.uk, tickets £7–15) does comedy, jazz and pop concerts, and contemporary (sometimes political) drama.

Catch an indie flick or pop/rock concert at the **Nerve Centre** (7-8 Magazine St., tel. 028/7126-0562, www.nerve-centre.org.uk, screenings £2, concerts £10–15), which also hosts the Foyle Film Festival every November. Part of a Bogside community regeneration project, the **Gasyard Centre** (128 Lecky Rd., Brandywell, tel. 028/7126-2812, www.freederry.org) sometimes hosts concerts in its multipurpose auditorium.

Shopping

Derry has two large shopping centers, the **Richmond** (tel. 028/7126-0525, www.richmondcentre.co.uk) on the diamond within the old city walls, and the **Foyleside** (tel. 028/7137-

7575, www.foyleside.co.uk) just without on Orchard Street. For a quieter, quainter shopping excursion, pop inside the **Derry Craft Village** (entrances on Shipquay St. and Magazine St.); a couple of small shops sell local crystal and jewelry beside a few cheap-and-cheesy souvenir stores. Even if you're not interested in either, it's nice to walk through this lovely little courtyard with its charming architecture and brightly painted doors, and **The Boston Tea Party** does simple but scrumptious desserts.

The place to go, if you're looking for a good book explaining the political situation in Northern Ireland, is **The Bookworm** (18-20 Bishop Street Within, tel. 028/7128-2727, www.bookwormderry.com), which also has a great café. Politically minded bibliophiles should stop by the Derry branch of **War on Want** (1B Carlisle Rd., tel. 028/7137-1520, waronwantni.org), with a nice selection of inexpensive used books and records and a stash of Fair Trade coffees, teas, and chocolate bars. All proceeds from War on Want Northern Ireland fund their African anti-hunger project. Another secondhand bookstore worth checking out is **Foyle Books** (12A Magazine St., tel. 028/7137-2530).

Sports and Recreation

Derry is the starting point of the 21-mile (34 km) **Foyle Valley Cycle Route,** which dips into Donegal briefly before delivering you to the Strabane tourist office in County Tyrone. The route is mostly off-road, making it a good choice for a peaceful, if strenuous, day's activity. Ask at the Derry tourist office for more information and a free map.

On **Foyle Cruises** (Harbour Museum, Harbour Sq., tel. 028/7136-2857, www.foylecruiseline.com) you can sail to Culmore Bay (at the mouth of the River Foyle) in the afternoon or to Greencastle on the east coast of the Inishowen Peninsula in the evening. Boats depart daily at 2 P.M. for the 75-minute Culmore Bay trip (£6), at 8 P.M. for the four-hour evening sail (£10).

Foyle International Golf Centre (12 Alder Rd., tel. 028/7135-2222, www.foylegolfcen-

HANG-GLIDING IN ULSTER

Northern Ireland offers a couple of opportunities to sightsee from above, as it were. In County Derry, the **Ulster Gliding Club** (tel. 077/0980-8276 for bookings, www.gliding.utvinternet.com, lessons given 9:30 A.M.–6 P.M. Sat.–Sun., trial lesson/1-day course £50/149), based in Bellarena, 36 kilometers east of Derry City, offers instruction for beginners as well as gliders of all experience levels. The same goes for the **Aerosports Paragliding School** (tel. 028/9334-1414, www.aerosports.co.uk, full-day "taster" course £130), which is affiliated with the **Ulster Hang-gliding and Paragliding Club** (tel. 028/3834-1544, www.uhpc.f9.co.uk), based in Craigavon in County Armagh, 22 kilometers northeast of Armagh City and 45 kilometers southwest of Belfast. Flying sites include mountains in the Sperrins in County Tyrone and the Mournes in County Down.

include continental breakfast and Internet access. The "fifth night free" policy and nightly barbecues (£2) April–September contribute to the phenomenon known around here as the "Derry vortex"—once here, you'll find it difficult to leave. The wonderfully friendly and helpful owners, Kylie and Steve, operate another townhouse with private rooms around the corner on Prince's Street, **Dolce Vita** (tel. 028/7128-0542, twins and doubles £17 pp, triples £11 pp). It's bright and airy, with a gorgeous kitchen and dining area and brand-new bathrooms, and the private room rates also include Internet access. For backpackers, it's definitely worth the splurge.

[**The Saddler's House** (36 Great James St., tel. 028/7126-9691 or 028/7126-4223, www.thesaddlershouse.com, £20–25 pp, s £20–30) is universally recognized as the best B&B in the city, and deservedly so. Dr. and Mrs. Pyne live in another townhouse around the corner, **The Merchant's House** (16 Queen St., £20–25 pp, s £20–30), which has more rooms with shared bath. Both Georgians have been restored to perfection—grandfather clocks, Hogarth prints, decorative plasterwork (and a lascivious young bulldog to boot). The breakfasts are outstanding. Be sure to book ahead, especially in high season, and call in to Saddler's when checking in.

If Saddler's and Merchant's are booked up, another option is the very homey **Sunbeam House** (147 Sunbeam Terrace, Bishop St., tel. 028/7126-3606, sunbeamhouse@hotmail.com, £22–24 pp, s £30), in an ordinary residential neighborhood teeming with lively schoolchildren. This is the kind of place where milk is still delivered daily on the doorstep in glass bottles.

It's surprising that the four-star **Tower Hotel** (Butcher St., tel. 028/7137-1000, www.towerhotelgroup.com, £35–55 pp, s £60–80), the first built within the old city walls, has such a modern design and impersonal ambience. That said, the location (at Magazine St. and Butcher St., just beside the western wall) is second to none—it's certainly reason enough to stay here. Check out the website for special deals; a weekend package (two nights B&B, dinner,

tre.co.uk) has two courses (one 18-hole championship course and a 9-hole par-3 course) as well as a floodlit driving range. The **City of Derry Golf Club** (49 Victoria Rd., Prehen, 3 mi/4.8 km west of Derry City, tel. 028/7134-6369, www.cityofderrygolfclub.com) also offers two courses.

They're over the border in County Donegal, but the **Lenamore Stables** (Muff, tel. 074/938-4022, www.lenamorestables.com) are only two miles (3.2 km) outside the city.

Accommodations

B&B accommodations are comparatively difficult to come by; you have more hotel choices. Luckily, the city's only hostel (outside of "Paddy's Palace," a magnet for tour groups) is a fine one. The **Derry City Independent Hostel** (44 Great James St., tel. 028/7128-0542, www.derry-hostel.co.uk, derryhostel@hotmail.com, dorms £11, private rooms £16 pp, laundry £2) is pleasantly bohemian and cozy, and prices

and guided city wall tour) can run you as little as €99 per person.

Also boasting four stars is the Great Southern **City Hotel** (Queen's Quay, tel. 028/7136-5800, www.greatsouthernhotels.com, rooms £60–70), which offers views of the Guildhall and the River Foyle and a deluxe leisure center (full-size pool, steam room, Jacuzzi, and gym).

It may not have the location, but the three-star **Ramada da Vinci's** (15 Culmore Rd., 1 mi/1.6 km north of the city, tel. 028/7127-9111, www.davincishotel.com, rooms £55–80, but as low as £40 at off-peak periods) more than compensates with comfortable business-class rooms, 21 cushy self-catering apartments, and free wireless Internet. While there aren't leisure facilities at the hotel, it offers discounted rates at the Templemore Sports Complex a mile away. You'll find above-average fare in the hotel restaurant and a lot of locals (always a good sign) in all of da Vinci's three bars.

Food

Derry may not compete with the capital when it comes to eating out, but you can have yourself a scrummy meal if you know where to go.

The coffee shop at the Nerve Centre, **Café Nervosa** (7-8 Magazine St., tel. 028/7126-0562, open 9:30 A.M.–5 P.M. Mon.–Sat., mains £3–5), facing the west wall, is a good place to chill out with a cup of coffee and surf the Net for no extra charge. The lunches are simple but hearty, with several vegetarian and gluten-free choices. The fare's more gourmet at **Café Artisan** (London St., tel. 028/7128-2727, open 8:30 A.M.–5 P.M. weekdays, 9 A.M.–5 P.M. Sat., mains £3–5), attached to the Bookworm, which does delicious (and super-fresh) salads, soups, and sandwiches. **The Boston Tea Party** (off Shipquay St., tel. 028/7126-9667, open 9 A.M.–5:30 P.M. Mon.–Sat., snacks under £3) inside the Derry Craft Village is a splendid little spot for lunch or afternoon tea.

The portions are on the dainty side, but **Badger's** (16-18 Orchard St., tel. 028/7136-0763, food served noon–7 P.M. Mon.–Thurs., noon–9:30 P.M. Fri.–Sat., noon–4 P.M. Sun., mains £5–11) does the best pub grub in town—the relatively creative menu features tasty Indian-inspired vegetarian dishes. The warm wood paneling, stained glass, whimsical wall murals, and second-floor nonsmoking section (with its own bar) make Badger's a comfy spot for lunch.

Two swanky but laid-back spots for lunch or dinner are **The Exchange** (Exchange House, Queen's Quay, tel. 028/7127-3990, www.exchangerestaurant.com, open noon–10 P.M. Mon.–Sat., 5:30–9 P.M. Sun., mains £8–15), a wine bar/restaurant, and **Fitzroy's** (3 Carlisle Rd. and 2-4 Bridge St., tel. 028/7126-6211, www.fitzroysrestaurant.com, open 9:30 A.M.–10 P.M. Wed.–Sun., 9:30 A.M.–7 P.M. Mon.–Tues., lunch £5–10, dinner £8–12, £13 3-course dinner Wed.–Thurs. after 7 P.M.). These are a couple of Derry's best eateries, offering imaginative dishes with fresh ingredients—no overpriced, microwaved appetizers here! Beware that another restaurant with a positive reputation in this town, Mange 2 on Clarendon Street, offers bland food that doesn't live up to the hype.

But Derry's finest restaurant is on the Waterside. The motto is "a little different" at **Spice** (162 Spencer Rd., tel. 028/7134-4875, open 12:30–2:30 P.M. Tues.–Fri. and Sun., 5:30–10 P.M. Tues.–Sat. and 5–9 P.M. Sun., mains £9–16), which doesn't refer to either the cuisine—it's more than a *little* different—or the nondescript decor. Any choice on the eclectic Continental menu makes for a truly memorable meal. Vegetarians shouldn't miss this one, as there's a whole different menu with a list of imaginative and totally mouthwatering options, asparagus tartlet and so forth. The service is first-class. Spice is a 20-minute walk over the Craigavon Bridge from the city walls.

Information

Tourist office (44 Foyle St., tel. 028/7126-7284, www.derryvisitor.com) hours vary seasonally (9 A.M.–5 P.M. weekdays all year, plus 10 A.M.–5 P.M. Sat. mid-Mar.–June and Oct.; 9 A.M.–7 P.M. weekdays, 10 A.M.–6 P.M. Sat., and 10 A.M.–5 P.M. Sun. July–Sept.).

The **Derry Journal** (www.derryjournal. com) is a good source for news and events in the Maiden City.

Services

Derry's banks (all with ATMs and bureaux de change) are clustered around Guildhall Square and Waterloo Place, including **Ulster Bank** and **Bank of Ireland.** The central **post office** is on Custom House Street behind the Guildhall.

Your best bet for a pharmacy is **Boots** (tel. 028/7126-0432) in the Foyleside Shopping Centre. Need your laundry done? **City Clean** (Waterloo Pl., tel. 028/7136-1962, closed Sun.) offers same-day service.

A couple of cafés in and around the old city offer speedy Internet access, but it's ridiculously priced at £4 an hour. Access on two old-school iMacs is free with purchase at **Café Nervosa** (7-8 Magazine St., tel. 028/7126-0562, open 9:30 A.M.–5 P.M. Mon.–Sat.). The excellent **central public library** (35 Foyle St., tel. 028/7127-2310) offers access to nonmembers for £0.75 per 15 minutes, and there are enough terminals that you shouldn't have to wait too long.

Getting There

Derry City is 72 miles (116 km) northwest of Belfast on the A6. Get here from the capital city via **Ulsterbus** (Foyle Street Depot, tel. 029/7126-2261, route #212, 32/day Mon.–Fri., 19/day Sat., 11/day Sun., travel time 1 hour 50 minutes, single/return £9.40/14). **Northern Ireland Railways** pulls into Waterside Station (tel. 028/7134-2228, www.translink.co.uk) across the Craigavon Bridge and offers service to/from Belfast (9/day Mon.–Sat., 3/day Sun., single/day return £9.80/14). At 2 hours and 10 minutes, the train actually takes longer than the bus!

Derry City Airport (Airport Rd., Eglinton, 7 mi/11 km northeast of Derry, tel. 028/7181-0784, www.cityofderryairport.com) offers direct flights from Dublin, Glasgow, and Manchester on British Airways, and Liverpool, London Stansted, and Nottingham on RyanAir. The **AIRporter** shuttle runs six times daily between the airport and the Quayside Shopping Centre.

For bus transport from the republic, Letterkenny-based **John McGinley** (tel. 074/913-5201, www.johnmcginley.com) operates a coach service linking Dublin (city and airport) with Derry before continuing on to Donegal. **Bus Éireann** can get you here from Donegal Town and Letterkenny (#64, 8/day daily).

Getting Around

Derry is small enough that you can walk everywhere you want to go. If you're just spending the afternoon, park your car at the multilevel Foyleside garage across the car park beside the tourist office (£0.80/hour).

For bicycle rental, try **Happy Days** (245 Lone Moor Rd., tel. 028/7128-7128, www .happydays.ie, £9/35 per day/week), a Raleigh agent.

For a cab, ring **Maiden City Taxis** (3 Lower Clarendon St., tel. 028/7126-1666); **Ace Cabs** (111 Strand Rd., tel. 028/7126-2020) and **Foyle Delta Cabs** (10a Market St., tel. 028/7127-9999 or 028/7126-3905) both offer 24-hour service.

◀ DOWNHILL ESTATE

Blink once and you might miss the loveliest spot in County Derry: Downhill is a tiny place, only on the map for the 18th-century clifftop estate of Bishop Hervey, now a huge and extremely eerie ruin. Beneath that cliff is a pristine beach popular with surfers.

The grand estate of the infamous Bishop of Derry and fourth Earl of Bristol, Frederick Augustus Hervey, has laid in ruin since World War II. More entrepreneur and playboy than holy man, he invented and grew wealthy on Hervey's Bristol Cream (ask for it instead of Bailey's while you're in the North) and built this rambling mansion in 1774. These ruins are among the very creepiest in all Ireland, especially if visited on a sunless day. Much of the original 395-acre Downhill Estate (Hezlett Farm, 107 Sea Rd., Castlerock, signposted from the A2, tel. 028/7084-8728, www.ntni.org.uk,

© CAMILLE DEANGELIS

The Mussenden Temple at Downhill Estate housed Bishop Hervey's library, mistress, or both.

open dawn–dusk all year, car admission £3.80) now makes up **Downhill Forest** (open 10 A.M.–dusk daily, free admission), which slopes eastward to the little ho-hum resort town of Castlerock. Perched on a cliff over the north coast, a short walk from the mansion ruin, is the delightful **Mussenden Temple** (open 11 A.M.–6 P.M. weekends Mar.–May and Sept.–Oct., daily Easter week and June, 11 A.M.–7 P.M. daily July–Aug.), which housed Hervey's library, mistress, or both, depending on whom you ask. This place is a favorite haunt of wedding parties, and a midsummer concert is performed on the lawn.

Just off the beach, the IHH, family-friendly ◖ **Downhill Hostel** (Glenhassan Hall, 12 Mussenden Rd., tel. 028/7084-9077, www .downhillhostel.com, open Easter–Oct., dorms £10, doubles £15 pp) is an absolute gem. A large restored Victorian nestled between cliff, stream, and sea, this place is the perfect getaway-from-it-all spot, especially if you're the outdoorsy type; not only can you rent wet suits and bodyboards here, but nearby Down-

hill Forest is ideal for a long walk or jog. The owners are a lovely young couple, William and McCall, who take pride in making ongoing improvements to an already fabulous hostel. As McCall is an accomplished potter, there's also a pottery attached where you can paint your own (but plan to spend at least two days or it won't be ready in time). This is literally the only accommodation in Downhill, but you won't care less about the lack of choice!

Downhill is 29 miles (47 km) east of Derry City on the A2. The **Ulsterbus** (tel. 028/9066-6630, www.ulsterbus.co.uk, 5/day Mon.–Sat., 2/day Sun.). Goldline Express route #234 between Derry and Coleraine can get you here.

DUNGIVEN

A market town on the A6 between Derry (19 mi/31 km) and Belfast (53 mi/85 km), Dungiven (Dún Geimhin, "Given's Fort") isn't a particularly attractive place, but it makes a fine base for exploring the Sperrin mountain range from the north. The ruins of a 12th-century **Augustinian priory** (tel. 028/7772-2074 for info, clearly signposted from Main St., always accessible) feature the resplendently Gothic 14th-century tomb of Cooey-na-Gal, a Gaelic chieftain, and a bullaun (a hollowed stone originally used for grinding grain—later folklore attributed wart-curing properties to rainwater caught in its hollow).

How'd you like to stay in a castle for the price of a couple of pizzas? **Dungiven Castle** (Upper Main St., tel. 028/7774-2428, www.dungivencastle.com, dorms £12, private rooms £16 pp) dates from the 1830s and has served many purposes over the decades (it was a barracks for American soldiers during World War II), but today it's a comfortable hostel. The neo-Gothic facade belies the mod cons inside: all the rooms are en suite (with bathtub) and offer views of the Sperrins (none face the ugly parking lot out front, luckily), and the private rooms are comfortably furnished to a near-B&B standard. Best of all are the 22 acres of conserved parkland out back, with an Italianate fountain and plenty of picnic tables; there's a one-mile loop walk as well as a path leading to Dungiven Priory. The castle also serves as the town's **tourist office,** open daily all year.

Ironically, the rest of the accommodations in Dungiven aren't nearly as dramatic or exciting. There is no hotel and only two small and fairly basic B&Bs; try **Edenroe** (32 Chapel Rd., signposted from the A6, tel. 028/7774-2029 or 077/5969-2122, margaretmonica@aol.com, £23 pp, s £28), with two en-suite rooms on the south side of town, or **Bradagh** (132 Main St., tel. 028/7774-1346 or 078/0108-8866, £18 pp, all with shared bath) in the town center.

Dungiven's main street is lined with uninspiring takeaways, leading one to despair of finding a decent spot for dinner. Never fear: **John T's** (at the bottom of Main St., tel. 028/7774-2170, open 12:30–9 P.M. daily, mains £6–15) feels extra-specially swanky after you've passed so many run-down chippers. Chicken and steak dishes dominate the menu, though the veggie options are solid, and the portions are huge. The staff are really friendly and helpful too.

Dungiven is serviced by **Ulsterbus** (tel. 028/9066-6630, www.ulsterbus.co.uk) on route #212 between Derry and Belfast (£8.20/12.50 single/return from Belfast). Or route #148 can get you here from the Foyle Street Bus Centre in Derry (4/day weekdays, 3/day Sat.) in about 50 minutes.

DOWN AND ARMAGH

There's truly something for everyone in County Down (An Dún, "The Fort"): some of the best golf courses on the island, the Mourne Mountains to challenge hikers and rock climbers, attractions like the Ulster Folk and Transport Museum perfect for family excursions, and delightfully out-of-the-way towns like Greyabbey and Saintfield with their reputations for top-notch antiques shops. You may also find that the people of Down are the friendliest in the north.

Partly because it's so rural and residential, Armagh ("ar-MAH," Ard Mhacha, "Macha's Height") ranks with County Tyrone as the least-visited of the six Northern counties. It's also the smallest of the six. But the atmospheric old "cathedral city," Navan Fort, and swaths of apple trees all a-blossom in May are all great reasons to make a special trip.

For more info before you go, check out the **Armagh Down Tourism** site (www.armagh-anddown.com).

HISTORY

Saint Patrick left his mark on these counties in a big way, founding his very first church in the hamlet of Saul, just east of Downpatrick, in 432; the building was a converted stable donated by a local chieftain, one of the saint's first converts. About 13 years later Patrick made Armagh his base, largely because of the pagan significance of the nearby fort of Emain Macha. (The city calls itself Ireland's "spiritual capital" not just for this, but because it's the seat of both Armagh archbishops—Anglican and Catholic—who also serve as primates of the whole of Ireland.) It's said

HIGHLIGHTS

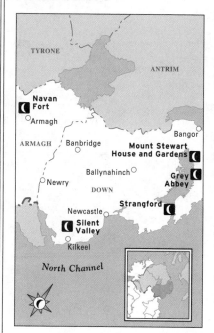

◖ Mount Stewart House and Gardens:
The highlight of this 18th-century manor is the 78-acre formal garden featuring a series of whimsical topiaries (page 467).

◖ Grey Abbey: Founded by the Welsh princess Affreca, bride of John de Courcy, in thanksgiving for her safe passage to Ireland despite a stormy sea, Grey Abbey is County Down's most important (not to mention spookiest) monastic ruin (page 467).

◖ Strangford: Possibly the loveliest spot in all of County Down, this seaside hamlet at the Strangford narrows offers short walks through picturesque woodland and nice eateries lining an almost unbearably charming main square (page 471).

◖ Silent Valley: So named for the absence of birdsong, this valley in the Mourne Mountains holds the Belfast reservoir, and there are picturesque walking trails all around it (page 473).

◖ Navan Fort: Rich in myth and legend, this hill just outside Armagh City has been called "Ireland's Mount Olympus" (page 479).

LOOK FOR ◖ TO FIND RECOMMENDED SIGHTS, ACTIVITIES, DINING, AND LODGING.

that Patrick returned to Saul in his "retirement" after three-plus decades.

These counties also have a few literary connections worth mentioning; Jonathan Swift is said to have written *Gulliver's Travels* at the old Gosford Castle outside Armagh City; and Patrick Brontë, father of that trio of novelist sisters, was born in Banbridge (in the western part of County Down) and taught at a school there as a young man.

PLANNING YOUR TIME

Since you'll be passing through Down on a trip from Dublin to Belfast, it makes sense to pause for a few days en route. Get to Belfast first if using public transport, because virtually all Ulsterbus routes come out of the capital (and traveling in between towns in Down may even require returning to Belfast). Don't waste time in towns like Newry and Lisburn; these are business-as-usual places with little to see.

Armagh is only 10 miles (16 km) west of the border, so you could make this small city your last stop before heading back into the republic. It's also roughly midway between Enniskillen and Belfast. Though Armagh's "orchard country" north of the city is pretty in springtime, there isn't much in terms of attractions and visitor amenities outside the county capital.

Because of their historical (or legendary)

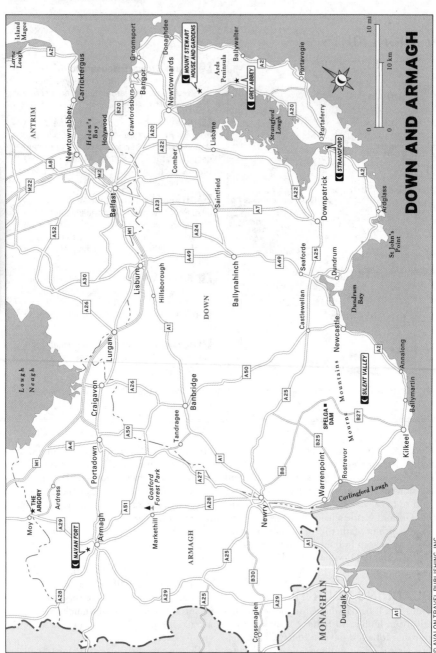

DOWN AND ARMAGH

associations with St. Patrick, many towns in Armagh and Down (Downpatrick especially) drag out his feast day into a weeklong carnival. Depending on your capacity for alcohol and crowds, you may want to either avoid these places in March—or make a beeline!

Down

Of the six counties in Northern Ireland, Down has the most to offer. Antrim may have the famous coastline, pretty glens, and capital city, but Down's smaller towns and villages are generally more upbeat and better maintained—and the mountain and coastal scenery is nearly as pretty.

BANGOR

A quintessential Victorian seaside resort, Bangor ("BANG-grr," Beannchor) began as a 6th-century monastery associated with St. Columbanus. Today it's a Belfast commuter suburb—and the third-largest town in Northern Ireland—with a bustling marina and a few good pubs and eateries. Base yourself here when visiting the capital city for lower-priced accommodations and prettier surrounds, or spend a couple days exploring the Ards Peninsula, south of here.

Sights

Now the headquarters of the North Down Borough Council, mid-19th-century **Bangor Castle** (Town Hall, Castle Park Ave., tel. 028/9127-0371, free admission to grounds) isn't generally open to the public, though you can ring for an appointment if you'd like to see inside.

Aside from a 15th-century bell tower, what's left of **Bangor Abbey** dates from the mid-19th century. You'll have to find someone in the adjacent Church of Ireland (tel. 028/9145-1087) to let you inside.

There's an eclectic range of exhibits at the **North Down Heritage Centre** (Castle Park Ave., tel. 028/9127-1200, open 10:30 A.M.–4:30 P.M. Tues.–Sat., 2–4:30 P.M. Sun. all year, and until 5:30 P.M. Tues.–Sun. July–Aug., free admission), one of which traces the abbey's history.

Like the Ulster-American Folk Park in County Tyrone, the **Ulster Folk and Transport Museum** (Cultra, A2 Belfast-Bangor road near Holywood, tel. 028/9042-8428, www.uftm.org.uk, train rides Sat. 2–5 P.M., admission £5.50 to either folk or transport, combo ticket £7) is a complex of reconstructed shopfronts with costumed craftspeople and other "villagers." Hours vary seasonally (10 A.M.–5 P.M. Mon.–Fri., 10 A.M.–6 P.M. Sat., 11 A.M.–6 P.M. Sun. Mar.–June; 10 A.M.–6 P.M. Mon.–Sat. and 11 A.M.–6 P.M. Sun. July–Sept.; 10 A.M.–4 P.M. Mon.–Fri., 10 A.M.–5 P.M. Sat., 11 A.M.–5 P.M. Sun. Oct.–Feb.).

Shopping

Bangor's mall, the **Flagship Shopping Centre,** has entrances on Main and Bingham Streets. The town's quaintest shops—antiques and artisans—are along Gray's Hill, just up from the marina. A few worth poking around in are **Annville Antiques** (28 Gray's Hill, tel. 028/9145-2522), **This&That** (32 Gray's Hill, tel. 028/9145-1799), and **Goldenage** (57A Gray's Hill, tel. 028/9127-0938).

Entertainment

Catch a trad session at **Jenny Watt's** (41 High St., tel. 028/9127-0401) on Tuesday, jazz on a Sunday afternoon (11 A.M.–3 P.M.), or acoustic rock on Sunday night. This is Bangor's oldest pub, established in 1780. **The Windsor** (24 Quay St., tel. 028/9147-3943) has folk music on Wednesdays, and **Donegan's** (37-39 High St., tel. 028/9146-3928) has a live rock band on Thursday, both gigs commencing soon after 10 P.M.

Sports and Recreation

The beautifully manicured **Ward Park** (Hamilton Rd., tel. 028/9145-8773 for bowling and

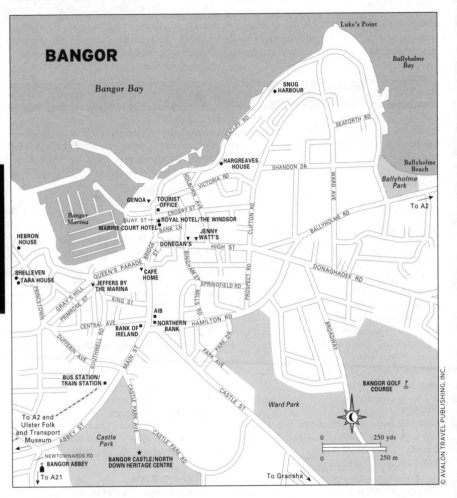

putting greens, tel. 028/9145-7177 for tennis, sporting facilities open daily Easter–Sept.) is one of the loveliest town parks anywhere in the country, with a brook cutting through it. You can play tennis or go bowling or putting for a nominal fee.

The **Bangor Marina** (tel. 028/9145-3297) is one of the biggest in Ireland. **John Erskine** (tel. 028/9146-9458 or 078/0157-1830) and the **Blue Aquarius** (tel. 077/7960-0607, www.

bangorboat.com) both offer fishing, bird-watching, and general sightseeing trips.

Gransha Equestrian Centre (10 Kerrs Rd., Six Road Ends, 3.7 mi/6 km southeast of Bangor off the A21, tel. 028/9181-3313, granshariding@utvinternet.com) has an indoor arena as well as 40 acres of cross-country trails. Or tee off at the 18-hole, 71-par **Bangor Golf Club** (Broadway, 1 mi/1.6 km east of town on the Donaghdee road/B21, tel. 028/9127-0922).

Accommodations

There aren't any hostels in Bangor, but for budget B&B (read: shared bath), Seacliff Road—right on the water—is the place to go. Try **Snug Harbour** (144 Seacliff Rd., tel. 028/9145-4238 or 078/3533-8252, £15–20 pp) or **Hargreaves House** (78 Seacliff Rd., tel. 028/9146-4071, ppeewee1@aol.com, £22 pp).

There are plenty of B&Bs to choose from along Princetown Road, and all of the following accept credit cards. **Tara** (51 Princetown Rd., tel. 028/9145-8820, www.taraguesthouse.co.uk, £23 pp, s £30) and **Shelleven** (61 Princetown Rd., tel. 028/9127-1777, www.shelleven-house.com, £28–30 pp, s £33–45) bookend a block of large, charming Victorian town-homes. These two offer all en-suite rooms and are large enough (11 and 14 rooms) to be your best bets if you haven't booked ahead. Shelleven may be more pricey, but it's a bit classier, and the breakfast menu offers more variety. Farther along on the other side of the street is the smaller, more upscale **Hebron House** (68 Princetown Rd., tel. 028/9146-3126, www.hebron-house.com, £32.50 pp, s £45), a smart brick home with views of the marina from the rear bedrooms and breakfast room, as well as wireless Internet access.

Because much of the clientele in Bangor's hotels is here for business in Belfast, rates are often lower over the weekend. The Victorian **Royal Hotel** (22-28 Quay St., tel. 028/9127-1866, www.royalhotelbangor.com, £35 pp, s £50), painted a queer shade of rusty orange, offers period atmosphere in its pub and reception areas, but the rooms are all modern. Another option right next door is the **Marine Court Hotel** (18-20 Quay St., tel. 028/9145-1100, www.marinecourthotel.net, £45 pp, s £80), also standard business-class (and with complimentary wireless Internet).

Food

It's no gastro-paradise, but Bangor still offers the best dining options in the county. Order yourself a cappuccino and a delicious sweet or savory crepe (or Belgian waffles) at **Café Home**

(2-3 Main St. at Queen's Parade, tel. 028/9147-3373, open 9 A.M.–5 P.M. Mon.–Tues., 9 A.M.–10 P.M. Wed.–Thurs., 9 A.M.–11 P.M. Fri.–Sat., 1–8:30 P.M. Sun., meals £2–5), a sleek and pleasant Fair Trade coffee shop with large windows facing the marina.

You'll find decent pub grub at **Jenny Watt's** (41 High St., tel. 028/9127-0401, food served noon–7 P.M. Mon.–Fri. and noon–9 P.M. Sat.–Sun., mains £5–8) or next door at **Donegan's** (37-39 High St., tel. 028/9146-3928, food served noon–2:30 P.M. weekdays and noon–9 P.M. weekends, mains £6–8), which also has a fine upstairs restaurant (open 5–9 P.M. Mon.–Fri., noon–9 P.M. Sat., 12:30–8 P.M. Sun., mains £6–16, 2-course Sun. lunch £10). It's quiet and low-key, though family-friendly, with efficient waitstaff and hefty portions. The menu's fairly standard—steaks and seafood—though the few meat-free options are surprisingly tasty.

A trendier option—for any meal—is **Jeffers by the Marina** (7 Grays Hill, tel. 028/9185-9555, open 9 A.M.–4:30 P.M. Mon., 9 A.M.–10 P.M. Tues.–Sat., 11 A.M.–8 P.M. Sun., mains £4–13), a mod café with a diverse and unusual menu that includes lamb burgers and curried prawn risotto.

Right on the pier in the old Harbour Master's office, **Genoa** (1a Seacliff Rd., tel. 028/9146-9253, open 11 A.M.–2:30 P.M. and 5:30–9 P.M. Tues.–Fri., 5:30–10 P.M. Sat., mains £10–18) does the freshest, tastiest seafood in Bangor in a quaint little dining room. There's a separate vegetarian menu, and the midweek couples' special—two meals and a bottle of wine for £40, Tuesday–Friday—is quite a good value.

Information

The **tourist office** (34 Quay St., tel. 028/9127-0069, www.northdown.gov.uk) resides in a 17th-century tower house beside the Royal Hotel. Hours vary seasonally (10 A.M.–7 P.M. Mon., 9 A.M.–7 P.M. Tues.–Fri., 10 A.M.–4 P.M. Sat. and noon–6 P.M. Sun. July–Aug.; 10 A.M.–5 P.M. Mon., 9 A.M.–5 P.M. Tues.–Fri., 10 A.M.–4 P.M. Sat. and 1–5 P.M. Sun. June and Sept.;

10 A.M.–5 P.M. Mon., 9 A.M.–5 P.M. Tues.–Fri. and 10 A.M.–4 P.M. Sat. Oct.–May).

Services

The **Bank of Ireland, Ulster Bank,** and **Northern Bank** are all on Main Street, and all have ATMs and bureaux de change. The **post office** is also on Main Street.

If you need a pharmacy, note the local branch of **Boots** (79/83 Main St., tel. 028/9127-1134). Suds your duds at **Bubbles** (43 Belfast Rd., tel. 028/9146-9991).

Check your email at the **public library** (Hamilton Rd., tel. 028/9127-0591, open 10 A.M.–8 P.M. Mon.–Wed., 10 A.M.–5 P.M. Fri., 10 A.M.–1 P.M. and 2–5 P.M. Sat., £1.50/30 minutes).

Getting There and Around

Bangor is 14 miles (22 km) east of Belfast on the A2. Get here from the capital via **Ulsterbus** (tel. 028/9066-6630) routes #B1 and #B2 (2/ hour Mon.–Sat., 8/day Sun., single/return £3/5.40) or **Northern Ireland Railways** (tel. 028/9066-6630, 2/hour Mon.–Sat., 13/day Sun., single/day return £3.80/6.80).

For a taxi, ring **North Down Cabs** (tel. 028/9147-0777). Strangely, there is no bike hire available in Bangor.

CRAWFORDSBURN

A couple miles west of Bangor—on the "gold coast," which refers as much to its wealthy Belfast commuters as the pristine beaches—is the charming village of Crawfordsburn, notable for its country park and 17th-century coaching inn. Established in 1614, **The Old Inn** (15 Main St., tel. 028/9185-3255, www.theoldinn.com, rooms £85–105) is awash in distinctions. It's Ireland's oldest hotel—naturally, it's also one of the most haunted. C. S. Lewis, a frequent guest, proclaimed it heaven on earth. And despite somewhat touch-and-go service, the restaurants—the posh **1614** and the less formal **Churn Bistro**— are the best in County Down (bar meals served noon–7 P.M. daily, 1614 open 7–9 P.M. Mon.– Sat. and 12:30–2 P.M. Sun., Churn open 7– 9:30 P.M. Mon.–Sat., 3-course dinner £25).

But first work up an appetite at the **Crawfordsburn Country Park** (Bridge Rd. S., Helen's Bay, 2 mi/3.2 km west of Bangor on the B20, tel. 028/9185-3621, open 9 A.M.– 8 P.M. daily Apr.–Sept., 9 A.M.–4:45 P.M. Oct.– Mar., visitors center open 9 A.M.–5 P.M. daily, free admission), with its two-mile (3.2-km) strand and wooded nature trails, one of which leads over an old railway viaduct to a waterfall near the Old Inn.

Crawfordsburn is just under two miles (3.2 km) west of Bangor on the B20, but you can get here on the Belfast–Bangor train via **Northern Ireland Railways** (tel. 028/9066-6630, 2–3/ hour). Get off at the Helen's Bay stop.

THE ARDS PENINSULA

Mourne Mountains aside, the area east of **Strangford Lough** (from the Norse Strang-fjörthr, "Strong Ford") is the loveliest part of County Down. A narrows connects the lake to the sea between the tips of the Ards (An Aird) and Lecale (Leth-Chathail, "Cathal's Half") Peninsulas. There's a frequent ferry connection between the two towns on opposite sides of the narrows (Portaferry and Strangford, respectively), so you can bypass the lough's less interesting western shore once you've explored the bucolic, low-lying Ards. The east coast is punctuated by caravan parks, and though there are a few pretty beaches, swimming in the Irish Sea is not recommended due to industrial pollution.

Newtownards

Gateway town to the Ards Peninsula, you'll find Newtownards' (Baile Nua na hArda) distasteful abbreviation—"N'ards"—on road signs all over northeast Down; the town itself isn't much more appealing. If you're passing through, you might want to stop at the **tourist office** and craft shop (31 Regent St., tel. 028/9182-6846, www.kingdomsofdown. com, open 9:15 A.M.–5 P.M. Mon.–Fri. and 9:30 A.M.–5 P.M. Sat.) if you have any questions about the peninsula, since the Portaferry office is only seasonal. From the A20/Belfast road, take the town center exit at the roundabout and turn right onto Church Street, which becomes Regent Street.

Scuba divers have another reason to stop in N'ards: **DV Diving** (138 Mountstewart Rd., tel. 028/9146-4671, www.dvdiving.co.uk), which caters to all experience levels (and provides accommodations).

Donaghdee

Claiming to be the oldest pub in Ireland, ◖ **Grace Neill's** (33 High St., tel. 028/9188-4595, food served noon–2:30 P.M. and 6–9:30 P.M. daily, mains £5–14) sure looks the part, from the gnome-sized entryway and low, rough wood ceiling to the cobwebby lace curtains and the dirt ground into the flagstone floor. Over the centuries, famous visitors have included Daniel Defoe, Franz Liszt, John Keats, and Peter the Great. During slow periods, you've got to ring the brass bell at the bar (stamped 1824) to obtain the bartender's attention. And with all the yellowed photographs on the walls and antique liquor bottles arranged in the glass cases, it might sound like Grace Neill's is a self-conscious tourist attraction, but it's not at all—and the staff are friendly as can be. Food is served in both the modern bistro and "library bar" adjoining.

Otherwise, the little seaside town of Donaghdee doesn't have much going on (and the beach isn't the greatest), but it's only a six-mile (9.6 km) drive east of Bangor, and Ulsterbus serves the town on its Belfast–Millisle route (#7 from Belfast, #3 from Bangor, 2–3/hour daily, single/return from Belfast £3.60/6.40).

◖ Mount Stewart House and Gardens

One of Ireland's most glorious manor houses overlooks Strangford Lough from the western side of the Ards. Now in care of the National Trust, the 18th-century Mount Stewart House and Gardens (on the A20 5 mi/8 km south of Newtownards, tel. 028/4278-8387, www.nationaltrust.org.uk, house and gardens/gardens-only admission £5.50/4.50) was the home of the marquess of Londonderry. The gardens are open year-round, but the house

Delightfully quaint, Grace Neill's in Donaghdee claims to be Ireland's oldest pub.

is not (house open noon–6 P.M. daily July–Aug.; noon–6 P.M. Wed.–Mon. Sept.; 1–6 P.M. Mon. and Wed.–Fri. and noon–6 P.M. Sat.–Sun. May–June; noon–6 P.M. weekends and holidays mid-Mar.–Apr. and Oct., gardens open 10 A.M.–8 P.M. daily May–Sept., 10 A.M.–6 P.M. Apr. and Oct., 10 A.M.–4 P.M. Nov.–Mar.). Inside you'll find a world-class collection of paintings and sculpture; outside is an equally stunning 78-acre formal garden dating to the 1920s, the highlight of which is the Dodo Terrace, featuring topiaries of mythical and long-extinct animals. A classical Greek folly set on a hill, the Temple of the Winds was built in 1780 and affords an excellent view of Strangford Lough.

Mount Stewart is a 15-minute drive south of N'ards, and the Belfast–Portaferry Ulsterbus routes #9A and #10 pass the gate six times a day Monday–Saturday, three times on Sunday.

◖ Grey Abbey

There are two great reasons to pause in Greyabbey, a small town just south of Mount

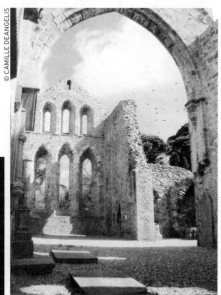

© CAMILLE DEANGELIS

DOWN AND ARMAGH

Grey Abbey is County Down's most important monastic ruin.

Stewart on the western Ards road: a charming stone courtyard lined with antiques stores, and the magnificent ruins of the 12th-century Grey Abbey (An Mhainistir Liath, Church Rd., tel. 028/9054-6552, visitors center open 10 A.M.–7 P.M. Tues.–Sat. and 2–7 P.M. Sun. Apr.–Sept., 10 A.M.–4 P.M. Mon.–Sat. and 2–4 P.M. Sun. Oct.–Mar., free admission). This Cistercian priory was founded in 1193 with the largesse of the Welsh princess Affreca, wife of Anglo-Norman adventurer John de Courcy, in thanksgiving for her safe passage from the Isle of Man. This is Ireland's first fully Gothic-style edifice—without a single rounded arch to be found—and there are a couple of interesting tomb effigies, a knight and a lady, incorrectly identified as Affreca (since the tomb style is late 13th century). Adding an element of spookiness even in fine weather is the largely 18th-century graveyard out front, with its otherwise dignified headstones tipped askew. This cemetery is more crowded than a U2 concert.

The abbey grounds are lush and immaculately maintained, an ideal spot for a picnic

lunch. If the sun's not shining, you can always enjoy a soup or sandwich at the splendidly old-fashioned tearoom at **Hoops** (Main St., tel. 028/4278-8541, open 9 A.M.–5 P.M. Tues.–Sat., daily July–Aug., tearoom open at 10 A.M., meals £3–6), a complex of more than a dozen antiques shops lining a cobblestoned courtyard.

Otherwise, the town of Greyabbey is a rather dull little place, with a proliferation of ugly pebble-dashed rowhouses. Plan on a visit of no more than a couple hours, as this is a quiet residential area with scarce accommodation.

Greyabbey is 14 miles (23 km) south of Bangor and is served on **Ulsterbus** route #9A or #10 (6/day Mon.–Sat., 3/day Sun.) between Belfast and Portaferry.

Portaferry

At the Ards' southern tip, quiet Portaferry (Port an Pheire, "Ferry Landing-Place") is still the most happening spot on the peninsula. With its seal sanctuary and displays of aquatic life from Strangford Lough and the Irish Sea, the **Exploris Aquarium** (Castle St., tel. 028/4272-8062, www.exploris.org.uk, open 10 A.M.–6 P.M. Mon.–Fri., 11 A.M.–6 P.M. Sat., noon–6 P.M. Sun. Apr.–Aug., until 5 P.M. Sept.–Feb., adult/family admission £6.70/18) makes a fine family excursion. Or go for a beach trek with the **Cherry Tree Riding Centre** (5 Newcastle Rd., tel. 028/4272-9639).

But frankly, Portaferry isn't as charming or atmospheric as the smaller Strangford across the narrows, though there are more accommodation options on the Ards side. Yet the ferry service is so convenient that you can have dinner in one town and sleep in the other (since the Lobster Pot in Strangford is better than the eateries in Portaferry).

Don't call it a hostel, but **Barholm** (11 The Strand, tel. 028/4272-9598, www.barholmportaferry.co.uk, £13–15 pp, credit cards accepted, 10 percent discount on midweek bookings) offers good-value budget accommodations in a well-kept Victorian right above the pier. It's popular with divers—there's an on-site compressor for air fills and full catering available for £16 per person—but there are single and double rooms on offer as well. Breakfast (£3.75) is served in a bright, clean, spacious conservatory overlooking the harbor.

It may be the hippest, coziest place to stay when in Portaferry, but **The Narrows** (8 Shore Rd., tel. 028/4272-8148, www.narrows.co.uk, B&B £45 pp, s £45–70, lunch £7–11, dinner £14–17) restaurant is a disappointment, as the main courses look like appetizers. The food is fine, but it's not good enough to justify such pretentiousness. For the typical old-fashioned, small-town hotel experience, stay at the **Portaferry Hotel** (7-10 the Strand, tel. 028/4272-8231, www.portaferryhotel.com, £55–65 pp, single in double room £75, lough view surcharge £10).

Portaferry's **tourist office** (Castle St., tel. 028/4272-9882, open 10 A.M.–5 P.M. Mon.–Sat., 2–6 P.M. Sun. Easter–Sept.) adjoins the ruin of a 16th-century tower house.

Portaferry is 23 miles (37 km) south of Bangor on the A2 (east side of the Ards) or A20 (lough-side). **Ulsterbus** (tel. 028/9066-6630, #9A or #10, 6/day Mon.–Sat., 3/day Sun.) can get you here from Belfast via N'ards and Greyabbey.

Zip across the narrows to Strangford on the **Strangford Lough Ferry** (tel. 028/4488-1637, www.roadsni.gov.uk, departs every half hour 7:30 A.M.–10:30 P.M. Mon.–Fri., 8 A.M.–11 P.M. Sat., 9:30 A.M.–10:30 P.M. Sun., single/day return £5.30/8.50 car and driver, £1.10/1.80 pedestrian or passenger).

WEST OF STRANGFORD LOUGH
Lisbane and Around

It's on the main A22 road between Bangor and Downpatrick, yet the hamlet of Lisbane (Lisbaun, "White Fort") is surprisingly quiet and pastoral. There are a few things of moderate interest in the area, including the scant remains of the 7th-century **Nendrum Abbey** (Mahee Island, 4.5 mi/7.2 km southeast of Lisbane, tel. 028/9754-2547, abbey ruins always accessible, visitors center open 9 A.M.–6 P.M. Tues.–Sat. and 1–6 P.M. Sun. Apr.–Sept., 10 A.M.–4 P.M. Sat. and 2–4 P.M. Sun. Oct.–Mar., free admission) and a nearby wildlife refuge, **Castle Espie** (Ballydrain Rd., tel. 028/9187-4146, www.wwt.org.uk, open 10:30 A.M.–5 P.M. Mon.–Fri., 11 A.M.–5:30 P.M. Sat.–Sun. Mar.–Oct., 11 A.M.–4 P.M. Mon.–Fri., 11 A.M.–4:30 P.M. Sat.–Sun., admission £4.70). Only the foundations remain of Nendrum's small churches and beehive huts (along with the diagonally shaped stump of a 12th-century round tower), but the interpretive displays and audiovisual at the adjacent visitor's center will help you imagine what this monastery must have been like a thousand years ago. Family-friendly Castle Espie is home to a flock of light-bellied Brent geese during the winter; the staff names each goose and keep close tabs on how each is doing. There's also an interpretive center here, though the views of Strangford Lough alone are reason enough to come. To get to Nendrum, turn onto Quarry Road opposite the Maxol Station in Lisbane, proceed 1.5 miles (2.4 km), and you'll see Nendrum signposted at a crossroads. After another three miles (4.8 km) you'll come to a small bridge with a castle ruin beyond it; cross this and you'll see the abbey car park on your right. The wildlife refuge is signposted on the A22 between Comber and Lisbane.

Even if you're just passing through Lisbane, stop for a snack at **The Old Post Office** (191 Killinchy Rd., the A22, tel. 028/9754-3335, open 9:30 A.M.–5 P.M. Mon.–Sat., mains £3–5), which includes a gallery, upscale gift shop, and cozy tearooms with loft seating and open fires.

But you really should consider spending the night here. One of the very best B&Bs on the island (if not *the* best) is [C] **Anna's House** (35 Lisbarnett Rd., 0.3 mi/0.5 km off the A22, signposted, tel. 028/9754-1566, www.annashouse.com, £40 pp, s £45, wireless Internet £5, credit cards accepted). Consider Anna's a destination in itself. This tranquil farmhouse overlooks a small lough, and has a fantastic two-acre garden dotted with whimsical clay busts and other neat sculptures by the owners' son. All the food is organic, down to the instant coffee on your hostess tray, and the breakfast menu is truly without equal. Each of the three double rooms is furnished with gorgeous antiques, a load of good books, pressed linen sheets, a minifridge for your milk, and a fully stocked medicine cabinet. As you would expect from such thoughtful gestures, the Johnsons are wonderfully kind and fascinating people with a genuine *mi casa e su casa* attitude; Anna periodically sleeps in her guest beds to ensure they're still comfortable. Plan to stay at least two nights—and even then you'll be reluctant to leave.

The best restaurant in the area is **Lisbarnett House** (on the A21, tel. 028/9754-1589, open 6–9 P.M. daily, 2-course early-bird special £13 6–7 P.M. daily and 6–9 P.M. Mon., mains £8– 17). The modern Irish here is fresh and deli-cious, if a bit unadventurous; though the staff are nice, the dining room is a bit on the stuffy side. There's live trad in the adjoining bar on Saturday nights.

For more atmosphere, drive a little farther to **Daft Eddy's** (Sketrick Island, Killinchy, tel. 028/9754-1615, food served noon–9 P.M. daily, mains £8–15), a well-established bar-restaurant with a quirky nautical theme (check out the overturned rowboat above your head decked out in Christmas lights, and the busty figure-head on the wall by the bar). The food is good (the token veggie dish is creative, if a bit dainty, but the steaks and seafood are hearty enough), the staff are cordial, but it's the lake views from the dining room and deck that make for a memorable meal. To get here from Lisbane, pass southward through the village and after 2.5 miles (4 km) or so, make a left onto Beech-vale Road (you'll see a signpost for Sketrick Castle). After another 2.5 miles you'll come to a narrow causeway with the ruins of Sketrick Castle on the far side; cross it to get to the res-taurant straight ahead, up a small hill.

Lisbane is 14 miles (23 km) south of Bel-fast off the A20, and unfortunately Ulsterbus doesn't serve this stretch of the A22.

Saintfield

A ho-hum town midway between Belfast and Downpatrick, Saintfield is worth a stop for its row of wonderful little antiques shops. A little over a mile south of town is the 52-acre

Rowallane Garden (signposted off the N7, tel. 028/9751-0131, www.ntni.org.uk, open 11 A.M.–6 P.M. Mon.–Fri., 2–6 P.M. Sat.–Sun. Apr.–Oct., 11 A.M.–5 P.M. Mon.–Fri. Nov.– Mar., admission £3.80) with its walled gardens and pretty fields of Himalayan poppies. The best time to visit is early spring, when the aza-leas and rhododendrons are in bright bloom.

As for the antiques shops, they're all on Saintfield's main street. **Christine Deane** (90 Main St., tel. 028/9751-1334 or 078/0197-9496) has an exquisite collection of Victorian and Edwardian jewelry. **Agar** (92 Main St., tel. 028/9751-1214) has some incredibly neat finds in the way of 19th-century furniture…if you're willing to pay to ship it home! Note that most of these shops close on Sunday and Monday.

Once they're done making the rounds, local antique-shoppers take lunch at ◖ **The March Hare** (Fairview, at the end of Main St., tel. 028/9751-9248, open 10 A.M.–4 P.M. Wed.– Fri., 10 A.M.–4 P.M. Sat., lunches £2–5), a tiny, unself-consciously old-fashioned tearoom with thoroughly delicious homemade soups, sand-wiches, quiches, and pies, and very friendly staff. The March Hare is so popular you may not get a table right away, but the food is defi-nitely worth the wait.

Saintfield is just over 15 miles (25 km) south of Belfast on the A24 and is served on the **Ulsterbus** (tel. 028/9066-6630, route #15, 2–4/hour daily) Belfast–Downpatrick route.

DOWNPATRICK

County Down's principal town may boast strong historical ties with the island's patron saint, but frankly Downpatrick (Dún Phád-raig, "Patrick's Fort") is a dismal place—and a dearth of quality dining options doesn't help matters. Across the River Quoile a mile outside town is the 12th-century **Inch Abbey** (sign-posted off the A7, always accessible), though it's not too remarkable as monastic ruins go. Stop to take in the Anglican **Down Cathedral** (The Mall, tel. 028/4461-4922, open 10 A.M.– 4:30 P.M. Mon.–Sat. and 2–5 P.M. Sun., free admission), which stands on the likely burial place of St. Patrick and so has been a place of

© CAMILLE DEANGELIS

George III donated this pipe organ to Down Cathedral in 1802.

6 P.M. Sun. June–Aug., 9:30 A.M.–5:30 P.M. Mon.–Sat. and 1–5:30 P.M. Sun. Apr.–May and Sept., 10 A.M.–5 P.M. Mon.–Sat. Oct.–Mar.) for tourist info and Internet access (free at time of writing), but don't waste time in the cheesy exhibition center.

Downpatrick is 20 miles (32 km) south of Belfast on the A7 and is served by **Ulsterbus** (tel. 028/4461-2384, route #15/A, hourly buses Mon.–Sat., 5/day Sun., single/return £4.70/8.40).

THE LECALE PENINSULA
◖ Strangford

The absolutely lovely harbor village of Strangford makes an ideal base for exploring the Lecale Peninsula; why stay in dreary Downpatrick when this seaside gem is a mere nine miles (14 km) northeast on the A25? From here you can also hop the ferry, with or without your car, across the lough to Portaferry.

The village's romantic atmosphere is defined by the sight of a fleet of colorful fishing boats, a small but perfectly manicured green, and the 16th-century **Strangford Castle,** a well-preserved ivy-clad tower house overlooking the harbor. Inside there isn't much to see but the bric-a-brac of ongoing neglect, but if you're really curious, the key is available from the caretaker at 39 Castle Street.

Head up Castle Street and hang a left at a shady stone staircase for the **Strangford Bay Path,** a Secret Gardenesque walk with woods on one side and the narrows on the other; the tide has heaved clumps of seaweed onto the grass. Eventually you'll come to the 18th-century, half-Gothic, half-neoclassical **Castle Ward Estate** (Park Rd., tel. 028/4488-1204, house open 1–6 P.M. Fri.–Wed. June, 1–6 P.M. daily July–Aug., 1–6 P.M. Sat.–Sun. mid-Mar.–May and Sept., grounds open 10 A.M.–8 P.M. daily May–Sept., 10 A.M.–4 P.M. daily Oct.–Apr., house and grounds/grounds only admission £5.50/3.80), which includes the Strangford Lough Wildlife Centre and a couple of older tower houses you spotted across the narrows from the bay path.

The old-fashioned facade of **The Lobster Pot**

pilgrimage for nearly a millennium and a half. An early church was destroyed in 1316 during the Scottish invasion, completely rebuilt 200 years later, destroyed again in the Tudor conquest, and fell into ruin before the Anglican diocese scraped up the funds to rebuild once more, at the turn of the 19th century. The cathedral's most striking feature is its splendid pipe organ, which sits atop a pulpitum separating the church vestibule from the choir. There are formal regency box pews and a few other things of mild interest, but all in all a 10-minute visit should suffice.

Just down the street is the **Down County Museum** (The Mall, English St., tel. 028/4461-5218, open 10 A.M.–5 P.M. Mon.–Fri. and 1–5 P.M. Sat.–Sun., free admission), which has a few interesting exhibits as well as a restored jail complete with mannequins representing real-life inmates, whose sad stories are posted outside each cell.

Then stop by the **St. Patrick Centre** (53a Market St., tel. 028/4461-2233, open 9:30 A.M.–7 P.M. Mon.–Sat. and 10 A.M.–

(9-11 The Square, tel. 028/4488-1288, www. lobsterpotstrangford.com, open 11:30 A.M.– 9 P.M. Mon.–Sat., 12:30–8 P.M. Sun., mains £8–15) belies a spiffy interior complete with aquarium (the fish aren't to eat), portholes in the ceiling, and the likes of Dean Martin on the stereo. The name is misleading too, for there are plenty of alternatives to the seafood dishes, and the chef is surprisingly vegetarian-friendly. The Sunday lunch menu (2/4 courses £11/14) is a better value than the à la carte, and a three-course lobster dinner will set you back £40. Another great thing about this place: It's absolutely nonsmoking. The adjoining pub has live trad most nights in the summertime.

Your other, equally delicious lunch or dinner option is a pub-cum-restaurant called **The Cuan** (The Square, tel. 028/4488-1222, www. thecuan.com, food served noon–8 P.M. daily in low season and until 9 P.M. Sun.–Thurs. and 9:30 P.M. Fri.–Sat. June–Aug., mains £7–15, B&B £35–40 pp, s £45–50), which also has nine smallish-but-comfortable (and super-clean) bedrooms on offer upstairs (not to mention complimentary wireless Internet) and a quaint little fish-and-chipper next door. Another accommodation option is **Strangford Cottage** (17 Castle St., tel. 028/4488-1208, open Apr.–Sept., £55–70 pp, s £60), an ivy-clad Georgian with three en-suite bedrooms and an award-winning breakfast.

Strangford is nine miles (14 km) northeast of Downpatrick on the A25. Get here from Belfast by **Ulsterbus** (#16E, at least 20/day, single/return fare £6.60/12).

The **Strangford Lough Ferry** provides a shortcut across the narrows to Portaferry on the Ards Peninsula (tel. 028/4488-1637, www.roadsni.gov.uk, departs every half hour 7:30 A.M.–10:30 P.M. Mon.–Fri., 8 A.M.–11 P.M. Sat., 9:30 A.M.–10:30 P.M. Sun., single/day return £5.30/8.50 car and driver, £1.10/1.80 pedestrian or passenger).

NEWCASTLE

Newcastle (An Caisleán Nua), County Down's other seaside resort, isn't as classy as Bangor. The main street, lined with the usual cheap-'n-greasy amusement arcades and takeaways, seems darn near endless. Newcastle's churches and public buildings seem to be struggling to retain some civic dignity, and it's well apparent that the town's best days are in the past. Yet Newcastle makes a logical base for exploring the Mourne Mountains, since the quiet coastal villages farther south have little in the way of beds, pubs, or eateries. If traveling by bus, you'll disembark on Railway Street; make a right onto Downs Road (where you can turn off for the beach), and you'll eventually hit Main Street, which becomes the Central Promenade; keep going and you'll be traveling south on the Mourne coastal road.

The northern end of the golden three-mile strand is marked by the **Murlough National Nature Reserve** (always accessible, free admission). Plus, there's the **Royal County Down Golf Club** (36 Golf Links Rd., tel. 028/4372-3314, www.royalcountydown.org), voted the island's #1 course, and the nearby **Castlewellan Forest Park** (Main St., Castlewellan, 5 mi/8 km northwest of Newcastle, tel. 028/4377-8664, open 10 A.M.–dusk, car admission £4). Inside the park you'll find the National Arboretum as well as the **Blue Lough Mountain & Water Sports Centre** (The Grange Yard, tel. 028/4377-0714, www.mountainandwater.com) offers the gamut of adventure sports "from the mild to the really really wild": kayaking, rock climbing, archery, you name it. The 1,200-acre **Tollymore Forest Park** is over a mile northwest of Newcastle, and its trails will take you through some of the Mourne foothills.

A Victorian in a nice location near the strand, the HINI **Newcastle Youth Hostel** (30 Downs Rd., tel. 028/4372-2133, www. hini.org.uk, dorms £11, credit cards accepted) is small enough (36 beds) to avoid attracting the noisiest school groups, and also offers a family room that sleeps four. The best B&B is the renovated 18th-century **Briers Country House** (29 Middle Tollymore Rd., 0.9 mi/1.5 km northwest of town, follow signs for Tollymore Forest Park, tel. 028/4372-4347, www. thebriers.co.uk, £23–28 pp, s £30–40, credit cards accepted) for its Mourne views, two-acre garden (and two-minute walk from the forest park), generous breakfast menu, and licensed restaurant for evening meals.

Pickings are slim when it comes to eating out here, unless you're in the mood for fast food. **Seasalt** (51 Central Promenade, tel. 028/4372-5027, open 10 A.M.–6 P.M. Tues.–Sun., until 10 P.M. Wed., Thurs. and Sun., until 11 P.M. Fri.–Sat., dinner reservations required, lunch mains £3–6, 2/3-course dinner £15/20) is Newcastle's best restaurant, with traditional dishes for lunch and fresh seafood dressed in Asian flavors.

Planning to explore the Mournes? Pick up an OS map and guidebooks at the **tourist office** (10-14 Central Promenade, tel. 028/4372-2222, open 9:30 A.M.–7 P.M. Mon.–Sat. and 1–7 P.M. Sun. July–Aug., 10 A.M.–5 P.M. Mon.–Sat. and 2–6 P.M. Sun. Sept.–June); the **post office** is directly across the street. There are a couple of banks with ATMs and bureaux de change on Main Street, including **Northern Bank.**

Newcastle is 30 miles (48 km) south of Belfast on the A24 and is served by **Ulsterbus** (#18 and #20, 13/day Mon.–Fri., 9/day Sat., 6/day Sun.) from Belfast.

◖ SILENT VALLEY

The granite-topped **Mourne Mountains** are the most spectacular scenery in County Down, no doubt about it. You'll drive past pretty gorse-dotted hills and unsettling sectarian road paint to the Silent Valley Reservoir (tel. 084/5744-0088, www.newryandmourne.gov.uk, open 10 A.M.–6:30 P.M. daily May–Sept., 10 A.M.–4 P.M. Oct.–Apr., visitors center open 10 A.M.–4 P.M. Apr.–Oct., car/pedestrian admission £3/1.50), the source of Belfast's drinking water since the Spelga Dam was built to span the Kilkeel River. As it should be, this is a beautiful, pristine park where you can walk right up to the reservoir and listen to the water lapping gently at the huge stone basin as you survey the surrounding peaks, each of them crossed by the 22-mile drystone **Mourne Wall.** Eight feet high and three feet thick, the wall was constructed between 1904 and 1922 to enclose the valley (and to provide much-needed work for hundreds

of local men, though most of them had to travel miles on foot to get here, and they weren't paid by the hour). As for how the Silent Valley got its name, it's said the noise of the rock-blasting frightened all the birds away—and they never returned. There are easy walking trails throughout; bring a picnic lunch.

Ulsterbus provides service in summertime (#405, 7/day, all-day ticket £5) to the Silent Valley, Atticall, and Tollymore; otherwise you'll need a car to reach the reservoir. If you're not here in high season, there are several ways to experience the mountains sans wheels, mostly by way of Newcastle. Take a walk through the foothills via the entrance at Tollymore Forest Park, or climb the 2,795-foot (852-meter) **Slieve Donard** via a route that begins three miles (4.8 km) south of town on the A2 (at a small car park carved into the hill) and winds through six miles (9.6 km) of County Down's most breathtaking scenery. Seeing as it's Northern Ireland's highest peak, Slieve Donard is a difficult four-hour climb—so take all the usual equipment and precautions. Take the Newcastle–Kilkeel **Ulsterbus** route (#37, 14/day Mon.–Fri., 11/day Sat., 6/day Sun.) from Newcastle to reach the starting point.

And if you don't have time for any of this, at least take the A2 coastal road south from Newcastle to Warrenpoint, wedged between gorse-strewn mountains and glittering sea.

You have several options if you'd like to experience the Mournes with a little help. For a guided walk or cycle, contact **Outdoor Ireland North** (14 Shimavale, tel. 028/4372-4372 or 079/7340-8056, www.outdoorirelandnorth.co.uk). **Mourne Cycle Tours** (13 Spelga Ave., Newcastle, tel. 028/4372-4348, www.mournecycletours.com) hooks you up with bikes, maps, and all equipment (delivered to your door). **Tollymore Mountain Centre** (Bryansford, tel. 028/4372-2158, www.tollymore.com) offers one-day mountaineering, rock-climbing, and canoeing courses. Nothing but rain? No worries: There's an indoor climbing wall.

You could base yourself on the Mourne coast, in Newcastle or Rostrevor; alternatively, there are a few accommodation options in the mountains, mostly in and around the village of Atticall. Located between the Silent Valley and Spelga Dam, the 28-bed, purpose-built, eco-friendly **Cnocafeola Centre** (Bog Rd., Atticall, 9 mi/14 km east of Rostrevor, 1.8 mi/2.9 km west of the Silent Valley entrance, tel. 028/4176-5859 or 028/4179-2952, www.mournehostel.com, dorms £13, twin/private rooms £16 pp) has two self-catering kitchens as well as a (bring your own bottle) restaurant serving three meals a day (packed lunches £4, 3-course dinner £13). All rooms are en suite. There's also a wonderfully friendly B&B, **Hill View House** (18 Bog Rd., Atticall, signposted from the B27, tel. 028/4176-4269, www.hillviewhouse.co.uk, £23–25 pp, s £25–30, credit cards accepted), that caters to hikers and cyclists. To get here, turn off the coastal road at Kilkeel, following signs for Atticall, and proceed through the village; Hill View and the Silent Valley are both signposted from there.

For more information, contact the **Mourne Heritage Trust** (87 Central Promenade, tel. 028/4372-4059, www.mournelive.com) or the local tourist office, both in Newcastle.

ROSTREVOR

A quieter, more dignified alternative to Newcastle, Rostrevor (Caisleán Ruairí, "Rory's Castle") is easily the most attractive town along the Mourne coastal road, with gorgeous views south over Carlingford Lough (just don't look west to the smokestacks of Warrenpoint). Spend the night here before heading up into the Mournes, and if time allows, go for a walk through the "fairy glen" in the hilltop **Kilbroney Forest Park** (Shore Rd., the A2, tel. 028/4173-8134, open 9 A.M.–10 P.M. daily

June–Aug., 9 A.M.–5 P.M. daily Sept.–May, free admission). Early July is a good time to be here, when some of the best traditional musicians in the north gather for the **Fiddler's Green Festival** (tel. 028/4173-9819, www.fiddlersgreenfestival.com).

It's a bit surprising there aren't many accommodations here—just a few nice but fairly basic B&Bs. You'll get a warm welcome at the cheerfully furnished and super-clean **Fir Trees** (16 Killowen Old Rd., signposted off the A2 1.8 mi/2.9 km east of town, tel. 028/4173-8602 or 077/1169-4089, www.firtrees.co.uk, £25 pp, s £30, credit cards accepted). There are three rooms, all en suite, and the twin room has a view of Carlingford Lough and Mountain; the breakfasts are fairly basic. Another option is the equally small and pleasant **An Tobar** ("The Well," 2 Cherry Hill, tel. 028/4173-8712 or 077/1118-9369, www.kilbroney.net, £25 pp, s £30), just a couple minutes' walk from the main street.

And for dinner, look no further than **The Kilbroney** (31 Church St., tel. 028/4173-8390, food served noon–9 P.M. daily, mains £5–9), which does fantastic bar meals—it's just burgers and paninis during the day, but the dinner fare is more sophisticated (including a mean mushroom risotto for vegetarians). Save room for the sticky toffee pudding, and ask if there'll be live music later in the evening.

Rostrevor is 22 miles (35 km) southwest of Newcastle on the A2 coastal road. **Ulsterbus** can get you here from Belfast (on route #238 then #39, 16/day Mon.–Sat., 3/day Sun., single/return fare £7.80/14), though a change is required at Newry. If coming from Newcastle, you'll have to change at either Newry or Kilkeel (#37).

Armagh

Known for its city cathedrals and apple orchards, mostly rural Armagh is the home of the only cider brewed in Northern Ireland, **Carson's** (www.armaghcider.com). A leisurely drive through northern Armagh's 4,000 acres of orchards in May is one of the highlights of a trip to Northern Ireland. You might even come upon a game of road bowling, a centuries-old sport that's still popular here and in parts of County Cork.

Being a border county with a high Catholic (and therefore republican) population, Armagh's southern towns are dotted with barracks and watchtowers, unsettling reminders of the Troubles. These days the area is perfectly safe, however—for locals as well as tourists.

ARMAGH CITY

Not that pleasant Armagh isn't pumping any money into its tourism industry, but it's clearly not a top priority—and the resulting atmosphere is one of laid-back ordinariness, a refreshing change from the slightly desperate, we're-safe-we-swear Tourist Board rhetoric of Belfast and Derry. You might even call Armagh Kilkenny's over-the-border twin (though it's more Georgian and less touristy than Kilkenny is). As in Kilkenny, you're never really sure if you should call this place a

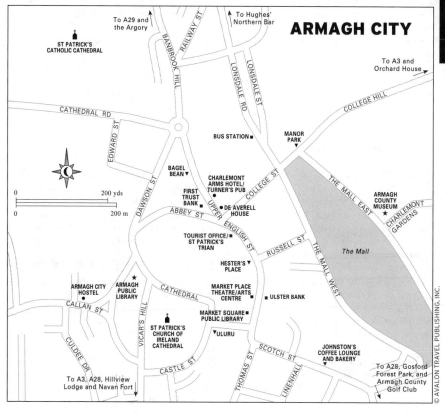

© AVALON TRAVEL PUBLISHING, INC.

DOWN AND ARMAGH

town or a city. It doesn't feel big enough to be a city, yet it has all the urban amenities.

A tidy Georgian green dotted with memorial statues on the eastern side of the city center, Armagh's Mall was a seedy racecourse and fairground until Archbishop Robinson (benefactor of the first public library) had it cleaned up and reopened as a public park in 1773. The city stretches west of the Mall, with curving streets shooting out from the central Market Square, presided over by the Anglican St. Patrick's. The main drag, English Street, heads north from the square, and after a few blocks you can make a left onto Cathedral Road for the Catholic St. Patrick's.

St. Patrick's Trian

St. Patrick's Trian (40 English St., tel. 028/3752-1801, open 10 A.M.–5 P.M. Mon.–Sat. and 2–5 P.M. Sun., admission £4.50) is an interpretive center in a converted Presbyterian church that uses cheesy life-size wax models to illustrate scenes from prehistory, the life of St. Patrick, and so on, as well as Jonathan Swift's *Gulliver's Travels*. For the usual eclectic collection of local artifacts, visit the **Armagh County Museum** (The Mall E., tel. 028/3752-3070, open 10 A.M.–5 P.M. Mon.–Fri., 10 A.M.–1 P.M. and 2–5 P.M. Sat., free admission).

St. Patrick's Church of Ireland Cathedral

The foundation of St. Patrick's Church of Ireland Cathedral (Cathedral Close, up the hill from Market Square, tel. 028/3752-3142, www.stpatricks-cathedral.org, open 10 A.M.–5 P.M. daily Apr.–Oct., 10 A.M.–4 P.M. daily Nov.–Mar., free admission) dates to the 13th century, though the present edifice dates to the 1830s. Legend states that Patrick founded his first church on this small hill in the year 445. Brian Boru is supposedly buried here, and there are several Celtic and Iron Age sculptures on display. Like many Anglican churches, this one is often closed in the low season—even during official opening hours—but between June and August there are guided tours at 11:30 A.M. and 2:30 P.M. daily (except Sunday).

St. Patrick's Catholic Cathedral

When you see the soaring twin spires of the hilltop neo-Gothic St. Patrick's Catholic Cathedral (Cathedral Rd., tel. 028/3752-2802, www.armagharchdiocese.org, free admission), you can fully understand why Armagh is "the Cathedral City." The cornerstone was laid in 1840, but the building dragged on for more than six decades, and the cathedral was finally consecrated in July 1904. Between the brilliant stained glass windows, gold mosaics, and flatscreen monitors anchored to the columns, the interior is visually overwhelming—but well worth a visit.

Armagh Public Library

Bibliophiles shouldn't miss the old Armagh Public Library (43 Abbey St., tel. 028/3752-3142, www.armaghrobinsonlibrary.org, open 10 A.M.–1 P.M. and 2–4 P.M. Mon.–Fri., free admission), established by the Protestant Archbishop Richard Robinson in 1771 to promote Armagh as a center of learning. The library houses the archbishop's private collection of 17th- and 18th-century tomes on every subject (including a first edition of *Gulliver's Travels,* which has Swift's annotations in the margins).

Tours

A 90-minute **walking tour** (tel. 077/4015-1442, www.armaghguidedtours.com, booking essential, £4) focusing on Armagh's history and architecture departs the tourist office on Saturday at 11 A.M. and 2 P.M. and Sunday at 2 P.M. June–September.

Entertainment and Events

Armagh has a lively pub scene, though there aren't as many traditional music venues as you'd expect. The Saturday session at **Turner's** (the Charlemont Arms, English St., tel. 028/3752-2028) starts at 10 P.M.; on Tuesday you'll find trad at the cozy **Hughes' Northern Bar** (100 Railway St., tel. 028/3752-7315), which attracts a fun, youngish crowd, and it has a live band on Saturday. Or see a play, concert, or comedy show at the **Market Place Theatre & Arts**

DOWN AND ARMAGH

Sports and Recreation

For a walking, cycling, golfing, or angling holiday, contact **Lurgaboy Adventure** (12 Gosford Rd., tel. 079/2114-3010, www.lurgaboylodge.com), which will hook you up with the equipment, a guide (if necessary), and a quaint, old-fashioned self-catering cottage with all the mod cons. Or just come for an afternoon of archery, tree-climbing, or raft-building. The owner, Richard Dougan, has climbed Mount Everest.

Tee off at the 18-hole **Armagh County Golf Club** (7 Newry Rd., tel. 028/3752-2501, www.golfarmagh.co.uk).

Accommodations

You can expect small dorms and B&B-quality private (twin) rooms at the modern, purpose-built **Armagh City Hostel** (39 Abbey St., tel. 028/3751-1800, www.hini.org.uk, dorms £13, twins £15 pp, credit cards accepted).

Without a doubt, the best B&B in the city center is **De Averell House** (47 Upper English St., tel. 028/3751-1213, http://deaverellhouse.net, £30 pp, s £35, Internet access £1.50/30 minutes), a restored, comfortable Georgian townhouse with four rooms and a self-catering apartment (not to mention one of Armagh's best restaurants on the ground floor).

There are some really nice B&Bs within a few miles of the city, but most have only two or three rooms, so be sure to book ahead. Golfers should stay at **Hillview Lodge** (33 Newtownhamilton Rd., 1.5 km south of Armagh, tel. 028/3752-2000, www.hillviewlodge.com, £25 pp, s £38, credit cards accepted), which has a driving range in the backyard as well as Internet access in the sitting room (there's wireless Internet, too). From town, follow the signs for the A3, and after you've passed the Armagh City Hotel on Friary Road (on the left), make a left at the fork in the road (following the signs for Keady), onto Irish Street, and then two more lefts at successive forks. The last fork will put you on Newtownhamilton Road, and the Hillview will be on your right.

Here's something even more out of the ordinary—a guesthouse with a pool! The spacious

© CAMILLE DEANGELIS

Madonna and Child at St. Patrick's Catholic Cathedral

Centre (Market St., tel. 028/3752-1821, www.marketplacearmagh.com, tickets £10–16).

The annual **St. Patrick's Festival** (tel. 028/3752-1800, www.st-patricksdayfestival.com) generally starts a week before the 17th and continues through the 20th. This is a fantastic (if hectic) time to be in Armagh, with a full calendar of folk and classical concerts, art exhibitions, special Masses and trad sessions, set-dancing performances—and of course, a carnival and parade on the day itself.

The **Apple Blossom Festival** (contact the tourist office for details, tel. 028/3752-1800, www.visitarmagh.com) takes place over the May bank holiday weekend, usually the first weekend in May. The weekend market is even more sprawling and colorful than usual, and you can sign up for a walking tour or bus tour of Armagh's "orchard country" north of the city.

A backroad pastime takes center stage at the **All-Ireland Road Bowls Finals,** generally held on the last weekend in July on Battleford Road.

and elegant **Orchard House** (76b Mullanasilla Rd., signposted on the A3, 4 mi/6.4 km north of Armagh, tel. 028/3887-1065, orchardhouse1@btinternet.com, £30 pp sharing) also has a hot tub and a snooker room. From Armagh, take the Portadown-bound A3 and make a right onto Mullanasilla road; Orchard House is down on the right.

It's a bit on the stodgy side, but the **Charlemont Arms Hotel** (57-65 English St., tel. 028/3752-2028, www.charlemontarmshotel.com, £40 pp, s £50) fits the bill for a traditional, family-run establishment in the city center. The restaurant is pretty prim, but there's a downstairs wine bar, and the hotel pub, **Turner's,** is one of the city's best spots for live trad. Conveniently, the bus station is just behind the hotel as well. The posh new **Armagh City Hotel** (Friary Rd., tel. 028/3751-8888, www.mooneyhotelgroup.com, rooms £84–108) prides itself on being refreshingly unpretentious, and since it's a business-class hotel you'll get a lower rate at the weekend (check the website for special weekend packages). With a swimming pool, sauna, and exercise room, who cares if it's on the impersonal side?

Food

Armagh isn't quite a gourmand's city, but there are several fine eateries if you know where to look. The trendiest spot for breakfast, dinner, or a gourmet coffee is the **Bagel Bean** (60 English St., tel. 028/3751-5251, open 7:30 A.M.–5:30 P.M. Mon.–Sat., mains £3–5). Popular with locals for its hearty, old-fashioned lunches is **Hester's Place** (12 Upper English St., tel. 028/3752-2374, open 9 A.M.–5:30 P.M. Mon.–Tues. and Thurs.–Sat., mains £3–6), comfortable despite all the bustle. It's cafeteria-style, but the atmosphere and food are much the same at **Johnston's Coffee Lounge and Bakery** (9 Scotch St., tel. 028/3752-2995, open 9 A.M.–5:30 P.M. Mon.–Sat., mains £3–6), whose owners pride themselves on using local produce.

De Averell (47 Upper English St., tel. 028/3751-1213, www.deaverellhouse.com, open 11 A.M.–9 P.M. Tues.–Sun., lunch £5–9, dinner

£6–15) has a deserved reputation for some of the best cuisine in town. It's straight-up Continental, with several delicious veggie options (pasta, mostly). Beware that the owners don't always stick to the posted opening times during the day, and though the atmosphere is pretty relaxed, reservations are essential at the weekend and pretty much every night in summer.

Even more upscale is **Manor Park** (2 College Hill, The Mall, tel. 028/3751-5353, www.manorparkrestaurant.com, open noon–2:30 P.M. Mon.–Fri. and noon–3 P.M. Sun., 5:30–10 P.M. daily, lunch £6–9, 2-course early-bird special £14 5–6:15 P.M., dinner mains £14–24), a fine French restaurant whose pretensions are more amusing than off-putting: the waitstaff (poor things) are forced to wear silly white jackets covered in brass buttons, the tablecloths are ironed between sittings, and the maître-d' informs with a smile that "we don't speak English here." Stained glass, tapestries, old stone walls, silver candlesticks and ornate place-settings—the atmosphere may sound a bit stuffy, but with the likes of Stevie Wonder on the stereo, this place isn't so easy to peg. The lunch menu is a surprisingly decent value, too—no dime-sized main courses here, thank goodness.

The chef and owner of ◖ **Uluru** (16-18 Market St., tel. 028/3751-8051, uluru_bistro@hotmail.co.uk, open noon–3 P.M. and 6–9:30 P.M. Tues.–Sat., mains £8–15) boasts, justifiably, that this Australian eatery is "turning cuisine upside down in Armagh." Aside from the requisite kangaroo steak, the menu is best described as Continental with a twist, and all ingredients are über-fresh. Votive candles, eclectic music on the stereo, and animated conversation at neighboring tables make for a great buzz any night of the week. The service is impeccable, the gourmet coffees sublime, and the dessert menu all but brings one to tears. In short, Uluru can more than compete with the hippest eateries in Belfast and Dublin.

Information

Armagh's **tourist office** (40 English St., tel. 028/3752-1800, www.visitarmagh.com, open

9 A.M.–5 P.M. Mon.–Sat. all year, 1–5:30 P.M. Sun. July–Aug. and 2–5 P.M. Sun. Sept.–June) is adjacent to the St. Patrick's Trian exhibition.

Services

For an ATM or bureau de change, visit **Ulster Bank** (Market St.), **Northern Bank** (Market Sq.), or **First Trust** (Upper English St.). The **post office** is also on English Street, opposite the tourist office.

Need an Rx? Try the local branch of **Boots** (15 Scotch St., tel. 028/3752-3199). Drop off your laundry at the **Squeaky Clean** (11a Cathedral Rd., tel. 028/3751-1408, closed Sun.).

Check your email at the **public library** (Market St., tel. 028/3752-4072, open until 8 P.M. Tues. and Thurs., till 5:30 P.M. Mon., Wed., Fri., and until 5 P.M. Sat., £1.50/30 minutes).

Getting There and Around

Armagh is 37 miles (60 km) southwest of Belfast on the A3 and 81 miles (130 km) northwest of Dublin on the M1, picking up the A29 in Dundalk. There is ample free parking on the east side of the Mall. **Ulsterbus** (tel. 028/3752-2266, route #551, 20/day Mon.–Fri., 15/day Sat., 8/day Sun.) can get you here from Belfast; the depot is on Lonsdale Road, on the Mall West.

Armagh seems like a city in name only, for it's easily walkable. Hire a bike from the **Lurgaboy Adventure Centre** (12 Gosford Rd., tel. 028/3755-2425, £10/day), or ring **Eurocabs** (tel. 028/3751-1900) if you need a ride.

AROUND ARMAGH CITY
𝗖 Navan Fort

The most important archaeological site in Northern Ireland is Navan Fort, or **Emain Macha** ("The Twins of Macha," 2 mi/3.2 km west of Armagh off the B115, tel. 028/3752-1801, www.navancentre.com, visitors center open 10 A.M.–5 P.M. Mon.–Sat. and noon–5 P.M. Sun. June–Aug., admission £5, free admission to site). As Ulster's pre-Christian capital (from 700 B.C.), the fort is comparable to the Hill of Tara in County Meath, and its

legends include all the heavy-hitters of Irish folklore; Macha, for whom the site (and Armagh itself) is named, was a queen/goddess who also built a fortress on the site of Armagh City's Church of Ireland long before St. Patrick. Archaeological excavations indicate Emain Macha was active as far back as 1150 B.C., but after this sacred place was burned and looted (by forces from the then-fifth province of Meath) in the 4th century A.D., it was never rebuilt. It must have retained some of its religious and ritual significance, however, if Patrick found it an important enough spot from which to start evangelizing. The fort itself—more an earthenwork—has a diameter of roughly 790 feet (240 meters), but all the fascinating finds at Navan, the stone temple ruins and the burial mounds, are either underground or in the Ulster Museum in Belfast. Also like Tara, what the site lacks in dramatic ruins it more than makes up for in a rich and spooky sense of history.

It takes less than an hour to walk here from the city, or you can take **Ulsterbus** (#73, 7/day Mon.–Fri., 3/day Sat.) to the village of Navan from the bus depot just north of the Mall.

Gosford Forest Park

The early 19th-century Gosford Castle, the first "Norman Revival" manor in the British Isles, has a rather unusual history: It was used as a military barracks after the castle's contents were sold in 1921, and it housed German POWs during World War II. Jonathan Swift was a guest of Lord and Lady Gosford in the original castle (which burned down in 1805), and it's said he wrote most of *Gulliver's Travels* here. Today the castle's 580 acres at Gosford Forest Park (7 Gosford Demesne, Markethill, tel. 028/3755-1277, www.forestserviceni.gov.uk, open 8 A.M.–dusk all year, car/pedestrian admission £4/1) are open to the public, complete with arboretum, walled garden, nature walks, and picnicking facilities. The sadly neglected house itself is closed to the public, however.

Gosford Forest Park is six miles (9.6 km) southeast of Armagh on the A28.

The Argory

Built in 1824, the Argory (144 Derrycaw Rd., 4 mi/6.4 km north of Moy off the A29, 11 mi/17 km north of Armagh, tel. 028/8778-4753, argory@nationaltrust.org.uk) *still* hasn't got electricity. And seeing as the National Trust has restored it to almost exactly the way it was at the turn of the 20th century (with its own acetylene gas plant), it probably never will. The grounds are open year-round (10 A.M.–4 P.M. daily Oct.–Apr., 10 A.M.–7 P.M. May–Sept.), while the house is open seasonally (1–6 P.M. weekends Apr.–May and Sept., 1–6 P.M. daily June–Aug. and Easter week). Admission to the grounds is £2.60 per car; the house tour costs £4.70. The highlight of the house tour is a cabinet organ dating to the time the house was built, and the old stable now serves as the estate's tearoom. It's worth a visit if you're interested in old manor houses, especially since there are some pretty gardens (including a rose garden and a Victorian arbor) and easy walking trails on the 200-acre estate.

TYRONE AND FERMANAGH

Where Northern Ireland tourism's concerned, the landscapes of landlocked Counties Tyrone (Tír Eoghain, "Land of Eoghan") and Fermanagh ("fur-MAN-ahh," Fir-Monach, "The Men of Monach") are generally overshadowed by the more dramatic scenery of the Derry and Antrim coasts. In Tyrone, especially, there are more ho-hum market towns than exciting tourist attractions. But the lakes of Fermanagh are rich in monastic ruins as well as trout, and Tyrone's Sperrin Mountains are a haven for hardcore walkers and cyclists looking to get off the beaten trail.

HISTORY

Memories of devastating IRA bombings in very recent history have marked the collective psyche of both Omagh and Enniskillen, these counties' principal towns. Eleven people lost their lives when a bomb went off on November 11, 1987, during a town center memorial service for those killed in the World Wars. Sixty-three people were injured, and another man would spend 13 years—the rest of his life—in a coma. The bomb was hidden in a nearby building.

As horrific as the Enniskillen bombing was, the Omagh tragedy was even bloodier. On August 15, 1998, 29 people were killed by a car bomb, making this the costliest act of terrorism since the Troubles began. The Royal Ulster Constabulary (RUC) unknowingly ushered people *toward* the bomb on a false tip. A few locals (both Protestant and Catholic) believe the police may have known more about the bomb before the fact than they ever let on; this

© CAMILLE DEANGELIS

HIGHLIGHTS

(Ulster-American Folk Park: Just north of Omagh, this is one of those rare museums that's primarily intended for children yet offers a very enjoyable experience for adults, too (page 484).

(Sperrin Mountains: Go on a long walk, cycle, or drive through these melancholy hills, dappled with gorse and heather, in northern Tyrone (page 486).

(Castle Coole: Cold and imposing, Fermanagh's most opulent manor house features nearly every stick of its original furniture; if you visit only one "big house" in these counties, let it be this one (page 492).

(Marble Arch Caves: Full of interesting, whimsically named formations and a network of subterranean rivers, these caves are some of the island's finest (page 492).

(Devenish Island: Take the ferry to this secluded Augustinian monastery on Lough Erne, which features a complete round tower – admire its original conical roof and decorated cornice, then step inside and climb it (page 493)!

LOOK FOR **(** TO FIND RECOMMENDED SIGHTS, ACTIVITIES, DINING, AND LODGING.

rumor was fueled by the subsequent investigation of why the RUC decided to heed the least reliable of the three tips they received in the hour before the bomb detonated. Though the investigation report, released in late 2001, confirmed that the RUC knew more than they chose to act upon, police officials have insisted that the report contained factual errors and questioned the reliability of the investigator's sources.

It must be noted that the perpetrators of these terrorist bombings were members of the "Provisional IRA" (in Enniskillen) and "Continuity IRA" (in Omagh), two splinter groups who disagreed with the IRA's conclusion that violence would never achieve their goal of a

united Ireland. Another salient point is the sense of common purpose that has arisen from these tragedies, uniting Protestants and Catholics who want only peace in their community and between one another.

PLANNING YOUR TIME

On a visit to Ulster you'll want to spend the bulk of your time in Down, Antrim, and Derry, visiting the Sperrin Mountains in Tyrone or the Lough Erne region of Fermanagh en route to Donegal. Or after visiting Derry City, you might drive south through the Sperrins, stopping at the Ulster-American Folk Park just north of Omagh before continuing to Enniskillen. If you get an early enough

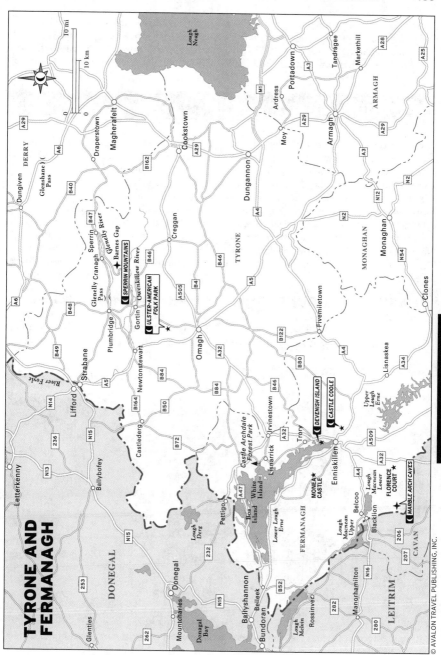

TYRONE AND FERMANAGH

Lough Neagh

DERRY

Dungiven
Glenshane Pass
Draperstown
Magherafelt
Cookstown
Moy
Potadown
Ardress
Armagh
ARMAGH
Markethill
Tandragee

Sperrin
Glenelly Cranagh
Glenelly Pass
Barnes Gap
Glenelly River
Owenkillew River
★ SPERRIN MOUNTAINS
◀ ULSTER-AMERICAN FOLK PARK
Gortin
Creggan
TYRONE
Dungannon
MONAGHAN
Monaghan
Clones

Strabane
Plumbridge
Newtonstewart
Omagh
Fivemiletown
Lisnaskea
River Foyle
Lifford
Castlederg
Irvinestown
◀ DEVENISH ISLAND
◀ CASTLE COOLE
Upper Lough Erne

Letterkenny
Ballybofey
Castle Archdale Forest Park
Lisnarrick
Trory
Enniskillen

DONEGAL
Pettigo
White Island
Boa Island
Lower Lough Erne
MONEA CASTLE ★
Lough Macnean Lower
FLORENCE COURT ★
◀ MARBLE ARCH CAVES
Belcoo
Blacklion

Lough Derg
FERMANAGH
Lough Macnean Upper

Donegal
Mountcharles
Glenties
Donegal Bay
Ballyshannon
Belleek
Bundoran
Rossinver
Manorhamilton
CAVAN
LEITRIM

Lough Melvin

10 mi
10 km

© AVALON TRAVEL PUBLISHING, INC.

start, you may not have to spend the night in Omagh, Tyrone's principal town—frankly it's not a very interesting place in itself. Not that Enniskillen's a party town either, but it defi- nitely has a lighter, friendlier vibe. Base your- self here and spend a couple days visiting the Marble Arch Caves, Devenish Island, Castle Coole, and Florence Court.

Tyrone

Between the bleak Sperrin mountain range and a proliferation of super-unionist Plantation towns, you may wonder how a trip through Ty- rone could be worthwhile. First, the Sperrins can be beautiful in fine weather (all sprinkled with yellow gorse and whatnot), and even if you don't have time for a long walk or cycle, you can still go for a scenic drive en route to or from Donegal or Derry. Plus, the Ulster-Amer- ican Folk Park just north of Omagh is one of the island's best museum/folk parks.

OMAGH AND AROUND

To be frank, Omagh ("OH-muh," An Ómaigh), Tyrone's principal town, is worth a stopover for convenience rather than for any inher- ent merit. Base yourself here and head north into the Sperrins for a long scenic drive, and spend most of another day at the excellent Ul- ster-American Folk Park. The town itself has a rather drab, mournful atmosphere.

Omagh straddles the River Strule, with most of what you'll need on the south side of the river. West to east, the main thorough- fare changes names from Abbey to Castle to George's to High to Market Street, with the tourist office where High becomes Market.

◖ Ulster-American Folk Park

When people tell you that the Ulster-American Folk Park (2 Mellon Rd., Castletown, 5 mi/8 km north of Omagh on the A5, tel. 028/8224-

Pittsburgh tycoon Thomas Mellon was born in this modest cottage, now a part of the Ulster-American Folk Park.

© CAMILLE DEANGELIS

TYRONE AND FERMANAGH

3292, www.folkpark.com, open 10:30 A.M.–6 P.M. Mon.–Sat. and 11 A.M.–6:30 P.M. Sun. Apr.–Sept., 10:30 A.M.–5 P.M. Mon.–Fri. Oct.–Mar., admission £4.50) is one of the best museums in the country, go on and believe them; it's a worthwhile excursion even if you don't have kids in tow. The extensive indoor museum spans the length of American history, focusing, of course, on the contributions of the Scots-Irish—providing something of a refresher course for Americans of all stripes. Outside, the folk park is divided into Old and New World villages, with a reconstructed port and emigrant ship ingeniously linking the two. The idea of a lady wearing a bonnet working at a spinning wheel sounds pretty hokey, but the "costumed interpreters" explain and demonstrate the traditional crafts in a clear, undramatic way. One of the highlights of the Old World park is the original cottage where Thomas Mellon, the Pittsburgh financier, was born in 1813. In the New World section you can tour a replica of the clapboard house his father built in Pennsylvania in 1822 (four years after emigrating), complete with rickety stairs and lumpy beds made with hand-sewn quilts. There's so much to see, both in and out of doors, that you should plan for a visit of three hours. And of course, try to get here as soon as the park opens—especially in the summer.

The folk park also hosts several special events throughout the year, like American Civil War reenactments, the Appalachian and Bluegrass Festival during the first weekend in September, and the three-day Hallowe'en Festival, when the ladies in bonnets tell ghost stories and dish out shoofly pie and other goodies. The adjacent **Centre for Migration Studies** (tel. 028/8225-6315, open Mon.–Fri. 10 A.M.–5 P.M.) offers an emigration database, though at time of writing it included only the shipping records from the Derry, Newry, and Belfast ports during the first half of the 19th century.

Sports and Recreation

The lovely **Gortin Glen Forest Park** (6 mi/9.6 km north of town signposted off the B48, tel. 028/8167-0666, open 10 A.M.–sunset daily, car admission £3) comprises nearly 3,800 acres of coniferous woodland, and it's only six miles outside town—you could even rent a bike and pedal there. And of course, there are the Sperrins farther north for serious cyclists.

Accommodations

The IHH, family-run **Omagh Independent Hostel** (9A Waterworks Rd., 3 mi/4.8 km northeast of Omagh on the B48, tel. 028/8224-1973, http://omaghhostel.co.uk, open Mar.–Oct., dorms £8, private rooms £10 pp, £6 per campsite, euros accepted) is a great little hostel in a tranquil spot surrounded by wild gardens. The friendly owners are happy to pick you up from the bus station.

For basic B&B (with a hearty Ulster fry) closer to town, try **Bankhead** (9 Lissan Rd., 2 mi/3.2 km south of town off the A5, tel. 028/8224-5592, £18 pp), on a working beef and sheep farm. All three bedrooms have a shared bath.

An authentically restored Georgian manor, **Mullaghmore House** (Old Mountfield Rd., 1 mi/1.6 km north of town, tel. 028/8224-2314, www.mullaghmorehouse.com, £34–39 pp) provides luxurious B&B accommodations (a plush drawing room with a fire in the hearth, a billiards room, strolling gardens—the lot) as well as courses in home and furniture restoration and interior design (clearly these people have a thing or two to teach), as well as crafts like stained glass, mosaics, and candle-making. Archaeological evidence indicates the house may have been built on the foundations of a medieval abbey, and a standing stone was recently excavated on the property. To get here, take the Gortin road out of Omagh and make a right onto Old Mountfield Road; Mullaghmore will be on the left.

An excellent guesthouse in a lovely bucolic setting a 15-minute drive from town, ◖ **Greenmount Lodge** (58 Greenmount Rd., 9 mi/14 km south of Omagh, tel. 028/8284-1325, www.greenmountlodge.com, £23 pp, s £27, credit cards accepted) has comfortable and well furnished rooms (with slouchy armchairs and complimentary wireless Internet), and the breakfast is ample. In high season Mrs. Reid serves hearty evening meals and will pack you a lunch if you ask the night before. All in all, it's a great value. To get here, take the A5 south out of Omagh and make a right onto Greenmount Road opposite Carrick-keel Pizza; you'll see the front gates down a mile and a half (2.4 km) on the left.

The family-run **Kelly's Inn** (232 Omagh Rd., on the A5 10 mi/16 km south of Omagh, Ballygawley, tel. 028/8556-8218, www.kellysinn.com, £30 pp), open since 1937, offers pretty much your run-of-the-mill hotel rooms. Seeing as the hotel restaurant is as good as (if not better than) the food in Omagh's eateries and the occasional pop, folk, or tribute concert, though, it sure makes sense to stay (and eat) here. It won't win any awards for outstanding architecture, but the nice thing about the modern **Silverbirch Hotel** (5 Gortin Rd./the B48, tel. 028/8224-2520, www.silverbirchhotel.com, £41–50 pp, s £58–68) is the private, mature garden, a nice way to work up an even bigger appetite before breakfast. It's also just a 10-minute walk from the center of town.

Food, Entertainment, and Shopping

Unlike Enniskillen, Omagh doesn't have much in the way of nice restaurants. The upstairs tearooms at **Serendipity** (22 Bridge St., tel. 028/8225-2230, open 10 A.M.–5 P.M. Mon.–Sat., lunches £2–4) are snug but cozy, a good spot for a cappuccino. Full of jewelry and sequined evening bags, the downstairs shop is a girlie-girl's paradise.

The **Watermill** at Kelly's Inn (on the A5 10 mi/16 km south of Omagh, Ballygawley, tel. 028/8556-8218, www.kellysinn.com, food served 8 A.M.–10 P.M. daily, mains £6–15) offers good seafood, chicken, and steak dishes, along with a few decent veggie options. Like the hotel itself, the restaurant is pleasant and spacious, if generic, and the waitstaff are nice and accommodating. The inn also offers a regular calendar of pop, folk, and tribute concerts.

You can find more surprisingly good hotel fare closer to town at the **Buttery Grill** at the

Silverbirch Hotel (5 Gortin Rd./the B48, tel. 028/8224-2520, www.silverbirchhotel.com, open 9:30 A.M.–9 P.M. Mon.–Sat., 7:30 A.M.–9 P.M. Sun., mains £8–18).

Information and Services

The **tourist office** (1 Market St., tel. 028/8224-7831, www.omagh.gov.uk, open 9 A.M.–5 P.M. Mon.–Sat. Apr.–Sept., until 5:30 P.M. July–Aug., 9 A.M.–5 P.M. Mon.–Fri. Oct.–Mar.) also offers **Internet access** (£1.50/30 minutes). Banks with ATMs and bureaux de change include **Ulster Bank** (High St.) and **Northern Bank** (5-7 Market St.).

Take care of business at **Carmen's Laundrette** (Main St., tel. 028/8076-1213) and **Boots the Chemist** (43/47 High St., tel. 028/8224-5455).

Getting There and Around

Omagh is 68 miles (109 km) west of Belfast (via the M1, A4, and A5) and 27 miles (44 km) northeast of Enniskillen on the A32. Get here via **Ulsterbus** from Belfast or Derry (#273, 8/day Mon.–Fri., 6/day Sat., 1/day Sun.), Enniskillen (#274, 7/day Mon.–Fri., 3/day Sat., 1/day Sun.), or Dublin (#274, 5/day daily). The bus depot is north of the river at Bridge Street and Drumragh Avenue.

Ring **James A.** (tel. 028/8284-0540) for a taxi.

◖ SPERRIN MOUNTAINS

Stretching north from Omagh to southern Derry, the moorland, gorse-dotted Sperrins are spooky and downright desolate in poor weather. In the more remote parts there's not a house, human, even sheep for miles on end. Then there's that howling wind, downright frightening at night. No wonder the Lord Deputy of Ireland was careful to avoid the area when giving a tour to London investors in 1609, which required a fair bit of spin-doctoring. Reports of gold aside, the English saw the Sperrins as a place to be avoided.

Today the Northern Ireland Tourist Board promotes the Sperrins as perfect for long-distance walking or cycling, yet there's almost no place to stay in the mountains (almost all accommodations are outside them); you can either camp or stay at a hostel (with self-catering apartments) on the southern fringes, **Gortin Accommodation Suite and Activity Centre** (62 Main St., Gortin, tel. 028/8164-8346, www.gortin.net, dorm beds £10, sheet rental £2.50). It's modern in a slightly depressing way, but they make it easy enough to organize abseiling, cycling, or canoeing excursions. Another option is a self-catering cottage at **An Creagan Visitor Centre** (Creggan, on the A505 12 mi/19 km northeast of Omagh, tel. 028/8076-1112, www.an-creagan.com, open 11 A.M.–6:30 P.M. daily Apr.–Sept., 11 A.M.–4:30 P.M. Mon.–Fri. Oct.–Mar., 1-bedroom cottage £70–90 per weekend, £110–180 per week, center admission £2), which offers an exhibition on the flora, fauna, and archaeology of the Sperrins. Bike rental is available as well (£5/7/40 per half-day/day/week), and in recent years they've also opened a pub-cum-restaurant serving lunch, tea, and dinner. There are regular weekend trad sessions.

One of the region's more popular cycling routes is the 47-mile (76-km), traffic-free **Sperrins Sprint,** a fairly tough circuit from Cookstown through the Glenelly Valley and back again. For more info on cycling excursions, contact **Sperrins Tourism** (tel. 028/8674-7700, www.sperrinstourism.com) or stop by the Omagh tourist office.

The Ulsterbus **Sperrin Rambler** service (#403, 2/day) connects Omagh with Gortin and Cranagh, where you'll find another resource: the **Sperrin Heritage Centre** (274 Glenelly Rd., Cranagh, on the B47 23 mi/37 km north of Omagh, tel. 028/8164-8142, open 11:30 A.M.–5:30 P.M. Mon.–Fri., 11:30 A.M.–6 P.M. Sat., 2–6 P.M. Sun. Apr.–Sept., admission £2.50). The center is situated just south of the Sperrins' highest peak, **Mount Sawel** (2,230 feet, 680 meters). Outside of the Rambler bus, those not walking or cycling will need a car to explore these mountains.

Fermanagh

Fermanagh is very much a lake county, as the Upper and Lower Loughs Erne (though "Lough Erne" generally refers to the larger lower lake) are central to its geography, commerce, and tourism. The nationalist writer William Bulfin cycled around the lakes near the turn of the 20th century, and he offered nought but praise. "You seldom hear of Fermanagh as being a picturesque district," he wrote, "and yet you could linger in it for weeks without tiring of it." *Weeks* may be a slight exaggeration, but it's certainly true that Lough Erne's beauty is underrated. Adding to its romance is a smattering of still-grand manor houses, equally forlorn castle ruins, and vast, lush forest parks.

ENNISKILLEN
Fermanagh's capital is the pleasant market town of Enniskillen (Inis Ceithleann), a natural base for exploring the islands of Lough Erne. The nightlife's not half bad either, and there are a few outstanding restaurants (all on Belmore Street, incidentally). The town's Irish name means "Ceithleann's Island," the name of an old Irish warrior (not "Cathleen").

Enniskillen is situated at the southern end of Lower Lough Erne, on an island at the mouth of a river with the same name, which eventually empties into the Upper Lough. Though it's easy to traverse by foot, the town is a maze of one-way streets; the main thoroughfare (changing names from Ann to Darling to Church to High to Downhall to East Bridge Street) moves east on Ann and Darling but west from Church Street. If driving, use the free parking lot by the Erneside bus station and explore the town on foot. Forthill Park is on the eastern end of town, off the Dublin roundabout at the end of Belmore Street.

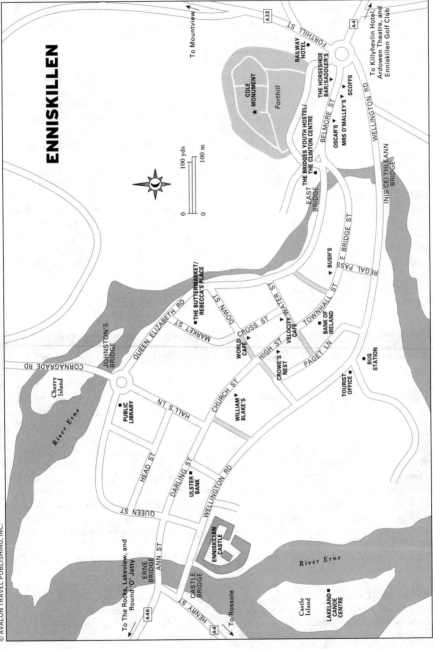

ENNISKILLEN

To Mountview

A32

FORTHILL ST

A4

To Killyhevlin Hotel, Ardowen Theatre, and Enniskillen Golf Club

RAILWAY HOTEL

COLE MONUMENT

Forthill

THE HORSESHOE BAR/SADDLER'S

BELMORE ST

OSCAR'S ▼

MRS O'MALLEY'S ▼

SCOFFS

WELLINGTON RD

INIS CEITHLEANN BRIDGE

EAST BRIDGE

THE BRIDGES YOUTH HOSTEL/ THE CLINTON CENTRE

0 100 yds
0 100 m

BUSH'S ▼

E BRIDGE ST

REGAL PASS

THE BUTTERMARKET/ REBECCA'S PLACE ■

QUEEN ELIZABETH RD

MARKET ST

DOWN ST

CROSS ST

WATER ST

VELOCITY CAFE

TOWNHALL ST

BANK OF IRELAND ■

WORLD CAFE ▼

HIGH ST

PAGET LN

JOHNSTON'S BRIDGE

CORNAGRADE RD

Cherry Island

River Erne

CROWE'S NEST ▼

TOURIST OFFICE ■

BUS STATION ■

PUBLIC LIBRARY ■

HALL'S LN

CHURCH ST

WILLIAM BLAKE'S ▼

HEAD ST

DARLING ST

ULSTER BANK ■

WELLINGTON RD

QUEEN ST

To The Rocks, Lakeview, and Round 'O' Jetty

ERNE BRIDGE

A46

ANN ST

HENRY ST

CASTLE BRIDGE

ENNISKILLEN CASTLE

River Erne

A4

To Rossole

Castle Island

LAKELAND CANOE CENTRE ■

Sights

Overlooking Lough Erne, the earliest parts of **Enniskillen Castle** (Castle Barracks, tel. 028/6632-5000, www.enniskillencastle.co.uk, open 10 A.M.–5 P.M. Tues.–Fri. and 2–5 P.M. Sat.–Mon. July–Aug., closed Sun. May–June and Sept., 2–5 P.M. Mon. and 10 A.M.–5 P.M. Tues.–Fri. Oct.–Apr., admission £2.50) date to the 15th century. The castle's most distinctive feature is a Scottish-style watergate of twin corbelled pepperpot bartizans—in other words, this section looks like it belongs in a fairy tale. The old keep houses a (crammed and creepy) military museum (the Regimental Museum of the Royal Inniskilling Fusiliers, to be precise), the arcaded barracks an exhibition on the monastic history of the Lough Erne islands, and the Fermanagh County Museum is also on the grounds, with small exhibits on Belleek and lace-making as well as the area's natural history. All in all, the castle is a fine rainy day activity, but in nice weather just admire the watergate—a misnomer, for it isn't actually a gateway—from a picnic bench in the park outside.

The watergate at Enniskillen Castle is fit for a fairy tale.

For a panoramic view of town and lake, climb the 108 steps of **Cole Monument** (Forthill Park, on the east end of town, tel. 028/6632-5050, open 1:30–3 P.M. daily Apr.–Sept., admission £1), erected in memory of the son of the first Earl of Enniskillen.

Opened in 2002 opposite the war memorial, **The Clinton Centre** (Belmore St., tel. 028/6634-0110, open 9 A.M.–4 P.M. Mon.–Fri., 11 A.M.–4 P.M. Sat., free admission) is a state-of-the-art conference center plus hostel, café, and gallery space. Pop in and see what's on display—you may find the art surprisingly avant-garde.

Entertainment and Events

The amiable barstaff at **William Blake's** (Church St., tel. 028/6632-2143) pour the best Guinness in the north; they also make the best Bailey's coffee. This gorgeous old pub retains much of its original Victorian detail—mahogany wall paneling and high ceilings, ornate pillar lamps sprouting out of the bar, and

real snugs in the back. As for trad, **Bush's** (26 Townhall St., tel. 028/6632-5212) is the town's best, with sessions Friday through Sunday nights all year. Or stop by the **Crowe's Nest** (12 High St., tel. 028/6632-5252) on Monday night (summer only). The Crowe's Nest has a nice beer garden out back, super-traditional pub grub, and live blues or rock every other night of the week.

Locals seem quite proud of Enniskillen's modern, lakeside theater, **Ardhowen** (Dublin Rd., 1.2 mi/2 km outside town, tel. 028/6632-5440, www.ardhowentheatre.com, tickets £7–15), which offers a diverse lineup of dance, concerts (jazz, pop, and the occasional tribute) and both classic and experimental dramatic productions. The town's annual amateur drama competition takes place here in early March.

Shopping

Got any room left in your suitcase? There are a couple of adorable little shops on Shore Road: **Cloughcor House Antiques** (tel. 028/6632-4805) sells a lot of neat stuff (bookends, clocks,

© CAMILLE DEANGELIS

wooden decoys, picture frames, and suchlike) that just *looks* antique, along with the real thing; next door, **The Crabtree Cottage** (tel. 028/6632-4333) stocks delightful, slightly quirky homewares. Just across the way is the Erneside Shopping Centre, with the usual offering of chain stores.

But no self-respecting shopper should miss the **Buttermarket** (Down St., tel. 028/6632-4499, closed Sun.), a quaint complex of small shops and galleries. The most extensive of these is the **Boston Quay Craft Shop** (tel. 028/6632-3837), selling lovely handmade greeting cards, French soaps, jewelry, candles, stationery, children's accessories, and fun housewares. Most of the stock is imported, however.

Sports and Recreation

Go for a waterbus cruise on Lough Erne with **Erne Tours** (Round 'O' Jetty, Brook Park, on the A46 just west of town, tel. 028/6632-2882, departures at 10:30 A.M., 2:15 P.M., and 4:15 P.M. daily July–Aug., 2:30 P.M. Tues.–Sat.–Sun. Sept., 2:30 P.M. Sun. May–June, tickets £8, 6:30 P.M. dinner cruise £20). The trip lasts just under two hours, and the highlight is a (however brief) stop at Devenish Island.

Anglers should head to **Home, Field & Stream** (18 Church St., tel. 028/6632-2114) for permits and tackle.

Opened in 1896, the 18-hole, par-71 **Enniskillen Golf Club** (1.5 mi/2.4 km southeast of town off the A4, tel. 028/6632-5250, www.enniskillengolfclub.com) is beside the Castle Coole estate.

The kid- and beginner-friendly **Forest Stables** (100 Cooneen Rd., Fivemiletown, 18 mi/26 km east of Enniskillen off the A4, tel. 028/8952-1991, one-hour beginner trek £15, two-hour scenic trek £35) is on the Fermanagh-Tyrone border.

Or go canoeing or windsurfing on Upper Lough Macnean at the **Corralea Activity Centre** (162 Lattone Rd., 14 mi/23 km west of town, tel. 028/6638-6123, www.activity-ireland.com). There are self-catering cottages available as well. To get here, take the A4 west out of town to Belcoo and make a right onto the B52; the center is three miles (4.8 km) down on the left. Canadian canoes are also up for rent at the **Lakeland Canoe Centre** (Castle Island, 0.5 mi/800 m, ring tel. 028/6632-4250 from the bus depot for ferry transport).

Accommodations

Part of The Clinton Centre, **The Bridges Youth Hostel** (Belmore St., tel. 028/6634-0110, www.hini.org.uk, dorms £12–13, private rooms £14 pp, credit cards accepted) offers private and small dorms so clean they're antiseptic, but no matter—the facilities here are unparalleled, and the staff are amazingly friendly and helpful. Even cooler are the futuristic solar panels on the facade.

Mountview (61 Irvinestown Rd., the A23, tel. 028/6632-3147, www.mountviewguests. com, £28 pp, s £37, credit cards accepted) is a charmingly faded ivy-covered Victorian overlooking the Race Course Lough with a well-tended garden, snooker table, and modern rooms with electric heating pads on the comfy beds. Wendy McChesney is an informative and efficient hostess who serves up a lovely breakfast. It's less than a 15-minute walk into town. A bit less dear, and perhaps more ideally situated, is **Rossole** (85 Sligo Rd., tel. 028/6632-3462 or 078/1245-2526, £23 pp, s £25), an imposing Georgian-style stone home with Lough Erne literally in the backyard (you can even borrow a boat from the owner).

If you're renting a car, consider staying a 20-minute drive west of Enniskillen at a farmhouse B&B along the scenic A46 to Belleek and Donegal. Two options are **The Rocks** (Cosbystown, signposted 8 mi/13 km west on the A46, tel. 028/6864-1230, £22 pp, s £25), on an organic farm, whose authentic Victorian furnishings will fool you into thinking the house was built long before the 1970s; and **Lakeview** (Drumcrow, Blaney, 10 mi/16 km west on the A46, tel. 028/6864-1263, open Feb.–Nov., kjhassard@yahoo.co.uk, £25 pp, s £27)—the house itself isn't quite as atmospheric, but the name says all you need to know. (Not all the rooms are en suite, but you'll appreciate the electric blankies.) The Rocks is a couple miles closer to town and also has a charming holiday cottage up for rent nearby.

The modern **Killyhevlin Hotel** (0.9 mi/1.5 km south of town on the A4, tel. 028/6632-3481, www.killyhevlin.co.uk, £60–70 pp, s £90–100) has a spa and leisure center as well as lake views from many of the rooms, but the walls are thin and the food is mediocre. The Victorian **Railway Hotel** (34 Forthill St., tel. 028/6632-2084, www.railwayhotelenniskillen.com, £35 pp) has better food and a more charming atmosphere.

Food

Did somebody say "fudge"? **Mrs. O'Malley's** (19-21 Belmore St., tel. 028/6632-2288, www.mrsomalleys.co.uk) is a delightfully old-fashioned confectionary and coffee shop. If you're shopping at the Buttermarket, the natural choice for lunch is cafeteria-style **Rebecca's Place** (tel. 028/6632-4499, open 9 A.M.–5:30 P.M. Mon.–Sat., mains £3–6), but at peak lunchtime hours it's mobbed with young families. Nearby is the **World Café Bar** (1 Middleton St., tel. 028/6632-2264, open 9:30 A.M.–6 P.M. Mon.–Sat., lunches £3–6), the trendiest coffee shop in Enniskillen. With the best cappuccino in town, it's also deservedly popular. For something a bit more formal, try the **Velocity Café** (2B Cross St. at Water St., tel. 028/6634-2616, open 8 A.M.–6 P.M. Mon.–Thurs., 8 A.M.–9 P.M. Fri. and Sat., mains £5–8), which does gourmet burgers and salads.

The Horseshoe Bar (66 Belmore St., tel. 028/6632-6223, www.horseshoeandsaddlers.com, food served 4–11 P.M. daily, until 10 P.M. Sun., mains £8–14) does terrific meat-and-potatoes pub grub. Be sure to save room for the amazing sticky toffee pudding. The food in the upstairs restaurant, **Saddler's** (open 5:30–11 P.M. Mon.–Sat. and noon–10 P.M., mains £10–18) is only slightly more sophisticated, but a fair bit pricier.

Enniskillen's top two restaurants are the swanky-but-relaxed ◗ **Scoffs** (17 Belmore St., tel. 028/6634-2622, www.scoffsuno.com, open 5 P.M.–late daily, 12:30–2:30 P.M. Sun., mains £10–17) and cozy, atmospheric **Oscar's** (29 Belmore St., tel. 028/6632-7037, www.oscarsrestaurant.co.uk, open 5–10:30 P.M. Wed.–Mon., mains £6–16). Candlelight dancing off the brazen Modigliani-style nude on the back wall, Scoffs has an inventive, oft-changing menu featuring kangaroo and ostrich filets, among other tamer fare. Named for Oscar Wilde (who attended the Portora Royal School here), Oscar's has an authentic Georgian bar, a "Dorian Gray Room," and an eclectic menu (though Scoffs has more creative veggie options). Reservations are recommended at weekends and in summertime, as both eateries are much loved by locals.

Information

Enniskillen's very helpful **tourist office** (Wellington Rd., tel. 028/6632-3110, www.fermanaghlakelands.com, open 9 A.M.–7 P.M. Mon.–Fri., 10 A.M.–6 P.M. Sat., 11 A.M.–5 P.M. Sun. July–Aug.; 9 A.M.–5:30 P.M. Mon.–Fri., 10 A.M.–6 P.M. Sat., 11 A.M.–5 P.M. Sun. Easter–June and Sept., 9 A.M.–5:30 P.M. Mon.–Fri. Oct.–Easter) also sells fishing licenses.

Services

You'll find ATMs and bureaux de change at **Ulster Bank** (16 Darling St.) and the **Bank of Ireland** (7 Townhall St.). The **post office** is inside Dolan's Centra on East Bridge.

Suds your duds at **The Wash Tub** (12 E. Bridge St., tel. 028/6632-5230) and get your Rx at **Belcoo Pharmacy** (15 Main St., tel. 028/6638-6931).

The **public library** (Hall's Ln., tel. 028/6632-2886, open 9:30 A.M.–5 P.M. Mon.–Fri., until 7:30 P.M. Tues. and Thurs., 9:30 A.M.–1 P.M. Sat.) offers Internet access for £0.75/15 minutes, and there are enough terminals that you shouldn't have to wait too long. Or try the super-speedy flatscreens at the **East End Restaurant** (tel. 028/6632-0883, open 8 A.M.–11 P.M. Mon.–Sat., 9 A.M.–10 P.M. Sun., £2/3.50 per 30 minutes/hour) on the ground floor of The Clinton Centre.

TYRONE AND FERMANAGH

Getting There and Around

Enniskillen is 42 miles (67 km) east of Sligo on the N16 and 50 miles (81 km) west of Armagh on the A4/A28. **Ulsterbus** (tel. 028/9066-6630) can get you here from Belfast (#261, 8/day Mon.–Sat., 2/day Sun.) or Derry (#296, 1/day Mon.–Fri.). **Bus Éireann** (tel. 01/836-6111) serves Enniskillen on its Dublin–Donegal route (#30, 4–5/day), and there's service from Sligo (#66, 5/day Mon.–Sat., 2/day Sun.) as well.

Ring **County Cabs** (tel. 028/6632-8888) for a taxi.

SOUTH OF ENNISKILLEN
◖ Castle Coole

One of Northern Ireland's grandest manors is the neoclassical Castle Coole (4 mi/6.4 km southeast of town on the A4, tel. 028/6632-2690, www.ntni.org.uk, grounds open 10 A.M.–8 P.M. Apr.–Sept., until 4 P.M. Oct.–Mar., house open noon–6 P.M. weekends mid-Mar.–May and Sept., Fri.–Wed. June, daily July–Aug., admission £4.20), the seat of the earls of Belmore. The saloon, bedchambers, and state rooms have been painstakingly restored by the National Trust to their Regency-era resplendence, with all the original furniture for which it was specially designed in the 1790s. It's said that the building costs so far exceeded estimates that the interior was decorated with restraint, yet the plasterwork and other period details are surely sumptuous enough—this is because the second earl was even more extravagant than his father had been. The most amusing part of a visit to the house is King George IV's bedroom, prepared for his visit in 1821 but never used. George was too busy with his mistress, Lady Conyngham of Slane Castle in County Meath.

Castle Coole is only four miles (6.4 km) from Enniskillen, a walk of 30–40 minutes south on the Dublin road. Even if you aren't all that interested in the manor itself, take a long walk around the tranquil 1,500-acre demesne, free for pedestrians (open 10 A.M.–8 P.M. May–Sept., until 4 P.M. Oct.–Apr., £2 for cars).

◖ Marble Arch Caves

In 1895 a French lawyer and speleologist named Edouard Martel ventured into a hitherto-unexplored cave in the Cuilcagh ("KWILL-kuh") Mountains, which locals swore was haunted. He found the Marble Arch Caves (Florencecourt, 11 mi/18 km southwest of town off the A32, tel. 028/6634-8855, www.marblearchcaves.net, open 10 A.M.–5 P.M. July–Aug., 10 A.M.–4:30 P.M. mid-Mar.–June and Sept., admission £6.50), one of Ireland's few subterranean sights as spectacular as hyped. After a 15-minute boat trip, during which you'll see the junction of the three smaller rivers that empty into the Cladagh, there's a one-hour walking tour jam-packed with geological tidbits. The guides have a clever name for every funny-looking formation. A specially designed cement walkway that parts the subterranean lake is known, appropriately enough, as "the Moses walk." Foam on the ceiling indicates how high the water was earlier in the day—even the Moses walk can flood.

While you're waiting for your tour to commence, check out the excellent 20-minute audiovisual on the geology, botany, and history of the area. The caves and the surrounding **Marlbank National Nature Reserve** have been designated a European Geopark, and the blanket bog on the Cuilcagh Mountains supports a great deal of flora and fauna.

Be smart and ring ahead to reserve a place on a tour in the summertime. To get here from Enniskillen, take the Sligo-bound A4, and after three miles (4.8 km) make a left onto the southbound A32. The caves are clearly signposted from there, and you'll pass Florence Court on the way. From Sligo, take the eastbound N16 and look for the Marble Arch signpost in Blacklion.

Florence Court

In the shadow of Benaughlin Mountain—from the Irish for "Peak of the Horse" because its limestone scree once resembled a horse's profile—Florence Court (7.5 mi/12 km southwest of town via the A4 and A32, tel. 028/6634-8249, grounds open 10 A.M.–8 P.M. Apr.–Sept., until 4 P.M. Oct.–Mar., house open noon–6 P.M. weekends mid-Mar.–May, 1–6 P.M. Mon. and Wed.–Fri., noon–6 P.M. Sat.–Sun. June, noon–6 P.M. daily July–Aug., Sat.–Sun. Sept., admission £4) offers a serene walled garden and wooded walking trails through the adjoining forest park. There are three circular trails, 2–7 miles (3–11 km) long; the shortest takes you past the Florence Court Yew, the tree from which all Irish yews the world over originated. The house itself is a Palladian manor, built in the 1740s by Sir John Cole and extended by his son William, the first Earl of Enniskillen, 30 years later. What's even more remarkable about the original 18th-century furniture and rococo plasterwork is that the place could be so well restored after the fire that broke out in 1955.

THE HOLY ISLANDS OF LOUGH ERNE
C Devenish Island

Devenish (Daimh Inis, "Ox Island") has the spectacular ruins of 6th-century Augustinian St. Molaise's Monastery. An astonishingly well-preserved 12th-century round tower, 30 meters high, sports a decorated cornice and its original conical roof. Best of all, you can climb it!

There are many legends surrounding this island, one of which concerns the building of 12th-century **St. Mary's Abbey** nearby; it's said that St. Molaise (who founded the monastery in the late 500s, mind you) listened to the birds singing, communing with the Holy Spirit. When he finally shook himself from his sacred reverie, half a millennium had passed, and his grand abbey stood all around him. The monastic community here flourished for another half a millennium, but despite its remote location it could not escape Henry VIII's decree of the late 1530s—that all the Irish monasteries be dissolved.

The Devenish **ferry** (tel. 028/6682-1588 or 028/6632-2882, sailings at 10 A.M., 1 P.M., 3 P.M., and 5 P.M. daily July–mid-Sept., weekends Easter–June, return fare £3) departs from Trory Point, three miles (4.8 km) north of Enniskillen on the A32. Those relying on public transport will have to hire a taxi; there is an early-morning Enniskillen–Irvinestown Ulsterbus service, but there's no way to get back again!

Boa Island

On the northern end of Lower Lough Erne is the largest of Lower Lough Erne's 97 islands, Boa Island (from Badh, an Irish war goddess), linked to the mainland by a bridge on either side and spanned by the A47. Boa is noteworthy for its two-faced Celtic idol (also known as the "Janus Stone"). Some 2,000 years old, the Janus Stone is located in the Caldragh cemetery, signposted off the A47. As if its freaky faces weren't enough to give you gooseflesh, just check out the hollow at the top of the stone; archaeologists believe it may have been used to hold sacrificial blood.

White Island

The spookiest of Lough Erne's "holy islands" is White Island. Walk through the plain Romanesque doorway of a 12th-century church, and you will find a row of six statues, pagan in aspect, attached to the interior wall. These are flanked by two pieces from a much later date: a mildly grotesque face on the right and a *sheila-na-gig* on the left. Though they were carved in a Celtic style, the six central stones were fashioned by the same hand sometime between the 7th and 10th centuries. Amazingly enough, they were used as ordinary stones during the building of the church, and were only discovered in the 19th century and arranged here for display.

White Island is accessible via a **ferry** (tel. 028/6862-1892, departures on the hour 11 A.M.–6 P.M. daily July–Aug., 11 A.M.–1 P.M. weekends Apr.–June, return fare £3) from the pier at the **Castle Archdale Country Park** (Lisnarrick, 10 mi/16 km northeast of Enniskillen on the B82, tel. 028/6862-1892, open 9 A.M.–dusk daily, free admission). The ferry allows you a sojourn of about 40 minutes.

BELLEEK

Renowned for its porcelain factory, Belleek (Béal Leice, "Flagstone Ford") is a pleasant one-street town on the western end of Lower Lough Erne. Shop to your heart's content at **Belleek Pottery** (on the A46, tel. 028/6865-9300, www.belleek. ie, open 9 A.M.–6 P.M. Mon.–Fri., 10 A.M.– 6 P.M. Sat., 2–6 P.M. Sun. Apr.–Sept.; open at 11 A.M. Sun. July–Aug.; 9 A.M.–5:30 P.M. Mon.– Fri., 10 A.M.–5:30 P.M. Sat., 2–6 P.M. Sun. in Oct.; 9 A.M.–5:30 P.M. Mon.–Fri. Nov.–Mar.). Tours take place every half hour (9:30 A.M.– 12:15 P.M. and 2:15–4:15 P.M. Mon.–Fri., admission £2.50). If you haven't maxed out your credit card, stop by **Fermanagh Crystal** (Main St., tel. 028/6865-8631).

There's more to do here besides the pottery, however. The **ExplorErne Gateway Centre** (on the A46 north of the river, tel. 028/6865-8866, open 11 A.M.–5 P.M. daily June–Sept., exhibition £1) houses a worthwhile geological and historical exhibition as well as a **tourist office.**

Accommodations aren't plentiful here, but luckily the **◖ Hotel Carlton** (Main St., tel. 028/6665-8282, www.hotelcarlton.co.uk, £45

pp, s £60, 2/3-course dinner £19/23) is excellent. The hotel fare is quite good, and though dinner is pricey, at least you can order a delicious gourmet coffee without surcharge to have with dessert. Best of all, the staff are genuinely affable and eager to please. Otherwise, the **Fiddlestone Pub** (15-17 Main St., tel. 028/6865-8008, £20 pp) does basic en-suite B&B. For a more casual meal, try the **Black Cat Cove** (28 Main St., tel. 028/6865-8942, food served noon–9 P.M., until 5 P.M. in low season, mains £5–12), a dark, spacious pub with a lot of crusty locals glued to the horserace on the telly.

Belleek is 24 miles (39 km) northwest of Enniskillen on the A46 and 18 miles (30 km) south of Donegal on the N3 (picking up the N15 in Ballyshannon). Ulsterbus service from Enniskillen is quite inconvenient, but fortunately **Bus Éireann** (#30, 7/day Mon.–Sat., 5/day Sun.) passes through Enniskillen and Belleek on the Dublin–Donegal route. Rent a bike from **Belleek Bicycle Hire** (Main St., tel. 028/6865-8181, £10/50 per day/week), or a rowboat from the **Belleek Angling Centre** (Main St., tel. 028/6865-8181).

BACKGROUND

The Land

GEOGRAPHY

Ireland is 84,079 square kilometers (32,477 square miles); as a size comparison, you might fit the island within the state of New York. The island lies between the Atlantic Ocean to the west and the Irish Sea to the east, which separates Ireland from Great Britain. The island's longest waterway is the River Shannon, stretching 259 kilometers from Lough Allen in County Leitrim south through Lough Derg (bordered by Clare, Tipperary, and Galway); then it empties into the 113-kilometer Shannon estuary, which forms the southern shore of County Clare. The largest lake is the 388-square-kilometer Lough Neagh in Northern Ireland, bordered by five of its six counties. Ireland's mountain ranges form a ring around the flat Midlands region, which features large swaths of bogland and many small lakes farther north, especially in County Cavan. Battered by the Atlantic, Ireland's west coast is far more rugged, characterized by peninsulas, islands, and headlands. The Irish coastline is estimated to be 5,800 kilometers long.

CLIMATE

The North Atlantic Drift, a warm ocean current in the north Atlantic, contributes to Ireland's temperate climate; its temperatures are among the least extreme in Europe, and it

© CAMILLE DEANGELIS

rarely snows and even more rarely freezes. Yes, it rains two days out of three, and as Heinrich Böll once wrote, "The rain here is absolute, magnificent, and frightening." But the mild winters and wet summers allow for a green landscape all year long.

May and June are the sunniest months, with an average of six hours of sunlight per day; July and August are the warmest (average temp 14–16°C/57–60°F), though the temperature sometimes climbs into the 20s C/lower 80s F. December and January are the rainiest (70–75 mm monthly rainfall), January and February the coldest (4–7°C/39–44°F). August–November is also a very wet time of year (66–70 mm), and July and August bring the highest risk of thunderstorms, especially in the west (which is the rainiest region overall). The southeast is Ireland's sunniest region, with Wexford boasting the title of "Ireland's Sunniest County."

ENVIRONMENTAL ISSUES

Ireland has its share of pollution, much of it the product of industry and irresponsible agricultural practices. There is also an acute nationwide litter problem. Those rolling green hills are deceptively pristine, and it's precisely this traditional image of Ireland that is preventing or delaying much-needed reforms. Though a majority of Irish rivers and lakes offer good water quality, the Irish Sea is highly polluted (and there is some evidence that regular bathing in it is a cause of cancer). Plus, several tests have confirmed fecal contamination in the groundwater, but one example of the consequences of improper agricultural practice. Ireland is also well behind much of Europe when it comes to recycling, though the government finally initiated county-run recycling programs in 2005. There are glass receptacles in every strip mall parking lot and home collection for plastic and paper, but because the counties charge for this service, many citizens are not as diligent as they should be. For more information, visit the **Friends of the Irish Environment** (www.friendsoftheirishenvironment.net) or **An Taisce** (www.antaisce.org) on the web.

© CAMILLE DEANGELIS

In springtime fuschia and foxglove spring from roadside hedges.

FLORA AND FAUNA

Ireland has comparatively few plant and animal species because of its geological "youth": The island was created at the end of the last ice age.

Vegetation

Bogs—blanket and raised—feature prominently on the Irish landscape (12,000 square kilometers in all). They were formed when Neolithic farmers first cleared forests for farming: The treeless soil gradually became more acidic, forming heather and rushes; these plants decayed and formed a layer of organic matter on which new growth could begin. Logs of turf—essentially bricks of peat sliced from the bog and laid out to dry—have been a source of fuel since the 17th century. Ireland was heavily forested before the Stone Age, and after the Norman invasion the English exploited many remaining Irish forests for timber for shipbuilding.

Fewer than 1,000 plant species are unique to Ireland. The Burren in County Clare is the most popular region for botanists, as there are

Also known as "bog dogs," sheep are ubiquitous on the Irish landscape.

both alpine and Mediterranean species growing alongside native species; the mild climate allows such nonnative varieties to flourish.

Mammals

There are only 31 extant mammal species in Ireland, most of which have been introduced by humans over the last 8,000 years. Native species include the red fox, hedgehog, stoat, and badger. Several species, though not endangered, are found mostly in the country's national parks and nature reserves: the pine marten, red deer, and Irish hare. It's speculated that Neolithic settlers first brought cattle and sheep to Ireland sometime around 6500 B.C. Rabbits were introduced by the Normans in the 12th century, and the two rat species and common mouse traveled here by boat as well.

Sealife

With all its lakes, rivers, tributaries, and coastlines, Ireland is an angler's paradise, and seafood is an integral part of the Irish diet. Salmon, pike, and brown trout are the primary freshwater species; marine species include bass, cod, haddock, hake, and turbot. Whales and dolphins frequent Irish waters, the common dolphin being the most frequently sighted species. Bottlenose dolphins are often very friendly, following boats for miles and lingering in harbors for long periods of time (Fungie in Dingle is the most famous example). There are dolphin-watching trips available in West Cork and Loop Head in County Clare.

Birds

Most of the island's 400 recorded bird species are migratory, and there are more than 60 bird sanctuaries. Many offshore islands are popular with bird-watchers, including Scattery Island in Clare, Rathlin Island in Antrim (one of few remaining homes of the endangered corncrake), the Saltee Islands in Wexford, and Small Skellig off the Iveragh Peninsula in County Kerry. For more information, contact the **Irish Wildbird Conservancy** (www.birdwatchireland.ie).

Reptiles and Amphibians

Ireland has very few reptiles. It's true that there are no snakes in Ireland, though St. Patrick probably had nothing to do with it! The island features only three amphibious species—the natterjack toad, smooth newt, and the common frog—and just one reptile, the common lizard. For everything else, you'll have to visit the zoo in Dublin or Belfast.

History

PREHISTORY

We know relatively little about pre-Christian Ireland, and what we do is extrapolated from archaeology, mythology, oral tradition, and Roman records. The first human hunter-gatherers arrived between 10,000 to 8000 B.C. as the ice age ended and the oceans rose to separate Ireland from Britain and Europe. They arrived in small boats, though some may have crossed a narrowing isthmus. Agriculture was introduced from the continent around 4000 B.C. Neolithic culture flourished, relics of which still punctuate the Irish landscape: large standing stones, dolmens, burial mounds, and stone circles, some cosmically aligned. The most impressive Neolithic passage tomb is **Newgrange** in County Meath, which predates the Great Pyramid in Egypt and features the famous tri-spiral motifs associated with Irish crafts to this day. Bronze Age artisans produced intricate gold work of a high quality renowned throughout Europe.

THE CELTS

Iron Age society in Ireland was dominated by druids, who functioned as spiritual leaders, doctors, poets, lawmakers, and teachers. The distinct rival kingdoms that began to emerge in Ireland at this time are survived today, more or less, in the traditional counties and provinces of Ireland. It is popularly believed that around this time Ireland underwent a large-scale invasion by the Celts, a creative if warlike race that originated in central Europe. It is more likely, however, that Celtic influences and culture were gradually adopted by the native Irish. Either way, from about 300 B.C. a strong Celtic society dominated Ireland over the following millennium, and their art and spiritualism are still considered an integral part of Irish culture. The Irish Celts followed an elaborate and surprisingly progressive civil legal system known as the **Brehon Laws,** though they were not above raiding the British coast and taking slaves.

While Ireland was never formally part of the Roman Empire, the island was influenced by, and engaged in trade with, the Romans. Frequent references to Hibernia, Ireland's Latin name, are found in Roman records, but it remains unclear what kind of relationship existed between Ireland and the vast empire.

EARLY CHRISTIAN IRELAND AND THE GOLDEN AGE

During the 5th century Irish pirates frequently raided the British coast, even forming colonies in Scotland, Wales, and England. Slaves were often taken, among them the adolescent who would become St. Patrick. Though popularly credited with single-handedly converting the Irish to Christianity, in fact there were other missionaries sent to Ireland long before and long after Patrick. And while he has had a lasting influence on Irish spirituality, Patrick cannot be solely credited with creating the particular variant of Christianity that embraced Irish traditions and laws (apart from those laws that directly contradicted Christian doctrine, of course). These influential clerics encouraged Ireland to unite its various rival kingdoms under a single authority, a high king.

Irish monasteries soon earned an excellent reputation as centers of Latin learning, and attracted scholars, scribes, and theologians from all over Europe. As scholarship and craftsmanship thrived in these monasteries, and as Christian values discouraged interkingdom warring, Ireland entered its Golden Age. The island's existing artisan traditions saw further advancement, and indeed the finest European artworks of the era were produced in Ireland's monasteries. Several impressive examples survive to this day, such as the delicately detailed **Ardagh Chalice,** on display in the National Museum, and the **Book of Kells,** an illuminated bible housed in Trinity College.

While the rest of Europe was ravaged by the Dark Ages, Latin learning (and Western civilization itself) was preserved in Irish monasteries like Glendalough in County Wicklow and Clonmacnoise in County Offaly. As Europe gradually stabilized, the "island of saints and scholars" sent missionaries back to mainland Europe, where they founded a great many monasteries.

THE VIKINGS

Such enormous wealth attracted barbarian attention, and in the 9th century Vikings from Norway arrived in their imposing longships, raiding the coasts and striking vulnerable towns and monasteries along the Shannon, Suir, and other strategic waterways.

The round tower, a style of refuge almost unique to Ireland, symbolizes this era. Eventually, some Vikings settled in Ireland, appreciating the milder winters. They founded towns along the coasts from which to attack the inland native strongholds, but successive generations embraced Irish culture and adopted Christianity, effectively becoming Hiberno-Norse. In the first decade of the 11th century, **Brian Boru** became high king. The title was mostly honorary for his predecessors, but Boru assumed actual authority over the island; he demanded tributes from the smaller kingdoms, which he used to rebuild churches and monasteries destroyed by the Vikings.

Brian Boru rallied the remaining Irish kingdoms in a bid to break Norse power over Ireland. His combined forces fought the climactic daylong **Battle of Clontarf** outside Viking Dublin in 1014, and Boru is traditionally credited with driving the Vikings "back into the sea." In reality, however, it was more a civil war between the Irish. (The "Viking" army was in the service of the king of Leinster and was composed mainly of Irish and Hiberno-Norse soldiers.) The elderly Boru did not survive the battle, and by this time the Viking and native cultures had already amalgamated. The Vikings had founded many of the seaports that would become Ireland's main towns and cities, including Dublin, Galway, and Cork. They also introduced the use of currency.

IRISH CASTLES

Many Irish castles are still inhabited, some by descendants of the original owners (who were members of the Protestant Ascendancy). Some of these families, like the owners of Dunsany Castle in County Meath, open a wing of their home to tour groups on weekends in the summer months, and others have beautiful gardens that are open to the public even if the manor itself isn't. Some castles are now hotels; others are made available for weddings, conferences, films, and other private events (a few even offer aristocratic holiday accommodations to the tune of €20,000-75,000 a week!).

Still others are ruins on private property – whether ivy-clad and picturesque, or literally a pile of rubble. The total number of Irish castles at all points in history would be no doubt staggering, if it were possible to catalog them all: In County Limerick alone there once numbered more than 400; in Cork nearly 300; Tipperary, Galway, and Clare had 200-300 each; and Kilkenny had almost 200. Of course, most of those castles are no longer extant.

Whether restored or in ruin, the castles covered in this book are easily accessible, and the few private homes listed can be visited by prior arrangement.

THE NORMANS

The second wave of invaders were to have an even more profound impact on Ireland's destiny. The Normans had previously settled in northern France, and in 1066 they conquered England. A century later Dermot MacMorrough, the exiled king of Leinster, petitioned England's Henry II to help him regain his kingdom. The Earl of Pembroke, Richard de Clare (popularly known as Strongbow) agreed to lead an invasion force in return for the hand of MacMorrough's daughter. By 1169 MacMorrough—often singled out as the greatest traitor in Irish history, which is no mean achievement—had retaken

Leinster, and upon his death his Norman son-in-law ruled it.

Henry II felt threatened by this rival Norman kingdom growing across the channel and secured a papal bull in order to land a fleet in Ireland. Soon after Henry II arrived in Waterford in 1171, the Normans, with their superior weapons, armor and tactics, conquered the entire east coast and divided the taken land into earldoms as rewards for their knights. They built many distinctive towerlike castles all around the country.

By the 13th century, however, the Normans had retreated to the territory surrounding Dublin, known as **The Pale,** due to several factors. In 1315 Edward Bruce of Scotland invaded England; a long and bloody war ensued throughout the British Isles, in which the Gaelic lords sided against the English. Also, the Black Death hit the more densely populated Norman towns harder than their scattered Irish counterparts. Disconnected from a troubled England, the settled Normans began to consider themselves natives, and became "more Irish than the Irish themselves." Toward the end of the 16th century, England had lost virtually all its control over Ireland "beyond the Pale."

THE REFORMATION AND PROTESTANT ASCENDANCY

For Ireland, the Reformation spelled enduring catastrophe. Henry VIII of England cut all ties with the Catholic Church following his divorce from Catherine of Aragon; while the majority of England, Scotland, and Wales converted to Protestantism relatively painlessly, the more independent Ireland retained its deep-rooted Catholicism. Henry increasingly feared an Ireland-based invasion of either French or Spanish Catholic forces. So the king sought to undermine the most powerful dynasty in Ireland, the Fitzgeralds, who were the earls of Kildare. In 1543 Dublin was stormed by Silken Thomas, son of the reigning earl. This rebellion was quashed, Thomas and his men executed, and the Fitzgeralds' lands confiscated. Henry next turned his sights on the Catholic Church and

pillaged several monasteries and churches, eventually "dissolving" them entirely (which is why virtually all of Ireland's pre-Reformation churches are Anglican). In 1541 Henry forced the Irish Parliament to declare him king of Ireland.

The Ulster province was last outpost of Irish Catholic power, where Hugh O'Neill, Earl of Tyrone, initiated a rebellion. This erupted into the **Nine Years' War,** which raged through the reigns of Elizabeth I and her successor, James I. In 1601 the earls marched south and gathered a large army to meet the English in the **Battle of Kinsale.** The Irish were aided by a Spanish fleet, which besieged Kinsale seaside. Due mainly to misguided tactics, O'Neill and the earls were defeated, though some survived and fled to Europe, a turning point known as the **Flight of the Earls.**

For the first time in the centuries since the Norman invasion, England had resoundingly conquered Ireland. Elizabeth I implemented the **Plantation of Ireland,** where huge amounts of land confiscated from the earls were given to Protestant settlers in a bid to assimilate the Irish. Unlike previous settlers, these Protestants did not integrate with the angry and powerless Catholic majority. The native Irish were further oppressed by the **Penal Laws,** which outlawed all faiths except Protestantism. The majority of Catholics continued to practice their religion in secret.

OLIVER CROMWELL AND THE PENAL LAWS

The disenfranchised Irish supported Charles I, a Catholic, during the English Civil War against the Protestant Parliamentarians. Charles was defeated, and Oliver Cromwell, leader of the Parliamentarians, decided to restore English control of Ireland. There are few historical figures on whom history is more divided than Cromwell. The English thought him a hero of democracy, but his actions in Ireland have rightfully branded him a monster. Cromwell's forces landed in Drogheda in 1649 and cut a swath of destruction upward through the country. Cromwell's brutal campaign left more than a third of Ireland's population either dead or in exile. More than 7,700 square miles were seized from Irish Catholics and divided amongst Cromwell's supporters. Many of the dispossessed Irish relocated to the wilder, less fertile west. Cromwell's own infamous words were "to hell or to Connaught."

In 1689 Ireland hosted a second conflict between English monarchists and Parliamentarians. James II, also Catholic, arrived in Ireland and was recognized as king by the Irish Parliament. Preparations were made to restore property and status to Catholics. They laid siege to the city of Derry, which caused mass starvation within the city walls. The siege ended when James II was defeated at the Battle of the Boyne by the forces of William of Orange. William was actually James's Protestant son-in-law, invited to the throne by the English Parliament after James's departure.

The Penal Laws were reapplied, though harsher this time: They prevented Catholics from owning land and essentially outlawed all traces of Irish culture.

THE BIRTH OF NATIONALISM

Most of the 18th century was relatively peaceful in Ireland, though unrest escalated as the economic situation worsened. This combined with two very cold winters caused the first **famine** of 1740–1741, which caused the deaths of 400,000 people. Also fueling unrest were the American and French Revolutions, which inspired liberal thinking—even in the "planted" Protestant population, who were beginning to consider Ireland their home. The **United Irishmen** (under the leadership of **Theobald Wolfe Tone,** a high-minded Dublin Protestant) initially sought reform through nonviolent means, but as the French Revolution became increasingly gruesome, the society took on a more militaristic approach. In retaliation the Protestants formed the Orange Society, named in honor of William of Orange.

Tone accompanied the French in a failed attempt to land a fleet in Bantry Bay. The English government began a full-scale nationwide hunt for the United Irishmen, which caused widespread panic among Catholics. In 1798 a rebellion erupted in the traditionally peaceful county of Wexford, led by Father John Murphy. The rebellion was bloodily suppressed after a run of minor victories. Later in 1798 Tone and a second French fleet were defeated at sea. He was captured and committed suicide in prison.

THE ACT OF UNION AND CATHOLIC EMANCIPATION

The Irish Parliament was composed of a increasingly anxious Protestant gentry, and in 1800 the ruling body dissolved itself and joined the House of Commons. This consolidated government, the United Kingdom of Great Britain and Ireland, was an attempt to secure British authority.

Meanwhile, **Daniel O'Connell,** a young Catholic lawyer from County Kerry (though Catholics were denied education, wealthier families would send their sons to study in Europe) fought a successful campaign for the repeal of the Penal Laws. The British Parliament conceded **Catholic Emancipation** in 1826 after O'Connell won a parliamentary seat for County Clare. Though Catholics were not allowed to become members of Parliament, the government feared mass protests and permitted O'Connell to sit in Westminster.

O'Connell, hailed then and now as "the Great Liberator," went on to campaign for more reforms for Catholics, most notably an attempt to repeal the Act of Union. Though O'Connell had the popularity to rally "monster meetings" that drew as many as half a million Catholics, he eventually lost influence over the nationalist movement as it grew impatient with nonviolent methods.

FAMINE AND EMIGRATION

In 1845 a blight caused the failure of potato crops all over the island. This, coupled with exploitative and selfish economic structures, led to Ireland's worst tragedy, the **Great Famine** (1845–1849). The island's population dropped from eight to five million because of mass starvation and emigration. Though there was more than enough food in the country, most of it was exported to Britain and overseas. As historian Roy Foster explains it, "Traditionally, the Famine was seen as at worst a deliberate English policy of genocide, at best willful neglect on the part of the British government."

Under the Poor Laws landlords were responsible for the welfare of their tenants, yet many landlords exercised a less expensive option: paying for their tenants' passage to America. The conditions of the overcrowded and poorly managed ships were atrocious, and many emigrants did not survive the journey on these "coffin ships." The British government eventually granted some aid, but it was far from adequate, and emigration continued. At the turn of the 20th century the population was down to four million.

During this time the Irish language fell out of popular use; famine and emigration more heavily impacted Irish-speaking areas. Also, the recently introduced National School system taught only through English by order of the British government. Many Catholics—weary of poverty and observing the economic prosperity of English-speaking America and Britain—began to see Irish as a dying language. Irish was still spoken in the country's more rural and remote reaches, however. The regions in which Irish is still spoken as the primary language—Dingle, Connemara, Gweedore, Ring, and others—are known as the Gaeltachtaí.

PARNELL AND HOME RULE

In the wake of the Great Famine, Ireland's resentment of the British government grew, and several minor rebellions were staged by organizations such as the Fenians and the **Irish Republican Brotherhood** (IRB, a secret society that was to play a considerable role in the struggle for independence). Impoverished Catholic tenants were granted more rights—like the option to purchase the land they rented—by consecutive British governments under pressure from the Land League, headed by the IRB's Michael Davitt and Protestant landowner **Charles Stewart Parnell,** who or-

ganized boycotts of landlords who didn't comply with the league's conditions.

Parnell's firm belief in Irish sovereignty led him to found the Home Rule League, and in 1875 he was elected to the British Parliament—where he caused a lot of trouble. Though Parnell was an overwhelmingly popular and charismatic leader (he was referred to as the Uncrowned king of Ireland, and he even convinced Prime Minister William Gladstone to back Home Rule twice), he fell from grace in 1890 when his affair with Kitty O'Shea, the wife of a fellow MP, became publicly known. The scandal greatly affected his health and he died the following year.

The wealthy Protestant population of eastern Ulster vehemently opposed the concept of Home Rule; as a heavily industrialized (rather than agrarian) society, they were spared the worst effects of the famine. Though Gladstone's second Home Rule Bill in 1892 had been defeated, they sensed the tides turning; in 1912 Sir Edward Carson founded the **Ulster Volunteer Force** (UVF, a vigilante offshoot of the Unionist Party). The UVF staged massive paramilitary rallies, threatening civil war in the face of Home Rule. In response to the UVF, Eoin O'Neill established the **Irish Volunteers** to defend Home Rule. But when World War I broke out in 1914, the threat of civil war was suspended.

THE EASTER RISING

In 1916 a small splinter group of Irish Volunteers, along with James Connelly's Irish Citizen Army, staged an armed rebellion. The nationalists marched into Dublin on Easter Monday and took several landmark locations in the city, making the General Post Office their headquarters. From the steps of the GPO the poet Patrick Pearse read aloud the **Proclamation of the Irish Republic,** declaring his group of insurrectionists the provisional government of a new republic, the Volunteers its legitimate uniformed army. Initially most Dubliners condemned the rising, as a week of intense fighting between the rebels and the British Army (who responded with superior firepower and

On Easter Monday, 1916, nationalist rebels used Dublin's General Post Office as their headquarters.

heavy artillery) had effectively wrecked the city. When the rebels finally surrendered to the British, they had to be protected from the mobs of angry Dubliners they had intended to liberate.

The British exacerbated the situation when they executed 15 of the rebels, including Patrick Pearse and James Connolly, and sentenced a further 77 to death. This effectively made martyrs of the rebels, creating the very blood sacrifice the rising had intended and sparking a new wave of Nationalism. Among the prisoners was Eamon de Valera, who was spared from execution by his American citizenship. He and his lieutenant, Michael Collins, a young civil servant from West Cork, were eventually released from prison on amnesty.

De Valera and other republicans formed a political party, **Sinn Féin** (meaning "We Ourselves"), and won the majority of the Irish seats in the 1918 general election. Rather than take their positions in Westminster, they declared Ireland independent and reformed the Volunteers into the Irish Republican Army (IRA),

simultaneously declaring war on British troops on Irish soil.

THE WAR OF INDEPENDENCE

This entrenched war commenced with the murders of two Royal Irish Constabulary (RIC) men, on the same day the Dáil (the new independent Irish Parliament) convened: January 21, 1919. The British government tried to regain order by deploying a combined force to Ireland to assist the RIC: regular infantry, Army Auxiliaries, and an RIC reserve force, better known as the **Black and Tans.** This was a vicious and undisciplined paramilitary group comprising mainly ex-soldiers and prisoners, whose unchecked deeds further cemented the general population's embrace of republicanism. The Black and Tans retaliated with excessive force, burning and sacking several towns, including the Cork city center. Unable to engage the better-armed British forces directly with a front line, the IRA pioneered guerrilla and urban warfare, creating "flying columns" to ambush their enemy.

This campaign was masterminded by Michael Collins, who in prison with other volunteers had effectively run a military training camp. Collins headed a delegation to London to negotiate, and in December 1921 both sides signed the **Anglo-Irish Treaty.** While granting Ireland considerable autonomy, the treaty allowed for the partition of the six counties that had a Protestant majority. This would create two new nations, each with Home Rule, though Northern Ireland would choose to remain part of the United Kingdom.

THE FREE STATE AND THE CIVIL WAR

The Dáil ratified the treaty in January 1922, forming the **Irish Free State,** and a general election that summer showed support for pro-treaty politicians. De Valera and his followers refused to accept the terms of the treaty, however, and stormed out of the Dáil. Soon afterward the Irish Free State erupted into a treacherous civil war. Arthur Griffith, who had helped negotiate the treaty, became president of the Free State.

Now commander-in-chief of the Free State Army (formerly the IRA), General Collins was forced to hunt down his former comrades and friends. This is an often unspoken chapter in Ireland's history, as uncompromising idealism turned the country against itself—it divided communities and even families down the middle—and atrocities were committed on both sides. Griffith died of anxiety and General Collins was shot dead in an ambush near his home parish in West Cork.

The anti-treaty forces laid down their arms in 1923, but the civil war had cast a long shadow over the young nation. De Valera eventually recognized the government and formed a rival political party in 1927, Fianna Fáil. They won several seats in the election of that year, and entered the Dáil without taking the oath of Allegiance to the British crown that had been a controversial condition of the treaty. (The Free State was still a member of the British Commonwealth.)

The Free State faced many difficulties in its early years. There was a global economic depression in the wake of the Wall Street crash of 1929, and several European states were turning to fascism to sustain themselves. Fianna Fáil came into power in 1932—and since it was a peaceful changeover, the Free State achieved a long-awaited sense of stability.

Though emigration, poverty, and unemployment levels were high, Ireland remained a democracy during the uncertain decade. De Valera's Ireland clung to several insular policies in an attempt at self-sufficiency. He oversaw the large-scale cultivation of the bogs for peat as well as the construction of the ambitious Ardnacrusha Hydroelectric Power Station (or "Shannon Scheme"); at the time it was the largest project of its kind ever attempted. De Valera also refused to pay land rates to Britain, contravening yet another condition of the treaty.

The Catholic Church was as influential as de Valera; it directed the Free State away from the liberal and inclusive ideals of the Proclamation of the Irish Republic and toward an oppressively conservative Catholic climate. The Church ensured the banning of contraception, divorce, and other so-called immoralities that affronted its dogma; at its bidding the Irish government censored and even banned a great many books and films. The Church also controlled the country's schools and hospitals. Many Protestants left the Free State feeling intimidated in an overwhelmingly Catholic environment. Indeed, during the 1920s, a great many Protestant "big houses"—seen as symbols of the Anglo-Irish Ascendancy—were burned to the ground.

In 1937 a new constitution was drawn up that affirmed Irish neutrality and spared it from the ravages of World War II. Many Irish fought in the war against fascism, however, and in truth the Free State was "neutral in favor of Britain." Idiosyncratically, World War II was known as "The Emergency" in Ireland, and heavy rationing was put in place.

THE IRISH REPUBLIC

After 16 years of political dominance, Fianna Fáil lost to Fine Gael, the successors to the original Free State government; Fine Gael quickly declared Ireland a republic and withdrew from the Commonwealth. Sean Lamass became Taoiseach (prime minister) in 1959, and he implemented sweeping new policies (such as free secondary education) to strengthen Ireland's economic prospects, competitiveness, and infrastructure—and to curb emigration. Successful and popular besides, Lamass was credited with laying the groundwork for Ireland's later economic vitality. Ireland also sought membership in the European Economic Community, but was not admitted until 1973 along with the United Kingdom. Membership initially proved beneficial, but toward the end of the 1970s a harsh downturn slowed the economy considerably. The 1980s were bleak indeed, characterized by high unemployment.

THE TROUBLES

Northern Ireland's first premier, James Craig, proclaimed it "a Protestant state for a Protestant people" in response to the overwhelmingly Catholic Free State south of the border. In the North, a policy of discrimination denied power, employment, and even decent housing to the Catholic minority. A corrupt electoral system and flagrant gerrymandering denied Catholics representation even in Derry, where they were in the majority by 10 percent.

A peaceful civil-rights movement emerged, following the example of Daniel O'Connell, Gandhi, and Martin Luther King Jr. But the Royal Ulster Constabulary and other militant unionists used violence to disperse a peaceful rights march in 1968, sparking counterviolence among the utterly disenfranchised Catholic population. Another march was attacked by a unionist mob in January of the following year, and the situation was only exacerbated by the police, who swept through the Catholic Bogside neighborhood of Derry City.

That August British troops were deployed to Northern Ireland to restore order. While the troops initially were welcomed by both sides, the Catholics soon realized the soldiers were an oppressive occupying force, an instrument of the Protestant majority. The situation came to a head with the events of January 30, 1972, **Bloody Sunday,** when 14 civilians were massacred by British troops during a civil-rights march. Many were shot in the back.

The IRA—not the original Irish Republican Army, but the ideological descendants of those who had rejected the Anglo-Irish Treaty—saw an exponential jump in recruitment and membership, as many Catholics believed these nationalist paramilitaries to be their lone, true defense force. In this poisonous atmosphere of sectarian hate and paranoia, the worst decade of the Troubles began.

DIRECT RULE AND THE NORTHERN QUESTION

The Troubles—a characteristically Irish euphemism—increased the size and power of various paramilitary groups on both sides, with various contrasting agendas. The IRA split into the Official IRA (OIRA) and the Provisional IRA (PIRA). In 1974 the more extreme Irish National Liberation Army was formed. On the unionist side, the UVF was joined by groups such as the Ulster Defense Association (UDA), the Ulster Freedom Fighters (UFF), and Red Hand Commandos.

The Northern Irish Parliament was dissolved in 1972, and a new power-sharing system was almost put into place. A widespread strike by Protestant workers derailed the process, though, and for the next 27 years, Northern Ireland was under Direct Rule by the British Parliament. The paramilitary campaigns of both sides now featured bombings, which often resulted in civilian casualties.

The violence also spread beyond the borders of Northern Ireland, with the PIRA (also known as "the provos") setting off several bombs in London from 1973, and the UVF perpetrating bombings in Dublin and Monaghan on St. Patrick's Day 1974. Groups on both sides regularly committed sectarian murders. All such terrorist acts were condemned from both communities and from the British and Irish governments, but the cycle of violence and retribution was well underway. The Troubles reached a climax in 1981, when republican inmates in the infamous "H-blocks"—including 27-year-old elected MP Bobby Sands—went on a hunger strike in a plea to be recognized as political prisoners. Sands and nine others fasted to death, and to this day they are hailed as martyrs to the nationalist cause. The hunger strikers are often commemorated by Sinn Féin: originally de Valera's political party, now socialist in bent, and oft-accused of being the political wing of the Provisional IRA.

The presence of the British Army reserve and the (predominantly Protestant) RUC seemed to discourage ongoing violence—yet IRA splinter groups were preparing for a full-scale "long war," going as far as to procure large arms shipments from Libya. Even the majority of Catholics, who totally condemned the IRA and their methods, were unwilling to trust the British soldiers who'd treated them so horribly in the past. Catholics also suspected collusion between the armed forces and unionist paramilitaries, and in recent years much evidence has come to light to confirm this.

In 1986 the British and Irish governments signed the **Anglo-Irish Agreement,** by which they would work together to bring peace to the North. The 1990s brought economic prosperity to both sides of the border—which, combined with the waning authority of the Catholic Church, helped depolarize attitudes in the North. The Northern Ireland demographics were also moderating, with Catholics now making up 40 percent of the population.

Significant advances in the peace process of the early '90s included the Downing Street Declaration, which formally declared that Britain had no self-serving strategic or economic interest in Northern Ireland. In August 1994, Gerry Adams, leader of Sinn Féin, announced that the IRA was on a ceasefire. Two months later loyalist groups also announced a ceasefire. Actual peace talks never began, though, as demands from both sides were not met. The IRA refused to surrender its weapons unless British troops were withdrawn from Northern Ireland and its political prisoners were freed, all of which were demands the British government considered too high. The bombing of London's Canary Wharf in February 1996 brought an end to the first ceasefire.

A second IRA ceasefire was secured in 1997, and on April 10, 1998, negotiations resulted in the Good Friday Agreement. For the first time since the implementation of Direct Rule, a system of power-sharing was brought to the North, with both nationalists and unionists receiving legislative control in several areas of government.

The Good Friday Agreement was overshadowed by riots during unionist marches through nationalist neighborhoods, a rising internal unionist murder rate, and the worst bombing since the start of the Troubles: on August 15, the Real IRA (founded by former members of the PIRA who refused to accept the terms of the Good Friday Agreement) detonated a car bomb in Omagh, County Tyrone. Twenty-nine people were killed, both Catholic and Protestant. The Real IRA's actions were condemned by all governments and parties, including Sinn Féin.

Peace talks have progressed slowly in recent years; many contentious aspects of the Good Friday Agreement have yet to be resolved, such as paramilitary decommissioning and British military withdrawal. Also, since 2002 the power-sharing agreement has been suspended as a result of distrust between nationalist and unionist politicians. Another contributing factor is the recent rise in popularity of the more extreme nationalist (Sinn Féin) and unionist (Ian Paisley's Democratic Unionist Party) political parties over their more moderate counterparts.

The most recent and promising development came in July 2005, when the Provisional IRA announced that its armed campaign had come to an end. In September an international weapons inspector from Canada, John de Chastelain, oversaw the destruction of the PIRA's arsenal.

More than 3,000 soldiers and civilians have lost their lives over the course of the Troubles.

RECENT DEVELOPMENTS IN THE REPUBLIC OF IRELAND

The 1980s were a period of high unemployment and emigration, though policies and reforms were introduced that built on the infrastructures of the '60s. Such policies finally paid off in the economic boom of the 1990s known as the "Celtic Tiger." The phrase, coined in 1994, refers to Ireland's remarkable period of economic growth between the early 1990s and 2001, which transformed the republic into one of Europe's wealthiest nations. This success has been attributed to a variety of factors, including financial support from the European Union, conservative government spending, and low corporate tax rates (which encouraged many international businesses to open Irish branches). The wealth is not evenly distributed throughout the population, however; the east coast, particularly Dublin, has benefited the most. The global downturn in 2001 was followed by a rebounding Irish economy in 2004, but some economists do not believe this second boom can sustain itself as well as the original "Celtic Tiger."

Birth control, illegalized in 1936, was made legally available again in 1992, and homosexuality was decriminalized the following year; divorce was legalized in 1996. Since these milestones of the mid-1990s Ireland has grown increasingly tolerant. The stigma associated with childbirth out of wedlock, for example, is pretty much a thing of the past in all but the most conservative circles. In keeping with these cultural shifts, Mass attendance has more than halved in the last two decades.

Another reversal is that immigration—rather than emigration—is now a feature of Ireland's increasingly diverse society. Many of the Eastern Bloc states (suffering from economic depression not unlike Ireland's in the '80s) gained European Union membership in 2004 and have modeled their policies on Ireland's successes. Furthermore, a significant percentage of Ireland's foreign-born workforce is from eastern Europe.

Government and Economy

GOVERNMENT
The Irish Republic

Adopted in 1937 by referendum (thus replacing the Constitution of the Irish Free State in place since 1922), the Constitution of Ireland guarantees a democratic republic for its citizens. There is a bicameral legislature (or parliament) known as the Oireachtas ("o-ROCK-tas"), which comprises a lower house, the Dáil Éireann ("doll AY-rinn"), and a Senate-like house known as the Seanad Éireann ("SHAN-add AY-rinn," informally known as "the Senate"); both houses meet at Leinster House in Dublin. Unlike in the U.S. Congress, however, the Dáil exercises significantly more power than the Senad. A member of the Oireachtas is known as a Teachta Dala ("TCHOCK-tuh DOLL-uh," abbreviated TD).

There are two primary political parties in the Irish system, the Fianna Fáil ("Soldiers of Destiny") and the Fine Gael ("Family of the Irish"). The former group was founded by Eamon de Valera in 1926 as a radical anti-treaty party, whereas the Fine Gael are the ideological descendants of the pro-treaty forces, founded in 1933 at the merging of three smaller parties. Fine Gael is traditionally considered moderate to conservative, while Fianna Fáil is moderate to liberal, though in reality the party lines are almost indistinguishable even to many native Irish. At time of writing the Fine Gael were the opposition party, holding 31 of the Dáil's 166 seats (Fianna Fáil holds 81).

Other minority parties include Labour (founded by Easter rebel James Connolly in 1912), the Progressive Democrats (founded in 1985), and the Green Party (founded in 1981 as the "Ecology Party of Ireland"). There is only one Socialist member of the Dáil.

Sinn Féin ("We Ourselves") is another minority

A guided tour of Belfast City Hall is a must for politics, history, and architecture buffs alike.

party in the republic, with five seats in the Dáil at time of writing; traditionally considered the political arm of the Irish Republican Army and often associated with Marxism, this party is a bigger player in North Ireland, where it is supported by most Catholic voters. Gerry Adams is the current leader of the Sinn Féin party, whose ultimate goal is a united Ireland.

The Irish prime minister is known as the Taoiseach ("TEE-shock"), meaning "chieftain," and the Tánaiste ("taw-NESH-tah") is the deputy prime minister. The Taoiseach is the leader of his or her party, appointed by the president from among the members of the Dáil for a five-year term—or until the Taoiseach "loses the confidence" of the Dáil, at which time he or she may be compelled to resign (though this has never occurred). An Taoiseach—the formal title— nominates the Irish cabinet (as well as 11 members of the Seanad), and all cabinet members must also be members of the Oireachtas. At time of writing, Ireland's Taoiseach was Bertie Ahern of the Fianna Fáil party; he took office in June of 1997 and was reelected in 2002.

The Irish president (Uachtarán na hÉireann in Irish) is essentially a ceremonial figure, elected for a maximum of two seven-year terms. Mary McAleese, also a Fianna Fáil member, was elected in 1997 and reelected in 2004. Eamon de Valera was the first Taoiseach (and third president) of the Irish Republic, in office 1937–1948 (and president 1959–1973); Douglas Hyde was the first president, in office 1938–1945.

Northern Politics

Northern Ireland is governed by the British Parliament. The North's loyalist parties include the Ulster Unionist Party and the Democratic Unionist Party (DUP), the latter of which is now the largest in the province. The DUP's leader, Ian Paisley, is an outspoken anti-Catholic (he is also a loud opponent of civil rights for homosexuals). Dr. Paisley is an MP for North Antrim and a Presbyterian minister. Sinn Féin is Northern Ireland's primary republican and nationalist political party, the second being the Social Democratic and Labour Party (SDLP). The SDLP distinguished itself during the Troubles as antiterrorism, while Sinn Féin supported IRA violence as a means of achieving a unified Ireland.

ECONOMY

Ireland is still enjoying its economic boom of the 1990s, as international companies are enticed with tax incentives (particularly information technology (IT) companies) and long-emigrated sisters and brothers return home to work. Ireland is now one of the richest nations in Europe, with a per capita wealth of nearly €150,000. Agriculture has been Ireland's traditional lifeline, though in the last couple of decades tourism has become the #1 industry (the island welcomes well over seven million visitors a year). Much of Ireland's white-collar workforce is engaged in the IT sector.

Economic stratification is less pronounced than in the United States, though not by much. Ireland's Gini coefficient—which measures disposable household income inequality on a scale of zero (perfect equality) to one (only one household having all the nation's income), based on data compiled between 1990 and 2000—is 0.33, same as Italy's but significantly higher than Germany (0.25) and the Scandinavian countries (0.24). America's coefficient is 0.37, and like the United States, Ireland's number is expected to rise. Ireland's statistics may seem surprising, but one might consider that many of its wealthiest citizens live "beneath their means" in relatively modest homes (though this, too, is changing).

People and Culture

DEMOGRAPHY

Ireland's population is on the swell. In fact, at 2.25 percent annual increase, it's Europe's fastest-growing country; in 2006 the figure was nearing six million. The current population is actually a fraction of that of 1840; before the Great Famine, there were eight million people living in Ireland. Of the 21st century population, approximately 1.7 million live in the six Northern counties (with 600,000 in the greater Belfast area), while the republic has about 4.1 million residents (estimated by the 2006 census). Though Dublin proper has roughly half a million inhabitants, more than 1.6 million Irish live in the greater metropolitan area, meaning that nearly 40 percent of the republic's population lives in the city and suburbs of the capital. The urban/rural population ratio is roughly 3:2, a reversal of the population distribution in the 1920s. Also, there are approximately 23,000 "travelers," the politically correct term for the island's itinerant populations; each region has slightly different customs and dialect.

The **Central Statistics Office** (www.census. ie) has more interesting stats: Seeing as agriculture is such a historically integral part of the Irish economy, it's worth noting that less than 20 percent of Irish farmers are under the age of 35. Another ominous statistic concerns divorce, which was legalized (by referendum) only in 1996; today one in six Irish marriages ends in divorce. The current life expectancy is just over 77 years: 75 for men and 80 for women.

IMMIGRATION

The influx of immigrants and refugees (from eastern Europe and Nigeria, mostly) since the advent of the "Celtic Tiger" economic boom is a remarkable irony: The Irish were so used to emigrating that they couldn't comprehend it when the foreigners started moving in! According to the 2002 census (the latest figures available at time of writing), about 11.5 percent of the republic's population were born outside the republic (and of these, 1.5 percent were born in Northern Ireland). Other British-born residents account for 5.7 percent, and African and Eastern European immigrants comprise 0.7 percent each. No doubt these figures will rise in subsequent censuses.

TRACING YOUR ROOTS

Looking for the names and old address of your great-great-grandparents from County Tipperary? Though each county has its own archive, it's more sensible to start at the **General Register Office** (Joyce House, Lombard St., Research Room, 2nd fl., tel. 01/635-4000, open 9:30 A.M.–4:30 P.M. Mon.-Fri.) in Dublin, where you can look up your ancestor's birth, marriage, or death certificate (all of which should list the addresses of the parties involved) no matter which county he or she came from; the records here start at 1864. The fees are nominal, though they can start to add up if you need to broaden your search: €2-4 per request (you can request up to five annual record books at a time), and €4 for a photocopy. Though the archive is always a hive of activity, the staff is willing to answer quick questions and offer search tips.

You can also check the census records and various databases at the **National Archives** (Bishop St., tel. 01/407-2300, www.nationalarchives.ie, open 10 A.M.–5 P.M. Mon.-Fri.). Another good starting point, particularly if you need help planning your search, is the

National Library Genealogy Service (Kildare St., tel. 01/603-0200, www.nli.ie, open 10 A.M.–4:45 P.M. Mon.-Fri. and 10 A.M.–12:30 P.M. Sat.), which at the time of writing had been relocated to the ground floor of the Heraldic Museum (2 Kildare St.). (Plans were underway for a return to their original offices upstairs at the National Library, though the move date had not yet been determined.) This office has a few databases on offer, but is worth a visit mainly for the knowledgeable staff, who will provide you with thorough advice.

The General Register Office in Dublin has birth, marriage, and death records for the Northern Ireland counties as well, but there is additional information available at the **Public Record Office of Northern Ireland** (66 Balmoral Ave., tel. 028/9025-5905, www.proni.gov.uk, open 9 A.M.–4:45 P.M. Mon.-Wed. and Fri., 10 A.M.–8:45 P.M. Thurs.).

If you don't have the time to conduct extensive genealogical research, you might want to consider hiring a professional. Ask at the National Library office for a list of private researchers; most are based in Dublin.

RELIGION

The population of the republic is 90 percent Catholic and 3 percent Protestant. The Northern Ireland population is roughly 46 percent Protestant and 40 percent Catholic, and that split continues to even out as strict Catholics keep on having larger families (the Catholic Church still forbids the use of contraception). Of course, these percentages vary by location; some areas (like Derry City and south Armagh) are predominantly Catholic and republican, and other areas (Plantation towns, mostly) are overwhelmingly Protestant and unionist. Of the North's Protestant population, most are Anglican (or Church of Ireland); the remainder are Methodist, Presbyterian, and many smaller, often evangelical sects. (You'll notice fire-and-brimstone-type notices and biblical quotations posted along the roadways when traveling in the North.) As

you'd expect, the percentages of Irish citizens who identify themselves as non-Christian or atheist is extremely small; 0.05 percent are Jewish, 0.004 percent Muslim, and 3.5 percent report no religious beliefs (a further 2 percent are "unspecified").

In recent decades Ireland has veered away from its traditionally conservative climate and attitudes, partly due to growing disillusionment with the Catholic Church. Divorce and homosexuality were legalized through several referenda, birth control was made legally available again (though the Church still does not sanction its use), and allowances for abortion have been made in extreme circumstances. Church attendance has plummeted in recent decades, from more than 90 percent in the mid-1970s to 60 percent in the mid-1990s to roughly 48 percent in 2001. As in the United States and several other European nations, child abuse

© CAMILLE DE ANGELIS

This leafy grotto in rural Waterford exemplifies Irish Catholic devotion.

scandals are a huge reason why so many disillusioned Irish Catholics are no longer going to church on Sunday.

LANGUAGE

Irish (or "Gaelic," as foreigners often call it) is the Republic of Ireland's first official language (though English is far more widely spoken, the Constitution recognizes it secondarily). Irish (*Gaeilge* in Irish) is an Indo-European language brought to the island by the Celts and related to the native tongues of Scotland, Wales, and the Isle of Man. The Gaelic language most similar to Irish is Scottish Gaelic; it is possible for a Donegal Irish speaker to hold an albeit halting conversation with a Scottish Gaelic speaker. Note that it is more precise to refer to the Irish language as "Irish" rather than "Gaelic," as "Gaelic" is more often used to refer to Scottish Gaelic.

Many people are working assiduously to avoid the death of the Irish language, and their hopes are looking up. The problem is that in the post-independence republic, students were "force-fed" Irish and punished if they did not speak it as well as they did English (a remarkable reversal from the age of the Penal Laws!), and as a result many middle-aged Irish retain a marked distaste for the language of their forebears. Outside the Gaeltachtaí, regions where Irish is the primary language, you'll hear it spoken fairly infrequently; another problem with sustaining the native tongue is that the Ulster (Donegal), Connaught (Mayo and Galway), and Munster (Cork and Kerry) dialects are different enough to incite confusion even among native speakers; there have been proponents of a standardized dialect, but unsurprisingly this movement has not progressed. Today there are approximately 70,000 native Irish speakers on the island, and though 40 percent of all those in the republic claim fluency in the language, most admit they use it pretty infrequently.

For more information on the Gaeltachtaí, check out the **Living Communities Movement** (tel. 097/88082, www.gaeltacht.info/living. html), and see the *Resources* chapter for a glossary and some useful Irish phrases.

IRISH PHRASEOLOGY

You will probably notice that the Irish have a unique way of responding to a question; for example, if you ask "Did you go to the match today?" they'll say "I did" rather than "yes." This is because there are no real words in the Irish language for "yes" and "no." Instead, Irish-speakers reply with the same verb that was used to ask the question.

You may also notice that the Irish often drop their apostrophes – Murphy's Pub may read "Murphys Pub" above the doorway. Perhaps this also stems from the absence of apostrophes in the Irish language.

Here are a few more expressions you may need to know:

"half-four" – 4:30 (i.e., the time of day)
"Monday week" – a week from Monday
"fair play to you" – good job, nice going
And "your man" just means the particular person the speaker is referring to, not your boyfriend or husband.

The first floor of a building is known as the "ground floor" in Ireland, and what Americans call a second floor is their first. Also, the Irish "ring" instead of "call" someone on their "mobile" rather than "cell phone." To "call on" people is to visit them in person.

Like the Brits, the Irish call french fries "chips" and potato chips "crisps." Soccer is "football" (which is not the same as Gaelic football), and fans are enthusiastic about "sport" rather than "sports."

The word *craic* (pronounced "crack") is fairly ubiquitous, and it has no direct translation – "fun" isn't quite adequate. "Fun with music and flowing pints" is more accurate. In any case, you'll brand yourself a tourist if you snicker when somebody uses it.

THE ARTS
Music and Dance

You may already be well acquainted with the music of U2, Van Morrison, the Cranberries, The Corrs, The Pogues, Enya, Damien Rice, and other popular Irish artists and groups, as well as the Riverdance phenomenon that began with the Eurovision performance in 1995 and all the other step-dance shows it's inspired since then. But you may not be as aware of the traditional music of Ireland.

The Irish traditional music session will always feature a fiddle, or two, or three, along with a bodhrán ("boh-RAWN"), a goatskin drum pounded with a two-ended wooden beater. Though they're not indigenous instruments—but to be accurate, very few quintessentially Irish instruments are—banjos, guitars, and bouzoukis are also common on the trad scene. The tin whistle is somewhat less popular despite its low startup (you can get a good whistle for under €10) and portability. Accordions (and concertinas for the ladies) are becoming somewhat less common as well. It takes decades of practice to master the uil-leann ("ILL-in") pipes, which is part of why uilleann pipers are few and far between these days. Harps are generally reserved for classical concerts and kitschy medieval banquets.

Regarding the music itself, most of the tunes you'll hear are jigs (6/8 time) and reels (4/4 time), with the occasional air—a song without time—thrown in for good measure (no pun intended). *Seán nós* is a traditional unaccompanied singing style, in Irish. Irish musicians have a strangely organic approach to their repertoires; oftentimes one in a group will begin to play and his or her fellow musicians will know which song it is, despite not having a name for it. Even if they don't know the song they will probably still be able to play along. There are no standardized names for traditional jigs and reels, either, as David A. Wilson has wryly noted: "Now one thing you can be sure of about session musicians is that they never know the names of the tunes they're playing; it's almost a point of honour with them not to know. But that never stops them from making up answers on the spot... 'That was "The Sow's Lament over the Empty Trough,"' said the piper. 'Not at all,' replied the fiddler; 'it was "My Mother Drowned in the Holy Water at Lourdes."'"

Traditional Irish dance consists of step dancing, in which dancers perform intricate tap dancing with stiff unmoving arms, and set dancing, a group dance resembling a quadrille. An evening of traditional music and dancing is called a ceilidh, though most of the ones you'll see as a tourist can have a somewhat over-the-top theatricality to them.

Literature

The Irish are consummate storytellers; just walk into a pub, sit beside a local, and wait for him or her to strike up a conversation. This longstanding reputation began with the bards of pre-Christian and medieval Ireland; they were some of the most revered members of society, patronized by petty chieftains and high kings. Until early Christian times Ireland's storytelling tradition was solely oral, but the first monks, learned in Latin as well as Irish, put nib to vellum and recorded many of the island's greatest epics, one of the more famous examples being the *Táin Bó Cúailnge* ("The Cattle Raid of Cooley").

Ireland's most famous writers have tended to be of the Anglo-Irish Ascendancy (not surprising, seeing as the vast majority of the dispossessed Irish were too busy trying to survive to produce much in the way of poetry and prose). Anglo-Irish writers of the 18th and 19th centuries still read today include Jonathan Swift (Dean of St. Patrick's Cathedral in Dublin, satirist, and author of the beloved *Gulliver's Travels*) and Maria Edgeworth, who produced fictions like *Castle Rackrent* to support her family estate in Longford. The 19th-century Anglo-Irish Gothic writers—Bram Stoker, Joseph Sheridan Le Fanu *(In a Glass Darkly)*, and Charles Maturin *(Melmoth the Wanderer)*—have been given short shrift in the realm of Irish literary criticism; it should be noted that Le Fanu's vampire novella *Carmilla* actually predates Stoker's enormously popular and influential *Dracula*. Maturin, an Anglican minister, was the great-uncle of Oscar Wilde, one of the country's greatest playwrights; Wilde would use the pseudonym "Sebastian Melmoth" when in exile in Paris.

Engineered by William Butler Yeats and his patron, Lady Augusta Gregory, the Irish Literary Revival of the early 20th century introduced more of the country's brightest luminaries, including John Millington Synge, George Bernard Shaw, and Sean O'Casey *(The Plough and the Stars)*. Today, James Joyce's doorstoppers, *Ulysses* and *Finnegan's Wake*, often eclipse the work of other fine writers of the early to mid-20th century on American college syllabi: Flann O'Brien, Sean O'Faolain, Patrick Kavanagh, Kate O'Brien, Elizabeth Bowen, and many others. Ironically, many of Ireland's greatest talents—Wilde, Yeats, Joyce, Samuel Beckett—spent most of their time abroad.

Playwright and author Brendan Behan *(The Borstal Boy)* was, like Wilde, a colorful figure renowned for his witty, self-revealing epigrams ("I only take a drink on two occasions: when I'm thirsty and when I'm not")—and prolific despite an early death in 1964, at age 41. The country's most important contemporary playwrights include Tom Murphy *(The Gigli Concert)* and Brian Friel *(Dancing at Lughnasa)*.

Seamus Heaney is Ireland's most famous contemporary poet, having translated *Beowulf* into English and produced an oeuvre worthy of the 1995 Nobel Prize in Literature. Other poets, like Nuala Ní Dhomnaill, write exclusively in Irish (their volumes have English translations by other Irish writers), and still other poets have gone back and forth between Irish and English, like Michael Hartnett and Mícheál Ó Siadhail.

Just looking for something to enjoy on the plane ride home? There are the bestsellers, of course (Frank McCourt has made a career out of his impoverished Limerick childhood, and Maeve Binchy is still the queen of Irish chick lit), but it's worth looking beyond the more famous names when cultivating an appreciation for contemporary Irish lit. For a list of recommended volumes of fiction and poetry (many by excellent yet lesser-known writers), see *Suggested Reading* in the *Resources* chapter.

Cinema

Until the founding of the Irish Film Board in 1981, British and American companies produced most of the movies made in Ireland. Though John Ford's *The Quiet Man*, filmed in Galway and Mayo in the summer of 1951, was seen as a Technicolor marvel at the time, the movie is thin on plot and rife with stereotypes and absurd brogues. Fortunately, Irish filmmakers have more than made up for such early American-made blunders with classics like *In the Name of the Father, The Field,* and *My Left Foot* (all directed by Jim Sheridan), as well as *Michael Collins* and *The Crying Game* (by Neil Jordan). Many American movies are filmed here each year too, Wicklow ("The Garden of Ireland") being the most-filmed county, and though Irish actors get plenty of work in Hollywood, they tend to remember their roots. Liam Neeson, a native of County Antrim, is the primary patron of the Lyric Theatre in Belfast, the theater in which he learned his craft back in the 1970s.

Handicrafts

Ireland's traditional cottage industries include lace, linen, tweed, and knitting. Kenmare in County Kerry was a center for the lace-making craft in the 19th century and today offers a historical lace exhibition in the heritage center. Virtually all the lace you find in stores now is machine-made, however.

The making of Irish linen goes back to the 11th century, when flax was first farmed here; from monastic annals we know that the fabric was worn by the upper classes. From the 17th through the 19th centuries, linen was an exclusively Northern industry, funded by the British government to encourage English and Scottish settlement; women and children toiled in the flax-spinning mills that lined Falls Road in Belfast, a staunchly Catholic neighborhood. Belfast's last linen factories closed in the early 1960s, though it's still possible to buy Irish-made linen products at upscale gift shops. Donegal is the island's center for tweed production, and you can see century-old looms still in use in Ardara, Donegal Town, and elsewhere.

Due to financial cutbacks, some of the county's tweed production is now completed abroad; look for the "made in" label when shopping for tweed (again, Donegal and Ardara are two of the best places to shop).

Knitwear is another quintessentially Irish craft. Women on the Aran Islands in County Galway still knit their intricately cabled sweaters by hand, as they have for centuries. The vast majority of the "Aran sweaters" you'll find in Irish gift shops are machine-knit, but it's well worth spending a great deal more on a hand-knit jumper, if you can afford it.

Ireland—County Waterford in particular—is also renowned for its crystal. Many counties besides Waterford have their own crystal factories, including Kilkenny (www.kilkennycrystal.com), Cavan (www.cavancrystaldesign.com), and Tipperary (www.tipperarycrystal.com), and there are smaller workshops all over the country (many of them run by former Waterford master craftspeople). Waterford may be the most famous, but the crystal produced elsewhere can be every bit as beautiful (and is sometimes less expensive).

Though pottery is also a very popular souvenir, most Irish potters import their clay from England. A few do use a local variety of red daub earthenware clay, though, and some glazes used by Irish potters are produced using local materials as well.

Architecture

Quaint thatched-roof whitewashed cottages aside, Ireland's most characteristic architecture belongs to the distant past: the Iron Age ring forts perched dramatically atop rocky promontories; the round towers and simple one-room churches of the early Christian monasteries; the solid medieval tower houses of the Gaelic chieftains and Norman conquerors. Because domestic architecture was often of the wattle-and-daub variety, what remains of the island's prehistoric buildings are found mostly within necropolises, the Brú na Bóinne site in County Meath being the most famous example. Archaeologists have also uncovered the stone foundations of Neolithic

AN ARCHITECTURAL GLOSSARY

From the Bronze Age to the opulent faux castles of the Victorian era, here's a rundown of the most common architectural terms. Architecture buffs should also check out **Archeire** (www.irish-architecture.com), an opinionated guide to Irish architecture from Norman castles to O'Donnell & Tuomey.

antae a pilaster forming the end of a projecting lateral wall, as in some Greek temples, and constituting one boundary of the portico

bailey a castle's outer wall

beehive hut a small circular stone building shaped like a beehive

caher a circular area enclosed by stone walls

cairn a prehistoric grave covered by a mound of stones

cashel a stone-walled circular fort

chancel the eastern end of a church, where the altar is located

cheveaux de frise a defensive field of sharp stone spikes around a fort, placed to impede the cavalry of an attacking army

clochán a dry-stone beehive hut usually used for monks' solitary cells in the early Christian period

corbel a triangular bracket, usually made of stone or brick, that projects from the face of a wall and is usually used to support a cornice or arch

cornice a horizontal molded projection that crowns a building or wall

crannóg an artificial island (piled up with rocks and debris) connected by a wooden bridge to the shore, usually containing a thatched house and barn surrounded by a palisade and created for ease of defense

cromlech a tomb with two upright stones covered by a capstone, synonymous with dolmens; literally a "bent flagstone"

curtain wall an exterior wall or a section of that wall between two gates or towers

dairtheach in a monastery, a small room reserved for private prayer

demesne the land surrounding a castle or manor house, often including gardens

dolmen a prehistoric tomb made of two vertical stones topped by a capstone, giving the structure the vague appearance of a toadstool

fulacht fiadh a Bronze Age hearth consisting of an earthen trough filled with water, into which fire-warmed stones would be placed, boiling whatever meats were submerged in the water; it is possible that such troughs were used for laundry, cloth-dyeing, and leather-making as well

gallery grave a burial chamber shaped like a tunnel

Georgian a relatively austere architectural style used from the 1710s to the 1830s, named for Britain's four King Georges and characterized by symmetry and proportion with a restrained use of classical Greek and Roman elements; examples abound in Irish domestic architecture, especially in Dublin and Limerick

Gothic an architectural style characterized by pointed arches, used in Irish castles and churches between the 12th and 16th centuries

keep a castle's main tower, also called a donjon

machicolation a projecting gallery at the top of a castle wall, supported by corbeled arches and having floor openings through which stones and boiling liquids were dropped on attackers

motte an early Norman fortification with a raised, flattened mound topped with a keep; many motte-and-bailey structures were erected in the early 1200s

neoclassical a movement beginning in the mid-18th century, inspired by ancient Greek and Roman architecture and a reaction against rococo and other ornate styles; examples include the Four Courts in Dublin

Palladian the early 18th-century English revival of the style of 16th-century Italian architect Andrea Palladio, characterized by an adherence to mathematical proportions as well as architectural features like loggias and porticos; the foremost example of Irish Palladian architecture is Castletown in County Kildare

(continues on next page)

AN ARCHITECTURAL GLOSSARY (continued)

passage grave a Celtic tomb reached by a passageway and buried beneath an earth and stone mound

ráth a circular fort surrounded by a wooden wall and earthen banks

reredos a decorative (usually wood-carved) partition in front of a church altar

ring fort a circular stone structure with an embankment on all sides, built between the Bronze Age and medieval times

Romanesque an architectural style characterized by rounded arches and vaulting, popular in Ireland in the 1100s; the style known as **Hiberno-Romanesque** incorporates Celtic motifs in its stone carvings as well as antae and high-pitched corbelled gables

round tower a tall circular tower built in Irish monasteries between the 9th and 11th centuries, used for a lookout and refuge from Viking invaders (which is why the tower entrance was virtually always at least one story off the ground)

sheila-na-gig a female effigy, similar to a prehistoric fertility figure in its exaggerated reproductive anatomy, carved in stone on the exterior of churches and castles (literally "Sheila of the teats")

souterrain an underground chamber or passageway, usually used in ring and hill forts to provide storage for food or an escape route in an emergency

standing stone a vertically placed stone set in the ground, dating across several time periods; their general purpose is unknown, though some were certainly used as grave markers

voussoir one of the wedge-shaped stones forming the curve of an arch or vaulted ceiling

farmhouses. Using such remains, some interpretive museums have been able to construct replicas of *crannógs*—artificial islands built up with rocks and topped by a round thatched house—and other ancient dwellings.

Though beehive huts, *clocháin,* are emblematic of the early Christian monastic period—used as the monks' cells, for sleep or solitary prayer—these corbelled structures were first erected in the Neolithic period. Round towers—which functioned as a defense against Viking raiders (not for the monks' lives so much as their treasures, jeweled reliquaries and illuminated manuscripts and suchlike) as well as a geographical touchstone for pilgrims—are unique not only to the Christian monastic period, but to Ireland as well. You won't find any round towers except on this island.

Though the Vikings established their port cities at Dublin, Waterford, Wexford, and elsewhere in the 9th and 10th centuries, their extant architecture is limited to chunks of city walls. The Normans left Ireland with a tremendous architectural heritage, mostly in the form of the fortified castles for which the country is perhaps best known. The Normans also brought the Gothic, which became the most pervasive style of ecclesiastical architecture in the centuries to follow—through the 19th century (and well into the 20th) Roman Catholic churches went up in the neo-Gothic style, sometimes with Hiberno-Romanesque flourishes.

The early 12th century heralded the popularity of the Romanesque style in Irish churches, the most famous example being the tiny, spooky Cormac Chapel at the Rock of Cashel. Irish stonemasons created an amalgam of Romanesque and Celtic motifs to create a distinctive "Hiberno-Romanesque" style; you'll find excellent examples of this fusion at the Nuns' Church at Clonmacnoise and Clonfert Cathedral in eastern Galway.

Opulent country houses built by English landlords run the gamut from neoclassical and Palladian styles (Emo Court in Laois and Castletown in Kildare being respective examples) to the neo-Gothic manors of Glenveagh Castle in Donegal and Kylemore Castle (now Abbey) in Connemara, to Victorian mansions like Muckross House in Killarney National Park (not to mention countless renovated boutique hotels and B&Bs). Ireland has a strong Georgian architectural heritage, and not just in cities like Dublin and Limerick. Many smaller market towns, like Birr in County Offaly, were planned by the local landlord, so the extant architecture lining those tidy tree-lined squares echoes the prevailing aesthetics of the time.

Dublin's grandest architecture is also in the neoclassical style; take for example the president's home in Phoenix Park (Áras an Uachtaráin), designed by Francis Johnston, and the Customs House and the Four Courts by James Gandon. Some architects, like William Chambers (who designed the Casino Marino for the Earl of Charlemont), never even set foot on Irish soil. Though such structures as neoclassical Dublin City Hall and the Palladian Leinster House are examples of imperialist style and construction, they are nonetheless some of Ireland's finest architecture of the last 300 years.

SPORTS

Though you'll find plenty of fans of the British football teams, most Irish love to watch Gaelic football and hurling (camogie is the ladies' version of hurling). Formed in 1884 to promote these uniquely Irish pastimes, the **Gaelic Athletic Association** (www.gaa.ie) is headquartered at Croke Park in Dublin. For want of a better comparison, hurling looks like a cross between field hockey, baseball, and lacrosse, with a broad-ended stick used to balance the ball briefly before hitting it; players can also handle the ball. Gaelic football looks more like soccer than anything else. Horse and greyhound racing are popular with bettors.

ESSENTIALS

Getting There

BY AIR

Air fares naturally vary greatly between seasons; when booking ahead for a summer holiday (round-trip, flying from the United States), expect to spend at least US$800; last-minute fares could cost you upward of US$1,000. Fares in shoulder season are in the neighborhood of US$600. The sooner you purchase your ticket, the better the deal; the only exception is in mid-January through February, when Aer Lingus and other carriers offer very good last-minute fares (less than US$400). Fares skyrocket again in the week leading up to St. Patrick's Day.

Orbitz, Priceline, and other websites will not necessarily offer the cheapest flights; you can often find the best prices on airline websites. Students will generally find the best deals on sites like **Student Universe** (www.studentuniverse.com) and **STA Travel** (www.statravel.com); the former is just for students, but the latter offers fare deals for nonstudents too. In any case, it's well worth spending the time comparing prices.

All ballpark figures noted above factor in taxes and fees.

From the United States and Canada

Aer Lingus (tel. 800/474-7424, www.aerlingus.com) and **Continental** (tel. 800/231-0856,

© CAMILLE DEANGELIS

www.continental.com) offer the best service and options when flying from the United States. Both offer direct flights from New York (JFK), Boston, Denver, San Francisco, Los Angeles, and many other cities. **Delta** (tel. 800/241-4141, www.delta.com) also offers direct flights.

Transatlantic flights are available to the island's three major airports: Dublin (tel. 01/814-1111, www.dublinairport.com), Shannon (tel. 061/712-000, www.shannonairport.com), and Belfast International (tel. 028/9448-4848, www.belfastairport.com), but not the smaller regional airports.

Air Canada (tel. 888/247-2262, www.aircanada.com) offers direct flights from Toronto to Shannon. **Delta** (tel. 800/221-1212, www.delta.com) and **Aer Lingus** (tel. 800/474-7424, www.aerlingus.com) are other options.

From the United Kingdom and Continental Europe

Despite the inconvenience of flying out of secondary airports, low-cost air carriers are the way to go when flying from the United Kingdom and mainland Europe. **RyanAir** (www.ryanair.com) is far and away the most popular option when flying to both the republic and the North, with **EasyJet** (www.easyjet.com) a close second. You can get a direct flight from Europe to several city and regional airports—Knock, Derry City, Belfast City, and Cork—and there is also more limited service available to Galway, Waterford, Donegal (near Gweedore), and Sligo. Aer Lingus offers frequent flights to Dublin from Heathrow, Gatwick, and London City, as well as Paris, Madrid, Milan, Rome, Naples, Frankfurt, Brussels, Amsterdam, Vienna, Budapest, Prague, Warsaw, Munich, and many more locations.

BY SEA

International ferry services are available, mostly from the United Kingdom: Liverpool, Holyhead, the Isle of Man, Fishguard, Pembroke, Heysham, Swansea, and a few other ports, as well as Roscoff and Cherbourg in France. Booking online can save you as much as 10 percent, but note that not all ferries accept pedestrian passengers.

Sail to Dublin from Liverpool or Holyhead via **P&O Irish Sea Ferries** (tel. 01/407-3434, www.poirishsea.com) or **Norfolk Line** (tel. 01/819-2999, www.norfolkline.com). **Irish Ferries** (tel. 01/638-3333, www.irishferries.com) also sails to Holyhead. **Steam Packet** (tel. 1800/805-055, www.steam-packet.com) sails to Dublin from the Isle of Man.

Ferry service is available to Dún Laoghaire, 13 kilometers south of Dublin, via **Stena Line** (tel. 01/204-7777 or 01/204-7799, www.stenaline.ie) from Holyhead in Wales.

Get to Rosslare Harbour from Fishguard in Wales via **Stena Line** (tel. 053/931-3997, www.stenaline.ie), or from Pembroke or France (Cherbourg or Roscoff, the latter Apr.–Sept. only) via **Irish Ferries** (tel. 053/913-3158, www.irishferries.com).

Service is available to Cork City from Swansea in Wales via **Swansea-Cork Ferries** (www.swansea-cork.ie).

Norfolk Line (tel. 01/819-2999, www.norfolkline.com) also operates a Belfast–Liverpool service.

Getting Around

BY AIR

To cut down on time in the car or bus, try flying from Dublin to one of the regional or city airports, usually on **Aer Arann** (www.aerarann.ie): Waterford (10 km south of the city, www.flywaterford.com), Cork (6 km south, tel. 021/431-3131, www.corkairport.com), Galway (8 km east, www.galwayairport.com), Sligo (Strandhill, 8 km west of Sligo Town, www.sligoairport.com), Donegal (Carrickfinn, 84 km northwest of Donegal Town, www.donegalairport.ie), Kerry (Farranfore, 16 km south of Tralee, www.kerryairport.com), or Knock (roughly equidistant between Sligo and Galway, both about 72 km away, www.knockairport.com). All airports host car-rental agencies.

BY BUS

The republic's national bus service, **Bus Éireann** (tel. 01/830-2222, www.buseireann.ie), has an extensive network of national and cross-border routes, as well as local service in the larger towns and cities. An **Open Road** ticket allows unlimited bus travel during a certain period, like 4 days out of 8 (€58), 7 days out of 14 (€97), and so forth. The **Irish Rover** bus-only pass (3 days out of 8 for €70) is valid on both sides of the border. You'll save yourself a fair bit of cash (and the farther you travel, the more you save).

Bus Éireann doesn't run everywhere, though, and several regional companies fill in the gaps. Others are commuter buses (also useful for tourists) that are often more comfortable and slightly less expensive than the national bus service. Bus Éireann covers much more of the country and is less expensive, but the railroad offers more speed and comfort. One independent company providing very useful Dublin–Galway and Galway–Shannon services is **Citylink** (tel. 01/626-6888, www.citylink.ie), preferable to Bus Éireann because the buses are newer, cleaner, and less crowded, yet comparable price-wise.

© CAMILLE DEANGELIS

The old Irish signposts give distances in miles.

Northern Ireland is served by **Ulsterbus** (tel. 028/9066-6630, www.ulsterbus.co.uk), which offers special sightseeing services on the Causeway Coast and the Sperrin Mountains, as well as a summer service through the Mourne Mountains. A steal at £7, the **Sunday Rambler** ticket will get you unlimited travel on all Ulsterbus services within Northern Ireland on Sunday.

BY TRAIN

The Irish national train network is Iarnród Éireann, a.k.a. **Irish Rail** (tel. 01/836-3333, www.irishrail.ie), which serves most of the larger towns and cities. For the most part, the railway map looks like a starfish, with all lines leading from Dublin—meaning that if you want to travel from, say, Sligo to Galway, a change is required. Return fares are always a better value, day return fares especially, though prices rise at the weekend. If you're planning on a lot of train travel, purchase an **Irish Explorer Ticket,** a combination bus-and-train ticket that allows you 8 days' travel out of 15 (€203) within the republic. There's also a **rolling ticket** (train/train and bus €14.80/16) for unlimited travel over a 3-day period. All tickets are available online or at any train station ticket desk. For the Eurail or other special travel pass, visit **The Travel Centre** (35 Lower Abbey St., Dublin, tel. 01/836-6222).

The **DART,** or Dublin Area Rapid Transit (www.dart.ie) is popular with commuters, and is very useful for visitors staying in Dublin who wish to see more of Counties Dublin and Wicklow. **Luas** (www.luas.ie) is a new light-rail service within the city designed to cut down on gridlock.

North of the border, the train operator is **Northern Ireland Railways** (tel. 028/9089-9411, www.translink.co.uk), which provides service from Derry to Belfast, Belfast to Bangor, and Belfast to Drogheda and Dublin.

BY CAR

Driving on the left is a downright scary proposition, and the idiosyncrasies of the Irish roads can leave even the best drivers anxious and stressed out. If you plan to stick to larger towns and cities, you're best off using public transportation. But the Irish bus and rail networks do not serve many remote locations, and many wonderful attractions are difficult, even impossible, to reach without a car (Clonmacnoise is one example). Weigh the stress involved in driving on Irish roads against the benefit of going anywhere you like, anytime you like, and make a decision from there.

Traffic Regulations and Tips

First off, you'll be driving on the left (and don't make any wisecracks about "driving on the wrong side" at the Europcar desk!). In keeping with this, the right lane is the "fast" lane. The dread of every foreign driver is the roundabout, a common substitute for an intersection; traffic proceeds in a clockwise direction, and you enter the circle only when there are no vehicles oncoming from your right. The larger roundabouts also have traffic lights. When approaching the roundabout, stay in the left lane if you intend to take the first exit, the right lane for subsequent exits; you'll know which exit you want by reading the big green sign posted before the roundabout.

Parking is generally free in smaller places, though the larger towns and cities operate a "pay-and-display" policy. You buy a ticket from a blue kiosk to leave on your dashboard, €0.60–3/hour depending on the size of the town (not all accept credit cards, so be sure to carry several euros in change). Still other parking lots are "disc-operated," meaning you'll have to duck into the nearest newsagent to purchase a disc for about the same price. In some towns it's worth seeking out free parking spaces a bit farther from the center; in other situations you'll just have to fork it over. Spend a few minutes when you first arrive in a new place just getting your bearings and scoping out free parking opportunities. Some lots charge €3–3.50 for the whole day. After 6:30 P.M., though, you won't have to feed the car park kiosk.

In the republic, distances and speed limits are given in kilometers, with the exception of some very old signs still in need of replacement in more remote locales (you'll have no difficulty recognizing them). Northern Ireland is still on the Imperial system, so in the Northern Ireland destination chapters all distances are listed in both miles and kilometers. Always trust your map over the road signs; they're sometimes pointed in the wrong direction (through age and weather, not necessarily mischief). Though this book lists roads by official number ("N" indicating a national road, "R" a regional road) for ease of navigation, the Irish don't really use them when giving directions—they say "the Dublin road" instead of "the N3." Also, brace yourself for a bottleneck every time you're entering a town; Ireland's few motorways (noted by an "M") are the only exception. There are tolls (€2–3) along the motorways, so be sure to carry extra change (otherwise you have to park on the side of the highway and visit the office to use your credit card).

It is polite to acknowledge the other drivers

© CAMILLE DEANGELIS

Warning – there's a roundabout ahead!

you pass on narrow backcountry roads, especially if they pull to the side to let you pass first. Raise a finger or two off the steering wheel in a sort of benediction.

Safety

This may be a generalization, but there's a great deal of truth in it: Irish drivers are reckless. They are impatient, they drive too fast, and they take ridiculous risks. Also, the speed limits off the national roads and motorways are too high: 100 kph (62 mph) on a narrow, winding road where even a good driver would apply the brake liberally. Ireland's roads claim many lives every weekend of the year, and until the government wises up, lowers the speed limits on regional roads, and then puts the guards on the streets to enforce them, these tragedies will continue to occur. Sadly, alcohol is often involved in such incidents. Avoid becoming a statistic by following all the usual common-sensible rules: Designate a sober driver who won't drink even a single beer, wear your seatbelts, and use the high beams on country roads

(be sure to dim them if you see a car ahead, though). Drive only as fast as you feel comfortable; Irish drivers have no qualms about passing you, anyway!

Car Rentals

To rent an automobile, you must be over 23 years old and have been licensed for at least two years. There are numerous rental companies, most of which are international (and have desks at all airports, even the smallest ones): **Europcar** (www.europcar.ie), **Avis** (www. avis.ie), **Budget** (www.budget.ie), and **Hertz** (www.hertz.ie).

Theft insurance is an option, but because car theft is practically nonexistent in Ireland you'd do well to opt out and save yourself a few euros a day.

Package Deals

You can find airfare-car rental combined rates on Expedia, Orbitz, and other websites. Otherwise, instead of booking directly through Avis, Europcar, or whichever, go through

AutoEurope (tel. 01/659-0500, www.autoeurope.com). Clerks at the rental agencies admit that booking through AutoEurope will get you a better rate.

Maps and Directions

Ordnance Survey (OS, www.osi.ie) publishes detailed scale maps of the national parks, cities, and the larger towns, which indicate one-way streets. Pick up a road atlas—the Collins or Ordnance Survey brands are recommended (about €9)—before leaving the airport, as the map the rental agency gives you isn't detailed enough.

BY BIKE

Bicycle hire will run you €10–15 per day (or £8–10 in North Ireland, and as much as €25 in Dublin). Weekly rental is a better value, roughly €50–60 per week. In addition, you're often required to leave a deposit and/or a form of ID. Some cycle shops provide one-way service for an additional fee; check out **Raleigh Rent-a-Bike** (www.raleigh.ie) for participating dealers. Serious cyclists will want to bring their own, of course; your bike will be factored into your baggage allowance. Irish buses usually allow bikes in the cargo hold, though you'll probably have to pay a surcharge. Especially with private companies, ring ahead to ensure you'll be able to bring your cycle along.

BY TOUR

Keep in mind that most tours follow the well-trod tourist tracks—the Cliffs of Moher, Killarney, Adare in County Limerick, Blarney Castle, and the usual spots in Dublin City. They are certainly convenient, but they generally provide only a very narrow tourist's view of Ireland. One of the most popular choices (popular with retirees) is **CIE** (www.cietours.com), offering coach tour packages in Ireland and elsewhere in Europe. The groups are smaller, but **EirTrail** (tel. 087/612-2501, www.eirtrail.com) offers 1–6-day tours covering the same ground. In contrast, Con Moriarty at **Hidden Ireland Tours** (tel. 064/22844 or 087/258-1966, www.hiddenirelandtours.com) offers active, often themed holidays. For the backpacking set, there's the Paddywagon (www.paddywagontours.com), a hop-on, hop-off bus tour, and **Shamrockers** (tel. 01/672-7651, www.radicaltravel.com).

Accommodations and Food

ACCOMMODATIONS
Hostels

Ireland has a rightful reputation for some of the best hostels in Europe. There are the inevitable stinkers, but the various hostelling organizations—**An Óige** (www.anoige.ie), the republic's youth hostel organization; **Independent Holiday Hostels in Ireland** (IHH, www.hostels-ireland.com); **Independent Hostel Owners of Ireland** (IHO, www.hostellingireland.com); and **Hostelling International of Northern Ireland** (HINI, tel. 028/9031-5435, www.hini.org.uk)—generally ensure that hostels operating under their banners offer cleanliness and hospitality. Some hostels also have an adjacent campground, where you pay less for a site than you would for a bed but have access to the kitchens, showers, and sitting rooms. Many hostels arrange outdoor activities and other events; some include a light breakfast in the room price, and the very best hostels offer additional meals at dinner. Cramped bunkbeds and communal showers can seem like negligible inconveniences when you consider how many new friends you can make while hostelling. Though most hostellers are under 30, generally travelers of all ages are welcomed. In recent years, some hostels have closed their doors to tourists to become immigrant or refugee housing (which is more profitable for the owner).

Also keep in mind that some hostels might start off with good management in the beginning, thus securing the IHH or IHO stamp of approval, only to decline after the business changes hands or for a number of other reasons. A personal recommendation from a fellow traveler is ideal, but if that's not possible and you have your doubts about a particular establishment, ask for a brief tour of the hostel (including the dorm room you'd be staying in along with the shower room) before you check in. Also, most hostels don't issue dorm room keys, so be very careful with your valuables. Checkout is generally 10 A.M.

Bed-and-Breakfasts

B&Bs, which are run out of a family home, are the most popular form of accommodation, and can be found in every nook and corner all over the country. Though B&B proprietors are among the friendliest, most knowledgeable, and helpful Irishpeople (after all, their livelihood depends upon it), there are several caveats here: There's less privacy here than in a hotel, and you may be forced to adjust to the owner's schedule, particularly regarding breakfast times. Also note that prices are per person, often with an unfortunate "supplement" for singles. Nevertheless, B&Bs are nearly always a better value than the hotels and much more comfortable than hostelling.

Also note that proprietors pay for those AA "diamond" ratings; if a B&B doesn't have one, it just means the owners didn't want to pay the AA inspector's fee. In the republic, the shamrock logo indicates the B&B has been approved by the tourist board, though many nonapproved B&Bs are excellent, too. By law, all Northern Ireland B&Bs must be approved by the N.I. Tourist Board.

In theory, B&Bs serve a full Irish breakfast, but most owners skip the time-consuming items like mushrooms, blood sausage, and fresh fried potatoes. (Tinned baked beans may not sound very appetizing now, but you'll grow to like them.) Vegetarians need only ask; proprietors are happy to skip the bacon, and most offer cereal, yogurt, and/or fruit salad. Most places have a set breakfast time of one or two hours between 6:30 A.M. and 10 A.M.;

your host will inform you of these hours. A few B&Bs serve evening meals, mostly in rural areas where there are few restaurants.

Most B&Bs do not accept credit cards, since the fees eat up a percentage of their profits, and those that do sometimes impose a small service charge (2–3 percent). It is customary to pay on the morning of your departure, though, so there's no need to search for the nearest ATM before you check in. Checkout time is generally 11 A.M.

Hotels

The more established Irish hotels can be quite grand, old-fashioned, and lovely, but compared to B&Bs they're generally not a great value for the money. Prices range from €40 in remote locales to well over €200 or €300 in converted castles or manor houses, though the higher price bracket is usually per room rather than per person. Some hotels have moved away from an inclusive full breakfast, so ask before making a reservation. Checkout time is generally at noon.

Self-Catering Accommodations

If you plan to "stay put" in one place for a week or more, taking day trips rather than moving from town to town, a self-catering cottage or apartment may be a good choice. Some self-catering digs are brand-new apartments or holiday homes; others are quaint thatched-roof cottages. Purpose-built "holiday homes" in highly touristed areas are often excessively priced, though, so look for individuals who rent out a few small properties as a way of making extra cash. Helpful websites with properties nationwide include **Self-Catering Ireland** (www.selfcatering.ie), **Trident Holiday Homes** (www.tridentholidayhomes.ie), and **Irish Cottage Holiday Homes** (www.irishcottageholidays.com). Another site, **Rent an Irish Cottage** (www.rentacottage.ie), offers rentals in the western counties from Mayo to Cork (excluding Galway). Note that some proprietors will charge you for the heat and electricity used over the week, so ask about this beforehand.

FOOD AND DRINK

Traditional Irish dishes like colcannon (mashed potatoes, butter, and cabbage or kale), boxty (potato pancakes), and lamb stew are fast disappearing off the pub menus, though black pudding, a sausage made from dried pigs' blood, is still served at B&Bs. When traditional meals do make an appearance, it's usually given the gourmet treatment in chic Continental restaurants, where your plate of bangers and mash (sausages and mashed potatoes) might come served with a sprig of some unidentifiable herb. This gourmet trend, encouraged by the Celtic Tiger, has resulted in hundreds of top-notch restaurants and "gastro-pubs" serving French- and Asian-inspired cuisine; the food is dubbed "Modern Irish" if it emphasizes local, often organic produce, meats (Kerry lamb, for instance), and seafood. Many native Irish chefs were trained on the Continent and have returned home to open their own eateries, and still other chef/owners are foreigners who recognize a growing market. Many pubs still serve defrosted fish-and-chips and gristly lamb stew, but they are becoming increasingly few and far between even in smaller villages. As ever, potatoes and brown bread are staples of the Irish diet.

Beverages

The Gaelic words for whiskey are *uisce beatha,* or "water of life"—which just goes to show you how much the Irish love to drink it. **Jameson** is the most popular brand, with **Bushmills** preferred by the Brits up North. Interestingly, it's said that you can tell the distillery's political affiliation by the shape of the bottle: square bottles are loyalist and round bottles (like Jameson's) are republican.

Of course, **Guinness** is far and away the most popular brand of Irish stout (also referred to as "porter" back in the day); **Beamish** and **Murphy's** are Cork brands, not readily available elsewhere in the country. Kilkenny-based **Smithwick's** is a popular ale (though it's now owned by Guinness). Imported beers are becoming increasingly commonplace in Irish pubs; favored brands include Stella Artois and Carlsberg. There are various cider brands available, though most of them are U.K. imports; Irish-brewed **Bulmer's** is the top brand (it's the same as Magner's in the United States).

Don't tip at the pub; unlike those back home, Irish bartenders make a regular wage. They'll actually be insulted if you try. Want to savor the music, but not the drink—or seriously short on cash? Try ordering a "blackcurrant," which is just a dollop of blackcurrant syrup in a pint glass of water. The bartender will charge you less than a euro for it, and it tastes like noncarbonated fruit soda.

The Irish do not use ice in their cold drinks, and if you ask for an "iced tea" they'll look at you like you're missing a few marbles (then inform you that "iced tea" is an oxymoron). Indeed, the Irish are fairly particular about their tea; few drink anything besides Barry's brand, and most people have at least one cup with pretty much every meal. Ireland's tea dependence originated in Britain; during the Industrial Revolution, English factory bosses recognized it as the ideal drink for their workers—inexpensive, caffeinated, and nonalcoholic. Low tea prices and comfort against the wet weather made it the natural choice in Irish homes as well. Despite declining tea sales (a 9 percent drop in 2005, compared with a 27 percent increase in coffee sales that year), Barry's is still Ireland's most popular beverage. Indeed, this island has the world's highest per-capita tea consumption (four cups per day and seven pounds a year, to be exact).

And though coffee drinking is on the rise, java-lovers beware: 99 percent of Irish B&Bs serve instant. In a nation of tea drinkers, very few people have ever seen (or heard of) a coffee grinder. Also, don't order a cocktail unless it's a posh sort of pub. Bartenders will often charge by the shot, meaning a Sex on the Beach could end up costing you €15.

Dining

Many bars offer a "pub grub" menu, featuring hearty traditional meat-and-potato meals at some places and more elegant, Continental-type fare at "gastro-pubs." Pub grub is less expensive than dinner at a regular restaurant, though most pub kitchens close by 9:30 P.M. The more upscale Irish restaurants generally offer a good-value two- or three-course early-bird menu.

Vegetarians, don't believe anyone who says you can't eat well in Ireland. Even halfway decent restaurants have at least one meat-free option, at worst an unimaginative pasta dish; gourmet eateries tend to offer only one choice, though it's generally as good as any other dish on the menu. Dublin has several vegetarian restaurants, most of them cafeteria-style, and Cork has two, the Quay Co-op and Cafe Paradiso (which is, hands down, the best vegetarian restaurant on the island). And in the off chance you find yourself in a rural watering hole—miles from the nearest proper restaurant, with nothing on the pub grub menu but meat and fish—just ask the staff what they can whip up for you; they'll be happy to help you out.

Tips for Travelers

VISAS AND OFFICIALDOM
Passports and Visas
Unless you are an European Union citizen, you'll need a passport to enter the country (and even if you are, it's smart to carry it anyway). At the customs desk at Shannon or Dublin, North American visitors' passports are stamped with a tourist visa, which allows them a stay of three months. If you plan to remain in the Republic of Ireland for longer than three months, contact the Irish police, the **Garda Síochána** (tel. 01/666-9100, www.garda.ie), to register for a student or work visa. If you ask at the customs desk, they'll provide you with the address of the *garda* station at your destination. Both the Garda National Immigration Bureau (GNIB) and the Irish Naturalisation and Immigration Service are at 13/14 Burgh Quay in the Dublin city center.

Border Crossings
Though there are still a few security checkpoints along the 360-kilometer border between Northern Ireland and the republic, only the most suspicious-looking travelers will be stopped; you as a tourist and a civilian will most likely cross the border without even realizing you've done so. If you intend to remain in Northern Ireland for longer than six months, contact the **U.K. Home Office** (www.ukvisas.gov.uk) for information on obtaining a visa or work permit.

Customs
When leaving Ireland, EU citizens have no limit to the monetary value of goods purchased while in Ireland, so long as the items purchased are not for commercial use. Citizens of the United States, however, are subject to U.S. Customs restrictions: You're only allowed $400 worth of goods tax free (that's $400 per person), and there's a 10 percent tax imposed thereafter. It's possible to mail up to an additional $200 worth of goods home without paying the duty, but your purchases in the duty-free shops in Irish airports count towards that $400 monthly total (that is, you're not paying tax in Ireland, but you may still be required to do so on those same goods upon return to the United States). There are also limits imposed upon cigarettes (200 maximum) and alcohol (one liter maximum). In addition, U.S. citizens should note that bringing fresh food or plants home is not permitted. For more information, visit the U.S. Customs website (www.customs.gov).

STUDY AND EMPLOYMENT OPPORTUNITIES
Irish universities are very popular with American students participating in study abroad programs; enrollment is generally arranged through one's home school. Irish-language summer schools also attract international participation, the most established being **Oideas**

Gael (tel. 074/973-0248, www.oideas-gael. com) in Glencolmcille, County Donegal.

E.U. citizens can work legally in Ireland, but the process is fraught with red tape for a noncitizen looking for a full-time position. For more information, contact the **Department of Enterprise, Trade & Employment** (Davitt House, 65a Adelaide Rd., Dublin, tel. 01/631-3333, www.entemp.ie) in the republic and the **U.K. Home Office** (www.ukvisas.gov.uk) in Northern Ireland. Six-month student work permits are available through **Council Exchanges** (tel. 888/268-6245 in the U.S., www.councilexchanges.org); seasonal work is available mostly in bars, restaurants, construction sites, and so forth.

ACCESS FOR TRAVELERS WITH DISABILITIES

Guesthouses, museums, and so forth are gradually becoming more accessible for visitors with disabilities. Bord Fáilte publishes an annual accommodations guide, available at any tourist office, that specifies which hotels and B&Bs offer special access. In the North, the booklet to ask for is *Accessible Accommodation in Northern Ireland*. The Dúchas website (www.heritageireland.ie) details which heritage sites are wheelchair-accessible.

Renting a car is probably the way to go, as navigating the public transportation systems can be difficult at best. Irish buses are not wheelchair-accessible, though the trains are possible to ride with some assistance. Iarnród Éireann official policy provides for this, but you must call ahead (tel. 01/836-3333).

For information or assistance, contact **Comhairle** (44 N. Great George's St., Dublin, tel. 01/874-7503, www.comhairle.ie), a national support agency in the republic, or **Disability Action** (Portside Business Park, 189 Airport Rd. W., Belfast, tel. 028/9029-7880, www.disabilityaction.org) in Northern Ireland. If you are in need of a wheelchair, contact **The Irish Wheelchair Association** (24 Blackheath Dr., Dublin, tel. 01/833-8241).

TRAVELING WITH CHILDREN

Ireland is the ideal choice for a family vacation. To simplify matters, you might want to consider making day trips from a single base town (you will find most B&Bs very accommodating) or renting a self-catering holiday cottage (the cooking is up to you, but then you don't have to conform to the serving times of restaurants and B&Bs). You might find the major cities too hectic if small children are involved—think about forgoing Dublin for a more relaxing holiday by lake, river, or sea, punctuated by day trips to heritage museums and medieval ruins. Virtually all sightseeing attractions offer a family admission rate, as do some modes of public transportation (with one or two adults and up to three children under the age of 16). Otherwise, B&Bs and hotels generally offer cots at no extra charge, as well as a children's discount of 20–50 percent.

By law, those under the age of 18 are not allowed in the pubs after 10 P.M. in the summertime and 9 P.M. in the winter. This cutoff time might be earlier depending on the establishment (look for a sign above the bar).

WOMEN TRAVELING ALONE

Ireland is one of the safest places on earth for the single female traveler. The psychological intricacies of the stereotypical Irishman aside, the men of this island are almost always genuinely friendly and eager to help you in any way they can.

Since you will need your sweaters even in July and August, the question of how revealing one can dress when out pubbing and clubbing is pretty much moot. While the occasional eccentric Englishwoman can be found sunbathing in the nude at some of the less touristy beaches, this kind of activity is not recommended. Nor is hitchhiking—though if you must, take a small dose of confidence in the knowledge that hitching in Ireland is safer than anywhere else. That said, caution and common sense are your greatest assets. Some parts of Belfast and Dublin simply aren't safe for lone women pedestrians after dark, and as you can hear on the local radio news, incidents can occur even in quiet suburban neighborhoods.

If you will be hostelling during your trip, note that many Irish hostels now offer predominantly mixed-gender dormitories. If you would prefer a girls-only dorm room, be sure to mention that when you check in.

GAY AND LESBIAN TRAVELERS

Ireland has grown increasingly tolerant and open minded regarding homosexuality. The pope's condemnations are disregarded, the local church is mum on the matter, and, thankfully, bigotry is limited to isolated incidents.

Needless to say, the largest cities—Dublin, Belfast, Cork, Galway, and Limerick and Waterford to a lesser degree—are the best places for socializing, though the smaller cities are slowly beginning to establish pubs and networking groups as well. An excellent resource is **Outhouse** (tel. 01/873-4932, www.outhouse.ie) and its directory site, **The Pink Pages** (www.pink-pages.org). The National Lesbian and Gay Federation's **Gay Community News** (tel. 01/671-9076, www.gcn.ie) offers news, message boards, and plenty of information on bars and special events all over the country. **QueerID** (www.queerid.com) is Dublin-centric, and Cork City's best resource is **Gay Cork** (www.gaycork.com). **Gaire** (www.gaire.com) is a news blog, and **Queer.ie** (www.queer.ie), a relatively new site, is heavy on the personals and disco annoucements. For information on the summer Gay Pride Parade in Dublin (and plenty more), check out **Dublin Pride** (www.dublinpride.org). A parade is also held annually in Belfast, although its participants have met with more hostility than their Dublin counterparts.

There are several switchboards in Dublin and Belfast, and though you can call from anywhere in Ireland the opening hours are quite restricted: **Gay Switchboard Dublin** (tel. 01/872-1055, open 8–10 P.M. daily, except for 3:30–6 P.M. Sat.); **Lesbian Line Dublin** (tel. 01/872-9911, open 7–9 P.M. Thurs.); **Mensline Belfast** (tel. 028/9032-2023, 7:30–10:30 P.M. Mon.–Wed.); and **Lesbian Line Belfast** (tel. 028/9023-8668, open 7:30–10 P.M. Thurs.).

Note that STD cases are on the rise, especially in Dublin, and be sure to take all necessary precautions. **The Gay Men's Health Project** (tel. 01/660-2189), which operates a clinic in the Baggot Street Hospital in Dublin, can offer more information, as can the sites listed above.

SENIOR TRAVELERS

Visitors over the age of 60 are entitled to discounts at museums and other sights as well as on most forms of public transit (including Bus Éireann and Irish Rail). The bus or train may be the best way to go, as car-rental companies will not rent automobiles to drivers over the age of 75 (and usually impose a surcharge for drivers ages 70 to 74).

SIGHTSEEING PASSES AND DISCOUNTS

If you plan to do much sightseeing, the **Dúchas Heritage Card** (www.heritageireland.com) is a must-have. For €21 (€8 for students!), you can get into any of the OPW's 70-plus sites for a full year. Seeing as Newgrange admission costs nearly €10 now (and many other sites are inching toward €6), you'll recoup that money in just a few visits. Obviously, students should pick up the card even if they're planning to use it only a few times. Purchase the card at the reception desk of any site.

In North Ireland, the **National Trust Touring Pass** (www.nationaltrust.org.uk), valid for 1–2 weeks (£17/22), gets you "free" admission to more than 300 manors, gardens, and suchlike throughout the British Isles. Couples' passes (£29/38) and family passes (£34/44) are also available.

Another option (island-wide) is the **Heritage Island Explorer Touring Guide** (www.heritageisland.com); buy the €6 info brochure and show it at more than 90 sites for a 2-for-1 or percentage discount. Most discounts are the former, though, so it makes more sense to buy this one if you're traveling in pairs.

BUSINESS HOURS

Irish banks are generally open 9 or 10 A.M. to 4 or 5 P.M. Monday to Friday; post offices keep the same hours, closing 1–2 P.M. for lunch. Many smaller businesses close during this hour, too, so keep this in mind when running errands. Bookstores, boutiques, and many other shops close at 6 P.M., and most stores still close on Sunday, especially in the smaller towns and villages.

LAUNDRY

Irish launderettes are mostly full service, and will run you €8–10 per load. Some offer a same-day tourist service. Many accommodations offer laundry service for an additional fee (often less than that of a launderette), so it makes sense to ask at your B&B before looking for a cleaners in town.

TOILETS

Most sizable Irish towns offer public toilets. Those not coin-operated are very basic (not to mention grotty), so always carry a bottle of hand sanitizer. Most establishments reserve their restrooms for customers only, though this rule is often bypassed in pubs by the truly desperate traveler.

The Irish words for "men" and "women" often appear on restroom doors: the men's room is labeled *fir* and the women's is *mna*. The Irish for "toilets" is *leithreas*.

CONDUCT AND CUSTOMS
Tipping

As bartenders are paid a regular wage in Ireland, there is no need to tip them.

At restaurants, your credit card slip will certainly include a gratuity line. Tip only if your service has been better than average (and if you aren't being served by the owner of the establishment), and do not feel compelled to leave 15 or 20 percent even for excellent service. (Remember that unlike American servers, your waiter is making at least minimum wage.) Also, if a restaurant has imposed a service charge (10–15 percent) and you weren't satisfied with the service, don't hesitate to request the charge be removed from your bill.

Though it isn't necessary to tip Irish taxi drivers, you might want to add a euro or two if he or she has been especially helpful. If you have luggage, there's an automatic surcharge of approximately three euros, which is fair considering the driver will almost always load and unload your bags, and may even carry them to the door for you unasked.

Social Situations and Etiquette

While the atmosphere in most pubs may seem informal enough, and plenty of people lapse into the use of excessive expletives when they've had too much to drink, you should always try to keep your language as clean as possible. The Irish make allowances for those silly drunkards, but they won't consider you very mannerly if you use the same language their inebriated friend does. It's also smart to avoid talking politics, unless you're sure your views won't clash with those of your companions—for example, you can agree wholeheartedly with a bunch of sentimental republicans when they drink to a unified Ireland, whereas you would absolutely avoid talking politics in a pub in Northern Ireland named the "Queen's" or "King's" anything.

During music sessions in the pub, it is polite to pause in conversation to clap for the musicians when a song ends. And if a new friend is kind enough to buy you a pint, it goes without saying that the next round is on you!

Visitors should never make assumptions about the sexual mores of their new friends—suggestive advertising, frank talk on TV and in social situations, and other purported signs of a sexually liberated culture can belie deep-rooted conservative values nevertheless.

Information and Services

HEALTH AND SAFETY

In the event of an emergency, dial 999 on your cell phone or nearest pay phone, which will connect you with the local police (or *gardaí*) and ambulance.

There is a choice of pharmacies even in the smaller Irish towns, though not all are open on Sunday; general hours of operation are 9 A.M.–6 P.M., and many places are open until 8 or 9 P.M. at least a few days a week. Your accommodation can direct you to the nearest seven-day pharmacy, if you end up needing medication over the weekend. Condoms are now available at any pharmacy.

Ireland is a very safe country—the vast majority of violent crimes are drug-related, and fortunately this is a world tourists seldom come into contact with. Your biggest safety concern regards your rental car, as there are a staggering number of motor accidents on a daily basis: 1,000 people are injured per month, with an average monthly death toll of 30. Drive conservatively no matter how many speed demons pass you on those narrow roads.

It goes without saying that you should never drink to excess—no matter if your B&B is a five-minute walk up the road, and regardless of how many free pints you're handed. If at all possible, avoid driving late at night even if you're the designated driver; many other motorists won't be so conscientious. And while it seldom happens that blackout drugs are slipped into nightclub drinks when a girl's back is turned, you should still keep your drink with you at all times.

MONEY
Currency

The Irish punt is no more—the euro has been the official currency here since February 2002. Check on the exchange rate before you leave with the **Universal Currency Converter** (www.xe.com/ucc); at time of writing the U.S. dollar was quite weak against the euro, €1 equaling $1.33. As part of the United King-

dom, Northern Ireland uses British sterling; the exchange rate at time of writing was £1 to $1.96. Many shops and accommodations along the border will accept either currency.

Using your credit or ATM card gets you the best exchange rate, but if you need to change money, visit a bureau de change at a bank. (Bureaux de change at tourist offices, hotels, and commercial agencies offer a poorer rate of exchange, plus commission.)

Taxes

You are entitled to a VAT (Value Added Tax) refund on all goods purchased in the republic upon departure, so long as you aren't an E.U. citizen—saving you 17.36 percent off the original price. Whenever you make a purchase at a gift shop, just ask for a voucher. (Note that it's the VAT on goods, not services, that is refundable.) Fill all your forms in before you get to the airport, then visit the Global Refund Desk, which is located between the security and immigration checkpoints. You'll receive a refund in cash or by credit card, though a credit refund can take as long as two months to process.

COMMUNICATIONS AND MEDIA
Telephone

Phone numbers in the republic can be five, six, or seven digits. The North has a single area code and eight-digit numbers. (When ringing Northern Ireland, use the area code 028 when dialing from within the U.K. or internationally, but 048 when dialing from the republic.) The area codes 085, 086, or 087 indicate the number belongs to a cell phone (Meteor, O2, and Vodafone, respectively).

When calling Ireland from the United States, note that the Republic of Ireland's country code is 353 and Northern Ireland is 44, and you must omit the zero from the area code when dialing. For example, to reach Galway City (area code 091) from the U.S., you would dial 011-353-91-555-555; to reach a location in Northern Ireland, you would dial 011-44-28-5555-5555.

If you are planning to stay for longer than a few weeks and need to use a phone regularly for reservations, taxis, and so forth, it might pay you to get your home cell phone "unlocked" (for a fee of €10) and then spend €10–20 for a new simcard and pay-as-you-go plan (though Vodafone has the widest service coverage, Meteor generally offers the best plans). This sounds like an involved process, but it's actually a bit cheaper and far more convenient than using your credit card on a pay phone.

Internet Access

There are Internet cafés in most Irish towns nowadays, though pricing varies greatly. Competition drives rates down in cities, but in smaller towns you may be charged as much as €8 (or £5) an hour. Free (or less expensive) access is sometimes available at the local public library (some do not offer access to nonmembers, some charge €2–3 per hour, and others are free to all). In North Ireland, you can check your email at any library, where the standard rate is £0.75 for 15 minutes.

Many accommodations offer wireless Internet (WiFi) access (and it's complimentary at most places); wireless service in pubs and cafés is generally through companies like BitBuzz or Eircom that charge a hefty monthly access fee. Twenty-minute vouchers are often available with any purchase, however.

Media

The Irish get their television and radio news from **RTÉ**, Radio Telefís Éireann. **TG4,** pronounced "tee gee CAH-her," is the Irish-language television network, though it does run some English-language programs (and includes subtitles for most of the rest).

The Irish Times (www.ireland.com) is the republic's primary newspaper, available at newsagents nationwide. The *Belfast Telegraph* (www.belfasttelegraph.co.uk) is Northern Ireland's national newspaper.

MAPS AND TOURIST INFORMATION

The tourist board in the Republic of Ireland is **Bord Fáilte** (www.ireland.ie), which literally means "Welcome Board." In the North, it's the **Northern Ireland Tourist Board** (www.discoverireland.com). Though these agencies provide information to visitors (tourist office clerks in the North tend to be particularly knowledgeable), they pretty much exist to arrange accommodations (for a small fee, of course), sell books and maps, and provide other profit-based services. Indeed, a tourist office always doubles as a gift shop. Tourist office opening hours vary from season to season; some are closed in winter, and many close for lunch (1–2 P.M.).

Ordnance Survey maps (www.osi.ie) are available at tourist offices and bookstores. The OS Discovery Series consists of 89 maps covering the country; at 1:50,000, they detail practically every stone in the road. If you are doing any walking, cycling, or in-depth sightseeing, be sure to pick up the appropriate map (they run about €8). Unfortunately, bookstores and tourist offices generally stock only maps covering the immediate area, though it is possible to order online.

WEIGHTS, MEASURES, AND TIME

Ireland is officially on the metric system, but in reality, measurements of weight and distance are inconsistent. Meat and produce is weighed and priced in kilograms, but Guinness will be poured in pints until the last day of the world. If you hear something like "I lost three stone on this new diet," know that one stone is roughly 14 pounds.

If driving, you will notice that locals are more likely to gauge distances in miles rather than kilometers, and the road signs seem to alternate in miles and kilometers. In the republic, all speed limit signs are still given in miles; the old white signposts give distance in miles, but the new ones (both green and white) list them in kilometers ("old" and "new" will be easy to distinguish once you're out on the road). The old white signs are being phased out, but gradually enough to cause ongoing confusion. In Northern Ireland, the Imperial system is still the norm—all distances are listed in miles.

Before you leave home, be sure to pick up a three flat-pin adapter from an electronics store so you can use your laptop and other electrical gadgets. Ireland's standard voltage is 220 volts at 50 hertz (Northern Ireland's is 230/240 at 50 hertz), and you will need to purchase a voltage converter if any of your appliances are not compliant (though most likely you'll be fine with just an adapter). If you have any doubts, contact the manufacturer of the device in question before departure.

Ireland is on Greenwich mean time (GMT) and uses daylight saving time (GMT plus one hour in summertime), though note that the country goes to daylight saving time two weeks ahead of the United States. Ireland is five hours ahead of America's east coast and eight hours ahead of the west coast, apart from those two weeks (when it is six and nine hours ahead).

Ireland is one hour behind Spain, France, and Italy, and nine and ten hours behind Australia (nine in Brisbane, ten in Sydney and Melbourne). To check the time difference between Ireland and other locations, you might try the helpful website **The World Clock** (www.time-anddate.com/worldclock).

RESOURCES

Glossary

This compilation includes slang and common cultural and historical references in both Irish and English.

advert short for advertisement

afters dessert

amadan (AH-mah-dahn) fool

Anglo-Irish a land-owning Protestant family of English descent, or any descendants thereof

Anglo-Irish Treaty the 1921 agreement that divided Ireland into British-controlled Northern Ireland and the independent republic in the south; the cause of the Irish Civil War (1922-1923)

ard rí (ard REE) high king

aubergine eggplant

bank holiday an official three-day weekend when banks close and everyone's off work on the Monday; expect crowds at pubs, restaurants, and hostels

banoffee pie a dessert made from toffee and bananas that originated in England and is now quite popular on Irish menus

banshee a female spirit whose shrieking and wailing augurs an impending death

bap a lunch roll, like a seedless hamburger bun

bawn a yard enclosed by a fortified house

beer mat coaster

big house a term used (usually disparagingly) to refer to the home of the local landlord, who would be a member of the Protestant ascendancy

biro ballpoint pen

biscuits cookies

Black and Tans a brutal and undisciplined British paramilitary force in 1920 and 1921, sent to Ireland to suppress all rebels (especially the IRA)

black pudding sausage made from dried pigs' blood

Blue Flag an "eco-label" awarded by an independent group, the Foundation for Environmental Education, that indicates the beach in question is very clean and safe

bodhrán (boh-RAWN) a hand-held goatskin drum used in traditional Irish music

bog wet terrain with thick spongy layers of moss and other vegetable matter; also slang for toilet

bollocks a more colorful way of calling someone a jerk; also used as an exclamation

bonnet the hood of a car

boot the trunk of a car

braces suspenders

bridle way path for walkers, cyclists, and horseback riders

brilliant a common exclamation, like "cool"

brolly umbrella

busker a street musician

camogie the women's version of hurling

caravan a trailer or mobile home

céad míle fáilte (kayd MEE-leh FAWL-cheh) traditional greeting, meaning "a hundred thousand welcomes"

ceilidh (KAY-lee) a session of traditional dance and music

champ mashed potatoes and onions

chemist pharmacist

chipper a fish-and-chips shop

cider alcoholic apple cider

clearway a road without a shoulder

coach long-distance charter bus, usually for large tourist groups

concession discounted admission

Connaught one of the four ancient Irish provinces, encompassing Counties Galway, Mayo, Sligo, Roscommon, and Leitrim

control zone the area of a town center where cars must not be left unattended

cotton buds cotton swabs

courgette zucchini

craic (crack) a fun time, good music and conversation; sometimes used in greeting, as in "What's the *craic*?"

culchie (CULL-chee) an urbanite's derogatory term for a person from the country; a "country bumpkin"

curragh a rowboat covered with tarred canvas, traditionally used for fishing

daft crazy

Dáil (Doll) the lower house of the Irish Parliament

DART Dublin Area Rapid Transit, the commuter train line running from Howth through Dublin south to Bray in County Wicklow

dear expensive

diamond town square

digestives round graham crackers taken with tea

dole Irish welfare or unemployment

drink alcohol (often called "the drink")

drisheen pudding made from pigs' blood, a traditional Irish breakfast food

dual carriageway a divided four-lane highway

Dubs short for Dubliners

DUP the Democratic Unionist Party, a hardline unionist (and exclusively Protestant) political group formed by Ian Paisley in the early 1970s

drumlin a gentle hill formed long ago by retreating glaciers

eejit fool, moron

Éire (Air) the Irish name for the Republic of Ireland

en suite with a private bathroom attached

eolas (OH-lahs) information

fáilte (FAWL-cheh) welcome

feis (fesh) a gathering

feis ceoil (fesh kyohl) a festival of music

Fenians a nickname for members of the Irish Republican Brotherhood (IRB), a militant nationalist group founded in 1858; predecessors of the IRA

Fianna (FEE-uh-nuh) a group of mythical warriors whose exploits feature in many Irish legends

Fianna Fáil (FEE-uh-nuh FALL) a centrist political party formed by those nationalists who did not want to accept the compromise of continued British rule in the North

Fine Gael (FEE-nuh GALE) a centrist political party formed by those nationalists who were willing to accept continued British rule in the North to be able to form an independent republic

fir (fihr) men; used on toilet doors (singular *fear*)

flannel a facecloth

fortnight two weeks

freephone number toll-free telephone number

full stop period

GAA abbreviation for the Gaelic Athletic Association, the organization founded in 1884 to promote the native pastimes of hurling, Gaelic football, and other sports.

Gaeltacht (GALE-tahckt or GWALE-tahckt) a region where Irish is the primary language spoken (plural Gaeltachtaí)

gangway aisle

gansey sweater, jumper

garda, gardaí (GAR-da, gar-DEE) the Irish police, the full name being An Garda Síochána, "Guardian of the Peace"

gas something funny; "a hoot"

grand good, well

H-blocks literally refers to the H-shaped layout of British prisons, though the term is generally used in regard to the IRA members who as H-block inmates conducted a widespread hunger strike in 1981 in hopes of being reclassified as political prisoners

Hibernia the Roman name for Ireland; literally "Land of Winter," so misnamed because the Romans thought they had discovered Iceland

homely cozy, homey, homelike (never means "ugly"!)

hooker a traditional Galway sailing ship, from the Irish *húicéir*

hurling a traditional Irish sport, one of the fastest games in the world; a cross between hockey, lacrosse, and soccer

IHH Independent Holiday Hostels of Ireland; a hostel's membership in this organization is indicative of high standards in safety, cleanliness, and hospitality

interval intermission

IRA the Irish Republican Army, the largest republican paramilitary group, founded in 1919 with the aim of a reunited Ireland, achieved by force if necessary

jacks toilet

jars alcoholic drinks

jumble rummage sale

jumper sweater

kerb just another spelling of "curb"

kipper smoked herring

knickers ladies' underwear

leabharlann (LORE-lahn) library

Leinster one of the four ancient Irish provinces, encompassing the southeastern section of the country from Louth down to Kilkenny and Wexford

left luggage baggage check (not necessarily the same as lost and found)

to let to rent

lift elevator

loo toilet

lorry truck

lough (lock) a lake or narrow sea inlet

loyalist one (usually a Protestant) who supports Northern Ireland's continued existence as part of Great Britain, another word for unionist

Luas the new light-rail system through suburban and downtown Dublin

lugs ears

mac trenchcoat (from "mackintosh")

manky dirty, unappealing

marching season the time of year between Easter and mid-June when the Northern Irish calendar is filled with loyalist marches in celebration of the victory of William of Orange at the Battle of the Boyne in 1690.

mate buddy, friend (usually male)

mean stingy

minced meat hamburger

mná (m'NAH) women; used on toilet door (singular *bean*)

mobile (MOH-bile) cell phone

MP member of Parliament (British)

Munster one of the four ancient Irish provinces, encompassing Counties Clare, Limerick, Kerry, Cork, Tipperary, and Waterford

musha (MUSH-ah) indeed (archaic)

naomh (nave) saint

nappy diaper

nationalism the belief that Ireland should be reunited; its proponents are called nationalists

off-license liquor store

ogham (OH-um) Ireland's earliest form of writing (dating from the 5th to the early 7th century), consisting of an alphabetic system of lines for consonants and notches for vowels, usually carved in stone

Oireachtas the bicameral Parliament of the Irish Republic, consisting of the Dáil (lower house) and the Seanad Éireann (upper house, or Senate)

OPW Office of Public Works, the republic's governmental agency for town planning as well as conservation and restoration efforts

Orange Order the largest Protestant group in Northern Ireland, established in 1795

OS Ordnance Survey, Britain's national mapping agency; Ordnance Survey Ireland (OSi) issues detailed region maps for all Ireland

Partition of Ireland the division of Ireland into Northern Ireland and the Irish Republic in 1921

pasty a meat pie with a crust

pay-and-display parking the paid hourly parking system in most Irish towns, whereby motorists are required to purchase a ticket from a blue kiosk to display on their "windscreens"

peat partially carbonized vegetable matter, found in bogs, that has traditionally been dried and used for fuel; now also comes in briquette form for household use (compressed, less smoke, and easier to light)

peckish hungry

Penal Laws laws passed in the 18th century that forbid all Catholics from gathering for Mass, owning land, holding public office, and so forth; officially known as "Laws in Ireland for the Suppression of Popery"

petrol gas (as in fuel)

Plantation the settlement of English immigrants on lands confiscated from Irish Catholic farmers in the 17th century

plaster a Band-Aid

poteen (PO-cheen) illegal whiskey, potent enough to kill in large quantities, that was usually brewed by dispossessed Irish farmers to make extra money; from the Irish *poitín*

Prod a Northern Irish Protestant

quay (key) a street along a river or harbor

queue (cue) a line (at the bank, the supermarket, etc.)

quid slang for pounds (now euros), though it isn't used as often since the conversion

rashers bacon

republicanism the militant belief in a reunited Ireland

return ticket a round-trip fare

roundabout traffic circle

Rover pass a euro-saving Bus Éireann bus pass good for 3 days' travel out of 8 consecutive days, 8 days out of 15, and so on

RTE Ireland's broadcast network, the acronym for Radio Telefís Éireann

rubber eraser

runners athletic shoes, sneakers

scrummy short for scrumptious

SDLP Social Democratic and Labour Party, the largest nationalist political party in the Northern Ireland assembly

sean nós (shawn NOHSS) a style of traditional song with three primary characteristics: the songs are unaccompanied, performed solo, and always sung in the Irish language; literally, "in the old way"

seisún a traditional music session

sellotape Scotch tape

single ticket a one-way fare

síbín (shuh-BEAN) an illicit tavern or speakeasy; "shebeen" in English

Sinn Féin a republican political party whose longstanding goal is a reunited Ireland; it is usually considered the political arm of the IRA despite its assertion that the two organizations are unaffiliated

slagging (off) making fun of someone

sláinte! (SLAWN-cheh) good health; cheers!

slí (shlee) literally "way," a hiking trail

slieve a mountain, from the Irish *sliabh*

smalls underwear

snog kiss

snug a booth tucked away in a pub, meant for a bit of privacy

solicitor lawyer

sound (as an adjective) very good

strand beach

subway an underground passageway for pedestrians

sultanas golden raisins

Taoiseach (TEE-shock) prime minister of the Republic of Ireland; literally, a chieftain

takeaway takeout food

taking the piss making fun of someone

Tánaiste (TAHN-ish-tcheh or TAHN-iss-teh) deputy prime minister of the Irish Republic

Teachta Dala (TCHOCK-tuh DOLL-uh) a member of the Irish Parliament, abbreviated TD

teach, tí, tigh (tchock, tchee) house (often used as in a public house, i.e., pub)

teampall (TCHYEM-pull) church

tinker a now politically incorrect (and even offensive) term for an Irish person who lives a nomadic lifestyle, traveling in caravans and often making a living as a smith; also (inaccurately) called gypsies

top up to fill up a drink, or to add credit to your mobile phone account

torc a neck or wrist ornament made of a band of twisted bronze or other metal, a type of jewelry introduced by the ancient Celts; most Irish examples date from the late Bronze Age and early Iron Age

torch flashlight

Tory the term for a conservative politician in Britain comes from the Irish *toiride*, meaning "pursuer," a word that originally referred to a highwayman

trad short for traditional music

trainers athletic shoes, sneakers

Traveller the politically correct word for one of a group of nomadic Irishpeople who travel in caravans and speak a separate language (called Shelta) in addition to English; there are approximately 25,000 Travellers in Ireland today

Tricolour the green, white, and orange Irish flag symbolizing peace between the (green) Catholic Irish and the (orange) Protestant Irish

turf another word for peat

turlough (TUR-lock) a small lake that disappears in dry weather

uilleann pipes (ILL-inn) the Irish bagpipes, which are inflated by a bellows and have a range of two octaves

uisce (ISH-keh) water

uisce beatha (ISH-keh BAH-hah) whiskey; literally, "water of life"

Ulster one of the four ancient Irish provinces, encompassing the six counties of Northern Ireland (Antrim, Armagh, Derry, Down, Fermanagh, and Tyrone) along with three counties in the republic (Cavan, Monaghan, and Donegal); sometimes used to refer to Northern Ireland (especially by the British government)

UVF Ulster Volunteer Force, a Unionist paramilitary group established in 1966

unionist one (usually a Protestant) who supports Northern Ireland's continued existence as part of Great Britain, synonym for loyalist

victualler butcher

Wellingtons knee-high rubber boots, also known as wellies

PLACE-NAMES

Here are Irish words that form place-names in English.

ard high

baile (BAL-ee or BALL-yuh) village, town

beag (beg) small

bothár (BOH-hir) road

caislean (CASH-lin) castle

carraig (KAR-rig) rock

cath (kah) battle

cill (kill) church

dún (doon) fort

gort field

lough (lock) lake

mór (more) big

slí (shlee) path, way

teach (tchock) house

Irish Phrasebook

You won't hear a whole lot of Irish spoken outside the Gaeltachtaí, but it's worth picking up a few phrases even if you aren't planning to venture into the farthest reaches of Donegal, Dingle, or Galway. There is now a "standard" dialect using a mix of the three dialects – Connaught (Galway and Mayo), Munster (Kerry, Cork, and Waterford), and Ulster (Donegal) – but Donegal tallies the most native speakers, so here's a quick primer using that dialect. (After all, who speaks textbook Irish outside the classroom? You should be understood wherever you go, and if someone feigns confusion just inform them you're trying out some Donegal Irish.)

There are 18 letters in the Irish alphabet. Others – *j, q, v, w, x,* and *z* – sometimes appear on loan from other languages.

PRONUNCIATION
Vowels

Vowels are divided into long and short. A long mark called a *fada* indicates a long vowel (short vowels are unmarked).

Short vowels are generally pronounced like short vowels in English. Long vowels are pronounced as follows:

á "aw," as in *áthas* (AW-huss, meaning "joy")

é "ay," as in *sé* (shay, meaning "he" or "it")

í "ee," as in *sí* (shee, meaning "she")

ó "oh," as in *bó* (boh, meaning "cow")
ú "ooh," as in *tú* (too, meaning "you")

Vowels are also divided into broad (*a, o,* and *u,* whether long or short) and slender (*e* and *i,* whether long or short). Whether a vowel is broad or slender can affect the pronunciation of the consonants before and after it.

Consonants

Most Irish consonants are pronounced as in English. Every consonant has broad and slender sounds, the rule being that a consonant preceding a broad vowel should be broad also (and vice versa). For example, a broad *d* sounds as it looks, but a slender *d* (as in *dearg,* JAR-ug, meaning "red") has a "j" sound. The other two consonants to watch out for are *s,* which has a "sh" sound before or after a slender vowel (as in *seo,* show, meaning "this"), and *t,* which has a "tch" sound before or after a slender vowel (as in *tine,* TCHI-nyeh, meaning "fire").

Some unfamiliar consonant clusters have pronunciations you'd never figure out on your own, such as the following:

bhf "w," as in *cá bhfuil tú* (cah will too, "where are you?")

bh "v," as in *mo bhean* (moh van, "my woman")

mh "v," as in *naomh* (nave, "saint")

dh "y," as in *dhá dhoras* (yah yorahs, "two doors")

gh "y," as in *mo gheansaí* (moh YAN-see, "my sweater")

Other familiar-looking clusters don't follow the English pronunciation; in words beginning with a *th,* for instance, the *t* is silent.

To show possession, when using the vocative, or with an adjective that modifies a feminine noun, the rule of **lenition** applies – that is, adding an *h* after the first consonant of a word. For instance, the word for house is *teach,* and "my house" is *mo theach;* girl is *cailín,* big is *mór,* and "big girl" is *cailín mhór.* (To get a full understanding of Irish and its grammatical rules, consult an Irish language textbook or take a language course.)

If you ever see a dot over a vowel in place of an *h,* like on a pub sign, it's called a *buailte* (BOOL-cheh), a throwback to old Irish.

BASIC AND COURTEOUS EXPRESSIONS

Hello *Dia duit* (GEE-a ditch; literally, "God to you")

Hello (to more than one) *Dia daoibh* (GEE-a deev)

Hello (response) *Dia is Muire duit* (GEE-a iss MAU-rya ditch; literally, "God and Mary to you")

Good morning *Dia duit ar maidin* (ar MAH-gin)

Good morning (to more than one) *Dia daoibh ar maidin* (GEE-a deev ar MAH-gin)

Welcome *Fáilte romhat* (FALL-cheh ROE-it)

Thank you *Go raibh maith agat* (go row MY AH-gut; literally, "may good be at you")

Thank you (to more than one) *Go raibh maith agaibh* (go row MY AH-give)

Thank you very much *Go raibh míle maith agat* (go row MEE-luh MY AH-gut)

Good night *Oíche mhaith* (EE-huh why)

Goodbye *Slán, slán go foill,* or *slán abhaile* (slawn, slawn go foll, slawn a-WALL-eh; literally, "safe," "safe yet," or "safe home")

Please *Le do thoil* (leh doe HULL)

Excuse me *Gabh mo leithscéal* (go mo LESH-cull; literally, "take my apology")

and *agus* (AH-gus)

but *ach* (ahkh)

or *nó* (no)

also *freisin* (FRESH-in)

How are you? *Conas atá tú?* (cunnas a-TAH too?)

I am . . . *Tá mé . . .* (tah may)

satisfied *sásta* (SAH-stah)

good *go maith* (go MY)

well enough *maith go leor* or *reasunta maith* (my go LORE, ra-SUN-ta my)

tired *tuirseach* (TER-shock)

terrible *go dona* (go DUN-uh)

wonderful *go hiontach* (HEEN-tock)

The weather is . . . *Tá an aimsir . . .* (tah ahn AM-shur)

fine *go breá* (go brah)

awful *go dona* (go DUN-uh)

We would like to go to . . . *Bá mhaith linn dul go dtí . . .* (bah why linn JUL go JEE)
here *anseo* (ahn-SHOW)
there *ansin* (ahn-SHIN)
I would like a pint *Bá mhaith liom pionta* (bah why lum PYUN-tah)
I would like another *Bá mhaith liom ceann eile* (kyawn ELL-eh)
He would like to buy . . . *Bá mhaith leis . . .* (bah why LESH)
Cheers! *Sláinte!* (SLAWN-cheh)
Happy Birthday! *Lá Breithe Sona duit!* (lah BREE-huh SUN-na ditch)
Happy Christmas and New Year to you! *Nollaig shona agus bliain nua duit!* (NUL-leg HUN-na a-GUS BLEE-un NEW-a ditch)

QUESTIONS

Where is . . . ? *Cá bhfuil . . . ?* (cah will)
the restroom *an leithreas* (ahn leh-riss)
the strand *an trá* (ahn trah)
the B&B *an leaba agus bricfeasta* (ahn LEE-bah a-gus brick-FAH-sta)
the hotel *teach ósta* (tchock OH-stuh)
my room *mo sheomra* (moh HOH-mra)
this restaurant? *bialann seo* (BEE-a-lahn show)
the pub *an teach tábhairne* (tchock tuh-VERN)
Which way? *Cén slí?* (ken shlee)
How many? *Cé mhéad?* (kay vayd)
What is that? *Cad é sin?* (kud AY shin)
Why? *Cén fath?* (ken fah)
I don't understand *Ní thuigim* (nee HIG-im)
I understand *Tigim* (TIG-im)
What's your name? *C'ainm atá ort?* (KEN-nim ata art?; literally, "what name is on you?")
My name is Charlie. *Charlie atá orm.* (AH-tah A-rum; literally, "Charlie is on me.")
Where are you from? *Cás tú?* (cahss too)
Where are you (plural) from? *Cás sibh?* (cahss shiv)
I am/we are from Canada. *Is as Ceanada mé/muid.* (iss ahss Canada may/mudge)

ARTICLES, ADJECTIVES, AND PREPOSITIONS

There is no indefinite article in Irish; to say "a thing" is just *rud*, while "the thing" is *an rud*.

small *beag* (beg)
big *mór* (more)
open *oscailte* (OSS-cultch)
closed *dúnta* (JUN-tuh)
inexpensive *saor* (sear)
expensive *daor* (deer)
nice *go deas* (jahss)
quiet *ciuin* (CUE-in)
other, another *eile* (ELL-uh)
white *bán* (bahn)
black *dubh* (doov)
gray *liath* (LEE-uh)
red *dearg* (JAR-ug), *rua* for red hair
green *glas* (glahs)
yellow *buí* (BOO-ey)
blue *gorm* (GORE-um), used to describe someone with dark skin; a "black man" is a "blue man" *(fear gorm)* in Irish.

Fifteen of the most common prepositions are conjugated for the pronoun to which they refer; for example, to say "with me," you must combine the words *lé* and *mé* to make *liom*. Here is a conjugation of one of the most common prepositions, *ag* ("at"), which is also used to say you "have" something (e.g., *Tá cóta nua agam*, "I have a new coat," literally, "A new coat is at me").

at me *agam* (AH-gum)
at you *agat* (AH-gut)
at him/it *aige* (EGG-eh)
at her *aici* (ECK-eh)
at us *againn* (AH-gin, with a hard "g")
at you (plural) *agaibh* (AH-give)
at them *acu* (AH-coo)

DIRECT ADDRESS

When speaking to someone directly, the person's name is pronounced (and spelled) differently, using the rule of lenition mentioned above. (It's like the vocative case in Latin, except it's the first letter rather than the ending that's altered.) To ask Maire how she is, for instance, you would say this: *Conás atá tú, a Mhaire?* (CUN-iss a-TAH too, ah WUR-yeh?)

PEOPLE

man *fear* (far), plural *fir* (fihr)
woman *bean* (ban), plural *mná* (m'NAH)
young boy *gasúr* (goss-UHR)
boy *buachaill* (BOH-khull)
girl *cailín* (kai-LEEN)
father *athair* (AH-hur)
my father *m'athair* (MAH-hur)
mother *máthair* (MAH-hur)
my mother *mo mhathair* (mo WAH-hur)
husband *fear cheile* (far HEH-leh)
wife *bean cheile* (ban HEH-leh)
son *mac* (mack)
daughter *iníon* (in-EE-un)
brother *deartháir* (JAR-har), plural
deartháracha (JAR-har, JAR-har-uh-HAH)
sister *driofúr* (JER-ih-fur), plural *driofúracha*
(JER-ih-fur-uh-HAH)
grandfather *seanathair* (shawn-AH-hir)
grandmother *seanmháthair* (shawn-WAH-hir)
granny *mamó* (mah-MOH)
friend *cara* (CAH-rah), plural *cairde* (CUR-jeh)
my friend *mo chara* (moh HAH-rah)
boyfriend *stócach* (STOH-cah)
girlfriend *cara mná* (CAH-rah m'NAH)
In Irish, when a woman's surname is prefaced
by *Ní*, it means it's her maiden name. The prefix
Uí indicates a married name. *Ní* ("nee") and *Uí*
("wee") are used instead of the male-only *Mac*
(meaning "son of") and *Ó.*

TERMS OF ENDEARMENT

The Irish word for love is *grá*, and it can be
used for friendly affection to familial bonds to
romance, and every shade in between.
friendship, companionship *cumann* (CUM-
ahn)
first love *céadsearc* (KAYD-shark)
I love (a thing or activity) *Is breá liom* (iss
brah lum; literally, "it is best with me")
kiss *póg* (as seen in the insult commonly
adopted by tourists, *póg mo thoin*, pohg moh
HOE-in, meaning "kiss my ass")
Give me a kiss *Tabhair dom póg* (TORE dum
pohg)
my little darling *a stóirín* (ah STORE-een, a
direct address)

my heart *mo chroí* (mo HREE), used as a term
of endearment
I love you *Tá mo chroí istigh ionat* (tah mo
HREE iss-TEE in-NIT; literally, "my heart is
within you")
I am in love with you *Táim i ngrá leat*
(TCHAY-im ih nrah laht)

NUMBERS

0 *náid* (nahdg)
1/2 *leath* (lah)
1 *haon* (heen)
2 *dó* (doe)
3 *trí* (chree)
4 *ceathair* (CAH-hur)
5 *cúig* (queeg)
6 *sé* (shay)
7 *seacht* (shock'd)
8 *ocht* (ockt)
9 *naoi* (knee)
10 *deich* (djayh)
11 *haon déag* (heen jayg)
12 *dó dhéag* (doe yayg)
For the remaining teens, add *dhéag* (yayg) to the
number in the ones column.
20 *fiche* (FEE-huh)
21 *fiche a haon* (FEE-huh a heen)
30 *triocha* (TREE-uh-hah)
40 *daichead* (DAY-hyayd)
50 *caoga* (KOW-gah)
60 *seasca* (SHAH-ska)
70 *seachtó* (SHOCK'D-oh)
80 *ochtó* (OKT-oh)
90 *nócha* (NO-hah)
100 *céad* (kayd)
1000 *míle* (MEE-luh)
a couple *cupla* (CUP-luh)
a lot *a lán* (ah lahn)
many, enough *go leor* (go LORE)
I am 29 years old *Tá mé naoi mbliana is fiche
d'aois* (tah may nee MLEE-uh-nuh iss FEE-huh
deesh)

TIME

What time is it? *Cén t-am é?* (ken tom ay)
It is nine o'clock *Tá sé a naoi a chlog* (tah
shay ah knee a hlog)

today *inniu* (in-YOU)
tomorrow *amáireach* (ah-MAR-ach)
yesterday *inné* (in-YAY)
now *anois* (uh-NISH)
soon *go luath* (go LOO-uh)
year *bliain* (BLEE-un)
month *mí* (mee)
week *seachtain* (SHOCK-tin)
this weekend *deireadh seachtaine seo* (JER-oo SHOCK-tin-eh show)
day *lá* (lah)
hour *uair an chloig* (OO-er ahn hlog)
minute *nóiméad* (NO-maydg)
second *soicind* (SHI-kihnd)
twenty past three *fiche i ndiaidh a trí* (FEE-huh ih NEE-eye ah chree)
half past three *leath i ndiaidh a trí* (lay ih NEE-eye ah chree)
quarter to four *ceathrú chun a ceathair* (KYAH-hroo khyoon ah KAH-hur)
five past four *a cúig i ndiaidh a ceathair* (ah KWEEG ih NEE-eye a KAH-hur)
midday *meán lae* (mahn lay)
midnight *meán oíche* (mahn EE-huh)
morning *maidin* (MAH-gin)
afternoon *tráthnóna* (truh-NO-nuh)
at night *san oíche* (sun EE-huh)

DAYS AND MONTHS

Sunday *Dé Domhnaigh* (jeh DOH-nee)
Monday *Dé Luaín* (jeh LOO-un)

Tuesday *Dé Máirt* (jeh march)
Wednesday *Dé Ceádaoin* (jeh KAY-jeen)
Thursday *Déardaoin* (JEER-doyn)
Friday *Dé hAoine* (jeh HEE-nyeh)
Saturday *Dé Sathairn* (jeh SAH-hurn)
January *Eanáir* (ANN-er)
February *Feabhra* (FAH-vrah)
March *Márta* (MAR-tah)
April *Aibreán* (EBB-rawn)
May *Bealtaine* (BAL-tin-yeh)
June *Meitheamh* (MEE-hiv)
July *Iúil* (ool)
August *Lúnasa* (LOO-nuh-suh)
September *Meán Fómhair* (meen FOE-er)
October *Deireadh Fómhair* (JER-ooh FOE-er)
November *Samhain* (SOW-in)
December *Nollaig* (NULL-ig)

SIGNS

city center *an lár* (ahn lahr)
men *fir* (fihr), used on toilet door
police *gardaí* (gar-DEE), full name An Gardaí Síochána (ahn GAR-da show-CHAH-nah)
post office *Oifig an Phoist* (OH-fig ahn fwisht)
toilet *leithreas* (LEH-riss)
tourist office *Oifig Fáilte* (OH-fig FAWL-cheh; literally, "welcome office")
trash *bruscar* (BRUSS-ker)
women *mná* (m'NAH), used on toilet door
go slowly *taisteal go mall* (TOSH-till go mahl)
yield *geill slí* (gel shlee, with a hard "g")

Suggested Reading

HISTORY

Connolly, S. J. J. *Oxford Companion to Irish History*, rev. ed. Oxford: Oxford University Press, 2004. With a collection of contributors that spans the political spectrum, this revised edition makes a solid primer—though the general tone is, as you'd expect, on the conservative side.

Harbison, Peter. *Guide to National and Historic Monuments of Ireland*, 3rd ed. Dublin: Gill & Macmillan, 1998. This guide will prove invaluable if you plan to visit a variety of archaeological sites.

LITERATURE

Here is an assortment of the contemporary and the classic. Ask at a local bookshop for more recommendations.

Banville, John. *The Sea*. New York: Knopf, 2005. The prolific Banville is one of today's best Irish literary novelists. *The Sea* won the 2005 Booker Prize.

Behan, Brendan. *The Complete Plays: The Hostage, the Quare Fellow, Richard's Cork Leg, Moving Out, A Garden Party, The Big House*. New York: Grove/Atlantic, 1978. Considering all the time he spent in jail (and in the pubs), hard-drinking IRA member Behan was able to write a load of plays and fiction in his 41 years; this volume is a must-have for theatergoers.

Joyce, James. *Dubliners*. Many consider Joyce the greatest Irish writer of all time and others find his work pretentious. If *Ulysses* isn't your cup of tea, try this collection of short stories. The final tale, *The Dead,* was inspired by the childhood love of his wife, Nora Barnacle, and the 1987 film version was director John Huston's last.

Keane, Molly. *Good Behaviour*. London: Virago Press, 2001. This ironically titled novel,

set in the 1920s, offers up black comedy at the expense of the Irish Ascendancy.

Kinsella, Thomas. *The Tain: from the Irish epic Táin Bó Cuailnge*. Oxford: Oxford University Press, 1969. The definitive translation of the 8th-century Irish epic featuring the hero Cúchulainn and his nemesis, Medb, the scheming queen of Connaught.

Le Fanu, Sheridan. *In a Glass Darkly* (Oxford World's Classics). Oxford: Oxford University Press, 1999. Dubbed "The Invisible Prince" by his Dublin neighbors, Le Fanu funneled his obsession with the occult into an awesome collection of horror stories, including the vampire tale "Carmilla" for which he is best known.

McCormack, Mike. *Notes from a Coma*. London: Jonathan Cape, 2005. A fine novel, described (albeit simplistically) as a cross between *1984* and *The X-Files,* from one of a younger generation of Irish prose writers.

McGahern, John. *By the Lake*. New York: Knopf, 2003. It may not have much of a plot, but in this gorgeously atmospheric novel (titled *That They May Face the Rising Sun* in Ireland and Britain) it's hardly a flaw. The much-revered McGahern, who passed away in 2006, is known for darker works than this (such as *The Dark,* which was banned in 1965).

Ní Dhomhnaill, Nuala. *Selected Poems: Rogha Dánta*. Dublin: New Island, 2000. Many of Ireland's finest poets are writing exclusively in Irish, and Ní Dhomhnaill is perhaps the most beloved among them. (Original Irish on the left page and the English translation on the right.)

O'Brien, Kate. *The Land of Spices*. London: Virago Modern Classics, 1988. Banned in Ireland in 1941 for its fleeting and euphemistic mention of a homosexual tryst, this is one of the best Irish novels of the 20th century.

O'Casey, Sean. *Three Dublin Plays: The Shadow of a Gunman, Juno and the Paycock, and the Plough and the Stars.* New York: Faber and Faber, 2000. These three early plays, generally considered O'Casey's best work, provide a window into inner-city life that only a man born there could have achieved.

Synge, John Millington. *The Aran Islands.* New York: Penguin, 1992. Synge's travel writing isn't as well known as his dramatic works, but this volume is a must-read for Aran enthusiasts and armchair travelers alike.

Synge, John Millington. *Playboy of the Western World and Other Plays.* Oxford: Oxford University Press, 1998. This edition features all of Synge's published plays.

Wilde, Oscar. *The Best of Oscar Wilde: Selected Plays and Writings.* New York: Penguin, 2004. This collection includes *An Ideal Husband* along with four more well-known plays and several pieces of Wilde's literary criticism.

Wilde, Oscar. *The Picture of Dorian Gray.* New York: Random House, 1998. This edition features an introduction by Pulitzer Prize winner Jeffrey Eugenides.

Yeats, William Butler. *Selected Poems and Four Plays,* 4th ed. New York: Scribner, 1996. If you buy only one compilation of Yeats's work, this is a solid choice.

ART HISTORY

Bowe, Nicola Gordon. *The Life and Work of Harry Clarke.* Dublin: Irish Academic Press, 1989. An illuminating study of Clarke, Ireland's greatest stained-glass artist, by a professor at the National College of Art and Design in Dublin.

THE IRISH LANGUAGE

Ó Siadhail, Mícheál. *Learning Irish: An Introductory Self-Tutor,* 3rd ed. New Haven: Yale University Press, 1995. This is one of the best introductory Irish textbooks; it uses Connaught Irish rather than the standard dialect.

PHOTOGRAPHY

O'Brien, Jacqueline, and Peter Harbison. *Ancient Ireland: From Prehistory to the Middle Ages.* New York: Oxford University Press, 1996. This is the third in a trilogy, the first two being *Great Irish Houses and Castles* and *Dublin: A Grand Tour.* The collection of aerial photographs in this volume is truly stunning.

FOOD AND DRINK

Cotter, Denis. *Cafe Paradiso Seasons.* Cork: Atrium, 2003, and Irvington, NY: Hylas, 2004. A fabulous cookbook from the owner/chef of Cork City's famous vegetarian restaurant, Cafe Paradiso.

NATURE AND WALKING GUIDES

Booth, Frank. *The Independent Walker's Guide to Ireland.* New York: Interlink, 1999. This guide features 35 day hikes nationwide, all 3–15 kilometers long.

Lynham, Joss, ed. *Best Irish Walks,* 3rd ed. Dublin: Gill & Macmillan, 2001. This volume offers 75 hiking routes that are generally longer and more challenging than those in the Booth guide.

LIVING IN IRELAND

Harvey, Steenie. *Living Abroad in Ireland.* Emeryville, CA: Avalon Travel Publishing, 2005. Whether you intend to stay six months or a lifetime, this book provides all the resources you need to put down roots.

Internet Resources

ENTERTAINMENT

www.culturenorthernireland.org
News and reviews of theater, books, music, fine arts, and sporting events in Northern Ireland.

www.entertainmentireland.ie
Entertainment Ireland has the lowdown on clubs, theaters, festivals, concerts, films, etc.

www.gigireland.com
Irish indie bands post info on upcoming gigs nationwide.

www.todayfm.com
One of the republic's most listened-to radio stations plays mostly "top 40" interspersed with lots of entertaining chitchat.

SIGHTSEEING AND TOURIST INFORMATION

www.discovernorthernireland.com
The official site from the Northern Ireland Tourist Board.

www.dublinblog.ie
The Dublin Community Blog has loads of insider sightseeing tips.

www.dublinks.com
Another excellent resource with entertainment listings and candid restaurant reviews.

www.dublintourist.com
"The definitive guide to Dublin on the web" lives up to its promise.

www.heritageireland.ie
Dúchas, Ireland's Office of Public Works, offers photos, background, and visitors' information on national parks and monuments on its official site.

www.map-ireland.com
Plug in your desired destinations (though the list isn't exhaustive), and this website will help you plan your itinerary more efficiently.

www.megalithomania.com
An informative and opinionated gazetteer on the country's megalithic and early Christian remains, including fine color photos.

www.ireland.ie
The official site of Bord Fáilte in the Republic of Ireland.

SPORTS AND ACTIVITIES

www.cavingireland.org
The official website of The Speleological Union of Ireland. Experienced cavers, start planning your Irish adventure here.

www.irelandwalkingcycling.com
This is your site if you're looking for a guided walking or cycling tour. All tour operators are Tourist Board–approved.

www.isasurf.ie
The official site of the Irish Surfing Association covers both sides of the border.

www.mountaineering.ie
Virtual home of the Mountaineering Council of Ireland.

www.mountainviews.ie
Before you go, view pictures and tips of individual mountains posted by seasoned hillwalkers.

www.npws.ie
For all you bird-watchers and walkers, the National Parks & Wildlife Service website

lists nature reserves and conservation sites in the republic.

www.walkireland.ie

The Irish Sports Council provides maps, trail descriptions, and other resources for long-distance walkers.

TRANSPORTATION

www.aaroadwatch.ie

The Automotive Association website includes a route planner, invaluable for mapping out your road trip.

www.irishtaxionline.com

Check out this site if you're not renting a car. It very helpfully provides a list of the maximum fares (by location) that a taxi driver can legally charge you.

NEWS AND PUBLICATIONS

www.bbc.co.uk

The BBC, many Northerners' primary news source.

www.breakingnews.ie

Just as it says, this slightly sensationalist news source lists Irish news first.

www.ireland.com

The *Irish Times,* the best source for nationwide news online and in print.

www.rte.ie

The official site of Radio Telefís Éireann, the republic's radio and television service.

www.unison.ie

This "portal" offers content from 27 Irish newspapers, making it the nation's largest virtual information resource.

Index

Acknowledgments

No one deserves greater thanks than my good friend Diarmuid O'Brien, who stepped in to write the history section when I realized I needed help making my deadline. He did a fantastic job, and I'm tremendously grateful for all his hard work in research and writing.

An adventure, in Ireland or elsewhere, is only as great as the people with whom you share it, and those kind and generous souls you encounter by providence. So I'll mention my traveling companions of the last six or so years—Kate DeAngelis, Kate Trainor, Aravinda Seshadri, Leah Smith, and Kelly Brown. I got to see and enjoy more of Ireland every time we slung on our backpacks.

Naturally, my time at the National University of Ireland, Galway better equipped me to tackle this guide, and I owe thanks to all the friends I made there: Ailbhe Slevin and Christian O'Reilly, Seanan McDonnell (and his wonderful family—Bán, J.P., and everyone), Megan Buckley, Patrick Curley, Lindsay and Trev Ward, Sinéad Ní Ghuidhir, Áine McHugh, Meg Ginnetty, Liam Kuhn, and Diarmuid O'Brien (again!). Whether you showed me around your hometown, tipped me off to your favorite pubs, put me up, drove me around, came out to dinner, made me laugh, or gave me absinthe: thanks a lot.

Way back in high school, Pamela Fisk encouraged my budding interest in Irish history. Thanks are also due to my professors in the Irish Studies program at NYU, Padraig ó Cearúill and Mick Moloney especially, as well as my teachers at NUI Galway—Adrian Frazier, Joe Woods, and Sinéad Mooney—and Mike McCormack in particular.

Jennifer Flores ("Ní Bhlathanna"), I am so lucky to have met you in Irish class at NYU. Our idyllic afternoon on the Causeway coast along with Natalie Mason and Genevieve Handy is always going to be one of my favorite memories of Ireland. Genevieve, thanks so much for your company (not to mention your photographs). Hanging out with you and Dave Wright in Dublin was another highlight—you started off as my hostel roommate, and now you're my friend for life!

As for those kind and generous souls one encounters by providence, I first have to mention Nora Coyne of Mount Gerard B&B, Limerick, who was nothing short of saintly in tending to me when I had a foot injury. I'll never forget her and her husband John's generosity. Other B&B owners who went above and beyond for me (not knowing what I was up to, mind!) include Teresa Keane (as well as her husband) of Whispering Pines, Listowel; Nancy O'Neill of Rosgal, Galway; Carmel and Mattie of the Rainbow Hostel and B&B in Doolin; and Anna and Ken Johnson of Anna's House in Lisbane.

Tom Sullivan, thank you for cheerfully changing my flat tire and feeding me delicious meals you pulled out of your hat. Kevin O'Cuinn, thanks for your company in Westport and elsewhere. You both made bumming around in Leenane one of the most memorable parts of my road trip. I am also grateful to Andrzej Syski for his company in Doolin and the Burren, John Renway Strohmeyer for allowing me to drag him all over Derry City, and to the lovely Susen from Germany for lending me her camera batteries in Ballycastle. Thanks to Brendan Stafford at Tintern Abbey, Michelle at Trim Castle, and all the other excellent tour guides who didn't think I was weird for taking notes. Many thanks also to Yvonne McEnnis of The Pottery Shop in Corofin for her help with getting my bearings in the area.

I am indebted to the works of Anthony Bailey, Heinrich Böll, Pat Boran, Brian de Breffny, William Bulfin, Roy Foster, Mike McCormack, Frank McDonald, H. V. Morton, Kate O'Brien, Patrick Pearse, George Bernard Shaw, Paul Theroux, David A. Wilson, and W. B. Yeats. I quoted these authors to add a little flavor to my write-ups, and I like to think the book is a much more entertaining read for all their wise observations.

As for the team at Avalon, thanks go to Rebecca Browning for giving me the opportunity to write *Moon Ireland;* to Grace Fujimoto and Kathryn Ettinger, who are both terrific editors; to Stefano Boni for his work on the photography; to Kevin Anglin for his cartography; and to everyone else who put so much time, energy, and enthusiasm into this guidebook. I'm also extremely grateful to my agent, Kate Garrick, who holds my hand whenever I need it.

A hundred thousand thank-yous to the Murphy family: Gene, Betty, Sharon, Yvonne, and Justin. They have overwhelmed me with their friendship, kindness, and generosity time and again, and I count myself incredibly privileged to be related to them. (Plus, Yve and Sharon gave me loads of great tips for dining and drinking in Dublin, and the book is so much better for them.)

Lastly but mostly, thank you to my sister Kate, my parents, my grandparents, and the rest of my family for their encouragement and support. Thanks to my mother for overcoming her (considerable) anxiety whenever I take off—I know it isn't easy for her. And my father deserves special thanks for fortifying me every summer morning with potatoes and eggs and half a dozen cups of gourmet java. Otherwise, with that deadline looming, I might've forgotten to eat altogether.

www.moon.com

For helpful advice on planning a trip, visit www.moon.com for the **TRAVEL PLANNER** and get access to useful travel strategies and valuable information about great places to visit. When you travel with Moon, expect an experience that is uncommon and truly unique.

HANDBOOKS | METRO | OUTDOORS | LIVING ABROAD

MAP SYMBOLS

▓▓▓	Expressway	〖	Highlight	✗	Airfield	⌁	Golf Course
▔▔▔	Primary Road	○	City/Town	✗	Airport	🅿	Parking Area
▬▬▬	Secondary Road	◉	State Capital	▲	Mountain	▰	Archaeological Site
⋯⋯	Unpaved Road	⊛	National Capital	✛	Unique Natural Feature	▐	Church
------	Trail	★	Point of Interest			🗑	Gas Station
··········	Ferry	•	Accommodation	⟋	Waterfall		Glacier
⊶⊶⊶	Railroad	▼	Restaurant/Bar	▲	Park		Mangrove
▓▓▓	Pedestrian Walkway	▪	Other Location	▣	Trailhead		Reef
⫶⫶⫶	Stairs	Λ	Campground	⚟	Skiing Area		Swamp

CONVERSION TABLES

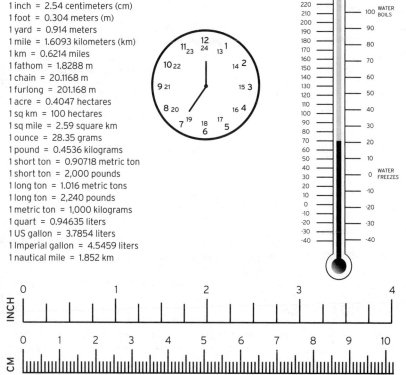

°C = (°F – 32) / 1.8
°F = (°C x 1.8) + 32
1 inch = 2.54 centimeters (cm)
1 foot = 0.304 meters (m)
1 yard = 0.914 meters
1 mile = 1.6093 kilometers (km)
1 km = 0.6214 miles
1 fathom = 1.8288 m
1 chain = 20.1168 m
1 furlong = 201.168 m
1 acre = 0.4047 hectares
1 sq km = 100 hectares
1 sq mile = 2.59 square km
1 ounce = 28.35 grams
1 pound = 0.4536 kilograms
1 short ton = 0.90718 metric ton
1 short ton = 2,000 pounds
1 long ton = 1.016 metric tons
1 long ton = 2,240 pounds
1 metric ton = 1,000 kilograms
1 quart = 0.94635 liters
1 US gallon = 3.7854 liters
1 Imperial gallon = 4.5459 liters
1 nautical mile = 1.852 km

MOON IRELAND

Avalon Travel Publishing

1400 65th Street, Suite 250
Emeryville, CA 94608, USA
www.moon.com

Editors: Kathryn Ettinger, Grace Fujimoto
Series Manager: Kathryn Ettinger
Acquisitions Manager: Rebecca K. Browning
Copy Editor: Deana Shields
Graphics Coordinator: Stefano Boni
Production Coordinator: Domini Dragoone
Cover Design: Stefano Boni
Cartography Manager: Mike Morgenfeld
Map Editor: Kevin Anglin
Cartographers: Kat Bennett, Chris Markiewicz
Proofreader: Meredith Sires
Indexer: Valerie Sellers Blanton

ISBN-10: 1-59880-048-5
ISBN-13: 978-1-59880-048-7
ISSN: 1936-1807

Printing History
1st Edition – May 2007
5 4 3 2 1

Text © 2007 by Camille DeAngelis.
Maps © 2007 by Avalon Travel Publishing, Inc.
All rights reserved.

Some photos and illustrations are used by permission
and are the property of the original copyright
owners.

Front cover photo: © Stephen Emerson/Alamy
Sunset on Kilclooney Dolmen, County Donegal

Title page photo: © Camille DeAngelis
Johnstown Castle

Printed in the United States by Worzalla

KEEPING CURRENT

If you have a favorite gem you'd like to see included in the next edition, or see anything
that needs updating, clarification, or correction, please drop us a line. Send your
comments via email to feedback@moon.com, or use the address above.